StandWithUs is pleased to present this copy of *Judaism, Zionism and the Land of Israel*, which has been donated by its author, Rabbi Yotav Eliach.

As Alan Dershowitz has stated about this book, "The case for Israel must be made anew in every generation and to every audience. Rabbi Eliach has been making the case to generations of high school students. Now he brings his insights and experience to a general public that is desperately in need of history and current realities."

Enjoy this substantial volume which will bring information and context to your libraries for years to come.

Roz Rothstein
StandWithUs
Co-founder and CEO

Special Thanks to Rabbi Yotav Eliach, Shalom Maidenbaum, Robert Koppel, Robert Segal, and Jack Doueck as well as Ilyse and Dr. Alex Sternberg.

Judaism, Zionism and The Land of Israel

Yotav Eliach

Dialog Press
Washington, D.C.

This book is printed on acid free paper.

ISBN: 978-0-914153-34-4
0-914153-34-X

First Edition, Second Printing
Printed in the United States of America
18   19   20   21   22   5   4   3

Cover designed by Tallgrass Studio
Pages designed and typeset by Wordsmithy, LLC
Maps courtesy of Martin Gilbert

Modern book text is produced using a variety of collaborative software, including automated spellcheckers and text revision tools. It is possible for such software to create typographical errors or other textual changes beyond the control of the author, editor, or publisher. Any changes, corrections or additions to this book should be reported to, and/or can be found at:

www.dialogpress.com

Web site addresses (URLs), titles, and statistics were accurate as of press time. Neither the author nor the publisher is responsible for URLs that have expired or moved since the manuscript was prepared.

Dedicated to my wife Hildy and our children,
Liam, Noa and Itai.

ACKNOWLEDGMENTS

The first pages of this book were actually typed in 1984. By 2004 I had a hundred-page version of what would be its outline. I began to write in earnest in the fall of 2013. Though I have written articles, op-eds, speeches, and co-wrote a short book on how to teach about terrorism, I had never before undertaken this type of project. Writing this book has been a wonderful and unique experience. It has been overwhelming, cathartic, instructive, humbling and life changing for me. I have many people to thank; I truly hope and pray that I will not have forgotten to mention anyone who was connected with this book. If I do, then I ask for their forgiveness.

I want to begin by thanking my wife Hildy and our children Liam, Noa and Itai for putting up with me for the last four years. When I was not working as a principal at Rambam Mesivta I was either writing, rewriting, researching, speaking or thinking about this book. I want to thank my friend Dr. Alex Grobman, a true scholar and author for pushing me to get top-notch professional editors so that my book would be a serious well-written scholarly book. Words are not sufficient when it comes to thanking Dr. Philip Sieradski who was the editor Dr. Grobman introduced me to. I am a speaker, a lecturer, a teacher and a writer of articles, but I had no experience when it came to writing a lengthy book, one I consider to be a scholarly book for non-scholars. Thanks especially to Phil for his skill, scholarship, knowledge, experience, patience and wizardry. *Judaism, Zionism and the Land of Israel* is a book that I am exceptionally proud of. Thank you! / *Todah Rabbah!*

I also want to thank Esther Gilbert, the wife of the late Sir Martin Gilbert, who connected me with the publishers of Sir Martin Gilbert's book of maps of Jewish history and of the Arab-Israeli conflict. Thanks to her I have over fifty of Sir Martin Gilbert's excellent and unique maps in this book.

I am lucky and privileged to be able to call Edwin Black, a world famous author of non-fiction bestsellers, a friend. He has taken the time to explain to me what is involved in publishing and distributing a book. Furthermore, he has been gracious enough to allow me to share the professionals he has been working with, including one of his publishers. You are most gracious!

I owe a debt of gratitude to my friend Rabbi Zev Meir Friedman, the Dean of Rambam Mesivta, as well as to Rambam Mesivta. For the last four years I have spent many nights, weekends and summer days sitting in my office writing and rewriting. I have printed thousands of pages of my book on the schools copy machine, both for editing purposes and for educational purposes. Rabbi Friedman and Rambam Mesivta have not only been encouraging and accommodating, but they have been my fans as well. Todah Rabbah!

Edwin Black explained to me that there is no money in the book business, especially when you write a historical book about a topic that you are passionate about. The only outcome will be your ending up investing a great deal of money. In my case it was not just my own money; I was fortunate enough to find people and organizations that were willing to invest in me and my book. I could not have written or published this book without their support:

Avi Chai Foundation – Thanks to Yossi Prager
Shalom Maidenbaum
Helene and Robert Rothenberg
Roz Rothstein
Anne Gontownik
Dr. Elliot Goldofsky
Rabbi Yamin Levy

Finally, I have been inspired my entire life by two people who raised me, taught me and led by example: my parents, Rabbi Dr. David Eliach and my late mother, Dr. Yaffa Eliach. This book is as much their book as it is mine.

Todah Rabbah!

Yotav Eliach
December 13 2017/25 Kislev 5778 Chanukah

TABLE OF CONTENTS

FOREWORD

Iwas born in the shadow of the Holocaust to Rabbi Dr. David Eliach, a sixth generation Jerusalemite whose family returned to *Eretz Yisrael* (the Land of Israel) in 1807. Since my father's family comes from a Chassidic dynasty called Karlin Stolin, and the *Rebbe* (Grand Rabbi who was the leader of the sect) said that it was time to return to *Eretz Yisrael*, the family did so because of a deep religious sense of obligation.

My mother, Dr. Yaffa Eliach, whose family had lived in Lithuania for generations and whose world was destroyed in September 1941 by the Nazis and their Lithuanian collaborators, had to endure over four years of living in ghettos, hiding under a pig sty, hiding in forests, and living with partisans. She watched her mother and two of her brothers murdered, and then walked across part of Europe until she found some sense of stability in a displaced persons camp. Eventually, she was allowed by the British to enter *Eretz Yisrael* in 1946. Seven years later she married my father in *Medinat Yisrael* (the Modern State of Israel). Their two stories have left a powerful impact on my life and world view.

The world I grew up in included many Holocaust survivors who spoke about the *Shoah* (the Holocaust) quite often, and in detail. Their stories were all quite horrible and unbelievable when compared to the world that I lived in. It was very clear to me that all these people, including my mother and many of my friends' parents, had experienced a form of brutality that is hard to imagine, and that they were abandoned by the world. Being Jewish between 1939-1945 in Europe and parts of North Africa meant you were being hunted and marked for extermination. The yellow *Magen David* (Star of David) these people were forced to wear was a sign of humiliation, and of being marked as a target.

It was also made crystal clear to me that I was exceptionally lucky to be born into a world where the *Magen David* was in the middle of a blue and white flag—the colors of the *talit* (Jewish prayer shawl)—that represented the first sovereign Jewish State since the days of the Maccabees, some 2,000 years past! The miraculous metamorphosis from the *Magen David* being a yellow star of shame to a symbol of a sovereign Jewish State, along with the metamorphosis of the Jewish people from a hunted, murdered, and dazed people to a proud, free, independent people, all occurred during a three-year period, 1945-1948!

This was the most remarkable positive change in the fortunes of the Jewish nation since the Maccabees entered the Second Temple in 165 BCE to cleanse it from the Greek defilement, and the re-establishment of Jewish sovereignty.

I have been truly fortunate to be born and live at a time in Jewish history where I get to realize the dream of the return to Zion for which Jews have prayed for nineteen centuries. To me, that is remarkable on a religious and a historical level. There are prayers I get to recite daily (some three times a day) that speak of the return of the Jewish people from all four corners of the Earth to *Eretz Yisrael,* that speak of the rebuilding of Jerusalem, that speak of a new light shining on Zion, that to past generations were aspirations for the future that for me are affirmations of my present!

The simplest way for me to share what the re-establishment of Jewish sovereignty has meant to the Jewish people from my perspective is by telling a story that involves relying on a principle from science fiction, namely, time travel. Imagine that time travel was possible. If it were, I would set my time machine to transport me back in time to the following dates and places: Southern Europe during the years 1095-1099, when the Crusaders were on their way to the Holy Land and killed tens of thousands of Jews; Spain, the summer of 1492, when after centuries of Jews being fully integrated into the country's life, all are expelled; parts of Ukraine (in the Jewish super-ghetto known as the Pale of Settlement) during the years 1882-1903, when horrible, violent riots, known as pogroms—that were either sanctioned by the Russian Government or ignored by it—took place in Jewish towns; finally, September 1939-May 1945, when the countries of Europe and North Africa and parts of Asia watched as the Nazis exterminated Jews in what we now call the *Shoah*, the Holocaust.

Since I have visited Israel well over fifty times and in total have spent over five very intense years in the country, on this trip I would take along an album of photos I took during my travels, as well as aerial photographs of Israel. At each stop, I would tell the Jews around me that I am from their future, and I would describe in detail what the sovereign, re-established Jewish State looks like and how many, and what types of, Jews live there. I would show them photographs of the country and its people. I would describe what the Kotel Plaza (Western Wall) looks like, and what it's like on Friday nights when thousands of different types of Jews come there to pray; what it looks like on Sukkot when thousands come to be blessed by the *Kohanim* (the priestly caste), and what it looks like when soldiers from the Israel Defense Forces (IDF) are sworn in there.

I would tell them about the Knesset, the Israeli flag, and the menorah which is the emblem of the Jewish State. I would tell them about the IDF and a little about what it has accomplished since 1948. I would show them my own swearing-in ceremony when I received my Tanach (Bible) and M16. I would tell them about the millions of Jews in Israel who come from well over one hundred and fifty countries, and how they have all returned to the land of their forefathers.

I would tell them about the many accomplishments of the Jewish State in science, technology, medicine, and its archeological finds that link the Jewish present to the Jewish past. They would see pictures of the green fields of the Hula Valley and the forests that surround Jerusalem, and of some of the thousands of synagogues and *yeshivot* (Jewish religious studies institutes/schools) in Israel.

I can guarantee that at each one of these historical stops the Jews I would be speaking to and showing pictures to would begin to weep with joy, and probably would just want to touch me as I would seem to represent something holy and unbelievable to them. Finally, I would not be surprised if some of them would probably ask me to describe the *Mashiach* (the Messiah), since surely, in their minds, he had arrived. I would smile and tell them we are still waiting for him, but that our present is the future they have all been dreaming of. The re-established State of Israel, with all of the problems running a sovereign state entails, is the embodiment of a 2,000-year-old dream!

The problems the re-established State of Israel has created—social, religious, economic, political, military—are the types of problems that only nations that govern themselves can experience. By definition, they are part and parcel of the package deal that comes with national sovereignty. If one studies the Tanach, s/he will find it replete with the issues in the ancient Jewish State. These issues were not reasons for the Jewish nation to avoid sovereignty then, and they are not reasons to avoid sovereignty today.

(The analogy I would use is personal. As a teenager I did not have a mortgage, credit card bills, utility and energy bills, insurances, car leases, yeshiva or college tuitions to worry about. All I had to do was go to yeshiva high school, spend my summers in sleep-away camp, play basketball, hang out with friends, watch TV, read books, and basically lead a worry-free life. Yet as much fun as that was, I prefer adulthood—where I have been raising a family, influencing the world around me, making a difference, as I undertake a variety of projects that benefit others, and me. My responsibilities, such as paying many bills and making decisions for my family and at my job, are part of being an adult, and I welcome these opportunities and challenges.)

The Jewish nation's mission is to be a light unto the nations of the world. This mission was not meant to be carried out on merely an individual level, but also in a world of nation states. The Jewish State was meant to be a nation state whose national behavior is to be an example for other nation states. By definition, running a state is a complicated and, at times, a messy endeavor. But the overall benefits of sovereignty clearly outweigh the negatives if one firmly believes that the Jewish people are a nation with a national purpose and mission.

Sadly, for some Jews on both extremes of the religious spectrum, the idea of Jewish statehood is abhorrent precisely because it entails the Jews returning to history as a functioning nation-state. After close to two millennium of Jewish statelessness—in and of itself an unnatural state for the Jewish nation from the Tanach's perspective and from a Jewish historical perspective—Jewish statelessness has been viewed as part of a punishment for not obeying the Ten Commandments and the laws of the Torah.

For many Jews on the extreme religious right, being Jewish is a religious experience devoid of any nationalistic aspects. They believe Jews need to keep personal and community commandments, the *mitzvoth*, while giving up those Jewish laws that can only be kept in *Eretz Yisrael*—which make up most of the laws—and they will wait until the Messiah arrives before they go to *Eretz Yisrael* to obey them.

For the extreme left of the religious spectrum, Judaism has morphed into a cosmopolitan-oriented culture where one has traded biblical, rabbinical and historical Judaism for the ideas and values of the Enlightenment, or as it is referred to today, liberalism or progressivism. To many of them, being Jewish means to be anti-religious and suspicious of governments and the military.

During the 2,000-year-old Jewish Diaspora, different Christian churches, European royalty, governments and militaries persecuted the Jews. For the extreme left, ironically, the Arab and Islamic view of the Jews is a correct one: The Jews are a religious/ethnic group that is not a nation and hence has no need for statehood. To them, being Jewish is being open-minded, being a person who questions authority and fights for the rights of all minorities and underdogs. If anything, Jewish statehood is abhorrent to them.[1]

For the majority of the world's Jews, however, the re-establishment of Jewish sovereignty in Israel is the answer to a 2,000-year-old prayer and the beginning of the fulfillment of a 2,000-year-old dream.

Another way to grasp what the reinstatement of the Land of Israel has meant is to imagine what it would have been like if Israel had not been re-established in 1948, and that the last event of great historical consequence for the Jewish people would have been the Holocaust and its immediate aftermath. What would a picture of world Jewry have looked like seventy years after the last concentration camp was liberated?

By May 1945, six million Jews, most of them Europeans, were murdered by the Nazis and their collaborators. Thousands of Jewish towns and neighborhoods were wiped off the map; millions were left homeless and further victimized. Being Jewish was a huge liability. Among the Holocaust survivors, many had deep philosophical questions about the wisdom of remaining Jewish.

In 1945, the second largest Jewish community—outside of Europe—was in the United States, where there were around five million Jews. If one reads about Jewish life in the U.S. in the first half of the 20th century, one will find that the overarching theme was that in order for Jews to succeed and be accepted into American society they had to assimilate or hide their Jewishness.[2] Thus, there were, comparatively, very few observant Jews in the U.S. in 1945. A handful of Orthodox Jewish men publicly wore *kippot* (skull caps) or dressed in overtly Jewish styles, and there were few kosher restaurants in the entire U.S. Most American Jews who considered themselves Orthodox went to synagogue on the Sabbath and then took off their *kippot* and went to work—which is prohibited—because they did not want to get fired. That was the accepted norm in the freest, most tolerant country on Earth![3]

I believe that after the Holocaust had there been no redemption via the creation of the Jewish State in the Land of Israel, American Jews would have accelerated their assimilation into American society and dropped as many trappings of Judaism as they could.

The few hard-core Orthodox Jews would have practiced in an almost Converso-like fashion (the Jews in Spain in the 15th century who openly converted to Christianity to avoid being killed but who practiced Judaism secretly).

But the re-establishment of Israel changed the world view of most Jews, and certainly the view of American Jews as well. Clearly the Holocaust was a horrific watershed in Jewish history that raised many philosophical, religious, sociological, and existential questions for the Jewish nation as a whole. But the events of 1948-1949, which included the Maccabee-like victory by the fledgling Jewish Army in defeating five better-equipped Arab armies, were seen by the overwhelming majority of the worlds' Jews as a modern-day miracle. Because it occurred only three years after the Holocaust, for many Jewish people it meant that the Almighty's message to the battered Jewish nation was that He had not abandoned them; that He had answered a 2,000-year-old prayer and re-established Jewish sovereignty in *Eretz Yisrael* and ushered in the ingathering of exiles. This changed the self-image of Jews all over the world. The images of skeleton-like, starved and tortured Jewish concentration camp survivors was replaced with images of brave IDF soldiers who raised the blue and white flag at the end of many battles in the War of Independence.

Thus the Jews reentered history as actors with speaking parts. They were no longer props. This lifted the spirits of American Jews and caused them to want to publicly identify themselves as Jews and to start living Jewish lives publicly. Holocaust survivors who were religiously Orthodox established themselves in distinct centers around America and acted to attract American Jews to Orthodoxy all over Brooklyn, in Los Angeles, in Lakewood, in Rockland County... *frum* (observant) Holocaust survivors and Chabad made a huge difference when they established yeshivas and day schools, *shuls* (synagogues) and *batei medrash* (houses of prayer) on every corner.

The second and perhaps more profound shift in American Jewry's self-image came after the 1967 Six-Day War. Israel defended itself against imminent annihilation and, as a result, was able to liberate the Old City of Jerusalem and Judea and Samaria. There was a sense that we had witnessed another epic modern-day miracle.

In essence, the Six-Day War was Israel's Second War of Independence, as well as the war that brought about the liberation of the Old City of Jerusalem where the Kotel, the Temple Mount, the Mount of Olives and the Jewish Quarter all sit. These are the holiest sites in Judaism, sites that had been desecrated and were off-limits after the Jordanian Army captured them in 1948. Also in Israeli hands were Judaism's holiest shrines, places like Ma'arat HaMachpela (the Tomb of the Patriarchs and Matriarchs) in Hevron, the burial spot of Rachel the Matriarch in Bet Lechem, the burial spot of Yosef (Joseph, the son of the Patriarch Yaacov/Jacob) in Shechem, the site where the *Mishkan* (Tabernacle) stood for several centuries in Eli, and many other places mentioned in the Tanach. Having the Jewish nation reunited with these places brought about a mystical and historical sense of pride and purpose that affected Jews all over the world, especially the American Jewish community.

Remarkably, American Jews began to publicly associate with the State of Israel and Judaism. The 1948 War of Independence and the Six-Day War became the theological and historical antidote to the horrible sense of loss and destruction of the Holocaust. Being Jewish in 1967 had very positive connotations, and together these two watershed events were seen as the Almighty's hand in action on behalf of the Jewish nation.

The net result was a prouder, more engaged, openly Jewish, and in many cases, a more openly religious Jewish community. In my opinion, this sense of pride and engagement has resulted in what I call "in-your-face Orthodoxy" that exists in the greater New York Metropolitan region and in a few other places around the United States where Orthodox Jews, whether centrist or *haredi*, have built large communities with hundreds of synagogues and *yeshivot*. Today in the U.S. there are a multitude of kosher restaurants and fast food establishments and dozens of kosher mega supermarkets, Jewish newspapers and radio stations, and thousands of Jewish websites. I do not believe that this type of Jewish life could have existed after the Holocaust if Israel had not been re-established.

Since 1979, I have been teaching yeshiva high school students about *Medinat Yisrael's* re-establishment as a tremendous miracle and how it has propelled the Jewish people back to the forefront of history and relevancy. Furthermore, we, unlike most Jewish generations in the last 2,000 years, have the privilege of saying many parts of the *Tefilot* (prayers) not as aspirations for a better future, but as affirmation of our remarkable day-to-day reality! I teach my students that we have a responsibility to *Am Yisrael* (the Nation of Israel) and to *Medinat Yisrael* to do whatever we can to help strengthen her—religiously, socially, economically, politically and defensively.

This book is my attempt to teach the Jews of the 21st century the story of the Jewish nation and *Eretz Yisrael*. Though the country celebrated its 69th birthday as I complete this work, the miracle of Israel's re-establishment is something Jews of all ages and backgrounds should never take for granted. It is heartening to see that for most young American Jews, certainly the more observant and traditional ones, Israel is a part of their lives as much as their local neighborhoods, *yeshivot* and day schools.

To many of these Jewish youngsters, however, Israel is an exotic Jewish "enclave" situated in a warm climate that offers many fun options for a teenager or a young adult. On the other hand, it is disheartening to see how little they know about how the modern Jewish State was established, its relationship to them on a personal, national and religious level, as well as its history. It is also disconcerting to find that when they arrive at college, the overwhelming majority of them are unprepared to respond to the barrage of lies and distortions about Israel and Zionism that, these days, have become part of campus reality.

A main goal of this book is to show the centrality of *Eretz Yisrael* in Judaism throughout the ages. The concept of Israel has been touched on for most religious and traditional Jewish youths since they have been in pre-school. However no single course ever attempts to make the connection between the Tanach, Mishna, Gemara, *Halacha* (Jewish Law), Jewish History, Jewish Philosophy, and the modern State of Israel. My attempt is to inform the reader of the role of Israel in the Jewish way of life/religion from the days of Avraham to the 21st century and to make the connections between the *Tefilot* that many Jews say every day, the *Chagim* (holidays) that many Jews observe, and the various Jewish texts that Jews study.

I will explain why the Jewish connection to *Eretz Yisrael* is not a modern phenomenon, but an idea that has existed for as long as there has been a Jewish people. I will also attempt to show the concept of Zion (Israel) as one of the pivotal and central ideas found in Judaism.

I do not intend to cover all the details of Jewish history in *Eretz Yisrael* these last 4,000 years. I will concentrate on what I believe are the most significant and relevant events in the remarkable story of the reappearance of the Jewish State as an actor on the world stage. There will be a bibliography and webography appendixed to the book so readers may further study the topic for which I offer a simple appetizer.

INTRODUCTION

From 1948 to 1981 Zionism was something U.S. Jewish teenagers received through osmosis. During those years, American Jewish communities were filled with Holocaust survivors raising children, running *shuls* (synagogues), schools, and Jewish organizations. The DNA of all of us that were brought up between the 1950s and the 1970s was infused with gratitude to the Almighty for the gift of Jewish sovereignty, and pride for the accomplishments of the gritty, tough, Jewish State that made the Tanach come alive for us.

The Western media was proud of the spunky "Dosh" (a cartoon character who represented Israel in newspapers from the 1950s to 1970s) who stood up to the legions of Arab despots and dictators who oppressed their own people and kept pointing to Israel to distract their people from their own misery, and continuously spoke of their goal to annihilate the Jewish State to anyone who was willing to listen. Their goal was openly and unabashedly to commit genocide. Everyone who followed events in Middle East knew that.

But since the first Lebanon War in 1982 and the birth of the relentless 24-hour TV news cycle, the image of Israel among American Jews has been tarnished and perverted. Holocaust survivors in leadership positions were retiring. The Holocaust itself and the 1967 and 1973 Wars were receding from our collective memories. For those born post-1967, Israel was not a miraculous gift, a break from 2,000 years of Diaspora, it was the Jewish community in the Jewish homeland in the far off Middle East, in the land of the Bible, in the Holy Land.

Though very few of us took formal courses on Zionism, its ideals and values were transmitted to us by words and deeds. We didn't Google the 1948 War of Independence, 1967 Six-Day War, the Munich Olympics, the 1973 Yom Kippur War, the Ma'alot Massacre in 1974, or the IDF Raid on Entebbe in 1976 to know what these events were and what they meant to the Jewish nation. We remember hearing about these events from our parents or experiencing them ourselves. To watch President Abdel Gamal Nasser of Egypt in late May and early June of 1967 call for the total annihilation of the Jewish State was not something the *New York Times* editorial board needed to interpret for us. Today, it is hard for those who do not know the history to figure out who the good guys and bad guys are.

It was taken for granted that students attending day schools and yeshivot in the '50s and '60s knew what was happening in Israel. There were few formal classes, but many students were exposed to special assemblies and programs about Israel. The assumption was that being in schools offering Israel-associated assemblies, programs, speakers and posters would create an atmosphere of identification and love of Israel, and would foster knowledge and commitment to and about Israel and Zionism.

Today, there are still few, if any, formal courses in Zionism and Jewish history that connect the dots from the days of Abraham to the present. Instead, most Americans learn about Israel from the instant images in the 1982 war with Lebanon, from media infatuated with the notion of "if it bleeds it leads," (an idea tied to Nielsen ratings), and since the advent of the Internet, to sticky-eye balls and hits. The media focused on the powerful Israeli Goliath putting a siege on Beirut, and the Christian Lebanese massacres of Palestinians in Sabra and Shatilla—for which Israel was blamed. There was no history mentioned, no depth and no context offered to audiences or readers.

During the 1987 Palestinian Intifada, the media broadcast pictures of young Arabs with slingshots facing huge Israeli tanks. Again there was no history or context offered. No one asked why the Palestinians were homeless. No one asked why, in 1947, the

Grand Mufti of Jerusalem rejected the idea of an Arab State next door to a Jewish one. No one asked why, from 1949 to 1967, the Jordanians never offered a state to the people living on the West Bank of the Jordan River in Judea and Samaria. No one asked who created the Palestinian cause or made Yasser Arafat its leader. Instead, it seemed that because Israel became a democratic state that could defend itself against mighty armies, her greatest sin was that she was no longer weak and vulnerable.

On the far left and in academic left-wing circles, Israel was tarred and feathered as a colonialist, imperialistic oppressor and occupier of Palestine and its indigenous Palestinian population. The Jews/Zionists were painted as European colonizers who colonized the free and sovereign State of Palestine, much like the British did in half of Africa and the Indian subcontinent in the 1800s.

Where did this distortion come from and who originated it?

In the last decade of the 20th century, Saudi Arabia and the Gulf sheikdoms began funding endowments for Middle Eastern Department Chairs staffed by students of Edward Said, a Palestinian-American literary theorist who helped found the critical-theory field of post-colonialism. He was an American-Christian Arab born in Jerusalem in 1935 to an Arab mother from Egypt and an American father, and spent much of his childhood in Cairo, where he was sent to elite British and American schools. He earned his BA at Princeton and his Ph.D. in English literature at Harvard. He joined the faculty of Columbia University in 1963 and became a professor of comparative literature in 1991.

Said's great claim to fame was his book, *Orientalism*. The work is based on his knowledge of literature, literary theory and colonialism. In that work he uses the word *Orientalism* to describe the West's patronizing attitudes to "the East"—meaning North Africa, Eastern, Middle Eastern and Asian societies. He claimed that these Western attitudes were directly linked to the imperialism of the 18th and 19th centuries, and that the scholarship they produced about these cultures was political, influenced by the power structure and therefore intellectually suspect.

His school of thought was contagious, and had enormous influence in Middle Eastern studies. Not everyone agreed with his theories; his strongest critic and debating partner was famed historian Bernard Lewis. Prior to Said's emergence, most people in academia looked to Lewis, the world famous chairman of the Middle East Studies Department at Princeton (now emeritus) and the father of Middle Eastern Studies, as well as a leading expert on Islam. Prof. Lewis speaks and reads English, Arabic, Hebrew, Turkish, Pharsi and Pashtu, served in the Middle East throughout World War II as a British Army intelligence officer, and spent years researching original documents throughout the Middle East. His insights and data he presented were all apolitical and not fueled by any agenda.

The same could not be said of Said who was a member of the Palestinian National Committee and a friend of Yasser Arafat. Many people believe he developed his agenda before writing *Orientalism* and that he bent and tortured the facts to fit his preconceived narrative. As such, Said claimed that all Middle Eastern historians and experts who did not understand and accept his *Orientalism* were bigoted, prejudiced, anti-Islam and anti-Arab because they were European (or American) with a Judaeo-Christian frame of reference. In his opinion, European scholars had a "Crusader" view of the Arab and Islamic world and viewed Arabs and Muslims as the "other"—dangerous, savage, wild; in need of taming and being controlled. In addition, the European/Christian view saw the Islamic and Arab world controlling Christianity's holy sites in the Holy Land when these areas should have been under Christian control, and he accused the West of plundering Middle Eastern natural resources, i.e., oil.

To complete his version of looking at the Middle East, Said "explained" that Israel and Zionism fit into his new overarching view of Middle East Studies when, in the late 19th century, naked, direct imperialism became embarrassing for the Western powers. According to him, they therefore conspired to create a phony "nationalist movement" ostensibly representing an indigenous people who were interested in re-establishing their homeland in the heart of the Arab and Islamic world. That movement, he wrote, was Zionism.[4]

Said said it was the reason the British Empire was pro-Zionist and why the other European powers, as well as the United States, supported it. He said it was a brilliant plan, in essence, to continue Western rule and control of the dangerous Arab and Islamic Middle East through a phony proxy movement.[5]

As Avner Shalit noted,

> ...Professor Edward Said and his students caused indescribable damage to the ability to think or speak the truth when it comes to the Arab world. Their wacky intellectual legacy did not permit talking about the region's residents as anything but victims. The grand Arab nation—with its rich history, profound culture and considerable economic power—was treated like a juvenile who isn't responsible for his actions. So all the ills of Arab politics were attributed to others—imperialists, colonialists, Zionists. So no real criticism of the Arab world was permitted and no one demanded it mend itself.[6]

Said died in 2003. Rashid Ismail Khalidi, a native New Yorker born to Palestinian parents, and who was educated at Yale and earned his Ph.D. at Oxford, is now the Edward Said Professor of Modern Arab Studies at Columbia and director of the Middle East Institute of Columbia's School of International and Public Affairs. He is also editor of the *Journal of Palestine Studies* and a member of the Council on Foreign Relations and the National Advisory Committee of the U.S. Interreligious Committee for Peace in the Middle East. He was teaching at the American University in Beirut in 1982 when the war broke out, and was thought to be a spokesman for the PLO, but denies that.

Khalidi shares Said's view of the colonial influences in Middle Eastern policy. In *Palestinian Identity: The Construction of Modern National Consciousness* (1997), he places the emergence of Palestinian national identity in the context of Ottoman and British colonialism as well as the early Zionist effort in the Levant, arguing that Arabs living in Palestine began to regard themselves as a distinct people decades before 1948, "and that the struggle against Zionism does not by itself sufficiently explain Palestinian nationalism."[7]

He is sharply critical of U.S. policies during the Cold War, writing that Cold War policies "formulated to oppose the Soviets, consistently undermined democracy and exacerbated tensions in the Middle East."[8] Khalidi has written, "It may seem hard to believe today, but for decades the United States was in fact a major patron, indeed in some respects the major patron, of earlier incarnations" of radical, militant Islam, in order to use all possible resources in waging the Cold War. He adds, "The Cold War was over, but its tragic sequels, its toxic debris, and its unexploded mines continued to cause great harm, in ways largely unrecognized in American discourse."[9]

Michael Oren, Israel's former ambassador to the United States and an historian, admitted that "Khalidi is mainstream" because "the stream itself has changed. The criteria for scholarship have become very political."[10]

Said's disciples now dominate most university Middle Eastern Studies Departments and influence many political science and history professors. They help explain the "compelling images" of Palestinians or Arabs being "brutalized" by the media to their gullible, uninformed students and to the many media outlets who rely on them as their Middle Eastern "experts."

Sadly, the overwhelming majority of university students, including most Jewish graduates of yeshiva high schools and day schools, do not have the historical or ideological backgrounds to respond or challenge what have become the mainstream views on many U.S. campuses. They already are the only view in almost all western European universities.

As someone who has been involved in educating Jewish youth formally and informally since 1978—in classrooms, weekend retreats, Israel advocacy training programs and tours to Israel—I can ask the question as to how many Jewish institutions have taken the time and effort to teach the Jewish historical and religious connection to *Eretz Yisrael?* How many Jewish institutions have taken the time to teach, in detail, the history of modern Zionism to our youth and community since the 1970s? The sad answer, I believe, is very few.

Hence, many Jewish university students are incapable of responding to the outlandish charges made against Israel and Zionism. Many American Jewish teens hear about Israel and they think of occupation, war, conflict, human rights violations, apartheid, check points, etc. Those are the "compelling images" and "terms" they have been watching and hearing about their entire lives, and that's what their professors of Middle Eastern Studies have taught (or will teach) them, so who can blame them?

The Jewish community has unwittingly given all of Israel's detractors, defamers and enemies an open field to play on. This has had a very deleterious effect on Israel's image and on the views held by a growing number of Jewish high school graduates, including those from yeshiva high schools and day schools.

FOOTNOTES

[1] Norman Podhoretz, *Why Are Jews Liberals?* (NY: Vintage Books, 2010), 1ff.

[2] Marshall Sklar, *America's Jews* (Waltham, MA: Brandeis University Press, 1971), 3ff.

[3] *Ibid.*, 110 ff; Edward S. Shapiro, *A Time For Healing* (Baltimore, MD: The John Hopkins University Press, 1992), 1ff.

[4] Edward Said, *The Question of Palestine* (NY: Vintage Books, 1980), 12-13, 63-70, 82.

[5] *Ibid.*

[6] Ari Shavit, "The Time Has Come to Open Our Eyes to the Arab Disaster," *Ha'aretz*, Sept. 11, 2015 (http://www.haaretz.com/opinion/.premium-1.675412?date=1441978762222).

[7] Evan R. Goldstein, "Rashid Khalidi's Balancing Act: The Middle-East scholar courts controversy with his Palestinian advocacy," *Chronicle of Higher Education* (March 6, 2009)(http://lists.econ.utah.edu/pipermail/marxism/2009-March/045483.html).

[8] *Ibid.*

[9] Rashid Khalidi, *Sowing Crisis: the Cold War and American Dominance in the Middle East* (Boston, MA: Beacon Press, 2009), 34.

[10] *Op. cit.*

Chapter 1

Defining Zionism

Zionism is Jewish nationalism or the national liberation movement of the Jewish nation. Nathan Birnbaum (1864-1937), co-founder in 1882 of "Kadimah," the first organization of Jewish nationalist students in the West, coined the words *Zionist* and *Zionism* in 1890. Its general definition means the national movement for the return of the Jewish people to their homeland and the resumption of Jewish sovereignty in the Land of Israel. Since the establishment of the State of Israel in 1948, Zionism has come to include the movement for the development of the State of Israel and the protection of the Jewish nation in Israel through support for the Israel Defense Forces (IDF).[1]

Only nations experience nationalism. To understand Zionism one must understand Judaism and the relationship Jews have with *Eretz Yisrael.* It is also important to understand why the Jews are a nation and how Judaism is one of the oldest forms of nationalism in recorded history.

In the Bible, the Jews are referred to as *Am Yisrael,* the Nation of Israel. This is at the heart of understanding what Judaism is and why Jews are inextricably linked to the Bible and to *Eretz Yisrael.* And it is the definition of Judaism that lies at the heart of the conflict between Jewish Zionists and non- and anti-Zionists. Most anti-Zionists, with the exception of certain Orthodox groups who have textual and spiritual issues with Modern Zionism but not "Torah Zionism"—the expressions of Zion in the Tanach— consider Judaism a religion and not a national identity.* The position of the anti-Zionist/anti-Israel camp is that the Jews are but a religious group and thus have no right to run their own state (which seems to fly in the face of an acknowledged Catholic city-state called the Vatican or Islam's dominance of Saudi Arabia). Article 20 of the Palestine Liberation Organization (PLO) Charter was written in 1968 and despite the 1993 Oslo Agreements crystallizes the anti-Zionist position:

> The Balfour Declaration, the Mandate of Palestine, and everything that has been based upon them, are deemed null and void. Claims of historical or religious ties of Jews with Palestine are incompatible with the facts of history and the true conception of what constitutes statehood. Judaism, being a religion, is not an independent nationality. Nor do Jews constitute a single nation with an identity of its own; they are citizens of the states to which they belong.[2]

The authors of the PLO Charter understood very well that the crux of the conflict rests on how one defines Judaism. If Judaism has a nationalistic component to it, and the Jews are a nation, they deserve a state of their own. But if they are "merely" a religion, then Jews should be happy to be citizens of the states in which they live (though Jewish history is replete with Jews being uprooted from the lands in which they lived whenever indigenous religious fervor and economic expediency mandated their expulsion).

---

*Even some Jews posited this position. The Reform Jewish movement, a form of Judaism initiated in Germany by the philosopher Moses Mendelssohn (1729-86), reformed or abandoned aspects of Orthodox Jewish worship and ritual in an attempt to adapt to modern changes in social, political and cultural life. This was as a direct result of the Emancipation led by Napoleon Bonaparte in France, which removed restrictions on the Jewish people living among the French. Other European nations soon followed. Mendelssohn, considered a heretic by his former Orthodox co-religionists, regarded Judaism as a religion, not as a nation. Relevant to Zionism and *Eretz Yisrael*, the movement would state in its 1885 Pittsburgh Platform:

Z ionism and Judaism are intertwined in the texts that make up the main sources of the religion: The Tanach/Jewish Bible (Old Testament); the Mishna, the Torah passed down from Sinai and the oral law written down from the first century B.C.E. until its codification in the 2nd century C.E., and the Talmud, completed in the 6th century C.E. containing Jewish Law/*Halakha*, which explains the Mishna in great detail. Scholars agree that the Jewish Bible is at the very least 2,100 years old—the age of the Dead Sea Scrolls. The same is true of Judaism. It is defined by looking at ancient Jewish sources and studying Jewish history and Jewish archaeology, all still relevant to millions of Jews today.

> We recognize, in the modern era of universal culture of heart and intellect, the approaching of the realization of Israel's great Messianic hope for the establishment of the kingdom of truth, justice, and peace among all men. We consider ourselves no longer a nation, but a religious community, and therefore expect neither a return to Palestine, nor a sacrificial worship under the sons of Aaron, nor the restoration of any of the laws concerning the Jewish state. (Central Conference of American Rabbis (ccarnet.org/rabbis-speak/platforms/declaration-principles/ (CCAR ed. 2014)

It would not be until the Union for Reform Judaism's 1937 Columbus Platform that a more nuanced endorsement of Zionism would be promulgated in response to pro-Zionist population shifts and the rise of fascist antisemitism:

> In all lands where our people live, they assume and seek to share loyally the full duties and responsibilities of citizenship and to create seats of Jewish knowledge and religion. In the rehabilitation of Palestine, the land hallowed by memories and hopes, we behold the promise of renewed life for many of our brethren. We affirm the obligation of all Jewry to aid in its upbuilding as a Jewish homeland by endeavoring to make it not only a haven of refuge for the oppressed but also a center of Jewish culture and spiritual life. (http://www.jewishvirtuallibrary.org/the-columbus-platform-1937)

Prior to the Six-Day War, Reform support for Zionism was lukewarm, but after the war its proponents fully joined the Zionist community and supported *Eretz Yisrael.*

Carefully studying the Five Books of Moses—the first five books of the Bible—one discovers that Judaism is a way of life covering all aspects of a person's existence. There is no distinction between religious life and non-religious life. The texts offer a blueprint for living to the individual and to the collective/national community.

Thus Judaism operates on three levels, as three concentric circles (like a bullseye) wherein each circle takes up more space and covers more areas of a Jewish individual's life and identity.

Level I – The Religious Level

The first level or circle in Judaism is the one that deals with the religious aspect.

Judaism has 613 commandments/laws/*mitzvot* centered on the belief in the one unseen, omnipresent, omnipotent God (*Hashem*), and how Jews worship Him. Many of these *mitzvot* deal with the *Mishkan/Beit HaMikdash* (Tabernacle/Temple) and everything connected to it: lifecycle rituals, prayers, holidays, religious garb and the Sabbath. There are also more religious-oriented commandments connected to the *Kohanim* (priests) who ran the Temple, those connected to the Sabbath and the Jewish holidays, those kept by Jews in their daily routines outside of the Temple and *mitzvot* directly connected to the Land of Israel. All of these together are the basis of Judaism, a very intricate and detailed religion.

Level II – The Social Level

Judaism also addresses rules for personal modesty, dress, body function, diet and behavior that have nothing to do with the performance of ritual, lifecycles, holidays, Sabbath, going to Temple, or being a priest or rabbi. These laws are meant for regular Jews leading their daily, routine lives. For example, matzo is connected to Passover and the matzo-eating Seder ritual, a religious dietary commandment that must be obeyed on Passover, although matzo can be eaten as normal food during the rest of the year.

Keeping kosher, a different commandment, means a Jew adheres to a specific diet which has no connection to specific holidays or rituals and is a law that must be followed daily. For example, one may never eat pork or shell fish, or mix milk products with meat products.

There are also laws regulating an individual's behavior in family settings, in business and in community affairs that have nothing to do with religious ritual. The Jewish people, for example, are asked to emulate God's behavior by behaving compassionately. The rabbis realized this when studying the texts where God clothes Adam and Eve; comforting Abraham in his illness; comforting Isaac at the death of Abraham, and comforting Moses as he died. These are only a few of the many examples of God's compassion in the Bible from which we learn that Judaism does not want us to simply think about compassion, it wants us to act compassionately and thereby emulate one of God's attributes.

Level III – The Nationalistic Level

The Torah, most notably the book of Deuteronomy (*Devarim*), is the basis for a constitution for running a Jewish State. In the Torah and the Talmud one will find a) criminal law, b) property law, c) liability law, d) business law, e) family law, f) rules regarding social welfare, g) governance and h) military law. They are laws meant to be kept by a society that runs its own state, laws for a Jewish republic. More than half of the 613 *mitzvot* are connected in one way or another to *Eretz Yisrael*. The following are the key five categories:

a) *Mitzvot* connected in any way to the Jewish Temple (*Beit HaMikdash*) which must be built in Jerusalem. This category includes the construction itself, the items found in the Temple—menorah, altars, etc., clothing and ornaments that the *Kohanim* wear—the many different types of sacrifices, and the pilgrimages to the Temple that all Jews are obligated to make at least three times a year (*aliya la regel*).

b) *Mitzvot* connected to the governing of a Jewish State: laws connected to kings and their responsibilities and privileges; military laws, tax laws, and the social welfare system only applicable in *Eretz Yisrael.*

c) *Mitzvot* connected to the Jewish court system, known as the *Sanhedrin*, which only apply in *Eretz Yisrael*. Every city had a *Sanhedrin* of 23 judges, and in Jerusalem there was the Grand *Sanhedrin* of 71 (the supreme court). The *Sanhedrin* system was entrusted with enforcing Jewish law throughout *Eretz Yisrael,* religious law and all aspects of Jewish law. These courts appointed prosecutors and defense attorneys.

d) *Mitzvot* dealing with purity—that includes dealing with purifying a person who has come into contact with a dead person, or with something impure that needs to go through a special "cleansing process" involving the *Kohanim* in the Temple in Jerusalem. All these laws are only applicable in Jerusalem.

e) Agricultural *mitzvot* applicable only in *Eretz Yisrael*. For example, there is *Shmita*—leaving the fields fallow once every seven years—the bringing of the new wheat harvest to the Temple called the *Omer*, or the bringing of fruits and vegetables to Jerusalem in the spring season, known as *Bikurim.*

If one adds up all of these commandments together they comprise more than half of the 613 that make up the canon of Jewish law. That is not a coincidence. By definition, Israel sits at the center of the biblical definition of what Judaism ought to be.

Shas/Mishna and Talmud also give us a sense of how central a role *Eretz Yisrael* plays in Judaism. The *Shas* is divided into six main sections. Each section deals with a different category of Jewish Law. Three of the sections are: *Zeraim*: agriculture; *Kadoshim*: sacrifices in the Temple, and *Taharot*, purification and other rituals connected to the Temple. With the exception of a tiny fraction of *Zeraim*, they are all connected to *Eretz Yisrael*. Of the remaining three sections, *Moed*, Jewish holidays; *Nizikin*, criminal, property, liability, contractual, labor, and the enforcing of religious law, and *Nashim*, family law, only *Nashim* can be kept by Jews, in its entirety, outside of Israel. Since *Moed* deals with Jewish holidays, and, by definition, has many laws that are connected to sacrifices and rituals that are connected either to the Temple or to Jerusalem itself, the majority of its laws are connected to *Eretz Yisrael*. *Nizikin*, which deals with the application of Jewish law throughout the Jewish Republic, the ordination of rabbis, and deciding when the lunar month begins (which sits at the heart of the Jewish calendar) among many other topics, all depend on the existence of the *Sanhedrin*. This entire court system can only exist in *Eretz Yisrael*.

Halakha (Written Law) mirrors the position of the Torah when it comes to the centrality of *Eretz Yisrael* in the implementation of Judaism. Thus, more than 70 percent of the Talmud deals with Jewish laws that are related to *Eretz Yisrael*. The Judaism described in the Torah and the Talmud is one that operates on a national level as a functioning nation state, a state with a Jewish government, army, court system, welfare and tax structure.

If one examines the Bible, the Mishna, the Talmud, the Rambam's *Yad Hachazaka* (written in the 12th century C.E. and the first complete compilation of all the laws found in the Talmud) and the *Shulchan Aruch* (written in the 16th century and practiced in the post-Temple era), clearly "authentic Judaism" can only be fully implemented when there is a Jewish State/National Home functioning in *Eretz Yisrael*.

The boundaries of Israel are readily found in the book of Genesis. The most specific geographic lesson in the Torah is in the 34th chapter of *Bamidbar*/Exodus in the chapter *Mas'a'ey*. The boundaries of Israel start at the bottom of the Dead Sea and move clockwise—spelled out over 12 verses in the chapter. There can be no mistake that the Torah does not see Judaism implemented in its entirety in any piece of real estate that the Jews happen to control other than in the holy boundaries of Israel.

The best definition for Judaism is that it is an all-encompassing way of life both for the individual and the nation based on the laws set forth in the Torah and the Talmud. Judaism and running a Jewish State go hand in hand. No one can re-define Judaism to fit his personal philosophy—he can observe it differently, but he cannot negate the basics as defined in the Torah. People who are against the right of the Jewish people to have a sovereign state are by definition going against the teachings of Judaism.[3]

Footnotes

[1] "Zionism" (https://www.jewishvirtuallibrary.org/jsource Zionism/zionism.html).
[2] "The Palestinian Charter" (http://www.pac-usa.org/the_palestinian_charter.htm)
[3] Many of Israel's foes love to point to Satmar Hasidim, who are known to be against the modern state of Israel. But Satmar Hasidim are not against the teachings of Judaism. They fully believe that *Eretz Yisrael* sits at the center of Jewish life. But because of their interpretation of a particular section of the Talmud in the tractate of *Ketubot* (Page 110 side B and Page 111 Side A) they do not believe that now is the right time to claim rightful sovereignty and are waiting for the Messiah before reclaiming sovereignty over *Eretz Yisrael*. The critics of Zionism, on the other hand, take the position that *Eretz Yisrael* was never, and should never be, the homeland of the Jews. The Satmar position is that *Eretz Yisrael* was a Jewish Republic in the past (in Biblical times) and will be again in the future (in Messianic times), but Jews should not establish a Jewish Republic in the present. This view is a minority view in the Orthodox world.

It should be further noted and clarified that the fringe group known as the Neturei Karta that demonstrates in front of AIPAC conferences, the New York Israel Day Parade, and has met with Iranian, Hamas, and PLO leaders while dressed in Hasidic garb, are considered beyond the pale even by Satmar Hasidim, since they literally give aid and comfort to enemies of the Jewish people.

Chapter 2

The Jewish Nation

The Jewish people are more than members of a religion, they are part of the Jewish nation. But what exactly is a nation? Different political scientists have different definitions, and over the last seventy years that definition has been in flux.

Prof. Béla Király, the renowned chairman of the history department at Brooklyn College (retired emeritus, 1982), taught that the definition of a nation is a group with a common language (preferably distinct); a common culture (preferably distinct), and a common land of origin—a location on Earth where a particular group developed its language and culture, and where this culture and language were dominant. It is a definition applied in the real world. The United Nations (UN) was founded in 1945 with approximately sixty founding nation-states; as of 2015 there are 193, and that number will no doubt climb as different national groups come forward and aspire to their own sovereignty.

Finally, common land of origin means where a people set up their state and ruled. In essence, one should be able to point to a map and through archaeology and historical documents show a distinct people coming from a certain place, and that their culture dominated and left an imprint on that geographical area. Earning sovereignty demonstrates proof of a history in a particular region. The nation of Israel, *Am Yisrael*, indisputably meets these criteria (despite the rhetoric of its enemies).

THE JEWS HAVE A COMMON LANGUAGE

Hebrew is the exclusive language of the Jewish nation that has been spoken and written for over 3,000 years. Today's "modern" Hebrew script is at least 2,100 years old and is the same alphabet used in the Dead Sea Scrolls. During the Biblical period when Jews had either independence or semi-independence—as Jewish republics ruled by Jewish governments—for close to fourteen centuries the official language of the Jewish people was Hebrew, the sacred language that bound the Israelites together, and was so much a part of their identity as a people that, in ancient times, Israelites were often called Hebrews.

Hebrew stayed as the major language of the Israelites until the various diasporas they underwent made Aramaic and, to a lesser extent Greek, the lingua franca of the day. And so, by the first century, the Jewish community was basically a three language community.

Still, when the Jews lost their independence, following the Bar Kochba Revolt in 135 CE, they did something remarkable: They kept Hebrew alive even though they no longer had sovereignty and were globally dispersed. This was because centuries earlier the center of Jewish life was transferred from the Temple to the synagogue and the yeshiva when Ezra the Scribe returned to Jerusalem from Babylon after the first dispersion and made Torah the center of Jewish life. When the Israelites began reading the Torah weekly in their local community synagogues (which replaced the Temple in Jerusalem), Hebrew was kept alive as the official language. It was used in the liturgy as well—the *Siddur* (Prayer Book) was written in Hebrew (nearly 2,000 years ago) and Hebrew became the language of Jewish study and scholarship. Since the time of Ezra, and everywhere in the Jewish Diaspora, Jews in Europe, Asia, Africa, North America, South America and Australia have taught their children to read and write Hebrew.

For almost 2,000 years, with the exception of the Talmud (written in Hebrew and Aramaic), almost all Jewish legal books and rabbinical *responsa* (a body of written decisions and rulings given by legal scholars in response to questions addressed to them) have been written in Hebrew. Until the Enlightenment and the emancipation of the Jews in Western Europe, all Jewish males (and a few females) were sent to *cheder* in early childhood to learn to read and write Hebrew. Thus, for millennia, Hebrew has been the undisputed language of the Jewish nation and knowledge of that language was necessary if one wished to be considered a literate Jew. As a result, if a Dutch Jewish businessman found himself traveling to Morocco in the 17th century to buy spices, he could converse with members of the local Jewish community and draw up documents in Hebrew that would be understood by Jews in Holland and in Morocco.* He could also pray in their synagogues and eat their kosher food.

THE JEWS HAVE A COMMON CULTURE

Judaism is a total way of life that includes a Biblical constitution, a calendar, special language, literature, a set of laws and customs, diet, dress codes and lifecycle ceremonies. All of these things, developed over five millennia, give Judaism its own culture. At the heart of this culture are the Torah and the Oral Law, and while the ancient Israelites, the ancestors of today's Jewish people, had customs similar to their neighbors, their covenant with the One God (*Hashem*) set them apart and created the Jewish people.

The Jewish Constitution

The Israelites' relationship to *Hashem* was based on a covenant binding God and Israel through a series of obligations. It is why the Bible draws a direct correlation between the patriarchs' prosperity and their fidelity to Him and why *Yitziat Mizraim*/the Exodus is conditional on obeying God—and why it describes the misfortunes that befell the Israelites as a result of failures to

---

* It should be mentioned that both Sephardic and Ashkenazic Jewish communities developed secondary languages. The European Ashkenazim spoke Yiddish, and the African/Eastern Sephardim spoke Ladino. Both these languages are still spoken in their respective communities, but both communities study and pray in the common Jewish language, Hebrew.

comply with terms of the Torah. The Torah/Constitution is the covenant of the Jewish people with *Hashem*.[1]

As historian Daniel J. Elazar states,

> ...[T]he book of Deuteronomy, known in Hebrew as *Devarim* (words or utterances; here best translated statements or stated laws), is Israel's ancient constitution. If it is indeed of Mosaic authorship as it is presented to be, it is certainly the oldest complete constitution in our possession, dating from the thirteenth or fourteenth century BCE. Even if it is younger than that, from as late as the time of Josiah (seventh century BCE), it still is a most venerable document. Those theories that claim an even later origin for it still place it in the period of the classic Greek constitutions.* Thus it, along with the Constitution of Athens,** are the two oldest such documents available to students of government and politics.[2]

Elazar maintains that Chapter 27 of Deuteronomy provides for writing everything down once the Israelites are in their land and quotes Chapter 28 (v. 69): "These are the words of the Covenant which the Lord commanded Moses to make with the Israelites in the land of Moab beside the Covenant he made with them at Horeb." Moses then makes a concluding summation of the covenant with its promises and obligations (Ch. 29-31), concluding with the formal designation of Joshua as his successor, the writing of the constitution and its placement in the Ark of the Covenant, and the provision for a public ceremony to renew the covenant

---

*For the various theories dating Deuteronomy, see: G.R. Berry, "Date of Deuteronomy," *Journal of Biblical Literature and Exgesis*, LIX (1940), 133-139; George Dahl, "The Currently Accepted Date of Deuteronomy," *Journal of Biblical Literature*, XLVII (1928), 358-379; M. Margolis, *Hebrew Scriptures in the Making* (Philadelphia: Jewish Publication Society,1922).

**On the Constitution of Athens, see Ernest Barker, *Greek Political Theory: Plato and His Predecessors* (New York: Barnes and Noble, 1960); Aristotle, *The Athenian Constitution, the Eemian Ethics, on Virtues and Vices*. Translated by Harris Rackman (Cambridge: Harvard University Press, 1981).

every seven years at the end of the sabbatical year during Sukkoth
(the Feast of Tabernacles).[3]

> [Moses] writes out the Torah and delivers it to priests, Levites,
> and elders; he establishes a covenant renewal ceremony to take
> place every seven years; God ratifies all this and the written
> Torah is placed in the Ark of the Covenant alongside of the
> commandments. Moses then presents his elaborate poem
> known as the Song of Moses, along with a final exhortation
> to the people to keep the commandments and to be faithful to
> their constitution (Chapter 32). In Chapter 33 he blesses the
> Bnei Israel before his death collectively and tribe by tribe. In
> Chapter 34 his death is described, as is Joshua's assumption of
> power. The book and the whole Pentateuch is closed with an
> evaluation of Moses' greatness and uniqueness as a prophet.[4]

Elazar concludes:

> The Book of *Devarim*, in sum, is presented as a covenant. The
> term itself is used in one-third (11 of 34) of its chapters and
> is implicitly present in virtually all of the others. It follows
> the standard formula: a historical prologue, a statement of
> responsibilities, specific provisions, blessings and curses
> with regard to its maintenance or violation, and a covenant
> ceremony accepting it with provisions for similar ceremonies
> for its periodic renewal.[5]

The Torah, the covenant and constitution, was a document
designed as the antithesis of the laws and practices of the cultures
surrounding the Israelites. Idol worship and human sacrifice
were banned. Whereas pagans worshipped many gods, Torah
laws commanded the belief in the One God. In addition, many
laws were written as the opposite of practices in the surrounding
cultures. For example, the Code of Hammurabi, in discussing
fertility rites, instructs that a goat must be cooked in its mother's
milk. The law in the Torah, in the section on fertility rites, makes it
explicitly clear the opposite is required: "Thou shalt NOT cook a
goat in its mother's milk."

By creating an operational norm via constitution and convenant, the Torah set the Israelites apart, established the Jewish religion and created a new, Israelite culture. Thus, when people in the ancient world traveled to Israel from Phoenicia or Egypt, they knew they were entering a country with a distinct and different culture, a culture able to withstand the destruction of the first Holy Temple in Jerusalem and the exile to Babylon, a portable culture that was able rebuild itself and that has endured through the ages.

Other Aspects of Jewish Culture

The official calendar of Israel was the Jewish calendar, and the Jewish holidays were the official state holidays. Jewish holidays, no matter where they are celebrated, are based on the seasons in Israel.

Jewish dress was based on laws of modesty. They wore specific items of clothing—like the fringed garment for men called *tzizit*. The arrival of the Greco-Roman empires marked the first concerted effort by a ruling party to impose their own culture upon the Jews. This culture, known as Hellenism, advocated physical beauty, arts and sciences and organized itself around the *polis* (city). This intervention in Jewish life led to revolts and to Jewish dispersal. But the Jews did not forget who they were and were often called "The People of the Book."

Jews in the diaspora taught their children to read and write Hebrew, and opened up special *yeshivot* (Jewish schools) and *mikvaot* (ritual baths) in their communities throughout the diaspora.

To keep the rules of *kashrut*, Jews all over the world had their own bakers, butchers, fishmongers and inns.

Sabbath was observed in places as disparate as Poland and Morocco.

All Jews studied the same Torah, the same Talmud and commentaries.

In every synagogue, the Ark that holds the Torah scrolls always faces toward Jerusalem. In Egypt, the arks were placed on a northern wall, in Syria on a southern one. In Persia they faced west and in Europe and America, they faced east. Many of the daily prayers mention Israel, Jerusalem and the ingathering of the exiles. Jews around the world have been praying for rain in Israel since the destruction of the Second Temple in 70 CE. And to remember the past, and hearken to Jerusalem, virtually all Jewish wedding ceremonies end with the groom breaking a glass to commemorate the destruction of the Holy Temples.

JEWS AND THE LAND OF ISRAEL

For the first three centuries, the Israelite State established by Joshua did not have a centralized monarchy. Governance was in the hands of judges, beginning with Joshua and ending with Samuel, who was also a prophet. During this time the Israelites were the majority of the population in *Eretz Yisrael* and their religion, culture, laws and language prevailed.

While the Israelites were still in the desert, after they received the Ten Commandments, they were commanded by God to build the *Mishkan* (also known as the Ark of the Covenant), the portable Tabernacle in which God resided with the Tablets of the Law. God spoke to the people and received their sacrifices at the *Mishkan*. Eventually, the *Mishkan* would be located inside the Temple, in the Holy of Holies. For almost 300 years, the *Mishkan* stood in Shilo, a city in Samaria, until King Solomon, son of King David, built the first Temple in Jerusalem, ca. 950 BCE, and placed it in the Holy of Holies at the center of the Temple.

The main enemies of Israel during this period were the Philistines (*Pelishtim*), a sea-faring people from the Aegean Sea near Greece who brought their culture and language with them. They conquered the southern coast of Canaan around 2,000 BCE and established a kingdom there that lasted until around 722 BCE, when the Assyrians swept into the area and destroyed most nations in their way. The Philistines ruled a fifteen mile-wide area that ran from what is today El Arish to Ashkelon. They were literally wiped out or exiled by the Assyrians and ceased to exist after the 8th century BCE.[6]

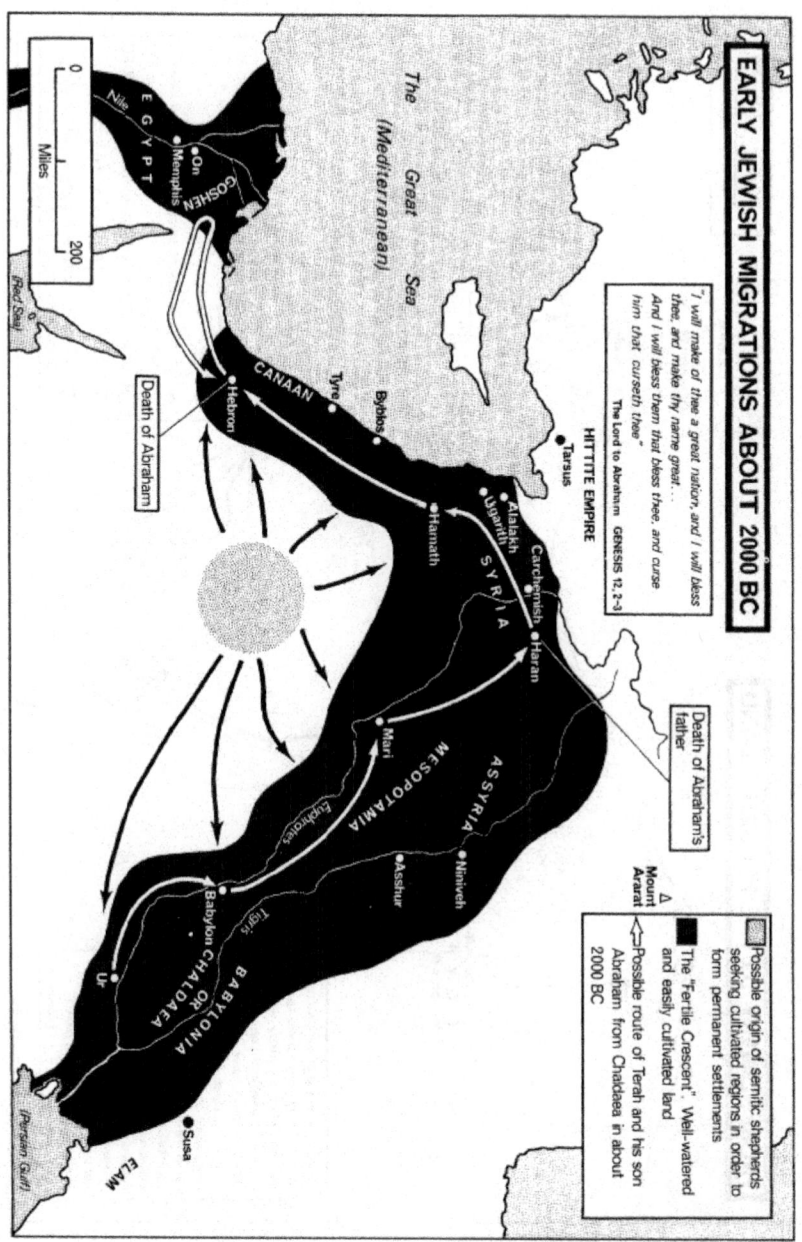

EARLY JEWISH MIGRATIONS ABOUT 2000 BC

Sir Martin Gilbert, © 2010. Reproduced by permission of Taylor
& Francis Books UK. www.martingilbert.com

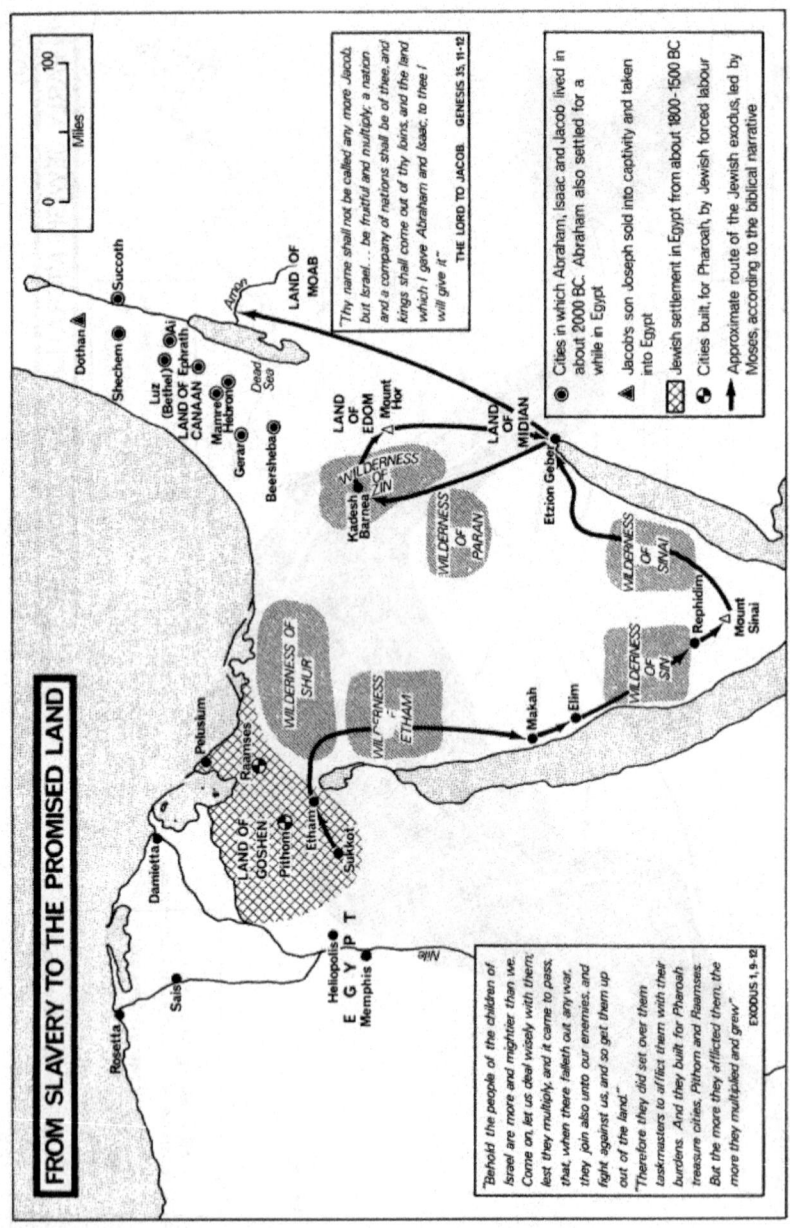

FROM SLAVERY TO THE PROMISED LAND

"Thy name shall not be called any more Jacob, but Israel... be fruitful and multiply; a nation and a company of nations shall be of thee, and kings shall come out of thy loins; and the land which I gave Abraham and Isaac, to thee I will give it."   THE LORD TO JACOB.   GENESIS 35, 11-12

● Cities in which Abraham, Isaac and Jacob lived in about 2000 BC. Abraham also settled for a while in Egypt

▲ Jacob's son Joseph sold into captivity and taken into Egypt

▨ Jewish settlement in Egypt from about 1800-1500 BC

◉ Cities built, for Pharoah by Jewish forced labour

→ Approximate route of the Jewish exodus, led by Moses, according to the biblical narrative

"Behold! the people of the children of Israel are more and mightier than we. Come on, let us deal wisely with them; lest they multiply, and it came to pass, that, when there falleth out any war, they join also unto our enemies, and fight against us, and so get them up out of the land"

"Therefore they did set over them taskmasters to afflict them with their burdens. And they built for Pharoah treasure cities, Pithom and Raamses: But the more they afflicted them, the more they multiplied and grew."   EXODUS 1, 9-12

Sir Martin Gilbert, © 2010. Reproduced by permission of Taylor & Francis Books UK. www.martingilbert.com

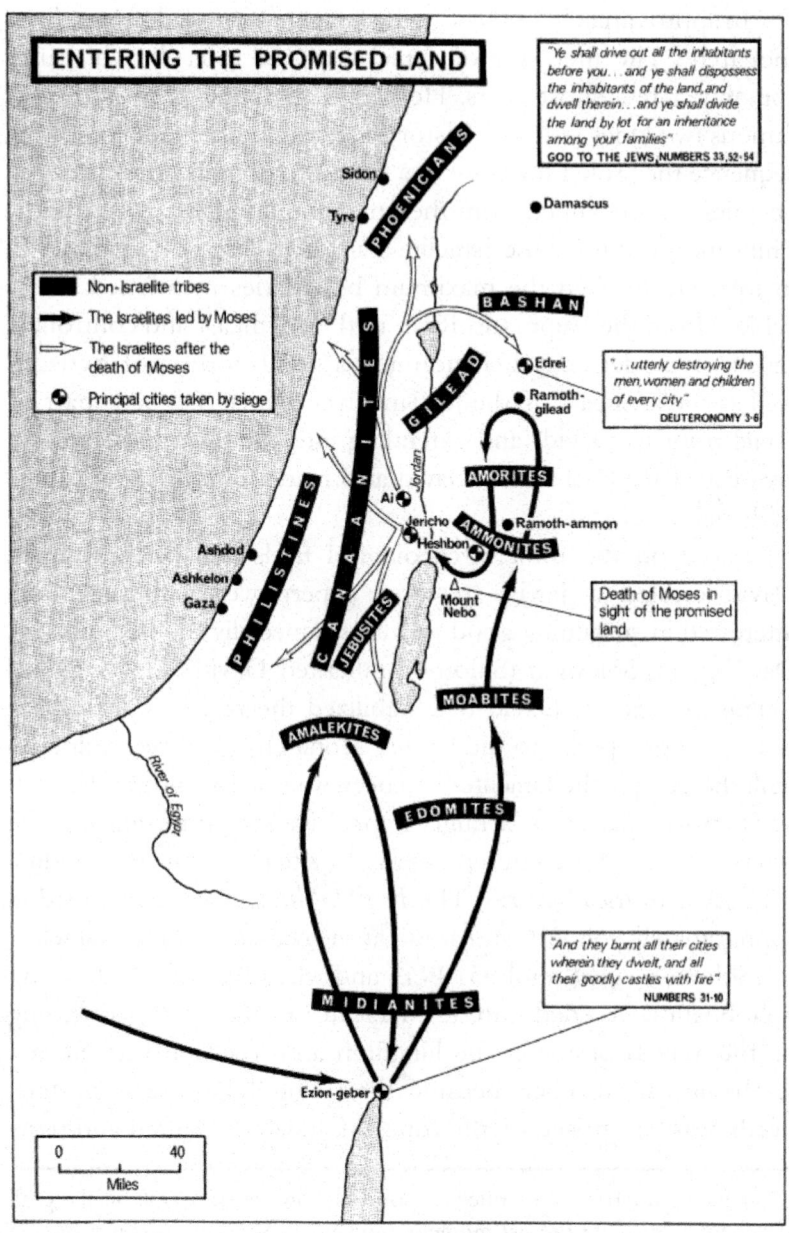

ENTERING THE PROMISED LAND

"Ye shall drive out all the inhabitants before you... and ye shall dispossess the inhabitants of the land, and dwell therein... and ye shall divide the land by lot for an inheritance among your families"
GOD TO THE JEWS, NUMBERS 33,52-54

Non-Israelite tribes
The Israelites led by Moses
The Israelites after the death of Moses
Principal cities taken by siege

"...utterly destroying the men, women and children of every city"
DEUTERONOMY 3-6

Death of Moses in sight of the promised land

"And they burnt all their cities wherein they dwelt, and all their goodly castles with fire"
NUMBERS 31-10

0   40
Miles

Sir Martin Gilbert, © 2010. Reproduced by permission of Taylor & Francis Books UK. www.martingilbert.com

In approximately 1,000 BCE, the Israelites founded a centralized monarchy. The first king of Israel was Saul (Sha'ul), who ruled for only a few short years. He was then followed by the most famous two kings in Jewish history, David and his son Solomon. In sequence they ruled for close to a century. King David vanquished enemies that remained from the time of the Judges, including the Philistines, and grew the Israelite state to its largest boundaries in history. He reached the maximum boundaries mentioned in the Bible—from the Euphrates River in the northeast and controlling much of modern-day Lebanon and a good portion of Syria, as well as the area east of the Jordan River (which had been part of Israel prior to David) and extending into the Sinai Desert to an area called Wadi El Arish. David also made Jerusalem the capital of Israel.[7]

Based on the Bible, archeological finds and other sources, David created a Jewish regional superpower with neighbors interested in sustaining good relations, especially the Phoenicians. David's son, Solomon (Shlomo), inherited David's kingdom and fought no wars as David had stabilized the region and brought peace and prosperity to the United Monarchy of Israel. Solomon built the Temple the Israelites had been waiting for and the *Mishkan* in Shilo was placed in a huge, impressive structure built on the top of Mount Moriah in Jerusalem, the site of Abraham's binding of Isaac centuries before.* The *Beit HaMikdash* was completed in approximately 950 BCE and stood at the center of united Israel.

Solomon ruled until 931 BCE, and when his son, Rechavom/Rehoboam succeeded him, the Israelites in the north, consisting of the Ten Tribes, split the kingdom and Yeravam ben Nevat/Jeroboam, his brother, became their king. The southern state, Judah, was comprised of the tribes of Judah, Benjamin and parts

---

*God asked Abraham to sacrifice his son Isaac on top of a rock on the peak of Mount Moriah. At the last moment, God asked Abraham to switch his son with a ram, and Isaac's life was saved. His mother, Sara, died of shock when she heard what happened, and Abraham then bought the Cave of the Patriarchs in Hebron/Chevron so that she could be buried properly inside the cave.

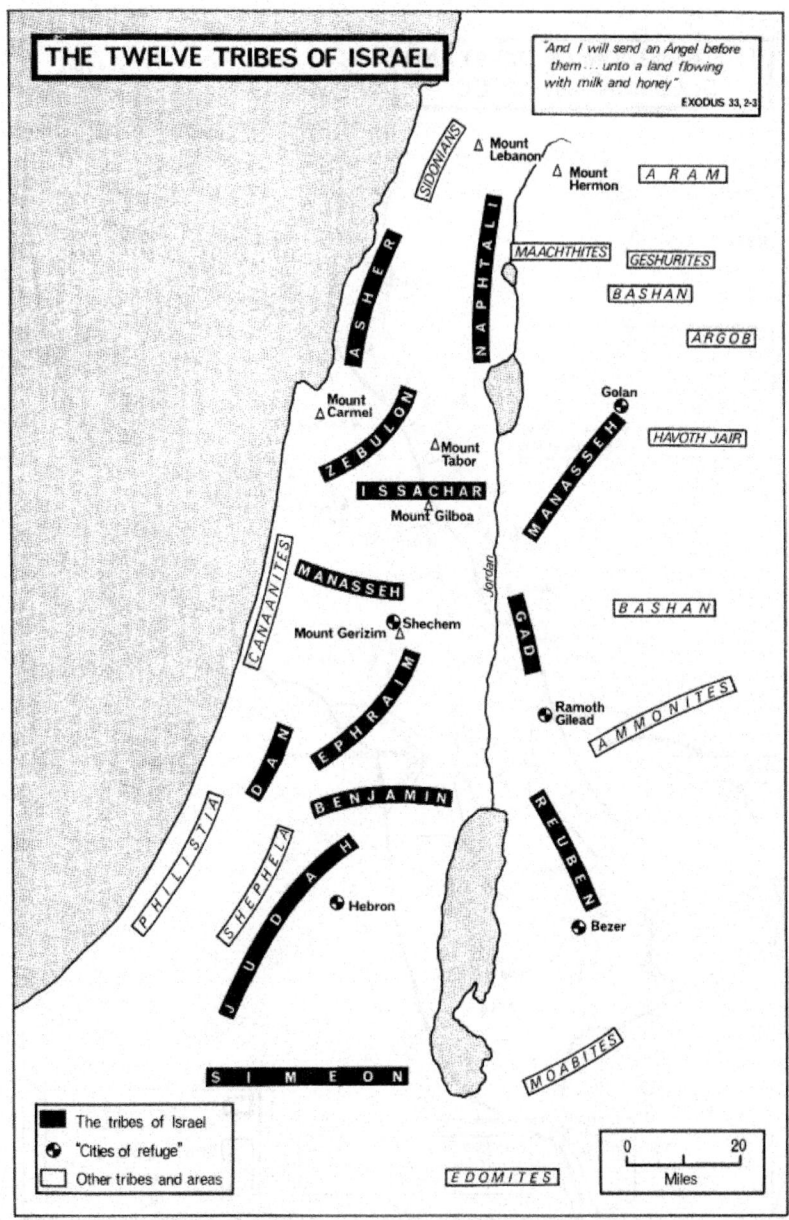

THE TWELVE TRIBES OF ISRAEL

"And I will send an Angel before them... unto a land flowing with milk and honey"
EXODUS 33, 2-3

Mount Lebanon
Mount Hermon
A R A M
SIDONIANS
MAACHTHITES
GESHURITES
BASHAN
ARGOB
ASHER
NAPHTALI
Golan
Mount Carmel
ZEBULON
Mount Tabor
MANASSEH
HAVOTH JAIR
I S S A C H A R
Mount Gilboa
MANASSEH
Jordan
BASHAN
CANAANITES
Mount Gerizim Shechem
GAD
EPHRAIM
Ramoth Gilead
AMMONITES
DAN
BENJAMIN
PHILISTIA
SHEPHELA
REUBEN
JUDAH
Hebron
Bezer
S I M E O N
MOABITES

The tribes of Israel
"Cities of refuge"
Other tribes and areas

0   20
Miles

EDOMITES

Sir Martin Gilbert, © 2010. Reproduced by permission of Taylor & Francis Books UK. www.martingilbert.com

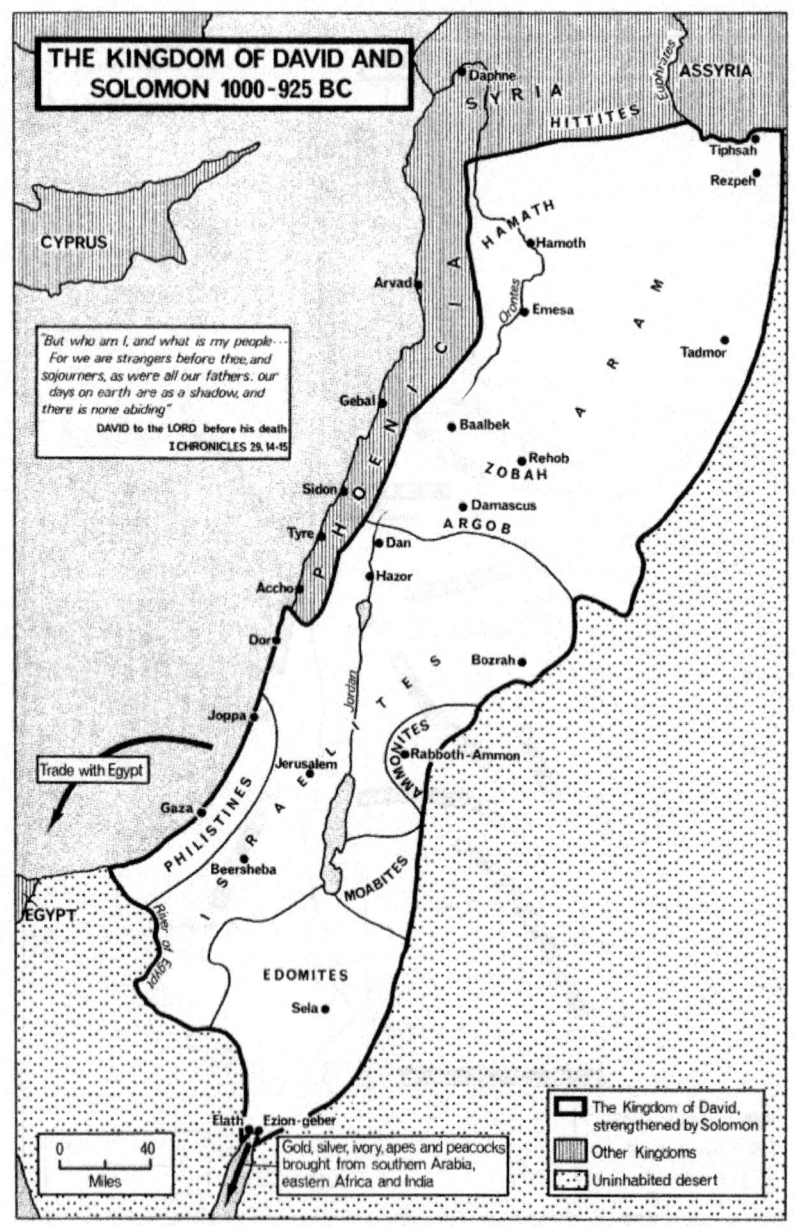

THE KINGDOM OF DAVID AND SOLOMON 1000–925 BC

CYPRUS

ASSYRIA

Daphne

SYRIA

HITTITES

Tiphsah

Rezpeh

HAMATH

Hamoth

Arvad

Emesa

ARAM

Tadmor

"But who am I, and what is my people...
For we are strangers before thee, and
sojourners, as were all our fathers. our
days on earth are as a shadow, and
there is none abiding"

DAVID to the LORD before his death
I CHRONICLES 29. 14-15

Gebal

Baalbek

Rehob

ZOBAH

Sidon

Damascus

Tyre

Dan

ARGOB

Accho

Hazor

Dor

Bozrah

Joppa

Jerusalem

Rabboth-Ammon

Trade with Egypt

Gaza

Beersheba

MOABITES

EGYPT

EDOMITES

Sela

Elath   Ezion-geber

0	40
Miles	

Gold, silver, ivory, apes and peacocks
brought from southern Arabia,
eastern Africa and India

The Kingdom of David,
strengthened by Solomon

Other Kingdoms

Uninhabited desert

Sir Martin Gilbert, © 2010. Reproduced by permission of Taylor & Francis Books UK. www.martingilbert.com

of Shimon. Though these two states at times were antagonistic towards each other and at times friendly, they were both Israelite states that existed side by side until the year 722 BCE when Assyria, the local superpower at the time, conquered them.

Assyria was located in Northern Mesopotamia (today's northern Iraq, northeastern Syria and southeastern Turkey), which became very powerful between the 21st and 18th centuries BCE. They were conquered briefly before they regained power between 1365 BCE to 1056 BCE, during which time they conquered the Hittites, the Egyptians and the Babylonians, as well as Judah and Israel.

Shalmaneser V (726-723 BCE) consolidated Assyrian power during his short reign and repressed Egyptian attempts to gain a foothold in the Near East, defeating and driving out Pharaoh Shoshenq V from the region. He is mentioned in Biblical sources as having conquered Israel and being responsible for deporting the Ten Lost Tribes of Israel to Assyria. He and his successor also brought the Samaritans, people originating from Babylon, Cuthah, Ava, Sepharvaim and Hamath, and settled them in the towns of Samaria to replace the Israelites (Kings 2, 17:24).

The ten tribes who populated the northern kingdom—Asher, Dan, Ephraim, Gad, Issachar, Manasseh, Naphtali, Reuben, Simeon and Zebulun—were exiled and eventually lost to the Jewish people, becoming forever "The Ten Lost Tribes of Israel."

Judah prospered under Assyrian vassalage (despite Hezekiah's revolt against the Assyrian king Sennacherib) but in 605 BCE the Assyrian Empire was defeated, and the ensuing competition between the 26th dynasty of Egypt and the Neo-Babylonian Empire for control of the Eastern Mediterranean led to the destruction of the kingdom in a series of campaigns between 597 and 582 BCE, the deportation of the elite of the Judean community, and the incorporation of Judah into a province of the Neo-Babylonian Empire.[8]

Nevertheless, Judah and Jerusalem survived a 20-year Assyrian siege. The independent Judean state would go on to last until 586 BCE, when it was finally destroyed by a new Middle Eastern power,

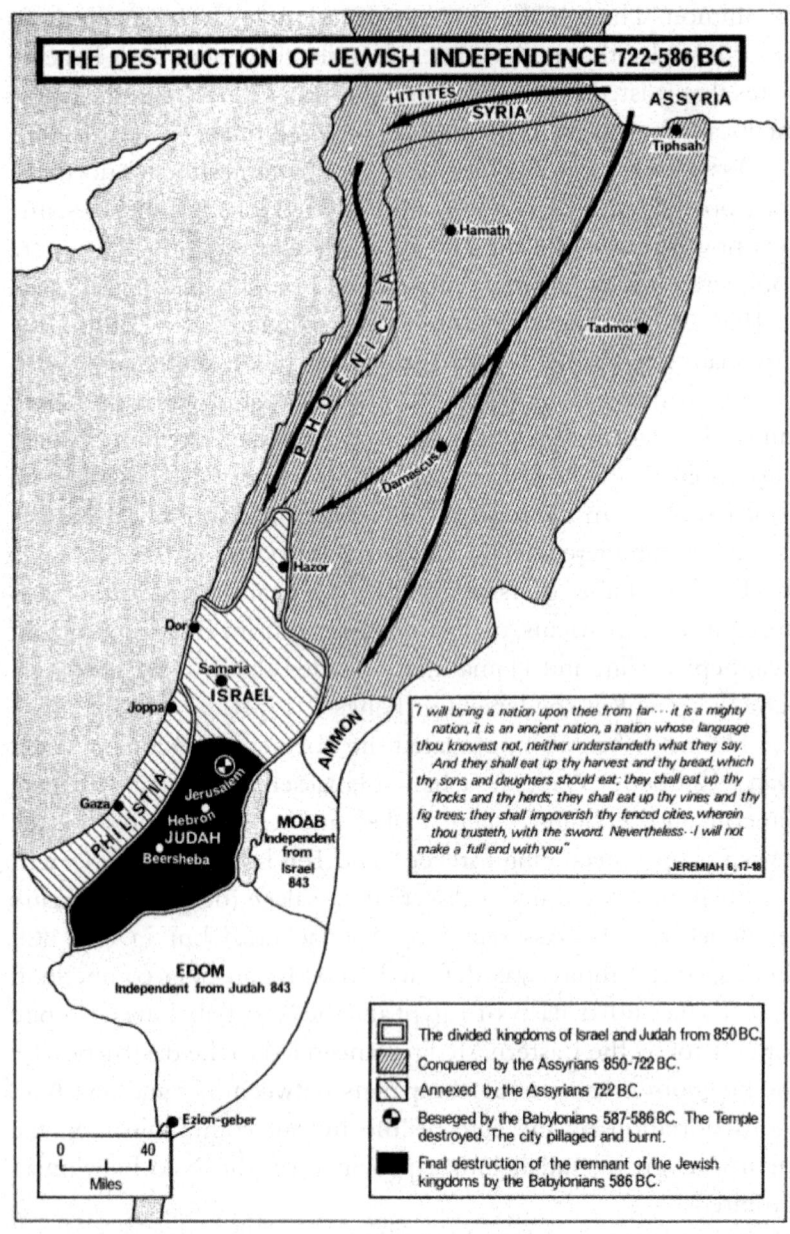

THE DESTRUCTION OF JEWISH INDEPENDENCE 722-586 BC

HITTITES

SYRIA

ASSYRIA

Tiphsah

Hamath

Tadmor

P H O E N I C I A

Damascus

Hazor

Dor

Samaria

ISRAEL

Joppa

AMMON

"I will bring a nation upon thee from far··· it is a mighty
nation, it is an ancient nation, a nation whose language
thou knowest not, neither understandeth what they say.
And they shall eat up thy harvest and thy bread, which
thy sons and daughters should eat; they shall eat up thy
flocks and thy herds; they shall eat up thy vines and thy
fig trees; they shall impoverish thy fenced cities, wherein
thou trusteth, with the sword. Nevertheless··· I will not
make a full end with you"

JEREMIAH 6, 17-18

Gaza

Hebron

Jerusalem

JUDAH

MOAB
Independent
from
Israel
843

Beersheba

P H I L I S T I A

EDOM
Independent from Judah 843

☐ The divided kingdoms of Israel and Judah from 850 BC.

▨ Conquered by the Assyrians 850-722 BC.

◩ Annexed by the Assyrians 722 BC.

◉ Besieged by the Babylonians 587-586 BC. The Temple
destroyed. The city pillaged and burnt.

■ Final destruction of the remnant of the Jewish
kingdoms by the Babylonians 586 BC.

Ezion-geber

0   40
Miles

Babylon. Judah was destroyed, and King Solomon's *Beit HaMikdash* was sacked and burned, along with Jerusalem. A sizeable percentage of the Jewish population was either exiled or left Judah to live in Babylon; only the lower classes remained in the ruins.

The Babylonian conquest and destruction of Judah ended 687 years of Jewish sovereignty in *Eretz Yisrael*. By all historical standards, seven centuries—from the days of Joshua, 1273 BCE, until 586 BCE, when Judah was destroyed—is a very long time for one nation to rule and dominate a particular area culturally, politically, religiously and demographically. During those 687 years, the Jewish State was at times small, at times large, at times it was powerful, at times it was weak, at times it was run by a monarch, at times it was run by tribal judges, at times it was a united kingdom and at times it was divided into two kingdoms. But throughout these 687 years the Israelite/Jewish nation was a sovereign state in *Eretz Yisrael*.

Shortly after the destruction of Judah by Babylon, the Babylonian Empire itself was destroyed by Persia, which replaced it as the strongest force in the Middle East. In 539 BCE the Persian Emperor Cyrus/Koresh issued a famous declaration allowing the Jews exiled in Babylon to rejoin their brothers in Judah, gave them permission to rebuild the Temple and offered them autonomy. This made Judah one of many states allowed to retain their own identities and cultures to make up what could be called the "United Persian Empire."

Three Jewish leaders led the Jewish people from Babylonia back to Judah, and became the leaders of the Judean Jewish community that incorporated those who had remained behind in the homeland. They were the prophet Zerubabel and the scribes Ezra and Nechemia. Between them, they brought 42,500 Jews from Babylon to Judah at different times and set up a Jewish autonomous republic as part of the Persian Empire. This autonomous republic had a Jewish Temple, a Jewish court system, operated on the Jewish calendar and Hebrew as its official language. On the other hand, the Jews did not have a king, could not coin money and did not

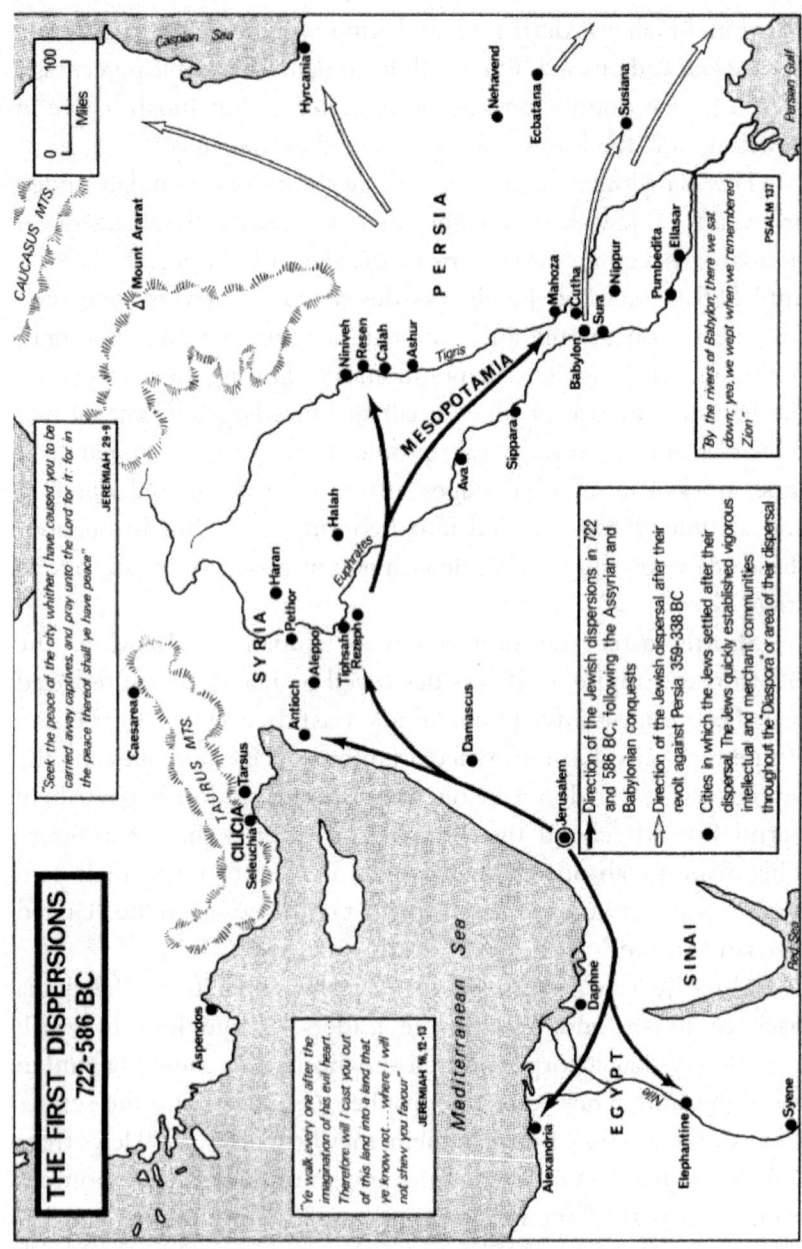

THE FIRST DISPERSIONS
722-586 BC

"Seek the peace of the city whither I have caused you to be carried away captives, and pray unto the Lord for it: for in the peace thereof shall ye have peace"
JEREMIAH 29:9

"Ye walk every one after the imagination of his evil heart. Therefore will I cast you out of this land into a land that ye know not... where I will not shew you favour"
JEREMIAH 16:12-13

→ Direction of the Jewish dispersions in 722 and 586 BC, following the Assyrian and Babylonian conquests

⇨ Direction of the Jewish dispersal after their revolt against Persia 359-338 BC

● Cities in which the Jews settled after their dispersal. The Jews quickly established vigorous intellectual and merchant communities throughout the "Diaspora" or area of their dispersal

"By the rivers of Babylon, there we sat down; yea, we wept when we remembered Zion"
PSALM 137

CAUCASUS MTS.
Caspian Sea
Mount Ararat
PERSIA
Hyrcania
Nehavend
Ecbatana
Susiana
Persian Gulf
Niniveh
Resen
Calah
Ashur
Tigris
Mahoza
Cutha
Babylon
Sura
Nippur
Pumbedita
Ellasar
MESOPOTAMIA
Sippara
Ava
Halah
Euphrates
Haran
Pethor
SYRIA
Aleppo
Tiphsah
Rezeph
Antioch
Damascus
Caesarea
TAURUS MTS.
Tarsus
CILICIA
Seleuchia
Jerusalem
Aspendos
Mediterranean Sea
SINAI
Red Sea
EGYPT
Nile
Daphne
Alexandria
Elephantine
Syene

0 100 Miles

Sir Martin Gilbert, © 2010. Reproduced by permission of Taylor & Francis Books UK. www.martingilbert.com

have an army. They paid taxes to the Persian Empire and Persian soldiers maintained garrisons in Judah. This reality continued until the arrival of Alexander the Great, a Macedonian who ruled the Greek Empire. In 333 BCE, when he conquered Judah from the Persians, he kept the same arrangements the Persians had made with the Jews. Judah, now named Judea, became an autonomous state in what could be called the United Greek Empire. The Jews had the same freedoms and rights as they had under the Persians.

When Alexander died, the Greek Empire was divided among generals who, in the early years, ran the empire with the same autonomy-oriented philosophy. But by the second century BCE, Judea fell under the rule of the Seleucid Dynasty (named after Seleucus I Nicator (c. 358-281 BCE) who ruled after Alexander's death). In 167 BCE, the Greek-Syrian king Antiochus Epiphanes changed the nature of the relationship between the Greek Empire and its subject states. He did not tolerate autonomy.

All Greek subject states had to adopt the Greek religion, language, alphabet and culture with all that that entailed. All local states accepted this decree except Judea. Antiochus, a pagan, could not understand why people would object to changing gods or language. To the pagan mind gods were as interchangeable as football teams. When they conquered Jerusalem, the Greek–Syrians entered the Holy Temple, brought in pagan gods and began sacrificing pigs on the altar. They also promised riches and power to any Jewish noblemen who publicly accepted Greek gods and dressed in Greek fashion.

The Jews of Judea, led by the Hasmonean priestly family from Modiin, began an open revolt against Antiochus' vastly superior armies. For the Jews of Judea the idea of giving up the One God, their way of life/religion, language and culture induced them to fight for their religion and their national identity. Many historians consider this the first revolt in the cause of freedom of religion and identity.

The commander of the Jewish revolt was Yehuda, who earned the designation as "*Ha Maccabee*"/The Hammer. He and his brothers, known as the Maccabees, led the nascent Jewish army. At first the Maccabees fought as guerrillas, using small groups for hit-and-run tactics. Their ranks swelled slowly but eventually the Maccabees raised a real army. They fought the seemingly invincible Greek army in a war that lasted two years, and in 165 BCE the Maccabees defeated the Greeks, liberated all of Judea and Jerusalem, cleansed the Temple and rededicated it. To this day the Jewish people commemorate this event by celebrating the eight-day festival of Chanukah.

Defeating the Greeks led to Jewish independence for the next 102 years. From 165-63 BCE, a fully sovereign Jewish State functioned in Judea, where the Hasmonean family created a ruling dynasty.

In 67 BCE, the last Hasmonean ruler, Queen Shlomtziyon/ Alexandra Salome, died. She had two sons, Hyrcanus, who she appointed king of Judea and High Priest/*Kohen Gadol* when her husband Alexander Jannaeus died in 63 BCE, and Aristobulus II, the younger brother, who lusted for the throne.

Salome was well aware of Aristobulus II's thirst for power and sent him to fight Ptolemy Mennai in 70-69 BCE to keep him from making war in her kingdom. He lost that war and came back ready to attack his mother, who, inconveniently, had died, so he attacked Hyrcanus. After Aristobulus II captured his brother in the Temple in Jerusalem, they negotiated a truce. The brief truce was broken when the Nabateans convinced Hyrcanus that his brother wanted him dead, and gave him shelter. At about that same time, the Romans sent their generals to conquer Seleucid Syria, which included Judea, and since the Hashmoneans were officially allied with Rome, both brothers asked them for help. But the Romans played them against each other.

Like his father, Hyrcanus supported the political party of the *rabbanim*, known as the Pharisees/*P'rushim*, who were against assimilating into Roman culture. Aristobulus II favored the Saducees/*Tzdukim*, as his mother had before him.

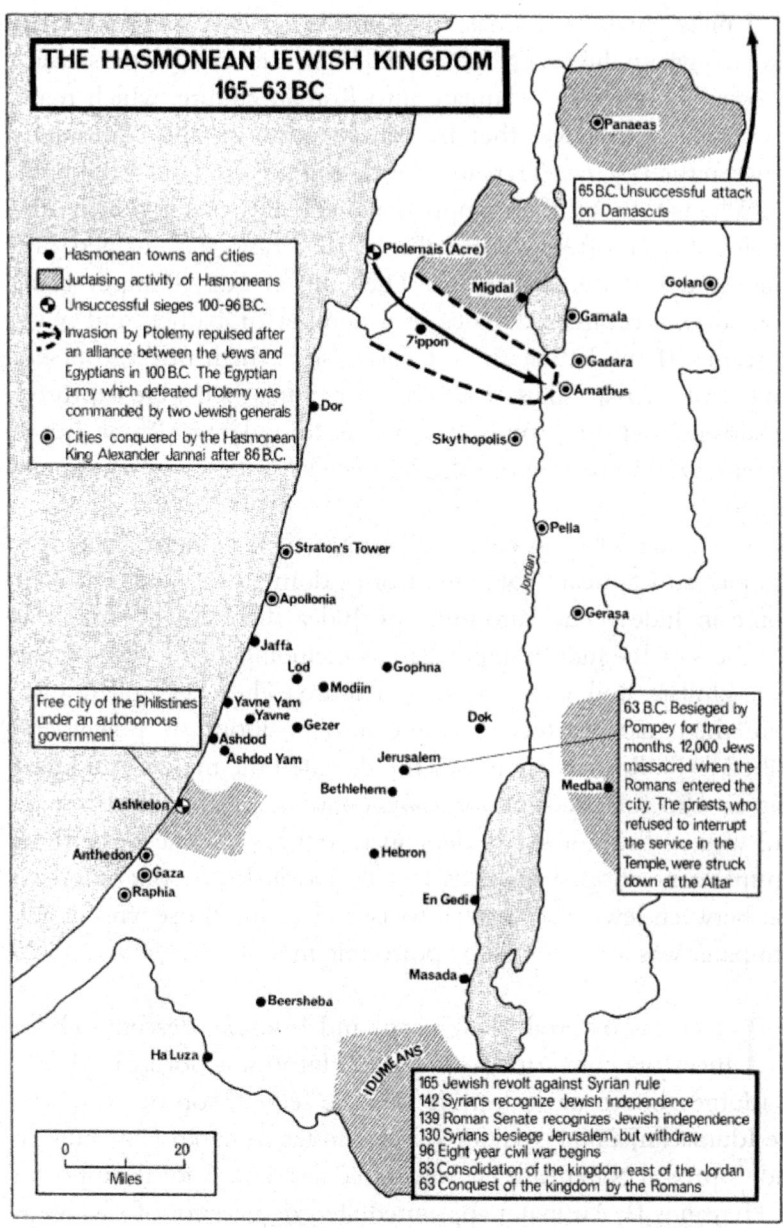

THE HASMONEAN JEWISH KINGDOM
165–63 BC

●Panaeas

65 B.C. Unsuccessful attack on Damascus

● Hasmonean towns and cities

▨ Judaising activity of Hasmoneans

◉ Unsuccessful sieges 100-96 B.C.

➡ Invasion by Ptolemy repulsed after an alliance between the Jews and Egyptians in 100 B.C. The Egyptian army which defeated Ptolemy was commanded by two Jewish generals

◉ Cities conquered by the Hasmonean King Alexander Jannai after 86 B.C.

●Ptolemais (Acre)

Migdal

Golan◉

◉Gamala

Zippon

◉Gadara

◉Amathus

●Dor

Skythopolis◉

◉Pella

Jordan

◉Straton's Tower

◉Apollonia

◉Gerasa

●Jaffa

Lod● ●Gophna

●Modiin

Free city of the Philistines under an autonomous government

●Yavne Yam
●Yavne ●Gezer
●Ashdod
●Ashdod Yam

Dok
●

Jerusalem●

Bethlehem●

Medba●

63 B.C. Besieged by Pompey for three months. 12,000 Jews massacred when the Romans entered the city. The priests, who refused to interrupt the service in the Temple, were struck down at the Altar

Ashkelon◉

Anthedon ◉
◉Gaza
◉Raphia

●Hebron

En Gedi●

Masada●

●Beersheba

Ha Luza●

IDUMEANS

165 Jewish revolt against Syrian rule
142 Syrians recognize Jewish independence
139 Roman Senate recognizes Jewish independence
130 Syrians besiege Jerusalem, but withdraw
96 Eight year civil war begins
83 Consolidation of the kingdom east of the Jordan
63 Conquest of the kingdom by the Romans

0   20
Miles

Sir Martin Gilbert, © 2010. Reproduced by permission of Taylor & Francis Books UK. www.martingilbert.com

Unlike previous regimes, the Romans decided not to force the Jews to give up their religion. Instead, they used cultural persuasion to convince Jews to assimilate into Roman culture, which many Jews found attractive, thereby causing strife in the community between the *Perushim* (Hyrcanus) and the *Tzedukim* (Aristobulus II).

When both brothers approached the Romans for help, and Aristobulus II offered them the better bribe, they helped him soundly defeat the Nabateans. Then, in 63 BCE, Pompey came from Rome, conquered Judea in a number of battles, and made Hyrcanus II the Ethnarch and *Kohen Gadol* (high priest), but not king. When Aristobulus II and his remaining men were captured, he surrendered and promised to deliver Jerusalem to Rome, but in the end could not because the *P'rushim* kept the gates to the city locked.

When Julius Caesar defeated Pompey, he appointed Antipater/Antipas, an Idumean (someone from Edom) as the Procurator of Rome in Judea. The autonomy of Judea then slowly eroded as members of the Judean upper classes, including the *Kohanim*, began to assimilate and adopt Roman culture. These assimilationists were then manipulated by Rome into positions of power and bribed to be Roman puppets. This alienated the middle and lower classes who followed the *rabbanim*, continued to live Jewish lives, and viewed their titular leadership as traitors. At the same time, Antipater positioned his sons to rule Judea. In the ongoing civil war between Jews who wanted to assimilate and those who didn't, Antipater was assassinated by poisoning in 43 BCE.

Herod was of Arab (Nabatean) and Edomite descent, whose ancestors converted to Judaism. Herod was born ca. 74 BCE in Idumea, south of Judea. He was the second son of Antipater the Idumaean, a high-ranking official under ethnarch Hyrcanus II, and Cypros, a Nabatean. He was raised as a Jew. A loyal supporter of Hyrcanus II, Antipater appointed Herod governor of Galilee at 25, and his elder brother, Phasael, governor of Jerusalem. Although he enjoyed the backing of Rome, his brutality was condemned by the *Sanhedrin* (the council of judges).

Herod was also a master builder who rebuilt the Holy Temple originally completed in 515 BCE by Ezra and Nechemia (Nehemiah). Herod took the simple structure that existed and turned it into an edifice as magnificent as King Solomon's. Herod also built the city of Caesarea, the fortress at Masada and the Herodion (a hollowed-out mountain fortress retreat), all of them built to curry favor with the local Jewish population and still visible as ruins today.

As King of the Jews, Herod generally respected Judaism in public, but made it clear he also represented non-Jews living in Judea. As such, he built temples for other religions outside of the Jewish areas of his kingdom, introduced foreign forms of entertainment and had a golden eagle erected at the entrance of the Temple, suggesting he did not truly represent the interests of the Jews.[9]

While the Jews were awed by the beauty of their remodeled *Beit HaMikdash* and Herod's palaces and fortresses, they were revolted by Herod's murderous behavior. Herod represented everything going wrong with Jewish life in Judea under Roman rule. Autonomy was being chiseled away; the Jewish upper classes were becoming Roman puppets; the posts of high priests (*Kohanim Gadolim*) in the *Beit HaMikdash*, the most holy positions in Judaism, went to the highest bidders, and Herod murdered them at will.

For the first time since the Babylonian exile, Judea fell into a deep despair. There appeared to be no saviors on the horizon to save them. Many disappointed Jews began focusing on the Messianic age promised by the Israelite prophets six centuries earlier. Messianic cults like the Essenes, who withdrew from normal life and set up a town in the caves overlooking the Dead Sea, were born anticipating the arrival of the Messiah. During this period, many Jews, including Jesus, known in Hebrew as Yeshu, declared themselves prophets and began to preach against Rome and the corruption in Jerusalem that was fostered by the Romans, Herod and his successors. The story of Jesus, who was Jewish and studying to be a rabbi, was used as the basis for the Christian Messiah, and in 50-60 CE, Paul, in Thessalonians, was the first to accuse the Jews, specifically, the *rabbanim*/Perushim, of killing the son of God. This was later made part of the Christian canon.

In ca. 10 CE, a group of grassroots Jews from the lower classes, who called themselves *Kanaim*/Zealots, and another, even more extreme group, the Sicarii, began to protest Roman rule and the corrupt Jewish elites. They organized their people and waited for the right moment to revolt.

It appeared that the revolt was going to start in the year 39 CE when the Roman emperor Caligula declared himself a god and was about to place a statue of himself in the *Beit HaMikdash*. Had he done so, there surely would have been a revolt, with the concomitant result that Caligula would have started his counterattack by destroying the *Beit HaMikdash*. But luckily for the Jews, Caligula was assassinated. But the Zealots and Sicarii continued building their strength and picking up more people as the years passed and as the hopelessness of the average Jew in Judea grew. By the year 66 CE, Judea was a tinderbox and someone just needed to throw a match to start the fire.

The Great Revolt began in 66 CE with tax protests and attacks on Romans by Zealots and Sicariis. The Romans then proceeded to plunder the *Beit Hamikdash* and murdered 6,000 Jews in Jerusalem, prompting a full-scale rebellion. As a result, the Roman military garrison of Judaea was overrun by rebels, and the Romans and their puppets fled. In response, the legate of Syria brought in the Syrian army and auxiliary troops to restore order, but the Syrian Legion was ambushed and defeated by Jewish rebels with 6,000 Romans killed, shocking the Roman rulers.

The Roman general Vespasian, with his son Titus as his second in command, was given the task of crushing the rebellion in 67 CE. Two factors helped the Romans defeat the Zealot armies in the Galilee: 1) The commander of the Judean Zealot forces, Yosef Ben Matityahu, became a traitor and surrendered the largest Jewish force in the Galil without a battle being fought. He switched sides and became known as Josephus Flavius, the man who would write the history of the revolt for the Romans and whose work became an essential historical documentation of this war, and 2) the Judean leadership in Jerusalem felt that the Zealots/Sicarii had started a war with Rome that the Jews could not possibly win, and so did not send reinforcements to Galilee.

Vespasian was called back to Rome to become Emperor in 69 CE. Then Titus began a seven-month long siege of Jerusalem in 70 CE, a Jerusalem fortified with a large population, a food supply designed to last for 20 years, and a sustainable water supply from the tunnel King Chizkiyahu had built in the 8th century BCE. The leaders of Judea in Jerusalem were dominated by rabbis, the *Perushim*, who felt strongly that the best course of action would be to wait out the Roman siege as their forefathers had done 800 years earlier in the war with the Assyrians.

But the Sicarii were rabid with rage and filled with a sense of betrayal. They were also deliberately suicidal. They declared war against the Judean leadership, many of them *Tana'im*, the men who began to compile the *Mishnah*. The Sicarii murdered most of them and burned the food supply in the city to force the Jews to fight the Romans or die. That was when Rabbi Yochanan Ben Yakkai faked his own death so he could leave Jerusalem to negotiate with Vespasian about saving Judaism after the oncoming Jewish rout.

After a horrific siege, the Roman Legions broke through the walls of Jerusalem on the 17th of Tammuz. Three weeks later, after bitter fighting, they entered the Temple Mount and on the 9th of Av began to loot and burn the second *Beit HaMikdash*. They killed most of the *Kohanim*, and then went on to slaughter most of the city's inhabitants and destroy what was left of the city.

This was the end of Jewish autonomy for close to 2,000 years. Since 70 CE, the 9th of Av, which is the same date ascribed to the destruction of the First Temple in Jerusalem, has become the saddest day of the Jewish calendar because on that day the two Jewish *Batei Mikdash* were destroyed, Jewish sovereignty was gone and the Jewish nation was scattered throughout the Roman Empire. For the first time since Joshua entered *Eretz Yisrael* and established the first Jewish State, the Jews who were left in Judea were a minority of the world's Jewish population. The majority of

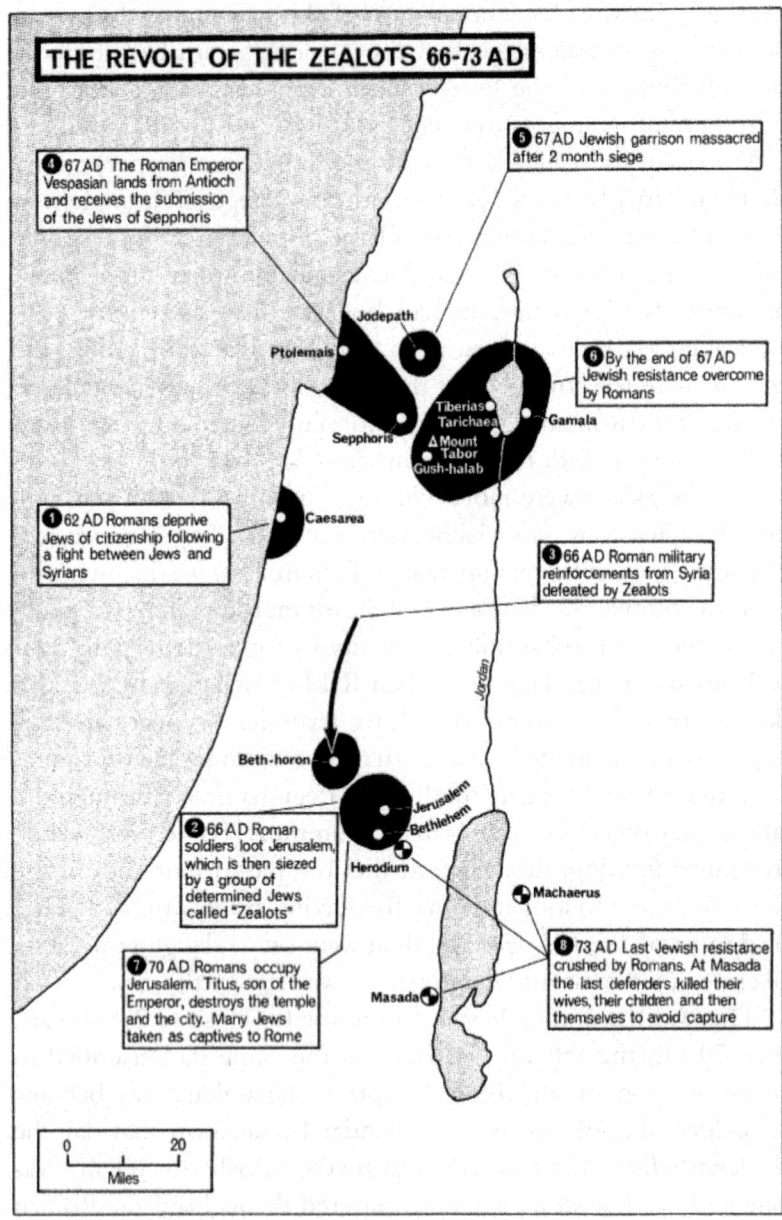

THE REVOLT OF THE ZEALOTS 66-73 A D

4 67 AD The Roman Emperor Vespasian lands from Antioch and receives the submission of the Jews of Sepphoris

5 67 AD Jewish garrison massacred after 2 month siege

6 By the end of 67 AD Jewish resistance overcome by Romans

Jodepath

Ptolemais

Tiberias
Tarichaea
Sepphoris   △ Mount Tabor
Gush-halab

Gamala

1 62 AD Romans deprive Jews of citizenship following a fight between Jews and Syrians

Caesarea

3 66 AD Roman military reinforcements from Syria defeated by Zealots

Jordan

Beth-horon

Jerusalem
Bethlehem

2 66 AD Roman soldiers loot Jerusalem, which is then siezed by a group of determined Jews called "Zealots"

Herodium

Machaerus

7 70 AD Romans occupy Jerusalem. Titus, son of the Emperor, destroys the temple and the city. Many Jews taken as captives to Rome

Masada

8 73 AD Last Jewish resistance crushed by Romans. At Masada the last defenders killed their wives, their children and then themselves to avoid capture

0   20
Miles

the Jewish nation was now in exile, forced to be concerned, first and foremost, with its very survival as a people.

MASADA

After Jerusalem fell, a group of Sicarii and their families escaped to Masada, Herod's abandoned mountain fortress near the Dead Sea. It was a self-sustaining mini-city/fortress, built on a 1500 x 900 foot mesa above tall cliffs. It had beautiful buildings, a synagogue, huge food storage areas, water cisterns and steep inclines that made it nearly impossible to capture. The Sicarii used Masada as their last stand in a Judea under Jewish rule, launching small guerilla attacks against Roman soldiers in the Judean Desert.

Eventually the Romans traced the source of these attacks to Masada. They sent a small unit to capture or kill the rebels, but they never returned. The Romans then assigned their best troops, the 10th Roman Legion and its legendary commander, Silva, to capture Masada.

Masada sheltered 960 men, women and children and had enough food and water to last years. Among the people were about 120 warriors. The 10th Legion, with its 12,000 soldiers, laid siege but Silva quickly discovered he couldn't supply his troops with enough water and food, so he changed his strategy. He ordered a ramp to be built along the cliffs leading to the fortress. When they got to the top, his troops could use a battering ram to breach the walls. At first the Romans used their own soldiers to build the ramp, but the Sicarii attacked with boulders from above, killing many. Silva then brought in thousands of Jewish slaves to force the Sicarii to kill their brethren to halt construction. But the Sicarii could not bring themselves to kill their fellow Jews.

Realizing that their days in their fortress were numbered, Sicarii commander Elazar Ben Yair called all his warriors together in the Masada synagogue to discuss how to end it. The following is taken from his speech that day:

> Since we long ago resolved never to be servants to the Romans,
> nor to any other than to God Himself, Who alone is the true

and just Lord of mankind, the time is now come that obliges us to make that resolution true in practice ... We were the very first that revolted, and we are the last to fight against them; and I cannot but esteem it as a favor that God has granted us that it is still in our power to die bravely, and in a state of freedom.[10]

After hearing these words, the Sicarii burned all their stores of food save one. Every warrior killed his own family, and then finally, by drawing lots, each man killed his friend. All their weapons were placed in a pile for the Romans to see that they had weapons, and then Eleazar Ben Yair killed himself.

In Judaism suicide is forbidden. Yet in the context of the rebellion against Rome, it was clear to Ben Yair and the others that when the Romans would overwhelm the tiny sliver of sovereign Judea they would make an example of the survivors. The women and children would be sold into of slavery and the men would be paraded through the streets of Rome as living trophies before they were crucified. To die as martyrs in God's name, to preserve their sense of freedom and the honor of their women, the Sicarii chose suicide as their only option.[11]

From the Roman perspective, the Jewish rebellion in Judea finally ended at Masada in 73 CE. But the rebellion was significant in that it highlighted Roman weaknesses. If a tiny province like Judea could defeat Rome's legions of warriors, its larger client states could do the same. The Romans thus implemented a scorched earth policy to let the Jews and all subjects of the Roman Empire know what happens when one, whether individuals or client states, rises against Rome.

We know what happened because it is recorded in Josephus' *The Jewish War* (c. 75 CE). Born Yosef ben Matityahu, he was born in Jerusalem to a *kohain* and a mother of royal Hashmonean descent. He fought against Rome during the first war and led the troops in the Galilee against them, but surrendered to Vespasian in 67 CE. He made a speech wherein he foresaw Vespasian's appointment as emperor of Rome, and so Vespasian kept him as a slave and interpreter until he was, indeed, appointed emperor in 69 CE. At that point, he granted Josephus his freedom and Roman citizenship. Josephus became an advisor to Titus, who led the siege of Jerusalem and oversaw the destruction of the Holy Temple.

Originally written in Aramaic, *The Jewish War* recounts the Jewish revolt against Roman occupation (66-70). Josephus later expanded the original into a seven volume work written in Greek. He also wrote the *Antiquities of the Jews* (ca. 94 CE) in Greek. It is a history of the world since the Creation as told from a Jewish perspective.[12]

Josephus wrote that there were four million Jews living in Judea on the eve of the rebellion, and that by the time Masada fell there were only one million left. (One million were killed by the Romans, one million were sold into slavery—flooding the Roman slave market—and one million fled.) The Romans were proud of their great victory and built the Arch of Titus in tribute to the general who also became Ceasar as his father had before him. The arch stands in the heart of Rome to this very day. Chiseled into its stone are images of Roman legionnaires carrying away the Temple's great menorah and other spoils.

The Romans also minted victory coins embossed with the legend *Judea Capta*—Judea has been defeated. They were circulated in Caesarea (Roman headquarters in Judea) and in Rome to celebrate their victory. The coin had a picture of a Roman legionnaire standing over a Jewish woman kneeling and weeping. The coin was meant to immortalize the end of Judea and, by association, the end of the Jewish nation.[13]

AFTER THE FALL OF JUDEA

For several decades after the fall of Jerusalem, the destruction of the *Beit HaMikdash*, and finally the defeat at Masada, Judea remained quiet as the Jewish community licked its wounds and found ways to survive as a nation without a state and religious and political centers.

Then, under the rule of Hadrian (117-138), Quintus Tineius Rufus (130-132) was appointed as the Governor of Judea. His strict enforcement of anti-Jewish laws only made the Jews angrier and they again prepared to revolt against Rome. The straw that broke the camel's back was the announcement by Rome that it intended to build a pagan temple to honor Jupiter on the site of the destroyed *Beit HaMikdash*. The second revolt against Rome was led by the charismatic Jewish warrior Bar Kochba, who was supported by the greatest and most respected rabbi of the time, Rabbi Akiva ben Joseph (ca. 50-135 CE).

The Jewish strongholds were in the regions in and around Jerusalem and the Judean Desert, but the rebellion spread throughout the country. Bar Kochba's army had most of its bases in caves, so it appeared to the Romans that their attackers simply vanished after every encounter. Eventually, the Romans figured out where Bar Kochba's caves were and they brought in twelve legions to teach the Jews a lesson. The Romans destroyed one Jewish fortress after the next and mercilessly demolished what was left of Judea. The last battle was fought in Betar, a few miles from Jerusalem, where Bar Kochba had established his stronghold.

On the 9th of Av in 135, Betar was razed to the ground and thousands of Bar Kochba's soldiers were killed. The second Jewish revolt was over, and Judea was eviscerated. Close to 1,000 Jewish towns were razed, and of the one million Jews left after the first revolt, 600,000 were either killed, sold into slavery, or fled. The Romans changed the name of Jerusalem to Aelia Capitalina, plowed the Temple Mount, salted the earth, and banned the Jews from Jerusalem. It would not be until the eighteenth century that Jews would begin reestablishing sovereignty in *Eretz Yisrael*.

Further retribution against the stiff-necked Jews occurred after the failed Bar Kochba Revolt, 132 -135 CE. Rome ordered its historians to change the name of the former Jewish Republic, to erase even the association between the Judeans/Jews and their homeland. Since the Romans knew the history of the Jews and their Bible, they renamed Judea for the Philistines, who had been wiped out by the Assyrians seven centuries earlier. The area would now be referred to as Syria Palaestina. This was to be a final slap in the face because the country named for the first monotheistic religion that had ruled for millennia would now be named for a dead nation that had been its enemy.

The 400,000 Jews who remained in Judea would remain the majority of the population until the arrival of the Arab armies in 636 CE. Judea remained a Jewish province; there were hundreds of synagogues, dozens of Jewish cities and towns, and even though the Romans outlawed the practice of Judaism, Jews continued to practice their religion. The center of Jewish life moved to the north of the country, to the Galilee and the Golan.

The status of the Jews changed after the Roman Emperor Constantine converted to Christianity in the fourth century. Once he converted, the entire Roman Empire went from being an enemy of Christianity to being the Holy (Christian) Roman Empire. As a Christian king, Constantine adversely affected the Jewish people: Other than Paul, who accused the Jews of killing Jesus in Thessalonians of the New Testament, the death of Jesus had been blamed on the Romans. But when Constantine became a devout Christian and spread the religion throughout his Empire, he could hardly champion Jesus as the Christ/Messiah if the Romans had killed him. So from his reign as Holy Roman Emperor until 1965, all Christians blamed the death of Jesus on the Jews.

The second change was that Syria Palaestina, a relatively unimportant province of the Roman Empire, was renamed as *Terra Sanctum*, the Holy Land, since it was the birthplace of Jesus and Christianity. Helena, Constantine's mother and a Christian convert, was moved by the Holy Spirit and during her visit to the Holy Land (326-328) claimed to have had visions that confirmed all of Jesus' experiences and the places where they happened 300 years earlier. Based on those visions, Constantine built the churches and sites that Christian pilgrims visit to this day: The Church of the Nativity, The Church of the Holy Sepulcher, the Via Delarosa, The Church of the Ascension, and other sites.

By the end of the fourth century, Israel was a center for Christian pilgrims, and the Jews, still the majority of the population, were kept from Jerusalem and its environs. Over the next two centuries, however, many synagogues were built and a flourishing Jewish life continued in the countryside.

In 636 CE, the newly formed Islamic *Umma* (nation) swept out of the desert of Arabia and began a 125-year-long war of conquest that eventually created the largest empire in human history. Syria Palaestina was one of the first areas to fall under Islamic rule and Arab Muslims built two holy shrines on the Temple Mount. One was a religious museum that surrounded the stone where, Muslims believe, Muhammad placed his foot during his famous night journey (dream) to the "farthest place," a story found in the last Sura (chapter) of the Koran, and interpreted by Islamic scholars as being in Jerusalem. This is the Dome of the Rock, not a mosque. About one hundred yards south of the Dome of the Rock is a mosque called the Al Aqsa, with its silver dome. Because it is closer to Mecca, it is there that Muslims pray, and it is designated as the third holiest site in Islam, after Mecca and Medina.

By 750 CE the Islamic Empire had conquered the entire Middle East, Turkey, all of central Asia, Western China and Western India, North Africa and Spain. Unlike all the previous conquerors who swept through Judea since the Assyrians in 722 BCE, the Arabs of the Islamic *Umma* brought their families with them and Arabized the entire Middle East. By the end of the seventh century the Jews became a minority in their own land. There were still some 300,000 Jews living there, but they made up just 35% of the population.

Under Muslim rule Jews were *dhimmis*, an Arabic word, loosely translated, meaning a subjugated—though protected—people. Since *dhimmis* are not Muslims, they must be inferior to Muslims in lands ruled by Islam.

In Islam, the Pact of Omar defined the Islamic Empire's attitude toward non-pagans, like Jews and Christians. Both religions were referred to as the *Umma El Kittab*, the People of the Book

(Bible). Under this pact Jews were officially second-class citizens. They had to wear yellow triangle patches, special hats, have their synagogues built below the height of the local mosque, ride donkeys—not horses—walk in the gutter so Muslims could walk on the sidewalks, and pay a collective tax called the *jizziya* as the Jewish community's fee for being tolerated and allowed to practice Judaism in the Muslim empire. Since Muslims did not accuse the Jews of deicide as did the Christians, it was actually easier to be a Jew under Islamic rule than it was under a Christian one.

For the next four centuries the Jews of Judea learned to live under Islamic rule. A vibrant Jewish life existed despite the status of second-class citizenship. But life slowly deteriorated within a century, as Palestina became a backwater far from the Islamic centers of power in Baghdad, Damascus, Cairo and Mecca. In 1072, the Turkish Seljuks took over the Islamic Empire from the Arabs and were zealous in their efforts to prevent Christians from making pilgrimages to the Holy Land.

For this and other reasons, the Catholic Church in Rome called for a crusade to recapture the Holy Land from the Muslims. The first Crusade began in 1095. Tens of thousands of Catholic warriors marched to the Holy Land via Southern Europe, Turkey, Syria, and Lebanon. Along the way they slaughtered tens of thousands of European Jews as well as tens of thousands of pagans. (The Lamentations—*Kinnot*—that are said on the 9th of Av were written about the Crusades.) In 1099, the Crusaders reached the Holy Land. The Jews fought alongside the Islamic armies, for they knew that life was better under Islamic rule.

After several bloody battles, the Crusaders captured the Holy Land in 1099. They created several Crusader-ruled areas: the Kingdom of Jerusalem, the County of Tripoli, the Principality of Antioch, and the County of Edessa. Jews lived mostly in the Kingdom of Jerusalem. Tens of thousands of Jews were killed in battles and in massacres (putting to death the killers of Jesus was a "bonus" in the war to capture the Holy Land). By the time the Crusaders were defeated and expelled, the Jewish population of the Holy Land had been reduced by murder and expulsion to approximately 35,000 souls. For the next 600 years, the Jewish population there hovered between 15,000-25,000. This was the most difficult and challenging time for Jews to continue keeping their community and collective presence alive in *Eretz Yisrael*.

After the Crusaders were defeated by the Islamic Mamlukes who hailed from Asia Minor (Kazakhstan, Uzbekistan, Tajikistan, etc.), the open antisemitism of the Crusaders was ended. But life in *Eretz Yisrael* became even more difficult. The area was neglected and there was almost no government except for tax collection. The few roads fell into disrepair and there was almost no new construction. Throughout the 13th to 16th centuries—the period of Mamluk rule and the beginning of Ottoman rule—even though it made no economic or political sense, thousands of Jews moved to *Eretz Yisrael* because of its religious and historical significance to the Jewish nation.

Regardless of how bad the situation was in post-Crusader *Eretz Yisrael*, Jews from all over the world continued to make *Aliyah*. which literally means moving to a higher place (in this context it means moving up spiritually). The famous scholar Nachmanides moved there in the 13th century and built a synagogue in Jerusalem that is still in use today. The famous Jewish poet and writer Rabbi Yehuda Halevi made *Aliyah* in the 14th century. Towards the end of the 15th and the beginning of the 16th century there was a relatively large *Aliyah* by Spanish Jews expelled from Spain in 1492. Many Spanish Jews made their way to northern *Eretz Yisrael* and settled in cities like Safed and Tiberias. In that small part of the Galilee the Jews became the majority of the population. During the 16th century, two major works of rabbinic literature were published in Safed. One was the *Shulchan Aruch*, literally the "Set Table," a collection of Jewish laws compiled over the centuries by Rabbi Yosef Caro. The other was the *Kabbalah*, the book of Jewish mysticism written by Rabbi Isaac Luria, known as the *Ari Hakadosh* (the Holy Ari.) In the late 1700s and early 1800s, students of the great Lithuanian rabbi, the Vilna Gaon, made *Aliyah*, as did followers of various Chassidic rabbis.

The Ottomans did complete one important task under the rule of Suleiman the Magnificent. They rebuilt the walls around the Old City of Jerusalem. Other than that, *Eretz Yisrael* fell into further decay during Ottoman rule from 1517 to 1917. Yet, throughout this period, a continuous flow of Jews made *Aliyah* because of the deep religious, historical and cultural connection that the Jewish people have with the land since the days of Abraham.

Jews always lived in the four holy cities of Jerusalem, Chevron, Tsfat and Teveria/Tiberias from the times the destruction of the Second *Beit HaMikdash*. Based on Ottoman Empire documents, the Jews were the largest group living in Jerusalem starting in 1859. By 1880 there were around 25,000 Jews living in the city.

The Jewish relationship with *Eretz Yisrael* is not theoretical, it is a historical relationship that goes back over 3,000 years. That is one of the reasons archaeology is so important in modern Israel. The more one digs, the more one finds a Jewish past. One can find the ruins of ancient Jewish kingdoms in and around the Old City of Jerusalem, Hatzor in the Galilee, Beit Jubrin in the Judean Desert and Katzrin in the Golan Heights. These are just a few of dozens of sites confirming Jewish presence in the land that goes back thousands of years.

From the destruction of Judea in 70 CE by the Roman Empire and again after the Bar Kochba Revolt in 135 CE, no sovereign nation-state was established on the ruins of what was once Israel or Judea. From the time of its destruction until the reestablishment of Jewish sovereignty on May 15, 1948/5th of Iyar 5708, the area the Jewish nation calls *Eretz Yisrael* and the Romans renamed Syria Palaestina, the land Christians refer to as the Holy Land, and the Islamic world, starting in 1920, called Palestine, always maintained a Jewish presence, albeit under a larger empire:

70 – 395	Roman Empire
395 – 614	Byzantine
614 – 629	Persian

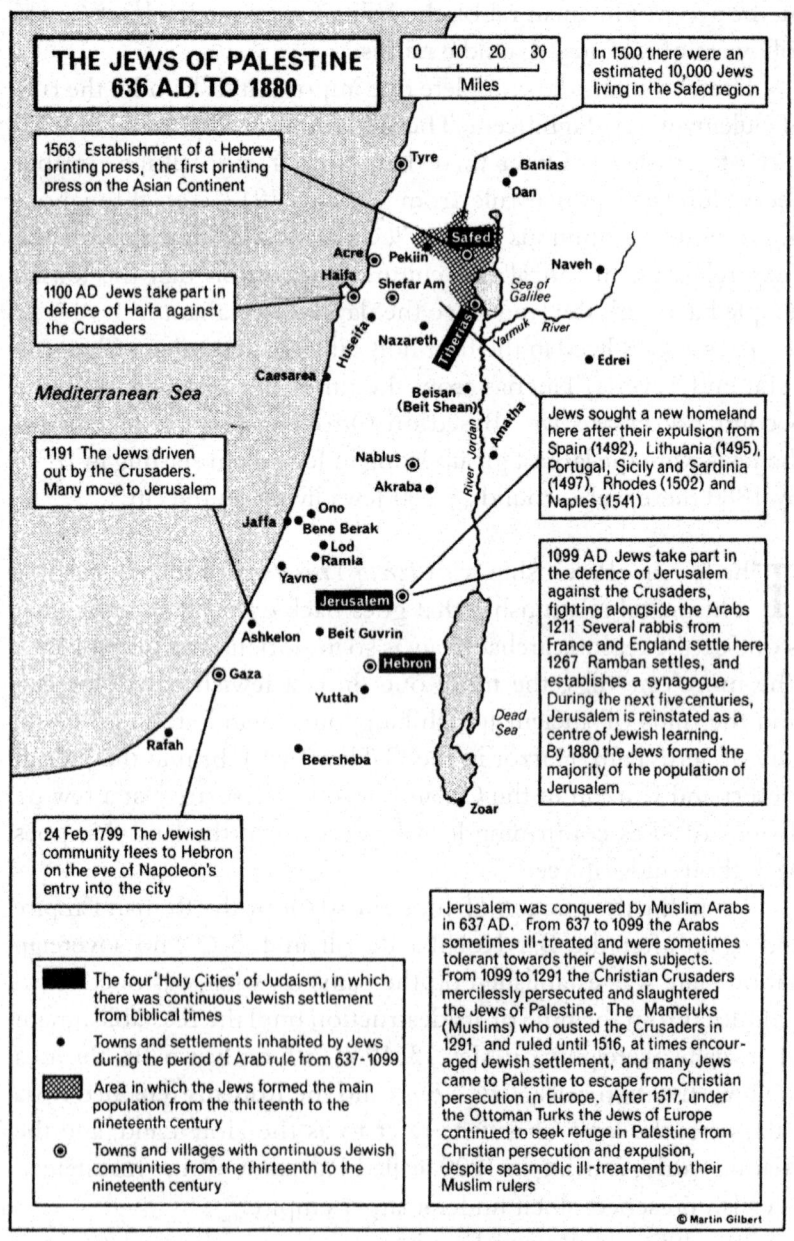

THE JEWS OF PALESTINE 636 A.D. TO 1880
0 10 20 30 Miles
In 1500 there were an estimated 10,000 Jews living in the Safed region
1563 Establishment of a Hebrew printing press, the first printing press on the Asian Continent
Tyre
Banias
Dan
Safed
Acre
Pekiin
Haifa
Shefar Am
Naveh
Sea of Galilee
1100 AD Jews take part in defence of Haifa against the Crusaders
Huseifa
Nazareth
Tiberias
Yarmuk River
Edrei
Caesarea
Mediterranean Sea
Beisan (Beit Shean)
Amatha
Jews sought a new homeland here after their expulsion from Spain (1492), Lithuania (1495), Portugal, Sicily and Sardinia (1497), Rhodes (1502) and Naples (1541)
1191 The Jews driven out by the Crusaders. Many move to Jerusalem
Nablus
River Jordan
Akraba
Jaffa
Ono
Bene Berak
Lod
Ramla
Yavne
1099 AD Jews take part in the defence of Jerusalem against the Crusaders, fighting alongside the Arabs 1211 Several rabbis from France and England settle here 1267 Ramban settles, and establishes a synagogue. During the next five centuries, Jerusalem is reinstated as a centre of Jewish learning. By 1880 the Jews formed the majority of the population of Jerusalem
Jerusalem
Ashkelon
Beit Guvrin
Hebron
Gaza
Yuttah
Dead Sea
Rafah
Beersheba
Zoar
24 Feb 1799 The Jewish community flees to Hebron on the eve of Napoleon's entry into the city
Jerusalem was conquered by Muslim Arabs in 637 AD. From 637 to 1099 the Arabs sometimes ill-treated and were sometimes tolerant towards their Jewish subjects. From 1099 to 1291 the Christian Crusaders mercilessly persecuted and slaughtered the Jews of Palestine. The Mameluks (Muslims) who ousted the Crusaders in 1291, and ruled until 1516, at times encouraged Jewish settlement, and many Jews came to Palestine to escape from Christian persecution in Europe. After 1517, under the Ottoman Turks the Jews of Europe continued to seek refuge in Palestine from Christian persecution and expulsion, despite spasmodic ill-treatment by their Muslim rulers
The four 'Holy Cities' of Judaism, in which there was continuous Jewish settlement from biblical times
Towns and settlements inhabited by Jews during the period of Arab rule from 637-1099
Area in which the Jews formed the main population from the thirteenth to the nineteenth century
Towns and villages with continuous Jewish communities from the thirteenth to the nineteenth century
© Martin Gilbert

Sir Martin Gilbert, © 2010. Reproduced by permission of Taylor & Francis Books UK. www.martingilbert.com

629 – 636	Byzantine
636 – 1072	Arab (Islamic)
1072 – 1099	Seljuk Turks (Islamic)
1099 – 1291	Crusader (Christian)
1291 – 1517	Mamluk (From Central Asia, Islamic)
1517 – 1917	Ottoman Empire (Islamic until 1908, then secular)
1917 – 1948	British Mandate under the League of Nations

During this entire period Jerusalem was never the capital of a ruling empire. During the 400-year rule by the Arabs, Mecca, Baghdad, Damascus and Cairo were all capitals, but Jerusalem was never one of their major cities. The Crusaders had two kingdoms along the Mediterranean coast, one of them the Jerusalem Kingdom. But even under the Crusaders, the seat of the Roman Catholic Church never moved to Jerusalem and the Crusaders never brought their families to live in the land or settle in Jerusalem. Rather, the Crusaders did military service in the Holy Land and then returned to homes and families in Europe. The only nation-state to occupy the borders of Israel/Judea/Syria Palaestina/ the Holy Land/Palestine was the Jewish nation, beginning with Joshua in 1273 BCE. And the only nation with Jerusalem as its administrative and religious capital was the Jewish nation, starting with King David in 1000 BCE.

Footnotes

[1] Daniel J. Elazar, "Deuteronomy as Israel's Ancient Constitution: Some Preliminary Reflections," Jerusalem Center for Public Affairs (http://www.jcpa.org/dje/articles2/deut-const.htm)

[2] *Ibid.*

[3] *Ibid.*

[4] *Ibid.*

[5] *Ibid.*

[6] Robert Drews, "Canaanites and Philistines." *Journal for the Study of the Old Testament* (1998) 81: 39–61.

[7] 2 Samuel 8:1–14:1.

[8] H. H. Ben-Sasson (Ed.), *A History of the Jewish People* (Cambridge, MA: Harvard University Press, 1976), 142.

[9] Shaye Cohen, "Roman Domination: The Jewish Revolt and the Destruction of the Second Temple," in *Ancient Israel*, ed. Hershel Shanks (Biblical Archaeology Society, 1999), 269-273.

[10] "Quotes on Judaism & Israel: Elazar Ben Yair Speech at Masada" (http://www.jewishvirtuallibrary.org/jsource/Quote/yairq.html)

[11] Fast forward 1,800 years to the period of the Modern Zionist movement when the story of Masada took on a new significance. In the 1960s, an expedition led by Israeli archeologist Yigal Yadin found Masada. From 1963-66 his team discovered that everything Josephus described in *The Jewish War* was there: the food storage bins, the synagogue, the cisterns, Herod's palaces, the *mikvah*, the steam room, the Roman ramp, weapons and the lots they drew to decide which warrior killed whom.

Today, Israeli Defense Forces (IDF) swear certain units into service at Masada. The swearing-in ceremony has an extra dimension: Masada is the metaphor for the Jewish return to Israel in the modern period. The Jewish people were declared dead after

Masada and they have returned vowing to never let a Jewish State be destroyed again. At the conclusion of the swearing-in ceremony, the soldiers add the line, "Masada shall not fall again!" For people unfamiliar with Jewish history or with the ideals and values of the Jewish nation, the idea of this affirmation sounds out of place and strange. But to those who know Jewish history and understand the significance of the re-establishment of Jewish sovereignty after 19 centuries of homelessness, the phrase "Masada shall not fall again" lies at the core of the ethos of the IDF and the modern State of Israel.

Masada is special because the IDF of today is made up of the descendants of the Judeans who were defeated at Masada and they are saying, "We are back! Judea has risen from the ashes like the phoenix. Judea has come back to life as the re-established Jewish State of Israel."

[12] Louis Feldman & Steve Mason, *Flavius Josephus* (Leiden, Netherlands: Brill Academic Publishers, 1999).

[13] To further emphasize what the re-establishment of a sovereign Jewish State has meant for the Jewish nation that longed and prayed for this event, in 1949, shortly after Israel won her war of independence against five Arab states, the government went back to Caesarea where the Romans had minted the *Judea Capta* and minted a new coin called "Judea has been Liberated." On the coin was a Jewish woman standing up under the same palm tree as the one on the Roman coin. Instead of crying, she is holding up a baby, while a Jewish man plants a new tree next to her.

Judea in the minds of Rome was destroyed for all time. For the Jewish nation it was a temporary destruction; the Jews knew that they were destined to return, it was just a question of time. The IDF's swearing-in ceremony at Masada and the minting of the "Judea has been Liberated" coin in 1949 are examples of the Jewish nation's relationship with *Eretz Yisrael* and its sense of commitment and belonging to it.

Chapter 3

Zionism: Ancient & Modern

The enemies of Zionism do not believe there is a Jewish nation, yet history, archeology and geography prove otherwise. The Jewish nation is one of the oldest on Earth, centered in what was the biblical land of Zion, today's modern State of Israel. Yet many of the countries who challenge Israel's status would have a hard time offering convincing arguments about their own statehood.

Can they prove common and exclusive language, common and exclusive culture and a common land of origin? Most likely that would not be the case, particularly since after the world wars the western powers divided their colonial territories around the globe into independent states that ignored existing ethnic and religious communities, creating conflict and civil/religious wars that endure to this day. Zionism and the Jewish nation have endured in their homeland for millennia, with or without sovereignty, but sadly, not without war.

Zion is a biblical word, meaning one of three things, depending on context. It can refer to a hill in Jerusalem called Mt. Zion; to the city of Jerusalem, and to *Eretz Yisrael*. In the Bible, Zion is where the Messiah will bring all Jews from the four corners of the Earth to live in peace and prosperity. Zion is a primary element of the traditional Jewish understanding of the Messiah, and is why Satmar and other Haredi sects disagree with Jews taking matters into their own hands—for creating their own Zion/Jewish state instead of waiting for the Messiah. There are also anti-Zionists on the left who claim that there is no connection between the Jewish people and *Eretz Yisrael.* Some of these people view Judaism as a religion, not as a nation, or they discount and reject the religion altogether—or both. Their goal is to delegitimize the State of Israel.

The political Zionist movement founded by Theodore Herzl in the late 19th century was a secular movement, and many religious Jews, like those in Hungarian Hasidic sects, were "turned off" because they considered the Zionists "secular messianists" who believed in creating their own future in the Jewish homeland. They did not see that secular Zionism had its roots in the Religious Zionism that simmered and churned beneath the surface for centuries before it emerged as a powerful and religious force in 19th century Modern Judaism and came to the forefront in the mid-20th century.

As noted in the previous chapter, Modern Zionism has its roots in the history of the rebellions against Greece and Rome, and in the return of Jewish leaders and others to *Eretz Yisrael* through the millennia. It has always been the hope and dream of the Jewish people to return to Zion. Religious Jews pray for that return daily and many modern Religious Zionists have taken the position that God helps those who help themselves. They moved to Israel and worked continuously to secure the reestablished Jewish State.

When Nathan Birnbaum (1864-1937, co-founder in 1882 of the Zionist youth group Kadimah) publicly coined the words Zionist and Zionism in 1892, he chose *Zion* to be the root word for his modern movement because it represented the ancient, classic and traditional relationship between the Jewish people, the Messiah and the return to Zion on the wings of eagles.

The yearning for Zion is not a new concept. Ever since the Jewish nation was forcibly exiled from Zion, from *Eretz Yisrael*, the Jewish people have yearned to return to the Land. Written close to 2,000 years ago, the *siddur*, the prayer book, with additions that were made during the Diaspora, is the Jewish text that gives poetic and constant voice to this collective yearning. Jews pray at least three times a day, and many prayers in the *siddur* beseech the Almighty to return the Jewish nation to Israel, to bring about the ingathering of the exiles and to rebuild the city of Jerusalem and the Holy Temple. There are also prayers Jews in the Diaspora recite to bless the climate and agriculture of *Eretz Yisrael.*

HOW AN ANCIENT IDEA OF JEWISH SOVEREIGNTY COMES TO LIFE AS A VIABLE OPTION FOR THE JEWISH NATION

For centuries after the exile from *Eretz Yisrael,* wherever they went, Jews were barely tolerated. Once Constantine converted, and when the office of the Emperor of Rome became the office of the Holy Roman Emperor, the charge of deicide was popularized and used to stir local populations against the Jews who settled among Christians and pagans in the realm, a realm which extended across most of Europe and England, as well as to Byzantium in the east. The charge that the Jews were eternally responsible for the murder of Jesus, the son of God and the Christian messiah, is at the basis of the ancient violent and virulent antisemitism that softened the ground for pogroms and expulsions—eventually setting the stage for the Holocaust and for the continued antisemitism that persists to this day.

In the Middle Ages, local populations turned on the Jews by forcing them to convert on threat of death. There were blood libels and pogroms, especially around Easter. Jews were said to be magicians who made a pact with the devil, and derogatory stereotypical images of Jews began to appear in Germany as early as the 12th century. The Crusades obliterated hundreds of Jewish communities in Germany, France and England. Once the Crusaders reached Jerusalem in 1099, the Jews tried to prepare themselves by gathering in the city's synagogue. Witnesses described how the Crusaders set the building ablaze and while singing "Christ, We Adore Thee" burned Jews alive.

Expulsions from England, France and Austria followed, with many Jews fleeing to the Pale of Settlement (which included all of Belarus, Lithuania and Moldova and much of present-day

Ukraine, a part of eastern Latvia and some parts of western Russia) in Eastern Europe. From 1290-1655 Jews were banned from England. In the mid-14th century, the Jews were blamed for the Black Plague that killed almost half of Europe's population. Though Pope Clement VI tried to protect them in 1389, more than 900 Jews were burned alive in Strasbourg before the plague even reached the city. In Catholic Spain, after the Inquisition (clerical insitutions to combat heresy) and the expulsion in 1492, Jews scattered around the globe, where the Inquisition, which had also spread to Portugal, pursued them even to the shores of the New World. Auto da fés, the burning of Jews as heretics, continued from 1481-1850 in Spain, Portugal, Peru, Brazil and Mexico.

Christians were not the only religious zealots who made it their business to forcibly convert people to their religions. Since the 9th century, Muslims imposed *dhimmi* status on their Jewish, Christian and pagan populations. While Jews under Muslim rule were permitted to practice their Judaism more than they could under Christian rule, they still were subject to strong restrictions, especially when the *Imams* (heads of Muslim communities) began treating *dhimmis* more harshly. For example, while Muslim Spain at first welcomed Jews, when the regimes changed in the 12th century and became harsher, many Jews, including Maimonides, fled to more tolerant Muslim lands, like *Eretz Yisrael*, Morocco and Egypt.

In Europe, Jews were prevented from joining guilds, or even apprenticing for professions like carpenters, blacksmiths, goldsmiths and silversmiths. They could not own land, open inns or do much more than collect taxes and rent for the powers that be—the churches and the nobility—and to act as moneylenders. Because people resented handing over their money to others, they also resented those who collected it, forgetting that the collectors were just doing what their employers ordered them to do.

Jews could not live in cities, and had to stay in their own neighborhoods outside town walls—and later were forced to live in ghettos (derived from the Venetian for a restricted area).

Jews in Europe paid extra taxes for being allowed to do so and were further humiliated by being required to wear badges or hats marking their status as Jews.

Adding insult to injury was the introduction of the blood libel, which involved accusing Jews of murdering Christian children and using their blood in the unleavened bread eaten on Passover—a purported mocking of the Eucharist.

In England, during the Middle Ages, the murders of William of Norwich, Hugh of Lincoln and Simon of Trent were excuses to level charges of blood libels against the Jews and to decimate and loot their communities.

> Altogether, there have been about 150 recorded cases of blood libel (not to mention thousands of rumors) that resulted in the arrest and killing of Jews throughout history, most of them in the Middle Ages. In almost every case, Jews were murdered, sometimes by a mob, sometimes following torture and a trial.[1]

In Spain, in the late 15th century, monarchs Ferdinand and Isabella, needing funding for mercantile expansion and not wanting to repay the Jewish moneylenders who had provided their court with funds, initiaited the Spanish Inquisition to force conversion to Roman Catholicism upon all who lived within Spain's borders or be forced to leave the country without any assets. Tomás de Torquemada (1420-1498), a Spanish Dominican friar, became the first Grand Inquisitor. Many Jews converted to avoid expulsion or death but remained secretly Jewishly observant. Called *Morranos* (pigs), today they are known as *Conversos*. For those who would not convert, in 1492 they were formally expelled from Spain, where the majority fled to Palestine, North Africa, Turkey, the Pale of Settlement and the Netherlands, and subsequently became merchants and tradesmen. A few made it to the New World via Holland and settled in Recífe, Brazil. But when the Portuguese Inquisition threatened them there almost 150 years later, they fled to New Amsterdam/Manhattan, arriving in 1654, to form the beginnings of the American Jewish community.

In the mid-16th century, the Reformation against the Catholic Church, led by Martin Luther, an Augustinian friar, put Jewish communities in jeopardy from Protestant communities. In addition to continuing the Catholic accusations of deicide and blood libels, Luther inveighed against them, inciting pogroms and ordering the genocide of the entire Jewish nation.*

From the mid-to late 17th century, the Jews who had fled to the Polish-Lithuanian Commonwealth and the Pale of Settlement were subjected to the Khmelnytsky uprisings (1648) against the Polish nobility and the Jews who served as their stewards. Jews were also murdered at the hands of the Ottoman Empire in places like *Eretz Yisrael* and Turkey and were expelled from Yemen.

The situation was so dire that many Jews pinned their hopes on Shabbtai Zevi, a Jew from the Ottoman Empire who declared himself the Jewish Messiah in 1665 and claimed he would bring everyone to Zion. He was a fraud who later converted to Islam and caused many Jews to lose their faith. He was not the first to make that claim.

In the 18th century, European populations began to rebel against the power structures that controlled them and began asserting their individual rights—and the issue of where the Jews would fit into this "civil rights" issue became known, early on, as The Jewish Question. Despite a quest for basic human rights, philosophers of the time, like Voltaire (François-Marie Arouet

---

*So heinous were the results of Luther's antisemitism and the resultant deaths of thousands upon thousands of Jews, that in 1998 the Land Synod of the Evangelical Lutheran Church in Bavaria issued a statement saying,

> "It is imperative for the Lutheran Church, which knows itself to be indebted to the work and tradition of Martin Luther, to take seriously also his anti-Jewish utterances, to acknowledge their theological function, and to reflect on their consequences. It has to distance itself from every [expression of] anti-Judaism in Lutheran theology" ("Christians and Jews: A Declaration of the Lutheran Church of Bavaria," November 24, 1998, also printed in *Freiburger Rundbrief,* 6:3 (1999), 191–197).

1694-1778), were vociferous in their rabid antisemitism. He, for example, had enormous influence on the French grassroots, which made antisemitism in France acceptable.

In 1744, all but ten Jewish families were locked out of Breslau, and Frederick II of Prussia recommended that all Jews be thrown out of Prussian cities. In 1752, Jews had to pay Maria Theresa (sovereign of Austria, Hungary, Croatia, Bohemia, Transylvania, Mantua, Milan, Lodomeria and Galicia, the Austrian Netherlands and Parma, 1740-1780) for the right to live in Austria. Russia increased its discrimination against Jews when it increased its Jewish population by conquering the Pale of Settlement from Poland in 1772, as Jews were trapped and prevented from returning to their homes in Poland proper by Catherine the Great (Empress of Russia, 1762-1796).

Major changes in the status of European Jewry began with the birth of the philosophical movement called the Enlightenment, a movement that had its roots in the Renaissance. The Enlightenment challenged over a thousand years of political and religious dogma that declared that Europe was destined to be ruled by two institutions: royal families/monarchies, and official Christian churches, mostly the Roman Catholic Church. These two institutions, royalty and religion, had dominated all aspects of European life for centuries.

Over previous centuries, these two power structures had a unique and mutually beneficial relationship. Monarchs were granted a form of divine right for their families to rule and their respective countries' chief clergyman would support that claim as representatives of God's will on earth—as long as the monarchy paid the church's bills through taxation of its subjects. This made people recognize that their meager incomes were being taxed to support a corrupt and immoral nobility sheltered by the church. Being hungry because they had no money for food while monarchs built extravaganzas like Versailles and L'Orangerie infuriated them.

At the same time, people began to believe in science and questioned religion. Secularism was born, and the fight for men's equality began.

In the British Colonies in North America, the American Revolution that began in 1776 set the standard for people seeking to free themselves from oppressive monarchies and religion, and pioneered in establishing a democratic republic where the people governed themselves and established religious freedom. The idea was to bring equal rights and privileges to the citizenry of all religions except, of course, their slaves.

The Revolutionary War inspired the French Revolution in 1789, which set in motion the "emancipation" of the Jews of Europe. Like their allies in the Colonies, French revolutionaries fought a battle against the monarchy and the church for individual freedom and self-governance.

The grassroots, via mob rule and at the incitement of the intellectual elites, overthrew the French monarchy, executed the king and queen, and stripped the Roman Catholic Church of all of its political and most of its economic power. The monarchs who ruled nearby countries, fearing for their own thrones, collaborated in an effort to take France back and reinstate the monarchy. In 1792, Austria, Spain, Portugal, Sardinia, Prussia and their allies attacked France. To their horror, their invasion did not destroy the French Republic; French armies counterattacked and by 1800 were in control of most of Western Europe. Once in control, they promoted democracy and self-governance, seen as anti-monarchy, anti-church and pro-individual rights. Eventually freed from French rule, these new entities established their own nation-states. For close to fourteen centuries most Europeans had defined themselves by monarch and church, not country. When the monarchies and churches were weakened, the new secular identity emrged as *nationalism*—dedication to their common language, common culture and common history. This new identity proved to be exceptionally powerful.

The Jews in France found themselves under the rule of a new secular French government prepared to view Jews as equal citizens. As Napoleon conquered city after city in Western Europe, he gave orders to blow up the ghetto walls wherever he found them. When living in ghettos, Jews were allowed to leave for work only during daylight hours and had to return by nightfall. When the French blew up the ghettos, it was the first time Jews were welcome to join society as equals, an opportunity that had not existed for 1,400 years. As a result, the Jewish community faced new challenges as it transitioned to the Modern Age, a transition that fostered a serious debate that continues to this very day.

Known as the Emancipation, there were three Jewish reactions: One was to accept this remarkable offer and take as little of the Jewish ghetto with you upon entering gentile society. Without converting to Christianity, one could try to assimilate to the new secular society as much as possible. The second was to reject the offer because it would lead to complete assimilation and intermarriage. The idea was to create invisible "fences" against assimilation by remaining separate and apart from gentile society and thus remaining true to Judaism. The third option was to cautiously accept the offer—leave the ghetto and take your Judaism with you. Do not be ashamed of your Jewish garb, traditions and culture. Bring it with you to the outside world and take from society what is worthwhile not in conflict with Jewish law, and reject what conflicts with Jewish law.

The overwhelming majority of Jews who entered the secular world of Western Europe assimilated within three generations (around the 1860s), or joined the newly formed Reform Jewish Movement, a form of Judaism that sought to embody the tenets of the Enlightenment.

As Arthur Hertzberg described Reform Judaism in *The Zionist Idea*,

> ...they denied that such absolute obedience to the commandments of the tradition was either possible, in the light of obligations imposed by equal citizenship, or intellectually defensible before the bar of rational criticism of the religious heritage. It, therefore, defined the religion of the Jew as an ethical creed, the moral heritage of the Bible. The traditional return to Zion could not be allowed to remain in

the liturgy as even a pious dream, for its presence might call into question the unqualified loyalty of the Jew to the state. It was replaced by the doctrine of the "mission of Israel," the belief that the Jews had been dispersed in the world by a beneficent Providence to act as its teachers and guides toward the ideals of justice and righteousness developed in the Bible. Nay, more, the Messiah was now to be identified with the vision of an age of individual liberty and universal peace...."[2]

The Reform movement also emphasized that the Jews are a religious group comprised of the citizens of the nation-states in which they live, and not a Jewish peoplehood. This was a break with 3,000 years of Jewish tradition and culture and it was a position restated at the Reform movement's international convocation in Pittsburgh in 1937.

There were many Jews who left the ghettos as proud *halacha*-keeping Jews; some were forerunners of today's Centrist or Modern Orthodox movements. Then and today they walk a tightrope between two worlds, and their ideological approach has created a universe of *halachic* literature and practice that shows how Judaism and Jews can and do contend with the ever-changing modern world.

And there are those who remained in the ghetto *halachically* and psychologically, those who wear distinctive clothing and practice ultra-strict observance, like the Hasidim.

By analyzing the results of the Emancipation on the Jews of Western Europe we see how the Modern Zionist Movement put into action the ideals and values that the Jews had been holding dear and praying for since the destruction of the Second Temple in 70 CE.

We know that by the mid-1800s there were Jewish politicians, millionaires, doctors, professors, lawyers, military officers, writers and journalists—an unprecedented Jewish presence in the dominant culture of nation-states—and some of them were in positions of influence.

There were now Jewish individuals who could pursue a Jewish agenda that until then they could only dream of but not pursue because of their previous legal inferior status. And one of the top items on the Jewish agenda had always been the goal of re-establishing Jewish sovereignty in *Eretz Yisrael*. Jewish nationalism could now be realized.

After seventeen centuries of seeing themselves as a nation in exile who prayed and longed to return collectively to their national home, the Jewish nation now had an audience to speak to in Western Europe. Long dreaming of renewing ancient Jewish nationalism, it wasn't until modern nationalism came into being that the peoples around them understood the Jewish longing for the homeland. Once modern-day nationalism was born and peoples throughout Western Europe saw themselves as members of nation-states, the idea of Jewish nationalism became a viable idea and spoken about by Jews. Additionally, there were now Jews in positions of power to help implement the age-old dream of the return to Zion.

THE PRE-MODERN ZIONIST THINKERS 1820s – 1860s

The first articles about the return to Zion appeared in the late 1820s, and said that the return was viable because of the new status of Jews in Western Europe and because nationalism was an accepted principle. The first to write about this was Rabbi Judah Ben Solomon Chai Alkalai (1798-1878), a Sephardic Kabbalist from Sarajevo, Bosnia.

Alkalai's view of a Jewish return to the Land of Israel was a religious one. He maintained, based on an ample body of religious literature, that the coming of the Messiah and divine redemption of the Jews require their return to the Promised Land. His Kabbalistic view made him specifically assert that the year 1840 was the Year of Redemption, which was not a single year, but "a century, from this day until 1939," representing the "days of the Messiah." Unless powerful practical steps were taken, this opportunity would be lost and the next extended "year" starting in 1940 would be one of great hardship when "with an outpouring of wrath will gather our

dispersed." The outcome—the return to the Promised Land—
would be the same, but under much harsher circumstances.[3]

Rabbi Alkalai raised the issue of Jewish political independence
and *Eretz Yisrael* for the first time in 1834, in a small booklet
entitled *Shema Yisrael* ("Hear, O Israel"). In his essay, he proposed
a beginning of Jewish settlement in *Eretz Yisrael* as a precursor
to messianic redemption. Such an idea was considered heretical
among many Jews who believed that messianic redemption would
come only through a miraculous event caused by God. Within
Alkalai's proposition of a natural process of redemption, there was
the inclusion of the rabbinic doctrine, expressed in the Midrash
and homiletic literature, that the Messiah, son of Joseph, would
first come to lead the people of Israel in the apocalyptic war of
Gog and Magog/Armageddon, and would then re-conquer *Eretz
Yisrael*, freeing it from foreign domination.

When the Damascus Blood Libel took place in 1840-41,
Rabbi Alkalai's community was shaken to its foundation when
thirteen Jews were arrested on charges of blood libel. They were
imprisoned and tortured. Four were murdered and one converted
before the survivors were released in 1841, after Ottoman Sultan
Abdulmejid (1823-1861) issued a *firman* (edict) against blood libels.
As a result of the trial, the synagogue in Damascus was pillaged, an
act that drew international condemnation. A delegation of Western
influential men, led by Sir Moses Montefiore (1784-1885) of Great
Britain, went to Alexandria in protest. Included in the delegation
were American Jews, marking the first time that members of an
American Jewish community, numbering but 15,000, united in
protest of treatment of fellow Jews elsewhere in the world. They
even persuaded the U.S. President, Martin Van Buren, to lodge a
protest.

Historian Hasia Diner writes that the Damascus Affair...

> "launched modern Jewish politics on an international scale,
> and for American Jews it represented their first effort at
> creating a distinctive political agenda. Just as the United States

had used this affair to proclaim its presence on the global scale, so too did American Jews, in their newspapers and at mass meetings, announce to their coreligionists in France and England that they too ought to be thought of as players in global Jewish diplomacy."[4]

It also resulted in the growth of Jewish newspapers in the capitals of Western Europe.

This blood libel convinced Rabbi Alkalai that freedom and security for the nation could and would only be achieved in the land of the forefathers, and that the redemption would only come about through positive action on the part of the Jewish community. He dreamed of establishing a worldwide organization along the lines of the various national organizations then prevalent among other nations of Europe. The purpose of these organizations would be to buy and reclaim land in *Eretz Yisrael*, ideas that were subsequently adopted by Theodor Herzl and the World Zionist Organization (W.Z.O.).

> Now we pray every day: Let our eyes behold Thy return to Zion in mercy and if we believe our own words, then upon whom will the Divine Presence become manifest? Upon the trees and the rocks? Therefore, as the first step to the beginning of redemption of our souls we must return to the Land 22,000 (Jews), the Holy One Blessed Be He to cause the Divine Presence to descend upon them. This most certainly will be followed by His showing us and all of Israel beneficial signs. Such an idea is hinted at in the Torah: And Jacob came in peace to the city of Shechem... and he bought the parcel of ground where he spread his tent. Why did Jacob buy the land if his only intention was to rest there for a time and then continue on to see his father, Isaac? It is apparent that this act was realized to teach his descendants that the redemption would come about by purchasing the land from its inhabitants. Because he bought the parcel of land it was as if he lived (permanently) on it. More so, the redemption from Egypt brought the people of Israel to a good and spacious land,

one whose wells were already dug, and whose vineyards and olive groves were already planted. Yet, because of our sins, the Land is now empty and desolate and we must, for this redemption, build the houses and dig the wells and plant the vineyards and the olive groves.[5]

Rabbi Alkalai speaks of massive *Aliyah* and mentions the Kabbalistic number of 22,000, not individuals or small groups making *Aliyah* who were the norm since the destruction of Judea. As it turned out, the First *Aliyah*, 1882–1903, consisted of 24,000 Jews. The purchase of land in Israel began in the 1880s, and was a cornerstone of modern Zionism.

Rabbi Alkalai also spoke of the need to revive Hebrew:

> I wish to attest to the pain I have always felt at the error of our ancestors, that they allowed our Holy Tongue to be forgotten. Because of this our people divided into seventy peoples; our one language was replaced by the seventy languages of the lands of exile. …We must redouble our efforts to maintain Hebrew and to strengthen its position. It must be the basis of our educational work.[6]

Finally, Rabbi Alkalai emphasized the need for the Jewish nation to create a Council of Elders, a group for global Jewish leadership.

> The Redemption will begin with the efforts by the Jews themselves, they must organize and unite, choose leaders, and leave the lands of exile. Since no community can exist without a governing body, they very first ordinance must be the appointment of the elders of each district, men of piety and wisdom, to oversee all the affairs of the community. I humbly suggest that this chosen assembly—the assembly of the elders—is what is meant by the promise to us of the Messiah, the son of Joseph.[7]

Rabbi Alkalai articulated the ideas of mass *Aliyah*, purchasing large tracts of land, reviving Hebrew as an everyday spoken language, and the creation of a Jewish governing body representing all the Jews of the world in 1843. Fifty-four years later in Basel, Switzerland, Theodor Herzl implemented these ideas. Rabbi Alkalai eventually made *Aliyah* himself and today there is a town in Israel named after him called Ohr Yehuda.

The second pre-Modern Zionist thinker was an Ashkenazi Orthodox rabbi, Rabbi Tzvi Hirsch Kalischer (1795–1874). Born in what today is Western Poland and was then under Prussian control, Rabbi Kalischer was also influenced by the changes taking place in Europe and the Damascus Blood Libel. Rabbi Kalischer was considered a *Talmid Chacham*—a master of Jewish religious studies, both Torah and Talmud. He gained fame by publicly debating Reform rabbis. In 1862, he wrote *Seeking Zion*, about the Jewish nation returning to *Eretz Yisrael*.

> The Redemption of Israel for which we long, is not to be imagined as a sudden miracle. The Almighty, blessed be His Name, will not suddenly descend from on high and command his people to go forth. He will not send the Messiah from heaven in a twinkling of an eye, to sound the great trumpet for the scattered of Israel and gather them into Jerusalem. He will not surround the holy city with a wall of fire and cause the Holy Temple to descend from the heavens. The bliss and miracles that were promised by His servants, the prophets, will certainly come to pass—everything will be fulfilled—but we will not run in terror and flight, for the Redemption of Israel will come by slow degrees, and the ray of deliverance will shine forth gradually.[8]

Rabbi Kalischer saw current events in the same light as Rabbi Alkalai: The Almighty was creating conditions that had not existed since the destruction of the Second Temple to allow the Jews to pursue their age-old dream of reconstituting Jewish sovereignty in *Eretz Yisrael*. He also believed that the return of thousands and tens of thousands of Jews was the beginning of the Redemption. All the supernatural events that the prophets spoke about would in fact occur, but first Jews had to go there, buy land and start building, just as God had indicated.

Can we logically explain why the Redemption will begin in a natural manner, and why the Lord, in His love for his people, will not immediately send the Messiah in an obvious miracle? Yes, we can. We know that our worship of God is in the form of trials by which He tests us. When God created man and placed him in the Garden of Eden, He also planted the Tree of Knowledge and then commanded man not to eat it. Why did He put the Tree in the Garden if not as a trial? Why did he allow the Snake to enter the Garden, to tempt man, if not to test whether man would observe God's command? When Israel went forth from Egypt, God again tested man's faith with hunger and thirst along the way. The laws given in the Torah about unclean animals which are forbidden us as food are also a continuous trial, else why did the Almighty make them so tempting and succulent? Throughout the days of our dispersion we have suffered martyrdom for the sanctity of God's Name; we have been dragged from land to land and have borne the yoke of exile through the ages, all for the sake of His holy Torah and a further stage of the testing of our faith.

If the Almighty would suddenly appear, one day in the future through undeniable miracles, this would be no trial. What straining of our faith would there be in the face of the miracles and wonders attending a clear heavenly command to go up and inherit the land and enjoy its good fruit? Under such circumstances, what fool would not go there, not because of his love of God, but for his own selfish sake? Only a natural beginning of the Redemption is a true test of those who initiate it. To concentrate all one's energy on this holy work and to renounce home and fortune for the sake of living in Zion before "the voice of gladness" and "the voice of joy" are heard—there is no greater merit or trial than this.[9]

Rabbi Kalischer also expanded upon Rabbi Alkalai's concept that the Jewish nation must, from a religious perspective, take part in its own redemption. This theme was later picked up by the leaders of the Religious Zionist movement, the most famous among them being Rabbi Avraham Yitzchak Kook and Rabbi Naftali Zvi Yehuda Berlin (known as the "Netziv").

By using the models in the Tanach, starting with Abraham and ending with Ezra and Nechemia, Jewish leaders began to take matters into their own hands. Like their forebears, they had great faith in the Almighty and took steps in the "real" world to change their reality. They believed in free will because they had faith in God. They believed that those who did not act, who waited for God to send miracles and signs, wonders and symbols, had less faith in Him.

A biblical example would be the time when Abraham heard Lot had been kidnapped. He gathered together three hundred and eighteen student/warriors and went on a successful rescue mission. Afterwards, he did not take credit for his military prowess. What he did was thank God for giving him the assistance he needed to succeed. This attitude in Jewish leaders is found in countless places in the Tanach.

Jewish leaders were pious, God-fearing, well-versed in the laws of the Torah, and at the same time were very involved in earthly realities. This is true of the Judges, the Prophets and leaders like Ezra and Nechemia. These people made political, military, social and economic decisions as leaders of the Jewish nation.

This was normal and natural. Judaism has a "natural" concept— *Yishuv Ha Olam*—settling the Earth. It comes from Genesis, when the Almighty commands man to inherit the Earth and settle it; to make it inhabitable and livable for mankind, physically and spiritually. Jewish kings were commanded to have a Torah scroll with them at all times. Judges and kings led armies into battles, ran the Jewish state and were involved in collecting taxes, building of cities and infrastructures. All of these were Jewish endeavors.

The Jewish generation that merited seeing the most miracles is the generation that left Egypt during the Exodus. That generation's entire existence was dependent upon one divine miracle after the next, starting with the ten plagues and the splitting of the Red Sea to the forty years they were sustained by manna in the Sinai Desert. The Torah tells us that this generation continually challenged the Almighty and kept speaking about wanting to return to Egypt where things were "great." There is a direct correlation between their constant complaining and challenging God and the number of divine miracles God sent their way.

This lack of faith is understandable because they had been slaves, and the children and grandchildren of slaves, who lived in demeaning and horrible conditions. Their lack of faith is not something to be judged by later Jewish generations. The next Jewish generation, the one born as free men and women in the Sinai and under the guidance of Moses and the laws of the Torah, had a very different relationship with God. They earned the privilege of entering and conquering *Eretz Yisrael*, and required less openly divine miracles to be performed for them. This is written in a positive light in the Book of Joshua, which praises the first free generation for its greater faith in God.

Rabbi Kalischer was trying to remind his Jewish brethren that the Diaspora is an unnatural state for Jews, and caused a mutation in terms of their understanding of their role regarding the Redemption. Sitting passively and simply waiting for a supernatural event to occur is not a Jewish idea or value. Jews are supposed to be the Almighty's partners on Earth. They must always give their best effort, not rely on miracles and hope that their efforts will warrant the Almighty to bless their efforts for a positive outcome.

Jews are not permitted to sit with a very sick person and just pray for a cure. They must bring him/her to the best doctor available while praying to the Almighty for a positive outcome. This is the parallel to Rabbi Kalischer's view of redemption. It involves the Jewish nation's active participation, and a redefinition of what constitutes faith and miracles.

The miracles in Tanach were steeped in a partnership between man and God. Joshua, David and the Maccabees knew for certain that when they entered into battle they could lose, yet they had enough faith to put their lives on the line. They believed that the Almighty would assist them in their battles against the enemies of the Jewish nation. Their victories were not of their own making. They praised the Almighty for their victories, seeing themselves as His tools.

This is the main point Rabbi Kalischer was making. He realized that by 1863 the world had changed so dramatically that the dream of returning to Zion could be achieved, thanks to the Almighty creating these conditions. Now it was up to the Jewish nation to recognize the remarkable opportunity and act as agents of change. This is the essence of Religious Zionism.

Later in his life, Rabbi Kalischer made *Aliyah*. A Religious Zionist kibbutz in the Beit She'an Valley was named after him, Kibbutz Tirat Tzvi.

The last of the three pre-modern Zionist thinkers was Moses Hess (1812–1875). Hess approached Zionism differently from the rabbis. Hess was an assimilated Western European Jew, a product of the Enlightenment and the Emancipation. A Jewish intellectual who saw himself as German first, European second, being Jewish was a distant third. He was a social historian involved in pushing for changes; Karl Marx (1818-1883) and Friedrich Engels (1820-1895) were personal friends. He understood the power of modern nationalism and the effect that it was having on the consciousness of many Europeans and the changing borders. Hess saw modern Italy being reborn as a combination of tiny states and provinces who felt a kinship to the ancient Roman Empire. He saw how a nationalist spark could ignite a flame in the hearts of millions.

Hess, unlike the rabbis who ran to embrace the idea of the return to Zion, backed into it, as did many of the non-Orthodox Zionist leaders of the late 19th century and the early and middle part of the 20th century. Hess saw all these great things happening around him and came to realize he had been estranged from his own history, culture, religion and all it had to offer. He saw that even in secular Europe antisemitism was still a powerful and growing phenomenon, and was also influenced by the Damascus Blood Libel. He saw antisemitism was alive in many parts of the world, but that Western Jews, if they truly desired, could work hard to challenge and perhaps defeat it. Events had convinced him it was time for him to be a member of the Jewish nation first, and to be concerned about his nation's future. He became an advocate of the Jewish nation returning to its ancient homeland and reestablishing sovereignty there. In *Rome and Jerusalem* (1862) he wrote:

> After twenty years of estrangement I have returned to my people. Once again I am sharing in its festivals of joy and days of sorrow, in its hopes and memories. I am taking part in the spiritual and intellectual struggles of our day, both within the House of Israel and between our people and the gentile world. The Jews have lived and labored among the nations for almost two thousand years, but nonetheless they cannot become rooted organically within them.
>
> A sentiment which I believed I had suppressed beyond recall is alive once again. It is the thought of my nationality, which is inseparably connected with my ancestral heritage, with the Holy Land and the Eternal City, the birthplace of the belief in the divine unity of life and of the hope for the ultimate brotherhood of all men.
>
> For years this half-strangled emotion has been stirring in my breast and clamoring for expression, but I had not the strength to swerve from my own path, which seemed so far from the road of Judaism, to a new one which I could envisage only vaguely in the hazy distance.
>
> Twenty years ago, when news came to Europe from Damascus of an absurd accusation against the Jews, a feeling of agony, as bitter as it was justified, was evoked in the hearts of all Jews. Once again we were face to face with the ignorance and credulity of the mobs of Asia and Europe, which are as ready today as they have been for the past two thousand years to believe any calumny directed against the Jews. I was painfully reminded, for the first time in many

years, that I belong to an unfortunate, maligned, despised, and dispersed people—but one that the world has not succeeded in destroying. At that time, though I was still greatly estranged from Judaism, I wanted to cry out in anguish in expression of my Jewish patriotism, but this emotion was immediately superseded by the greater pain which was evoked in me by the suffering of the proletariat of Europe.[10]

Toward The Jewish Restoration

Have your eyes ever read the words of the prophet Isaiah? "Comfort ye, comfort ye My people, saith your God. Bid Jerusalem take heart, and proclaim unto her, that her time of service is accomplished, that her guilt is paid off; that she hath received of the Lord's hand double for all her sins... Clear ye in the wilderness the way of the Lord, make plain in the desert a highway for our God.

Every valley shall be lifted up, and every mountain and hill shall be made low; and the rugged shall be made level, and the rough places a plain. And the glory of the Lord shall be revealed, and all flesh shall see it together; for the mouth of the Lord hath spoken it."

Do you not believe that in these opening words of the prophecies of Second Isaiah, as well as in the closing verse of the book of Obadiah (1:21), the conditions of our day are depicted? Is not everything being made even and prepared; is not the road of civilization being laid in the desert by the digging of the Suez Canal, and by the work on a railroad which will connect Europe and Asia? To be sure, none of this reflects any intention to re-establish our nation, but you know the proverb: Man proposes and God disposes.

What we have to do at present for the regeneration of the Jewish nation is, first, to keep alive the hope of the political rebirth of our people, and, next, to reawaken that hope where it slumbers. When political conditions in the Orient shape themselves so as to permit the organization of a beginning of the restoration of a Jewish state, this beginning will express itself in the founding of Jewish colonies in the land of their ancestors, to which enterprise France will undoubtedly lend a hand. France, beloved friend, is the savior who will restore our people to its place in universal history.[11]

Hess did not make *Aliyah* to *Eretz Yisrael*, but he was the first of many assimilated Western European Jews to be inspired by Jewish history and the remarkable story of the Jewish nation which felt the time was right to return to *Eretz Yisrael* and re-establish Jewish sovereignty.

Unfortunately, the very conditions in the West that created the fertile religious and intellectual atmosphere for the Jewish nation to act on its 2,000-year-old return to Zion also created conditions that almost guaranteed that these three pre-Modern Zionist thinkers would not have a large following.

The vast majority of post-French Revolution and emancipated Western European Jews were happy to integrate into Western European society. The path to acceptance, however, was not conversion to Christianity, it was enough to be less Jewish. This was compounded by nationalism in countries where Jews lived. Western European Jews fervently embraced their new identities as Frenchmen, Germans, Italians and so forth. The idea that they would now remind their gentile neighbors that they, loyal citizens well-integrated into society, would be members of the Jewish nation longing to return to their ancestral homeland was absurd to most of them.

Though the ideas of Modern Zionism were articulated in Europe as early as 1843, the Modern Zionist Movement with tens of thousands of members would not be born until the 1880s in another part of the world.

EASTERN EUROPE AND THE BIRTH OF THE MODERN ZIONIST MOVEMENT

Though all the conditions necessary for the birth of Modern Zionism existed in Western Europe by the 1840s, Jews as a whole were very content with their situation there and were not interested in Jewish nationalism. In Eastern Europe, however, where none of the requisite conditions existed, Modern Zionism found a receptive audience.

Eastern Europe in the late 1800s was, for the most part, Russia, a country ruled by Czars that had not yet experienced anything remotely close to the Enlightenment. And Russia still had a powerful church (the Russian Orthodox Church) that was seen as part of the Russian government and its national identity.

As such, old-fashioned Christian-inspired official antisemitism thrived there. Deliberate government antisemitism required most Russian Jews to live within a clearly defined area known as the Pale of Settlement. Until 1917, it comprised about 20 percent of European Russia and corresponded to much of present-day Belarus, Lithuania, Moldova, Poland, Ukraine and parts of western Russia.

At first, Jews were simply forbidden to live outside the Pale. Later, main cities in the Pale itself were also declared out of bounds. Inside the Pale, Jews lived in tight clusters containing anywhere from a few hundred to a few thousand people. Mostly, they lived in small towns known as *shtetls*. The people of the *shtetl* were primarily Orthodox Jews whose lives revolved around family, synagogue, yeshiva and *mikvah*. Though their lives overall were not wonderful by any stretch of the imagination, they had learned to live under dire conditions.

The seven million Jews who lived in Russia in 1880 were somehow comforted by the thought that as unpleasant as life was, things could get worse—but then they did. In the late 1870s, a group of radical Russians reasoned that the French had their revolution a hundred years previously and now it was time for Russia to rid itself of its monarchy and free the peasants.

This small group of revolutionaries, despite the fact that they didn't have the kind of grassroots support that drove the French Revolution, decided to assassinate the Czar to spark a revolt, mistakenly believing that the masses were a silent majority who were on their side.

When Czar Alexander II was murdered in 1881, nothing changed when Alexander III came into power. His agents caught and convicted one of the few Jewish radicals, who was made to look like the instigator of the plot to prevent the former Czar from initiating economic reforms. After several weeks of newspaper editorials and articles attacking Jews, and speeches made by government and non-government officials, the populace was whipped into a frenzy. Pogroms against the Jews in Russia began and continued for years. Bands of local Russians would attack Jewish *shtetls*, maim, rape, burn and murder, while the police were nowhere to be found. Sometimes, the local police took off their uniforms and participated, as did some Cossacks.

And so it came time for Russia's Jews to re-evaluate their situation. Until then they'd known their lives were not perfect, but somehow one could survive in Russia as a Jew. Now that was becoming impossible.

The Jews reacted in three ways:

1) Hundreds of thousands emigrated to the West in search of a better life, most of them going to the United States. Between 1882 and 1914 close to 2.5 million Russian/Eastern European Jews moved to the U.S. Another half million moved to Western European countries like England, France and Germany;

2) Some Jews (mostly young and relatively assimilated) got involved in the radical politics of the new Russian underground, whose goal was to overthrow the Czar and establish a new liberal Russian republic. Eventually, many leaders of the successful Bolshevik Revolution of 1917 were Jewish. But, for the most part, this involved only a small group.

3) Many young Jews turned to Zionism (Jewish nationalism).

Eventually tens of thousands of Jews concluded that they must leave Russia, but had no intention of immigrating to a gentile country. Their answer was the solution to the Jewish homelessness problem. It was time for Jews to return to *Eretz Yisrael* and establish the foundations of what could become an independent Jewish State. In 1882, these young Russian Jews formed an organization called Lovers of Zion, *Hovevei Zion*, and moved to *Eretz Yisrael*.

The founder was Rabbi Samuel Mohilever (1824-1898), an Orthodox rabbi from Vilna, who was involved in public discussions about pogroms with Jewish leadership. In 1881, Rabbi Mohilever, who lived in Lvov (Lemberg/Lviv) at the time, was the first to suggest that Jews start resettling *Eretz Yisrael*. His greatest personal achievement was to found the first modern Zionist organization, the Merkaz Haruchni, that eventually became the Mizrachi Party, the oldest Orthodox Zionist party. Because he enjoyed a close relationship with Baron Edmond de Rothschild, a wealthy French Jew who agreed to bankroll this new *Aliyah* to *Eretz Yisrael*, he realized that even though he was an Orthodox rabbi it was still important to work with all Jews, observant or not, since the resettlement of *Eretz Yisrael* was such an important *mitzvah*.

While Rabbi Mohilever was the founder of the Hovevei Tzion movement, there were two philosophers who had huge influence in the movement: Moses Lilienblum and Dr. Leo Pinsker.

MOSES LEIB LILIENBLUM

The Jews who chose to either join or identify with the Hovevei Tzion were very influenced by the writings of Moses Leib Lilienblum (1843-1901), a man who was raised Orthodox but chose to try to assimilate into Russian society and culture. Though he had heard of pogroms, he had never witnessed one. At the age of 37, during the Odessa pogrom of 1881, that changed.

Seeing and hearing the brutality personally, was a life-changing experience for him. "I am glad I have suffered," he wrote in his diary on May 7, one day after the riots. He described what happened as the rioters approached his house:

> The women shrieked and wailed, hugging their children to their breasts, and did not know where to turn. The men stood by dumbfounded. . . . At least once in my life I have had the opportunity to feel what my ancestors felt every day of their lives. Their lives were one long terror, why should I experience nothing of that fright? ... I am their son, their suffering is dear to me and I am exalted by their glory.[12]

What was particularly shocking to Lilienblum was that it was not only Cossacks and peasants who were participating in the pogroms, but cultured, educated Russians as well. As a result, he returned to the Jewish community he had forsaken and became an ardent Zionist. One could say that unlike Rabbis Alkalai and Kalischer who ran towards Zionism, Lilienblum, like Moses Hess, backed into it. He finally understood that the Jews of Russia had no chance of ever being accepted by Russian society as equals. "It was not a lack of high culture that was the cause of our tragedy," he wrote, "for aliens we are and aliens we shall remain, even if we become full to the brim with [Russian and secular] culture."[13]

This realization pushed him to reach the conclusion that the Jews are in fact a nation that needs to return to its ancestral homeland, *Eretz Yisrael*, if they want to live a life of normalcy.

> "Why should we be aliens in foreign lands," he wrote, "when the land of our forefathers is not yet forgotten on the face of the earth, is still desolate and capable ... of receiving our people. We must purchase much land and innumerable estates and slowly settle them."[14]

LEO PINSKER

Unlike Lilienblum, Leo Pinsker (1821-1891) did not leave the Russian Orthodox Jewish community to assimilate into Russian society. He was one of the very few Russian Jews who, in the 19th century, received a secular upbringing. Pinsker even attended medical school and became a doctor and a decorated officer in the Russian Army for his service in the Crimean War (1853 – 1856). Thus antisemitism was not something that was remotely part of Pinsker's life. But that all changed when a wave of pogroms began in 1881. Like Lilienblum, Pinsker was shocked and horrified by the fact that supposedly educated and cultured Russians participated in the vicious attacks. And Pinsker reached the same conclusions that Lilienblum did, but being a physician, he used medical terms to describe the problem. He diagnosed antisemitism as an incurable disease, and the reason that the Jews were so susceptible to this disease was the fact that they were homeless as a nation.

The Jewish people has no fatherland of its own, though many motherlands; no center of focus or gravity, no government of its own, no official representation. They home everywhere, but are nowhere at home. The nations have never to deal with a Jewish nation but always with mere Jews. The Jews are not a nation because they lack a certain distinctive national character inherent in all other nations, which is formed by common residence in a single state. It was clearly impossiblr fot this national character to be developed in the Diaspora; the Jews seem rather to have lost all remembrance of their former home. Thanks to their ready adaptability, they have all the more easily acquired characteristics, not inborn, of the people among whom fate has thrown them. Often to please their protectors, they recommend their traditional individuality entirely....In seeking to fuse with other peoples they deliberately denounced to some extent their own nationality. Yet nowhere did they succeed in obtaining from their fellow-citizens recognition as natives of equal status.... [T]o the living the Jew is a corpse, to the native a foreigner, to the homesteader a vagrant, to the proprietary a beggar, to the poor an exploiter and a millionaire, to the patriot a man without a country, for all a hated rival.[15]

Thus, according to Pinsker, the remedy was for the Jews to cease being homeless and establish their own state. Because Pinsker did not come from an Orthodox or traditional Jewish background he was not acquainted with the biblical, religious, or historical connection the Jewish nation had with *Eretz Yisrael*. Hence, at the outset, Pinsker did not speak of a return, but rather about the Jewish nation acquiring its own piece of territory someplace on earth; the Land of Israel was but one option. (Eventually, Pinsker was persuaded by the members of Hovevei Tzion, when he attended the movement's first convention in 1884, that Zionism meant an interest in Zion—the Land of Israel—not just a piece of territory.)

Soon after, Pinsker wrote a pamphlet in 1882 entitled "Auto-Emancipation—An Appeal to His People by a Russian Jew." Pinsker then took the pamphlet with him on a tour through

Western Europe, where he tried to impress his ideas on those he met. Not everybody was impressed. A typical view was that of Rabbi Adolf Jellinek, the chief rabbi of Vienna, who wrote:

> Since the days of Moses Mendelsohn and particularly since the great historic revolution in France, the Jews have sent out their best men to fight for their recognition and equality in the European states, and they have marshaled their intellectual resources in numerous writings, on the speaker's platform, and in the pulpit for the lofty goal of emancipation. Have they done all this in order to abandon, in this year of 1882, everything they have achieved, to give up all they have fought for and achieved, to declare that they are aliens, people without a homeland or a fatherland—or, as you put it, vagrants—the wanderer's staff in hand, to set out for an uncertain new fatherland? No! That would mean to accept the view of our implacable foes who deny that we have any true patriotic feelings for Europe. In fact, we are not even capable of doing this. We are at home in Europe and regard ourselves as children of the lands in which we were born and raised, whose languages we speak, and whose cultures make up our intellectual substance. We are Germans, Frenchmen, Magyars, Italians and so forth with every fiber of our being, We have long ceased to be true thoroughbred Semites, and we have long ago lost the sense of Hebrew nationality.[16]

Sadly, until Herzl published his famous work, *The Jewish State* in 1896, Western European Jews, in fact world Jewry, remained, with the exception of Baron Rothchild, disinterested in the Hovevei Tzion movement in particular and the Zionist movement in general.

THE FIRST ALIYAH (1882-1903)

Between 1882-1903, 25,000 young Russian Jews left Russia and moved to *Eretz Yisrael.* These *olim* were referred to as *Biluim*, coming from the Hebrew acronym for *Beit Yaacov Lechu Ve Neylcha.* What distinguished them from the past generations of brave *olim* was that they wanted to live in *Eretz Yisrael*, and they wanted to rebuild the land.

The BILU Manifesto written in 1882 stated:

> To our brothers and sisters in Exile!
> "If I do not help myself, who will help me?"
> Nearly two thousand years have passed since, in an evil hour, after an heroic struggle, the glory of our Temple vanished in fire and our kings and chieftains exchanged their crowns and diadems for the chains of exile. We lost our country where our beloved ancestors had lived. Into the Exile we took with us, of all our glories, only a spark of the fire by which our Temple, the abode of the Great One, was engirdled, and this little spark kept us alive while the towers of our enemies crumbled into dust, and this spark leapt into the celestial flame and illuminated the heroes of our race and inspired them to endure the horrors of the dance of death and the tortures of the autos-da fe. And this spark is again kindling and will shine for us, a true pillar of fire going before us on the road to Zion, while behind us is a pillar of cloud, the pillar of oppression threatening to destroy us. Are you asleep, O our nation? What have you been doing until 1882? Sleeping and dreaming the false dream of assimilation. Now, thank God, you have awakened from your slothful slumber. The pogroms have awakened you from your charmed sleep. Your eyes are open to recognize the obscure and delusive hopes. Can you listen in silence to the taunts and mocking of your enemies?
>
> Where is your ancient pride, your old spirit? Remember that you were a nation possessing a wise religion, a law, a constitution, a celestial Temple whose wall is still a silent witness to the glories of the past...
>
> Your state in the West is hopeless; the star of your future is gleaming in the East. Deeply conscious of all the foregoing, and inspired by the true teaching of our great master, Hillel, "If I do not help myself, who will help me?" we propose to form the following society for national ends:
>
> 1. The society will be named BILU, according to the motto, "House of Jacob, come let us go." It will be divided into local branches according to the numbers of its members.

2. The seat of the Committee will be Jerusalem.

3. Donations and contributions shall be unfixed and unlimited.

WE WANT:

1. A home in our country. It was given to us by the mercy of God; it is ours as registered in the archives of history.

2. To beg it of the Sultan himself, and if it be impossible to obtain this, to beg that we may at least possess it as a state within a larger state; the internal administration to be ours, to have our civil and political rights, and to act with the Turkish Empire only in foreign affairs, so as to help our brother Ishmael in his time of need.

We hope that the interests of our glorious nation will rouse the national spirit in rich and powerful men, and that everyone, rich or poor, will give his best labors to the holy cause.

Greetings dear brothers and sisters!

HEAR O! ISRAEL! The Lord is our God, the Lord is one, and our land Zion is our only hope.

GOD be with us! The Pioneers of BILU.[17]

Though they were not all Orthodox Jews, it is clear from the above document that what inspired them was their connection to Jewish history, religious sources, ideals and prayers. They wanted to implement a 2,000-year-old dream, and they faced formidable obstacles. In those days there were no eleven-hour flights across the skies. It took five to six weeks to get there via trains, boats, buses, trucks, whatever it took to get to a port with ships heading for Yaffo.

When they finally arrived in *Eretz Yisrael*, they were, for the most part, in deep shock when they saw how miserable the Promised Land was. In the 1880s, the Ottoman Empire was decaying. There were few paved roads or telegraph lines, hospitals or anything remotely modern. And the province was one of the more neglected areas of the empire. In the modern period, post-1948, after Israel was declared an independent state, the Arab world tried to refute Jewish claims that Israel was a backward and decaying area. Arabs claimed that this was Jewish Zionist propaganda and that in fact the land was a flourishing paradise exporting its goods to the rest of the world.

Here is famed author Mark Twain's description of his journey to the Holy Land in 1867, fifteen years before the first *Aliyah*:

> Of all the lands there are for dismal scenery, I think Palestine must be the prince. The hills are barren, they are dull of color, and they are picturesque in shape. The valleys are unsightly deserts fringed with a feeble vegetation that has an expression about it of being sorrowful and despondent. The Dead Sea and the Sea of Galilee sleep in the midst of a vast stretch of hill and plain wherein the eye rests upon no pleasant tint, no striking object, no soft picture dreaming in a purple haze or mottled with the shadows of the clouds. Every outline is harsh, every feature is distinct, there is no perspective—distance works no enchantment here. It is a hopeless, dreary, heartbroken land.
>
> Small shreds and patches of it must be very beautiful in the full flush of spring, however, and all the more beautiful by contrast with the far-reaching desolation that surrounds them on every side. I would like much to see the fringes of the Jordan in springtime, and Shechem, Esdraelon, Ajalon, and the borders of Galilee—but even then these spots would seem mere toy gardens set at wide intervals in the waste of a limitless desolation.
>
> Palestine sits in sackcloth and ashes. Over it broods the spell of a curse that has withered its fields and fettered its energies. Where Sodom and Gomorrah reared their domes and towers, that solemn sea now floods the plain, in whose bitter waters no living thing exists—over whose waveless surface the blistering air hangs motionless and dead—about whose borders nothing grows but weeds, and scattering tufts of cane, and that treacherous fruit that promises refreshment to parching lips, but turns to ashes at the touch.
>
> Nazareth is forlorn; about that ford of Jordan where the hosts of Israel entered the Promised Land with songs of rejoicing, one finds only a squalid camp of fantastic Bedouins

of the desert; Jericho the accursed lies a moldering ruin today, even as Joshua's miracle left it more than three thousand years ago; Bethlehem and Bethany, in their poverty and their humiliation, have nothing about them now to remind one that they once knew the high honor of the Saviour's presence; the hallowed spot where the shepherds watched their flocks by night, and where the angels sang, "Peace on earth, good will to men," is untenanted by any living creature and unblessed by any feature that is pleasant to the eye.

Renowned Jerusalem itself, the stateliest name in history, has lost all its ancient grandeur and is become a pauper village; the riches of Solomon are no longer there to compel the admiration of visiting Oriental queens; the wonderful temple which was the pride and the glory of Israel is gone, and the Ottoman crescent is lifted above the spot where, on that most memorable day in the annals of the world, they reared the Holy Cross. The noted Sea of Galilee, where Roman fleets once rode at anchor and the disciples of the Saviour sailed in their ships, was long ago deserted by the devotees of war and commerce, and its borders are a silent wilderness; Capernaum is a shapeless ruin; Magdala is the home of beggared Arabs; Bethsaida and Chorazin have vanished from the earth, and the "desert places" round about them, where thousands of men once listened to the Saviour's voice and ate the miraculous bread, sleep in the hush of a solitude that is inhabited only by birds of prey and skulking foxes.[18]

Despite revisionist claims of an Arab land flowing with verdant green pastures and opulent orchards, the actual physical condition of Palestine was dismal, neglected, uncultivated; a desert—arid, depressing and barely populated.

But what of the actual population when the *Biluim* first arrived in 1882? Again here, as in the case of the condition of the land, there is wild disparity between the reality and the picture painted by detractors. From the Arabs perspective Palestine was some sort of independent country filled with Palestinians, millions perhaps, living a wonderful life, in a beautiful country that had its own distinct political and national identity. In these versions, "the Zionist invasion of 1882" was the beginning of the destruction of the Arab Palestinian State. However, based on all the information that exists in the archives of what was then the Ottoman Empire, there appears a very different picture.

As far as Palestine being an independent country, this is mere fiction. Palestine never existed as anything but a province in someone's empire, at this time the Ottoman Empire. No one has ever produced any document or archeological evidence of the existence of a country called Palestine. When was this State founded? Who were its presidents? Kings? Rulers? What official documents did this State produce? Where are the coins they minted? The money they printed? What does the Palestinian language sound like? What was its flag? Emblem? Insignia? Are there any maps pre-1882 of the country of Palestine? Where was the capitol? What was the ruling government body called? What were its laws? No one can answer any of these questions, because there simply was no state called Palestine in the annals of recorded history.

The Arabs that lived in *Eretz Yisrael* in the 1880s were citizens of the Ottoman Empire. During the 1880s, the Arab world was not divided into Syrians, Lebanese, Jordanians, Palestinians, Iraqis, etc. During the 400-year rule by the Ottoman Empire, there were no accurate censuses taken by the Ottomans, so population numbers are based on Ottoman registers. There were about 350,000 Arab Muslims, Christians, Druze and other groups and 25,000 Jews. The 350,000 or so Arabs living in the province of the empire known as Palestine represented about one percent of the world's Arab population.

Finally, these approximately 350,000 Arabs lived in only a few cities: Acco, Haifa, Nazereth, Jenin, Shechem (Nablus), Qalqilya, Tulkarem, Ramallah, Ramle, Yaffo, Jerusalem, Bet Lechem, Hevron, and Gaza, and approximately 500 villages that were clustered near these cities. These cities and villages comprised less than five percent of *Eretz Yisrael*, and most of these Arab settlements were in the interior part of the land—in Judea and Samaria.[19]

The members of the First *Aliyah* had no intention of living in Arab towns or villages; they would build their settlements in the remaining ninty-five percent of the country. Under these extremely adverse conditions, the members of the Lovers of Zion arrived in Israel and began the almost impossible task of rebuilding the land.

These pioneers—*halutzim*—purposely did not settle in the four holy cities of Jerusalem, Hevron, Teveriya, and Tzfat. Instead, they wanted to build new Jewish settlements. It should be noted that many of the members of the existing Jewish community (numbering about 25,000 on the eve of the First *Aliyah*) were not very happy about the arrival of these new *olim*. For the most part, being very observant Jews, they were suspicious of these mostly secular young Russians, who did not seem to share their ideas about waiting for *Mashiach* to build Israel. Thus, the two groups of Jews did not have much to do with each other at first.

The *halutzim* took their meager supplies and their abundant enthusiasm and set out from Yaffo (the port city at which they had all arrived) to rebuild the land. In the next twenty years they were to build eighteen new settlements, many of them on what were formerly swamps. The names of these settlements reflected their ideas and enthusiasm: Rishon LeZion (The First in Zion), Petach Tikvah (The Gates of Hope), Zichron Yaacov (Remembering Jacob), and Rosh Pina (The Corner Stone) among others. Life in these settlements was harsh, but they persevered. They worked long, unbearable hours draining swamps, removing rocks, building irrigation ditches, digging wells, building houses, paving roads and tending the soil.

BARON EDMOND DE ROTHSCHILD

For all their enthusiasm, energy and sacrifice, the First *Aliyah* would not have been able to achieve what it did were it not for Baron Edmond de Rothschild, a descendant of the famous family of financiers.

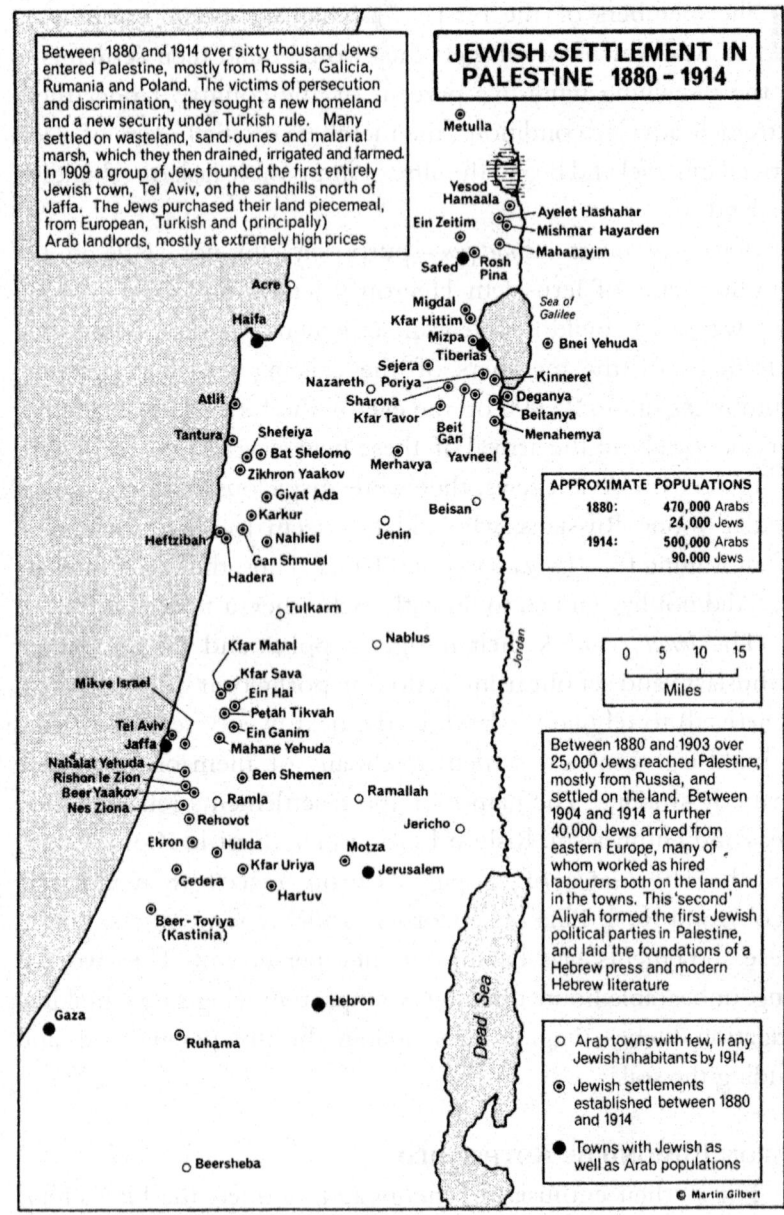

Between 1880 and 1914 over sixty thousand Jews entered Palestine, mostly from Russia, Galicia, Rumania and Poland. The victims of persecution and discrimination, they sought a new homeland and a new security under Turkish rule. Many settled on wasteland, sand-dunes and malarial marsh, which they then drained, irrigated and farmed. In 1909 a group of Jews founded the first entirely Jewish town, Tel Aviv, on the sandhills north of Jaffa. The Jews purchased their land piecemeal, from European, Turkish and (principally) Arab landlords, mostly at extremely high prices

JEWISH SETTLEMENT IN PALESTINE 1880 - 1914

APPROXIMATE POPULATIONS

1880:	470,000 Arabs 24,000 Jews
1914:	500,000 Arabs 90,000 Jews

Between 1880 and 1903 over 25,000 Jews reached Palestine, mostly from Russia, and settled on the land. Between 1904 and 1914 a further 40,000 Jews arrived from eastern Europe, many of whom worked as hired labourers both on the land and in the towns. This 'second' Aliyah formed the first Jewish political parties in Palestine, and laid the foundations of a Hebrew press and modern Hebrew literature

○ Arab towns with few, if any Jewish inhabitants by 1914

◉ Jewish settlements established between 1880 and 1914

● Towns with Jewish as well as Arab populations

© Martin Gilbert

Sir Martin Gilbert, © 2010. Reproduced by permission of Taylor & Francis Books UK. www.martingilbert.com

Over the course of his life Rothschild purchased some 500,000 dunams of land in what is today Israel and financially helped in the creation of thirty settlements. It is estimated that Rothschild spent over $50 million in supporting the settlements, backed research in electricity by engineers and financed development of an electric generating station.

Though his interest was in promoting Jewish rebirth in *Eretz Yisrael*, ...

> Rothschild recognized that the overriding interest of the Jews of Palestine was the confidence and the friendship of their Arab neighbours. The interests of the Arab cultivators of the land he bought were never overlooked, but by development he made this land capable of maintaining a population ten times its former size.[20]*

In October 1882, Rothschild willingly responded to a plea by the settlers of Rishon le-Zion for a modest loan of 25,000 francs toward the digging of wells in the colony. He did so because...

> ...[i]t was not a simple act of charity, but an undertaking of quite a different nature from the moral point of view. At that time I felt grave anxiety regarding the future of Judaism. Our unfortunate coreligionists in Eastern Europe, where they are so numerous, were suffering under the most crushing oppression and were beginning to give way to the deepest despair...I finally came to the conclusion that we must look towards Palestine to save Judaism, by creating over there centers where the Jewish moral and intellectual culture could be fully developed.[21]

Between Baron Rothschild's money and business support, and the actual work and physical sacrifice of the *Hovevei Zion* and

---

*In a 1934 letter to the League of Nations, Rothschild stated that "the struggle to put an end to the Wandering Jew, could not have as its result, the creation of the Wandering Arab." https://streetsofisrael.wordpress.com/2013/03/27/10-things-you-need-to-know-about-baronedmondderothschild/.

Billuim, the First *Aliyah* was a success. The ice had been broken. When new *olim* arrived, *Eretz Yisrael* was still a backwater province of the Ottoman Empire, but as hard as life would be, they had the comfort of staying at Rishon LeZion, and knowing that their dream could come true.

THE BIRTH OF MODERN POLITICAL ZIONISM

The father of the idea that *Eretz Yisrael* is the homeland of the Jewish nation was the Patriarch Abraham. The visionary who led the Jewish people to the banks of the Jordan River and prepared them to enter the Land of Israel was Moses. The man who established the first Jewish State was Joshua; Ezra the Scribe re-established the Second Jewish Commonwealth. Judah the Maccabee established sovereignty for the second Jewish State. Sixty years after the second Jewish State was destroyed in 70 CE by the Romans, Bar Kochba and Rabbi Akiva launched a failed rebellion to re-establish a third Jewish State. The most Zionist book written in the post-Biblical period was the *Siddur*, the Jewish prayer book that is replete with references to the Jewish nation returning to the Land of Israel and Jerusalem, written by members of the Great Knesset in the waning days of the second Jewish State. In the beginning and middle of the 19th century, Rabbis Alkalai and Kalischer wrote that the time ordained to begin the mass return by Jews to the Land of Israel had arrived. Finally, in 1882, Hovevei Tzion began the process of settling in the ancient Jewish homeland.

The point is that those who focus on Herzl as the father of Zionism forget the 4,000-year Jewish connection to the Land of Israel. That is not to say that Herzl was not a visionary who played an enormous role in the re-establishment of the third Jewish State. Herzl was a very important link in a 4,000-year-old chain, but he was not the first link.

Theodor Herzl

Theodor Herzl was born in Budapest, Hungary in 1860. He was brought up in an assimilated household, viewing himself as citizen of the Austro–Hungarian Empire and a part of the enlightened Western European world. Being a Jew did not hold any special significance for Herzl for a good part of his life, not because he rejected Judaism but rather that he was never really exposed to it. Herzl was a lawyer by education and a writer by trade. In 1892 he was hired by a paper in Vienna, the *Neue Freie Presse* (the New Free Press), a very respectable paper at the time, where he eventually became the paper's French correspondent.

In 1894 a huge scandal rocked France. Known as the Dreyfus Affair, the French Army made claims that it had caught a Jewish Captain Alfred Dreyfus stealing, and then handing over to the hated German enemy, French military secrets. Herzl covered the trial not only as a writer but as someone who was a lawyer and understood what was involved in making a case against someone in court. He found the case against Dreyfus at best flimsy, at worst made up. Also the idea that a captain in the French Army had access to high-level top secret information was highly questionable. The trial was a speedy one and Dreyfus was found guilty and sentenced to life in France's worst penal colony, Devil's Island, off the coast of French Guyana, South America.

Besides the flimsy evidence and speed of the trial, Herzl was most horrified by the reaction of the large French crowds in the courthouse, as well as those lining the streets outside. There were constant chants of "Death to the Jews!," "Dirty Jew!," "Traitor!" The fact that Dreyfus had been even more assimilated than Herzl and the idea that his being a Jew engendered such an outpouring of antisemitism in the country that gave Western Europe and the world the Enlightenment and the Emancipation of the Jews, was stunning and frightening to him.

> [Herzl) lamented that such an event could occur even "in republican, modern civilized France, one hundred years after the declaration of the Rights of Man." He discerned in those bloodthirsty chants ["Death to the Jews"] "the wish of the enormous majority in France to damn a Jew, and, in this one Jew, all Jews," and concluded that in that call "the edict of the

Great Revolution"—which had granted Jews full citizenship rights more than half a century before any other country— "has been revoked." The implied question was clear—if this is what is done to a Jew in France, what will they scruple to do to him in Austria, Germany, Poland, and the Ukraine?[22]

Herzl watched closely, absorbing all that was happening. Within a year after the conviction, a French intelligence officer uncovered evidence that cast doubt on the testimony produced at the trial. The new evidence strongly suggested that Dreyfus had served as a scapegoat; the treason had actually been committed by others. But when this came to no avail, liberal journalists took up the cause. The famous French novelist Emile Zola, in an open letter to the president of the Republic, accused (*J'accuse!*) the military of antisemitism and of falsely imprisoning Dreyfus. The incident soon caused an international furor.

France quickly divided into two camps, the so-called Dreyfusards and anti-Dreyfusards. The Dreyfusards were mostly liberals, democrats and republicans anxious to uphold the principles proclaimed by the French Revolution in the "Declaration of the Rights of Man." Their opponents, the anti-Dreyfusards, were mostly conservatives, monarchists, militarists and militant Catholics who opposed the separation of church and state.. In the end, the Dreyfusards were victorious.

The Dreyfus trial was a watershed event in Herzl's life. All that he was brought up to believe had been shattered by the conviction of Dreyfus and the antisemitic reactions of the French public. It was time for Herzl to reassess many things in his life.

Dreyfus, thanks to the tireless work of Zola, was exonerated and reinstated into the French Army in 1906 after serving a decade on Devil's Island. He retired in 1935. But this happy ending to the Dreyfus story did not change the devastating effect it had on Herzl. Herzl left his job at the New Free Press and spent over a year working on a book which was to change the trajectory of his life, as well as that of the Zionist movement and the Jewish nation.

While Herzl was not a religious man by any stretch of the imagination, after the Dreyfus trial he was a changed man. He went from being a European first to being a Jew first and foremost, and a proud one at that. He became acquainted with the Jewish nation and its history and culture and knew that re-establishing Jewish sovereignty in *Eretz Yisrael* was a necessity for the Jewish nation.

As a result, in 1896, Herzl published his most famous work, *Der Judenstaat (The Jewish State)*, in which he urged the orderly departure of Jews from the lands where they were being persecuted to their own land, *Eretz Yisrael*. He spoke of the Jewish need for a homeland, and how, in essence, the Jewish people are a nation and hence have the legitimate historical right to establish a state. Herzl warned that the Jewish problem (antisemitism) would not go away by way of assimilation or acceptance by the gentile world, rather the problem would only be solved when the Jewish people achieved the status of a nation with its own state: Israel. It should be noted that Herzl never read the works of Lilienblum or Pinsker prior to his writing of *The Jewish State*; he came to his conclusions independently.

> The idea I have developed in this pamphlet is an ancient one: It is the restoration of the Jewish State. . . The decisive factor is our propelling force. And what is that force? The plight of the Jews. . . I am profoundly convinced that I am right, though I doubt whether I shall live to see myself proved so. Those who today inaugurate this movement are unlikely to live to see its glorious culmination. But the very inauguration is enough to inspire in them a high pride and the joy of an inner liberation of their existence. . .
>
> The plan would seem mad enough if a single individual were to undertake it; but if many Jews simultaneously agree on it, it is entirely reasonable, and its achievement presents no difficulties worth mentioning. The idea depends only on the number of its adherents. Perhaps our ambitious young men, to whom every road of advancement is now closed, and for whom the Jewish state throws open a bright prospect of

freedom, happiness, and honor, perhaps they will see to it that this idea is spread. . .

It depends on the Jews themselves whether this political document remains for the present a political romance. If this generation is too dull to understand it rightly, a future, finer, more advanced generation will arise to comprehend it. The Jews who will try it shall achieve their State; and they will deserve it. ...

I consider the Jewish question neither a social nor a religious one, even though it sometimes takes these and other forms. It is a national question, and to solve it we must first of all establish it as an international political problem to be discussed and settled by the civilized nations of the world in council.

We are a people—one people.

We have sincerely tried everywhere to merge with the national communities in which we live, seeking only to preserve the faith of our fathers. It is not permitted us. In vain are we loyal patriots, sometimes superloyal; in vain do we make the same sacrifices of life and property as our fellow citizens; in vain do we strive to enhance the fame of our native lands in the arts and sciences, or her wealth by trade and commerce. In our native lands where we have lived for centuries we are still decried as aliens, often by men whose ancestors had not yet come at a time when Jewish sighs had long been heard in the country. . .

Oppression and persecution cannot exterminate us. No nation on earth has endured such struggles and sufferings as we have. Jew-baiting has merely winnowed out our weaklings; the strong among us defiantly return to their own whenever persecution breaks out. . . Wherever we remain politically secure for any length of time, we assimilate. I think this is not praiseworthy. . .

Palestine is our unforgettable historic homeland. . . Let me repeat once more my opening words: The Jews who will it shall achieve their State. We shall live at last as free men on our own soil, and in our own homes peacefully die. The world will be liberated by our freedom, enriched by our wealth, magnified by our greatness. And whatever we attempt there for our own benefit will redound mightily and beneficially to the good of all mankind.[23]

Even though many of the ideas expressed by Herzl were not new, his work was very significant and had a far greater impact than any of the previous works on Zionism. Herzl's work had a profound impact because unlike the religious Zionist leaders, Herzl's name was already well known and respected because he was a journalist for a famous newspaper. Herzl's material was well written and his credibility was enhanced because he was seen as a Western European Jew. The typical Western European Jew, at that time, was in a position of power and scorned Eastern European Jews, who they considered to be backwards, uneducated and too "Jewish." The writings of Lilienblum and Pinsker, and the BILU Manifesto were seen by Western Jews as the works of hysterics. Herzl's work, on the othere hand, stressed the need for worldwide cooperation among the Jewish people as the only realistic way of bringing about the establishment of a Jewish state; it embodied a clear sense of mission and destiny.

Herzl's *Der Judenstaat* had an immediate impact on world Jewry, particularly in Europe. His work inspired passionate debate in the Jewish community; for many assimilated Jews, Herzl's blunt assertion that Jews will never be fully accepted in the gentile world was offensive and threatening. To other Jews (assimilated and traditional), Herzl wrote openly about many of the thoughts they had privately. For Eastern European Jews, Herzl's work was a welcome acknowledgement that they were right, and no longer alone.

Thus, Herzl became the international focal point for Zionism. He began to receive letters from all over the world informing him that his message had touched a nerve among Jews everywhere. Zionist clubs and groups began to spring up all over the world.

In 1896 Herzl began publishing a monthly journal called *The World* as a forum for Zionist ideas. By 1897 he realized he was sitting on a vast untapped reservoir of Jewish nationalism and that the time had come to turn Zionism into a worldwide Jewish political cause.

Herzl rented a hotel in Basel, Switzerland, and sent invitations to the leaders of the different Zionist organizations and clubs that had sprung up all over the world. It is ironic that he chose Basel, a city without a large Jewish community, as the site of the gathering. Herzl wanted to hold the First World Zionist Congress in London, Paris, or Berlin, but local Jewish leadership threatened to demonstrate in front of the site so they could send the message to their gentile neighbors and fellow countrymen that they had no connection to the Zionist/Jewish nationalist movement. They wanted it to be crystal clear that they were very happy, well-integrated citizens of England, France, or Germany.

And so, the First World Zionist Congress was held on August 29-31, 1897. On that day, 167 delegates representing tens of thousands of Jews from all over the world arrived in Basel. The largest contingent was the Eastern European delegation of *Hovevei Zion*. Herzl had single-handedly turned Zionism into a worldwide political movement.

The official statement of Zionist purpose adopted by the First World Zionist Congress stated:

> The aim of Zionism is to create for the Jewish people a home in Palestine secured by public law.
>
> The Congress contemplates the following means to the attainment of this end:
>
> 1. The promotion, on suitable lines, of the colonization of Palestine by Jewish agricultural and industrial workers.
>
> 2. The organization and binding together of the whole of Jewry by means of appropriate institutions, local and international, in accordance with the laws of each country.
>
> 3. The strengthening and fostering of Jewish national sentiment and consciousness.
>
> 4. Preparatory steps towards obtaining government consent, where necessary, to the attainment of the aim of Zionism.[24]

In his diary Herzl wrote at the completion of the W.Z.O. Congress:

> Were I to sum up the Basle Congress in a word—which I shall guard against pronouncing publicly—it would be this: "At Basle [sic], I founded the Jewish State. If I said this out loud today, I would be answered by universal laughter. If not in 5 years, certainly in 50, everyone will know it."[25]

At Basel, the blue and white flag with the *Magen David* in the middle was adopted as the flag of the World Zionist Movement, and Hatikva, "The Hope," was adopted as the official national anthem of the Zionist Movement.

> Thus Zionism stepped out into the open, announcing itself as a political movement with a definite object to be achieved only through political negotiations. Two financial institutions were at once contemplated and before long created: the Jewish Colonial Trust (1899) and the Jewish National Fund (1901).[26]

After Basel, the W.Z.O. became the organization responsible for the implementation of the Basel Program, its business Zionism day in and day out. Shortly after Basel, the W.Z.O. opened offices in all the countries that had large Jewish populations. It also opened a branch in Palestine. From 1897 until 1948, the W.Z.O. functioned as the center of Zionism; in 1948 it was replaced by the government of the State of Israel.

POLITICAL ZIONIST PARTIES

Shortly after the 1897 meeting it became clear that while many Jews clearly wanted the establishment of an independent Jewish State, there were vast differences as to what type of Jewish State should be established. There were those who wanted a religious state, while others wanted a secular one. There were those who wanted a capitalist economy, and others who wanted a socialist one. And there were differences of opinion as to what form of political system should be adopted. All of this led to the emergence of different Zionist parties that reflected these different ideologies. Those differences still exist today in modern Israel.

After years of the Jewish nation being dispersed throughout the world, of being exposed to different cultures, different political systems, political ideas, and the Enlightenment, it was not logical to assume that even the Jews who embraced the Zionist ideal had the same vision of what the Jewish State should look like. That is the essence of Zionist political parties. They are a reflection of the different political, religious, social, and economic views of different segments of the Jewish nation.

Since 1897, though the Jewish State has been re-established and Israel has a representative government, there are still many parties in the Knesset, Israel's Parliament. When you look at them carefully, with the exception of the Arab Parties, they fall into one of three different forms of Zionism. While each one may have different offshoots, these three cover the spectrum: Socialist or Labor Zionism, Religious Zionism and Revisionist Zionism.

Socialist or Labor Zionism

Socialist Zionism (or Labor Zionism) strove to achieve Jewish national and social redemption by fusing Zionism with socialism. Its founder was Nachman Syrkin, who promulgated this view shortly before the Third Zionist Congress (1899).

Its philosophy was based on the assumption that the problem of Diaspora Jewry would remain unsolved even after the socialist revolution, and that the solution to the anomaly of Jewish existence was the immigration of Jews to, and their concentration in, a territorial base. Dov Ber Borochov, a prominent advocate of Socialist Zionism, argued that the development of capitalism would inevitably prompt Jews to immigrate to Palestine, and that only there could the economic structure of the Jewish people be reconstituted as a base for the class struggle of the Jewish proletariat. Zionism, he asserted, is a historic-economic necessity for the Jewish people and the historic role of spearheading the Jewish national liberation process is reserved for the Jewish proletariat.[27]

Disagreements about the conceptual and philosophical foundations of Socialist Zionism, the methods to use in achieving it in Palestine and relations with socialist organizations and parties in other countries, led to the formation of many and sundry Socialist Zionist parties. Some of these entities eschewed Marxist terminology and refrained from explicitly terming themselves socialist. Others, considering themselves more socialist and less Zionist, forswore membership in the Zionist Organization at various times.

The Socialist Zionist idea gave rise to many pioneering youth movements, such as Hashomer Hatz'air and Hehalutz. The leaders of the Socialist Zionist parties were among the most prominent in the pre-independence Palestine community. Socialist Zionism was the progenitor of most of Israel's settlement movements and the Israel Labor Party, one of Israel's two main political parties. In the 1890s and early 1900s Socialist or Labor Zionism was represented by parties like Poaley Tzion, and later in the 1940s–1960s by parties called Mapam and Rafi, to name a few. Finally from the 1970s on they go by the name the Labor Party.[28]

Socialist or Labor Zionism attracted many young people from Czarist Russia who saw no future for the Jews there but were still enthralled by the ideas of socialism. They made up the vast majority of those who made *Aliyah* between 1904-1924, were the founders of the kibbutz movement, created the Histadrut, the first and most powerful union in Israel during the Third *Aliyah* (details to follow), and were the dominant form of Zionism both in *Eretz Yisrael* and in the W.Z.O. for close to 80 years.

The different Socialist or Labor Zionist parties were for a centralized economy, powerful unions, universal medical insurance, and frowned upon capitalism. As a movement they took a more dovish approach to the growing Arab hostility to Zionism, but as the years passed and the hostility increased, they became more hawkish. Finally, since the movement was interested in creating a new Jew almost entirely divorced from the Diaspora, they were not for a religious Jewish State or even a traditional one, but rather a Hebrew-speaking state that exemplified the ideals and values of the Tanach. In essence, they wanted a cultural Jewish State. The father of the modern State of Israel, David Ben-Gurion, was a Socialist Labor Zionist.

Religious Zionism

Religious Zionism stands for the concept of *Eretz Yisrael*, for the people of Israel, according to the Torah of Israel. Modern Religious Zionism can be traced to the "Augurers of Zion" (*Mevasrei Zion*, precursors of *Hibbat Zion*), including Rabbis Yehudah Alkalai, Zvi Kalischer, Samuel Mohilever, and Naftali Zvi Yehudah Berlin (the Netziv). Religious Zionism aims to restore Jewish political freedom and a functioning modern Jewish State that would model itself on the first two Jewish States that existed in Biblical and post-Biblical times, while adjusting to the realities of the modern period. For Religious Zionism, Judaism based on the commandments is a *sine qua non* for Jewish national life in the homeland.

In 1902, in response to the decision of the Fifth Zionist Congress (1901) to consider cultural activity as part of the Zionist program, Rabbis Yitzchak Yaacov Reines (1839-1915) and Ze'ev Yavetz (1847-1924) established the Mizrachi organization (Mizrachi being the Hebrew abbreviation of *merkaz ruhani*, "spiritual center"). Mizrachi held its first world convention in 1904 and composed the movement's platform, which concerned itself principally with observance of the commandments and a return to Zion. In *Eretz Yisrael*, Rabbi Avraham Yitzchak Kook, who was the student of the Netziv, gave Religious Zionism his personal and spiritual endorsement regarding settlement in the Land as the beginning of redemption. Rav Kook's teachings and ideals permeate the growing and overall successful Religious Zionist movement in modern day Israel.

Religious Zionism has pledged much of its efforts and resources to constructing a national-religious education system, and infusing as much Jewish culture and ideals into the DNA of the modern state. It has also been very active in the country's rabbinate and the rabbinate of the modern state's military, the IDF. The main goal is to keep the Jewish State as Jewish as possible. Hapoel Hamizrahi branched away from the main movement in 1922 to focus on Orthodox rural settlement in Palestine under the slogan, "*Torah va-'Avodah*" (Torah and Labor). In 1956, the two movements, Mizrachi and Hapoel Hamizrahi, united under the umbrella of the National Religious Party (NRP). In 2008 the NRP merged with a group of small right of center Zionist parties to form Bayit Hayehudi (the Jewish Home).[29]

Religious Zionism believes in working with other Zionists in promoting its ideals and strengthening the Jewish nature of the State. To the Religious Zionist movement all Zionist groups were by definition involved in a holy endeavor, since they were rebuilding the holy Land of Israel. So even if they were not outwardly Orthodox, they were to a certain extent religious. Hence, the Religious Zionist movement was always comfortable working with other Zionist parties and groups, though there were, and remain, ideological differences between Religious Zionists and other Zionist parties.

There are other religious parties that exist in the Knesset that pre-existed the State of Israel. Most famous among them is the Agudath Israel Party, originally founded as an anti-Zionist party by a segment of the ultra-Orthodox community which felt that it should have an organized voice to speak with to the W.Z.O. As the years passed, and the disaster of the *Shoah* became all too real, the Agudah began to see the practical utility of a Jewish State and hence became non-Zionist as opposed to anti-Zionist. If the Zionist movement could establish a Jewish State, then the Agudah should be the voice of ultra-Orthodoxy helping shape the religious policies of said state. By the 1980s, the name of the party was changed to Degel HaTorah (the Flag of Torah). Shortly after, a

Sephardic ultra-Orthodox party, Shas, was also formed. Together they represent the non-Zionist ultra-Orthodox voice in the State of Israel, along with United Torah Judaism, another ultra-Orthodox party.

Revisionist Zionism

Revisionist Zionism is an outgrowth of Herzl's Political Zionism, augmented by the ideas of Vladimir (Ze'ev) Jabotinsky (1880-1940). In 1925, Jabotinsky established the Revisionist Zionist Alliance, which advocated a revision, i.e., reexamination, of the principles of Political Zionism. The party's principal aim was to change moderate policies toward the British Mandatory regime.

The declared goals of Revisionist ideology included relentless pressure on Great Britain, including petitions and mass demonstrations, for Jewish statehood on both banks of the Jordan River, a Jewish majority in Palestine, a reestablishment of the Jewish regiments and military training for youth.

The Revisionists waged a heated debate in the Zionist organization [W.Z.O.] concerning the immediate and public stipulation of the final aim of Zionism. When their approach was rejected, they seceded from the W.Z.O. (1935) and established the New Zionist Organization. They returned to the W.Z.O. in 1946, explaining that this became possible after the Biltmore Program (1942) had proclaimed the establishment of a Jewish commonwealth in Palestine as the goal of Zionism.[30]

The true ideologue behind Revisionist Zionism was Ze'ev Jabotinsky, who, among other things, believed that the Arab resistance to Zionism that began in earnest in 1920 would only increase. He predicted that the Zionist State would have to erect a metaphorical Steel Wall (he could not have predicted the reality of the suicide bombing war of 2000–2002 when he made that statement) to protect itself from the non-stop hostility of the Arab world. His testimony at the Peel Commission (1937) hearings clearly articulated his views of the Arab war against Zionism and what the Zionist response should be. Revisionist Zionism stands for a capitalist economy, a state that is very Jewish in its character (not religious, but traditional), and takes a tough stance toward the Arab world.

The National Military Organization (Etzel or Irgun) and some members of the Jewish Freedom Fighters (Lehi) came from the ranks of the Revisionists. After the State of Israel was established, the Revisionist Zionist Organization merged with the Etzel-founded Herut movement to form the Herut party, a component of the Likud, one of Israel's two main political parties.

THE QUEST FOR A CHARTER

Once the W.Z.O. had been founded and Herzl elected as its president, it was time to get to the task at hand: reestablishing a Jewish State. Offices were opened where there were Jewish communities, money was raised and *Aliyah* encouraged. Herzl, as president of the W.Z.O., had one very important task only he could carry out: getting a charter to establish a Jewish State in *Eretz Yisrael*. After the W.Z.O. was founded, Herzl was treated as the closest thing to a Jewish president/prime minister, which allowed him to meet with heads of state.

Between 1897 and 1899, Herzl met twice with Sultan Abdul Hamid II (1842-1918) of the Ottoman Empire. He hoped to gain a charter, but the Sultan, who at first let Herzl believe he could possibly buy one, changed his mind. Herzl tried to influence the Sultan by meeting with his most important ally, Kaiser Wilhelm (1859-1941) of Germany. The meeting took place in Jerusalem in 1899 and was held without interpreters since Herzl was fluent in German. It lasted about an hour, and although it appeared to be a positive meeting, nothing came of it.

By 1903, Herzl was feeling desperate; he was no closer to getting a charter than he was in 1897. To make matters worse, in 1903 there was a pogrom in Kishinev, the worst pogrom in twenty years. Approximately thrity-five Jews were killed, 1,000 wounded and many synagogues destroyed. Because Kishinev was close to the German border, there were photojournalists from the West who covered the tragedy. The Western world now knew what a pogrom was. There was outrage and a call on the Russian government to stop the government-sanctioned riots.

As far as Herzl was concerned the Kishinev pogrom was a call for him for further urgency in getting a charter as the lives of Jews in Eastern Europe were at stake. As Jews in Eastern Europe exposed to danger began a tide of immigration, whether to the U.S. or elsewhere, Herzl began in earnest to urge them to make *Aliyah*.

Out of desperation, Herzl turned to the British, knowing full well that they did not control Palestine, nor did they have influence over the Turks—if anything they were enemies. But England, at the time, was the world's foremost power; it owned colonies all over the world. If anyone could help, maybe England could. The English were sympathetic for several reasons. Some in the government were genuinely sympathetic to Jews; 2) some in the government were antisemitic, and were interested in a Jewish State as a way of solving England's Jewish problem, and 3) the British realized that a Jewish State would be a loyal ally in a turbulent and economically vital region.

Thus, the British were sympathetic and made Herzl an offer. While they could do nothing with regard to Palestine, they did make an offer regarding a colony they had right next door to Israel: Egypt and Sinai. The British offered Herzl a charter for the city of El-Arish in northwestern Sinai. If they could irrigate this land (the plan was to divert waters from the Nile), they could settle up to 100,000 people there. Herzl was very thankful for the offer but rejected the idea because of the historical negative undertones Sinai carries for the Jews (forty years spent there after the Exodus from Egypt), and the fact that it could only hold 100,000 Jews maximum. At no time did Herzl view his British options as a replacement for *Eretz Yisrael*; the options were to be entertained only until it would be feasible to get a charter for *Eretz Yisrael* itself.

The British then came back with a very interesting proposal: the British East Africa Protectorate (the future Kenya), a colony in East

Africa. Herzl said that this proposal was worthy of consideration and brought it up at the Sixth World Zionist Congress (1903). At the opening of the conference Herzl clearly stated that the reason they were considering the mislabeled "Uganda Proposal" was not as a replacement for the Zionist goal of *Eretz Yisrael* but as a temporary solution. When the proposal was made, the conference exploded! Herzl never contemplated the controversy such a proposal would foster. The Uganda question divided the W.Z.O. along geographic lines. While the Eastern Europeans opposed it, the Western Europeans supported the idea. Even though the Eastern Europeans were the ones in physical danger, it was they who were outraged by the proposal.

To the Eastern Europeans (who, for the most part, came from traditional backgrounds), the quest for a state was not about any piece of land the Jews could get, it was about a return home to Zion. They were not interested in a piece of good real estate, nor were they interested in charters. They wanted to continue a relationship with Zion that began 4,000 years earlier. On the other hand, the Western Zionists (who on the whole came from assimilationist backgrounds) felt that to continue to settle *Eretz Yisrael* (the way the *Hovevei Zion* were doing without a charter) would be very dangerous, since the Turks could suddenly turn around and say that the settlement had gotten out of hand and they wanted it stopped. They were also concerned about the plight of Russian Jewry.

Behind these two positions, something more fundamental was going on: a different approach as to how one goes about getting a state. The Eastern Europeans felt that the way to get *Eretz Yisrael* was by physically going there, settling, and building up the land. In short, you create facts on the ground, not negotiate them. The Western European approach was to get the legal backing of a powerful state, or states, in order to set up a Jewish republic. That back-up is legal, political and economic, and you cannot have a state without it.

As Rabbi Ari Zivotofsky explains it:

At the beginning of the 1900s, Palestine was under Turkish rule, and negotiations between the Turks and the Zionists concerning the creation of a Jewish state in Palestine failed to progress. Desperate to find a sanctuary for Eastern European Jews suffering from poverty, discrimination and deadly pogroms, Zionist leaders, particularly Herzl's assistant Leopold Greenberg, began meeting with Joseph Chamberlain and other British leaders in search of a solution within the British Empire.

Starting in 1895, the British East Africa Protectorate (called Kenya since the 1920s) was administered by the British Foreign Office, but development of the region was stagnant due to a lack of European settlers. In December 1902, Chamberlain, then the British colonial secretary, visited the protectorate. He conceived of the notion of offering it to the Jews and proposed his idea to Herzl in April, and then again in May, 1903. By August of that year, just before the Sixth Zionist Congress, the British-Zionist talks seemed to have borne fruit.

On Sunday, August 23, 1903, Herzl stunned the nearly 600 delegates of the Sixth Zionist Congress with his proposal to settle Jews in East Africa. The proposal led to heated, often acrimonious, debate among both the Zionists and the East African settlers...

It was clear that the Zionists preferred Palestine as a refuge for the Jews. Chamberlain realized this, as he stated in his notes:

If Dr. Herzl were at all inclined to transfer his efforts to East Africa there would be no difficulty in finding land suitable for Jewish settlers, but I assume that this country is too far removed from Palestine to have any attractions for him.

The historic longing for the Promised Land certainly motivated the Zionists, but they were also driven by the pressing need to save Jewish lives. Leo Pinsker (1821-1891; Encylopaedia Judaica 13:545-8) articulated this territorialist position:

The goal of our present endeavors must not be the "Holy Land" but a land of our own. We need nothing but a large piece of land for our poor brothers; a piece of land which shall remain our property from which no foreign master can expel us...

In fact, the first non-Palestine option seriously considered was El Arish, Egypt. Lying adjacent to Palestine, the area was therefore not viewed as a repudiation of the ultimate goal, but rather as a temporary stepping stone to an ultimate move to Palestine...

Herzl's immediate response to Chamberlain's offer of present-day Kenya, as recorded in his diary, was the following: "Our base must be in or near Palestine. Later on we could also settle in Uganda [confused with Kenya], for we have masses of people ready to emigrate".

The East Africa proposal led to one of the fiercest controversies in Zionist history and nearly destroyed the still young and fragile Zionist movement. Chaim Weizmann (1874-1952), who was to become the first president of the State of Israel, recalled that that was the only time in his life there was a coolness between him and his pro-Kenya father and brother. Max Nordau (1849-1923), a defender of the Africa plan, insisted that the goal was, and always would be, Zion, but that there were Jews who needed a haven now and could not wait. The event that ultimately moved the plan along was the horrific Kishinev Pogrom on April 6-7, 1903. Though it was not the only, nor even the largest, pogrom, it occurred in a city that by 1897 was 46 percent Jewish.

In Herzl's concluding speech to the Sixth Zionist Congress on erev Shabbat, August 28, 1903, he dramatically displayed his commitment to Palestine by raising his right hand and solemnly declaring in Hebrew, "If I forget thee, O Jerusalem, may my right hand forget its cunning" (Psalms 137:5-6). Despite this pledge, Avraham Menachem Mendel Ussishkin (1863-1941) and other Russian Zionists continued to oppose the plan, as did the British Sephardic Chief Rabbi and Vice President of the First Zionist Congress, Rabbi Moses Gaster (1856-1939).

Surprisingly, one of the blocks of support for the Uganda Plan was the Religious Zionist Mizrachi movement, under the leadership of the esteemed Talmudic sage Rabbi Isaac Jacob Reines (1839-1915). For the Religious Zionists, unlike the secular Zionists, there was no fear of forgetting Jerusalem. Even if the Jews found a temporary refuge in East Africa, the Religious Zionists would continue to pray for the return to Zion, and thus would never forget the ultimate goal of returning to the Land of Israel. Rabbi Reines is said to have voted with Herzl for the Uganda Plan in an effort to prevent the Zionist movement from splintering.

However, not all Religious Zionists supported the plan. Rabbi Yitzchak Nissenbaum (1868-1942), known as the "traveling Zionist preacher," served as the link between Herzl and the Chovevei Tzion movement, and attended the First Zionist Congress. In order to fight the Uganda Plan, he temporarily moved to Palestine, later returning to Poland, where he refused to leave during the Nazi occupation and was murdered in the Warsaw Ghetto in 1942.

So too Rabbi Meir Berlin (Bar Ilan; 1880-1949), son of the famed Netziv (Rabbi Naftali Tzvi Yehuda Berlin), who attended his first Zionist congress as a delegate in 1905, voted against the Uganda Plan. Nonetheless, he attended many future congresses...Despite being approved for consideration by the Zionists, the Uganda Plan was almost killed in December 1903 due to difficult negotiations between Zionist leaders and the British Foreign Office regarding, among other things, the exact size and location of the East Africa allocation. The region finally settled upon was an area known as the Uasin Gishu plateau. It also became clear that England was offering the Jews only limited autonomy, on par with that of an English county.

Even the very Jews who most needed to be saved were passionately opposed to Kenya or any place other than the Land of Israel. As Herzl said, "These people have a rope round their necks and still they refuse".

Not only were Jews being persecuted and murdered, but England, for example, was considering legislation to ban aliens. In the midst of the Zionist movement's internal wrangling over the East Africa plan, its intense negotiations with England and the renewed contact with Turkey about Palestine, the movement was dealt a stunning blow—on July 3, 1904, Herzl died at the young age of forty-four.

David Wolffsohn (1856-1914) succeeded Herzl as president of the World Zionist Organization.

The Uganda Plan was officially rejected at the Seventh Zionist Congress (1905) in Basel, and the decision was conveyed to the British government by Greenberg on August 8, 1905.[31]

Eventually England, for its own reasons, withdrew the offer.

After Herzl's death, the W.Z.O. was able to continue to function because another great leader, who had learned positive lessons from the Uganda debate, appeared on the scene. Chaim Weizmann (1874-1952) was born in Eastern Europe and educated in Western Europe. He was a scientist by profession and an ardent Zionist. He emerged from the Uganda debate as one of the new leaders, realizing that the key to survival was to admit that both approaches, the Eastern European called Practical Zionism (because of its emphasis on *Aliyah* and building the land) and the Western European approach called Political Zionism (because of its emphasis on getting a charter through political means) were both right! Settlement of Israel, while at the same time working towards getting a charter, was paramount. And, indeed, that was to be the course of action taken by the W.Z.O. over the next decade.

THE SECOND ALIYAH (1904-1914)

After the Uganda debate, Zionism moved forward. Between the years 1904-1914, some 30,000 Jews settled in Ottoman Palestine. Most of these were young Russian Jews who were Labor Zionists. The term *Yishuv* is short for *Ha Yishuv Ha Yehudi Beh Eretz Yisrael*, which means the Jewish Settlement of, and in, *Eretz Yisrael*. This term is used to describe *Eretz Yisrael* from 1904 to 1948.

During the Second *Aliyah*, several very important contributions were made to the development of the *Yishuv*. With the arrival of 30,000 Jews, the Jewish population was increased to 90,000 by 1914. For 700 years, the Jewish population of *Eretz Yisrael* had been between 15,000-25,000. Approximately thirty-five new settlements were added during the Second *Aliyah*.

The new immigrants introduced a new philosophy centering on a new work ethic. The author of this philosophy was A.D. Gordon, who was a philosopher and thinker of the Labor Zionist movement. The philosophy was built on the premise that the Jews' return to *Eretz Yisrael* had two purposes: a) to physically transform *Eretz Yisrael* from its sorry state into a beautiful flourishing state, and b) to transform the Jewish people into a people who can be totally self-reliant in their own land; a people who do not make up one level of society, but all of society from ditch diggers to president. Conquest of labor spoke of the importance of the Jews doing as much physical labor as possible in *Eretz Yisrael*.

Besides changing the Jewish peoples' perspective of themselves as being able to do everything themselves, building something yourself gives a person a great sense of accomplishment and ownership.

As Gordon stated:

> What are we seeking in Palestine? Is it not that which we can never find elsewhere—the fresh milk of a healthy people's culture? What we are come to create at present is not the culture of the academy, before we have anything else, but a culture of life, of which the culture of the academy is only one element. We seek to create a vital culture out of which the cream of a higher culture can easily be evolved. We intend to create creeds and ideologies, art and poetry, and ethics and religion, all growing out of a healthy life and intimately related to it; we shall therefore have created healthy human relationships and living links that bind the present to the past. What we seek to create here is life—our own life—in our own spirit and in our own way. Let me put it more bluntly: In Palestine we must

do with our own hands all the things that make up the sum total of life. We must ourselves do all the work, from the least strenuous, cleanest, and most sophisticated, to the dirtiest and most difficult. In our own way, we must feel what a worker feels and think what a worker thinks—then, and only then, shall we have a culture of our own, for then we shall have a life of our own.[32]

In the spirit of the Jews transforming themselves to be once again a free and independent nation in their own land, the Hebrew language took on a new significance. The members of the Second *Aliyah* felt that they should revive Hebrew and use it as a day-to-day language. Thanks to the work of Eliezer Ben Yehuda, who compiled a Modern Hebrew dictionary, the people of the Second *Aliyah* were able to speak Hebrew daily. The children born during this period were the first Jewish children born in hundreds of years who spoke Hebrew as their first language. By 1914 there were schools that taught everything in Hebrew, and there were daily newspapers in Hebrew as well.

In 1909, *Hashomer* (Hebrew for the Watchman), the first Jewish self-defense organization since the days of Bar Kochba, was founded. Most of the members were veterans of the Russian Army. Two became famous: Yosef Trumpeldor was a military hero, and Yitzhak Ben-Zvi, who became one of Israel's presidents. *Hashomer* was founded to develop military skill to protect the nation-state, and to be the police in a dangerous neighborhood with many thieves. The new Jewish settlers were very tempting targets because of their livestock, supplies and other goods. With the Ottoman administration reluctant to protect new residents, a need had arisen for a self-defense organization.

The *kibbutzim* were founded during the Second *Aliyah*. A *kibbutz* is a collective settlement based on the principles of communal living. The establishment of *kibbutzim* was one of the greatest achievements of the Labor Zionist Movement because they took the ideas expressed by many socialist and communist thinkers and implemented them democratically, without creating a "ruling class." In the *kibbutz*, all property is owned collectively, all work is divided equally and all profits are divided equally. There have been many experiments in communal living over the years in many places around the world. To date, only the *kibbutz* has lasted as a working model for over 100 years.

Over the years, different types of *kibbutzim* were established, including religious ones. What makes *kibbutzim* so interesting are their contributions to Israeli society over the years. Even though *kibbutzim* never made up more than 14 percent of Israel's population (that was in 1949), and today make up less than two percent, yet pilots, politicians, writers, and professors have come from these collective farms and *kibbutzniks* have been very well represented in all high-profile areas of Israeli life, including a very high percentage of them as high ranking officers in the army.

By 1914 the *Yishuv* was reestablishing itself as *Eretz Yisrael*. Zionism was no longer an idea, it was reality.

WORLD WAR I (1914 – 1918)

Though many people think of World War I as a European conflict, it had profound effects on the Middle East, and Zionism in particular. The Zionist movement had been on a forward march since 1882, but during World War I it was stopped and even reversed.

There were two major camps in World War I: The Central Powers—Germany, Austria-Hungary and the Ottoman Empire, who fought The Triple Alliance—England, France, and Russia. Russia bordered Turkey, which was the first front. The border that concerned the Jews was the border between the Ottoman and British Empires: Palestine.

Eretz Yisrael was the Ottoman Empire's southwestern border with Sinai part of the British Empire. Suddenly, this once neglected outpost became a center of attention. If there was going to be a second front against the Ottoman Empire, it would be here. The British had to protect the Suez Canal, a strategic waterway connecting the Mediterranean to the Red Sea and the Indian

Ocean, from possible Turkish attack. Thus, the British brought in many troops and supplies into the Sinai. As a result, thousands of Turkish troops poured into Palestine at the end of 1914. And with the rise of the industrial revolution, oil—all of it controlled by Arabs in the region—was a factor as well, one still important to international Middle Eastern strategy in the 21st century.

Initially, the people in the *Yishuv* supported the Ottoman Empire, because they felt the Turks better understood the Zionist effort in Israel from 1882-1914. Many Jews volunteered for military service in the Turkish Army, some even for officers' training. Unfortunately, after the war began, Turkish authorities became hostile to members of the *Yishuv*.

The Ottoman Empire found itself facing a well-organized, well-equipped foe in Britain. Its own forces were anything but. They desperately needed supplies and bases, and the Jewish settlements were ripe for the pickings. The Ottomans seized all the supplies and livestock and drafted all able-bodied men into their army.

Then things got worse for the *Yishuv*. All public displays of Zionist feelings were outlawed. The Zionist flag could no longer fly, and Hashomer was disbanded. The only flag that flew was the Turkish flag, and the only armed men were members of the Turkish Army. The final blow to the *Yishuv* came when the Turks expelled 16,000 Jews on the grounds that they were spies for the Russians, the other hated enemy of the Ottoman Empire. Considered spies because they carried Russian papers, the Ottomans did not realize that these Jews hated the Russian government for the way they'd been treated by Mother Russia. (These 16,000 Jews went to Egypt.)

The *Yishuv* also suffered because of the British blockade of the Turkish Empire. A big part of the British war effort was to starve the Ottomans and deprive them of resources, but part of their empire was the *Yishuv*. So, in addition to suffering because of the Ottomans, the Jews also suffered at the hands of the British. *Aliyah* stopped. There were no supplies, no medicines and no food. By 1915, the situation in the *Yishuv* was desperate.

This caused a shift in the *Yishuv*'s political alliances. With growing hunger, outbreaks of epidemics, and discrimination, almost everyone prayed for a swift British victory. In addition to praying, the Jews took concrete steps to aid the British. They formed a pro-British intelligence underground and passed information about the Ottoman Army to them. The underground group was called Nili, a Hebrew acronym which stood for *Netzach Yisrael Lo Yishaker*, which means that the eternity of the Jewish nation will not be forsaken.

Sarah Aaronsohn, her brother Aaron, and their sister Rivka, together with their friend Avshalom Feinberg formed and led Nili. So effective were their contribution to the British cause that the Chief of British Military intelligence at the War Office, Major General George Macdonogh, admitted:

> You will no doubt remember the great campaign of Lord Allenby in Palestine and perhaps you are surprised at the daring of his actions. Someone who is looking from the side lines, lacking knowledge about the situation, is likely to think that Allenby took unwarranted risks. That is not true. For Allenby knew with certainty from his intelligence (in Palestine) of all the preparations and all the movements of his enemy. All the cards of his enemy were revealed to him, and so he could play his hand with complete confidence. Under these conditions, victory was certain before he began.[33]

Once the Turks found out about Nili, they arrested most of the leadership and then executed them. Sarah Aaronson managed to commit suicide after four days of torture.

In the meantime, the 11,000 exiled Jews in Egypt organized a volunteer unit, the Zion Mule Corp, to aid the British. A combat resupply unit, they saw action in a failed British attack on Turkey in Gallipoli. Jews from around the world also joined the war effort by joining the British volunteer unit in Egypt known as the Jewish Legion. David Ben-Gurion and Ze'ev Jabotinsky were both in this unit.

The Balfour Declaration

Chaim Weizmann (who had worked out the compromise between Eastern and Western European Zionists at the Sixth World Zionist Congress) was in England during World War I. By profession a chemist, he offered his services to the War Department, where he worked on weapons development. In the course of his work there he did two very important things: He developed a form of acetone that was used in explosives, and befriended his boss, Arthur Balfour, then a high-ranking official in the War Department. Balfour became a committed Zionist because of his friendship with Weizmann.[34]

By 1916, the Zionist movement was clearly in England's corner in its struggle against the Ottoman Empire. In the reshuffle of England's cabinet, Arthur Balfour became the new Foreign Minister, and his friend and former Minister of Defense, David Lloyd George, became the new Prime Minister. The two most important people in the British Empire were now individuals very sympathetic to the Zionist cause. Both, and in particular Arthur Balfour, worked to persuade the British government to issue the charter for a Jewish homeland that the Zionist movement had been craving since 1897.

Thus, on November 2, 1917 the British government issued the Balfour Declaration. This declaration was to open a new chapter in the Jewish people's relationship with *Eretz Yisrael*, the international community, and the Arabs who lived in the Middle East. Presented as a letter to Lord Lionel Rothschild, a former member of Parliament, a peer of the realm, friend of Chaim Weizmann, and ardent Zionist, it stated:

Foreign Office
November 2nd, 1917

Dear Lord Rothschild,
I have much pleasure in conveying to you, on behalf of his Majesty's Government, the following declaration of sympathy

with Jewish Zionist aspirations which has been submitted to and approved by the cabinet.

His Majesty's Government view with favour the establishment in Palestine of a national home for the Jewish people and will use their best endeavors to facilitate the achievement of this object, it being clearly understood that nothing shall be done which may prejudice the civil and religious rights of existing non-Jewish communities in Palestine, or the rights and political status enjoyed by Jews in any other country.

I should be grateful if you would bring this declaration to the knowledge of the Zionist Federation.

Sincerely,

Arthur Balfour[35]*

Since the British offered El Arish and then the British Protectorate to Herzl in 1903, there had been clear interest on part

---

* Britain carried out incoherent and contradictory policies within the Middle East. It used questionable diplomatic maneuvering to satisfy both Arab and Jewish claims whilst avoiding a serious analysis of the current and foreseeable problems in the region.

• In issuing the Balfour Declaration, the British believed that the Jews could finance part of the war effort whilst the British also persuaded the United States to engage in World War I.

• The Balfour Declaration was undoubtedly a milestone in the modern history of the Jewish people since for the first time it officially recognized the natural right of the Jews to return to their ancestral homeland. However, the document cast many complex doubts, as well as embarrassing questions, to which, at this stage, the British government could not provide specific answers...

o In order to restore calm, the British made repeated gestures in favor of the Arabs, and adopted a reserved, ambiguous, and often hostile approach towards the Jews, resulting in the creation of a series of White Papers.

o The Balfour Declaration made no reference to the future establishment of a sovereign, independent Jewish state:

a. No details nor even suggestions were made as to the parameters of the State: its territory and borders as well as political, administrative and military character.

b. No commitment was made on the autonomy of the national home.

c. No mention was made on the links with Great Britain.

• The Balfour Declaration was declared and confirmed in the (cont'd)

of the British leadership to accommodate the Zionist movement's quest to attain a Jewish homeland in the Land of Israel. Some of this support came from people who genuinely believed for religious and ideological reasons that the Jewish nation deserved its old ancestral homeland back, and others believed—for antisemitic reasons—that having a place to send all of Britain's Jews would be a win-win for Britain as well as its Jews. World War I created a real opportunity for Britain to act on these beliefs. Ottoman Palestine was now available, and the Zionist Movement had shown, beyond a shadow of a doubt, its support of England during the war to end all wars.

As Prime Minister David Lloyd George wrote in his memoirs;

> There has been a good deal of discussion as to the meaning of the words "Jewish National Home" and whether it involved the setting up of a Jewish National State in Palestine. I have already quoted the words actually used by Mr. Balfour when he submitted the declaration to the Cabinet for its approval. They were not challenged at the time by any member present, and there could be no doubt as to what the Cabinet then had in their minds. It was not their idea that a Jewish State should be set up immediately by the Peace Treaty without reference to the wishes of the majority of the inhabitants.
>
> On the other hand, it was contemplated that when the time arrived for according representative institutions to Palestine, if the Jews had meanwhile responded to the opportunity

preamble to the text of the Mandate for Palestine (July 24, 1922), and in the same vein, with the British government memorandum on the implementation of this mandate in Transjordan, and approved by the Council of the League of Nations on September 16, 1922. The memorandum initiated by Winston Churchill in fact reduced the original territory of Palestine by three-quarters. It was arbitrarily detached from the rest of Palestine and King Abdullah Emir was recognized as Emir by the British. Later he became King of the Hashemite Kingdom of Jordan, which also included the West Bank of the Jordan, or Cisjordan.(Freddy Eytan, "The Failures of the International Community in the Middle East since the Sykes-Picot Agreement, 1916-2016," Jerusalem Center for Public Affairs (http://jcpa.org/the-failures-in-the-middle-east-since-the-sykes-picot-agreement/#sthash.pNywq0aO.dpuf)

afforded them by the idea of a National Home and had become a definite majority of the inhabitants, then Palestine would thus become a Jewish Commonwealth. The notion that Jewish immigration would have to be artificially restricted in order to ensure that the Jews should be a permanent minority never entered into the heads of anyone engaged in framing the policy. That would have been regarded as "unjust and as a fraud on the people to whom we were appealing."[36]*

The issuing of the Balfour Declaration was a major turning point in modern Jewish history. The immediate effect was very positive: a new wave of *olim* began to arrive. These *olim* were badly needed because *Eretz Yisrael* was in dire straits. Approximately 16,000 Jews had been expelled, thousands more had died of starvation and disease, and many settlements were destroyed. The population and settlements needed to be rebuilt.

The conquest of Palestine began two days after the declaration was issued, on November 9, 1917, when a large British force attacked Gaza from Sinai under the command of General Sir Edmund Henry Hynman Allenby (1861-1936). On December 11/25 Kislev, on Chanukah, General Allenby captured Jerusalem

---

* There are critics of Zionism who use one sentence in the Balfour Declaration to prove it was not intended to be a promise for the creation of a Jewish State. That sentence is:

"It being clearly understood that nothing shall be done which may prejudice the civil and religious rights of existing non-Jewish communities in Palestine, or the rights and political status enjoyed by Jews in any other country." "Balfour Declaration: Text of the Declaration (November 2, 1917)," Jewish Virtual Library (http://www.jewishvirtuallibrary.org/jsource/History/balfour.html)

They claim that the above statement means that the political rights of the non-Jews, namely Arabs and Muslims, cannot be touched. And that is not possible with a Jewish State for it would, by definition, hamper Arab political rights. But the authors did not use the term political rights, they spoke of civil and religious rights for the non-Jews who would live in the Jewish national home, a term purposely used in the document. (Wallace Edward Brand, "The Exclusive Political Rights Granted To Jews In 1920 At San Remo," Israeli Frontline, December 30, 2012 (http://www.israelifrontline.com/2012/12/the-eexclusive-political-rights-granted.html

and brought 400 years of Ottoman rule to an end. By August 1918, all of Palestine was under British rule, along with most of the Ottoman Empire.

THE BALFOUR DECLARATION IN LIGHT OF OTHER INTERNATIONAL AGREEMENTS

During World War I there was an exchange of letters between the British High Commissioner of Egypt, Sir Henry McMahon and the most respected Arab tribal leader in the Arabian Peninsula, the Sharif of Mecca, Hussein Ibn Ali. This exchange occurred between July 14, 1915 and January 30, 1916.

Unlike the Zionists who understood it was clearly in their interests to support the British, the Arabs did not reach the same conclusion. At that time, there was no serious Arab nationalist movement. The closest the Arab world came to return to Arab collective political control was in 1905, when Negib Azouri proposed his "Program of the League of the Arab Fatherland." His appeal did not spark a movement or conferences; Arabs were content to be ruled by the Ottomans. It was the British who prodded the Arabs into starting some sort of revolt in the Arabian Peninsula in order to create a second front against the Ottoman Empire, where the British could confront the enemy on the important Sinai/Palestine front. It was in this context that McMahon reached out to Hussein Ibn Ali, with the promise to help the Arab nation gain its independence, if he helped them in the war.

McMahon offered some military help, and a military advisor on site. In exchange, Britain would consider handing over parts of lands conquered from the Ottomans to create one large Arab state or two smaller ones. Hussein's terms for helping the British included certain territorial demands and McMahon let him know what terms he was authorized to agree to and which terms he could not meet.

These letters created the basis for the Arab revolt by forces loyal to Hussein. As a result, his followers attacked the Ottoman Turkish rail supply line with the help of British arms and a British

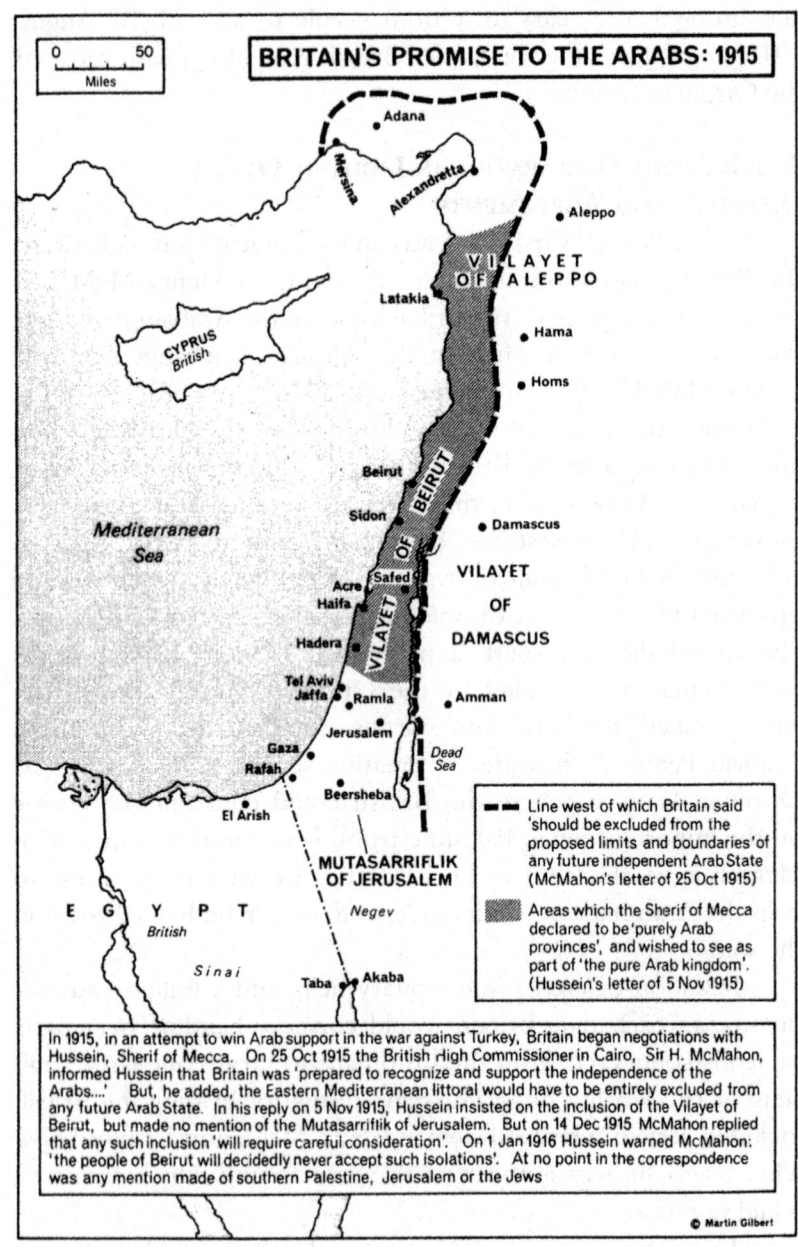

BRITAIN'S PROMISE TO THE ARABS: 1915

0 — 50 Miles

Adana

Mersina

Alexandretta

Aleppo

VILAYET OF ALEPPO

Latakia

Hama

Homs

CYPRUS British

Beirut

Sidon

VILAYET OF BEIRUT

Damascus

Mediterranean Sea

Acre
Haifa

Safed

VILAYET OF DAMASCUS

Hadera

VILAYET OF

Tel Aviv
Jaffa

Ramla

Amman

Jerusalem

Gaza
Rafah

Dead Sea

El Arish

Beersheba

MUTASARRIFLIK OF JERUSALEM

Line west of which Britain said 'should be excluded from the proposed limits and boundaries' of any future independent Arab State (McMahon's letter of 25 Oct 1915)

Areas which the Sherif of Mecca declared to be 'purely Arab provinces', and wished to see as part of 'the pure Arab kingdom'. (Hussein's letter of 5 Nov 1915)

E G Y P T
British

Negev

S i n a i

Taba   Akaba

In 1915, in an attempt to win Arab support in the war against Turkey, Britain began negotiations with Hussein, Sherif of Mecca. On 25 Oct 1915 the British High Commissioner in Cairo, Sir H. McMahon, informed Hussein that Britain was 'prepared to recognize and support the independence of the Arabs....' But, he added, the Eastern Mediterranean littoral would have to be entirely excluded from any future Arab State. In his reply on 5 Nov 1915, Hussein insisted on the inclusion of the Vilayet of Beirut, but made no mention of the Mutasarriflik of Jerusalem. But on 14 Dec 1915 McMahon replied that any such inclusion 'will require careful consideration'. On 1 Jan 1916 Hussein warned McMahon: 'the people of Beirut will decidedly never accept such isolations'. At no point in the correspondence was any mention made of southern Palestine, Jerusalem or the Jews

© Martin Gilbert

Sir Martin Gilbert, © 2010. Reproduced by permission of Taylor & Francis Books UK. www.martingilbert.com

officer, one T.E. Lawrence, who was very fond of Arab culture and an expert in desert warfare. He would later come to be known as "Lawrence of Arabia."

After the Balfour Declaration was issued, some in the Arab world began to argue that Ottoman Palestine had already been promised to the Arabs in the Hussein-McMahon correspondence. They claimed that Hussein made it clear that he would never agree to an Arab State that did not include Palestine. These contentions were proven false in 1937 when the British published the hitherto secret letters. Clearly, Hussein never requested Palestine be included in any future Arab State and McMahon was clear that Britain never intended to place Palestine under Arab control.

Sir,

Many references have been made in the Palestine Royal Commission Report and in the course of the recent debates in both Houses of Parliament to the "McMahon Pledge," especially to that portion of the pledge which concerns Palestine and of which one interpretation has been claimed by the Jews and another by the Arabs.

It has been suggested to me that continued silence on the part of the giver of that pledge may itself be misunderstood.

I feel, therefore, called upon to make some statement on the subject, but I will confine myself in doing so to the point now at issue—i.e., whether that portion of Syria now known as Palestine was or was not intended to be included in the territories in which the independence of the Arabs was guaranteed in my pledge.

I feel it my duty to state, and I do so definitely and emphatically, that it was not intended by me in giving this pledge to King Hussein to include Palestine in the area in which Arab independence was promised.

I also had every reason to believe at the time that the fact that Palestine was not included in my pledge was well understood by King Hussein.

Yours faithfully,
Henry McMahon

5, Wilton Place, S.W.
July 22 1915[37]

Hussein had never requested Palestine by name in any of his letters, though he did mention a request to include the Vilayet of Beirut, an area that included the northern tip of Palestine and Southern Lebanon up to and including the city of Beirut. But McMahon replied that Britain had interests to protect in what he referred to as the "Eastern Mediterranean Littoral," an area stretching along the entire shore of the Mediterranean from Turkey through Sinai. Therefore the entire area was excluded from any Arab State or States that were to be carved out for the Arabs after the Ottoman Empire was defeated. And since the local population consisted of many non-Muslim peoples—Jews, Druze, Maronite Christians, Circassians, and other Christian minorities—Arab hegemony was not on the British agenda for the area.

As Lord Balfour stated in a memorandum addressed to new Foreign Secretary Lord Curzon (George Nathaniel Curzon (1859-1925),

> [I]n Palestine we do not propose to even go through the form of consulting the wishes of the present (majority) inhabitants of the country though the American [King-Crane] Commission is going through the form of asking what they are...The Four Great Powers [Britain, France, Italy and the United States] are committed to Zionism. And Zionism, be it right or wrong, good or bad, is rooted in age-long traditions, in present needs, and future hopes, of far profounder import than the desires and prejudices of the 700,000 Arabs who now inhabit that ancient land.[38]

But governments change and the pertfidious British were duplicitously negotiating with the French to retain large swathes of former Ottoman territory as colonial possessions based on the final draft of the secret Sykes–Picot Agreement of 1916 (named after the British and French negotiators).

And with those colonialist ambitions also came a revision of the commitment to the Jewish homeland.

The [British] Eastern Committee of the Cabinet, previously known as the Middle Eastern Committee, had met on 5 December 1918 to discuss the government's commitments regarding Palestine. Lord Curzon chaired the meeting. General Jan Smuts, Lord Balfour, Lord Robert Cecil, General Sir Henry Wilson, Chief of the Imperial General Staff, and representatives of the Foreign Office, the India Office, the Admiralty, the War Office, and the Treasury were present. T. E. Lawrence also attended. According to the minutes Lord Curzon explained the Hussein, Sykes-Picot, and Balfour commitments:

"The Palestine position is this. If we deal with our commitments, there is first the general pledge to Hussein in October 1915, under which Palestine was included in the areas as to which Great Britain pledged itself that they should be Arab and independent in the future...Great Britain and France—Italy subsequently agreeing—committed themselves to an international administration of Palestine in consultation with Russia, [and the Sharif of Mecca] who was an ally at that time...A new feature was brought into the case in November 1917, when Mr Balfour, with the authority of the War Cabinet, issued his famous declaration to the Zionists that Palestine 'should be the national home of the Jewish people, but that nothing should be done—and this, of course, was a most important proviso—to prejudice the civil and religious rights of the existing non-Jewish communities in Palestine.' Those, as far as I know, are the only actual engagements into which we entered with regard to Palestine."[39]

There are those who claim that the Balfour Declaration was issued to appease the American Jewish community which, they maintain, stood in the way of the U.S. joining World War I as England's ally. According to their argument, the American Jewish community was happy to see Russia being pummeled by the Germans and the Austria-Hungarian armies because of what

Russia had done to its Jews during its pogroms (1881-1903). Thus, the Balfour Declaration was an attempt to bribe the American Jewish community into agreeing to let the U.S. enter World War I.

This argument is totally without merit. In 1880 there were a mere 230,000 Jews living in America. By 1917 there were approximately 3 million. The overwhelming majority of these Jews were either immigrants who had fled from Russia and other Eastern European countries or were first generation Americans.

American Jews at that time were not a political force of any kind and had no lobbying groups. Most were poor and not politically active. In 1917, there were five Jewish congressmen and no Jewish senators. Claiming that Jews controlled the United States government was at the very least fictitious. The only powerful, well-connected American Jew in Washington, D.C. at that time was Supreme Court Justice Louis Brandeis, an unabashed Zionist who nevertheless had no control over Congress or the Administration.

Another argument centers on the Russian Revolution of 1917. The Bolsheviks (Communists) overthrew the Czar of Russia on October 25, 1917. The following day, Vladimir Lenin, who led the Revolution, signed "The Decree of Peace" and began extracting Russia from World War I, while making many concessions to Germany. The notion that on November 2, 1917 the British issued the Balfour Declaration as a bribe to the nonexistent, powerful American Jewish Lobby again doesn't wash. What may indeed have been relevant was not the Jewish lobby but rather the Jewish Bolshevik presence.

> ...England, according to Winston Churchill...desired to win over the Jews in Russia, many of them in the Bolshevik government, so that they might influence the new Marxist government to remain in battle with the Germans and Ottomans in WWI on the side of the Allies. He thought that the Balfour Declaration could sway them in British favor.[40]

But Bolshevik Russia's surrender had already begun and became official when the Treaty of Brest-Litovsk was signed on March 3, 1918.

There were, however, two groups in America opposed to the U.S. entering World War I who were much more powerful politically than American Jews and demographically much larger. They were German and Irish Americans. For German Americans, World War I was an agonizing time. The Kaiser's Germany of World War I was not the Germany of Hitler in World War II. World War I pitted their adopted land against their homeland. The Irish, who had no love for England, had no desire to see the U.S. defend their age-old antagonist from suffering defeat at Germany's hands. These two groups, and not American Jews, lobbied for America to stay out of the war.

Nevertheless, the U.S. entered World War I officially on April 2, 1917, seven months before the Balfour Declaration was issued. Although President Woodrow Wilson (1856-1924) pledged in 1914 to keep the U.S. out of the war, reality forced him to change his mind.

Germany's resumption of submarine attacks on passenger and merchant ships in 1917 became the primary motivation behind Wilson's decision to lead the United States into World War I. Following the sinking of an unarmed French boat, the Sussex, in the English Channel in March 1916, Wilson threatened to sever diplomatic relations with Germany unless the German Government refrained from attacking all passenger ships and allowed the crews of enemy merchant vessels to abandon their ships prior to any attack. On May 4, 1916, the German Government accepted these terms and conditions in what came to be known as the "Sussex pledge."

By January 1917, however, the situation in Germany had changed. During a wartime conference that month, representatives from the German Navy convinced the military leadership and Kaiser Wilhelm II that a resumption of unrestricted submarine warfare could help defeat Great Britain within five months. German policymakers argued that they could violate the "Sussex pledge" since the United States could no longer be considered a neutral party after supplying munitions and financial assistance to the Allies. Germany also

believed that the United States had jeopardized its neutrality
by acquiescing to the Allied blockade of Germany.[41]

In addition, in January 1917, the U.S. government uncovered
the secret Zimmerman Telegram, a German attempt to convince
the Mexican government to join Germany as an ally and to open a
front on the U.S. border in exchange for the territory (Texas, New
Mexico and Arizona) lost in the Mexican American War of 1845-
1846.

Thus, when in March 1917 the Germans sank four U.S.
merchant ships on their way to England, a U.S. entry into the war
became a foregone conclusion. Finally, on June 26, 1917, the first
14,000 U.S. troops arrived in France to begin training for combat.[42]

GLIMMERS OF COOPERATION BETWEEN ZIONISM AND ARAB NATIONALISM THAT FADED QUICKLY

Within the framework of the Paris Peace Conference,
a political accord was signed on January 3, 1919 by Dr. Chaim
Weizmann, in the name of the World Zionist Organization, and by
the Emir Feisal, son of the Sharif of Mecca. Under the terms of
the agreement, the Arabs would recognize the Balfour Declaration
and would encourage Jewish immigration and settlement in
Palestine. Freedom of religion and worship in Palestine was set
forth as a fundamental principle, and the Muslim holy sites were
to be under Muslim control. The W.Z.O. promised to look into
the economic possibilities of an Arab state and to help it develop
its resources. Unfortunately, the Arabs and their representatives
repudiated the agreement. The Weizmann-Feisal agreement was
never implemented.

As we see from this remarkable document, early on there was
an actual agreement between the Zionist movement and one of
the most prominent Arab nationalists of the time that spoke of
mutual respect and about areas of cooperation between the two
nationalist movements. Throughout the document, Palestine is
referred to as Jewish. There was also a letter of understanding
between Emir Feisal (son of Hussen Ibn Ali, Sharif of Mecca) to
Felix Frankfurter, associate of Dr. Chaim Weizmann:

Delegation Hedjazienne
Paris Peace Conference
March 3, 1919

Dear Mr. Frankfurter:

I want to take this opportunity of my first contact with American Zionists to tell you what I have often been able to say to Dr. Weizmann in Arabia and Europe.

We feel that the Arabs and Jews are cousins in having suffered similar oppressions at the hands of powers stronger than themselves, and by a happy coincidence have been able to take the first step towards the attainment of their national ideals together.

The Arabs, especially the educated among us, look with the deepest sympathy on the Zionist movement. Our deputation here in Paris is fully acquainted with the proposals submitted yesterday by the Zionist Organization to the Peace Conference, and we regard them as moderate and proper. We will do our best, in so far as we are concerned, to help them through: We will wish the Jews a most hearty welcome home.

With the chiefs of your movement, especially with Dr. Weizmann, we have had, and continue to have, the closest relations. He has been a great helper of our cause, and I hope the Arabs may soon be in a position to make the Jews some return for their kindness. We are working together for a reformed and revived Near East, and our two movements complete one another. The Jewish movement is national and not imperialist. Our movement is national and not imperialist, and there is room in Syria for us both. Indeed I think that neither can be a real success without the other.

People less informed and less responsible than our leaders and yours, ignoring the need for cooperation of the Arabs and Zionists, have been trying to exploit the local difficulties that must necessarily arise in Palestine in the early stages of our movements. Some of them have, I am afraid, misrepresented your aims to the Arab peasantry, and our aims to the Jewish peasantry, with the result that interested parties have been able to make capital out of what they call our differences.

I wish to give you my firm conviction that these differences are not on questions of principle, but on matters of detail such as must inevitably occur in every contact of neighbouring peoples, and as are easily adjusted by mutual good will. Indeed nearly all of them will disappear with fuller knowledge.

I look forward, and my people with me look forward, to a future in which we will help you and you will help us, so that the countries in which we are mutually interested may once again take their places in the community of civilised peoples of the world.

Believe me,

Yours sincerely,

(Sgd.) Feisal[43]

Letter of reply from Felix Frankfurter to Emir Feisal:

Paris Peace Conference

March 5, 1919

Royal Highness,

Allow me, on behalf of the Zionist Organization, to acknowledge your recent letter with deep appreciation.

Those of us who come from the United States have already been gratified by the friendly relations and the active cooperation maintained between you and the Zionist leaders, particularly Dr. Weizmann. We knew it could not be otherwise; we knew that the aspirations of the Arab and the Jewish peoples were parallel, that each aspired to re-establish its nationality in its own homeland, each making its own distinctive contribution to civilization, each seeking its own peaceful mode of life.

The Zionist leaders and the Jewish people for whom they speak have watched with satisfaction the spiritual vigor of the Arab movement. Themselves seeking justice, they are anxious that the just national aims of the Arab people be confirmed and safeguarded by the Peace Conference.

We knew from your acts and your past utterances that the Zionist movement—in other words the national aim of the Jewish people—had your support and the support of the

Arab people for whom you speak. These aims are now before the Peace Conference as definite proposals by the Zionist Organization. We are happy indeed that you consider these proposals "moderate and proper," and that we have in you a staunch supporter for their realization.

For both the Arab and the Jewish peoples there are difficulties ahead—difficulties that challenge the united statesmanship of Arab and Jewish leaders. For it is no easy task to rebuild two great civilizations that have been suffering oppression and misrule for centuries. We each have our difficulties we shall work out as friends, friends who are animated by similar purposes, seeking a free and full development for the two neighboring peoples. The Arabs and Jews are neighbors in territory; we cannot but live side by side as friends.

Very respectfully,
(Sgd.) Felix Frankfurter[44]

Sadly, though Jewish-Arab cooperation exists to the present day on local levels, it would ultimately be Palestinian leadership that condemned its people to years of enmity and war. From the days of the Mufti to the Palestinian Authority (PA) and Hamas, it nvariably falls to this selfsame leadership to always choose the path of no coexistence and no acceptance of Jewish nationhood. Thus, where an Arab Palestinian people could have arguably enjoyed a prosperous and advanced Arab state, instead the PA areas and Hamas-ruled Gaza offer little but irredentism and misery to their inhabitants.

THE BRITISH MANDATE 1917-1948

The British were the last in a long line of foreign conquerors of the territory that began with the Roman conquest of Judea in 70 CE.

Shortly after World War I, the League of Nations, a forerunner of the United Nations, was established. Its job was to work toward world peace to prevent the horrors witnessed during World War I. One of the tasks of the League was to decide the fate of all the territories captured by the Allies from Germany, Austria-Hungary and Ottoman Turkey. The league appointed countries on the victorious side to administer these territories. England was chosen to administer most of the territories taken from the Turks. In particular, Palestine became Britain's responsibility. The official term for this overseeing of land is *mandate*, and hence Britain's control of Palestine is referred to as the period of the British Mandate and the land was referred to as Mandate Palestine.

The League of Nations meeting at San Remo officially adopted the ideas of the Balfour Declaration into the language of the document handing over Ottoman Palestine to Britain as a Mandate. This meant that the international community accepted the right of the Jewish nation to re-establish its homeland in the Land of Israel/Mandate Palestine.

(This international commitment to the re-establishment of a Jewish State was transferred by the League of Nations to the United Nations on April 18, 1946, when the League was dissolved. The British Palestine Mandate officially, at the outset, included what today is the State of Israel, Judea and Samaria, Gaza and Jordan. Initially, the Mandate was a very promising time for the Zionist movement. But, the relationship with Britain would quickly change to a more confrontational one.)

Though the terms of the Mandate and the agreement at San Remo were specific as to the intent of a Jewish homeland, it did not take long for England to renege on her responsibilities vis-á-vis the established Trust.

Perfidious Albion did not maintain [the] 1920 form of its trust for very long. Circumstances changed, British interests changed, and the British Government also changed. Italy's opposition had delayed the issuance of the mandate as proposed in the initial draft submitted to the WWI Allies at San Remo. In the meantime, England had installed Feisal as the King of Syria. After the Battle of Maysalun, in which the French Armed Forces defeated the Syrian Army, the French deposed Feisal. Abdullah, Feisal's brother, was furious. He marched his troops

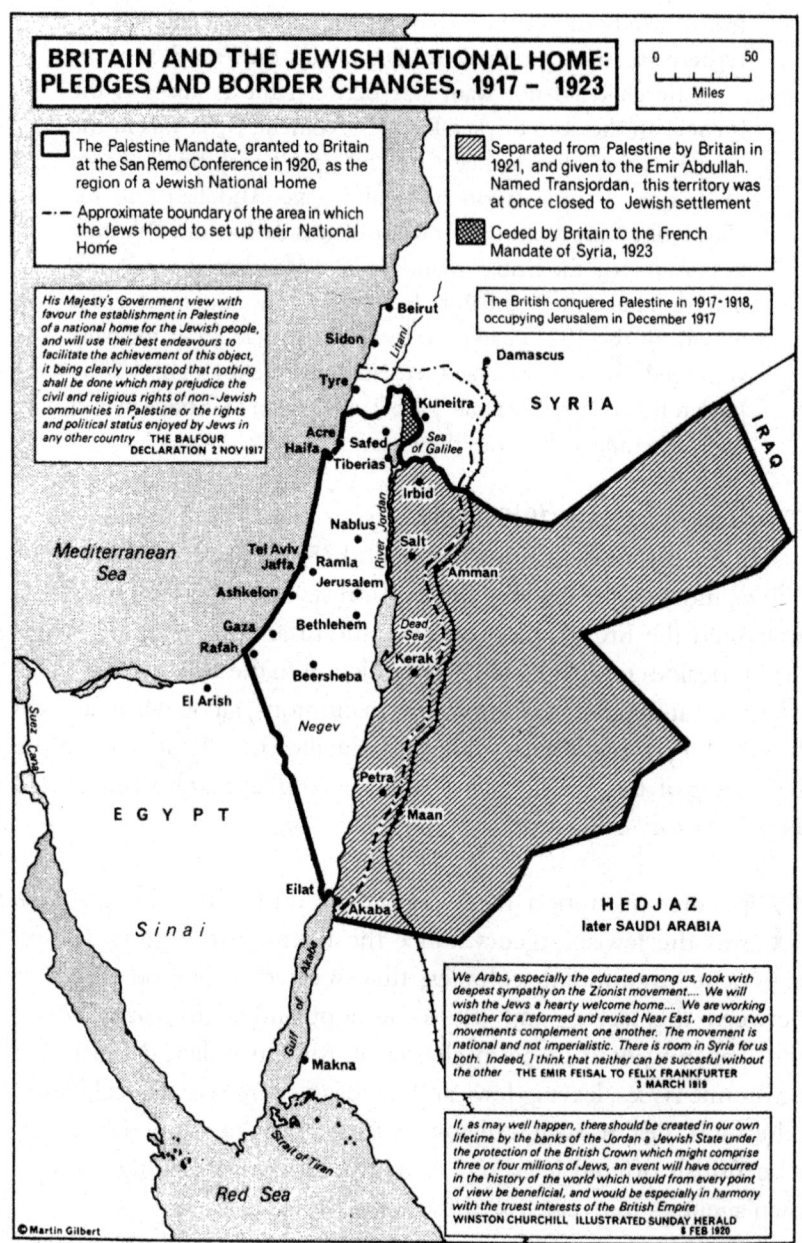

BRITAIN AND THE JEWISH NATIONAL HOME:
PLEDGES AND BORDER CHANGES, 1917 – 1923

0   50
Miles

☐ The Palestine Mandate, granted to Britain at the San Remo Conference in 1920, as the region of a Jewish National Home

–·– Approximate boundary of the area in which the Jews hoped to set up their National Home

▨ Separated from Palestine by Britain in 1921, and given to the Emir Abdullah. Named Transjordan, this territory was at once closed to Jewish settlement

▨ Ceded by Britain to the French Mandate of Syria, 1923

His Majesty's Government view with favour the establishment in Palestine of a national home for the Jewish people, and will use their best endeavours to facilitate the achievement of this object, it being clearly understood that nothing shall be done which may prejudice the civil and religious rights of non-Jewish communities in Palestine or the rights and political status enjoyed by Jews in any other country   **THE BALFOUR DECLARATION 2 NOV 1917**

The British conquered Palestine in 1917-1918, occupying Jerusalem in December 1917

Beirut
Sidon
Litani
Damascus
Tyre
Kuneitra   S Y R I A
Acre   Safed   Sea of Galilee
Haifa
Tiberias
Irbid
IRAQ
Nablus   River Jordan
Salt
Tel Aviv   Jaffa   Ramla   Amman
Jerusalem
Ashkelon
Gaza   Bethlehem   Dead Sea
Rafah   Kerak
Beersheba

Mediterranean Sea

El Arish
Negev

Petra
Suez Canal
E G Y P T   Maan

Eilat
Akaba

Sinai

HEDJAZ
later SAUDI ARABIA

We Arabs, especially the educated among us, look with deepest sympathy on the Zionist movement.... We will wish the Jews a hearty welcome home.... We are working together for a reformed and revised Near East, and our two movements complement one another. The movement is national and not imperialistic. There is room in Syria for us both. Indeed, I think that neither can be successful without the other   **THE EMIR FEISAL TO FELIX FRANKFURTER 3 MARCH 1919**

Makna
Gulf of Akaba
Strait of Tiran

Red Sea

©Martin Gilbert

If, as may well happen, there should be created in our own lifetime by the banks of the Jordan a Jewish State under the protection of the British Crown which might comprise three or four millions of Jews, an event will have occurred in the history of the world which would from every point of view be beneficial, and would be especially in harmony with the truest interests of the British Empire   **WINSTON CHURCHILL ILLUSTRATED SUNDAY HERALD 8 FEB 1920**

Sir Martin Gilbert, © 2010. Reproduced by permission of Taylor & Francis Books UK. www.martingilbert.com

from their home in the Hejaz (in the Arabian Peninsula) to Eastern Palestine and made ready to attack the French in Syria.

Churchill did not want war between the Arabs and the French. In the secret Sykes-Picot Agreement, Syria was in the French sphere of influence. Churchill gave Feisal the Kingdom of Iraq as a consolation prize and gave Abdullah and his Hashemite tribe from the Arabian Peninsula Eastern Palestine in violation of the British Mandate. The Mandate at San Remo had prohibited the Mandatory from ceding any land to a foreign nation. In the 1922 change, with a new Article 25, it formally approved delaying organized settlement by the Jews East of the Jordan River and informally gave TransJordan to Abdullah and his Hashemite Tribe from the Hejaz.[45]

THE THIRD ALIYAH (1919-1923)

In the meantime, during this period 35,000 Jews arrived in *Eretz Yisrael*, most of them young Labor Zionists from Russia. This *Aliyah* re-ignited the fire of Zionism after the disastrous years of World War I. Besides raising the Jewish population to the 100,000 mark, this *Aliyah* created three very important institutions, all of which are still functioning in one form or another. Finally, this *Aliyah* marked the beginning of the Arab-Israeli Conflict, a conflict that has dominated Israel's history ever since.

The first institution that was set up during the Third *Aliyah* was the Jewish Agency. Since the British had a great deal of experience in running colonies, they wanted a division of labor between themselves and the local populations. In *Eretz Yisrael*, the British wanted to be in charge of foreign policy, defense and economic issues, leaving Jews and Arabs in charge of all local issues: education, health, mail, religious affairs, immigration and housing. The British offered Jews and Arabs the option of setting up their own agencies to oversee all these social and civil issues.

The Jewish community accepted the offer, while the Arabs rejected it. The Arabs wanted one super Palestine Agency to run the affairs of all of Palestine, with the Arabs in charge. Since they were the majority of the population of Palestine, they rejected the Balfour Declaration and the British Mandate. Thus Palestinian Arabs began playing the very dangerous game of "double or nothing" and always ended up with nothing—and then blamed the Jews for their own poor choices.

The Jewish Agency, established in 1920, became the nerve center of world Zionism, surpassing the W.Z.O. in importance. It ran the day-to-day affairs of the *Yishuv* as the unofficial government of the unofficial state of Israel, until Israel became a state in 1948. The first Executive Director of the Jewish Agency was Chaim Weizmann. Since Israel became a state with a democratic government, the Jewish Agency has been in charge of *Aliyah* and absorption and other social programs.

The Histadrut*, the Jewish Federation of Labor, was also founded in 1920. Twenty-eight years before Israel became a state, it had a strong labor union—further proof of how well-organized the Jews were.

The Histadrut had two main functions. It acted as an employment agency/union. It speeded up the effort to develop the land by keeping files on all the types of workers available—plumbers, ditch diggers, electricians, masons and so forth. Instead of spending days or weeks putting together a labor force for a particular project, they were able to assemble a workforce for a project in one or two days just by checking their lists of workers. If you registered with the Histadrut, it would find work for you in your field at a guaranteed wage. The Histadrut also offered medical and life insurance to its members.

---

*Today, the Histadrut is Israel's largest and only union. But with the idealism of the *kibbutz* movement almost gone, and capitalism as the main economic engine, there are Israelis who feel that the Histadrut has outlived its usefulness and stifles the economy because it controls wages and benefits for its members. Businesses resent it, and want to hold on to profits while depriving workers of their rights and benefits—in a climate of growing income inequality that has become a front-burner issue in today's Israel.

Thanks to the Histadrut, the Land of Israel was developed at an incredible pace. Israel became a Western-style modern country in less than 50 years.

The Haganah, the Jewish self-defense underground army, was formed in 1920. The Haganah was the father of the Israeli Army.

During the Third *Aliyah* it became apparent that the Arab world was opposed to the establishment of an independent Jewish State and would do everything in its power to prevent it. This opposition was violent and deadly at times. Since the British were not about to risk their men's lives, they opted not to involve themselves in the defense of Jews. If the Jewish people intended to run an independent Jewish State, they needed to create a nucleus of an army.

Unlike Hashomer, whose main concern was to stop thieves, the Haganah was intended to be a military force capable of dealing with terrorism. Hashomer, at its height, had approximately 200 members in the country; the Haganah was initially set up with more than 1,000 men, most of them Jews who had served in the British and Russian armies. The Haganah became the unofficial army of the unofficial state of Israel, and lasted until 1948 when it, together with the other smaller undergrounds, formed Tzahal/the Israel Defense Forces (IDF).

During the 28 years that the Haganah operated as an underground army, it was commanded by the civilians of the Jewish Agency. This was a very significant development because in many similar situations around the globe underground armies become independent operations responsible only to themselves. In Israel, the tradition of civilian control of the military began in 1920.

From this point on the Arab-Israeli conflict would come to dominate modern Jewish history. Arab hostility had turned violent, and Jewish properties all around Israel were becoming targets.

The conflict became a very intense and fierce one; in a sense it helped mold Israel more than any other factor or events. It was a development none of the early Zionist leaders had predicted or prepared for. One cannot fully understand the history of modem Israel or Zionism without examining the roots of the Arab-Israeli conflict, in particular the roots of the Arab hostility to Zionism.

Footnotes

[1] Walter Laqueur, *The Changing Face of Antisemitism: From Ancient Times to the Present Day* (Oxford: Oxford University Press, 2006), 56.

[2] Arthur Hertzberg, *The Zionist Idea: A Historical Analysis and Reader* (Philadelphia: Jewish Publication Society, 1997), 23.

[3] Yitzhak Kraus "Rabbi Alkalai on Returning to Zion and Returning to the Lord." Bar-Ilan University, Parshat Hashavua Study Center, 20 September 2014.

[4] Hasia R. Diner, *The Jews of the United States, 1654 to 2000* (Berkeley, CA: University of California Press, 2004), 175.

[5] Hertzberg, *The Zionist Idea*, 105.

[6] *Ibid.*, 106.

[7] *Ibid.*, 107.

[8] *Ibid.*, 111.

[9] *Ibid.*, 112.

[10] *Ibid.*, 119.

[11] *Ibid.*, 132-133.

[12] Ksharim, "The Origins of Zionism," Lesson 41 (http://makomisrael.org/blog/the-origins-of-zionism-2/ http://makomisrael.org/wp-content/uploads/2011/10/lesson41.pdf.), 402.

[13] *Ibid.*

[14] *Ibid.*

[15] Zionist Library, http://www.geocities.com/Vienna/6640/zion/pinsker.html

[16] Jellinek and Pinsker, *Ein Zwiegespäch*, reprinted in Robert S. Wistrich, "Zionism and its Religious Critics in fin-de-siècle Vienna," in Shmuel Almog, et. al., *Zionism and Religion* (Waltham, MA: Brandeis University Press, 1998) pp. 140-158, 142-143.

[17] "Zionism: BILU Manifesto," Jewish Virtual Library (https://www.jewishvirtuallibrary.org/jsource/Zionism/BILU_Manifesto.html)

[18] Mark Twain, *The Innocents Abroad, or The New Pilgrims' Progress, Volume 2* (New York: P. F. Collier & Son, 1911), 357-359.

[19] See Bernard Lewis, "Studies in the Ottoman Archives—I", *Bulletin of the School of Oriental and African Studies*, University of London, Vol. 16, No. 3, 1954, pp. 469–501; Alexander Scholch. "The Demographic Development of Palestine, 1850–1882." *International Journal of Middle East Studies* 17 (4), (November 1985): 485–505; Justin McCarthy, *The Population of Palestine: Population History and Statistics of the Late Ottoman Period and the Mandate* (New York: Columbia University Press, 1990.)

[20] Albert M. Hyamson, *Palestine: A Policy* (London:: Methuen, 1942), 58.

[21] "Without Settlers Initiative Rothschild Would Not Have Undertaken Colonization," JTA, August 13, 1928 (http://www.jta.org/1928/08/13/archive/without-settlers-initiative-rothschild-would-not-have-undertaken-colonization)

[22] Wesley Yang, "The End of the Affair," *Tablet*, September 4, 2009 (http://www.tabletmag.com/jewish-arts-and-culture/books/15116/the-end-of-the-affair)

[23] Theodore Herzl, *Der Judenstaat*, 1896, Jewish Virtual Library (http://www..jewishvirtual library.org/jsource/Zionism/herzl2.html)

[24] "Zionist Congress: First Zionist Congress & Basel Program (August 1897)," Jewish Virtual Library (http://www.jewishvirtuallibrary.org/jsource/Zionism/First_Cong_&_Basel_Program.html)

[25] "The Jewish State: Theodor Herzl's Program for Zionism" (http://www.zionism-israel.com/js/Jewish_State.html)

[26] Max L. Margolis & Alexander Marx, *A History of the Jewish People* (Philadelphia: The Jewish Publication Society of America, 1927), 707.

[27] "Zionism: Socialist Zionism," Jewish Virtual Library (https://

www.jewishvirtuallibrary.org/jsource/Zionism/Socialist_
Zionism.html)

[28] *Ibid.*

[29] Matthew Wagner, "As NRP folds to create united front, signs of dissent emerge," *The Jerusalem Post*, Nov 19, 2008 (http://www.jpost.com/Israel/As-NRP-folds-to-create-united-front-signs-of-dissent-emerge)

[30] *Ibid.*

[31] Rabbi Ari Zivotofsky, "What's the Truth about ... the Uganda Plan?", Jewish Action, March 1, 2008 (https://jewishaction.com/jewish-world/history/whats_the_truth_about_the_uganda_plan/)

[32] Arthur Hertzberg, *The Zionist Idea:A Historical Analysis and Reader.* (Philadelphia: Jewish Publication Society, 1997), 374.

[33] Mark Belt, "Unsung Heroes," *Horsefeathers*, June 8, 2005 (https://web.archive.org/web/20090611041943/http://doctor-horsefeathers.com/archives2/000437.php)

[34] "The Balfour Declaration November 2, 1917" (http://www.zionism-israel.com/Balfour_Declaration_1917.htm)

[35] "Balfour Declaration: Text of the Declaration (November 2, 1917)," Jewish Virtual Library (http://www.jewishvirtuallibrary.org/jsource/History/balfour.html)

[36] David Lloyd George, *Memoirs* (London: Odhams Press Limited, 1933), 736-7.

[37] Alfred Bonné, *State and Economics in the Middle East: A Society in Turmoil* (London: Routledge, 2001), 83.

[38] Wallace Edward Brand, "The Exclusive Political Rights Granted To Jews In 1920 At San Remo," Israeli Frontline, December 30, 2012 (http://www.israelifrontline.com/2012/12/the-eexclusive-political-rights-granted.html)

[39] Doreen Ingrams, *Palestine Papers 1917-1922*, page 48 and UK Archives PRO. CAB 27/24

[40] *Op. cit.*

[41] "U.S. Entry into World War I, 1917," Office of the Historian (Milestones: 1914–1920 - Office of the Historian of the U.S. Govt. pdf)

[42] "April 06, 1917: America Enters World War I," History.com (www.history.com/this-day-in-history/america-enters-world-war-i/print)

[43] "Pre-State Israel: Feisal-Frankfurter Correspondence (March 1919)," Jewish Virtual Library (https://www.jewishvirtuallibrary.org/feisal-frankfurter-correspondence-march-1919)

[44] *Ibid.*

[45] Wallace Edward Brand, "The Exclusive Political Rights Granted To Jews In 1920 At San Remo."

Chapter 4

The Arab World

There was once a popular TV show about the White House called *West Wing*, which ran from 1999-2006. Many episodes covered the crises in the Middle East, and one in particular resounded with audiences Jewish and Arab. The plot involved the White House being locked down due to a terror threat, and among those "trapped" in the White House was a group of high school students put into the care of the First Lady, who kept them distracted in the cafeteria while the NSA dealt with the situation. The students asked her questions and one of them wanted to know where the conflict between Jews and Arabs began. After a thoughtful pause she responded, "It began with Sarah and Hagar."

These two women, and the stories of what happened to them and their sons, sits at the foundation of the religious conflict between Muslims and Jews. It is very much a product of the tribal culture from which it came, a tribal culture that continues to play a role in contemporary history. But let us begin with *Bereishit*/Genesis.

The story is about Avraham, the first patriarch of the Jewish people, his wife, the first Jewish matriarch, Sarah, and his concubine, Hagar, an Egyptian. Here is the story according to Genesis and its commentaries (*Chumash* and *midrashim*).

Hagar, who was Sarah's maid, became Avraham's concubine, (some would say second wife) and bore him a son, Ishmael, a man the Bedouin and Arabs consider their patriarch. The *Midrash* says Hagar was the daughter of an Egyptian Pharoah, who had witnessed how God saved Sarah from her father's hands. The

Midrash reports Hagar to have said, "It is better to be a slave in Sarah's house than a princess in my own," and joined Avraham's household as Sarah's servant.

The relationship changed as Sarah grew older and despaired of giving birth. Desperate to be a mother, she gave Hagar to Avraham as a concubine to bear him a son as her surrogate. Hagar is acknowledged as being the mother of Avraham's son in all Avrahamic faiths. She appears in *sefer Bereishit*, and in the Christian New Testament, yet is only alluded to in the Qur'an. While the Torah considers Hagar Avraham's concubine, Hagar is considered Avraham's second wife in the Islamic faith.

The relationship with Sarah changed when Hagar discovered she was pregnant, and became arrogant and disrespectful to her mistress. Sarah asserted her authority and treated Hagar cruelly, so Hagar fled into the desert while still pregnant. There, an angel of God appeared and told her to return to Sarah so that she may bear a child who "shall be a wild ass of a man: his hand shall be against every man, and every man's hand against him; and he shall dwell in the face of all his brethren" (Genesis 16:12). Her son was to be given the name Ishmael (God will hear him). Hagar went back to the camp and gave birth to Ishmael when Avraham was 86 (Genesis 16:7-16). Later, when God commanded Avraham to have a *brit milah*, Ishmael was also circumcised.

When, in her old age, Sarah gave birth to Isaac—the son God had promised her—there was another confrontation between the two women when Ishmael, then a teenager, taunted the infant Isaac/Yitzhak at his weaning ceremony. Furious, Sarah went to Avraham and demanded that Hagar and Ishmael be banished. Though Avraham was upset, he was commanded by God to do as Sarah asked, was told by God that Isaac/Yitzhak would carry the Avrahamic line, and that Ishmael would also be a patriarch of a nation (Genesis 21:9-13).

And so Hagar and Ishmael were banished. Almost perishing in the wildnerness, they were rescued by an angel who led them to a well and told Hagar that God "will make a great nation" of her son. Hagar eventually found Ishmael a wife from Egypt and they settled in the Desert of Paran (Genesis 21:14-21).[1]

THE ARABIAN PENINSULA

All of this took place in the ancient Near East, cradle of civilization, a region that now covers what we call the Middle East. It consisted of Mesopotamia, Anatolia, the Armenian highlands, Asia Minor, the Levant—basically covering all the territory today that stretches from Georgia and Azerbaijan, from Turkey, Iraq and Iran to Lebanon, Syria, Jordan, Egypt and the entire Arabian Penninsula to Kuwait, including the State of Israel.

In ancient times this was a region where the basic institutions of civilization were created and developed—from organized religion (monotheistic and pagan) to centralized governments, writing systems, rule of law, and the basis for astronomy and mathematics, as well as the invention of the wheel. It was also the region where Avraham was sent on his mission to spread the word of the One God.

The history of the Arabian Peninsula goes back to the beginnings of human habitation in an area that covers approximately 1.25 million square miles.

> In our earliest sources Arabia signifies the steppe and desert wastes bordering on the territories of the states and principalities of Egypt and the Fertile Crescent. For Herodotus (d. c.430 BC) Arabia chiefly designates parts of eastern Egypt, Sinai and the Negev..., which accords with the note of Pliny the Elder (d. AD 79) that "beyond the Pelusiac [easternmost] mouth of the Nile is Arabia, extending to the Red Sea"... In Persian administrative lists, mostly from the reign of Darius (521-486 BC), a district called Arabâya is usually included between Assyria and Egypt, which is probably Herodotus' Arabia plus parts of the Syrian desert. The latter corresponds to Pliny's "Arabia of the nomads", lying to the east of the Dead Sea... In order to seize the Persian throne from his brother, the young Cyrus led his army of ten thousand Greeks

on an epic journey from Sardis to Babylon in 401 BC. On the way "he marched through Arabia, keeping the Euphrates on the right" (Xenophon, An. 1.4.19), the reference here being to the province of Arabia in central Mesopotamia. This is qualified by Pliny as "the district of Arabia called the country of the Orroei" to the east of the Euphrates and south of the Taurus mountains....

Herodotus knew of south Arabia as well: "Arabia is the most distant to the south of all inhabited countries and this is the only country which yields frankincense and myrrh".... He had little information about it, however, and it remained for him a land of mystery and legend, abounding with aromatics, "vipers and winged serpents". This was to change after the voyage of Scylax of Caryanda commissioned by Darius (Herodotus 4.44) and particularly after the journeys of exploration dispatched by Alexander the Great (d. 323 BC), which made the Arabian peninsula much better known to the outside world. Theophrastus of Eresus (d. 287), interested in botanical matters, gives it only a passing mention..., but Eratosthenes of Cyrene (d. c.202 BC), chief librarian to the Ptolemies of Egypt, furnishes a proper description. "The northern side", he says, "is formed by the above-mentioned [Syrian] desert, the eastern by the Persian Gulf, the western by the Arabian Gulf, and the southern by the great sea that lies outside both gulfs" (cited in Strabo 16.3.1; cf. Pliny 6.143).[2]

ARABS

But who were the "Arabs" who inhabited this area?

The Greco-Roman and Persian terms for Arabia derive from the word "Arab", which is the name of a people. "Arabia" is thus equivalent to the Assyrian expression "land of the Arabs" (*mât Aribi*)... They are first mentioned in Biblical and Assyrian texts of the ninth to fifth centuries BC where they appear as nomadic pastoralists inhabiting the Syrian desert. The fact that the name begins to be used by both cultures during the same period suggests that "Arab" was how these pastoralists designated themselves. What its original significance was we do not know, but it came to be synonymous with desert-dweller and a nomadic way of life in the texts of settled peoples. "You waited by the roadside for lovers like an Arab in the desert", says the prophet Jeremiah (3.2). "Babylon...will be overthrown by God," prophesies Isaiah (13.19-20), "never again will the Arab pitch his tent there or the shepherds make their folds." "Do not show to an Arab the sea or to a Sidonian the desert, for their occupations are different", opined a seventh-century BC sage (Ahiqar 110). And the Assyrian king Sargon II (721-705 BC) speaks of "the Arabs who live far away in the desert and who know neither overseers nor officials" (AR 2.17).[3]

For most of that time the Arabs were a pagan, nomadic people who were divided into hundreds of tribes. Having to forage for survival, pre-Islamic Arab culture was tribal because the arid, hot desert weather conditions and lack of rain prevented nomadic tribes from settling down. But because the peninsula was on a number of trade routes running to different continents, urban trading settlements, such as Mecca and Medina, came into being. Recent discoveries of pre-Islamic societies in the area, including that of Sheba and the Kingdom of Aswan, among others, have added to the recognition of fixed societies.

Ubaid, Umman-Nar, and Sabr culture originated in the pre-historic age (circa 5300 BCE). The A'adids established themseleves in Yemen, where they settled beside the Qahtan tribe. The Thamud, a people of Arabia, flourished from 3000 BCE to 200 BCE. The Minaean Kingdom of northwestern Yemen existed from 600 to 100 BCE., while the kingdon of Saba in southwestern Yemen ruled from 800 BCE to 275 CE. The kingdom of Hadhramaut existed from 700 BCE to 200 CE. Subsequet kingdoms of Aswan and Qataban flouished from 700 BCE to 200 CE in Yemen. In Northern Arabia there existed the Achaemenids and the Nabateans, with the Ghassanids, the Lahkhmids and the Kindites the last major migration from Yemen by the 6th century CE.[4]

Overall,

...Arab traditions relating to the origins and classification of the Arabian tribes is based on biblical genealogy. The general consensus among 14th-century Arabic genealogists was that Arabs were three kinds:

"Perishing Arabs": These are the ancients of whose history little is known. They include ʿĀd, Thamud, Tasm, Jadis, Imlaq and others. Jadis and Tasm perished because of genocide. ʿĀd and Thamud perished because of their decadence. Some people in the past doubted their existence, but Imlaq is the singular form of ʿAmaleeq and is probably synonymous to the biblical Amalek.

"Pure Arabs" (Qahtanite): These are traditionally considered to have originated from the progeny of Yaʿrub bin Yashjub bin Qahtan so were also called Qahtanite Arabs.

"Arabized Arabs" (Adnanite): They are traditionally seen as having descended from Adnan.*[5]

ARAB CULTURE

Arab culture built Mecca, and created one of the world's oldest written Semitic languages, Arabic. Pre-Islamic literature produced a classic masterpiece, *A Thousand and One Arabian Nights.*

According to many non-Islamic historians and archeologists, a meteorite fell to earth several thousand years ago on the spot where Mecca stands today. Pagan Arab tribes saw a fiery streak of light from the heavens crash to earth. It is assumed they believed one or many of the gods threw a stone at the Earth, making it holy. People wanted to see the holy rock, touch it, pray to it, and worship there. Priests from different tribes built shrines next to

---

* Contemporary historiography unveiled the lack of inner coherence of this genealogical system and demonstrated that it finds insufficient matching evidence; the distinction between Qahtanites and Adnanites is even believed to be a product of the Umayyad Age, when the war of factions (al-niza al-hizbi) was raging in the young Islamic Empire. (Gianluca P. Parolin, *Citizenship in the Arab World: Kin, Religion and Nation-State* (Amsterdam Univeristy Press, 2009), 30.)

the meteorite and attracted followers. Normally, Arab tribes did not cooperate with each other and, in fact, more often than not, were rivals and enemies. Mecca became the religious and economic center for the different tribes, and while no one set of laws governed these many tribes, there appears to have been certain laws in Mecca to allow worship and business to be conducted in a fashion that was acceptable to most Arabs—though many of these laws were harsh and favored the rich and powerful tribes and tribal leaders. This rich world of successful merchants in Mecca was the world Muhammad was born into.

THE PROPHET MUHAMMAD AND THE RISE OF ISLAM

In 570 CE, Muhammad—who Muslims consider the last prophet in a line of prophets from Moses to Jesus—was born into the Quraish tribe, the most powerful tribe in Mecca. The city was a major stop on a number of trade routes where the Quraish controlled the west coast of Arabia, from Syria to Yemen. The religious life in Mecca was split between two pagan cults whose gods were thought to provide their wealth. Muhammad worked in his family's business and eventually married a rich woman who had hired him to secure her trade caravans to Syria.

Muhammad was a thinker and spiritual person who apparently had contact with Jewish and Christian traders in Mecca who taught him about the Jewish Bible and the Christian New Testament. He learned about Jewish monotheism and the concept of God-given law to govern mankind. He found these ideas to be fascinating, alluring and something lacking in Arab tribal culture.

Until the late sixth and early seventh century, Judaism and Christianity had not penetrated the Arabian Desert. Muhammad would change this. He would become the Avraham, Moses and, to an extent, the Jesus of the Arab world. He would introduce the Arabs to monotheism, the ideas of justice and law.

In creating Islam Muhammad borrowed heavily from the Tanach/Old Testament and, to a lesser extent, from the New Testament. Non-Islamic historians believe that the actual first

Qur'an was written and completed by Muhammad's followers some 50 to 100 years after his death in 632.

THE QUR'AN

The Qur'an is divided into chapters called Suras. They are arranged in size order. The first Sura, called the "Cow," is the longest, and the last Sura, called "Men," is the shortest. There are 114 Suras in the Qur'an. Throughout its passages there are many references to Judaism, Jews, Moses (Musa), Avraham (Ibrahim) and other figures from the Tanach. The references to Judaism are mostly positive. The Qur'an accepts the idea that the Tanach and the New Testament were also revelations made by Allah to prophets who predated Muhammad, but that the Jews and the Christians had lost their way, and hence Allah had to reveal himself one last time to Muhammad. This last revelation is the greatest and final word of Allah.

Muhammad was familiar with stories and ideas that originated from the Tanach and the New Testament, but it is clear he didn't read the Hebrew or Greek texts. Many of the references to events from the Tanach are incorrect and could only be made by someone unfamiliar with the text. [It is unlikely Muhammad had access to any existing Biblical scrolls, hence his knowledge of the Bible would have come solely from the oral tradition from which most adherents learned.] For example, in Sura 28, Verse 38, Muhammad has Pharaoh from the Book of Exodus, who lived in the 14th century BCE, ask Haman from the Book of Esther, who lived in the sixth century BCE, to build the Tower of Babel, which appears in the beginning of Genesis, around 3,000 BCE.

The overall sense one gets from reading the Qur'an is that Muhammad liked many of the ideas and values of Judaism and its biblical prophets, but was angry at the Jews who he felt had abandoned Allah's teachings and were hence punished. But it appears that the main reason for Muhammad's anger at the Jews was because of the reactions of the Arabian Jews who lived in and around Medina to Muhammad's message that he was indeed a prophet of Allah's in the true tradition of the Tanach. The Jews simply did not accept Muhammad as a prophet, any more than they had accepted Jesus as the Christian Messiah. At best, Muhammad was an enlightened Arab who embraced some Jewish values and ideals found in the Tanach and taught his hybrid new faith to the Arab tribesman of the Arabian Desert. At worst, he was a false prophet.

At the outset of Muhammad's quest to gain converts to Islam, non-Islamic historians claim that it was so important for Muhammad to win over the Jews of Medina he decreed that when his followers prayed they should face Jerusalem, which he knew to be the center of the Jewish faith. But the Jews were not impressed by this gesture and the Arabs, as much as they had accepted Muhammad's Islam, faced Mecca when they prayed. Based on many versions in the Qur'an that speak of the Jews, it is clear Muhammad did not forgive them for rejecting him. For example, in Sura 5, Verse 33 it says:

> The punishment of those who wage war against Allah and His apostle and strive to make mischief in the land is only this—that they should be murdered or crucified or their hands and their feet should be cut off on opposite sides or they should be imprisoned; this shall be as a disgrace for them in this world, and in the hereafter they shall have a grievous chastisement.

In Sura 5, Verse 54 it says:

> And the Jews say: The hand of Allah is tied up! Their hands shall be shackled and they shall be cursed for what they say. Nay, both His hands are spread out, He expends as He pleases; and what has been revealed to you from your Lord will certainly make many of them increase in inordinacy and unbelief; and We have put enmity and hatred among them till the day of resurrection; whenever they kindle a fire for war Allah puts it out, and they strive to make mischief in the land; and Allah does not love the mischief makers.

In Sura 111, Verse 112 it says:

> Ignominy shall be their portion [the Jews] wheresoever
> they are found... They have incurred anger from their Lord,
> and wretchedness is laid upon them... because they disbelieve
> the revelations of Allah and slew the Prophets wrongfully...
> because they were rebellious and used to transgress.

There are many other verses in the Qur'an that speak of the Jews as being cursed and having been the killers of prophets.

Islam has a very definite view of Judaism: The Jews used to be the chosen people, but because they sinned against Allah they no longer are. This was illustrated in laws passed during the height of the Arab-Islamic Empire known as the "Pact of Omar" (ninth century, CE) that defined what the Islamic attitude towards the Jews should be in light of the fact that Islam had a very uncompromising policy towards dealing with pagan peoples, namely, "Convert or Die!"

Since Jews were the "People of the Book" (in Arabic, *Umma El Kittab*), they would be allowed to live even if they are foolish and do not convert to Islam. However, their position as second-class citizens was clear and codified: Jews are *dhimmis*, protected second-class citizens in the Islamic Empire.

The Pact of Omar states that Jews have the right to live their lives, study and practice the Torah on a community level but:

a) they must wear distinctive clothing;

b) synagogues must not be taller than the local mosque;

c) Jews must ride donkeys, while Muslims ride horses; and,

d) the community must pay a special tax to the government known as the *dhimmi* tax or the *jizya*.

Qur'an Sura 9 Verse 29 on this matter states:

> Fight those who believe not in Allah nor the Last Day, nor
> hold that forbidden which hath been forbidden by Allah and
> His Messenger, nor acknowledge the religion of Truth (even

if they are) of the People of the Book, until they pay the jizya with willing submission and feel themselves subdued.

In the final analysis, Jews were to be tolerated in the Islamic world as long as they knew their place, and accepted it. Compared to Christian Europe, the Islamic Middle East was far more tolerant.

In general, Jewish life under Muslim rule was best during times of political, economic, and social stability, notably the eighth to the twelfth centuries in the Middle East under the Abbasid and Fatimid caliphates, the tenth and eleventh centuries under the Umayyads and Taifa rulers in Iberia, and the fifteenth to the seventeenth centuries under the Ottomans in the Balkans, Anatolia, and the Middle East. Jewish culture developed and flourished during these periods, when, up until the beginning of the seventeenth century, the majority of world Jewry actually lived in the Islamic world.[6]

THE FIVE BASIC PILLARS OF ISLAM

1) *Shahada*: Testifying to God's One-ness: The declaration, "There is no God but Allah and Muhammad is His prophet."

2) *Salat*: Prayer. Praying five times a day facing Mecca.

3) *Zakat*: Giving charity, originally a free-will donation that is now called *Sadaqah* (similar to the Hebrew word for charity, *tzedakah*). This is usually 2.5% of one's income that is given to either the Islamic government or to the Islamic community.

4) *Sawm*: Fasting during the month of Ramadan.

5) *Hajj*: The pilgrimage a Muslim must make to Mecca at least once in his life.

Islam wants its adherents to be constantly aware that while there are other monotheistic religions, only Islam has the final word of the last and greatest of all the prophets, Muhammad. A Muslim prays five times a day so that s/he is reminded of the presence of Allah all day, as well as the significance of Mecca. There is a community obligation to take care of the poor and community upkeep of the mosque, the Islamic place of worship. Fasting during

Ramadan is from dawn to dusk for an entire month. In the evening you eat and actually feast. The purpose of the fasting is to cause one to be self-introspective, and to appreciate the significance of self-control. When Ramadan ends there is a festive holiday called *Eid al Fitr*, which begins on the first day of the next month, Shawwal. The Muslim calendar is a lunar calendar, like the Jewish one. The Jewish lunar calendar, however, has to align with the solar calendar, so every two to three years a thirteenth month is added. But the Islamic lunar calendar creates a 354-day year, so that over the course of a decade, Ramadan and all the other months fall out at very different times throughout the solar calendar.

In addition to the Qur'an—the main source of laws, faith, ideology and theology for Islam—there is the Islamic body of jurisprudence collected and codified over the last 14 centuries by Islamic judges and legal scholars, called the *Sharia*—the Islamic version of Judaism's *Halacha*. There is also a collection of stories connected to Muhammad called the *Hadith*. In aggregate, the Qur'an, the *Sharia* and the *Hadith* make up the texts that guide Islamic thinking and practice.

THE BIRTH OF ISLAM

When Muhammad was about 40 years old he began having religious visions and hearing voices. Muslims believe the Archangel Gabriel revealed himself to Muhammad when he was on one of his meditative retreats in the mountains around Mecca and instructed him to recite "in the name of your lord." This could be a parallel to God revealing himself to Moses at the burning bush. His revelations spoke of the only God, Allah, the All Powerful, who negated the local idolatrous cults of the pre-Islamic period.

Muhammad began to write down his revelations and they became the basis of the Qu'ran, Islam's holy book. As God's prophet and messenger, Muhammad's followers, the Muslims, try to follow his ways. In addition to the Qur'an, there are the *Hadith*, which consists of the sayings of Muhammad, and the *Sunna*, which describes Muhammad's way of life.

Muhammad's monotheistic views were anathema to the merchants of Mecca who worried that he was angering the pagan gods, and thus would destroy their businesses. Until their deaths, Muhammad's uncle, head of the tribe, and Muhammad's rich and influential wife were able to prevent him from being harmed. But after they died, he and his followers were forced to flee Mecca for Medina, where they were promised religious freedom. This exodus, the *Hegira*, took place in 622, and is considered year one on the Islamic calendar.

As Muhammad continued to develop Islam in Medina, there were still problems with his tribe in Mecca until *jihad* (literally *struggling* or *striving* but more often used for "holy war") was declared and Mecca surrendered to Muhammad in 629. Muhammad and his followers took over the entire city, destroying all its idols. Allah thus became the one and only god.

MECCA

How and why did Mecca become so holy? In order to gain acceptance Muhammad had to accommodate the very strong traditional—and pagan—holiness and specialness of Mecca that predated Islam by thousands of years. The black meteorite that had fallen to earth and become an Arab holy site had to be transformed into an Islamic holy site. In pre-Islamic times pagan Arab tribes had built a square building around the black stone and called it the Kabba (cube). Mohammad appropriated the site as the spot where the first Muslim in history, Ibrahim (Avraham), and his son Ishmael built the first prayer site to Allah.

From the information we have from the Old Testament, Avraham traveled from Ur, in present-day Iraq, to Haran (in present-day Syria), settled in Canaan (present-day Israel), and traveled to Egypt during a famine. But there is no mention of him traveling anywhere near Mecca or even in the Arabian Desert. Nevertheless, when Muhammad conquered Mecca he cleansed the Kabba and declared it the holiest shrine in Islam. It is so holy that all Muslims must face it when they pray and, to this day, only

Muslims may enter the city of Mecca. Finally, because the city is so holy, every Muslim adult who has the means and the ability must make the pilgrimage to Mecca, the *Hajj*, at least once in his or her life.

Medina, Muhammad's safe haven after being banned from Mecca, and the city wherein he created a community of Muslims, is Islam's second holiest city. There is no specific law connected to Medina except the *Hegira*.

Below Medina in holiness is Al Quds or Jerusalem. The holiness of Jerusalem comes from Sura 17, Verse 1 in the Qur'an that speaks of the night the Archangel Gabriel appeared to Muhammad and took him on a journey to Jerusalem, Heaven and Hell and then returned him to Earth. In Jerusalem, Muhammad was said to have prayed with Moses and Jesus.

> Glory to (Allah) Who did take His Servant for a Journey by night from the Sacred Mosque to the Farthest Mosque (*Masjid al Aqsa*), whose precincts We did bless, in order that We might show him some of Our Signs: for He is the One Who heareth and seeth (all things).

Islamic scholars interpret the entire Sura to mean that Muhammad was flown to Al Quds/Jerusalem on a creature that had wings, the body of a donkey and the face of a woman called Al Buraq. Muhammad flew to the site of the Temple Mount, dismounted from Al Buraq and placed his foot on the rock considered by many to be the rock of the *Akedah Yitzhak* (the binding of Isaac (Genesis 22)) and where had once stood the First and Second Jewish Temples. He then climbed back on Al Buraq and ascended to heaven. It is based on this Sura that Al Quds became holy in Islam.

The Islamic armies conquered Palestine in 636 and built two structures on the site of the two Jewish Temples. In 691, at the order of Umayyad Caliph Abd al-Malik, an Islamic shrine was built over the rock that Muslims believe Muhammad stepped on during his night journey. The shrine is called the Dome of the Rock, the structure with the golden dome seen in many photographs of Jerusalem. It is not a mosque. It is a religious museum that surrounds the holy rock itself. Several hundred feet to the south of the Dome of the Rock is the Al Aqsa Mosque, which literally means the "farthest mosque," because Islamic tradition believes that Muhammad led prayers toward Mecca during his night journey from that spot. He picked that spot because it is closer to Mecca than the Dome of the Rock. The Al Aqsa Mosque was completed in 705 by the Caliph Abd al-Malik; it was destroyed by an earthquake in 754 and rebuilt in 784.

The Temple Mount area where these two Islamic structures stand is called the Al Haram Al Sharif—the noble sanctuary. The Dome of the Rock and the Al Aqsa Mosque were built seventeen centuries after the first *Beit HaMikdash* and eleven centuries after the Second Temple were built, and five centuries after the Second *Beit HaMikdash* was destroyed by the Romans. The Dome of the Rock has no special religious standing in the Islamic world. There is no Islamic law or tradition that necessitates a visit to the Al Aqsa Mosque.

The Al Aqsa Mosque and the Dome of the Rock would be the equivalent of the third holiest city in *Eretz Israel* (Jerusalem first and Hebron second.) At no point during the 400 years of the Arab-Islamic Empire (632-1072) was Jerusalem/Al Quds ever designated as the capitol of the Islamic empire, unlike Mecca, Cairo, Damascus and Baghdad, which all took turns as being the capital of the Arab Islamic Empire.

THE DEATH OF MUHAMMAD

Muhammad died in 632. At the time of his death, he had founded Islam—a monotheistic faith that replaced the multiple pagan gods worshiped in the Arabian Peninsula—and united the hundreds of Arab and Bedouin tribes into one united nation known in Arabic as the *Umma*. That unity did not last.

Because Muhammad did not name a successor before his demise, there was a split in the Muslim world. The Shiites or Shi'a, believe that the true leader of Islam must be a direct descendant of Muhammad, and that was Ali Muhammad, Muhammad's son-in-law. The Sunnis believed the leader should be determined by consensus, and appointed three caliphs in a row who had been Muhammad's closest advisors. They were succeeded by Ali, who became the fourth caliph.

The Sunni branch continues to recognize the heirs of the four first caliphs of the *Umma* as legitimate religious leaders. They regard themselves as the orthodox and traditionalist branch of Islam. The word *Sunni* comes from *Ahl al-Sunna*, the people of the tradition. The tradition in this case refers to practices based on precedent or reports of the actions of the Prophet Muhammad and those close to him.

Sunnis venerate all the prophets mentioned in the Qur'an, but particularly Muhammad, as the final prophet. All subsequent Muslim leaders are seen as temporal figures. In contrast to Shi'a, Sunni religious teachers and leaders have historically come under state control. The Sunni tradition also emphasizes a codified system of Islamic law.

In early Islamic history, the Shiites were a political faction, literally "Shiat Ali" or the party of Ali, Muhammad's son-in-law and the fourth caliph of the *Umma*. Ali was killed as a result of intrigues, violence and civil wars that marred his caliphate. His sons, Hassan and Hussein, were denied what they believed was their legitimate right of succcession to the caliphate. Hassan was supposedly poisoned by Muawiyah, the first caliph of the Umayyad dynasty. Hussein was killed on the battlefield with members of his family, after being invited to Kufa (the seat of the caliphate of Ali) where supporters had promised to swear allegiance to him.

These events gave rise to the Shi'a concept of martyrdom and rituals of grieving—including self-flagellation with chains—as well as their deep distrust of Sunnis. They also have a distinctive messianic element in their faith and a hierarchy of clerics who practice independent and ongoing interpretation of Islamic texts.

The *Mahdi* is considered to be the Muslim Messiah, The Rightly Guided One (a messiah of sorts), who will lead a new global Islamic Empire (Caliphate). The Sunni believe he has yet to arrive; the Shi'a believe he has come once, and will return from hiding. This parallel between Christianity and Judaism is notable. Whereas the Christians believe the Messiah has been here already and are waiting for him to return, the Jews believe he has not yet come.

The schism between Sunni and Shi'a is enormous; each considers the other a corrupted version of Islam, or even as apostates. It is estimated that between 85-90 percent of the world's Muslims are Sunni. The remaining 10-15 percent are Shi'a. Shi'a Muslims are the majority in Iran, Iraq, Bahrain, Azerbaijan and, according to some estimates, Yemen. There are large Shi'a communities in Afghanistan, India, Kuwait, Lebanon, Pakistan, Qatar, Syria, Turkey, Saudi Arabia and the UAE.

In countries governed by Sunnis, Shi'a make up the poorest sections of society and are often victims of discrimination and oppression. Some extremist Sunni doctrines even preach hatred of Shi'a. The Iranian revolution of 1979 launched a radical Shi'a Islamist agenda perceived as a challenge to conservative Sunni regimes, particularly in the Persian Gulf. Tehran's policy of supporting Shi'a militias and parties beyond its borders is a main cause of instability and war in the Middle East—as part of a centuries'-old effort to diminish or even destroy the Sunni domination of Islam.

JIHAD

There are some non-Islamic historians who say it is possible that Muhammad's intention in creating Islam was to introduce a form of monotheism to fit the Arab and Bedouin culture of the Arabian Desert and did not mean to spread Islam throughout the world. We will never know his intention. We know the *Umma* spread Islam by the sword in a holy war, known in Arabic as *jihad*, across much of the globe. There is also the personal spiritual concept of *jihad* which refers to a Muslim's inner struggle against bad thoughts, traits and actions. *Jihad* became a concept that divided the world into two groups: the *dar al harab*, the territory of war, and the *dar al Islam*, the territory of Islam, the Muslim land where Islamic law reigns. *Jihad* is a normal state of being in the *dar al harab* which will only end with the conversion of the entire world to Islam.

In the early era that inspired classical Islam (Rashidun Caliphate—the first four caliphs after Muhammad) and lasted less than a century, *jihad* spread the realm of Islam to include millions of subjects and an area extending "from the borders of India and China to the Pyrenees and the Atlantic."[7]

Two empires impeded the advance of Islam, the Persian Sassanian Empire and the Byzantine Empire. But by 657 the Persian Empire was conquered and by 661 the Byzantine Empire was reduced to a fraction of its former size.

The role of religion in these early conquests is debated. Medieval Arabic scholars believed the conquests were commanded by God, and presented them as orderly and disciplined, under the command of the caliph.[8] Many modern historians question whether hunger and desertification, rather than *jihad*, were motivating forces in the conquests. Historians argued that,

> "Most of the participants in the [early Islamic] expeditions probably thought of nothing more than booty ... There was no thought of spreading the religion of Islam." Another argued that the motivations of the Arab conquests were certainly not "for the propagation of Islam...Military advantage, economic desires, [and] the attempt to strengthen the hand of the state and enhance its sovereignty...are some of the determining factors."[9]

Over the next 125 years Islamic armies conquered half of the known world. They captured all of the Middle East, including Palestine from the Persians in 636, Central Asia, North Africa and Spain. Millions of non-Arab and non-Islamic people were conquered and forced to convert. In the process, the entire Middle East was Arabized and the official sacred language of Islam gave them a sense of superiority that they exercised over others.

MUSLIMS AND JEWS IN THE MODERN WORLD

As has been mentioned, the *dhimmi* relationship between Muslims and Jews existed under varying degrees of comity for nigh a thousand years. This changed with the European Enlightenment which afforded Jews greater avenues of liberty and education. It also changed definitively with the importation of antisemitc Western themes into Muslim lands.

> With few exceptions, the present-day Islamic world exhibits a marked general hostility toward Israel and Jews. This hostility is found among most mainstream Muslims, both secular and religious, irrespective of whether they are the majoritarian Sunnis, who constitute approximately 90 percent of the world's billion Muslims, or the minority Shi'ites. It is found as well as among the militant Islamists, who hold both a political and religious vision of Islam. Although in discourse aimed at Western consumption, a distinction has often been made between Jews and Zionists, claiming that it is only the latter who are enemies, not Jews per se, this distinction is almost never maintained in speech or writing aimed at the Muslim public. What is even more disturbing is that contemporary Islamic anti-Israel and anti-Jewish animus is replete with the tropes and themes of both European medieval and modern post-Enlightenment anti-Semitism. These notions are found among the principal tenets of virtually every contemporary Islamist group, whether dubbed "militant" or "moderate" by Western governments and pundits. These include the various Sunni groups such as the Muslim Brotherhood, Dā'ish (also known as ISIS and ISIL), al-Qā'ida, al-Jamā'a al-Islāmiyya, and Hamas in the Middle East, or Jamī'at al-'Adl wa'l-Ihsān and al-Nahda in the Maghreb, or Hizb al-Tahrīr in Europe, or the Shi'ite ones such as the Khomeinists in Iran and Hizbollāh in Lebanon. These groups hold a wide variety of theological views and doctrines. However, they all share a rejection of Western secularism and the utopian goal of establishing a society that is completely Islamic in culture and governed by Islamic law, first in their own countries and eventually

throughout the entire world. They also tend to see the world as a Manichaean dichotomy between good and evil and maintain the traditional vision of the world as divided into the Dār al-Islām and the Dār al-'arb (the Domain of War), which is that part of the world that has yet to be subjugated to Islam and with which there is perpetual conflict under the obligation of jihād, or holy war. Although a temporary cease-fire (Ar. hudna) may be negotiated between the two domains, there can be no permanent peace between them. No less significant as far as Jews and Israel are concerned, virtually all contemporary Islamists share a number of anti-Semitic beliefs among their principal tenets.[10]

Footnotes

[1] Moshe Reiss, "Ishmael, Son of Abraham," *Jewish Bible Quarterly*, Vol. 30:4, 2002 (http://jbq.jewishbible.org/assets/Uploads/304/304_ishmael5.pdf)

[2] Robert G. Hoyland, *Arabia and the Arabs: From the Bronze Age to the Coming of Islam* (London: Routledge, 2001), 2-3.

[3] *Ibid.*, 5,8.

[4] "Preislamic Arabia" (https://www.saylor.org/site/wp-content/uploads/2011/08/HIST351-1.1-Pre-Islamic-Arabia.pdf)

[5] Gianluca P. Parolin, *Citizenship in the Arab World: Kin, Religion and Nation-State* (Amsterdam: Amsterdam Univeristy Press, 2009), 30.

[6] Norman A. Stillman, "Perceptions and Understandings of Israel within Islam," *Essential Israel: Essays for the 21st Century*, S. Ilan Troen; Rachel Fish, Eds., (Bloomington, IN: Indiana University Press, 2017), 317.

[7] Majid Khadduri, "Doctrine of Jihad," *War and Peace in the Law of Islam* (Baltimore: Johns Hopkins Press, 1955), 60.

[8] Michael Bonner, "Jihad" in *Islamic History: Doctrines and Practice* (Princeton: Princeton University Press, 2006), 60-61.

[9] Ahmed Al-Dawoody, *The Islamic Law of War: Justifications and Regulations* (London: Palgrave Macmillan, 2011), 87.

[10] Norman A. Stillman, 312-313.

Chapter 5

Mixing Politics and Religion:
Jews & Muslims

Middle East peoples take religion very seriously. The over-whelming majority of the Arabs are practicing Muslims, and every Arab state defines itself as an Islamic country. The same is true of non-Arab Islamic states in the Middle East like Turkey, Afghanistan, Pakistan and Bangladesh. When couched in religious and political terms, Islamic resistance to Israel/Zionism is deadly serious.

Modern Muslims are fond of saying that until Herzl's Zionism emerged, Arabs and Jews had no problems getting along. Arabs point out that Jews were treated far better in the Islamic world than they were in Christian Europe, and, there is truth to both statements.

It is true that the Arab and Muslim world got along with the Jews of the Middle East until the advent of the Modern Zionist movement. That's because Jews accepted their place as second-class citizens, with all the taxes and restrictions that came with that "tolerance." Zionism instilled in Jews a sense that they had the right to be first-class citizens in their sovereign homeland. The majority of the Arabs and Muslims in the Middle East reject the notion of Jews (and Christians) as a people who are their equals. They reject the notion of Jews being God's "chosen people" because the concept of Jews being "chosen" challenges a basic Islam premise: Islam is meant to supersede Judaism and Christianity, to rise above the two other Avrahamic faiths and replace them.

This was originally a premise of Christianity as it spread through the Middle East and Europe in the third century and is called replacement theology, or supersessionism. Churches were built on the highest point of of land to reflect their superior position to other faiths, and many were subsequently destroyed and replaced with mosques during the *jihads* that spread Islam into Europe and throughout the Middle East where there were ancient Christian communities. Synagogues, incidentally, were forbidden to be taller than either.

As Muslim conquest proceeded, those who were not Muslim were considered infidels, with Jews and Christians—as monotheists who predated Muhammad and were people of "The Book"— given limited dispensation. Still, Christians are particularly hated because of the Crusades. [More recently, the animosity toward them by Islamists was reiterated and strengthened by the religious political wars between Christians and Muslims in the Balkans at the turn of the 21st century.]

Theoretically, if the territory that constitutes Israel today would be a Christian, Hindu or any other religious nationalistic state, Islamic animosity would still exist, and there would be efforts to eliminate the "other" in the region. However, there is no religion and culture more offensive to many Muslim clerics and their followers than Judaism.

All people are motivated to some extent by honor and shame but...

> ...in some cultures the dominant voices openly promote honor/shame values in a way that militates against liberal society and progress. Arab political culture, to take one example—despite some liberal voices, despite noble dissidents—tends to favor ascendancy through aggression, the politics of the 'strong horse,' and the application of "Hama rules"...[1]

For almost 1,000 years, Muslim honor was vested in the humiliation of Jews and Christians, their *dhimmis*, their second-class citizens. Any enlightened Muslim leader who sought to equalize their legal status "struck a heavy blow to Muslim honor."

It gave them a sense of superiority that they exercised over others. They believed that Christians, and even more so Jews, were inferior to them. To "honor driven Arab and Muslim political players, an autonomous Jewish political entity was blasphemy against Islam and an insult to Arab virility."[2]

Humiliation of Muslims could not be felt more deeply than those who became the "subjects" of former *dhimmis* in the newly resurrected Jewish State rebuilt on land once controlled by the Caliphate.*

PAN-ARAB NATIONALISM

After the collapse of the Ottoman Empire in 1918 (after its defeat in World War I), the Arab world expected independence by the creation of one or more distinctly Arab states because, to the Arabs, the entire region between Morocco and Iraq is Arab territory conquered a millennium ago.

Thus, before the creation of the State of Israel, the Arab world viewed Palestine as an integral part of the larger Arab homeland. But arguing that a mere 8,000 square miles compared to 3-5 million square miles of pan-Arab territory would prevent Arabs from realizing their nationalist dreams did not seem valid. Yet in 1948, six Arabs states did exactly that. When their armies failed, twenty-one Arab nations claimed that Israel had stolen the land from the twent-second nation, the Palestinians, and until the Palestinians were given back their "national homeland" Arab nationalism would not have achieved its goals.

Understanding the above reasons for anti-Zionism and anti-semitism from Islamists is the key to understanding Arab and Islamist resolve to destroy the State of Israel.

The Balfour Declaration had made it clear that the intentions of Zionism were to establish a Jewish state in Israel. To make matters worse, the Zionist movement had the backing of a foreign European, Christian state, England, homeland to many of the

Crusaders who pillaged Arab lands in the past. Thus, the Zionist movement was supported by all the elements that the Arab/Islamic world detested. The alarm was sounded in 1917, and the Arabs heard it.

HAJ AMIN AL HUSSEINI

Haj Amin Al Husseini, an Islamist clergyman and Arab nationalist from a wealthy and powerful family in Palestine, ran the anti-Zionist movement in Israel for 31 years. Al-Husseini was largely responsible for riots that started on April 20, 1920 on Nebi Musa, a Muslim holiday honoring Moses. He was jailed, subsequently released and elected Grand Mufti of Jerusalem, a position created by the British. His election is widely believed to have been rigged by Sir Herbert Samuel, the British High Commissioner, who thought to co-opt Al Husseini's radicalism by placing him on the British payroll. But this became a disaster of epic proportions.

As Grand Mufti of Jerusalem, Al Husseini accrued a great deal of religious and political power. Because of his position and family connections, the Mufti had access to about £200,000 annually, much of which was used to finance terror campaigns and to advance his own position. In 1921 he organized Arab bands to attack isolated Jewish settlements around Palestine, the most famous being the Battle of Tel Hai where Yosef Trumpeldor*, the first Zionist modern military hero, was killed. The battle marked the beginning of violence and terror that continues to this day to plague the people of *Eretz Israel.*

---

* Joseph Trumpeldor (1980-1920) was an early Zionist activist and war hero. He was the most decorated Jewish soldier in the Russian army during the Russo-Japanese War (1904-1905), losing an arm in the process. During World War I he helped organize the Zion Mule Corps to fight the Turks and afterwards helped bring Jewish immigrants to Israel. He died defending the Tal Hai settlement and subsequently became a national hero. (Idith Zertal, *Israel's Holocaust And The Politics Of Nationhood,* (Cambridge, UK: Cambridge University Press, 2005), pp.13-15).

THE 1922 WHITE PAPER

After the terrorist attacks in 1920 and 1921, the British were forced to reevaluate their position on the Balfour Declaration, since they had miscalculated Arab opposition to the establishment of a Jewish State. The British thus decided to appease the Arabs, since their violence stemmed from a legitimate Arab grievance about being overwhelmed by Jewish immigrants, in particular when it came to job opportunities.* Perhaps the Balfour Declaration was a step too far for England to take.

To rectify the situation, the British government issued a White Paper modifying its position on the Mandate. In this reassessment of the Balfour Declaration and of the Mandate, the British ignored all the openly antisemitic speeches and articles written by Hajj Amin Al Husseini and others, and instead turned Arab and Islamic hostility into something connected to economics.

The White Paper of 1922 stipulated that Jews would no longer have unlimited immigration to *Eretz Yisrael*. Immigration would be tied to the ability to provide jobs for new immigrants in the *Yishuv*.

Palestine as designated in the League of Nations Mandate— namely present-day Israel, Judea and Samaria, Gaza and Jordan —was divided. Originally, the Balfour Declaration applied to the

---

* "Not until the Zionists had arrived in numbers did the Arab population begin to augment itself. The introduction of European standards of wage and life acted like a magnet on the entire Near East. Abruptly, Palestine became an Arab center of attraction. By 1922, after a quarter century of Jewish colonization, their numbers mushroomed to 488,000...If the English contention were accurate, we should expect to find an exodus of Arabs from areas where Jews are settled into purely Arab regions. But exactly the opposite is true: It is precisely in the vicinity of these Jewish villages that Arab development is most marked. Arab Haifa, profiting by the Zionist boom, grew from 1922 to 1936 by 130%, Jaffa by 80%, and Jerusalem by 55%. The Arab rural settlement in the Tel Aviv district increased by over 135%. The all-Arab city of Nablus, which held 33,000 before the war, has fallen to less than 12,000. Safed which had 20,000, dropped to less than 9,000." (William Ziff, *The Rape of Palestine*, 1st ed. (London: Longmans, Green and Co., 1938. Reprint. Mansfield Centre, (Conn.: Martino Fine Books, 2010), 385-6. (http://www.meforum.org/6275/were-the-arabs-indigenous-to-mandatory-palestine)

entire area; after 1922 it applied only to the area west of the Jordan River. The area to the east was designated as Transjordan, a new state to be given to the Arabs, to placate them and the Grand Mufti. Transjordan represented 77% of what was formerly called Mandate Palestine.

As a result, all Jewish settlement was forbidden in TransJordan; 30 Jewish settlements that were there were dismantled. And the British imported Abdullah, one of the sons of Hussein Ibn Ali, the Sharif of Mecca, to be its new king. Thus began the slow but sure appeasement of the Arab and Islamic world by the British at the expense of the Zionist movement. The Grand Mufti learned that violence pays when dealing with the Jews/Zionists of Mandate Palestine. Transjordan was to be the land of the Palestinians.

THE FOURTH ALIYAH (1924-1929)

From 1924-1929, 35,000 more Jews arrived in *Eretz Israel*, most of them middle-class Poles who were looking to expand their economic opportunities. They were carpenters, shoemakers, electricians, small business people. Some even arrived with capital to invest, and all of them worked to create a stable economy.

Members of the *Yishuv* made sure the economy was strong enough to absorb all the new immigrants who settled primarily in the new city of Tel Aviv on the shore of the Mediterranean and in Jerusalem in the Judean hills. By 1929, there were over 150,000 Jews living in the Mandate. Well over 100 new Jewish towns and cities had been built since 1882. Tens of thousands of acres of swamp land, purchased for exorbitant prices from Arab and Turkish land owners, were drained and turned into prime farm land by the hard-working and dedicated pioneers. Sand dunes near Yaffo were tranformed into the city of Tel Aviv. Hundreds of miles of roads were paved, electrical lines went up. Hospitals, schools, *yeshivot* and a university (Hebrew University in Jerusalem) were built.

And soon there was a thriving Jewish culture. Thousands of books were published in Hebrew. There was a Hebrew theater and cinema. The Jewish Agency, Histadrut and Haganah all grew in significance and size. The *Yishuv* began to resemble a Jewish state.

This *Aliyah* also saw the expansion of the Arab-Israeli conflict. By the late 1920s the Grand Mufti felt comfortable enough to use his pulpit to preach hatred against the Jews. He gave sermons about how the Jews were planning to steal all of Palestine from the Arabs, and kill them.

THE KOTEL

In the summer of 1929, the Grand Mufti focused on the large numbers of Jews praying at Judaism's holiest remnant, the *Kotel* (also known as the Wailing Wall and the Western Wall)—the outer retaining wall on the west side of the Second *Beit HaMikdash*, (Herod's Temple, destroyed by the Romans in 70 A.D.). Jews had been praying there since its destruction. The *Kotel* sits at the foot of The Temple Mount, where the *Beis HaMikdash* once stood and where today the Dome of the Rock and Al Aqsa are situated. Since the destruction of the *Beit HaMikdash* Jews found it difficult to gain access to the *Kotel**, and when they could it was not always possible to conduct proper prayer services because of interference by Christians and Muslims.

Though Muslims have said that *Har HaBayit* was holy to Islam—since the seventh century and Muhammad's conquest of Jerusalem—they used the site as a garbage dump and said it was where Muhammad stabled the famous magical steed that took him to heaven, hell and back. They named the area after the horse, Al Buraq.

In the 1920s, the Mufti gave his antisemitic and anti-Zionist sermons on the Temple Mount in the Al Asqa Mosque. He said that the Jews, who had been too timid to show up at the *Kotel* for centuries, were now so confident and so powerful they intended to destroy the mosque and build a third Holy Temple.

The reaction among Muslims was, and continues to be, horror and anger. After one of the Mufti's particularly vicious speeches on August 23, 1929, riots broke out in Jerusalem and soon spread across *Eretz Israel*. Jewish communities that had long existed peacefully side by side with Arab communities were attacked by Arabs. Typically, the British were slow to react.

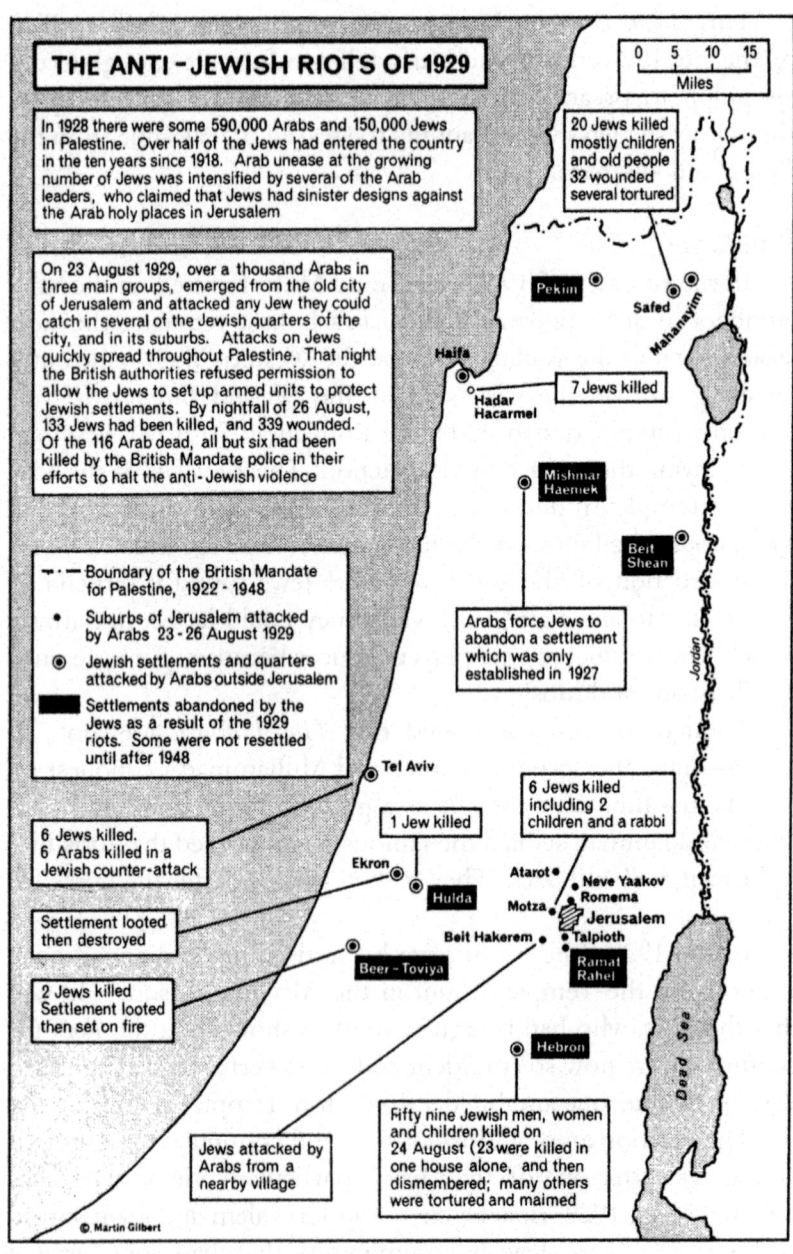

THE ANTI - JEWISH RIOTS OF 1929

0   5   10   15
Miles

In 1928 there were some 590,000 Arabs and 150,000 Jews in Palestine. Over half of the Jews had entered the country in the ten years since 1918. Arab unease at the growing number of Jews was intensified by several of the Arab leaders, who claimed that Jews had sinister designs against the Arab holy places in Jerusalem

20 Jews killed mostly children and old people 32 wounded several tortured

On 23 August 1929, over a thousand Arabs in three main groups, emerged from the old city of Jerusalem and attacked any Jew they could catch in several of the Jewish quarters of the city, and in its suburbs. Attacks on Jews quickly spread throughout Palestine. That night the British authorities refused permission to allow the Jews to set up armed units to protect Jewish settlements. By nightfall of 26 August, 133 Jews had been killed, and 339 wounded. Of the 116 Arab dead, all but six had been killed by the British Mandate police in their efforts to halt the anti - Jewish violence

Pekiin

Safed

Mahanayim

Haifa

Hadar Hacarmel

7 Jews killed

Mishmar Haemek

Beit Shean

▪ ▪— Boundary of the British Mandate for Palestine, 1922 - 1948

● Suburbs of Jerusalem attacked by Arabs 23 - 26 August 1929

◉ Jewish settlements and quarters attacked by Arabs outside Jerusalem

■ Settlements abandoned by the Jews as a result of the 1929 riots. Some were not resettled until after 1948

Arabs force Jews to abandon a settlement which was only established in 1927

Jordan

Tel Aviv

6 Jews killed including 2 children and a rabbi

1 Jew killed

6 Jews killed. 6 Arabs killed in a Jewish counter-attack

Ekron

Atarot ●

Neve Yaakov

Hulda

Motza ●

Romema

Jerusalem

Settlement looted then destroyed

Beit Hakerem ●

Talpioth

2 Jews killed Settlement looted then set on fire

Beer - Toviya

Ramat Rahel

Hebron

Dead Sea

Jews attacked by Arabs from a nearby village

Fifty nine Jewish men, women and children killed on 24 August (23 were killed in one house alone, and then dismembered; many others were tortured and maimed

© Martin Gilbert

Sir Martin Gilbert, © 2010. Reproduced by permission of Taylor & Francis Books UK. www.martingilbert.com

When the riots ended three days later, there were 133 Jewish dead and over 300 wounded. The worst riots occurred in two cities where the Jews did not have Haganah chapters: Tsfat (Safed) and Hebron, two of the original four Jewish holy cities where Jews had been living since biblical times, where the ultra-Orthodox communities there had inveighed against the idea of a Zionist military operating among them. As a consquence, 20 men, women and children were murdered in Tsfat, and in Hebron 67 were butchered and hundreds wounded. By the end of the three days of rioting the survivors of the massacre in Hebron fled to Jerusalem.

The following is a from the testimony of the British Police Commander of the 18-man police force in Hebron during the 1929 riots, Raymond Cafferata, who was not known to be friendly to Jews:

> On hearing screams in a room I went up a sort of tunnel passage and saw an Arab in the act of cutting off a child's head with a sword. He had already hit him and was having another cut, but on seeing me he tried to aim the stroke at me, but missed; he was practically on the muzzle of my rifle. I shot him low in the groin. Behind him was a Jewish woman smothered in blood with a man I recognized as a[n Arab] police constable named Issa Sherif from Jaffa in mufti. He was standing over the woman with a dagger in his hand. He saw me and bolted into a room close by and tried to shut me out shouting in Arabic, "Your Honor, I am a policeman." ...I got into the room and shot him."[3]

From 1929-1967 Hebron was empty of Jews for the first time in 3,000 years; it would take ther Six-Day War to bring them back.

While the Grand Mufti told the British that he was worried about the economy and didn't want too many Jews coming in, in 1929 he exhorted his followers with this: "Arise, O sons of Arabia. Fight for your sacred rights. Slaughter Jews wherever you find them. Their spilled blood pleases Allah, our history and religion. That will save our honor."[4] [It is precisely this hate speech, which has been magnified via social media, that is at the source of the violence that has since plagued Jews and Muslims.]

After the 1929 riots, the Jewish relationship with the Arabs soured. The riots showed Jews in the *Yishuv* that the British would only go so far in their efforts to protect Jewish lives and property. For the sake of their own survival, Jews of would have to handle their own security.

After the riots, the British once again reassessed their commitment to the Balfour Declaration and "blamed" the *Yishuv* for the events of 1929. The *Yishuv*, the British claimed, was growing too rapidly, causing great alarm in the Arab community. And so they issued another White Paper in 1930.

1930 WHITE PAPER

In October 1930, the British Colonial Secretary, Lord Passfield (Sidney Webb), issued a formal statement of policy on Palestine on behalf of his Majesty's Government ("HMG"), a document known as the Passfield White Paper.*

...The White Paper restates British policy in relation to

---

* "The Passfield White Paper, issued October 20, 1930, by colonial secretary Lord Passfield (Sidney Webb), was a formal statement of British policy in Palestine, which previously had been set by the Churchill White Paper of 1922. The new statement resulted from the Hope-Simpson Commission's investigation into the deeper causes of the 1929 Palestine riots, that initially started over access to the Wailing Wall. The white paper limited official Jewish immigration to a much greater degree.

"The paper's tone was decidedly anti-Zionist since several of its institutions were severely criticized, including the Histadrut (General Federation of Labor) and the Jewish Agency, which both promoted Jewish employment of only Jewish labor, thereby supporting the ejection of Arabs from purchased land, most who previously worked under a tenant farming system. Like the Hope-Simpson Report, the Passfield White Paper found this Zionist policy damaging to the economic development of the Arab population. It concluded that Jewish immigration to Palestine was taking land from the Arab fellahs; sales of land to Jewish settlers should in future be restricted, and Arab unemployment levels should be a factor in considering permitted levels of Jewish immigration (cont'd)

the governance of Palestine, emphasising in strong terms that, pursuant to Britain's obligations under the Balfour Declaration, Arabs and Jews were to be treated equally. The White Paper proposed the establishment of a Legislative Council that would include representation from all communities, giving them all a say in the governance of Palestine.

The White Paper was critical of Zionist organizations for their policy of only employing Jewish labour, to the detriment of the Arab population; and for meddling in the governance of Palestine. It recommended that Jewish immigration be greatly reduced because there was not sufficient arable land, and because of high unemployment among the Arab community.

The White Paper presumed that Jews would remain a minority in Palestine, enjoying some measure of autonomy, and that only another few tens of thousands of immigrants (some of them Arabs) would be allowed to enter the country.[5]

The 1930 White Paper was primarily based on the assumption that the continued level of Jewish immigration was causing "economic problems" for the Arabs of Palestine.

From the British point of view, linking immigration to the Arab as well as the Jewish economy and making a statement of equal support for Palestine's Arabs was a logical move. The events of the summer of 1929 had made clear the costs of supporting Zionism.[6]

---

to Palestine. Furthermore, a legislative council should be formed which would represent the (Arab) majority of its population....Zionists claimed it backtracked from what they felt were commitments in the Balfour Declaration and, if implemented, would limit Jewish immigration to Palestine. Contrary to these claims, the White Paper states that the development of a Jewish National Home in Palestine is a consideration, which would enjoy continued support, but it was not central to mandate governance. The paper states that the British intend to fulfill their mandate obligations to both Arabs and Jews, and they would resolve any conflicts that might surface as a result of their respective needs." (https://en.wikipedia.org/wiki/Passfi eld_white_paper)

The British completely ignored the blatant antisemitic nature of the bloody 1929 massacres in Hebron and Tsfat and the very clear antisemitic speeches by the Grand Mufti that inspired them.

Zionist leadership had remained silent in 1922 when 77 percent of Mandate Palestine was taken away to create Transjordan, but after the 1929 riots leaders of the *Yishuv* reacted with widespread demonstrations.

In London there were battles inside the government against the harsh measures against the Jews listed in the 1930 White Paper.* Chaim Weizmann, enraged by the British perfidy, sent his letter of resignation as Director of the Admiralty Laboratories to the British government.

Prime Minister Ramsay MacDonald sent Weizmann a response as a result of that resignation. In his letter, he assured Weizmann the 1930 White Paper was only a temporary measure to calm the Arab population, and that very soon all the restrictions against the *Yishuv* would be lifted.

February 13, 1931
Dear Dr. Weizmann:

In order to remove certain misconceptions and misunder-

---

* "Lloyd George called the White Paper antisemitic and said its authors wished to see the Balfour Declaration and the British Mandate overturned. He opposed restraints on Jewish immigration to Palestine, and turned the complaint of the Arabs concerning the exclusive use of Jewish labour by Jewish employers and organizations on its head, justifying the policy thus: 'They are extraordinarily anxious that the Jew with his capital behind him should not be tempted to become an effendi and exploit cheap Arab labour, of which there is plenty, in a way which is discreditable to the country—that the Jew should not come there with capital in his pocket, exploit cheap Arab labour and reap the profit. So they say you must not be allowed to do that.' Lloyd George said it was the Zionists' capital and if the government wanted them to invest in Palestine it could not dictate terms. ("Palestine 1930: The Passfield White Paper," Canadians for Justice and Peace in the Middle Eeast, Factsheet No. 135, August 2011 (https://d3n8a8pro7vhmx.cloudfront.net/cjpme/pages/1146/attachments/original/1433363533/135-En-Passfield-White-Paper-v3.pdf?1433363533))

standings which have arisen as to the policy of his Majesty's Government with regard to Palestine, as set forth in the White Paper of October, 1930, and which were the subject of a debate in the House of Commons on Nov. 17, and also to meet certain criticisms put forward by the Jewish Agency, I have pleasure in forwarding you the following statement of our position, which will fall to be read as the authoritative interpretation of the White Paper on the matters with which this letter deals.

It has been said that the policy of his Majesty's Government involves a serious departure from the obligations of the mandate as hitherto understood; that it misconceives the mandatory obligations, and that it foreshadows a policy which is inconsistent with the obligations of the mandatory to the Jewish people....

His Majesty's Government desires to say, finally, as they have repeatedly and unequivocally affirmed, that the obligations imposed upon the mandatory by its acceptance of the mandate are solemn international obligations from which there is not now, nor has there been at any time, an intention to depart. To the tasks imposed by the mandate, his Majesty's Government have set their hand, and they will not withdraw it. But if their efforts are to be successful, there is need for cooperation, confidence, readiness on all sides to appreciate the difficulties and complexities of the problem, and, above all, there must be a full and unqualified recognition that no solution can be satisfactory or permanent which is not based upon justice, both to the Jewish people and to the non-Jewish communities of Palestine.

Ramsay MacDonald[7]

As the former prime minister David Lloyd George stated in 1931:

The Jews surely have a special claim on [Palestine]. They are the only people who have made a success of it during the past 3,000 years. They are the only people who have made its name immortal, and as a race, they have no other home. This was their first; this has been their only home; they have no other home. They found no home in Egypt or in Babylon. Since their long exile they have found no home as a people in any other land, and this is the time and opportunity for enabling them once more to recreate their lives as a separate people in their old home and to make their contribution to humanity as a separate people, having a habitation in the land which inspired their forefathers. Later on it might be too late.[8]

By 1932 *Aliyah* was back to pre-1930 levels, but the situation in Mandate Palestine was tense and dangerous because Arabs and Jews could no longer trust each other and were suspicious of each other. Neither group trusted the British, who were seen as having reneged on commitments made to both sides: The Arabs felt the 1930 White Paper was violated and the Jews felt that the 1917 Balfour Declaration and the 1922 League of Nations Mandate for Palestine had been violated.

Footnotes

[1] Richard Landes, "Why The Arab World Is Lost In An Emotional Nakba, And How We Keep It There," *Tablet,* June 24, 2014 (http://www.tabletmag.com/jewish-news-and-politics/176673/emotional-nakba)

[2] *Ibid.*

[3] Benny Morris, *Righteous Victims: A History of the Zionist-Arab Conflict, 1881–1998* (NY: Knopf Doubleday, 2001), 114 as quoted in https://en.wikipedia.org/wiki/1929_Hebron_massacre

[4] https://en.wikiquote.org/wiki/Haj_Amin_al-Husseini

[5] "Palestine 1930: The Passfield White Paper," CJPME, Factsheet No. 135, August 2011 (https://d3n8a8pro7vhmx.cloudfront.net/cjpme/pages/1146/attachments/original/1433363533/135-En-Passfield-White-Paper-v3.pdf?1433363533)

[6] Tom Segev and Haim Watzman, *One Palestine, Complete: Jews and Arabs Under the British Mandate* (NY: Metropolitan Books, 2000), 334-335.

[7] "British White Papers: The MacDonald Letter (February 13, 1931)," Jewish Virtual Library (http://www.jewishvirtuallibrary.org/jsource/history/macdonaldtext.html)

[8] Richard Kemp, "Balfour Declaration, November 2016," Gatestone Institute, November 6, 2016 (https://www.gatestoneinstitute.org/9273/balfour-declaration)

Chapter 6

The Holocaust
1933-1945

The Fifth *Aliyah*, 1933-1939, changed the face of the *Yishuv* as no *Aliyah* had done since the Hovevei Tzion in the 1880s. In the seven years of this *Aliyah* close to 240,000 people arrived in *Eretz Yisrael*. That is more people than the previous four *Aliyot* combined. By 1939, the population of the *Yishuv* was well over 400,000. But more than that, this *Aliyah* was the first to attract people from Western Europe, in particular Germany and Austria. The reason for this sudden interest from the West came after 1933, when the Nazi Party won election in Germany and Adolf Hitler became Chancellor. Though most people at the time did not take him seriously enough, or did not believe he (and the Nazis) would last, some Jews knew it was time to leave their European homelands.

What motivated tens of thousands of German Jews, many of whom were very well integrated into German society and had lived in Germany for generations, to leave? Hitler's own words in his autobiography, *Mein Kampf*, are illuminating:

> The Jew's rule in the State now appears secured to such an extent that he may not only again call himself Jew, but ruthlessly admits his final thoughts as regards nationality .and politics. A part of his race even admits quite openly that it is a foreign people, however, not without again lying in this respect. For while Zionism tries to make the other part of the world believe that the national selfconsciousness of the

Jew finds satisfaction in the creation of a Palestinian State, the Jews again most slyly dupe the stupid goiim. [Jewish colloquial expression: Gentile men or women.] They have no thought of building up a Jewish State in Palestine, so that they might perhaps inhabit it, but they only want a central organization of their international world cheating, endowed with prerogatives, with drawn from the seizure of others: a refuge for convicted rascals and a high school for future rogues.[1]

To Hitler, the Jew was the embodiment of all evil. Hitler wrote *Mein Kampf* in 1925 and became Chancellor of Germany in 1933. He had every intention of dealing with the Jewish problem exactly as he had spelled it out now that he was the leader of Germany. Sadly, most Jews in Germany didn't realize how serious Hitler and his Nazi Party were about destroying the Jewish people until it was too late. Everyone laughed and thought he was a joke. No one believed the Nazi party would sweep the elections in parliament and then vote Hitler in as Chancellor, marking the end of democracy and the emancipation of Jews in Germany.

The Nazis began their program by stripping Jews of their legal and commercial rights, and separating them from the rest of the German population by enacting laws to make that happen—in other words, they made it legal to discriminate aginst Jews.

By initiating a campaign of lies about the Jewish people and spreading them on the radio, in newspapers, in newsreels and feature films, the Nazis convinced Germans to stand idly by as Jews were targeted for destruction or to become active participants in the solution to the Jewish problem.

In the face of such activity and with the goal of moving as many Jews as possible out of Germany, Hanotea, a citrus growing company in the *Yishuv*, made a deal with the German government in May 1933 to transfer people and goods from Germany. Because it was successful, it led to the Haavara Agreement, a transfer agreement led by Hanotea consultant Sam Cohen.[2]

On August 25, 1933, the Anglo-Palestine Bank, operating under instructions from the Jewish Agency and the Zionist Federation of

Germany signed an agreement to allow German Jews to leave for the *Yishuv*. Those who were able to emigrate had to leave behind their possessions in Germany, ostensibly on a temporary basis. They were to be returned by transferring them to the *Yishuv* as German exports.[3] [See note with footnote.]

The following is the transfer agreement used by PALTREU, an acronym for Palaestina Treuhandstelle, established specifically for Jews wishing to emigrate under the Haavara Agreement, advising how to deal with the bureaucracy.

> The Trust and Transfer Office "Haavara" Ltd. places at the disposal of the Banks in Palestine amounts in Reichmarks which have been put at its disposal by the Jewish immigrants from Germany. The Banks avail themselves of these amounts in Reichmarks in order to make payments on behalf of Palestinian merchants for goods imported by them from Germany. The merchants pay in the value of the goods to the Banks and the "Haavara" Ltd. pays the countervalue to the Jewish immigrants from Germany. To the same extent that local merchants will make use of this arrangement, the import of German goods will serve to withdraw Jewish capital from Germany.
> The Trust and Transfer Office,
> HAAVARA, LTD.[4]

Immigrants had to pay The Haavara Company with, at the very least, £1000 sterling to put into the bank. This money would then be used to buy German exports for import to Palestine—the goods that the German Jews left behind. In other words, they were paying for their own property.

Once Poland was invaded in September 1939, continuing the program became impossible. According to the United States Holocaust Memorial Museum, under the agreement 60,000 German Jews came to the *Yishuv* between 1933 and 1939, 25 percent of the total number (240,000) who arrived in the *Yishuv* during those years.[5]

The Nuremberg Laws

The first wave of Nazi legislation against the Jews, from 1933 to 1934, focused largely on limiting their participation in German public life. The first major law to curtail Jewish rights as German citizens was the "Law for the Restoration of the Professional Civil Service" of April 7, 1933, decreeing that Jewish and "politically unreliable" civil servants and employees were to be excluded from state service.

The law was the Nazi application of the "Aryan paragraph," the clause inserted in legislation and by-laws of organizations, corporations or real estate entities and other contractual agreements that reserves civilian rights solely for members of the "Aryan race" and excludes from such rights any non-Aryans. These regulations were in effect in varying degrees in Austria and Germany from as early as 1885 to 1945.

In April 1933 German law restricted the number of Jewish students at German schools and universities and sharply curtailed Jewish participation in the medical and legal professions. Subsequent laws and decrees restricted reimbursement of Jewish doctors from public (state) health insurance funds. Locally, the mayor of Munich disallowed Jewish doctors from treating non-Jewish patients, and the Bavarian Interior Ministry denied admission of Jewish students to medical school; the city of Berlin forbade Jewish lawyers and notaries to work on legal matters. Local governments also issued regulations that affected religious Jewish life: In Saxony, Jews could no longer slaughter animals according to ritual purity requirements, effectively preventing them from obtaining kosher meat.

At the national level, the Nazi government revoked the licenses of Jewish tax consultants; imposed a 1.5 percent quota on admission of "non-Aryans" to public schools and universities; fired Jewish civilian workers from the army, and, in early 1934, forbade Jewish actors from performing on stage or screen.

At an annual party rally held in Nuremberg in September 1935, Nazi leaders announced new laws to institutionalize the racial theories prevalent in Nazi ideology. The Nuremberg Laws excluded

German Jews from Reich citizenship and prohibited them from marrying or having sexual relations with persons of "German or German related blood." Ancillary ordinances to these laws deprived them of most political rights. Jews were disenfranchised (that is, they had no formal expectation to the right to vote) and could not hold public office.

The Nuremberg Laws did not identify a "Jew" as someone with particular religious beliefs. Instead, the first amendment to the Nuremberg Laws defined anyone who had three or four Jewish grandparents as a Jew, regardless of whether that individual recognized himself or herself as a Jew or belonged to the Jewish religious community. Many Germans who had not practiced Judaism or who had not done so for years found themselves caught in the grip of Nazi terror. Even people with Jewish grandparents who had converted to Christianity could be defined as Jews.

The Nuremberg Laws of 1935 heralded a new wave of antisemitic legislation that brought about immediate and concrete segregation: Jewish patients were no longer admitted to municipal hospitals in Düsseldorf; German court judges could not cite legal commentaries or opinions written by Jewish authors; Jewish officers were expelled from the army, and Jewish university students were not allowed to sit for doctoral exams.

Other regulations reinforced the message that Jews were outsiders in Germany; for example, in December 1935, the Reich Propaganda Ministry issued a decree forbidding Jewish soldiers to be named among the dead in World War I memorials.

Government agencies at all levels aimed to exclude Jews from the economic sphere of Germany by preventing them from earning a living. Jews were required to register their domestic and foreign property and assets, a prelude to the gradual expropriation of their material wealth by the state. Likewise, the German authorities intended to Aryanize all Jewish businesses—handing them over to pure Germans—a process involving the dismissal of Jewish workers and managers, as well as the transfer of companies and enterprises to non-Jewish Germans, who bought them at prices officially fixed well below market value. From April 1933 to April 1938, Aryanization effectively reduced the number of Jewish owned businesses in Germany by approximately two-thirds.

To avoid bad publicity, in the weeks before and during the 1936 Winter and Summer Olympic Games held in Garmisch Partenkirchen and Berlin, the Nazi regime toned down much of its public anti-Jewish rhetoric and activities. The regime even removed some signage saying "Jews Unwelcome" from public places. Hitler did not want international criticism of his government to result in the transfer of the Games to another country. Such a loss would have been a serious blow to German prestige. Nazi leaders also did not want to discourage international tourism and the revenue it would bring during the Olympics year.

After the Olympics, however, the Nazis reverted to their program of Jewish discrimination. By 1937 it became nearly impossible for Jews to leave Germany, and that is why the number of *olim* to the *Yishuv* dropped off greatly that year. In addition, German authorities stepped up legislative persecution of German Jews. By 1938 the Nazis forbade Jewish doctors to treat non-Jews and revoked the licenses of Jewish lawyers to practice law.

Following the Kristallnacht Pogrom (the Night of Broken Glass) of November 9-10, 1938, Nazi leaders stepped up Aryanization efforts and enforced measures that succeeded increasingly in physically isolating and segregating Jews from their fellow Germans. That night is often considered the first official night of the Holocaust because it was the first time government approved violence was permitted and encouraged. Thousands of synagogues and Jewish shops were destroyed, and when the damaged was assessed, the German Jewish communities were forced to pay for all the damages, plus additional taxes and fines. Moreover, Jews were now barred from all public schools and universities, as well as from cinemas, theaters, public parks and sports facilities. In many cities, Jews were forbidden to enter designated Aryan zones.

In addition, the government required Jews to identify themselves in ways that would permanently separate them from the rest of the population. In August 1938, German authorities decreed that by January 1, 1939, Jewish men and women bearing first names of "non-Jewish" origin had to add "Israel" and "Sara," respectively, to their given names. All Jews were ordered to carry identity cards indicating their Jewish heritage, and, in the autumn of 1938, all Jewish passports were stamped with an identifying letter "J" (for *Jude*).*

THE PEEL COMMISSION AND THE ARAB REVOLT

The arrival of the German Jews in the *Yishuv* led to the development of heavy industry and manufacturing. The *Aliyah* also brought many professionals—doctors, lawyers, engineers, professors—to the *Yishuv* as had the Fourth *Aliyah*. These individuals also gravitated to the cities; by 1939 the population of Tel Aviv was 150,000. During the Fifth *Aliyah* over 120 new settlements were established. By the end of the Fifth *Aliyah* there were more than 400,000 Jews living in the *Yishuv*.

But, as in Germany, Arab hostility became a major issue. The Grand Mufti, outraged at the influx of Jews to Mandate Palestine, became more outraged when some 60,000 German Jews arrived in 1935. This was considered the Zionist invasion the Mufti had feared, and so it was time for drastic action. The Grand Mufti called for a six-month general strike by all Arabs in Israel. They were not to work for Jews, hire Jews, nor were they to buy from or sell to Jews. The idea was to sever Arab-Jewish business relations and

---

* "Ironically, this came at the behest of the leaders of the Swiss Jewish community and the representative of the American Jewish Joint Distribution Committee in Switzerland, one Saly Mayer, who foresaw serious issues for the local Jewish community if it was flooded with German Jewish refugees." (David Kranzler, "Orthodox Ends, Unorthodox Means," *Goldberg Commission report on The Role of the American Jewish Community in the Rescue of European Jewry* (New York: City University, 1984.) See also Prof. Yehuda Bauer, *Jews for Sale* (New Haven: Yale University Press, 1996).

strangle the Jewish economy. The strike lasted six months, from April through September 1936. It was accompanied by a sharp rise in Arab violence against Jews and Jewish property.

On the surface, the Grand Mufti failed in his objective. The *Yishuv* did not collapse and, if anything, became more powerful economically, being forced to become totally self-reliant. But the Grand Mufti made life most unpleasant for Jews and the British, and intended to do so until his demands were met: 1) an immediate end to all Jewish immigration to Palestine; 2) an immediate end to all purchase of land by Jews in Palestine, and 3) the creation of an Arab state in all of Palestine.

When the Grand Mufti called for the strike, and when he called for revolt against the British and the *Yishuv*, there was no State of Israel, nor were there settlements in Judea and Samaria. His calls for violence were based on his total and complete rejection of any state for the Jews.

The Jews and the British reacted differently to Arab violence and had done so since the Third *Aliyah* and the riots of 1920-1921. This time was no different. The Jewish reaction had been to become even more determined to achieve a nation-state of Israel. Paradoxically, Arab pressure made the *Yishuv* stronger. The British, on the other hand, viewed all Arab violence as proof of a mistaken reality in 1917, when they issued the Balfour Declaration. In addition, the former allies, especially Britain, had a vested interested in cheap fossil fuels for expanding their post-war economy and industry.

In that spirit, the British sent Lord William Robert Wellesley Peel to head a commission to Palestine in November 1936. Their mission was to investigate the workings of the Mandate and recommend any helpful changes.

The Peel Commission arrived in Israel and began hearings almost immediately. Jews and Arabs were asked to testify about each other's grievances and aspirations. The British were trying to get a clear picture as to what it was the Jews wanted and what it was the Arabs wanted. At the same time, they wanted to know what were the political, social, economic and religious issues dividing these two communities.

Hundreds of people gave testimony, Arabs and Jews, leaders from all the different Jewish parties, and leaders from all the various Arab communities. The commission also visited dozens of Jewish and Arab cities and towns. In total, over 100,000 of pages of testimony were compiled.

Ze'ev Jabotinsky, leader of the Revisionist Zionists, was one of many who testified. What distinguishes his testimony is that he spoke of the religious, historical and political rights of the Jewish people to the land of Israel, and the impending doom that awaited them in Europe. He spoke of the horrors in Germany and was sure they would soon spread to the rest of Europe. His case was that the Jewish right for a state was steeped in biblical history and that acknowledged history and archaeology were all being ignored by those denying the desperate need Jews had in 1937 for a state of their own:

> Perhaps the greatest gap in all I am going to say and in all the Commission have heard up to now is the impossibility of really going to the root of the problem, really bringing before you a picture of what Jewish hell looks like, and I feel I cannot do it. I do hope the day may come when some Jewish representative may be allowed to appear at the Bar of one of these two Houses just to tell them what it really is, and to ask the English people: "What are you going to advise us? Where is the way out? Or, standing up and facing God, say that there is no way out and that we Jews have just to go under." But unfortunately I cannot do it, so I will simply assume that the Royal Commission are sufficiently informed of this situation, and then I want you to realize this: The phenomenon called Zionism may include all kinds of dreams—a "model community," Hebrew culture, perhaps even a second edition of the Bible—but all this longing for wonderful toys of velvet and silver is nothing in comparison with that tangible momentum of irresistible distress and need by which we are propelled and borne....

I am very much afraid that what I am going to say will not be popular with many among my co-religionists, and I regret that, but the truth is the truth. We are facing an elemental calamity ... We have got to save millions, many millions. I do not know whether it is a question of re-housing one-third of the Jewish race, half of the Jewish race, or a quarter of the Jewish race; I do not know; but it is a question of millions ...

It is quite understandable that the Arabs of Palestine would also prefer Palestine to be the Arab State No. 4, No. 5, or No. 6—that I quite understand. But when the Arab claim is confronted with our Jewish demand to be saved, it is like the claims of appetite versus the claims of starvation.[6]*

After hearing all the testimony, the Peel Commission issued the following in its report of July, 1937:

An irrepressible conflict has arisen between two national communities within the narrow bounds of one small country. About 1,000,000 Arabs are in strife, open or latent with some 400,000 Jews. There is no common ground between them. The Arab community is predominantly Asiatic in character, the Jewish community predominantly European. They differ in religion and in language. Their cultural and social life, their ways of thought and conduct are incompatible as their national aspirations. These last are the greatest bar to peace. Arabs and Jews might possibly learn to live and work together in Palestine if they would make a genuine effort to reconcile and combine their national ideals and so build up in time a joint or dual nationality. But this they cannot do. The War and its sequel [World War I] have inspired the Arabs with the hope of reviving a free and united Arab world the traditions of the Arab golden age. The Jews similarly are inspired by

---

* Jabotinsky was literally a prophet of doom as he went from town to town in Poland in 1938 with a copy of *Mein Kampf* in hand warning the Jews that the now-Chancellor of Germany meant to implement his virulent antisemitic ideas. He would tell his audiences, "Eliminate the Diaspora, or the Diaspora will surely eliminate you." Sadly, he was thrown out from almost every town he spoke at by the local Jewish leadership.

their historic past. They mean to show what the Jewish Nation can achieve when restored to the land of its birth. National assimilation between Arabs and Jews is thus ruled out. In the Arab picture the Jews could only occupy the place they occupied in Arab Egypt or Arab Spain. The Arabs would be as much outside the Jewish picture as the Canaanites in the old land of Israel. The National Home as we have said before cannot be half national. In these circumstances to maintain the Palestinian citizenship has any moral meaning is a mischievous pretense. Neither Arab nor Jew has any sense of service to a single State....[7]

As had happened since the issuance of the Balfour Declaration, the British once again recanted on their promise of a Jewish homeland. The Peel Commission called for another partition of Palestine. The first partition took place in 1922, when seventy-seven percent of Palestine was cut off to create Transjordan. According to this plan, of the remaining twenty-three percent, 70 percent would go to the Arabs, twenty-five percent to the Jews and five percent would remain in the hands of the British, a slice running from Yaffo to Jerusalem. The Zionist movement was offered twenty-five percent of the remaining twenty-three percent, in essence some eight percent of the original area called Mandate Palestine designated to be the national home of the Jewish Nation.

The plan was submitted to the Jewish Agency and to the Muslim Supreme Council. The Jewish Agency, after a bitter debate, accepted the plan because of the terrible news from Nazi Germany; the Muslim Supreme Council rejected it. For the Arabs there was to be no compromise on the issue of Palestine. The Grand Mufti called for an open revolt against the British while increasing terror attacks against the Jews.

For the next twenty-two months, terrorism raged on both sides, Lehi and the Irgun going against the Jewish Agency and the World Zionist Congress in their attempts to force the British out of Mandate Palesine and to avenge Arab acts of terror against Jews.

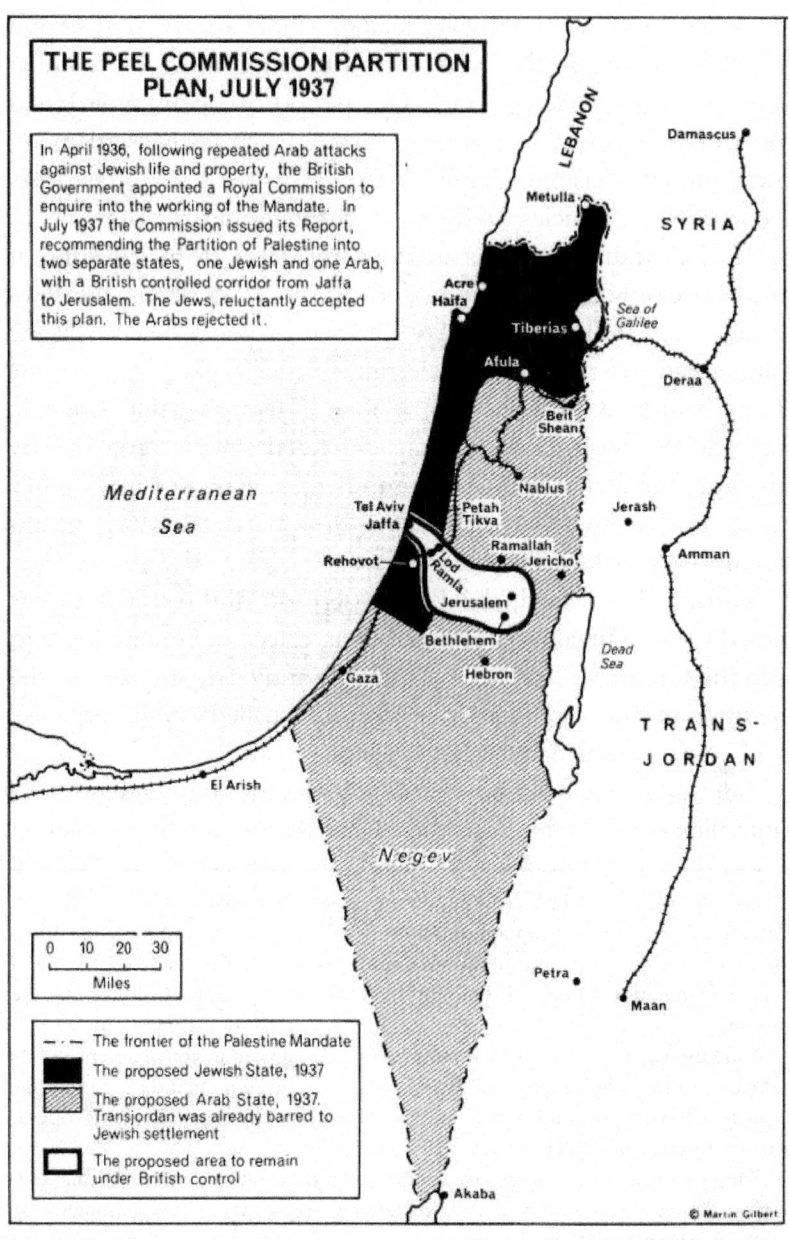

THE PEEL COMMISSION PARTITION PLAN, JULY 1937

In April 1936, following repeated Arab attacks against Jewish life and property, the British Government appointed a Royal Commission to enquire into the working of the Mandate. In July 1937 the Commission issued its Report, recommending the Partition of Palestine into two separate states, one Jewish and one Arab, with a British controlled corridor from Jaffa to Jerusalem. The Jews, reluctantly accepted this plan. The Arabs rejected it.

Damascus

LEBANON

Metulla

SYRIA

Acre
Haifa

Sea of
Galilee

Tiberias

Deraa

Afula

Beit
Shean

Mediterranean

Sea

Nablus

Jerash

Tel Aviv
Jaffa

Petah
Tikva

Amman

Ramallah

Rehovot

Lod
Ramla

Jericho

Jerusalem

Bethlehem

Dead
Sea

Gaza

Hebron

T R A N S -
J O R D A N

El Arish

Negev

0 10 20 30

Miles

Petra

Maan

— · — The frontier of the Palestine Mandate

The proposed Jewish State, 1937

The proposed Arab State, 1937. Transjordan was already barred to Jewish settlement

The proposed area to remain under British control

Akaba

© Martin Gilbert

Every day there were bombings, killings, sniper attacks, destruction of property. The British were forced to bring in 15,000 combat troops to begin policing Israel. This period of open revolt lasted until the spring of 1939. In the meantime, every Jewish settlement, town, and city became a target for Arab terrorists. Arab terrorists also ambushed vehicles on the roads throughout the country.

If the Arab revolt was to drive the Jews from Palestine, it failed miserably. During the period of the Arab revolt, the Jews of the *Yishuv* took responsibility for their own self-defense. Many volunteered to serve in the Palestine Border Police, special units of the British. With thousands of men in its ranks, the Haganah, the official Jewish army, actively defended Jewish property. By this time, the Haganah had thousands of men active in its ranks and moved from strict defense to "hot pursuit," which meant preemptive attacks on terrorist bases.

During this period, the British sent an anti-terrorist expert named Orde Wingate to put together an effective fighting force to keep the Grand Mufti's men off balance and bring the fight to the enemy. Wingate put together special units called "Night Squads" that proved effective in the battle against Arab terror.*

During the Arab Revolt of 1936-39, the Irgun, an underground paramilitary unit, split from the Haganah for not being militant

---

* "In 1936, at the height of the Arab terror campaign known as the Arab Revolt, Wingate was serving as a captain in British intelligence. Assigned to British units posted in Mandatory Haifa, he quickly came to admire the Jewish people and their determination to reclaim the land that had been promised to them by the Creator.

Wingate began training Jewish volunteers, who served in active defense units that came to be called the Special Night Squads. They launched daring missions to protect Jewish communities from Arab terrorists, often undertaking operations that penetrated deep into Arab villages.

Wingate drew on his deep love and profound knowledge of the Bible, employing strategy and tactics he had distilled from studying the campaigns of Joshua, Gideon and King David. As an officer, he emphasized the need for preemptive strikes, and insisted upon taking the fight to the enemy's territory. Both of these principles later came to serve as central tenets of Israel's defensive posture and military doctrine. (cont'd)

enough, and went out to extract an eye for an eye from even innocent Arabs. The Irgun was politically linked to the Herut Party (Revisionist Zionism) while the Haganah was linked to the Mapam Party (Labor Zionism). All remained rivals until the declaration and establishment of the modern State of Israel.

The Irgun was condemned for its terrorism by the Jewish Agency leadership and by many leading figures in the *Yishuv*. The same cannot be said of Arab terrorism led and inspired by the Grand Mufti. Arab leaders in and out of Mandate Palestine lauded the actions of the Mufti and his men. The one clan daring to question the actions of the Grand Mufti, the Nashishibi clan, had many of its leaders murdered by the Grand Mufti's men, often in front of their horrified families.

Still, the Jews of the *Yishuv* did not back down and added 50 more settlements during this period. Erected literally overnight because of new British restrictions, these settlements were purposely erected very close to Arab areas. Called "Stockade and Tower" settlements, they were built as small fortresses.

Wingate organized special training courses at Ein Harod, where some of the future leaders of Israel's military were schooled. He dreamt of one day leading a Jewish army, and befriended various Zionist leaders such as Chaim Weizmann and Moshe Sharett.

To Jews living in pre-state Israel, Wingate came to be known as "Hayedid," or "the friend," but many of his British colleagues looked askance at his fondness for the Jewish cause. Fellow officers criticized him, forcing Wingate in 1939 to submit a formal appeal in which he wrote, "I am not ashamed to say that I am a real and devoted admirer of the Jews.... Had more officers shared my views, the [Arab] rebellion would have come to a speedy conclusion some years ago."

As a result of his stance, Wingate was unceremoniously recalled to England, where the authorities went so far as to bar him from ever returning to the land of Israel." (Michael Freund, "Remembering a Christian Warrior for Zion," *The Jerusalem Post*, March 24, 2012 (22:43) (http://www.jpost.com/Opinion/Columnists/Remembering-a-Christian-warrior-for-Zion).

Wingate was transferred out of the Middle East in May 1939 and sent to East Africa to fight the Italians at the outbreak of World War II. When those units were dissolved, he was sent to the Far East to fight in Burma, where, in 1944, he was killed in a plane crash with nine others.

The 1939 White Paper

By 1939 the British had stationed some fifteen thousand combat troops in Israel, and built many forts and prisons. The Grand Mufti became an outlaw (becuase of his anti-British actions from 1936-1939) who had to operate mostly from outside the Mandate; on the surface it appeared the Zionist movement and England were on the same wavelength. However, a great deal was happening beneath the surface which was to change the entire nature of England's relationship to Zionism and the nature of Zionism itself.

By May of 1939 it was becoming clear to the leaders of England that all the efforts to appease Hitler by British Prime Minister Neville Chamberlin were a disastrous failure and had, in fact, emboldened *Der Führer* since it was clear to him that Western European leaders had no stomach for war.

On September 30, 1938, in an act of appeasement to German territorial claims, Adolf Hitler, Benito Mussolini, French Premier Edouard Daladier and British Prime Minister Neville Chamberlain signed the Munich Pact. Upon return to Britain, Chamberlain declared that they had achieved "peace in our time"—a slogan that rang hollow and helped usher in World War II and the Holocaust.

The pact sealed the fate of Czechoslovakia by handing the resource-rich Sudetenland, populated with more than three million ethnic Germans, over to Germany. Czechoslovakia had to turn over sixty-six percent of its coal, seventy percent of its steel and iron and seventy percent of its electrical generating power to the German war machine. Once the Sudetenland was handed over it wasn't long before Bohemia, Moravia, Slovakia and Ukraine were all absorbed into the Third Reich. In each region, Germany set up pro-Nazi regimes that served Hitler's military and political ends. By the time of the invasion of Poland in September 1939, the nation called "Czechoslovakia" no longer existed.

By May of 1939 it was clear that Hitler's intent was to continue grabbing more territory in Europe thereby forcing England to realize she would shortly be at war with Nazi Germany. The British had no way to know how long and deadly a struggle it would turn out to be, but they knew it would be great and bitter. In addition, in the late 1930s, British colonies in Asia were under attack by the Japanese Empire which had already invaded Chinese Manchuria in 1937. Thus, they were justifiably worried about a world war. As such, the question of Palestine and the Balfour Declaration were not even considered at the time; everything was subordinated to the forthcoming war effort. In fact, the issue of the Jewish Homeland and the entire Middle East, for that matter, could only be dealt with in the context of the world war England was about to fight. From England's perspective, these were the new realities as of May 1939.

Vast reserves of oil had been discovered in the Persian Gulf in the 1930s that changed the entire calculus of the Arab-Zionist conflict going forward. This oil was essential in war and had to be protected at all costs. The Suez Canal, which linked the Middle East and its oil to Britain and its Asian empire, had to be kept open at all costs. Since there were forty million Arabs in the Middle East who could easily side with Nazi Germany and sabotage the oil fields and the Suez Canal, Britain issued a White Paper on May 17, 1939 that caved into most of the Mufti's demands, including one limiting *Aliyah*.

> Jewish immigration during the next five years will be at a rate which, if economic absorptive capacity permits, will bring the Jewish population up to approximately one-third of the total population of the country. Taking into account the expected natural increase of the Arab and Jewish populations, and the number of illegal Jewish immigrants now in the country, this would allow of the admission, as from the beginning of April this year, of some 75,000 immigrants over the next five years.
>
> After the period of five years, no further Jewish immigration will be permitted unless the Arabs of Palestine are prepared to acquiesce in it.[8]

In addition, the sale of land to Jews was severely restricted; there would be very few areas that Jews would be able to still buy land. Basically, this would freeze the size of the *Yishuv*.

> The Administration of Palestine is required, under Article 6 of the Mandate, "while ensuring that the rights and position of other sections of the population are not prejudiced," to encourage "close settlement by Jews on the land," and no restriction has been imposed hitherto on the transfer of land from Arabs to Jews. The Reports of several expert Commissions have indicated that, owing to the natural growth of the Arab population and the steady sale in recent years of Arab land to Jews, there is now in certain areas no room for further transfers of Arab land, whilst in some other areas such transfers of land must be restricted if Arab cultivators are to maintain their existing standard of life and a considerable landless Arab population is not soon to be created. In these circumstances, the High Commissioner will be given general powers to prohibit and regulate transfers of land. These powers will date from the publication of this statement of policy and the High Commissioner will retain them throughout the transitional period.[9]

An additional decree of the White Paper indicated that after a five-year period the British would establish a government in Palestine based on majority rule. Since immigration would be capped at 75,000 Jews, this meant that the British intended on creating an Arab government in Israel.

> The independent State should be one in which Arabs and Jews share government in such a way as to ensure that the essential interests of each community are safeguarded.
>
> The establishment of the independent State will be preceded by a transitional period throughout which His Majesty's Government will retain responsibility for the country. During the transitional period the people of Palestine will be given an increasing part in the government of their country. Both sections of the population will have an opportunity to

participate in the machinery of government, and the process will be carried on whether or not they both avail themselves of it.

As soon as peace and order have been sufficiently restored in Palestine steps will be taken to carry out this policy of giving the people of Palestine an increasing part in the government of their country, the objective being to place Palestinians in charge of all the Departments of Government, with the assistance of British advisers and subject to the control of the High Commissioner. Arab and Jewish representatives will be invited to serve as heads of Departments approximately in proportion to their respective populations. The number of Palestinians in charge of Departments will be increased as circumstances permit until all heads of Departments are Palestinians, exercising the administrative and advisory functions which are presently performed by British officials. When that stage is reached consideration will be given to the question of converting the Executive Council into a Council of Ministers with a consequential change in the status and functions of the Palestinian heads of Departments. His Majesty's Government make no proposals at this stage regarding the establishment of an elective legislature.[10]

In essence, there would be only one state in Mandate Palestine in 1944 (after the five-year period of Jewish immigration was over) and it would be based on majority rule. This edict ignored the 1937 Peel Commission report that concluded there could be no one Palestinian State where Jews and Arabs could live together. The 1939 White Paper was an abrogation of everything the British promised in the 1917 Balfour Declaration and a violation of the Mandate received from the League of Nations.

The 1939 White Paper, for all intents and purposes, buried the Balfour Declaration and ended England's commitment to the establishment of a Jewish Homeland. Coming as it did directly on the eve of World War II and the Holocaust, made it doubly horrible.

From 1939-1945, millions of Jews were trapped in Europe. No free countries, including the United States, would take them in. European, Asian and North African Jews would be hunted by the Nazis and murdered, while, after the Bermuda Conference* the gates were locked around the world to keep Jewish refugees out.

The story of the *SS St. Louis*, loaded with Jewish refugees headed for Cuba, typified worldwide repsonse to Jewish attempts to escape certain death at Nazi hands. When refused permission to land her passengers despite their having paid for legitimate visas, even the United States refused to allow them in as the ship sat

---

* "The Bermuda Conference was an Anglo-American Conference on Refugees in 1943.

During World War II, Jewish and general public opinion in the U.S. and the British Commonwealth urgently demanded that the Allied governments rescue the victims of the Nazi regime. Under pressure from parliament, churches, and humanitarian organizations, the British Foreign Office, on Jan. 20, 1943, proposed joint consultation between Britain and the U.S.A. to examine the problem and possible solutions. After an exchange of diplomatic notes, the Anglo-American Conference on Refugees was held in Bermuda from April 19 to 30, 1943.

"The American delegation was headed by Harold Willis Dodds, president of Princeton University; the British delegation, by Richard Law, parliamentary undersecretary of state for foreign affairs. No private organizations or observers were admitted but interested Jewish organizations in America and England prepared memoranda proposing rescue measures. Chaim Weizmann submitted a document on behalf of the Jewish Agency for Palestine, underlining the importance of Palestine in the solution of the problem of Jewish refugees, and demanding abandonment of the policy based on the British White Paper policy of May 1939. The delegates, however, anxiously avoided referring to the Jews as the Nazis' major victims. Disagreement between the two governments about continuing the Intergovernmental Committee of Refugees, founded at the Evian Conference in July 1938, took up most of the time but it was decided eventually to extend its mandate to deal with postwar problems. British plans for opening up camps in North Africa as a haven for refugees during the war proved impracticable.

"After seven months—on Dec. 10, 1943—the report of the conference was published. Its only positive decision—to revive the Evian Committee—came too late to save a single Jew from the Nazi Holocaust." ("U.S. Policy During WWII: The Bermuda Conference (April 1943), Jewish Virtual Library (https://www.jewishvirtuallibrary.org/jsource/Holocaust/bermuda.html)

off the coast of Florida after being forced from Cuban waters. Eventually the ship sailed back to Europe where many were murdered by the Nazis.[11]

The Jews of the *Yishuv* were crushed by the 1939 White Paper. The dream of a sovereign Jewish State which was so close to being realized had been snatched away at the darkest hour in the Jewish nation's history since the destruction of the Second *Bet HaMikdash*.

David Ben-Gurion – Israel's Founding Father

In 1935 it was becoming apparent to the Jewish leadership in Palestine, to leaders of the Jewish Agency, that the main obstacle to statehood was not the lack of a charter, but Arab opposition to Zionism. The man who led the Jewish Agency since its founding in 1920 was Chaim Weizmann. His major strengths were his contacts with high ranking British officials and his diplomatic style.

By 1935, he was no longer familiar with British leadership and two White Papers had been issued. Diplomacy was pointless. The leaders of the Jewish Agency were looking for a new Executive Director, one who would be tougher and perhaps less diplomatic. They chose David Ben-Gurion.

Born in Russia in the 1886, David Grün came to Israel during the Second *Aliyah*. While studying law in Turkey* in 1912, he changed his name to David Ben-Gurion. Ben-Gurion was part of the Labor Zionist movement, had a Turkish law degree, and spent some time in the British Army/Jewish Legion, during World War I. He had worked his way up in the Labor Zionist movement the hard way, by earning a reputation as a tough and tenacious individual. Though he was small physically, he was very much like his name, Ben-Gurion, "Son of a Lion."

Ben-Gurion led the Jewish Agency, the quasi-governmental organization that ran the *Yishuv*, through the Arab Riots of 1936, the Peel Commission investigations, the Arab Revolt, the 1939

---

* The Ottoman Empire, i.e., the Turks, was still the ruling government and, hence, its legal system prevailed in Palestine.

White Paper, World War II, the Jewish Revolt against Britain, the UN Partition, the 1948 War of Independence and the declaration of the State of Israel. He went on to become Israel's first Prime Minister (1948-1963) (with an exception of a two-year period). He is considered the founding father of modern Israel.

In 1939, Ben-Gurion rose to the challenge of the White Paper. The choices before the Jews were between bad and worse. He responded by proclaiming: "We will fight the war as if there is no White Paper and we will fight the White Paper as if there is no War!"[12] By this Ben-Gurion meant that the Jews of the *Yishuv* would have no choice but to fight both. When it came to fighting against the Nazis, the Jews of the *Yishuv* would do everything in their power to help the British win. Jews volunteered for the British Army and many volunteered for commando units to fight behind enemy lines. The Jewish *Yishuv* would produce anything they could to help the British war effort. (Moshe Dayan, the famous general, archeologist and defense minister lost his eye fighting the Germans in Syria.)

At the same time, however, they did everything possible to subvert the White Paper, including sneaking as many Jews from Europe into *Eretz Yisrael* and purchasing land anywhere in Palestine they could. This kept the Zionist movement alive and full of hope during the war years.

JEWISH AND ARAB REACTION TO THE 1939 WHITE PAPER

There was an implicit cynicism in the White Paper because the British were dismissing the Zionist dream and implementing harsh policies knowing full well that the Jews had no choice but to remain loyal to their protectors—the alternative was to support the Axis nations, to support the Nazis. Indeed, Lehi, splitting with everyone, did try to do precisely that because they believed the British were more dangerous to the Jews than the Germans.

Almost 30,000 Jews from Mandate Palestine volunteered in the British Army during the course of World War II, with the overwhelming majority serving in combat units. In addition to the

Jewish people in the *Yishuv*, 4,000 Arabs from Mandate Palestine also fought on the side of the British.

A special commando unit, known as the Palmach, was created to fight the Germans on the local front. Rommel, the Nazi general known as the Desert Fox, was at Egypt's door by 1942. The Palmach also trained troops in guerilla warfare against the Germans, and a group with blue eyes and blond hair was sent as an undercover sabotage unit to infiltrate Tobruk, Libya, to create havoc behind German lines.

Thirty-two Jews from the *Yishuv* who spoke Eastern European languages or who came from those countries volunteered to be guerillas deep behind German lines. Their mission was to organize Jewish resistance to the Nazis and do as much damage as possible.

The *Yishuv* itself was mobilized to support the British in any way possible, including manufacturing whatever they could for the war effort against the Axis powers. Despite the 1939 White Paper and the attempts to destroy all vestiges of the Balfour Declaration, there were Jews who wanted to serve. At the urging of Winston Churchill, the British Prime Minister, qualified members of the *Yishuv* could join the Jewish Brigade.*

And while the British had been concerned enough to capitulate to Arab demands lest leaders turn to Germany, in the end there were only two Muslim leaders in the Middle East who did that: Rashid Ali, the self-proclaimed Iraqi Prime Minister (1941–1942), and the Grand Mufti of Jerusalem.

---

* "In 1940, the Jews of Palestine were permitted to enlist in Jewish companies attached to the East Kent Regiment (the 'Buffs'). These companies were formed into three infantry battalions of a newly-established "Palestine Regiment." The battalions were moved to Cyrenaica and Egypt, but there, too, as in Palestine, they continued to be engaged primarily in guard duties. The Jewish soldiers demanded to participate in the fighting and the right to display the Jewish flag.

"In a letter to Chaim Weizmann in 1944, British Prime Minister Winston Churchill stated that his government was prepared 'to discuss concrete proposals' in the matter of the formation of a Jewish Fighting Force. While Jews were dispersed throughout the British army, the Jewish Agency wished to concentrate them into one unit, flying the Jewish national flag. (cont'd)

In April 1941, the pro-British Iraqi government of General Nuri as-Said was overthrown by Rashid Ali, an anti-British general who proceeded to cut off British oil supplies. Britain countered with a military response that defeated a 9,000-man Iraqi division. Ali retaliated by sealing off the British airbase at Habbaniya. Hitler, "elated" at the effect Ali was having on Britain's war capabilities, began sending arms (via Syria) and military experts to aid Ali.

On the run from Palestine since the Arab Revolt of 1936-1939...

Al-Husseini used his influence and ties with the Germans to promote Arab nationalism in Iraq. He was among the key promoters of the pan-Arab Al-Muthanna Club, and

---

"Churchill was much more receptive to the idea than his predecessor, Neville Chamberlain. Chamberlain disapproved of an all-Jewish Brigade, fearing that it would give more legitimacy to the Jewish yearning for national independence. British policy since the White Paper of 1939 no longer favored partition, and therefore symbols of Jewish independence were not encouraged. As more and more information came to light over the tragedy in Europe, however, the British bowed to Zionist demands for a Jewish military unit.

"It was not until September 1944, after six years of prolonged negotiations, that the British government agreed to the establishment of a Jewish Brigade. It consisted of Jewish infantry, artillery, and service units. After a period of training in Egypt, the Jewish Brigade Group—approximately 5,000 soldiers—took part in the final battles of the war on the Italian front under the command of the Canadian-born Jew, Brigadier Ernest Benjamin. In May 1945, the Brigade was moved to North East Italy where, for the first time, it encountered survivors of the Holocaust. In the summer of 1946, the British authorities decided to disband the Brigade.

"Skills gained in the Jewish Brigade and in the British army in general was experience that would be put to use again during Israel's War of Independence. More than its military value, however, the Jewish Brigade served as a symbol of hope for renewed Jewish life in Eretz Israel. The soldiers of the Jewish Brigade met with survivors of the Holocaust in Displaced Persons camps, bringing them Jewish and Zionist culture. The Jewish Brigade was also instrumental in bringing many of the survivors to Palestine, by Bericha [sic] and 'illegal immigration.'" ("Jewish Defense Organizations: The Jewish Brigade Group," (1944 - 1946)) (http://www.jewishvirtuallibrary.org/jsource/History/brigade.html)

supported the coup d'état by Rashid Ali in April 1941. The situation of Iraq's Jews rapidly deteriorated, with extortions and sometimes murders taking place. When the Anglo-Iraqi War broke out, al-Husseini used his influence to issue a fatwa for a holy war against Britain. As the British advanced on the capital, the Farhud pogrom in Baghdad, led by members of the Al-Muthanna Club, which had served as a conduit for German propaganda funding, erupted in June 1941, following the Iraqi defeat and the collapse of Rashid Ali's government. The pogrom was rooted in antisemitic incitement during the preceding decade against the backdrop of the conflict between Arabs and Jews in Palestine.

When the war failed for the Iraqis...al-Husseini escaped to Persia (together with Rashid Ali), where he was granted legation asylum first by Japan, and then by Italy. On 8 October, after the occupation of Persia by the Allies and after the new Persian government of Shah Mohammad Reza Pahlavi severed diplomatic relations with the Axis powers, al-Husseini was taken under Italian protection and conveyed through Turkey to Axis Europe in an operation organized by Italian Military Intelligence (Servizio Informazioni Militari, or SIM).[13]

Once in Germany, he met with Hitler to gain approval for his plan for the future of Palestine. In addition, he broadcast propaganda speeches to Muslims in Germany and German-occupied territories and was useful in the creation of the Serbian Handschar units.

Among the Nazi leadership, the greatest interest in the idea of creating Muslim units under German command was shown by Heinrich Himmler, who viewed the Islamic world as a potential ally against the British Empire...Himmler had a romantic vision of Islam as a faith 'fostering fearless soldiers', and this probably played a significant role in his decision to raise three Muslim divisions under German leadership in the Balkans from Bosnian Muslims and Albanians: the 13th Handschar, the 21st Skanderbeg, and the 23rd Kama

(Shepherd's dagger). Riven by interethnic conflict, the region's Jewish, Croat, Roma, Serb and Muslim communities suffered huge losses of life, Bosnian Muslims losing around 85,000 from a genocidal Chetnik ethnic cleansing operations alone. The Muslims had three options: to join the Croatian Ustaše, or the Yugoslav partisans, or to create local defense units. Following a tradition of service in the old Bosnian regiments of the former Austro-Hungarian army, they chose an alliance with Germany, which promised them autonomy. Husseini, having been petitioned by the Bosnian Muslim leaders, was well informed of their plight. Dissatisfied with low enlistment, Himmler asked the mufti to intervene. Husseini negotiated, made several requests, mostly ignored by the SS, and conducted several visits to the area. His speeches and charismatic authority proved instrumental in improving enlistment notably.[14]

WORLD WAR II AND THE HOLOCAUST: SEPTEMBER 1939-MAY 1945

World War II officially began when Germany invaded Poland on September 1, 1939 and lasted until April of 1945. More than 60 million people died around the world and most of the European continent was devastated. Historians generally divide it into two phases: Phase I: September 1939-December 1942 and Phase II: January 1943-May 1945.

During Phase I the Nazi war machine was unstoppable, as it crushed every army in its path. With Russia as its ally, based on the Ribbentrop-Molotov Non-Aggression Pact signed on August 23, 1939, the Nazis were able to capture most of Western and all of Eastern Europe, and once they captured all of North Africa, they ruled over 10 million square miles. Germany broke the pact in June 1941 by invading Russia, quickly capturing about one-third of the country.

The second phase began after the Nazi's Axis allies, in this case the Japanese, attacked Pearl Harbor in December 1941, and the Americans entered the war as allies of France, Britain and Russia. During Phase II, the Allies began to drive the Nazi armies back on all fronts. In June 1944 the American and British forces launched an invasion on the beaches of Normandy, France (D-Day) with more than one million men. This was the beginning of the end for Germany. Eleven months later the Russian, American and British armies finally stopped the Third Reich.

THE HOLOCAUST AND THE FINAL SOLUTION

During the years 1939-1945, the Nazis fought two separate wars: one, an armed conflict against other sovereign states and another against the Jewish people, who at that time possessed no country and no army. Hidden among the mass movement of refugees across Europe, millions of Jews were gathered, deported to labor and death camps and murdered. More than 3 million Jews had lived in Poland for more than 1,000 years, and the Germans and their collaborators killed more than ninety percent of them, as well as sixty percent of the rest of European Jewry. They deported the Jews of Rhodes and were getting ready to deport the Jews from North Africa and the Middle East when their troops ran out of gas in the North African desert. Though he wanted to annihilate every Jew in the world, Hitler managed to destroy thirty-three percent of the Jewish people, and many of those who survived did so because they had hope—hope to be taken on the wings of eagles to the Promised Land. In the camps, ghettos and in hiding, Zionists encouraged people to hope for a future in the Holy Land.

POLAND AS A MILITARY TARGET OF THE NAZIS

On September 1, 1939, the Nazis invaded Poland with bombers, heavy artillery and tanks against an unprepared Polish cavalry. The Nazi attack relied heavily on nonstop bombing that pounded away at Poland's major cities without distinguishing between civilian and military targets.

Within a month Poland was brought to her knees, her army destroyed, most of her cities in ruins, tens of thousands of civilians killed, and hundreds of thousands wounded and/or refugees. Dazed and bloodied by the German *blitzkrieg*, it became Nazi-occupied territory. Germany was declared the Gouvernement

Generale as the Polish government fled into exile in London.

Under Nazi occupation life was terrible, and for the Jews it would only get worse, as they were registered, gathered in ghettos and deported to labor and death camps.

B efore the Germans conquered Polish territory and had to deal with 3 million Jews, the plan was to ship them out of Europe, perhaps to Madagascar or even to Manchuria. But the sheer overwhelming size of the Jewish community in Poland pushed the Nazis into deciding to eliminate a people they had turned into "the other," a contaminated race that controlled the world on one hand and were beneath contempt and consideration as humans on the other. The Germans positioned themselves as a pure race, the superior race, the Master Race, and even set up breeding programs to produce perfect people with blond hair and blue eyes, strong bodies and clean minds.*

The Nazis considered Jewish blood impure, which is why they defined Jews by how many grandparents were Jewish. Once they invaded Poland, they put the same laws into place against the Jews, just as they had in Germany, and as they took over each country the laws against the Jews, and the consequences of those laws, began to take effect. Jews were systematically gathered, used as slave labor and deported to death camps where they were gassed and cremated.

---

* "Some 8,000 children were born in Germany and around 12,000 in Norway as part of Lebensborn, formed by SS leader Heinrich Himmler to encourage women of 'pure blood' to bear blond, blue-eyed children.

Historians have refuted the public's perception that it was a system of Nazi stud farms where SS zealots mated with each other. But it was an integral part of a murderous racial policy that stretched from the forced sterilization of people with hereditary diseases to the killing of 6 million Jews.

Founded in 1935, Lebensborn was designed to halt the high rate of abortions in Germany which rose as high as 800,000 a year in the inter-war years because of a chronic shortage of men to marry after World War I. Its aim was to prevent 100,000 abortions and its statute stated that it was to support 'racially and genetically valuable families with many children.' (cont'd)

THE FINAL SOLUTION

Towards the end of 1941 when close to one and a half million Jews had been killed, the Nazi high command called a conference to discuss a more efficient and cheaper way to exterminate them. The Nazis had reached the conclusion that the methods they were using were very inefficient; it would take well over a decade to kill all of Europe's Jews at the rate they were going, and it was costly.

The Wannsee Conference was held on January 20, 1942 in a Jewish mansion that had been confiscated by the Nazis. They thought it just to hold such a meeting in the former home of a Jew. Chaired by Reinhard Heydrich, a high ranking Nazi official, it was run like a business meeting for some corporation trying to improve its sales. This conference was about a faster, more efficient, cheaper way to exterminate the Jews. The man who presented the agreed upon "plan" was Adolf Eichmann.

At the conference the Nazi's reached the following conclusions; collectively they became known as the Final Solution to the Jewish Problem:

a) First, Jews would be rounded up and put into ghettos, overcrowded small sections of a city (named after Venetian restricted Jewish areas created in 1516). That way the Nazis could first take inventory of how many Jews there were. In these ghettos the Jews would feed and clothe themselves, thus avoiding any Nazi expenditure for upkeep. Many, of course, would die of malnutrition and disease, but that was part of the process, after all.

It enabled unmarried pregnant women to avoid social stigma by giving birth anonymously away from their homes, often under the pretext of needing a long-term recuperation. About 60 percent of Lebensborn mothers were unmarried. Lebensborn ran children's homes and an adoption service if the mother didn't want to keep the child.

It even had its own registry office system to keep true identities secret. Most documents were burnt at the end of the war. That, together with the refusal of many Lebensborn mothers to tell their children about the program, has made it very difficult to find the truth." (David Crossland, "Lebensborn Children Break the Silence, *Der Spiegel* (November 7, 2006) (http://www.spiegel.de/international/nazi-program-to-breed-master-race-lebensborn-children-break-silence-a-446978.html))* To learn more about the Holocaust, visit www.ushmm.orfg and www.yadvadshem.org.

b) Then the ghettos would be emptied, i.e., liquidated. The survivors would be shipped off to special camps. There would be two types of camps: labor camps and death camps. The Jews would be transported to these camps by the cheapest most efficient method, railway, and stuffed into cattle cars with standing room only, about 100 to a car. Each locomotive would haul at least twenty to thirty cars. The journey to these camps would take on average three days, with many of the transportees dying along the way.

c) Once at these camps, a *selektion* (a selection of the captives designated for labor or extermination) would take place. Very young, women and the elderly would be sent to the death camps immediately. Those over thirteen or fourteen, and those who looked stronger, would be sent to labor camps to become slave labor for the Nazi war machine. These slaves would work eighteen hours a day and receive perhaps 300-400 calories a day of substandard food. (A normal healthy working person consumes between 2,000-3,000 calories a day.) This way the Nazis could get about six to nine months of work out of a slave at no cost until s/he was ready to be executed in the death camps.

d) The death camps were to operate cheaply and quickly. It was decided that the cheapest and most efficient way to kill Jews was by using a very deadly insecticide called Zyklon B gas. The Jews would be hoarded into large windowless holding pens, called showers by the Nazis to fool their victims, 100-300 at a time. Then the gas would be injected into the chamber until everyone inside was asphyxiated, usually in about twenty minutes. Since these gas chambers would operate around the clock, too many bodies would be created to bury, so they had to be disposed of in some way. The answer was special high intensity ovens that cremated the bodies quickly. To allow the Nazis to come out ahead financially on this venture they collected all the Jews' belongings, collected their shaved hair, eyeglasses, shoes and clothing, and even yanked all the gold fillings out of corpses' teeth. Finally, the ashes of the cremated bodies were to be used as fertilizer—nothing was to be

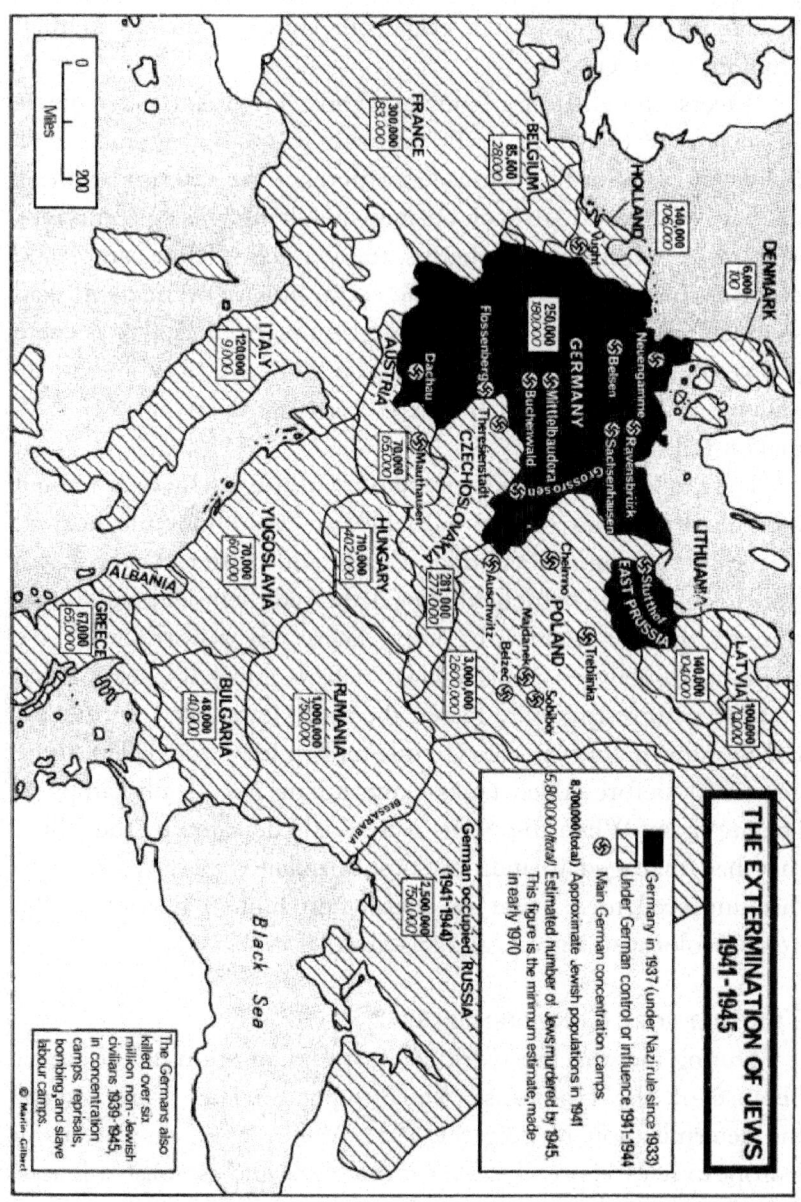

Sir Martin Gilbert, © 2010. Reproduced by permission of Taylor
& Francis Books UK. www.martingilbert.com

wasted, so the Nazis could come out ahead financially in their program of execution.

Overseen by Adolf Eichmann, whose job was to exterminate all the Jews of the world, his first mission was the extermination of Polish Jewry. After the Wannsee Conference the extermination of the Jews became a high-tech business involving tens of thousands of Nazi SS executioners, ghettos, train systems, labor camps and death camps. Never before in the entire history of mankind had so much premeditated thought and planning been used to execute people. Between January 1942 and May 1945 over four and a half million more Jews were murdered, among them another 2.25 million Polish Jews.

For the Jews the second phase of World War II was not about the Allied victories on the battlefield, it was about the horrors of the Final Solution becoming clearer and clearer. As the Nazis were losing on the battlefield, they dedicated themselves to at least winning the war against the Jews! There was a horrible inverse relationship between Nazi military defeats and Jews being killed in death camps; the more losses, the more Jews killed. In the last five months of the war, close to one million Jews were killed, some just hours before Allied tanks came rolling into death camps to liberate them. When the Nazis were finaly defeated by the Allies, they had managed to murder some 6 million Jews! We refer to this unprecedented event in Jewish and human history as the *Shoah*/Holocaust; a great, all-consuming fire.

THE BILTMORE CONFERENCE, 1942

During the war, the World Zionist Organization did not meet because of the Holocaust, which superseded all issues except the determination to defy the 1939 White Paper, save as many European Jews as possible, defeat the Nazis and establish a Jewish State in *Eretz Yisrael* as soon as possible. A special meeting of the Zionist leadership from the *Yishuv* and American Zionist leaders met at the Biltmore Hotel in New York, May 6–11, 1942. The purpose was to send a message to world Jewry, to the world at large, and especially to the United States, that the Zionist Movement was determined to establish a Jewish State in Mandate Palestine after the war regardless of the 1939 British White Paper. That position, as presented, made the establishment of a State the first priority and placed rescue lower on the agenda.

Declaration adopted by the Extraordinary Zionist Conference at the Biltmore Hotel of New York City, May 11, 1942. The following programme was approved by a Zionist Conference held in the Biltmore Hotel, New York City:

1. American Zionists assembled in this Extraordinary Conference reaffirm their unequivocal devotion to the cause of democratic freedom and international justice to which the people of the United States, allied with the other United Nations, have dedicated themselves, and give expression to their faith in the ultimate victory of humanity and justice over lawlessness and brute force.

2. This Conference offers a message of hope and encouragement to their fellow Jews in the Ghettos and concentration camps of Hitler dominated Europe and prays that their hour of liberation may not be far distant.

The Conference sends its warmest greetings to the Jewish Agency Executive in Jerusalem, to the Va`ad Leumi, and to the whole Yishuv in Palestine, and expresses its profound admiration for their steadfastness and achievements in the face of peril and great difficulties ...

4. In our generation, and in particular in the course of the past twenty years, the Jewish people have awakened and transformed their ancient homeland; from 50,000 at the end of the last war their numbers have increased to more than 500,000. They have made the waste places to bear fruit and the desert to blossom. Their pioneering achievements in agriculture and in industry, embodying new patterns of cooperative endeavour, have written a notable page in the history of colonization.

5. In the new values thus created, their Arab neighbours in Palestine have shared. The Jewish people in its own work of national redemption welcomes the economic, agricultural

and national development of the Arab peoples and states. The Conference reaffirms the stand previously adopted at Congresses of the World Zionist Organization, expressing the readiness and the desire of the Jewish people for full cooperation with their Arab neighbours.

6. The Conference calls for the fulfillment of the original purpose of the Balfour Declaration and the Mandate which recognizing the historical connection of the Jewish people with Palestine' was to afford them the opportunity, as stated by President Wilson, to found there a Jewish Commonwealth. The Conference affirms its unalterable rejection of the White Paper of May 1939 and denies its moral or legal validity. The White Paper seeks to limit, and in fact to nullify Jewish rights to immigration and settlement in Palestine, and, as stated by Mr. Winston Churchill in the House of Commons in May 1939, constitutes `a breach and repudiation of the Balfour Declaration'. The policy of the White Paper is cruel and indefensible in its denial of sanctuary to Jews fleeing from Nazi persecution; and at a time when Palestine has become a focal point in the war front of the United Nations, and Palestine Jewry must provide all available manpower for farm and factory and camp, it is in direct conflict with the interests of the allied war effort.

7. In the struggle against the forces of aggression and tyranny, of which Jews were the earliest victims, and which now menace the Jewish National Home, recognition must be given to the right of the Jews of Palestine to play their full part in the war effort and in the defence of their country, through a Jewish military force fighting under its own flag and under the high command of the United Nations.

8. The Conference declares that the new world order that will follow victory cannot be established on foundations of peace, justice and equality, unless the problem of Jewish homelessness is finally solved. The Conference urges that the gates of Palestine be opened; that the Jewish Agency be vested with control of immigration into Palestine and with the necessary authority for upbuilding the country, including the development of its unoccupied and uncultivated lands; and that Palestine be established as a Jewish Commonwealth

integrated in the structure of the new democratic world. Then and only then will the age old wrong to the Jewish people be righted.[15]

Zionist leadership made it clear that the Jews would no longer wait politely for England to fulfill the promise of the Balfour Declaration, reaffirmed by the League of Nations. The Zionist movement was going to build a state when the war was over, and hoped that allied countries such as the U.S. would come to see that the re-establishment of a Jewish State was a historical and moral imperative.

The Biltmore Declaration openly charged Britain with helping send the Jews of Europe to their deaths because it closed the gates of Mandate Palestine to Jewish immigration during the Holocaust. The case was also made that the Jews of Mandate Palestine had fought the Nazis like any other Allied Nation and they deserved to have their own fighting force and be treated like an ally country after the war was over.

BEN-GURION AND THE HOLOCAUST

Much has been written on the dearth of efforts by the Jewish Agency to aid in the rescue of European Jewry. Modern-day historians have...

> ...accused the leaders of the Zionist movement of "Palestinocentrism," caring little about the Jews in the Diaspora, and giving little priority to the rescue of Jews under Nazi occupation. This obsession with the creation of a Jewish state, according to the critics, meant that all energies and resources were devoted to that goal. What is more, the critics charge, while doing little to help Hitler's victims, Ben-Gurion and his fellow Zionist leaders cynically exploited the Holocaust and its survivors for political purposes in the struggle for the creation of the State of Israel.*[16]

Newly revealed documents indicate this may not have been entirely the case.

[M]any rescue schemes [were] attempted by Ben Gurion and the Jewish Agency Executive beginning in 1942, when confirmation of mass murder reached them. These initiatives included the attempt to rescue children from Vichy France, Bulgaria, and Romania, and various actions undertaken to ransom Jews from Transnistria, Slovakia, and Hungary, including the controversial Joel Brand mission in the spring of 1944. These efforts virtually all failed, despite the expenditure of considerable talent, energy, and money...The attempts at rescue failed for a variety of reasons: British obstructionism, the pressure of Germany on its allies not to release Jews, the failure of the Allies to support negotiations that might strengthen the Nazis and prolong the war, and the physical problem of getting refugees into (often unhelpful) neutral countries....[These] failures were not for want of trying, and that the rescue of Jews was always a top priority for Ben Gurion. There were some modest successes as well, the most notable being the smuggling of perhaps 20,000 immigrants to Palestine from Romanian ports or via Turkey, in which the (right-wing) Revisionists played an important role, and the rescue of a few thousand Jewish children.[17]

Despite these activities, Ben-Gurion still provides fodder for his naysayers with remarks such as his response to news of the 1938 Kindertransport:

Were I to know that all German Jewish children could be rescued by transferring them to England and only half by transfer to Palestine, I would opt for the latter, because our concern is not only the personal interests of these children, but the historic interest of the Jewish people.[18]

---

* For example, see S. B. Beit-Zvi, *Post-Ugandan Zionism on Trial* (Tel Aviv: Zahala, 1991 [trans. of 1977 Hebrew edition]); Tom Segev, *The Seventh Million* (New York: Hill & Wang, 1993). Zeev Sternhell, *The Founding Myths of Israel* (Princeton, NJ: Princeton University Press, 1999)

All in all, the best answer to the debate about Ben-Gurion's actions during the Holocaust may best be summed up with the following:

> It is easy to forget that there was no sovereign Jewish state during the Holocaust, that the British ruled Palestine (and blocked immigration as well as rescue efforts that might result in such immigration), and that ultimately Ben Gurion had precious few cards to play, whatever his thoughts, feelings, and schemes. The Allied decision to give priority to winning the war and not to civilian rescue, and British policy toward the Arab world, may have doomed his efforts from the start.[19]

In addition, despite the naysayers declaring *J'accuse*, it should be recognized that during the *Shoah* all regular norms of civilized behavior were suspended for the Jews. This was not their choice; it was a barbaric and surreal reality that was imposed upon them by the Nazis and their collaborators.

Life for Jews under Nazi rule was capricious, cheap, fleeting and horrific. They were literally living in a real Dante's *Inferno*. Decisions that Jewish grandparents, parents, children, relatives and friends made on a daily or even hourly basis were all in line with the terrible choice that was featured in the movie *Sophie's Choice* (1982), where a Jewish mother had a few seconds to decide which of her two children would live and which one die. To judge or try to score any political points based on the behavior of any single Jew or Jewish group or organization is at best pointless or, at worst, a form of someone practicing wickedness masquerading as moral superiority. There are many questions that are best not asked and, if asked, no one should expect a cogent, clear unambiguous answer. It is not just Ben-Gurion who had to make "Sophie's Choice" but hundreds of thousands of Jews, and certain lucky Jewish groups of individuals.

As Theodore Roosevelt stated in a speech at the Sorbonne in 1910:

It is not the critic who counts; not the man who points out how the strong man stumbles, or where the doer of deeds could have done them better. The credit belongs to the man who is actually in the arena, whose face is marred by dust and sweat and blood; who strives valiantly; who errs, who comes short again and again, because there is no effort without error and shortcoming; but who does actually strive to do the deeds; who knows great enthusiasms, the great devotions; who spends himself in a worthy cause; who at the best knows in the end the triumph of high achievement, and who at the worst, if he fails, at least fails while daring greatly, so that his place shall never be with those cold and timid souls who neither know victory nor defeat.[20]

The people who have made a point of putting Ben-Gurion and the Zionist movement under a microscope and making it appear as if they were involved in a unique type of behavior should be a little more intellectually honest and just accept the fact that many Jews and Jewish organizations saved family, friends, rabbis, colleagues, and members of specific Jewish organizations or sects during the *Shoah*. Finally, those who make accusations should think long and hard about what they would have done under these horrific conditions.*

---

* Ironically, since the War of Independence, the treatment of Holocaust survivors in *Eretz Israel* continues to be a national disgrace. Called "bars of soap" by indigenous Israelis; their Yiddish language torn from them and disavowed by Ben-Gurion as an acceptable lingua franca of the nascent state; their future German reparations assigned to the government which has persistently failed to provide for them adequately as promised; the fact that the national bank of Israel, Bank Leumi, to this day is parsimonious in its distribution of over 65,000 accounts of Holocaust survivors or their dependents as it holds out (cont'd)

waiting for the claimants to die, all of this reflects an official ideology that may act to counter some who would excuse the government's attitude toward survivors in general. "While the nascent state of Israel provided refuge for the Holocaust survivors and offered them a new identity and opportunity to rebuild their lives, it also demanded that they abnegate their former identities, their Holocaust experiences above all, and repress all the emotional problems that the Holocaust created. In the nearly 5 decades since the first survivors arrived on Israel's shores with their accounts of barely imaginable horror, society's attitudes toward the survivors have traced a tortured course...." [Solomon Z., "From denial to recognition: attitudes toward Holocaust survivors from World War II to the present," *Journal of Trauma Stress*, April 1995, 8(2): 215-228 (https://www.ncbi. nlm.nih.gov/pubmed/7627438)]

Footnotes

[1] Adolf Hitler, *Mein Kampf* (New York: Reynal & Hitchcock, 1939) 447-448.

[2] Edwin Black, *The Transfer Agreement: The Dramatic Story of the Pact Between the Third Reich and Jewish Palestine* (Washington, DC: Dialog Press, 2009).

[3] Yf'aat Weiss, "The Transfer Agreement and the Boycott Movement: A Jewish Dilemma on the Eve of the Holocaust," Yad Vashem Shoah Resource Center (http://www.yadvashem.org/odot_pdf/Microsoft%20Word%20-%203231.pdf)

In contemporary times the head of the Palestinian Authority, Mahmoud Abbas, expounded on this agreement in his doctoral thesis and couched this arrangement as a Zionist collaboration with the Nazi regime. He also wrote, in that only a million Jews were killed between the years, 1939-1945.

The following is from a *Daily Beast* article, posted on January 23, 2013, by David. N. Myers:

"I was reminded of this upon hearing the statement attributed...to Mahmoud Abbas, the president of the Palestinian Authority, suggesting that one would be foolhardy "to deny the relationship between Zionism and Nazism before World War II."

The oft-quoted figure of six million dead, he maintains, was but a myth, foisted on the world by the singularly demonic Zionists. It is they, Abbas further claimed, who collaborated with the Nazis during the War to incite hatred of European Jews in order to validate their own ideology. And it was they who then sought after the War to exploit the death of Jews to their own advantage."

Characteristically, the blatant hypocrisy of this claim neglects to mention the overt Nazi affiliation of the Grand Mufti of Jerusalem with the Nazi regime.

[4] *Op. cit.*

[5] "Refugees: Key Facts," *Holocaust Encyclopedia*, USHMM (https://www.ushmm.org/wlc/en/article.php?ModuleId= 10005139)

[6] V. Jabotinsky, "A Jewish State Now" in Walter Laqueur and Barry Rubin (eds.), *The Israel-Arab Reader* (NY: Penguin Books, 4th revised and updated edition, 1984), at 58-61. See also, http://spengler.atimes.net/viewtopic.php?t=12002

[7] "British Palestine Mandate: Text of the Peel Commission Report (July 1937), Jewish Virtual Library (http://www.jewishvirtuallibrary.org/jsource/History/peel1.html)

[8] "British White Paper of 1939," Yale Law School, Lillian Goldman Library, The Avalon Project (http://avalon.law.yale.edu/20th_century/brwh1939.asp)

[9] *Ibid.*

[10] *Ibid.*

[11] "U.S. Policy During the Holocaust: The Tragedy of S.S. St. Louis (May 13 - June 20, 1939), Jewish Virtual Library (https://www.jewishvirtuallibrary.org/jsource/Holocaust/stlouis.html)

[12] Michael Berkowitz, *The Crime of My Existence: Nazism and the Myth of Jewish Criminality* (Berkeley: Univ. of California Press, 2007), 116.

[13] https://en.wikipedia.org/wiki/Amin_al-Husseini as derived from: Haya Gavish, *Unwitting Zionists: The Jewish Community of Zakho in Iraqi Kurdistan* (Detroit: Wayne State University Press, 2010 239; Erik Davis, Erik, *Memories of State: Politics, History, and Collective Identity in Modern Iraq* (Berkeley: University of California Press, 2005) 70; Liora Lukitz, *Iraq: The Search for National Identity* (Abingdon-on-Thames: Routledge, 1995), 96; Charles Tripp, *A History of Iraq* (2nd.(rev.) ed.), (Cambridge: Cambridge University Press, 2000), 105; Henry Laurens, *Une mission sacrée de civilisation. La Question de Palestine. 2* (Paris: Fayard, 2002), 463-4; Robert Fisk, *The Great War for Civilisation: The Conquest of the Middle East* (NY: HarperPerennial, 2006), 442; Renzo De Felice, *Mussolini l'alleato: 1. L'Italia in guerra 1940-1945. 1* (Torino: Einaudi, 1990), 247.

[14] *Ibid.* as derived from: Marko Attila Hoare, *The Bosnian Muslims in the Second World War: A History* (London: C. Hust and Co., 2013)

p. 53; Jozo Tomasevich, *War and Revolution in Yugoslavia, 1941-1945: Occupation and Collaboration* (Stanford: Stanford University Press, 2001), 496; George Lepre, *Himmler's Bosnian Division; The Waffen-SS Handschar Division 1943-1945* (Atglen, PA: Schiffer Military History, 1997), 12, 310; George H. Stein, *The Waffen SS: Hitler's Elite Guard at War, 1939-1945* (Ithaca, NY: Cornell University Press, 1984), 184-5; Lepre (1997), 228, n. 28; Lepre (1997), 47; Paul Mojzes, *Balkan Genocides: Holocaust and Ethnic Cleansing in the Twentieth Century* (Lanham, MD: Rowman & Littlefield Publishers, 2011), 78; Lepre (1997), 313; Mojzes (2011), 97-98; Lepre (1997), 31; Lepre (1997), 26-28; Lepre (1997), 34; Lepre (1997), 313. See Carl Savich, "Dagger and Swastika: The Handschar Division in the German Media in World War II, 1943-1944." (http://serbianna.com/analysis/archives/2151)

[15] "Zionist Congresses: The Biltmore Conference (May 6 - 11, 1942)," Jewish Virtual Library (http://www.jewishvirtuallibrary.org/jsource/History/biltmore.html)

[16] Severin A. Hochberg, "Arrows in the Dark: David Ben Gurion, the Yishuv Leadership, and Rescue Attempts during the Holocaust," *The Middle East Journal*, 60 (2) Spring 2006, 385+.

[17] *Ibid.*

[18] Shabtai Teveth, *Ben Gurion and the Holocaust* (NY: Harcourt Brace & Co., 1996), 47.

[19] *Op. cit.*

[20] Theodore Roosevelt, "Man in the Arena," *Citizenship in a Republic*, April 23, 1910 (http://www.theodore-roosevelt.com/images/research/speeches/maninthearena.pdf)

Chapter 7

Militant Zionism
1945 - 1947

When World War II ended in 1945 there was nothing left to do but mourn the millions who were robbed, tortured, enslaved and murdered because they were Jews. There were no victory celebrations to speak of for anyone, other than a short spasm of joy of knowing the fighting had stopped and that for some life could go back to normal. Not so for the Jewish people.

There were over ten million Displaced Persons (DPs) after World War II, among them some 250,000 Jewish Holocaust survivors liberated from the camps. Many had lost family members; parents, spouses, children and friends forever disappeared. Thousands were orphans. Interred in DP camps scattered throughout Western Europe and Germany because they had nowhere else to go, most possessed only the rags on their backs. In Bergen-Belsen alone more than 17,000 died of disease and debilitation after the liberation. Of those who tried to go back to their homes in Central and Eastern Europe, many were murdered by neighbors who had taken over their homes and valuable properties.

In Poland, for instance, scores of antisemitic attacks led to the death of many Jews who had survived the war:

> Poles were feeling guilty: so implicated were they in the Jewish tragedy, aiding and abetting and expropriating, that the mere sight of those wraiths returning from the camps or exile or

hiding, people who knew the Poles' dirty secrets and held title to their property, was too much to bear. So they murdered Jews or chased them away.[1]

Unable to return to their native lands, and still blocked from entry to countries around the world, Jewish displaced persons came to present significant problems for allied occupation forces.

Some of the problems that the Jews posed for the Allies included their legal status; their need for food, clothing, shelter, rehabilitation, and medical care; and their desire to reestablish contact with relatives and friends. After years of systematic persecution and mass murder by the Nazis, the Jews assumed that the Allies would provide special treatment for them. In particular, they expected separate camps where they would not have to share facilities with their former guards and tormentors. But the Allies didn't treat them any better than anyone else, and the British refused to do so, in case the Jews would use special status to force immigration to Mandate Palestine.[2]

Still, thousands hoped to make their new homes in the *Yishuv*. The hope of a return to Zion kept them going, kept them alive throughout their ordeals.

Famed Nazi hunter Simon Wiesenthal, a Holocaust survivor, told the following story:

It was 10 o'clock In the morning, with a bright sun shining down to help us to celebrate the moment of liberation. The American tanks entered the camp, and every prisoner struggled to get to them. I was about 150 yards from the first tank. The soldiers who had come were surrounded by prisoners sinking into their arms, crying, laughing at the same time, exulted beyond their ordinary feeling. I covered the first 100 yards, but then I collapsed on the ground. I was lying there, trying to get up again, panting and staring, fascinated as the American flag fluttered on the top.

I could not take my eyes from the stars of the flag, symbols not only of the States of the Union, but of all the things we had lost in the Holocaust. Every star had acquired a meaning of its own: One was the star of hope, and that of justice, of tolerance, friendship, of brotherly love, of understanding, and so on.

A little later, we saw prisoners from other blocks marching by, carrying their national flags—Czechs, Poles, Italians, and many others. They had secretly prepared them for the day of liberation. I looked around me, we were all Jews; I asked: "Why don't have we a flag?" I was longing for such a symbol of liberty and national dignity for us Jews. One of us had a blue shirt, I had one which had once been white. We took them off, and another prisoner managed to make them into something like a blue-and-white flag.

We were much too weak to attempt a parade like the other nationalities, and so we just sat there in the sun, ... waving our makeshift flag. Jews from other blocks came over to us and cried, some of them kissed the flag, a symbol of hope amidst the dead and the dying.[3]

Though now liberated from Nazi persecution, the life of a displaced person was far from liberating. American armed forces chaplain, Reform Rabbi Abraham Klausner, who ministered to 10,000 Dachau survivors, put it this way:

> Liberated but not free, that is the paradox of the Jew. In the concentration camp, his whole being was consumed with the hope of salvation. That hope was his life, for that he was willing to suffer. Saved, his hope evanesces, for no new source of hope has been given him. Suffering continues to be his badge.[4]

THE ROLE OF THE AMERICAN JEWISH CHAPLAINS

Klausner and other chaplains worked to alleviate Jewish suffering in the DP camps and let Jewish organizations, mainstream media and politicians see what was going on. Pressure to change the situation mounted and, as a result, the State Department and U.S. President Harry Truman (1884-1972) sent Earl G. Harrison, the dean of the University of Pennsylvania Law School, to Europe to investigate the situation. The result was front-page headlines in the States. Harrison charged that,

> As matters now stand, we appear to be treating the Jews as the Nazis treated them, except that we do not exterminate them. They are ill in large numbers under our military guard, instead of the SS troops. One is led to wonder whether the German people, seeing this, are not supposing that we are following or at least condoning Nazi policy.[5]

Harrison's solution was for the United States to support a plan to settle the DPs in Palestine. "With respect to possible places of resettlement for those who may be stateless or who do not wish to return to their homes," Harrison declared, "Palestine is definitely and preeminently the first choice." He informed the president that "there is no acceptable or even decent solution for their future other than Palestine," although he pointed out that some people felt that the United States or other countries were options.

In particular, Harrison asserted that "some reasonable extension or modification of the British White Paper of 1939," which limited Jewish emigration to Palestine to 75,000 over a five-year period beginning in that year, "ought to be possible without serious repercussions." In arguing for Palestine as the solution to the problems of Jewish statelessness, Harrison pointed out that "this is said on a purely humanitarian basis with no reference to ideological or political considerations so far as Palestine is concerned."[6]

A decision on this issue had to be made shortly, Harrison insisted, because certificates for immigration to Palestine would be exhausted by August, 1945. ... He then noted that the ...

> Jewish Agency for Palestine has submitted to the British government a petition that 100,000 additional immigration

certificates be made available. A memorandum accompanying the petition makes a persuasive showing with respect to the immediate absorptive capacity of Palestine and the current, actual manpower shortages there....

"While there may be room for difference of opinion as to the precise number of certificates which might tinder the circumstances be considered reasonable," Harrison observed, "there is no question but that the request thus made would, if granted, contribute much to the sound solution for the future of Jews still in Germany and Austria and even other displaced Jews, who do not wish either to remain there or to return to their countries of nationality. No matter is, therefore, so important from the viewpoint of Jews in Germany and Austria and those elsewhere who have known the horrors of the Concentration Camps as is the disposition of the Palestine question."[7]

Truman knew that British restrictions for Palestine had to be lifted and urged American Jewish leaders to pressure the British to open the gates. In the summer of 1945, 37 out of 48 state governors asked that the doors be opened in a special proposal to the British. Truman also met with British Prime Minister Winston Churchill about the issue, but a few days later, Clement Atlee became the prime minster and he resolved nothing with Truman, who urged Atlee to grant 100,000 entry certificates to the Jewish survivors and pointed out that "if it is to be effective, such action should not be long delayed."[8]

The British responded with a resounding "no"! The 1939 White Paper was still in effect. As a matter of fact, the five-year immigration period was over, and the gates of Israel were shut.

The British logic for refusing DP entry into Mandate Palestine was logical from their perspective. After World War II England ceased being a world power. The last thing England was capable of doing was running a vast empire that stretched all around the globe. So, towards the end of the war, England began to grant independence to many of her colonies, wanting to part on good terms since she still wanted an economic and political relationship with them. The Arabs fell into this category, particularly since they sat on 50 percent of the planet's known oil reserves and hosted the Suez Canal. England was not about to jeopardize her relationship with twelve brand new Arab states (all former colonies) for the sake of some goodwill from the Jewish people or public opinion. Hence, the same way England told the Jews "no" in 1939, she said "no" again in 1945.

Thus Truman's request was initially rejected, but then the British called for an Anglo-American Committee of Inquiry after Truman made his demands public on September 24, 1945. Foreign Secretary Ernest Bevin hoped that the committee would enable the British to delay a resolution and involve the United States in the process of finding a solution. After some discussion, the Anglo-American Committee was set up in November, 1945.[9]

But this was not the first group to involve itself in the fate of post-war Jews. In the spring of 1944, small groups of survivors in the Russian sector organized to decide their future. They came to Lublin in January 1945, and met with former Warsaw Ghetto fighters. Together they formed a secret organization called Berihah (Flight). Berihah in Poland soon began smuggling Jews to points on the Mediterranean coasts, where they would be in a better position to reach Palestine. They also worked with the Jewish Agency, the British Jewish Brigade, with Allied chaplains and Jewish soldiers and officers in the American armed forces and with Jewish groups, including the American Jewish Joint Distribution Committee. All these British and American chaplains and soldiers risked everything to help the survivors—their lives, the possibility of a court martial and dishonorable dismissal from service.

From then on the *Yishuv* and the *Shearith Hapletah* (the Surviving Remnant) were inseparable members of the Brigade. In a speech to the leaders of the DPs, Major Yigal Kaspi of the Brigade declared: "You are bone of our bone, flesh of our flesh. Our families are overjoyed to know you have survived, and are waiting to welcome you with open and loving arms.... Unite! Be organized and disciplined!"[10]

The efforts of the Berihah resulted in the arrival of a large number of Jews into the American zone of Germany on their road to Palestine. Many had reached Italy, but there was no room for all of them there. The Palestinians decided to divert as many of them as possible to the American zones of Germany and Austria. They would remain there until they could be taken to Palestine, despite the British ban on Jewish immigration. The American zone was chosen because it was a temporary transit area for the refugees and because they would be treated better there than in the other zones. But it should be noted that the DPs were not always well treated in the American zone.* The situation improved only after

---

* "As Germany and Austria came under Allied military administration, the commanders assumed responsibility for the safety and disposition of all displaced persons. The Allies provided for the DPs according to nationality, and initially did not recognize Jews as constituting a separate group. One significant consequence of this early perspective was that Jewish DPs sometimes found themselves housed in the same quarters with former Nazi collaborators. Also, the general policy of the Allied occupation forces was to repatriate DPs to their country of origin as soon as possible, and there was not necessarily sufficient consideration for exceptions; repatriation policy varied from place to place, but Jewish DPs, for whom repatriation was problematic, were apt to find themselves under pressure to return home.

General George Patton, the commander of the United States Third Army and military governor of Bavaria, where most of the Jewish DPs resided, was known for pursuing a harsh, indiscriminate repatriation policy. However, his approach raised objections from the refugees themselves, as well as from American military and civilian parties sympathetic to their plight. In early July 1945, Patton issued a directive that the entire Munich area was to be cleared of displaced persons with an eye toward repatriating them. Joseph Dunner, an American officer who in civilian life was a professor of political science, sent a memorandum to military authorities protesting the order. When 90 trucks of the Third Army arrived at Buchberg to transport the refugees there, they refused to move, citing Dunner's memo." (https://en.wikipedia.org/wiki/Sh%27erit_ha-Pletah as derived from Angelika Königseder and Juliane Wetzel, *Waiting for Hope: Jewish Displaced Persons in Post-World War II Germany*, Trans. John A. Broadwin (Evanston, IL: Northwestern University Press, 2001), 16; Zeev W. Mankowitz, *Life between Memory and Hope: The Survivors of the Holocaust in Occupied Germany* (Cambridge, UK: Cambridge University Press, 2002), 12-16; Michael Brenner, *After the Holocaust: Rebuilding Jewish Lives in Postwar Germany*, Trans. Barbara Harshav (Princeton, NJ: Princeton University Press, 1997), 15.

survivors protested about being treated badly by the American military. In the British zone no additional refugees with a DP status were accepted. This caused many problems for the U.S. Occupying Forces.[11]

As early as October 1945, Ben-Gurion, then chairman of the Jewish Agency Executive in Palestine, was in Germany to meet with the survivors and representatives of the Jewish Agency, as well as with Generals Dwight D. Eisenhower (1890-1969) and Walter Bedell Smith (1895-1961), Eisenhower's chief of staff. Ben-Gurion hoped that by "concentrating a quarter of a million Jews in the American zone" it would "...increase the American pressure [on the British] to allow them to enter Palestine." It was "not because of the financial aspects of the problem," he declared; "that does not matter to them, but because they see no future for these people outside of Eretz Yisrael."[12] But the Americans wanted this done quietly so as not to arouse the British.

At the end of 1945, Truman attempted to admit some Jews into the United States. His efforts were unsuccessful. Despite the suffering endured by European Jews, the United States Congress was in no mood to relax restrictive immigration laws. Rather than initiate a protracted fight to change these statutes, Truman issued an Executive Order on December 22, 1945, which gave the Jews priority on existing quotas already available to DPs. The Polish, Austrian, and German quotas came to approximately 39,000.

The major factor contributing to the increased influx into the American zone was the Kielce pogrom. It has already been noted that assaults against Jews were not uncommon in Poland. Several hundred Jews had been murdered between November, 1944, and October, 1945; the worst massacre occurred on July 4, 1946, with the pogrom at Kielce, when forty-two Jews were murdered in a blood libel. Within three months, 100,000 Jews fled Poland and the surrounding countries. Led by the Berihah, Jews were brought through Czechoslovakia to Bratislava and Vienna. From Vienna they were taken to Salzburg and then either to Italy or the American zone of Germany. Another Berihah route went from Stettin

(Szezecin) to Berlin and from there to the West. Berihah operators from Poland, Rumania, Hungary, Czechoslovakia and Yugoslavia continued into 1948, transferring approximately 250,000 survivors into Austria, Germany and Italy. It was the "largest organized illegal mass movement in the twentieth century."[13]

In the meantime, the Jews in the *Yishuv* did not take Britain's "no" with equanimity and diplomacy, as they had in 1922, 1930 and 1939. After waiting for millennia to return to the Zionist homeland, and particularly after the Holocaust when no nation was particularly willing to take in the DPs, the Jewish Agency decided to declare war on Britain.

After the war the British were distracted in trying to administer their colonies, grant independence and rebuild their own cities and industries. Britain had very little time to deal with Mandate Palestine as a priority and, after the Holocaust, the Jews looking to settle in the *Yishuv* figured Europe had done its worst and what the British would inflict would be negligible compared to what had gone before. These Jews were determined, they were armed, and they wanted their homeland back with a passion.

The first front, according to Ben-Gurion, was to attempt to smuggle thousands of Jews into Israel from Europe via Aliyah Bet. This was a concerted effort to have people escape or be smuggled to cities with harbors on the Mediterranean in places like Italy, Portugal and France. The *Maapalim*, the boats they boarded, were on their last legs, freighters built for carrying coal and a crew of twenty were outfitted below deck to carry 400 people; old ferries built to carry 400 passengers had 2,000 people crammed on board. The DPs were snuck on to these boats at night, then set sail with false papers and flags supposedly carrying cargo, with their passengers below deck in horribly crammed conditions. These boats would than zigzag towards Mandate Palestine trying to avoid the British Navy, whose full time job in the eastern Mediterranean was to catch them. If they got by the British Navy, they would drop anchor about a mile off the shore of *Eretz Yisrael* near some deserted beach, and there the Haganah would be waiting to pick them up and bring them ashore to their new lives in Mandate Palestine. These new arrivals were then scattered among several settlements so as not to create suspicion the next day. They were all taught the same first line in Hebrew should they be stopped and asked who they were: "I am a Jew from *Eretz Yisrael*."

Thousands of Jews were smuggled in this way in 1946, but thousands more were caught by the British Navy, sometimes just offshore. Once that happened, the boats were boarded and the passengers taken to British prison camps waiting for them on Cyprus (a British island colony about 300 miles west of Mandate Palestine). After surviving the Holocaust and the long, tortured journey to their homeland, these people found themselves once again behind barbed-wire. Clearly these camps in Cyprus were not Nazi death camps, but they were still prisons..

There are numerous sources that tell incredible stories of rescue and heroism, cunning and success to be told about the men and women who helped the DPs realize their dreams of a return to Zion.

The second front Ben-Gurion wanted to open was one that used sabotage and violence to drive the British out of Mandate Palestine once and for all. To accomplish this, by 1946, there were three underground groups using weapons directed against both British and Arabs. Each group had its own leaders and its own ideologies.

The Haganah, which included elite Palmach units, was militarily headed by Yitzhak Sadeh (1890-1952), who received his orders from Ben-Gurion. The Haganah had about 35,000 men under its command at this time. Their targets were purely military targets and did not go after military personnel or any officials connected to the running of the Mandate. They tried to minimize loss of life.

Irgun (*Irgun Tzvaee Le'umee* – IT"L in Hebrew, *Etzel*) was founded during the Arab revolt and was commanded by Menachem Begin (1913-1992), a Ze'ev Jabotinsky devotee. The Irgun had about 3,000 men under its command. Their targets were anything connected to the British military rule in Mandate

Palestine, including British soldiers and those who were involved in the running of the Mandate. The Irgun would sometimes warn of an upcoming attack if civilians could be in the line of fire.

Lehi (*Lohamei Herut Yisrael*-Fighters for the Freedom of Israel), a splinter group from the Irgun, included some former Haganah people. Avraham Stern (1907-1942) was their commander; second in command was Yitzhak Shamir (1915-2012). Also known as the "Stern Gang," Lehi had about 500 men. To Lehi, anyone who opposed the creation of an independent Jewish State—be it British officials or UN officials—was a target. They specifically targeted individuals. When they targeted civilians, Zionist leadership considered those acts of terror, and condemned them as such. But the acts of terror were minor in the operations carried out by Lehi.

In 1945, to some degree, all these factions agreed to put many of their ideological differences aside and make the British pay for keeping the gates of Israel closed to Jews. Thus came into existence the Jewish Resistance Movement (*Tnuat Hameri*). The British had never experienced anything remotely like this in their thirty-year stay in Palestine. Every day there was something done by one of the Jewish undergrounds: a bombing of a headquarters, an attack on a British outpost, the blowing up of bridges and train tracks—it was relentless. The British responded with martial law, curfews, sweeping arrests of hundreds of people, filling the prisons, sentencing people to death—and carrying out the sentences swiftly! As the Palestine Mandate became a battleground, the *Yishuv* did not back down under British pressure but rather stepped up its resistance.

From autumn 1945 to July 1946 these forces sabotaged airfields, railroads, radar stations, oil refineries, bridges, lighthouses and other military targets. Even so, the Irgun and the Haganah avoided attacking civilians and most of the time warned the British of an impending assault to prevent casualties.

On June 12, 1946, the Haganah blew up all the bridges connecting Mandate Palestine to the surrounding Arab countries. The main purpose was to cut off the British Army from all of its land-based lines of logistical support. But it was also to send a message to the British that the Haganah had the capacity to carry out such a large, well-coordinated attack right under their noses. The blowing up of all of these bridges caused a very harsh British response. They launched Operation Agatha, known to the *Yishuv* as the Black Shabbat (Sabbath). All the leaders of the Jewish Agency were arrested and held without trial. All of the *Yishuv* was placed under a harsh curfew; dozens of *kibbutzim* were raided and torn apart by British soldiers looking for illegal weapons. This harsh reaction caused the Haganah to back away from direct engagement with British forces in the *Yishuv* and instead to intensify the fight to break the British blockade and attempt to sneak in as many Jews into the *Yishuv* as possible. The Irgun and Lehi, on the other hand, felt that a very strong response to the British was in order. Hence they planned a very dramatic and painful response: They would blow up the headquarters of the British High Command in Mandate Palestine located in the southern wing of the world famous King David Hotel in Jerusalem. At first the Irgun had the green light from the Haganah, but the Haganah claimed that it later rescinded its green light. This operation was run by Menachem Begin himself.

On July 22, 1946, British Headquarters was blown up. A phone call was made by a female member of the Irgun twenty-five minutes before the explosion warning the British to evacuate the King David. A similar phone call was made to the French Consulate next door. The British, presuming the warning a prank, did not evacuate. The massive explosion took down one third of the building. In total 91 people were killed. Among the dead were many civilians.

The British were outraged and further stepped up their war against the Jewish undergrounds. Ben-Gurion also condemned the attack, even though the Irgun claimed that Moshe Sneh (1909 -1972), Chief of Haganah General Headquarters, had approved the attack. The mood in Mandate Palestine was one of war between the British and the *Yishuv* who now in the post-Holocaust era was determined to establish a Jewish State in Israel one way or another.[14]

The British further retaliated against the *Yishuv* in August by beginning to expel illegal immigrants to detention camps in Cyprus. Approximately 51,000 Jews spent nearly two years in these camps. The Jews, however, were not intimidated by British countermeasures. Their resolve to reach Palestine was only strengthened. Moreover, the image of crisp British naval uniforms rounding up a motley crew of starved and emaciated civilians (including women and children) rebounded against them.

While British forces in Palestine were trying to quell Jewish resistance and place illegal immigrants in detention camps, the Anglo-American Committee of experts was completing its report. On July 31, the report and its recommendations, known as the Morrison-Grady Plan, after Dr. Henry F. Grady and Herbert Morrison (the heads of the two delegations), was released to the British Parliament. The committee proposed that the country be divided into separate Jewish and Arab provinces and that each community have self-rule in domestic affairs, but that Britain retain control over foreign relations, defense, police, courts, customs and communications. A hundred thousand refugees would be admitted to Palestine during the first year the plan was to be implemented, but the British would determine the extent of any future immigration.[15]

The British government reacted favorably to the Morrison-Grady Plan, but the Zionists realized it would be a disaster and would prevent the establishment of a Jewish independent state. Dr. Nahum Goldmann (1895-1982) of the Jewish Agency argued that partition was the best of three possible options: bi-nationalism, trusteeship and partition.

Bi-nationalism was impractical, Goldmann asserted, because the Arabs would not agree to parity. And even if they did agree to this arrangement, there would be no unanimity on political decisions. Trusteeship would require a British presence, and the English were clearly anti-Zionist. Partition was, therefore, the only viable solution, he concluded, because it would separate the Jews and the Arabs, thus reducing conflict and simultaneously promoting economic competition.[16]

On August 30, 1946, Goldmann asked for a statement from Truman or Dean Acheson (1893-1971), acting U.S. Secretary of State, endorsing partition. The State Department and the Joint Chiefs of Staff opposed the idea for fear of antagonizing the British and alienating the Arabs.

1947 – THE YEAR GREAT BRITAIN ASKS THE UN TO SOLVE THE PROBLEM OF MANDATE PALESTINE

In 1947, one *Maapalim* ship, the *Exodus*, made world headlines. The dilapidated vessel, originally built for 400, was crammed with 4,500 DPs who were caught by the English trying to enter Mandate Palestine. The boat was sent back to Europe and the Jews went on a hunger strike that gained international media coverage. Finally, everyone saw how desperate the Jews were to return to their homeland. By the end of 1946 England was reeling from the effect of the Jewish revolt:

1) Though she just finished close to six years of WII and was trying to demobilize armies, over 100,000 British troops were now stationed in and around Palestine, where barely 600,000 Jews lived. In 1938, at the height of the Arab Revolt, there were never more than 15,000 British troops in Palestine.

2) Keeping Palestine closed and running the camps at Cyprus was costing millions of pounds that England simply could not afford.

3) World public opinion was turning against England. It did not look good that one year after WWII the English were fighting Holocaust survivors and putting them again in some sort of camp.

For all these reasons, in early 1947, England got so fed up with the Palestine Mandate problem that it literally dumped it into the lap of the fledgling United Nations. In doing so, the British hoped that the United Nations would ultimately adopt their Morrison-Grady solution. They expected no western European opposition; furthermore, the Soviets, who were anti-Zionists, would be against a Jewish State, and Latin American countries would not want this new state, in line with the Vatican's opposition to Jewish sovereignty in Palestine.[17]

Despite British plans, during the summer of 1947 a United Nations Special Committee on Palestine visited Europe and Palestine to recommend a solution to the Palestine question. On August 31, 1947, the committee completed its report, which called for the partition of Palestine. On November 29, 1947, the General Assembly of the United Nations voted by a two-thirds majority to approve the partition plan. The Arabs opposed this decision and the Israeli War for Independence began. On May 14, 1948, the State of Israel was established.

In early 1949, the war ended with an armistice. By that time, 6,500 Palestinian Jews, about one percent of the Jews in the country, had died. By 1950-1951, two-thirds of the survivors had come to Israel; the rest went to other countries.

The Jews paid dearly for their political independence and their return to world history. The establishment of the State of Israel in 1948 resulted from several factors. The United States, through President Truman, played a decisive role in keeping the British from implementing their anti-Zionist policy; Truman had been motivated by his desire to help the remnants of Europe's Jews. American Jews, in turn, maintained pressure on American officials and cultivated American public opinion. This meant that the "establishment of the State of Israel and the consequent achievement of a political base for the Jewish people was made possible, to a large degree, by the Jews in the Diaspora: the survivors who organized groups like the Berihah, and American Jewry." It also corrected...

> "the impression that the main factor leading to statehood was the activity of the Jewish underground movements in Palestine. All these developments, of course, had built on the fundamental contribution of the prewar Zionist movement—the building up of the Yishuv by three generations of Zionist immigrants."[18]

Footnotes

[1] David Margolick, "Postwar Pogrom," *New York Times*, July 23, 2006 (http://www.nytimes.com/2006/07/23/books/review/23margolick.html)

[2] Alex Grobman, "From the Holocaust to the Establishment of the State of Israel" (9 Aftermath), Museum of Tolerance (http://motlc.wiesenthal.com/site/pp.asp?c=gvKVLcMVIuG&b=394681)

[3] *Ibid.*

[4] *Ibid.*

[5] *Ibid.*

[6] *Ibid.*

[7] *Ibid*

[8] *Ibid.*

[9] *Ibid.*

[10] *Ibid.*

[11] *Ibid.*

[12] *Ibid.*

[13] *Ibid.*

[14] I want to address the claim made by many of Israel's detractors that the Haganah, Irgun and Lehi were no different than the myriad of Palestinian Arab and Islamic terror groups that have been operating since the 1950s. These people like to repeat the slogan: "That one man's terrorist, is another man's freedom fighter."

One man's terrorist is not another man's freedom fighter. I draw a very clear distinction between the type of violence that the Jewish undergrounds used in the 1945-1948 battles against the British and the Arabs, and the terrorism of Hamas, Islamic Jihad, Al Aqsa Martyr Brigades, Tanzim, etc. of today.

In today's world almost everything related to morality has become subjective. What once was considered a crime is now someone's line of work. What was once considered deviant behavior is now merely one's lifestyle. Immorality and deviant behavior are no longer acceptable terms in today's culture. What constitutes an act of terror or terrorism has also been redefined and is considered to be a subjective term or concept. The phrase "One man's terrorist is another man's freedom fighter" has been quoted by many a political spokesman and university political science professor and repeated so often in print and on TV that it is fair to assume that most people probably accept this as a truth or as a new norm described by Senator Daniel Patrick Moynihan in *Defining Deviancy Down*.

Morality and uncivilized behavior is not a subjective concept; and that terrorism is most certainly not freedom fighting. A basic part of the Orwellian nightmare can be detected in today's society. The meaning of words has been perverted when we say a terrorist is a freedom fighter. The way we define words determines how we interpret and define events, news and history. If terms lose all objective meaning, then it becomes impossible to judge and evaluate the actions of an individual, group, nation or government. No one side can ever be right or wrong because everything is considered to be subjective.

Therefore, morality is not subjective; that words and terms do in fact have very clear and objective definitions, and that, in fact, there are actions that are inherently immoral and cannot be justified because the cause is just. There are very forthright definitions that clearly distinguish the differences between a soldier, guerrilla fighter, terrorist and freedom fighter, all who are connected with armed conflict. It must be clearly understood that:

a) Murder, as opposed to killing as a result of armed conflict between combatants, constitutes criminal behavior.

b) Unfortunately, the killing of people clearly is one of the goals of armed conflict. A soldier killing an enemy soldier in war is not a criminal murderer, but he may be a state sanctioned killer. If that same soldier captures an enemy soldier and then kills him, he has committed murder, since he killed an unarmed captive.

b) The killing and maiming of unarmed civilians as a goal of an operation, as opposed to unarmed civilians being killed because they are unfortunately in the proximity of a military target, is murder.

c) Targeting and the premeditated killing of unarmed civilians who clearly are not part of an army or fighting force, and who are clearly not in or part of an army or any other form of fighting forces base or headquarters, is a criminal and immoral act of murder.

Based on these four assumptions, it becomes clear that it is only the terrorist who specifically murders innocent non-combatant civilians to further his agenda.

1. Soldier

Soldiers serve in a sovereign state's armed military force. They work for their country, wear their country's uniform and insignia, and are bound to that country's laws, military codes and ideals. Furthermore, all soldiers, in theory, are held to a standard called the Geneva Convention, which outlines what countries consider to be the rules for state-sponsored armed conflict or war. A soldier operates on orders received from superior officers and ultimately through the chain of command from the head of that state. Hence, all actions taken by a soldier reflect a given government policy. Soldiers' actions are held up to the standards of his/her country, as well as those of the international community as a whole. In the past, soldiers and even entire armies have violated all the norms of society. The Nazi SS 70 years ago, and more recently many soldiers of the Serbian Army, have done just that. But when this occurs an outcry in the international community against such behavior leads to soldiers and their leaders being brought up on charges as war criminals.

2. Guerrilla Fighter

There are two types of guerrilla fighters:

a) Soldiers in a state-sponsored military/army organized into small units who fight behind enemy lines and who use tactics that are considered unconventional. These include: surprise attacks deep inside enemy territory, not operating out of regular bases, living off the land, and hiding "in-country" for long periods of times. In armies they are generally referred to as special forces or commando units. (Green Berets, Navy Seals, etc.) The targets of these units are military; unarmed civilians are not targeted.

b) Underground militia that do not represent an official state but rather an ethnic group fighting for a state, or a group with a distinct political or religious ideology with an agenda they are willing to be violent for. These groups use the same tactics and methods that army commando units do, but they do not represent a state military, they are not bound as an army commando unit is by the same laws, codes, discipline and international scrutiny. The targets of these forces are military, not unarmed civilians. (Haganah pre-1948 Israel.)

3. Terrorist

A terrorist belongs to a militia that does not abide by the norms of war as outlined in the Geneva Convention. A terrorist does not want to clearly separate himself from civilians. Rather, he wants to blend in with civilians so as to be able to use violence for a distinct political or religious ideology. What separates the terrorist from the guerrilla is the willful and calculated choice to use force/violence as a weapon against specifically unarmed nonmilitary related civilians. A terrorist does not choose military targets; he specifically wants to kill and maim as many as possible of his enemy's unarmed civilians while they are engaged in non-military/normal day-to-day activities. "Terrorism is the deliberate and systematic murder, maiming and menacing of the innocent to inspire fear for political ends." Terrorists are trained to kill unarmed civilians while they are riding buses, shopping in stores or malls, driving their cars, working, attending school, movies or sporting events. In short, they consider anyone belonging to their adversary's universe the enemy and legitimate target—infant, child, handicapped person, are all equally targeted for death and destruction. (Al Aqsa Martyrs Brigades: Affiliated with the Palestinian Authority that took responsibility for dozens of suicide bombings in Israel 2001-2002, as well as dozens of drive-by shootings that continue to the present day; Hamas: firing rockets at Israeli schools, hospitals, civilian dwellings, using suicide bombers to attack shopping centers, buses, restaurants; Hezbollah: firing rockets into dozens of Israeli cities attempting to hit as many civilian targets as possible as in the 2006 Second Lebanon War.)

We live in a world where armed conflict has been part of our history since the dawn of time. Obviously, the world would be a better place if there were no wars and people were able to solve their differences peacefully. That has not been the case, and we have to come to accept the fact that there will be continued armed conflict between nations and groups. However, there are differences between levels of violence, methods and targets. Within the context of war and armed struggle there is a notion of acceptable and moral behavior and unacceptable, immoral behavior. I reject the moral equivalency argument that all killing is murder, and hence there can be no differentiation between those who participate in armed conflict/wars. There are clearly moral and practical differences between a soldier, guerrilla and terrorist. Finally, I reject the notion that one man's terrorist is another man's freedom fighter. By definition, a terrorist is one who operates against all the ideals of freedom, morality and civilized behavior.

[15] *Op. cit.*

[16] *Op. cit*

[17] *Op. cit*

[18] *Op. cit.*

Chapter 8

The UN Partition and its Aftermath

PRELUDE

In February of 1947 the United Nations (UN) received its first serious challenge. But two years old, full of idealism and promise, the UN was confronted for the first time with what would become the never-ending Middle East problem. A special committee, called the United Nations Special Commission on Palestine (UNSCOP), representing eleven UN members* considered to be relatively impartial to the Arab-Israeli conflict, was created. The job of UNSCOP. was to investigate the goings on in and around Palestine and then recommend a viable course of action.

Following the model set by the Peel Commission in 1936-1937, UNSCOP arrived in Mandate Palestine prepared to hear testimony and to visit many Jewish and Arab villages and settlements. But there were three major differences with this commission: 1) This time an outside international group investigated the Mandate; it was not an internal British affair; 2) the Peel Commission had only the power to recommend to the British government; UNSCOP had the power to recommend a solution that the UN could vote on as in a binding arbitration case, and 3) this time the investigation was not limited to Mandate Palestine. Commission members also traveled to surrounding Arab countries, European DP camps and the detention centers in Cyprus.

---

*Australia, Canada, Czechoslovakia, Guatemala, India, Iran, Netherlands, Peru, Sweden, Uruguay and Yugoslavia. "Report of UNSCOP - 1947: September 1, 1947," Mideast Web (http://www.mideastweb.org/unscop1947.htm)

Both the *Yishuv* and the Palestinian Arab leadership were given the opportunity to have special representatives be part of the UNSCOP process and present their side of the story.

While the Jewish Agency and the Jewish National Council cooperated with UNSCOP in its deliberations, the Arab Higher Committee charged UNSCOP with being pro-Zionist, and decided to boycott it. It announced a one-day general strike to protest its arrival, and Arab opposition figures were threatened with death if they spoke to UNSCOP. It first heard evidence from two British representatives and the head of the Jewish Agency's Political Department, Moshe Shertok, who submitted documents and were questioned by the committee's members.

From June 18 to July 3, the committee embarked on a tour of Palestine, visiting Jerusalem, Haifa, the Dead Sea, Hebron, Beersheba, Gaza, Jaffa, the Galilee, Tel Aviv, Acre, Nablus, Beit Dajan, Tulkarm, Rehovot, Arab and Jewish settlements in the Negev, and several Jewish agricultural communities. When visiting Jewish areas, committee members were warmly welcomed. Jewish Agency officials also ensured that they met with Jews who spoke the native languages of committee members such as Swedish, Spanish, and Persian. By contrast, committee members were ignored and faced hostility in Arab areas. It then held 12 public hearings from July 4 to July 17, during which 31 representatives from 12 Jewish organizations gave testimony and submitted written depositions, totaling thirty-two tons of material. Jewish Agency representatives such as David Ben-Gurion, Moshe Shertok, and Abba Eban testified, along with Chaim Weizmann, a former senior Zionist official who held no office at the particular time and testified as a private citizen. Anti-Zionist Jewish representatives from the Palestine Communist Party and Ichud party were included.

Despite the Arab boycott, several Arab officials and intellectuals privately met committee members, among them AHC member and former Jerusalem mayor Husayn al-Khalidi.[1]

By the end of August 1947 the committee had a report ready for the United Nations General Assembly. Below is the introductory statement of the UNSCOP findings:

1. The Committee held a series of informal discussions during its deliberations in Geneva as a means of appraising comprehensively the numerous aspects of the Palestine problem. In these discussions the members of the Committee debated at length and in great detail the various proposals advanced for its solution.

2. In the early stages of the discussions, it became apparent that there was little support for either of the solutions which would take an extreme position, namely, a single independent State of Palestine, under either Arab or Jewish domination. It was clear, therefore, that there was no disposition in the Committee to support in full the official proposals of either the Arab States or the Jewish Agency as described in Chapter IV of this report. It was recognized by all members that an effort must be made to find a solution which would avoid meeting fully the claims of one group at the expense of committing grave injustice against the other.

3. At its forty-seventh meeting on 27 August 1947, the Committee formally rejected both of the extreme solutions. In taking, this action the Committee was fully aware that both Arabs and Jews advance strong claims to rights and interests in Palestine, the Arabs by virtue of being for centuries the indigenous and preponderant people there, and the Jews by virtue of historical association with the country and international pledges made to them respecting their rights in it. But the Committee also realized that the crux of the Palestine problem is to be found in the fact that two sizeable groups, an Arab population of over 1,200,000 and a Jewish population of over 600,000, with intense nationalist aspirations, are diffused throughout a country that is arid, limited in area, and poor in all essential resources. It was relatively easy to conclude, therefore, that since both groups steadfastly maintain their claims, it is manifestly impossible, in the circumstances, to

satisfy fully the claims of both groups, while it is indefensible to accept the full claims of one at the expense of the other.

4. Following the rejection of the extreme solutions in its informal discussions, the Committee devoted its attention to the binational State and cantonal proposals. It considered both, but the members who may have been prepared to consider these proposals in principle were not impressed by the workability of either. It was apparent that the binational solution, although attractive in some of its aspects, would have little meaning unless provision were made for numerical or political parity between the two population groups, as provided for in the proposal of Dr. J. L. Magnes. This, however, would require the inauguration of complicated mechanical devices which are patently artificial and of dubious practicality.

5. The cantonal solution, under the existing conditions of Arab and Jewish diffusion in Palestine, might easily entail an excessive fragmentation of the governmental processes, and in its ultimate result, would be quite unworkable.

6. Having thus disposed of the extreme solutions and the binational and cantonal schemes, the members of the Committee, by and large, manifested a tendency to move toward either partition qualified by economic unity, or a federal State plan. In due course, the Committee established two informal working groups, one on partition under a confederation arrangement and one on the federal State, for the purpose of working out the details of the two plans, which in their final form are presented in Chapters VI and VII of this report, with the names of the members who supported them.

7. As a result of the work done in these working groups, a substantial measure of unanimity with regard to a number of important issues emerged, as evidenced in the forty seventh meeting of the Committee. On the basis of this measure of agreement, a drafting subcommittee was appointed to formulate specific texts.

8. In the course of its forty-ninth meeting on 29 August 1947, the Committee considered the report of the drafting subcommittee, and unanimously approved eleven

recommendations to the General Assembly, the texts of which are set forth in section A of this chapter. A twelfth recommendation, with which the representatives of Guatemala and Uruguay were not in agreement, appears in section B. Section A. Recommendations approved unanimously.[2]

It is clear that the UNSCOP committee weighed all possibilities including the unrealistic idea of a bi-national state, something the Peel Commission looked into in 1937 and also concluded was unrealistic and even dangerous. Hence, once again, the idea of partition was brought up as the only solution to the Jewish/Arab conflict.

To recap, in 1922 the British unilaterally partitioned Mandate Palestine that was allotted to them by the League of Nations by cutting off seventy-seven percent and creating the new country of Transjordan. The idea was to appease Haj Amin al Husseini, who was to become the Grand Mufti. Keep in mind the Arab world had been promised most of the Arabian desert, Mesopotamia (Iraq) and Syria by the British post-World War I, all of which had been run by the Ottoman Turks, all areas where there had been no Arab independent states since 1072. Transjordan was a bonus, a bribe at the expense of the Zionist Movement. As pointed out earlier, this did not work and led to the 1937 Peel Partition plan, which offered the Arabs of Mandate Palestine seventy-five percent of what was left after the 1922 Partition. Again, this was rejected out of hand by the Mufti, which led to the Arab Revolt, the 1939 White Paper and eventually to the 1947 UNSCOP Partition plan, which was the third partition plan for Mandate Palestine.

The Zionist leadership accepted, albeit reluctantly, the 1922 Partition and the 1937 offer of partition. It was clear they accepted that there was another entity that the Jews needed to take into account when it came to the Land of Israel The Zionist movement always recognized the reality that Arabs, but not necessarily as a special and unique sub-category called Palestinians, had a connection to the land. Hence, they were open to some compromise. The same cannot be said of the Arab world and certainly the Mufti. To them, the Zionists/Jews had no right to sovereignty in any part of the land of Mandate Palestine. This position did not change with the issuance of the UNSCOP recommendation.

Essentially, the report called for a two-state solution, a partition of Palestine into a Jewish state and an Arab state. The Jews would receive about fifty-two percent of the land—most of the Galil, the Coastal Plain and most of the Negev, basically, mostly desert—while the Arabs would receive forty-eight percent—part of the Galil, a small part of the coastal plain including what became the Gaza strip, Samaria and Judea. Both states would be in three sections. As far as Jerusalem was concerned, the UN plan saw this city remaining under the control of the UN as an international city. Both the Jews and the Arabs did not get what they wanted; both felt the plan was unfair—perhaps that itself was proof that the UN plan was really an attempt at a compromise.

The Partition Plan was scheduled to be voted on by November 29, 1947. In order for the plan to be adopted, two-thirds of the countries voting would have to vote in its favor. Though the leaders of the Zionist movement across the spectrum did not like this plan at all, they realized two very important aspects that it contained: a) it would officially end the British Mandate once and for all, and b) as bad as the boundaries were, it still would establish an independent Jewish State.

On November 29, 1947, every Jew in the *Yishuv*, in Cyprus, in DP camps and all over the world were glued to their radios counting the votes as they were cast by the UN members. One of the turning points was the surprising speech given by Andrei Gromyko, the USSR Ambassador to the UN. He spoke of the historical right of the Jewish people to have a state of their own. (This is one of the few times during the Cold War that the USSR and the U.S.A. were on the same side of an issue.) There were two main reasons that the USSR favored a Jewish State: 1) The fact that the Arab States were closely aligned with England meant that a vote for a Jewish State was a vote against the interests of England, who was considered an enemy of the USSR, and 2) the leaders of the *Yishuv* were overwhelmingly Socialist Zionists, which led the Russians to believe that the new Jewish State would probably be aligned politically with the USSR.

The final vote was thirty-three countries in favor of partition, ten abstained, and thireteen against. Thiry-three was more than two-thirds of forty-six, so the resolution passed! Every Arab State at the UN voted against the plan. England abstained.

It was clear that implementing this partition plan would be very difficult. Nevertheless, in Israel, there was euphoria. David Ben-Gurion, speaking on behalf of the Jewish Agency, accepted the resolution; the Arabs totally rejected it, with the Grand Mufti (though a war criminal, he was now residing in Egypt where he conspired to control Palestine) vowing to fight against it with all resources. It is very important to note that by accepting the 1947 partition resolution Israel de-facto recognized that there would be yet another Arab state in the Middle East, this one called Palestine. It was the Arabs who once again continued to play the dangerous game of double or nothing.

According to the provisions of the plan, the English, together with the UN, were to remain in Mandate Palestine for a short period; the exact amount of years is not mentioned, but the following language was used:

> A transitional period, however, would in all likelihood only serve to aggravate the present difficult situation in Palestine unless it were related to a specific and definitive solution which would go into effect immediately upon the termination of that period, and were to be of a positively stated duration, which, in any case, should not exceed a very few years.[3]

During that time the infrastructure of both states (Jewish and Arab) were to be built and their political and economic structures organized properly. It was also made clear that each state would have a minority of the others' population, with the Jewish State

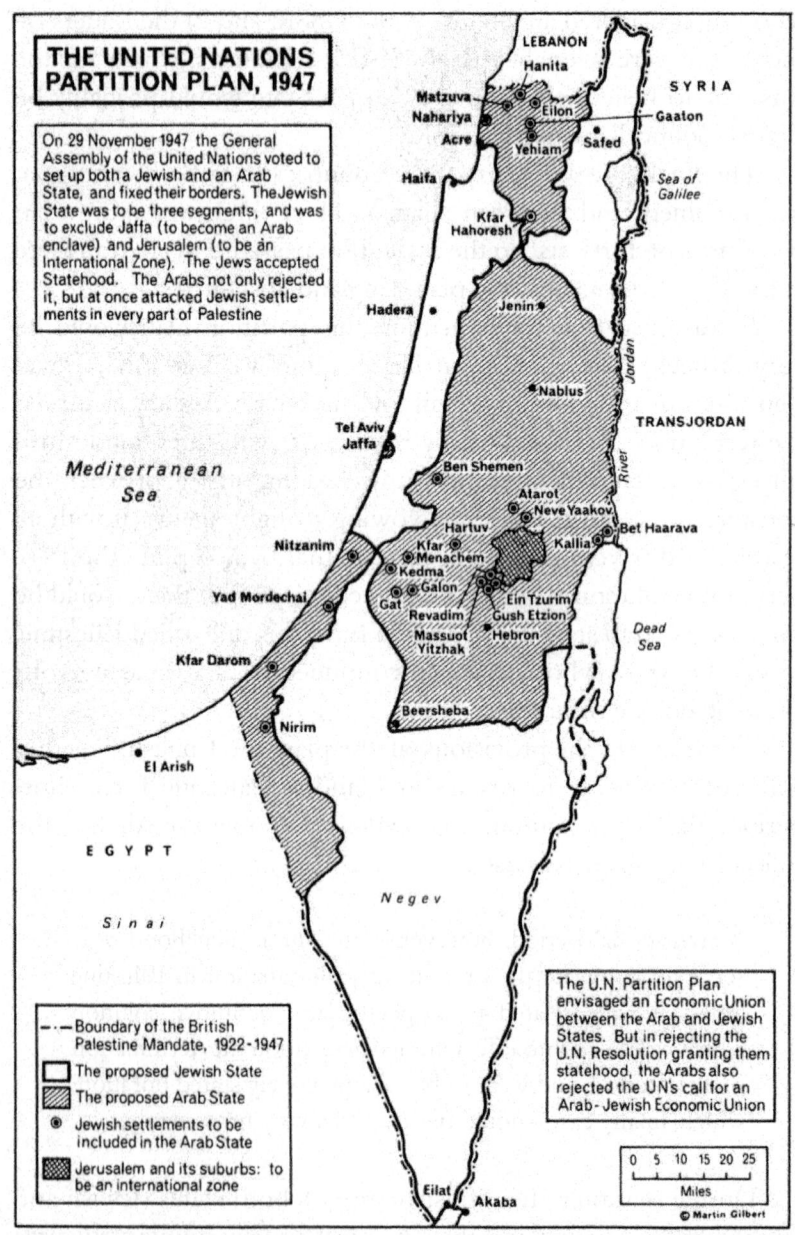

THE UNITED NATIONS PARTITION PLAN, 1947

On 29 November 1947 the General Assembly of the United Nations voted to set up both a Jewish and an Arab State, and fixed their borders. The Jewish State was to be three segments, and was to exclude Jaffa (to become an Arab enclave) and Jerusalem (to be an International Zone). The Jews accepted Statehood. The Arabs not only rejected it, but at once attacked Jewish settlements in every part of Palestine

LEBANON
Hanita
Matzuva
Nahariya
Acre
Haifa
Kfar Hahoresh
Hadera
Tel Aviv
Jaffa
Nitzanim
Yad Mordechai
Kfar Darom
Nirim
El Arish

Eilon
Yehiam
Safed
SYRIA
Gaaton
Sea of Galilee

Jenin
Nablus
TRANSJORDAN
Jordan River

Ben Shemen
Atarot
Neve Yaakov
Hartuv
Kfar Menachem
Kedma
Galon
Gat
Revadim
Massuot Yitzhak
Kallia
Bet Haarava
Ein Tzurim
Gush Etzion
Hebron
Dead Sea

Beersheba

Mediterranean Sea

EGYPT
Sinai
Negev

The U.N. Partition Plan envisaged an Economic Union between the Arab and Jewish States. But in rejecting the U.N. Resolution granting them statehood, the Arabs also rejected the UN's call for an Arab-Jewish Economic Union

- ·- Boundary of the British Palestine Mandate, 1922-1947
☐ The proposed Jewish State
▨ The proposed Arab State
⊛ Jewish settlements to be included in the Arab State
▨ Jerusalem and its suburbs: to be an international zone

Eilat Akaba

0 5 10 15 20 25
Miles
© Martin Gilbert

Sir Martin Gilbert, © 2010. Reproduced by permission of Taylor & Francis Books UK. www.martingilbert.com

having close to a forty percent Arab minority. In theory, by 1949 or early 1950, there would be two new states functioning side by side. The British, however, announced shortly after the adoption of the partition plan that they had no intention of staying on as "babysitters." As far as they were concerned, their job was done in Mandate Palestine; their only concern was packing up and going back to England. Hence, England announced that as of May 14, 1948, the British mandate in Palestine would come to an end. It would be on that date that they would lower the Union Jack for the last time and leave Palestine. England had no intention of helping establish two new independent states. If the UN wanted there to be a Jewish and Arab state in Palestine, it had best send a huge force to implement such a program, since the Arab world was overwhelmingly opposed to it. The UN, of course, was not prepared, nor did it have the resources to send such a force. The only real practical result of the November 29, 1947 UN vote was that it brought to an end Britain's 31-year control of Palestine.

CIVIL WAR IN ISRAEL (NOVEMBER 30, 1947 - MAY 14, 1948

In a sense, the Arab-Israeli conflict became an independent entity on November 30, 1947—from that day on it would be the Jews in Israel and the Arabs who would decide the future of the struggle, not the British nor the United States. The land of Israel was plunged into a civil war because the Arabs rejected partition totally and vowed to push the Jews into the sea. From that day on the future of the Zionist state would be determined by facts on the ground more than anything else. The Arabs had decided to make the question of ownership of land in Palestine a military question.

From November 30, 1947 to May 14,1948 the Arab war against the *Yishuv* was waged by the Mufti's men, a war of guerilla warfare, terrorism, sabotage, ambushes and planting bombs in Jewish civilian areas. The goal was to make life in the *Yishuv* a living hell, while the strategic goal was to cut off each Jewish settlement from the other, causing them to be abandoned or surrendered. The focal point of this war would be control of the roads of the Palestine

Mandate. Since neither side had an air force, all supplies were moved overland by truck. Control of the roads would determine which areas would be Jewish or Arab. Thus, the civil war became a war for control of all the major roads, with the most important road being the Tel-Aviv to Jerusalem highway. The overall goal was to physically destroy the *Yishuv* so that when May 14 arrived the Jews would not be in a position to declare an independent state.

What would make this war almost impossible to wage for the *Yishuv* was the fact that its forces were virtually unarmed! All the Jewish forces were undergrounds and illegal. The British, for their part, were (since 1939) affiliated with the Arabs throughout the Middle East, in particular Jordan, Iraq, Kuwait and all the small sheikdoms of the Persian Gulf. The British would not openly fight the Jews and prevent them from getting a state, but they would do everything in their power to insure that the Arab world, as a whole, would enjoy the upper hand in this already one-sided battle. Hence, the British, even as they were leaving Mandate Palestine, continued to enforce a strict embargo against all arms flowing to the Jews, and confiscated all ammunition that they could find in Jewish sectors. At the same time, the British openly sold huge quantities of ammunition to Jordan and Iraq, and turned a blind eye when neighboring Arab countries (notably Jordan) snuck in men and ammunition into the Mandate area to help the Arab irregular forces of the Mufti.

THE BATTLE FOR THE ROADS

The war itself would pit the undergrounds of the *Yishuv* (Haganah, Palmach, Irgun and Lehi) against the Arab irregular forces loyal to the Grand Mufti. The battleground was every Jewish area that the Arabs felt they could either conquer or isolate and force to surrender. But the one area that the Arab forces wanted to concentrate on was the Tel Aviv to Jerusalem road. At the time, the majority of the *Yishuv's* population was concentrated along the coast, and Jerusalem was an island of Jews surrounded by Arab villages up on the Judean Mountains. The total Jewish

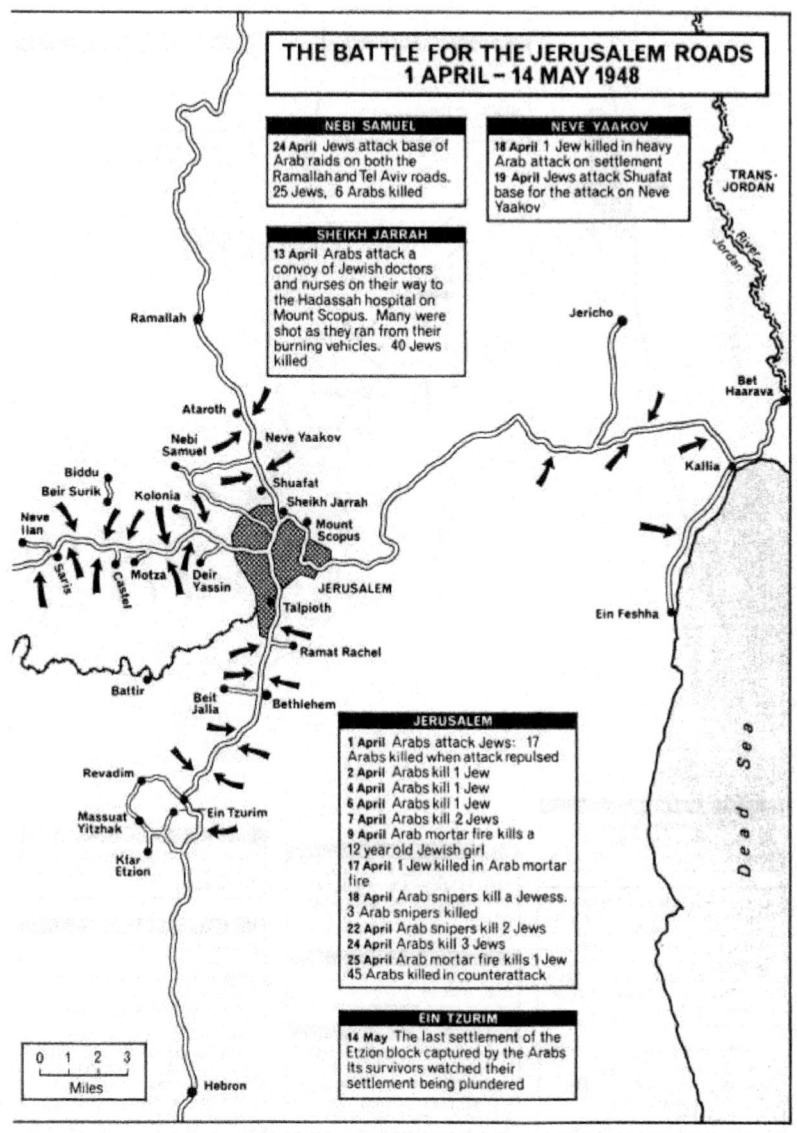

THE BATTLE FOR THE JERUSALEM ROADS
1 APRIL – 14 MAY 1948

NEBI SAMUEL
24 April Jews attack base of Arab raids on both the Ramallah and Tel Aviv roads. 25 Jews, 6 Arabs killed

NEVE YAAKOV
18 April 1 Jew killed in heavy Arab attack on settlement
19 April Jews attack Shuafat base for the attack on Neve Yaakov

SHEIKH JARRAH
13 April Arabs attack a convoy of Jewish doctors and nurses on their way to the Hadassah hospital on Mount Scopus. Many were shot as they ran from their burning vehicles. 40 Jews killed

JERUSALEM
1 April Arabs attack Jews: 17 Arabs killed when attack repulsed
2 April Arabs kill 1 Jew
4 April Arabs kill 1 Jew
6 April Arabs kill 1 Jew
7 April Arabs kill 2 Jews
9 April Arab mortar fire kills a 12 year old Jewish girl
17 April 1 Jew killed in Arab mortar fire
18 April Arab snipers kill a Jewess. 3 Arab snipers killed
22 April Arab snipers kill 2 Jews
24 April Arabs kill 3 Jews
25 April Arab mortar fire kills 1 Jew 45 Arabs killed in counterattack

EIN TZURIM
14 May The last settlement of the Etzion block captured by the Arabs. Its survivors watched their settlement being plundered

TRANS-JORDAN
River Jordan
Ramallah
Jericho
Bet Haarava
Ataroth
Nebi Samuel
Neve Yaakov
Kallia
Biddu
Beir Surik
Kolonia
Shuafat
Neve Ilan
Saris
Castel
Motza
Deir Yassin
Sheikh Jarrah
Mount Scopus
JERUSALEM
Talpioth
Ein Feshha
Battir
Beit Jalla
Ramat Rachel
Bethlehem
Revadim
Dead Sea
Massuat Yitzhak
Ein Tzurim
Klar Etzion
Hebron

0 1 2 3
Miles

Sir Martin Gilbert, © 2010. Reproduced by permission of Taylor & Francis Books UK. www.martingilbert.com

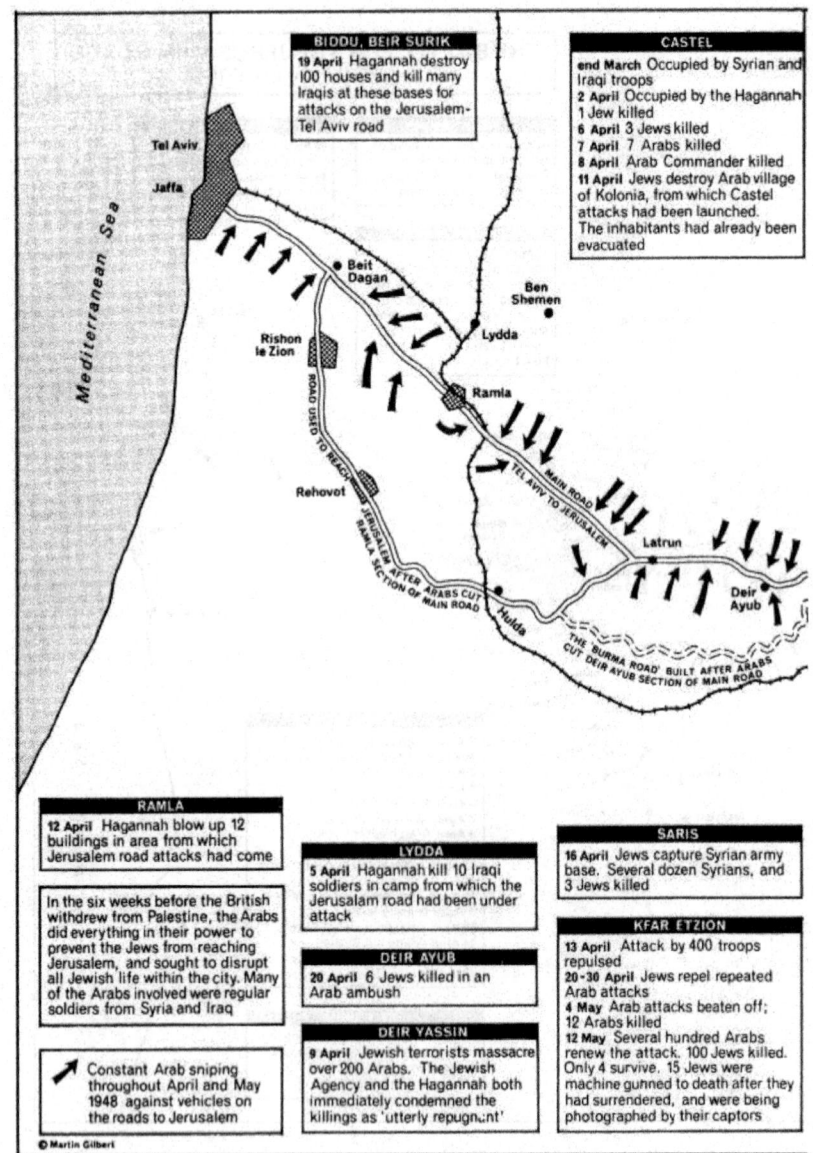

BIDDU, BEIR SURIK
19 April Hagannah destroy 100 houses and kill many Iraqis at these bases for attacks on the Jerusalem-Tel Aviv road

CASTEL
end March Occupied by Syrian and Iraqi troops
2 April Occupied by the Hagannah 1 Jew killed
6 April 3 Jews killed
7 April 7 Arabs killed
8 April Arab Commander killed
11 April Jews destroy Arab village of Kolonia, from which Castel attacks had been launched. The inhabitants had already been evacuated

RAMLA
12 April Hagannah blow up 12 buildings in area from which Jerusalem road attacks had come

In the six weeks before the British withdrew from Palestine, the Arabs did everything in their power to prevent the Jews from reaching Jerusalem, and sought to disrupt all Jewish life within the city. Many of the Arabs involved were regular soldiers from Syria and Iraq

Constant Arab sniping throughout April and May 1948 against vehicles on the roads to Jerusalem

LYDDA
5 April Hagannah kill 10 Iraqi soldiers in camp from which the Jerusalem road had been under attack

DEIR AYUB
20 April 6 Jews killed in an Arab ambush

DEIR YASSIN
9 April Jewish terrorists massacre over 200 Arabs. The Jewish Agency and the Hagannah both immediately condemned the killings as 'utterly repugnant'

SARIS
16 April Jews capture Syrian army base. Several dozen Syrians, and 3 Jews killed

KFAR ETZION
13 April Attack by 400 troops repulsed
20-30 April Jews repel repeated Arab attacks
4 May Arab attacks beaten off; 12 Arabs killed
12 May Several hundred Arabs renew the attack. 100 Jews killed. Only 4 survive. 15 Jews were machine gunned to death after they had surrendered, and were being photographed by their captors

© Martin Gilbert

population of the *Yishuv* was about 600,000, and 80,000 of them were in Jerusalem. In addition to the size of the Jewish population of Jerusalem, the Arabs recognized its religious, historical and symbolic significance to the Jews. They theorized that if their forces could cut off Jerusalem and capture it, they could probably so demoralize their enemy that they might not declare a state once the British left.

Traveling east from Tel-Aviv towards Jerusalem, one soon finds onself in Arab areas like the city of Ramla. From that point on the road begins to climb into the Judean hills—a 3,000 foot climb. At the time it was a narrow road, barely one lane in each direction, and on both sides of the road were Arab villages that dominated the mountain tops. The terrain in this area clearly favored Arab forces. To top it all off, all over the Mandate the British Army and police did their best to coordinate their departures from strategically located forts with the arrival of Arab forces, in particular the British-trained and led Arab Legion of Jordan. In the Ayalon Valley, for instance, where the Coastal Plain ends and the Judean Mountains begin, the British built Latrun, a fort to control this vital axis point. Latrun was handed over to the Arab Legion.

Under these conditions the civil war began. The Jewish forces were at a serious disadvantage, with the Arab forces having the open support of the surrounding Arab countries, as well as the tacit support of England. Finally, the terms of the battle also favored the Arab forces, as they were on the offensive and the Jews on the defensive.

The war began with Arab assaults on all the major roads in Israel that linked Jewish towns. All over Mandate Palestine the forces of the Mufti attacked Jewish vehicles on the main highways that linked one Jewish city to the next, such as the Tel-Aviv to Haifa road, Haifa to Tsfat road, Tsfat to Teveriya, and of course the Tel-Aviv to Jerusalem road, the most important road of all. Together with the pressure on the roads, there began to be attacks on the isolated Jewish towns that were surrounded by Arab villages throughout all of Mandate Palestine. But to the Arabs' surprise and to the surprise of the British, Jewish forces held their own. While there was a great deal of damage done to Jewish property, and the Jews suffered many casualties, especially in the Jerusalem area, no settlements were captured and no roads were really effectively cut off by the Arabs. As a matter of fact, the Arab forces found themselves suffering many more casualties than they had expected. Furthermore, during this period, the Irgun and Lechi stepped up their reprisal raids against the Arabs; every time there was an Arab terrorist bombing of Jews (and there were many in the weeks following the November 29, 1947 UN partition vote) either the Irgun or Lehi responded with a bombing of their own aimed at Arab civilians. The Haganah condemned these Jewish reprisals and labeled them terrorist attacks. This further exasperated the already tense relationship that existed between the Haganah, Irgun and Lechi.

THE BATTLE FOR JERUSALEM AND THE LAST DAYS OF THE BRITISH MANDATE

By late February 1948 most of the Arab forces in Mandate Palestine were concentrating on sealing off the road to Jerusalem and keeping the 80,000+ Jews living there under siege. Since early December 1947, the Arab forces had cut off the water and electricity of Jewish Jerusalem (the Western part of the city) and kept Jewish vehicles from resupplying the city from the Tel Aviv coastal area. The British, for their part, were interested in packing up and leaving and were not going to officially get involved in the Arab-Jewish conflict. However, as was mentioned earlier, the British did try to transfer strategic positions to the Jordanian Arab Legion whenever they could.

The initial response of the Jews to the siege of Jerusalem was to try to break the siege by employing convoys of armored trucks manned by armed members of the Palmach and Haganah. Large numbers of vehicles were gathered in the Tel-Aviv area and loaded with supplies, with the heaviest vehicle in the lead. They would then drive straight up the road to Jerusalem hoping to break the siege. The strategy here was very simple: Go straight at the Arabs strength vs. strength. This tactic was partially successful; some supplies did reach the city of Jerusalem, enough to barely keep the city alive and full of hope. But there was a very high price to pay. Dozens of soldiers were killed and hundreds wounded from these convoys, and most of the supplies never made it to the city. In addition, more and more of these armored vehicles were destroyed. (It should be noted that throughout this period all the Jewish forces were technically illegal and certainly all the arms were illegal as well. The British were arresting Haganah, Palmach, Irgun and Lehi members and confiscating ammunition until the day they left. All the armored vehicles used in the convoys to Jerusalem were civilian vehicles that were armored illegally, and at that time constituted the Jewish forces only form of heavy armor.) This strategy could not offer the Jews a victory of any sort; at best it could delay an Arab victory in the Jerusalem area. But, by its very nature religiously, historically and emotionally there was no way the leadership of the Jewish Agency could have allowed the fall of Jerusalem!

In early April 1948 Ben-Gurion, as Executive Director of the Jewish Agency, made a very crucial and historical decision: Jewish forces would now attempt to capture the road to Jerusalem, and that meant controlling both sides of the road as well—at least a mile or two on each side of the road. For the first time in the history of the Arab-Israeli conflict, and for the first time in the history of the Modern Zionist movement, Jews were going to go on the offensive and take by force Arab territory. This was an extremely important decision since it would be fulfilling what had long been part of Arab propganda, namely that the Zionist movement was dedicated to ousting the "native" Arabs of Palestine and settling "their land."

From the days of the First *Aliyah* in 1881 until April of 1948 the Jewish immigrants to *Eretz Yisrael* had purchased from Arab or Turkish landowners every acre of land that they settled on.

Furthermore, Jewish *olim* had made a point of not living where Arabs lived, rather they built brand new Jewish towns and villages with names like Rishon Le Tzion, Petach Tikva, Nes Tziona, Rosh Pina, Rechovot, etc. Almost all the Jewish settlements were built not only in areas that the Arabs did not inhabit, but in areas that the Arabs either did not want to live in or never considered developing—because of the poor quality of the area, i.e., swamps or deserts. If one looks at the map of Jewish and Arab villages in March of 1948 one would find that the Arabs lived for the most part in the same twelve cities and 500 villages they had lived in since 1882, and that the Jews had settled the Coastal Plain, the Eastern Galil and areas south and west of Jerusalem, as well as creating the new city of Jerusalem that for the most part was built to the west of the walled ancient "original" Jerusalem. Finally, and perhaps most important, the so called "Zionist Invasion" not only did not touch Arab inhabited areas, but it created a reality that attracted tens of thousands of Arabs to move to Palestine. In 1882 the Arab population of Turkish Palestine was about 350,000; sixty-five years later it stood at 1,100,000!

Ben-Gurion decided that the Jews must sadly end a decades-old trend of acquiring land peacefully. The reason was simple and clear: By April of 1948 the Arabs of Mandate Palestine and of the entire Middle East had made it clear in print, speech and action that it was now a zero-sum game. In Palestine there was only room for one state to be declared, and it would be an Arab one; there was no room for a Jewish state. The embryo of this Jewish state must be aborted!

If that was the case as the siege of Jerusalem made clear, the time had come to remind the Arab world that making war on the Jews, a centuries-old sport, was now governed by new rules: Now the Jews could and would make war against those who chose to make war against them. The Haganah and the Palmach received the orders to open the road to Jerusalem by capturing that entire corridor that stretched from the Coastal Plain up until the city of Jerusalem itself.

In April 1948, the Arab world was shocked to learn that in trying to dislodge the Jews from *Eretz Yisrael* it would be them who would pay the price of being pushed out of their Palestine. In a series of night-time attacks from west to east, named Operation Nachshon, the Palmach captured and emptied of its inhabitants two Arab cities (Ramla and Lod) and over two dozen Arab villages. By late April it was finally true and correct to say that the Zionists had pushed Arabs out of a part of Mandate Palestine and had taken over their villages.

Footnotes

1 https://en.wikipedia.org/wiki/United_Nations_Special_Committee_on_Palestine as dervied from "Report of UNSCOP - 1947: September 1, 1947," Mideast Web (http://www.mideastweb.org/unscop1947.htm); Benny Morris, *1948: A History of the First Arab-Israeli War* (New Haven: Yale, 2009); R. Judah Magnes Urges U.N. Committee to Recommend Bi-national State in Palestine, *JTA*, July 15, 1947 (http://www.jta.org/1947/07/15/archive/r-judah-magnes-urges-u-n-committee-to-recommend-bi-national-state-in-palestine); "Munists Ask Independent Jewish-arab State in Testimony Before U.N. Probers," *JTA*, July 14, 1947 (http://www.jta.org/1947/07/14/archive/munists-ask-independent-jewish-arab-state-in-testimony-before-u-n-probers)

2 "Report of UNSCOP - 1947: September 1, 1947," Mideast Web (http://www.mideastweb.org/unscop1947.htm)

3 *Ibid.*

Chapter 9

The Rebirth of the State of Israel

Deir Yassin was an Arab village closest to the entrance to Jerusalem. Like many other Arab towns along the road from Tel Aviv to Jerusalem, the townspeople participated in the attacks upon the armored convoys coming to West Jerusalem with vital supplies, including water and ammunition. Deir Yassin had 600 -750* inhabitants at the time.

The Irgun and Lehi finally had enough of these attacks and initiated Operation Nachshon on April 6, with the major attack on April 9. Approximately 120 fighters fought the battle. They met stiff resistance, and a house-to-house battle raged in the village for several hours. When the smoke cleared there were four dead Irgun fighters and thirty-seven wounded. The Arabs suffered one hundred and seven civilian dead, and thirteen Arab fighters killed (based on a study done at the Arab-founded Bir Zeit University in Judea.)[1]**

Yet this was not a battle of annihilation. An escape corridor created by the Irgun was used by two hundred Deir Yassin residents. When the battle was over, the Irgun rounded up the Arab civilians and fighters, trying to separate one group from the other. Some Arab fighters acted as if they were surrendering but then

---

*Sharif Kanani and Nihad Zitawi, "Deir Yassin," Monograph No.4, *Destroyed Palestinian Villages Documentation Project* (Bir Zeit: Documentation Center of Bir Zeit University, 1987), 67.

** A later study done at Bir Zeit University in 1998 suggests the numbers of Arab casualties may have been smaller. (Sharif Kanaana, "Reinterpreting Deir Yassin," Bir Zeit University, April 1998).

opened fire. Other Arab fighters tried to disguise themselves as female civilians. Upon being approached, one pulled out a weapon and killed the Irgun commander. As a result, some Irgun fighters opened fire on any Arabs they saw, since from their perspective they could not determine who was a civilian or a fighter and who had surrendered and who had not. As a consquence of the confusion, Arab civilians were killed in this operation, including some women and children.[2]

Immediately after the battle, the Irgun invited the Red Cross to investigate what happened at Deir Yassin. This was done to make sure that there would be no false reports or claims made by the Arab side. At the time, the *New York Times* reported that two hundred Arabs were killed, forty captured and seventy women and children released.

Instead of reporting facts, the Palestinian and Jordanian media wildly exaggerated what had happened. They described a huge massacre of hundreds of innocent Palestinian civilians in a quiet and serene Arab village that was viciously attacked by blood thirsty Zionist killers. They spoke of multiple rapes. Years later, Hazam Nusseibi, who worked for the Palestine Broadcasting Service in 1948, admitted being told by Hussein Khalidi, a Palestinian leader, to fabricate the atrocity claims: "This was our biggest mistake. We did not realize how our people would react. As soon as they heard that women had been raped at Deir Yassin, Palestinians fled in terror.[3]

The exaggerated claims frightened tens of thousands of Arabs to flee the Jerusalem Corridor and from other parts of Mandate Palestine.

Sensing that the story and myth of Deir Yassin could cause international political danger to the Jewish Agency, Ben-Gurion, the two chief rabbis, the Haganah and responsible Jewish leadership accused the attackers of the violation of the Jewish principle of purity of arms. Ben-Gurion also sent an apology letter to King Abdullah of Jordan, who rejected the apology and warned that future actions like that one could cause serious consequences.

Four days after Deir Yassin, following a clearly premeditated plan, an unarmed convoy of Jewish doctors and nurses, headed for the besieged Hadassah Hospital on Mount Scopus was ambushed by the Mufti's men. They massacred and mutilated the bodies of seventy-deven Jews whose mission was to save lives. There were no condemnations of the massacre.

THE BEGINNING OF THE PALESTINIAN ARAB REFUGEE SELF-INFLICTED WOUND.

Five weeks after the attack, other Arab governments got involved in the crisis. Having exaggerated the realities of the Battle of Deir Yassin, the Arab media created a panic in many parts of Mandate Palestine. So while the Palmach created the first Palestinian refugees with their attacks on Arabs who ambushed the convoys, approximately 50,000 Arabs left Mandate Palestine during April and May because of Arab propaganda.

> In mid-April, units of the Golani Brigade captured the city of Tiberias. When they cut the city in two, isolating a major part of the Arab population, the Arabs chose to evacuate the city and, with the assistance of units of the British Army, were transported East to Jordan.[4]

At the same time there would be an even larger more disastrous, (from a Palestinian perspective) exodus. While some were battling in the Jerusalem Corridor, Jewish underground troops and Arab forces were facing off in the Galil and in the large coastal city of Haifa. The Haganah, the main fighting force outside the Jerusalem area, was doing well against the Mufti's forces and troops from other Arab states.

At the end of the 19th century there were maybe one thousand residents in Haifa, by 1947 that number had ballooned to 145,000, comprising some 70,910 Arabs and 74,230 Jews.[5] Because the Arab media created a panic due to its fabricated stories of massacres and rapes in Deir Yassin, many Arabs from Haifa fled, even though the Zionist leadership pleaded with them to stay. As the British

District Superintendent of Police in Haifa commented in April 1948: "Every effort is being made by the Jews to persuade the Arab population to stay and carry on with their normal lives, to get their shops and businesses open and be assured that their lives and interests will be safe."[6]

To add insult to injury, most of the political and business leaders of the Arab Haifa community fled, leaving the community leaderless. By the end of April 1947 there were barely three thousand Arabs left in Haifa![7] In total, during the five and a half month Arab-initiated civil war in Mandate Palestine, 335,000 Palestinian Arabs had fled their homes. Most had fled to either Lebanon or parts of Judea and Samaria.[8] On November 29, 1947 there was not one Arab Palestinian refugee!

By the end of April 1948, the siege of Jerusalem had been broken. The Mufti's goal of terrorizing the Jews into leaving the budding state of Israel had failed. The first wave of Palestinian Arab refugees, one group pushed out by the Irgun and Palmach, and a far larger group who fled because of the lies broadcast by the Arab media, was now complete. The five-and-a-half month civil war was about to come to an end, and the British were poised to leave. Right before they did, there was one more battle to be fought before the Jews could declare an independent state. That was the Battle for Gush Etzion.

THE FALL OF GUSH ETZION

In the early 1940s four Jewish settlements were built south of Jerusalem in an area rich in biblical history: Kfar Etzion, Masuot Yitzchak, Ein Tzurim and Revadim. Based on the UN Partition Plan, these four settlements were in the area of the proposed Arab state. But since the Mufti and the Arab leadership rejected the partition plan, facts on the ground would determine the boundaries of each state. The population of Gush Etzion was determined to stay and become part of the Jewish state once the British left.

By January 1948, the Arab assaults on the Gush settlements and the siege of the roads leading to the Gush were so severe that women and children were evacuated, and only male volunteers stayed to defend the settlement. It was clear to the defenders that they were hopelessly outnumbered and cut off from other Jewish areas. They realized that their role was to act as a "lightning rod" to attract and pin down as many Arab fighters as possible, keeping those Arab fighters from participating in the siege of Jerusalem. They held out until May 13, the day before the British left and the State of Israel was re-established.

On May 13, 1948 a thousand local Arab fighters and members of the Arab Legion broke through the perimeter of Kfar Etzion and massacred the defenders. Gush Etzion fell. The Arab Legion took twohundred and sixty men and some women defenders as prisoners and brought them to Jordan, where they were kept in POW camps for eleven months.

The Gush defenders had done their job. By holding out until May 13, they had deprived the Arabs of having enough forces to strangle Jerusalem. Ben-Gurion said everyone in Israel owed a debt of gratitude to these defenders. When their mutilated bodies were brought to Jerusalem for burial, many Jews attended the funerals. Everyone knew that these people had sacrificed their lives for the sake of Jerusalem and the Jewish State. Gush Etzion fell on 4 Iyar 5708. That is why that day, the day before *Yom Ha'atzmaut*, Israel's Independence Day, was chosen to be Israel's Memorial Day, *Yom HaZikaron*.

To avoid a full scale invasion the day the British left, Ben-Gurion sent one of his most capable and smartest aides, Golda Meir (born in Russia, educated in the U.S.; made *Aliyah* in 1921), to secretly meet with King Abdullah of Jordan on May 11, 1948. Unfortunately, the meeting was a failure. King Abdullah made it clear he could not sit back as other Arab armies invaded for fear he would be branded a traitor and assassinated. His move was disastrous for both countries.

By May 14, 1948 Jewish forces maintained control of the major roads and captured the towns of Safed and Tiberias in the Upper

Galilee. But the most important achievement was the capture of the road to Jerusalem, though the battle for the Jerusalem Corridor continued after independence was declared and the Jewish State established. Enough supplies were brought in during April and May to keep Jerusalem alive and capable of holding back Arab forces.

The Arabs did not succeed in aborting the birth of a Jewish State, but they were still in control of seventy-five percent of the area that was Mandate Palestine. And just as the Jews were able to declare the State of Israel on twenty-five percent of the land they were once promised, the Mufti and the Arabs could have declared a State of Palestine on their seventy-five percent of the land, more than the UN promised them. But they chose not to, creating the meme of rejectionism of a two-state solution that persists today.

DECLARING A JEWISH STATE AFTER 1,878 YEARS OF DIASPORA

At 4:00 p.m., Friday May 14, 1948/5 of Iyar 5708, the British Empire's presence in Palestine came to an end, leaving a vacuum. In the last days of the British Mandate local Palestinian forces, with the help of some outside Arab troops, vowed to destroy the budding state and had five Arab armies waiting to attack.

As impressive as the Jewish military achievements were in the last days of the Mandate, it was against mostly guerilla forces and some organized Jordanian military units. The Jews were now facing five armies supplied with armor, artillery and air power. The Jews possessed nothing of the kind, and on average were controlling areas that were but four to five miles wide. There was nowhere to retreat and regroup.

The international community urged Ben-Gurion and the leaders of the Jewish Agency to give up the fantasy of an independent Jewish state because they would be instantly wiped off the map. It was suggested that the UN take over Palestine as a trusteeship until a permanent safe solution could be found. Ben-Gurion made it clear that after waiting 1,878 years, suffering countless expulsions, inquisitions, Crusades, pogroms and a Holocaust, it was time to declare a Jewish State. Ben-Gurion often said a Jew who does not believe in miracles is not a realist.

Against almost half the leadership of the Jewish Agency Ben-Gurion pushed for establishing a Jewish State as soon as the British exited. The only concession he was willing to make to the dangerous and seemingly hopeless reality was to declare the State from Tel-Aviv instead of Jerusalem, since it was too dangerous to bring the entire Jewish leadership of the *Yishuv* to the beleaguered city in the hills.

At 4:00 p.m. on May 14, as the British flag came down, the leadership of the *Yishuv* gathered at the Tel Aviv Museum. In an emotionally charged voice, Ben-Gurion read the Jewish Declaration of Independence. Citing the Jewish peoples' historical, religious, and spiritual connection to *Eretz Yisrael*, he declared the first independent Jewish State in almost 2,000 years, and that the state's name would be *Medinat Yisrael*. When he finished, Chief Rabbi Yehuda Leib Fishman (alss known as Yehuda Leib Hacohen Maimon) got up and, weeping, recited the *"Shehechiyanu"* blessing.

THE DECLARATION OF THE ESTABLISHMENT
OF THE STATE OF ISRAEL

ERETZ-ISRAEL [(Hebrew) - the Land of Israel, Palestine] was the birthplace of the Jewish people. Here their spiritual, religious and political identity was shaped. Here they first attained to statehood, created cultural values of national and universal significance and gave to the world the eternal Book of Books.

After being forcibly exiled from their land, the people kept faith with it throughout their Dispersion and never ceased to pray and hope for their return to it and for the restoration in it of their political freedom.

Impelled by this historic and traditional attachment, Jews strove in every successive generation to re-establish themselves in their ancient homeland. In recent decades they returned in their masses. Pioneers, ma'pilim [(Hebrew)— immigrants coming to Eretz-Israel in defiance of restrictive legislation] and defenders, they made deserts bloom, revived the Hebrew language, built villages and towns, and created a thriving community controlling its own economy and culture, loving peace but knowing how to defend itself, bringing the blessings of progress to all the country's inhabitants, and aspiring towards independent nationhood.

In the year 5657 (1897), at the summons of the spiritual father of the Jewish State, Theodore Herzl, the First Zionist Congress convened and proclaimed the right of the Jewish people to national rebirth in its own country.

This right was recognized in the Balfour Declaration of the 2nd November, 1917, and re-affirmed in the Mandate of the League of Nations which, in particular, gave international sanction to the historic connection between the Jewish people and Eretz-Israel and to the right of the Jewish people to rebuild its National Home.

The catastrophe which recently befell the Jewish people —the massacre of millions of Jews in Europe—was another clear demonstration of the urgency of solving the problem of its homelessness by re-establishing in Eretz-Israel the Jewish State, which would open the gates of the homeland wide to every Jew and confer upon the Jewish people the status of a fully privileged member of the comity of nations.

Survivors of the Nazi holocaust in Europe, as well as Jews from other parts of the world, continued to migrate to Eretz-Israel, undaunted by difficulties, restrictions and dangers, and never ceased to assert their right to a life of dignity, freedom and honest toil in their national homeland.

In the Second World War, the Jewish community of this country contributed its full share to the struggle of the freedom and peace-loving nations against the forces of Nazi wickedness and, by the blood of its soldiers and its war effort, gained the right to be reckoned among the peoples who founded the United Nations.

On the 29th November, 1947, the United Nations General Assembly passed a resolution calling for the establishment of a Jewish State in Eretz-Israel; the General Assembly required the inhabitants of Eretz-Israel to take such steps as were necessary on their part for the implementation of that resolution. This recognition by the United Nations of the right of the Jewish people to establish their State is irrevocable.

This right is the natural right of the Jewish people to be masters of their own fate, like all other nations, in their own sovereign State.

Accordingly we, members of the people's council, representatives of the Jewish community of Eretz-Israel and of the Zionist movement, are here assembled on the day of the termination of the British Mandate over Eretz-Israel and, by virtue of our natural and historic right and on the strength of the resolution of the United Nations General Assembly, hereby declare the establishment of a Jewish state in Eretz-Israel, to be known as the State of Israel.

WE DECLARE that, with effect from the moment of the termination of the Mandate being tonight, the eve of Sabbath, the 6th Iyar, 5708 (15th May, 1948), until the establishment of the elected, regular authorities of the State in accordance with the Constitution which shall be adopted by the Elected Constituent Assembly not later than the 1st October 1948, the People's Council shall act as a Provisional Council of State, and its executive organ, the People's Administration, shall be the Provisional Government of the Jewish State, to be called "Israel".

THE STATE OF ISRAEL will be open for Jewish immigration and for the Ingathering of the Exiles; it will foster the development of the country for the benefit of all its inhabitants; it will be based on freedom, justice and peace as envisaged by the prophets of Israel; it will ensure complete equality of social and political rights to all its inhabitants irrespective of religion, race or sex; it will guarantee freedom of religion, conscience, language, education and culture; it will safeguard the Holy Places of all religions; and it will be faithful to the principles of the Charter of the United Nations.

THE STATE OF ISRAEL is prepared to cooperate with the agencies and representatives of the United Nations in implementing the resolution of the General Assembly of the 29th November, 1947, and will take steps to bring about the economic union of the whole of Eretz-Israel.

WE APPEAL to the United Nations to assist the Jewish people in the building-up of its State and to receive the State of Israel into the comity of nations.

WE APPEAL—in the very midst of the onslaught launched against us now for months—to the Arab inhabitants of the State of Israel to preserve peace and participate in the upbuilding of the State on the basis of full and equal citizenship and due representation in all its provisional and permanent institutions.

WE EXTEND our hand to all neighbouring states and their peoples in an offer of peace and good neighbourliness, and appeal to them to establish bonds of cooperation and mutual help with the sovereign Jewish people settled in its own land. The State of Israel is prepared to do its share in a common effort for the advancement of the entire Middle East.

WE APPEAL to the Jewish people throughout the Diaspora to rally round the Jews of Eretz-Israel in the tasks of immigration and upbuilding and to stand by them in the great struggle for the realization of the age-old dream—the redemption of Israel.

PLACING OUR TRUST IN THE "ROCK OF ISRAEL", WE AFFIX OUR SIGNATURES TO THIS PROCLAMATION AT THIS SESSION OF THE PROVISIONAL COUNCIL OF STATE, ON THE SOIL OF THE HOMELAND, IN THE CITY OF TEL-AVIV, ON THIS SABBATH EVE, THE 5TH DAY OF IYAR, 5708 (14TH MAY,1948).*

---

* Published in the Official Gazette, No. 1 of the 5th, Iyar, 5708 (14th May, 1948).

David Ben-Gurion

Daniel Auster

Mordekhai Bentov

Yitzchak Ben Zvi

Eliyahu Berligne

Fritz Bernstein

Rabbi Wolf Gold

Meir Grabovsky

Yitzchak Gruenbaum

Dr. Abraham Granovsky

Eliyahu Dobkin

Meir Wilner-Kovner

Zerach Wahrhaftig

Herzl Vardi

Rachel Cohen

Rabbi Kalman Kahana

Saadia Kobashi

Rabbi Yitzchak Meir Levin

Meir David Loewenstein

Zvi Luria

Golda Myerson

Nachum Nir

Zvi Segal

R. Yehuda Leib Hacohen

Fishman

David Zvi Pinkas

Aharon Zisling

Moshe Kolodny

Eliezer Kaplan

Abraham Katznelson

Felix Rosenblueth

David Remez

Berl Repetur

Mordekhai Shattner

Ben Zion Sternberg

Bekhor Shitreet

Moshe Shapira

Moshe Shertok

The Israeli Declaration of Independence encapsulates all the basic ideas of the Zionist Movement. It begins by speaking of the biblical and historical connection between the Jewish nation with the land of Israel from ancient times to the present. It then continues by telling the story of the Jewish nation's attachment to the land throughout the years of the long Diaspora, and the story of the Modern Zionist movement. It speaks of the effect that the Holocaust had on the Jewish nation and that even the British restrictions did not stop the influx of Jews into their homeland. It says that since the Jews of Mandate Palestine—*the Yishuv*—had its own combat unit in the Jewish Brigade, an "Allied Force," under the charter of the UN they were entitled their own sovereign state.

The document speaks of the right of the Jewish nation to reestablish sovereignty in its ancestral homeland, *Eretz Yisrael*, and declares the reborn state *Medinat Yisrael*, and appeals to the UN and the nations of the world to recognize *Medinat Yisrael*.

The Jewish people in the Diaspora are then asked to support *Medinat Yisrael* in a variety of ways. *Medinat Yisrael* extends its hand in peace both to the Arabs living in its boundaries and to its neighboring Arab states. The document ends with the Zionist leadership placing its trust in the Almighty. The name used in the document was *"Tzur Yisrael,"* which means the Rock of Israel, one of the many Hebrew names for the Almighty.

Thanks to the lobbying efforts of Chaim Weizmann, U.S. President Harry S. Truman recognized the new Jewish State shortly after it was declared, even though most of his advisors were against such a move. In the streets of Tel Aviv and around the reborn Jewish State people were dancing and singing. But this euphoria was to be short-lived. One hour after Ben-Gurion declared Israel's independence, the five Arab armies that had been lying in wait invaded.

MAY 14 1948 - JANUARY 1949 - ISRAEL'S WAR OF INDEPENDENCE
MAY 14 – JUNE 1, 1948

The War of Independence began in earnest when the Egyptian Air Force bombed Tel Aviv one hour after the declaration of *Medinat Israel*. And then the Lebanese, Syrian, Iraqi, Jordanian and Egyptian armies attacked with the goal of annihilating the Jewish State and committing genocide, as announced by the Mufti and all Arab leadership and clerics.

During the first week of May 1948, the chiefs of staff of the five invading armies convened in Damascus to approve the invasion plans. King Abdullah of Jordan was chosen as commander-in-chief...in name only. Each army had its own strategy. The Lebanese Army was to capture the Northwestern coast of Israel, up to the city of Naharia. The Syrian Army was to attack along the Sea of Galilee to conquer and occupy the entire Galilee. The Iraqi Army was to invade from the South of the Sea of Galilee and grab the northern coastal center of Israel up to Netanya. But since

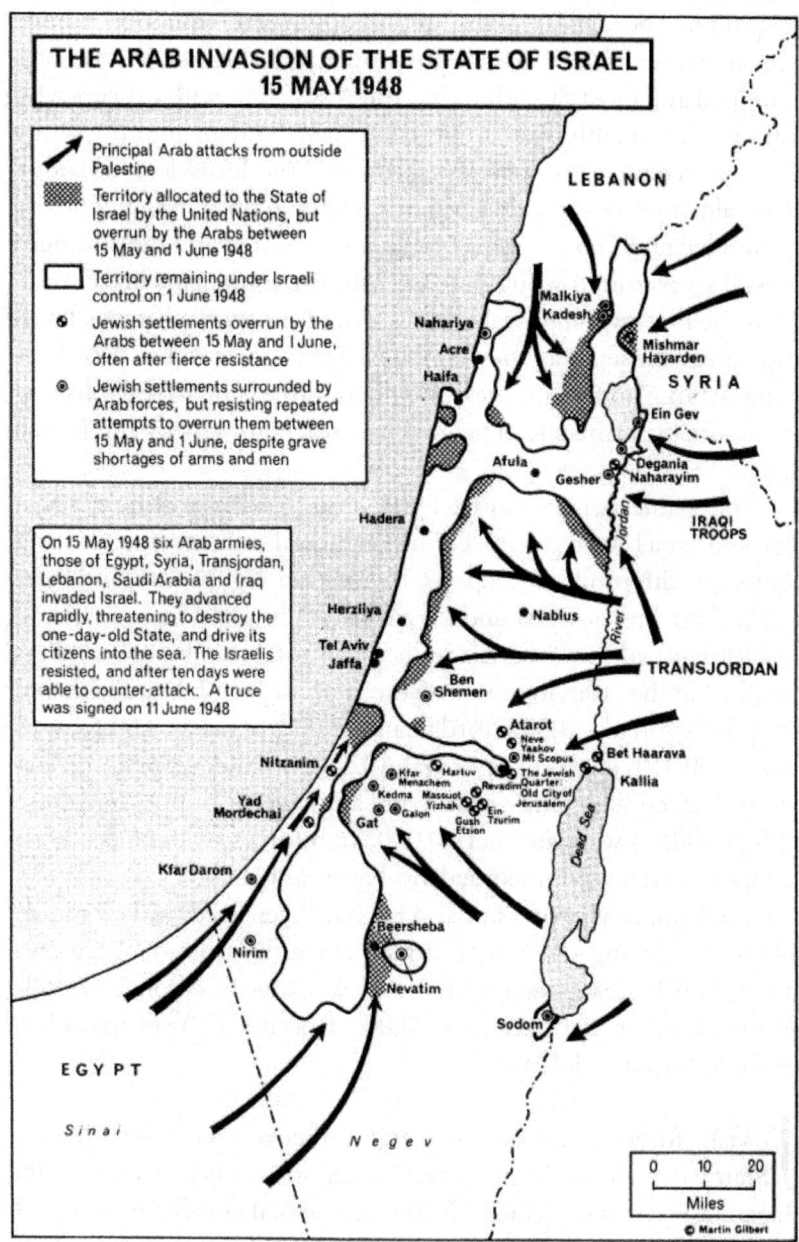

THE ARAB INVASION OF THE STATE OF ISRAEL
15 MAY 1948

Principal Arab attacks from outside Palestine

Territory allocated to the State of Israel by the United Nations, but overrun by the Arabs between 15 May and 1 June 1948

Territory remaining under Israeli control on 1 June 1948

Jewish settlements overrun by the Arabs between 15 May and I June, often after fierce resistance

Jewish settlements surrounded by Arab forces, but resisting repeated attempts to overrun them between 15 May and 1 June, despite grave shortages of arms and men

On 15 May 1948 six Arab armies, those of Egypt, Syria, Transjordan, Lebanon, Saudi Arabia and Iraq invaded Israel. They advanced rapidly, threatening to destroy the one-day-old State, and drive its citizens into the sea. The Israelis resisted, and after ten days were able to counter-attack. A truce was signed on 11 June 1948

LEBANON

Malkiya
Kadesh
Nahariya
Acre
Mishmar Hayarden
Haifa
SYRIA
Ein Gev
Afula
Degania Naharayim
Gesher
IRAQI TROOPS
Hadera
Herziliya
Nablus
Tel Aviv
Jaffa
Ben Shemen
TRANSJORDAN
Atarot
Neve Yaakov
Mt Scopus
Bet Haarava
Nitzanim
Kfar Menachem
Hartuv
The Jewish Quarter Old City of Jerusalem
Kallia
Kedma
Revadim
Massuot
Yad Mordechai
Galon
Yizhak
Ein Tzurim
Gush Etzion
Gat
Kfar Darom
Dead Sea
Beersheba
Nirim
Nevatim
Sodom
EGYPT
Sinai
Negev

| 0 | 10 | 20 |
Miles

© Martin Gilbert

Sir Martin Gilbert, © 2010. Reproduced by permission of Taylor & Francis Books UK. www.martingilbert.com

Iraq did not border Israel the areas it conquered would be handed over to Syria and Jordan. The Jordanian Arab Legion was the best equipped and most disciplined of the Arab units, with officers who were predominantly British. It was to take Samaria and the entire Tel Aviv region, as well as Jerusalem and the Jerusalem Corridor. It would then occupy that region. The Egyptian Army, coming from Sinai and Gaza, was to conquer the Negev and the southern coastal areas until it would link up with the Jordanians in Tel Aviv. Thus the five invading Arab armies would carve up what was Israel and annex those areas they conquered into their states. Nowhere in the Arab plan of conquest was there discussion of establishing a Palestinian Arab state. The goal was solely to destroy the Jewish State.

The armies of Lebanon, Syria, Iraq, Jordan and Egypt that attacked Israel were organized into standard military brigades and equipped with modern weapons. In addition, Egypt, Iraq and Syria had real air forces, Syria and Egypt had tanks, and Iraq, Lebanon and Jordan had armored car units.[9] The total number of soldiers involved in the Arab invasion of the nascent Jewish State included 10,000 Egyptians, 4,500 Jordanians, 7,000 Syrians, 8,000 Iraqis and 3,000 Lebanese, in aggregate 32,500 well-equipped combat troops backed by artillery, armor and air power.[10] Supporting these 32,500 soldiers were another 10,000 Arab forces of the Palestinian Liberation Army commanded by Fawzi al-Qawuqji (1890-1977), a trained military professional who had been leading Palestinian forces in carrying out terror attacks since the riots of 1936 and during WWII was a Nazi acolyte and Wehrmacht colonel. On top of this number were another 50,000 Palestinian Arab irregulars available for local defense.[11]

Jewish forces available to defend the re-established Jewish State were divided into several categories: There were 29,900 Haganah fighters of which 16,400 were actual combat troops and 13,500 civilians organized into special fighting units to defend their towns and villages. It should be noted that only sixty percent of these 29,900 fighters had personal weapons.[12] Adding Palmach units and Irgun and Lehi fighters, the fledgling State of Israel had a total of 40,000 fighters that could be deployed to blunt the Arab invasion.[13]

> Apart from the large variety of small arms, the heaviest equipment of any consequence in the Israeli forces was the 3 inch mortar, of which there were 195, while the "artillery" units acquired some Hipano-Suiza 20mm guns and some French 65mm howitzers without sights dating from the beginning of the century…. Armored units included some scout cars and a number of crudely homemade armored vehicles.[14]

Israel had no air force. The only aircraft available were non-military British-style Piper Cubs called Austers.[15] All in all, the Israeli forces had no real artillery, armor or air force.

Objectively and logistically the invading Arab armies should have made short work of the State of Israel. With no allies or military support—the UN remained passive and the U.S. maintained a posture of neutrality—Israel's back was literally up against the Mediterranean Sea. Thus, the Arab world had every reason to believe that it would finally destroy the hated Zionist enemy. But that was not what occurred. What did happen was the modern-day equivalent of the victory the Maccabees achieved twenty-two centuries earlier. The order of the day for all Israeli military forces was in effect: No retreat and no surrender. In essence, after 2,000 years of waiting for a Jewish State, this was the first opportunity and perhaps the last to make this reality come true. Coming on the heels of the Holocaust, the motivation was even higher than it otherwise may have been.

THE BATTLE FOR YAD MORDECHAI

One of the pivotal sieges of the War of Independence was the battle at Kibbutz Yad Mordechai. Yad Mordechai had been founded in the 1930s but renamed after the commander of the 1943 Warsaw Ghetto Uprising, Mordechai Anilevetz. Dominating the roadway between Gaza and today's Ashkelon, and a strategic point between Gaza and Tel-Aviv, it was deemed too important a logistical site to avoid.[16] Thus, on May 19, 1948 an Egyptian force of some 2,500 men, several tanks, artillery and air cover attacked a Jewish force of some one hundred thirty defenders. "On the eve of battle, Yad Mordechai had the following arms: thirty-seven rifles and semi-automatic rifles, a PIAT (Projector, Infantry, Anti-Tank) gun, two light mortars and two machine guns.[17] The Egyptian military allocated an hour to conquer the kibbutz and believed that within twenty-four hours Egyptian forces would be in Tel Aviv. Much to the shock and surprise of the Egyptian commanders and soldiers, the Battle for Yad Mordechai lasted five full days.

The defenders fought with remarkable heroism and courage. They continued fighting as long as they had ammunition, and enough defenders who were not killed or wounded. The stunned Egyptians had between 300-400 casualties, counting dead and wounded.[18] The five days were crucial because the Egyptians were slowed in their march to Tel Aviv, and the Jewish State was able to import relatively large amounts of ammunition, including four Czech Avia S199s (Messerschmitt 109 aircraft) from black market arms dealers. This materiel was handed out quickly to newly formed units that then were able to move south to engage the Egyptian Army and stop its advance.

The story of the fierce defense of Kibbutz Yad Mordechai spread throughout the country and became an inspiration for the Jewish defenders of *Eretz Yisrael*. It also made the Egyptian and other Arab forces realize that the information they'd received from their superiors about the war being a "cakewalk" was false.

THE LOSS OF THE JEWISH QUARTER IN THE OLD CITY

Following the partition decree of the UN, Jerusalem was to be placed under international domain, referred to as a *corpus separatum*. Neither Arabs nor Jews favored this position.

Part of the United Nations Partition Plan for Palestine, which the Jews of Mandatory Palestine accepted and the Arabs of Mandatory Palestine and neighboring states rejected, was that Jerusalem would be a *corpus separatum*, meaning that the United Nations would assume responsibility for the city and it would not be a part of either the proposed Arab or Jewish states. Israel argued that the partition plan regarding Jerusalem was "null and void" due to the UN's "active relinquishing of responsibility in a critical hour" when the UN did not act to protect the city. The Arabs, who had been against Jerusalem's internationalization all along, felt similarly.[19]

Under the command of Abd al-Qadir al-Husayni*, Arab forces in November of 1947 began a blockade of the road to Jerusalem in an attempt to starve out the city's Jewish inhabitants. Reinforced by the Arab Legion in Latrun**, and despite repeated attempts to capture that stronghold by Israeli militia, the Jewish Quarter of the

---

* Abd al-Qadir al-Husayni (1907-1948) was "a Palestinian Arab nationalist and fighter who in late 1933 founded the secret militant group known as the Organization for Holy Struggle (Munathamat al-Jihad al-Muqaddas), which he and Hasan Salama commanded as the Army of the Holy War (Jaysh al-Jihad al-Muqaddas) during the 1936–39 Arab revolt and during the 1948 war." (https://en.wikipedia.org/wiki/Abd_al-Qadir_al-Husayni as derived from Ted Swedenburg, "The role of the Palestinian peasantry in the Great Revolt (1936-9)," in Ilan Pappé (Ed.) *The Israel/Palestine Question* (London: Routledge, 1999), 150 (129–168); Yezid Sayigh, *Armed Struggle and the Search for State: The Palestinian National Movement, 1949-1993* (Oxford: Oxford University Press, 2000), 35.

** "The Battles of Latrun were a series of military engagements between the Israel Defense Forces and the Jordanian Arab Legion on the outskirts of Latrun between 25 May and 18 July 1948, during the 1948 Arab-Israeli War. Latrun takes its name from the monastery close to the junction of two major highways: Jerusalem to Jaffa/Tel Aviv and Gaza to Ramallah. During the British Mandate it became a Palestine Police base with a Tegart fort. The United Nations Resolution 181 placed this area within the proposed Arab state. In May 1948, it was under the control of the Arab Legion. It commanded the only road linking the Yishuv-controlled area of Jerusalem to Israel, giving Latrun strategic importance in the battle for Jerusalem. (cont'd)

Despite assaulting Latrun on five separate occasions Israel was ultimately unable to capture Latrun, and it remained under Jordanian control until the Six-Day War. The battles were so decisive that the Israelis decided to construct a bypass surrounding Latrun so as to allow vehicular movement between Tel Aviv and Jerusalem, thus avoiding the main road. Regardless, during the (cont'd)

Old City of Jerusalem was annexed by Jordan until its reconquest in the Six-Day War of 1967.

The city had been short of water, food, medicine and ammunition since the latter days of the British Mandate, when Ben-Gurion finally gave the order to capture the road to Jerusalem.

Colonel David Daniel "Mickey" Marcus (1901-1948), a Jewish West Point graduate and veteran of World War II, was conscripted by Ben-Gurion to unite the various factions of the nascent state's military. One of his assignments was to open the road to Jerusalem. Marcus had men bulldoze a road through the Judean mountains out of range of the Arab troops. This road was named the Burma Road after the famous road that the British had built in the jungles of Burma during World War II. This Burma Road would keep Jerusalem supplied even when parts of the main road were under attack or being shelled. [Marcus was involved in writing the first field manual for the new IDF based on his experience in World War II. He also helped the IDF draw up battle plans to deal with the five invading Arab armies. Ben-Gurion assigned him the rank of *Aluph*, which is Hebrew for Major General. He was the first *Aluph* in over 2,000 years! Sadly, Marcus was mistakenly killed one evening by an IDF soldier because the non-Hebrew speaking Colonel Marcus didn't know the Hebrew password that evening.]

With the construction of the Burma Road and the killing of Abd al-Qadir al-Husayni, the Arab ability to besiege Jerusalem

---

Battle for Jerusalem, the Jewish population of Jerusalem could still be supplied by a new road, named the 'Burma Road', that bypassed Latrun and was suitable for convoys. The Battle of Latrun left its imprint on the Israeli collective imagination and constitutes part of the 'founding myth' of the Jewish State. The attacks cost the lives of 168 Israeli soldiers, but some accounts inflated this number to as many as 2,000. The combat at Latrun also carries a symbolic significance because of the participation of Holocaust survivors." (https://en.wikipedia.org/wiki/Battles_of_Latrun_(1948) as derived from: Kenneth M. Pollack, Arabs at War: Military Effectiveness 1948–1991, University of Nebraska Press, 2003), 278; Anita Shapira, L'imaginaire d'Israël: histoire d'une culture politique (Paris: Calmann-Lévy, 2005), 91; Itzchaki, Ariè, Latrun. The *Battle for the road of Jerusalem*, Jerusalem, 1982.

decreased. Still, the Jewish Quarter in the Old City was literally sealed off from the rest of Jewish Jerusalem by the ancient wall built by Suleiman the Magnificent in the 16th century.

There were three hundred Jewish fighters with light arms, some machine guns and grenades inside the Jewish Quarter, as well as some 2,000 civilians. Against them stood the well-equipped, well-trained and British-led Jordanian Arab Legion. While the Jewish forces were doing well in Western Jerusalem in spite of the non-stop bombardment and were advancing on the Jewish Quarter, it was forced to surrender on May 28 when only 36 of the 300 fighters were still left standing. The surrender was made to the Commander of the Jordanian Arab Legion, Sir John Bagot Glubb.* A detailed agreement was signed which allowed the Jewish civilians to march down the Zion Hill road to Jewish Jerusalem with whatever belongings they could carry. The Jewish fighters were taken prisoner by the Jordanian Arab Legion. There was also an agreement that the Jewish homes, belongings and any Jewish holy sites would not be be touched. Within 24 hours all the Jewish homes were looted and many were burned. The synagogues of the Jewish Quarter of the Old City were desecrated. For the next nineteen years the holiest sites to Judaism, which are all in and around the Old City of Jerusalem, were both desecrated and off-limits to Jews.

The June 11, 1948 Cease Fire That Changed the Balance of Forces

After a month of fierce fighting, the invaders achieved only limited success: the capture of the Jewish Quarter of the Old City of Jerusalem and the capture of small *kibbutzim* in the Negev, like Kibbutz Yad Mordehcai. Everywhere else they were met with defeat and paid an exceptionally heavy price in dead and wounded.

---

* Sir John Bagot Glubb, KCB, CMG, DSO, OBE, MC, KStJ, KPM (1897-1986) was commanding general of the Jordanian Arab Legion from 1939 to 1956. Known as Glubb Pasha, this British officer was reputed to have made the Legion into the best Arab fighting force of its day.

The flood of Palestinian refugees multiplied during the Arab invasion of Israel. Now it was not just the exaggerated claims of Jewish atrocities and the collapse of the Arab Palestinian elite, but it was the Arab armies' calling for Arab Palestinian residents to get out of the way so that they could do battle without having to worry about which areas were Arab and which were Jewish that added to the Palestinian diaspora. Finally, Arab Palestinian residents were promised they would be away from their homes for a very short period, since after the Arab victory they would return to their homes and have the property of the vanquished Jews as well.

By the end of the first month of the 1948-1949 War of Independence, there were hundreds of thousands more Arab Palestinian refugees.

After the first month of battle both armies were ready for a UN-sponsored three-week cease fire. The Israeli forces were simply exhausted and depleted. They had put up a fierce and desperate defense and were in need of a break. They were literally out of ammunition and had suffered many dead and wounded. The Arab armies were literally in shock. They had prepared for a one-week war with minimum casualties, and after a month of fighting they had thousands of dead and wounded and had captured just a few square miles of Jewish territory.

The UN brokered cease-fire forbade outside countries from rearming either side. In reality, this only hurt the Israeli forces, since the Arab armies went back to their bases in their countries of origin to pick up more weapons and fresh soldiers. The Israeli forces had used up everything at their disposal.

Still, the three-week cease fire turned out to be the turning point of the War of Independence. While the Arab armies resupplied, the Israelis purchased ammunition on black markets all over the world, mostly in Europe and the U.S. *Yishuv* agents was charged with the task of making these purchases and slipping the munitions into Israel under the watchful eyes of UN monitors. What these agents were able to purchase and smuggle in changed the entire balance of forces and the nature of the war going forward.

As a new nation, Israel had no credit or cash to pay for the arms it needed. The funds were raised mostly by Israelis donating anything they could, such as engagement rings, wedding bands, Kiddush cups, family silver and, of course, money that Israelis had saved in banks and safes. Money was also raised in the American Jewish community, mostly via the Jewish Federations around America, who used Holocaust survivors and U.S. service chaplains to pitch to potential donors. Golda Meir (née Myerson) was sent to the U.S. to raise money because she was fluent in English, as she had grown up in Milwaukee and was once a school teacher there.

---

* "The demobilization that followed World War II afforded the Zionists enormous opportunities to procure weapons in the United States. American factories had produced massive amounts of weaponry during the war. Hundreds of thousands of tons of surplus military equipment, from mess kits to tanks, airplanes, machine guns, artillery, and even warships, were now being offered for sale as scrap by the War Assets Administration (WAA). Regulations required that all the weapons be rendered inoperable, but in many cases the soldiers awaiting discharge who performed the neutralization did a far from thorough job; the damage done to disable weapons was often only superficial. Moreover, as the material was only "junk," anyone could buy it legally. However, on 14 December 1947—just weeks after the UN passed the partition resolution that in effect touched off the military confrontation in Palestine—President Truman invoked the Neutrality Act, imposing a unilateral embargo on weapons to both sides in the Zionist-Arab conflict. From then on, exporting American arms to Palestine was illegal. By that time, however, a highly sophisticated arms-smuggling scheme was already in place and was taking full advantage of the opportunities offered by demobilization...The closest to a comprehensive account existing today is investigative journalist Leonard Slater's book, *The Pledge*, written as a heroic tribute to the participants and published in 1970.

"According to Slater, who interviewed many of those involved, the conspiracy began with a meeting on 1 July 1945 in the New York penthouse apartment of Rudolf Sonneborn, scion of a wealthy American Jewish family that had made its fortune in the oil and chemical business. Besides Sonneborn, those present at the meeting were Henry Montor, director of United Jewish Appeal, the fundraising arm of the Jewish Agency in the United States; David Ben-Gurion, chairman of the Executive of the Jewish Agency and essentially the head of the Yishuv; and seventeen prominent American Jews whom Slater did not name...All were prominent members of the Jewish community; all were wealthy... (cont'd)

Her goal was to raise $25,000,000, and she came back to Israel with $50,000,000.[20]

The Mossad went on a shopping spree in Europe where there were still stockpiles of World War II leftover ammunition for sale, and bought whatever they could get their hands on.* The IDF used the three-week cease fire for training its troops and established a clear command and control system. It divided its forces into different brigades and commands. Many Jewish volunteers with World War II combat experience showed up to fight for Israel from the U.S. and Britain. Most importantly, combat pilots arrived and, under the cover of night, so did airplanes from Central Europe (they were lucky they made it to Israel, practically flying in on fumes). The IDF smuggled in tanks, armored vehicles, jeeps, artillery, anti-tank weapons, heavy machine guns, grenades, heavy mortars, and enough rifles for every IDF soldier and millions of rounds of ammunition by sea and by air.

Ben-Gurion changed the role of the IDF. If the Arabs broke the cease-fire, he said he would order the IDF to go on offense. The Arab states and the Mufti made it clear repeatedly that the May 14, 1948 borders were irrelevant to them. From their perspective there were no borders to a state that should be wiped out. Hence, Israel felt no need to be restrained by those boundaries either, especially since they represented less than half of what the UN November 29, 1947 Partition Plan called for.

THE ALTALENA AFFAIR

As the State of Israel came into being and before the rival militia

---

Sonneborn and his associates eventually adopted the legal cover of a charity, the Sonneborn Institute, dedicated to the relief of European Jews. In fact, the group became the fundraisers, facilitators, and behind-the-scenes masterminds of the Haganah's illegal armaments procurement effort in the United States, operating separately from the Jewish Agency and thereby shielding it from direct involvement in unlawful activities." (Ricky-Dale Calhoun, "Arming David: The Haganah's illegal arms procurement network in the United States 1945-1949," *Journal of Palestine Studies*, Vol. XXXVI, No. 4 (Summer 2007), 22–32.)

factions officially merged into what was to become the IDF, Irgun agents operating in Europe purchased ammunition to be brought to Israel. The ship carrying the munitions was named the *Altalena* after Ze'ev Jabotinsky's pen name. The *Altalena*, docked in France, was scheduled to arrive in Israel on the day of the declaration of independence, with nine hundred and forty Irgun fighters and tons of weapons that had been funded by the French government.

For a variety of reasons the vessel only set sail on June 11, 1948, by which time Menachem Begin, the Irgun commander, had signed an agreement that incorporated the Irgun into the IDF. As fate would have it, the *Altalena* had set sail for Israel during the UN sponsored cease-fire which placed an embargo on the acquisition of arms. In desperate need of the munitions, the provisional government, informed by Begin of the shipment, decided to ignore the embargo and smuggle the weapons into the country.

Because of the continuous internecine squabbling, there were issues concerning where the *Altalena* could land and unload and who would get the arms. Would they go to the Irgun or the IDF?

Eventually, the *Altalena* landed on a remote beach near Kfar Vitkin, between Netanya and Hadera, on the night of June 20, 1948. After the men on board had unloaded about a third of the shipment, things unraveled. The local IDF Haganah commander, under orders from the provisdional government headed by Ben-Gurion, gave the Irgun crew an ultimatum: They had 10 minutes to surrender the *Altalena* or be fired upon. Before the Irgun members could return to the *Altalena*, he ordered his men to open fire. Six Irgun members were killed. The *Altalena* then proceeded to hoist anchor and sail south to the Tel Aviv beach, where Begin was hoping to work out an agreement with Ben-Gurion to allow the remaining two thirds of the desperately needed ammunition to be unloaded.

That did not happen. The Tel Aviv beach was a highly visible and crowded area with UN observers who were there to stop the smuggling. Ben-Gurion did not want the opposition to control any arms, and he certainly didn't want them risking future smuggling operations by unloading in plain sight of the authorities.

The *Altalena* dropped anchor on June 22, 1948, about 700 yards from the Dan Hotel on the Tel Aviv beach.

> The IDF transferred heavy guns to the area and at four in the afternoon the next day, Ben-Gurion ordered the shelling of the Altalena...Yitzchak Rabin commanded the IDF and Palmach forces on the shore. One of the shells hit the ship, and it began to burn. Yigal Allon later claimed only five or six shells were fired, as warning shots, and the ship was hit by accident. IDF troops on the shore also directed heavy small-arms fire towards the ship, and employed heavy machine guns with armor-piercing rounds...Menachem Begin, hoping to avert civil war, ordered his men not to shoot back, and the ship raised the white flag. However, the firing continued, and some Irgun men on board reportedly returned fire. The Israeli corvettes also fired at the Altalena during the battle, and one crewman later claimed that IDF troops on the beach were hit by fire from one of the corvettes, which had aimed at the Altalena but overshot its target. On the beach, a battle between the IDF and Irgun forces along the shore erupted, and clashes between IDF and Irgun units also took place throughout Tel Aviv, mainly in the south and center.[21]

Begin was the last to leave the sinking ship. That evening he went on the radio in tears and bore witness to the day's horrible events. He swore he would not allow a Jewish civil war just when Jews had finally reestablished their own state. He exhorted Irgun members not to seek revenge, and told them the task at hand was the fight against the five invading armies waiting for the cease-fire to end. His emotional appeal probably avoided what could have been a disastrous civil war.

The animosity between Irgun members and Haganah members lasted for decades. Begin and Ben-Gurion only spoke to each other in 1967, on the eve of the Six-Day War, when Begin was brought into a national unity government.

THE ASSASSINATION OF FOLKE BERNADOTTE

Count Folke Bernadotte, a Swedish diplomat who had made a name for himself for having rescued thousands of POWs during WWII, was assigned by the UN as a mediator in the newly partitioned former British Mandate of Palestine. He recommended a peace plan before the cease-fire ended. It called for the dissolution of the Jewish State, limited Jewish immigration, with the Negev and Jerusalem to be handed to the Arabs. In addition, he posited:

> It is...undeniable that no settlement can be just and complete if recognition is not accorded to the right of the Arab refugee to return to the home from which he has been dislodged by the hazards and strategy of the armed conflict between Arabs and Jews in Palestine. The majority of these refugees have come from territory which...was to be included in the Jewish State. The exodus of Palestinian Arabs resulted from panic created by fighting in their communities, by rumours concerning real or alleged acts of terrorism, or expulsion. It would be an offence against the principles of elemental justice if these innocent victims of the conflict were denied the right to return to their homes while Jewish immigrants flow into Palestine, and, indeed, at least offer the threat of permanent replacement of the Arab refugees who have been rooted in the land for centuries.[22]

The Israeli government rejected this "peace plan" out of hand, and continued to prepare for the post cease-fire assaults on their state. On July 8, 1948, Israel evacuated a small town, Kfar Darom, on the Gaza Strip. That same day the Egyptian Army broke the cease-fire and mounted an offensive operation in Gaza heading toward the Negev. The IDF, with fresh munitions and training, responded. For the following ten days, the Israelis took one town after another because it finally had use of arms and planes, as dilapidated and old as some of them were.

The Arab cities of Lod and Ramle, two cities in the Jerusalem Corridor, were captured and emptied of Arab inhabitants. Even with the success of the April offensive that captured the road to Jerusalem and with the Burma Road, Jerusalem was still in a precarious position since Ramle, Lod and the fortress of Latrun were occupied by the Arabs. By capturing Lod and Ramle, convoys could be sent to Jerusalem with supplies. Lod was also strategically important because the International Airport was there. The Arabs who were pushed out of Lod and Ramle were the few who remained after many fled.

The IDF also captured Rosh Ha'ayin and Migdal Tzedek in the center of Israel, and the entire southern Galilee—including the city of Natzeret (Nazareth), a city historically important to Christians and Jews. On the northern coast, Acco was captured, and in the south the IDF pushed the Egyptians into an area called the Faluja Pocket. Finally,the newly formed IDF Air Force did a great deal of damage to the Arab armies. On July 18th, a second UN cease-fire went into effect. From that point on, the Arab armies were pushed back and the IDF captured more territory. Again the time was used to rearm, retrain and regroup.

The Arabs began to grasp the enormity of their mistakes, beginning with the rejection of the November 29, 1947 Partition Plan. Then there was their support of the Mufti's plan to abort the birth of a Jewish State by launching a terror war against all Jewish towns, roads and settlements on November 30 1947, with all that followed as a result of that. Their ultimate mistake was the invasion of the Jewish State on May 14, 1948.

Having endured enough of the Count's interference, on September 17, 1948 Folke Bernadotte was assassinated in Jerusalem by members of Lehi. In response to his murder, the Israel government outlawed the organization's branch in Jerusalem and shut down its publication, *Hamivrak*. The leaders of Lehi, Natan Yellin Mor and Mattityahu Shmuelevitz, were sentenced to long jail terms by a military court, but were released in a general amnesty.

Bernadotte, who had been instrumental in also saving Jews during the Holocaust, had made recommendations that adopted many previous British proposals that had long ago not found muster by Palestine's Jewish inhabitants. Nevertheless, this did not deter the UN General Assembly from passing Resolution 194 on December 11, 1948.

United Nations General Assembly Resolution 194 (III) (11 December 1948)

The General Assembly, Having considered further the situation in Palestine,

1. Expresses its deep appreciation of the progress achieved through the good offices of the late United Nations Mediator in promoting a peaceful adjustment of the future situation of Palestine, for which cause he sacrificed his life; and Extends its thanks to the Acting Mediator and his staff for their continued efforts and devotion to duty in Palestine;

2. Establishes a Conciliation Commission consisting of three States members of the United Nations which shall have the following functions:

(a) To assume, in so far as it considers necessary in existing circumstances, the functions given to the United Nations Mediator on Palestine by resolution 186 (S2) of the General Assembly of 14 May 1948;

(b) To carry out the specific functions and directives given to it by the present resolution and such additional functions and directives as may be given to it by the General Assembly or by the Security Council;

(c) To undertake, upon the request of the Security Council, any of the functions now assigned to the United Nations Mediator on Palestine or to the United Nations Truce Commission by resolutions of the Security Council; upon such request to the Conciliation Commission by the Security Council with respect to all the remaining functions of the United Nations Mediator on Palestine under Security Council resolutions, the office of the Mediator shall be terminated;

3. Decides that a Committee of the Assembly, consisting of China, France, the Union of Soviet Socialist Republics, the United Kingdom and the United States of America, shall

present, before the end of the first part of the present session of the General Assembly, for the approval of the Assembly, a proposal concerning the names of the three States which will constitute the Conciliation Commission;

4. Requests the Commission to begin its functions at once, with a view to the establishment of contact between the parties themselves and the Commission at the earliest possible date;

5. Calls upon the Governments and authorities concerned to extend the scope of the negotiations provided for in the Security Council's resolution of 16 November 1948(1) and to seek agreement by negotiations conducted either with the Conciliation Commission or directly, with a view to the final settlement of all questions outstanding between them;

6. Instructs the Conciliation Commission to take steps to assist the Governments and authorities concerned to achieve a final settlement of all questions outstanding between them;

7. Resolves that the Holy Places including Nazareth religious buildings and sites in Palestine should be protected and free access to them assured, in accordance with existing rights and historical practice; that arrangements to this end should be under effective United Nations supervision; that the United Nations Conciliation Commission, in presenting to the fourth regular session of the General Assembly its detailed proposals for a permanent international regime for the territory of Jerusalem, should include recommendations concerning the Holy Places in that territory; that with regard to the Holy Places in the rest of Palestine the Commission should call upon the political authorities of the areas concerned to give appropriate formal guarantees as to the protection of the Holy Places and access to them; and that these undertakings should be presented to the General Assembly for approval;

8. Resolves that, in view of its association with three world religions, the Jerusalem area, including the present municipality of Jerusalem plus the surrounding villages and towns, the most eastern of which shall be Abu Dis; the most southern, Bethlehem; the most western, Ein Karim (including also the built up area of Motsa); and the most northern, Shu'fat,

should be accorded special and separate treatment from the rest of Palestine and should be placed under effective United Nations control; Requests the Security Council to take further steps to ensure the demilitarization of Jerusalem at the earliest possible date; Instructs the Conciliation Commission to present to the fourth regular session of the General Assembly detailed proposals for a permanent international regime for the Jerusalem area which will provide for the maximum local autonomy for distinctive groups consistent with the special international status of the Jerusalem area; The Conciliation Commission is authorized to appoint a United Nations representative, who shall cooperate with the local authorities with respect to the interim administration of the Jerusalem area;

9. Resolves that, pending agreement on more detailed arrangements among the Governments and authorities concerned, the freest possible access to Jerusalem by road, rail or air should be accorded to all inhabitants of Palestine; Instructs the Conciliation Commission to report immediately to the Security Council, for appropriate action by that organ, any attempt by any party to impede such access;

10. Instructs the Conciliation Commission to seek arrangements among the Governments and authorities concerned which will facilitate the economic development of the area, including arrangements for access to ports and airfields and the use of transportation and communication facilities;

11. Resolves that the refugees wishing to return to their homes and live at peace with their neighbours should be permitted to do so at the earliest practicable date, and that compensation should be paid for the property of those choosing not to return and for loss of or damage to property which, under principles of international law or in equity, should be made good by the Governments or authorities responsible; Instructs the Conciliation Commission to facilitate the repatriation, resettlement and economic and social rehabilitation of the refugees and the payment of compensation, and to maintain close relations with the Director of the United Nations Relief for Palestine Refugees

and, through him, with the appropriate organs and agencies of the United Nations;

12. Authorizes the Conciliation Commission to appoint such subsidiary bodies and to employ such technical experts, acting under its authority, as it may find necessary for the effective discharge of its functions and responsibilities under the present resolution; The Conciliation Commission will have its official headquarters at Jerusalem. The authorities responsible for maintaining order in Jerusalem will be responsible for taking all measures necessary to ensure the security of the Commission. The Secretary General will provide a limited number of guards to the protection of the staff and premises of the Commission;

13. Instructs the Conciliation Commission to render progress reports periodically to the Secretary General for transmission to the Security Council and to the Members of the United Nations;

14. Calls upon all Governments and authorities concerned to cooperate with the Conciliation Commission and to take all possible steps to assist in the implementation of the present resolution;

15. Requests the Secretary General to provide the necessary staff and facilities and to make appropriate arrangements to provide the necessary funds required in carrying out the terms of the present resolution.*

---

[8] "Resolution 194, adopted by the UN General Assembly on December 11, 1948, addressed a host of issues, but only one paragraph out of 15 dealt with refugees created by the conflict. Resolution 194 attempted to create the tools required to reach a truce in the region. It established a conciliation commission with representatives from the United States, France and Turkey to replace the UN mediator. The commission was charged with achieving "a final settlement of all questions between…governments and authorities concerned."

The Resolution's "refugee clause" is not a standalone item, as the Arabs would have us think, nor does it pertain specifically to Palestinian Arab refugees. Of the 15 paragraphs, the first six sections addressed ways to achieve a truce; the next four paragraphs addressed the ways that Jerusalem and surrounding villages and towns should be demilitarized, and how an international (cont'd)

* * *

At the 186th plenary meeting on 11 December 1948, a committee of the Assembly consisting of the five States designated in paragraph 3 of the above resolution proposed that the following three States should constitute the Conciliation Commission: France, Turkey, United States of America.

The proposal of the Committee having been adopted by the General Assembly at the same meeting, the Conciliation Commission is therefore composed of the above mentioned three States.[23]

---

zone or jurisdiction would be created in and around Jerusalem. The resolution also called on all parties to protect and allow free access to holy places, including religious buildings.

One paragraph has drawn the most attention: Paragraph 11, which alone addressed the issue of refugees and compensation for those whose property was lost or damaged. Contrary to Arab claims, it did not guarantee a Right of Return and certainly did not guarantee an unconditional Right of Return – that is the right of Palestinian Arab refugees to return to Israel. Nor did it specifically mention Arab refugees, thereby indicating that the resolution was aimed at all refugees, both Jewish and Arab. Instead, Resolution 194 recommended that refugees be allowed to return to their homeland if they met two important conditions:

1. That they be willing to live in peace with their neighbors
2. That the return takes place "at the earliest practicable date."

The resolution also recommended that for those who did not wish to return, "Compensation should be paid for the property…and for loss of or damage to property" by the "governments or authorities responsible."

Although Arab leaders point to Resolution 194 as proof that Arab refugees have a right to return or be compensated, it is important to note that the Arab States: Egypt, Iraq, Lebanon, Saudi Arabia, Syria, and Yemen voted against Resolution 194. Israel is not even mentioned in the resolution. The fact that plural wording also is used—"governments or authorities"—suggests that, contrary to Arab claims, the burden of compensation does not fall solely (cont'd)upon one side of the conflict. Because seven Arab armies invaded Israel, Israel was not responsible for creating the refugee problem. When hundreds of thousands of Arab Jews, under threat of death, attack and other forms of persecution, were forced to flee Arab communities, the State of Israel absorbed the overwhelming majority of them into the then-fledgling nation." (Eli Hertz, "An Analysis of Resolution 194," *Myths and Facts* (http://www.mythsandfacts. org/conflict/10/resolution-194.pdf))

THE FORGOTTEN JEWISH REFUGEES

For a host of reasons—practical to parochial—Israel has failed to raise the issue of the mammoth injustice done to almost a million Jews from Arab countries. The scale and the premeditated state-sponsored nature of persecution that prompted the 1948 flight of close to 900,000 Jews from their homes has only recently begun to emerge. These Sephardic Jews had their synagogues burned, businesses looted and in many places were murdered. It was made clear that they were no longer welcome in the Arab world, even as second class citizens; and the faster they left the better. They left with the shirts on their backs and the few possessions they could carry. They left behind billions of dollars worth of real estate and property, especially the Jews who left Iraq.

Two days after Israel declared independence an article appeared in the *New York Times*:

> For nearly four months, the United Nations has had before it an appeal for "immediate and urgent" consideration of the case of the Jewish populations in Arab and Moslem countries stretching from Morocco to India.
>
> The country-by-country table estimated the Jewish population-at-risk as 899,000 souls. The article cited the dismissal of Jews in the civil service in Syria, per capita ransom payment of $20,000 by Iraqi Jews seeking to leave Iraq, a forced levy on the Lebanese Jewish community to support the Arab war effort parallel to incitement and physical attacks on Jews, and Jews fleeing to India from Afghanistan. It quoted the UN Economic and Social Council report as saying:
>
> 'The very survival of the Jewish communities in certain Arab and Moslem countries is in serious danger, unless preventive action is taken without delay.'
>
> Hostility and oppression only grew, ultimately leading to the exodus of almost all Jews from all Arab and Moslem countries from Casablanca to Karachi. Arab claims that Israel is required to allow refugees a Right of Return are groundless.[24]

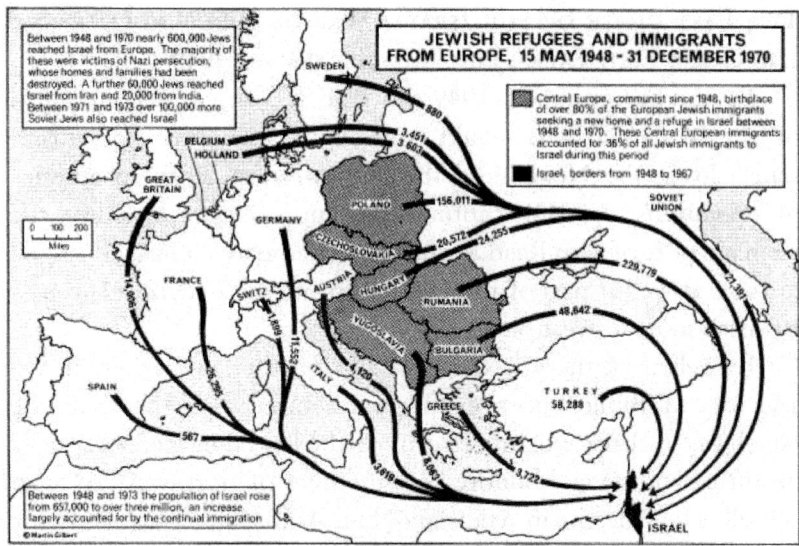

Sir Martin Gilbert, © 2010. Reproduced by permission of Taylor & Francis Books UK. www.martingilbert.com

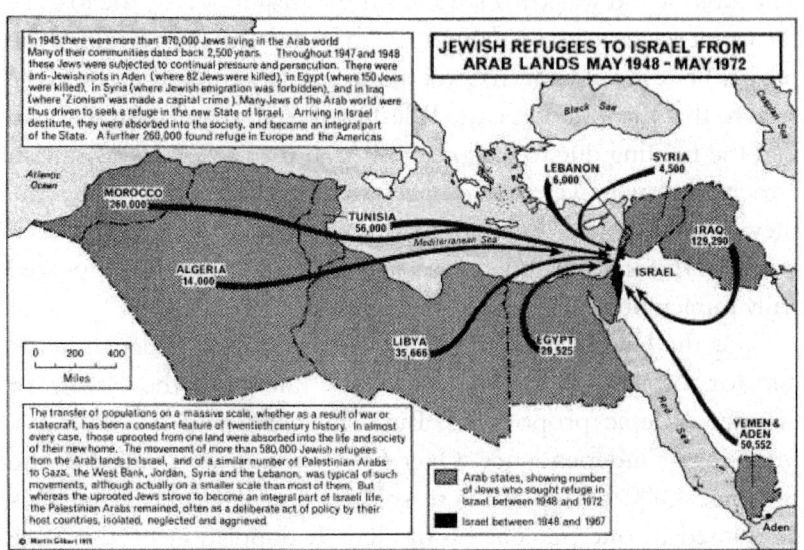

Sir Martin Gilbert, © 2010. Reproduced by permission of Taylor & Francis Books UK. www.martingilbert.com

THE LAST PHASE OF THE ISRAELI WAR OF INDEPENDENCE AND THE CEASE FIRE TALKS, JANUARY - SEPTEMBER 1949

By the beginning of 1949 the IDF was in complete control of the battlefield and would continue its offensive operations, especially in the Negev and the northwestern Sinai. In a series of operations, the IDF captured the entire Negev including the strategic port of Um Rash Rash, whose name was quickly changed to Eilat, as well as part of the Gaza Strip and the area in and around El Arish in northwest Sinai.

By February, the war was over and for the Jewish State it was a victory of Biblical portions. By late February 1949 the State of Israel was in control of 65 percent of the land they were originally promised and several hundred square miles of northwestern Sinai as well. The Palestinian Arabs and their Arab allies controlled only thirty-five percent.

No one in the Israeli leadership, including the overly optimistic David Ben-Gurion, dreamed this would be how the war would end. The Arab world was truly stunned at the magnitude of the loss. In the worst scenario assessment of Arab leaders, no one imagined the Jewish State would survive, yet alone actually expand its borders. Add to that the loss of a large Palestinian Arab population that had fled the fighting due to exaggerated Arab media reports of Jewish atrocities, or who were led to believe that by getting out of the way they were hastening an Arab victory, or because they were forced out by IDF forces in some areas, and the war's outcomes appeared truly miraculous.

For the Jewish State this war was the War of Independence, and for the Arab world this was to be known as the *Nakba*, or disaster of epic proportions. But Israel had paid a very heavy price for its independence. Over 6,000 Israelis were killed in the fighting, 4,000 of whom were soldiers and 2,000 civilians. This amounted to one percent of the Jewish population of the State of Israel. To put this percentage in perspective, it would be as if the U.S. had lost 1.5 million people in World War II, one million soldiers and 500,000 civilians. During World War II the U.S. lost

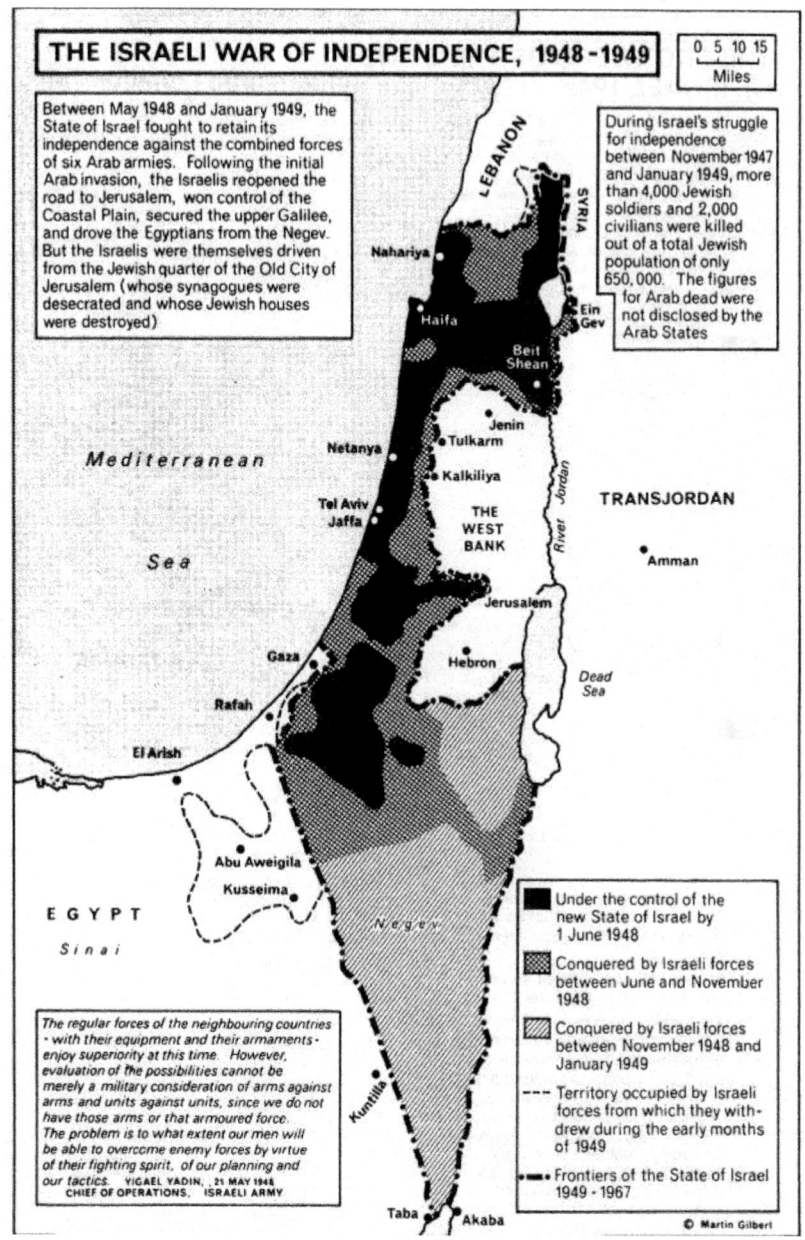

THE ISRAELI WAR OF INDEPENDENCE, 1948-1949

0 5 10 15 Miles

Between May 1948 and January 1949, the State of Israel fought to retain its independence against the combined forces of six Arab armies. Following the initial Arab invasion, the Israelis reopened the road to Jerusalem, won control of the Coastal Plain, secured the upper Galilee, and drove the Egyptians from the Negev. But the Israelis were themselves driven from the Jewish quarter of the Old City of Jerusalem (whose synagogues were desecrated and whose Jewish houses were destroyed)

During Israel's struggle for independence between November 1947 and January 1949, more than 4,000 Jewish soldiers and 2,000 civilians were killed out of a total Jewish population of only 650,000. The figures for Arab dead were not disclosed by the Arab States

The regular forces of the neighbouring countries - with their equipment and their armaments - enjoy superiority at this time. However, evaluation of the possibilities cannot be merely a military consideration of arms against arms and units against units, since we do not have those arms or that armoured force. The problem is to what extent our men will be able to overcome enemy forces by virtue of their fighting spirit, of our planning and our tactics. YIGAEL YADIN, 21 MAY 1948 CHIEF OF OPERATIONS, ISRAELI ARMY

Under the control of the new State of Israel by 1 June 1948

Conquered by Israeli forces between June and November 1948

Conquered by Israeli forces between November 1948 and January 1949

Territory occupied by Israeli forces from which they withdrew during the early months of 1949

Frontiers of the State of Israel 1949 - 1967

© Martin Gilbert

Sir Martin Gilbert, © 2010. Reproduced by permission of Taylor & Francis Books UK. www.martingilbert.com

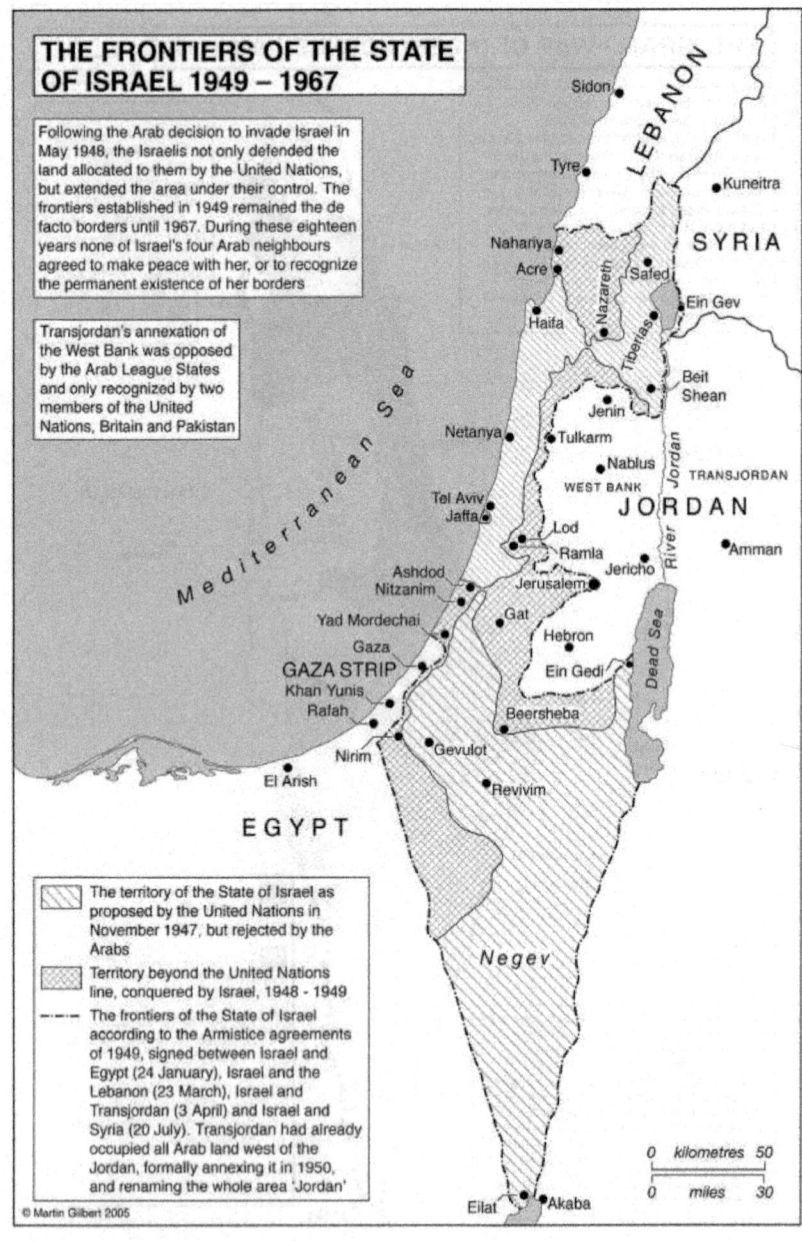

THE FRONTIERS OF THE STATE OF ISRAEL 1949 – 1967

Following the Arab decision to invade Israel in May 1948, the Israelis not only defended the land allocated to them by the United Nations, but extended the area under their control. The frontiers established in 1949 remained the de facto borders until 1967. During these eighteen years none of Israel's four Arab neighbours agreed to make peace with her, or to recognize the permanent existence of her borders

Transjordan's annexation of the West Bank was opposed by the Arab League States and only recognized by two members of the United Nations, Britain and Pakistan

LEBANON

Sidon

Tyre

Kuneitra

Nahariya

SYRIA

Acre

Safed

Ein Gev

Haifa

Nazareth

Tiberias

Mediterranean Sea

Beit Shean

Jenin

Netanya

Tulkarm

Nablus

TRANSJORDAN

Tel Aviv
Jaffa

WEST BANK

JORDAN

Lod

Ramla

Jericho

Amman

Ashdod
Nitzanim

Jerusalem

Jordan River

Yad Mordechai

Gat

Gaza

Hebron

Dead Sea

GAZA STRIP

Ein Gedi

Khan Yunis
Rafah

Beersheba

Nirim

Gevulot

El Arish

EGYPT

Revivim

The territory of the State of Israel as proposed by the United Nations in November 1947, but rejected by the Arabs

Territory beyond the United Nations line, conquered by Israel, 1948 - 1949

------ The frontiers of the State of Israel according to the Armistice agreements of 1949, signed between Israel and Egypt (24 January), Israel and the Lebanon (23 March), Israel and Transjordan (3 April) and Israel and Syria (20 July). Transjordan had already occupied all Arab land west of the Jordan, formally annexing it in 1950, and renaming the whole area 'Jordan'

© Martin Gilbert 2005

Negev

0   kilometres   50
0   miles   30

Eilat   Akaba

Sir Martin Gilbert, © 2010. Reproduced by permission of Taylor & Francis Books UK. www.martingilbert.com

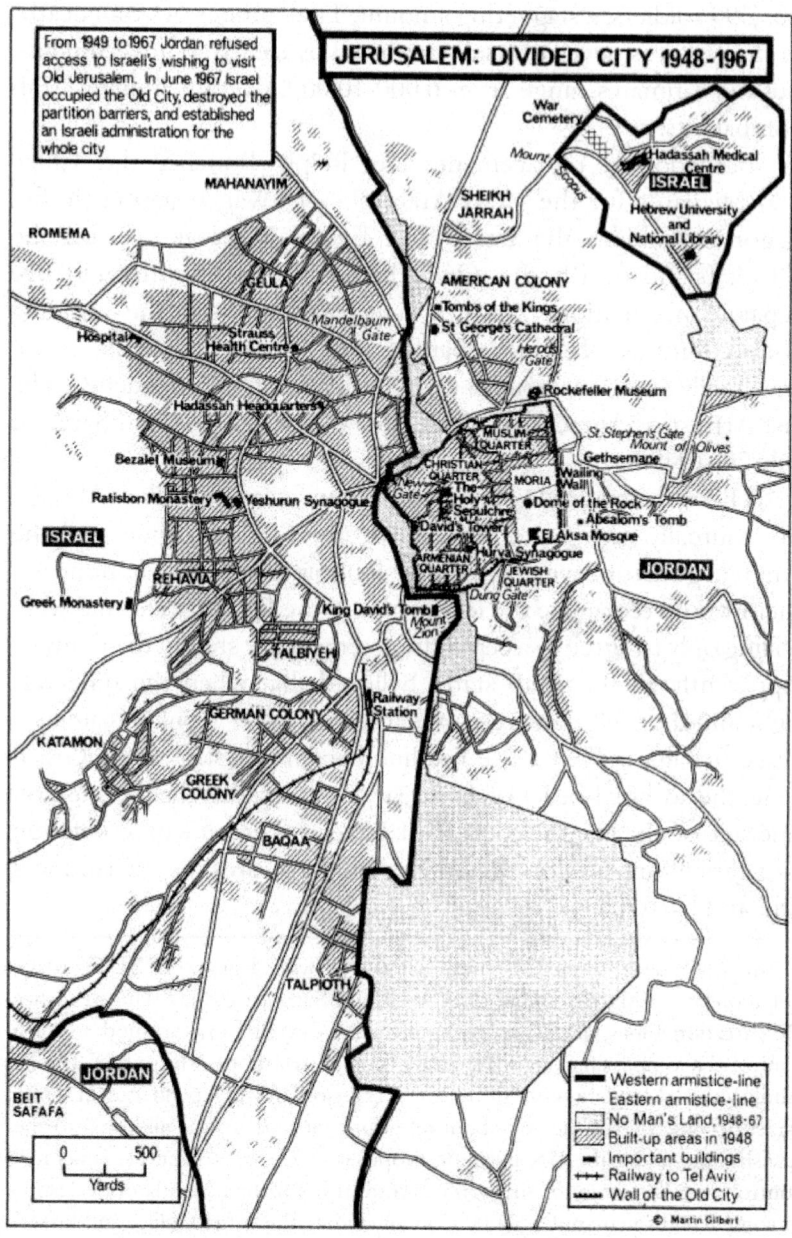

JERUSALEM: DIVIDED CITY 1948-1967

From 1949 to 1967 Jordan refused access to Israeli's wishing to visit Old Jerusalem. In June 1967 Israel occupied the Old City, destroyed the partition barriers, and established an Israeli administration for the whole city

War Cemetery

Mount Scopus

Hadassah Medical Centre

ISRAEL

Hebrew University and National Library

MAHANAYIM

SHEIKH JARRAH

ROMEMA

AMERICAN COLONY

GEULA

Tombs of the Kings

St George's Cathedral

Mandelbaum Gate

Herod's Gate

Hospital

Strauss Health Centre

Rockefeller Museum

Hadassah Headquarters

MUSLIM QUARTER

St Stephen's Gate

Mount of Olives

Bezalel Museum

CHRISTIAN QUARTER

Gethsemane

Ratisbon Monastery

Yeshurun Synagogue

New Gate

The Holy Sepulchre

Walling Wall

MORIA

Dome of the Rock

ISRAEL

David's Tower

El Aksa Mosque

Absalom's Tomb

REHAVIA

ARMENIAN QUARTER

Hurva Synagogue

JORDAN

Greek Monastery

JEWISH QUARTER

Dung Gate

King David's Tomb

Mount Zion

TALBIYEH

Railway Station

GERMAN COLONY

KATAMON

GREEK COLONY

BAQAA

TALPIOTH

JORDAN

BEIT SAFAFA

	Western armistice-line
	Eastern armistice-line
	No Man's Land, 1948-67
	Built-up areas in 1948
	Important buildings
+++	Railway to Tel Aviv
	Wall of the Old City

0   500
Yards

© Martin Gilbert

405,399 soldiers, a staggering amount. The number of Arab deaths in the war was never officially reported by the Arab governments, but the estimates range from 6,000-10,000, overwhelmingly Arab combatants.

Bernadotte's replacement, Dr. Ralph Bunche, the Chief UN Mediator for the Israel Arab 1948-49 War, began cease-fire negotiations with the Israeli and Egyptian delegations on the Greek Island of Rhodes. Over the next seven months and five separate negotiations between Israel and each of the invading Arab countries—Egypt, Lebanon, Iraq, Jordan and Syria—there was finally an official end to the Israeli War of Independence. The last Armistice Agreement was signed between Israel and Syria on July 20, 1949.

These Armistice Agreements set up cease-fire lines though not mutually recognized borders of the State of Israel. All the Arab negotiators were emphatic in pointing out that none of them would recognize the legitimacy of the Jewish State, and were willing only to agree to a cease-fire, a temporary stop in the fighting. Apparently all the Arab states believed that when the time was right and they felt they were militarily ready they would create new cease-fire lines. That cease-fire line became known as the Green Line, the ad-hoc border of Israel, and it was called that because on one side of the line the country of Israel was green with vegetation and agriculture, and on the other side, the Arab side, the land was arid and barren.*

---

* "In 1949 Israel signed separate armistices with Egypt on 24 February, Lebanon on 23 March, Jordan on 3 April, and Syria on 20 July. The Armistice Demarcation Lines, as set by the agreements, saw the territory under Israeli control encompassing approximately three-quarters of the prior British administered Mandate as it stood after Transjordan's independence in 1946. Israel occupied territories of about one-third more than was allocated to the Jewish State under the UN partition proposal. After the armistices, Israel had control over 78 percent of the territory comprising former Mandatory Palestine or some 8,000 square miles (21,000 km), including the entire Galilee and Jezreel Valley in the north, whole Negev in the south, West Jerusalem and the coastal plain in the center.

"The armistice lines were known afterwards as the "Green Line". (cont'd)

THE PALESTINIAN REFUGEES FROM THE 1948 – 1949 WAR OF INDEPENDENCE

As we have seen, on November 29th 1947, when the UN voted to partition Mandate Palestine into two states, one Jewish and one Arab, there was not one Arab Palestinian refugee. There were 1.1 million Arabs in Mandate Palestine on the day of the partition vote. More than 600,000 fled because of what had happened at Deir Yassin and because of the resultant propaganda from their leaders; some had fled from Arab (and some Jewish) expulsions during the War of Independence.

But it goes beyond that. Arab leaders were so convinced that they would wipe Israel off the map that they broadcast and published articles in newspapers urging the Palestinian Arabs to get out of the way of the Arab invasion so as not to become collateral damage as Israel was being destroyed. They told Palestinian Arabs they would be back in their homes in a matter of a few short weeks.

The Gaza Strip and the West Bank (including East Jerusalem) were occupied by Egypt and Jordan respectively. The United Nations Truce Supervision Organization and Mixed Armistice Commissions were set up to monitor ceasefires, supervise the armistice agreements, to prevent isolated incidents from escalating, and assist other UN peacekeeping operations in the region.

Just before the signing of the Israel-Jordan armistice agreement, General Yigal Allon proposed to conquer the West Bank up to the Jordan River as the natural, defensible border of the state. Ben-Gurion refused, although he was aware that the IDF was militarily strong enough to carry out the conquest. He feared the reaction of Western powers and wanted to maintain good relations with the United States and not to provoke the British. More, the results of the war were already satisfactory and Israeli leaders had to build a nation. (https://en.wikipedia.org/wiki/1948_Arab%E2%80%93Israeli_War as derived from http://lawcenter.birzeit.edu/lawcenter/ar/homepage/2013-08-31-07-08-03): Maurine and Robert Tobin (2002). *How Long O Lord?: Christian, Jewish, and Muslim Voices from the Ground and visions for the future in Israel–Palestine* (Cambridge, MA:Cowley Publications, 2002), Anita Shapira. *Ben-Gurion: Father of Modern Israel* (New Haven: Yale University Press, 2014), 173–; Benny Morris, *One state, two states: resolving the Israel/Palestine conflict* (New Haven: Yale University Press), 79; Zaki Shalom, *David Ben-Gurion, the State of Israel and the Arab World, 1949-1956* (Eastbourne, UK: Sussex Academic Press (2002), 174-)

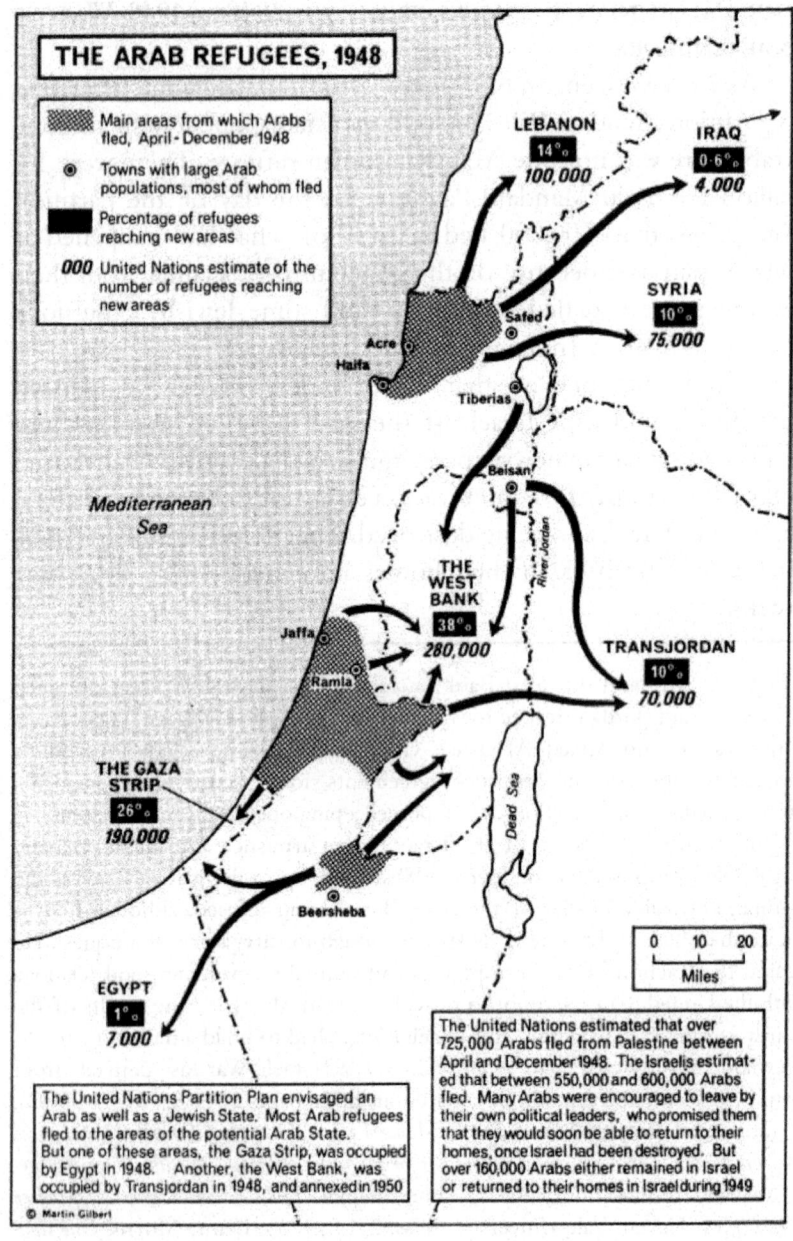

THE ARAB REFUGEES, 1948

Main areas from which Arabs fled, April - December 1948

Towns with large Arab populations, most of whom fled

Percentage of refugees reaching new areas

000 United Nations estimate of the number of refugees reaching new areas

LEBANON 14% 100,000

IRAQ 0.6% 4,000

SYRIA 10% 75,000

Acre
Haifa
Safed
Tiberias
Beisan

Mediterranean Sea

THE WEST BANK 38% 280,000

TRANSJORDAN 10% 70,000

Jaffa
Ramla

THE GAZA STRIP 26% 190,000

Dead Sea

Beersheba

0 10 20 Miles

EGYPT 1% 7,000

The United Nations Partition Plan envisaged an Arab as well as a Jewish State. Most Arab refugees fled to the areas of the potential Arab State. But one of these areas, the Gaza Strip, was occupied by Egypt in 1948. Another, the West Bank, was occupied by Transjordan in 1948, and annexed in 1950

The United Nations estimated that over 725,000 Arabs fled from Palestine between April and December 1948. The Israelis estimated that between 550,000 and 600,000 Arabs fled. Many Arabs were encouraged to leave by their own political leaders, who promised them that they would soon be able to return to their homes, once Israel had been destroyed. But over 160,000 Arabs either remained in Israel or returned to their homes in Israel during 1949

© Martin Gilbert

Sir Martin Gilbert, © 2010. Reproduced by permission of Taylor & Francis Books UK. www.martingilbert.com

Who gave such orders? Leaders such as Iraqi Prime Minister Nuri Said, who declared: "We will smash the country with our guns and obliterate every place the Jews seek shelter in. The Arabs should conduct their wives and children to safe areas until the fighting has died down."[25]

The Secretary of the Arab League Office in London, Edward Atiyah, wrote in his book: "This wholesale exodus was due partly to the belief of the Arabs, encouraged by the boastings of an unrealistic Arabic press and the irresponsible utterances of some of the Arab leaders that it could be only a matter of weeks before the Jews were defeated by the armies of the Arab States and the Palestinian Arabs enabled to re-enter and retake possession of their country."[26]

"The refugees were confident their absence would not last long, and that they would return within a week or two," Monsignor George Hakim, a Greek Orthodox Catholic Bishop of Galilee told the Beirut newspaper, *Sada al-Janub* (August 16, 1948). "Their leaders had promised them that the Arab Armies would crush the 'Zionist gangs' very quickly and that there was no need for panic or fear of a long exile."

"The Arab States encouraged the Palestine Arabs to leave their homes temporarily in order to be out of the way of the Arab invasion armies," according to the Jordanian newspaper *Filastin* (February 19, 1949).

One refugee quoted in the Jordan newspaper, *Ad Difaa* (September 6, 1954), said: "The Arab government told us: Get out so that we can get in. So we got out, but they did not get in."

An Arab resident of a Palestinian refugee camp explained why his family left Israel in 1948:
"The radio stations of the Arab regimes kept repeating to us: 'Get away from the battle lines. It's a matter of ten days or two weeks at the most, and we'll bring you back to Ein-Kerem

[near Jerusalem].' And we said to ourselves, 'That's a very long time. What is this? Two weeks? That's a lot!' That's what we thought [then]. And now 50 years have gone by.[27]

Mahmoud Al-Habbash, a Palestinian journalist wrote in the Palestinian Authority's official newspaper:

. . . The leaders and the elites promised us at the beginning of the "Catastrophe" in 1948, that the duration of the exile will not be long, and that it will not last more than a few days or months, and afterwards the refugees will return to their homes, which most of them did not leave only until they put their trust in those "Arkuvian" promises made by the leaders and the political elites. Afterwards, days passed, months, years and decades, and the promises were lost with the strain of the succession of events . . . ["Arkuvian" is a reference to Arkuv, a figure from Arab tradition known for breaking promises and lying.][28]

It must thus be undertood that the self-inflicted wound called by Palestinians the *Nakba*, literally the *disaster* or *catastrophe*, was primarily of their own doing.*

---

*New Historians dispute this contention. Newly released state documents reveal that there was an intent on the part of the Israeli hierarchy to transfer Arab populations out of Israel, in essence "ethnic cleansing.".

"Most leaders of the Zionist movement publicly opposed such transfers. However, a study of their confidential correspondence, private diaries and minutes of closed meetings, made available to the public under the 'thirty year rule', reveals the true feelings of the Zionist leaders on the transfer question. We see from this classified material that Herzl, Ben-Gurion, Weizmann, Sharett and Ben-Zvi, to mention just a few, were really in favour of transferring the Arabs from Palestine. Attempts to hide transfer proposals made by past Zionist leaders has led to a 'rewriting of history' and the censoring and amending of official documents!" [Chaim Simons, *A Historical Survey of Proposals to Transfer Arabs from Palestine 1895 - 1947* ((Hoboken, NJ): KTAV Pub Inc., 1988), 298]

This is disputed by more traditional historians who claim:

"[R]ecent studies, based on official Israeli archives, have shown that there was no official policy or instructions intended to bring about the expulsion and that most of the Palestinians who became refugees had left their homes (cont'd

When the war was over, when one looks at where the Palestinian Arab refugees fled, it is clear that close to two-thirds of them fled into areas that were supposed to be part of the Palestinian Arab State that was never created. Thirty-eight percent fled to Judea and Samaria and 26 percent fled to the Gaza Strip. The Arab world could have proclaimed a Palestinian Arab State in Judea and Samaria and Gaza and given citizenship to the Palestinian Arabs who fled there, ending their status as refugees. It did not do so.

After the War of 1948-1949, Egypt declared Gaza as an Egyptian military district and Jordan formally annexed Judea and Samaria in 1950. This 35 percent of post-1922 Mandate Palestine became part of two existing Arab States, Egypt and Jordan. There was no declaration of a Palestinian State.

An Arab government for all of Palestine was created on October 1, 1948 by the Arab High Command. Haj Amin Al-Husseini, the Mufti, was named its president. Ahmad Himi Abd al Bagi was named prime minister, and Jamal al Husayni was named foreign minister. They issued a flag, taken from the Arab Revolt of 1916, designed by the British Diplomat Mark Sykes to help the Arabs have a banner to fight under when they revolted against the Ottoman Empire in World War I. It was only later, when the Palestine Liberation Organization was formed by the Egyptian Government in 1964, that this flag, with one modification, became the official Palestinian flag. This Arab government had no power and was never recognized even by the Arab world as having any say in the affairs of the Arabs of Palestine during or after the 1948-1949 war.

---

on their own initiative, before they came face to face with Israeli forces, especially in the period between late 1947 and June 1948. Later on, Israel's civil and military leadership became more decisive about preventing refugees from returning to their homes and more willing to resort to coercion in expelling the (cont'd) Palestine Arabs from their homes. This was not uniformly implemented in every sector and had much to do with decisions of local military commanders and circumstances, which might explain why some 156,000 Palestinians remained in Israel at the end of the war." [Moshe Efrat, "Refugees," *The Continuum Political Encyclopedia of the Middle East*, Ed. Avraham Sela. (NY: Continuum, 2002), 727]

The tragedy of the Palestinian Arab refugees is compounded further by how they were treated by the Arab states. Two-thirds of the Palestinian Arabs traveled around twenty to thirty miles from their homes to other parts of Mandate Palestine and the majority of the remaining thirty-five percent traveled around fifty miles to Jordan, Syria and Lebanon, where they found themselves with people who shared the same language, dialect, culture, religion and values. And yet, they were not integrated into any of these societies. Palestinian refugees were not re-settled as a matter of policy and kept in refugee camps administered by the United Nations, not by the Arab League. The United Nations Relief Workers Association (UNRWA) remains in operation while all other UN refugee agencies folded their tents long ago.

Since 1949 the Palestinians have been the planet's oldest unresolved refugee problem. World War II created close to forty million refugees, the India Pakistan War in 1947 created around twelve million and the Vietnam War created around three million. In all these cases, within a decade, almost everyone was resettled and able to start new lives. There is something remarkable about a group of 600,000 people who fled to countries run by their kinsmen, where they share the same culture and language, and who happen to be sitting on half the world's known oil reserves, yet those states cannot find the resources and space to resettle these people. Worse yet, the refugees are considered pariahs who for the most part must stay in designated refugee camps and are not granted local citizenship. Jordan is the exception. But the sight of Palestinian Arabs suffering in refugees camps clearly helped portray the Arabs as the victims of Zionist aggression. Thus, the Palestinian "problem" became the most effective tool in the Arab world's ongoing war against a sovereign Jewish State.

This callous treatment of the Palestinians by their "brother" Arabs is contrasted sharply by how the State of Israel treated the Jewish refugees who flooded the newborn Jewish State during its first decade of independence. In 1949, Israel was a third-world country that had just been through a devastating war during which one percent of her population was killed and her economy devastated. The total population of Israel was 760,000, of whom 600,000 were Jews. Between 1949-1959 Israel accepted approximately one million refugees and within a decade integrated them into Israeli society. All this absorption was done by taxing Israelis to the extreme and receiving donations from Jewish organizations and Jews around the world. The cultural, social, psychological and economic challenges involved in a brand new, poor Jewish country absorbing more than its existing population was monumental, yet it was done.

The Arab world continuously claims Jews are not a nation but rather a religious group who are the citizens of the states that

---

* "[A]longside the nakba (catastrophe) that struck hundreds of thousands of the Arab inhabitants of the former British Mandate Palestine, we find yet another, much greater psychological catastrophe that struck the entire Arab world and especially its leaders: a humiliation so immense that Arab political culture and discourse could not absorb it. Initially, the refugees used the term nakba to reproach the Arab leaders who started and lost the war that so hurt them. In a culture less obsessed by honor and more open to self-criticism, this might have led to the replacement of political elites with leaders more inclined to move ahead with positive-sum games of the global politics of the United Nations and the Marshall Plan. But when appearances matter above all, any public criticism shames the nation, the people, and the leaders.

"Instead, in a state of intense humiliation and impotence on the world stage, the Arab leadership chose denial—the Jews did not, could not, have not won. The war was not—could never—be over until victory. If the refugees from this Zionist aggression disappeared, absorbed by their brethren in the lands to which they fled, this would acknowledge the intolerable: that Israel had won. And so, driven by rage and denial, the Arab honor group redoubled the catastrophe of its own refugees: They made them suffer in camps, frozen in time at the moment of the humiliation, waiting and fighting to reverse that Zionist victory that could not be acknowledged. The continued suffering of these sacrificial victims on the altar of Arab pride called out to the Arab world for vengeance against the Jews. In the meantime, wherever Muslims held power, they drove their Jews out as a preliminary act of revenge. (cont'd)

they live in, while the Arabs are a large united nation who treat each other as brothers. Yet the Arab world would not integrate its Palestinian brothers.*

"The Arab leadership's interpretation of honor had them responding to the loss of their own hard zero-sum game—we're going to massacre them—by adopting a negative-sum strategy. Damaging the Israeli 'other' became paramount, no matter how much that effort might hurt Arabs, especially Palestinians. 'No recognition, no negotiations, no peace.' No Israel. Sooner leave millions of Muslims under Jewish rule than negotiate a solution. Sooner die than live humiliated. Sooner commit suicide to kill Jews than make peace with them." Richard Landes, "Why The Arab World Is Lost In An Emotional Nakba, And How We Keep It There," *Tablet*, June 24, 2014 (http://www.tabletmag.com/jewish-news-and-politics/176673/emotional-nakba))

Footnotes

[1] Sharif Kanaana and Nihad Zitawi, "Deir Yassin," Monograph No. 4, *Destroyed Palestinian Villages Documentation Project Bir Zeit*: (Documentation Center of Bir Zeit University, 1987), 55.

[2] "Israel War of Independence: The Capture of Deir Yassin (April 9, 1948)," Jewish Virtual Library (http://www.jewishvirtuallibrary.org/the-capture-of-deir-yassin)

[3] *Ibid.*

[4] Chaim Herzog, *The Arab Israeli Wars* (NY: Vintage Books, 1984), 33.

[5] Efraim Karsh, *Palestine Betrayed* (New Haven: Yale University Press, 2014) 124.

[6] *Ibid.*

[7] *Ibid.*, 137.

[8] *Ibid.*, 264.

[9] Herzog, 48.

[10] Howard M. Sachar, *The History of Israel from the Rise of Zionism To Our Time* (NY: Alfred Knopf, 1996), 317.

[11] Herzog, 47-48.

[12] Efraim Karsh, *The Arab-Israeli Conflict: The Palestine War 1948* (London: Osprey Publishing, 2014), 50.

[13] Herzog, 48.

[14] *Ibid.*

[15] Martin Gilbert, *Israel A History* (Toronto: Key Porter Books, 2008), 189.

[16] Benny Morris, *1948: A History of the First Arab-Israeli War* (New Haven: Yale University Press, 2008), 237.

[17] Ami Isseroff, "Battle of Yad Mordechai, 1948," *Zionism and Israel - Encyclopedic Dictionary* (http://zionism-israel.com/dic/Yad_Mordechai_battle.htm).

[18] *Ibid.*

[19] https://en.wikipedia.org/wiki/Battle_for_Jerusalem_(1948) as derived from "Statements of the Prime Minister David Ben-Gurion Regarding Moving the Capital of Israel to Jerusalem (https://www.knesset.gov.il/docs/eng/bengurion-jer.htm); Dore Gold, *Tower of Babble: How the United Nations Has Fueled Global Chaos* (New York: Three Rivers Press, 2004), 48-52; Mark A. Tessler, *A History of the Israeli-Palestinian Conflict* (Bloomington: Indiana University Press, 2009), 23; "Jerusalem: This City Needs UN Government," *LIFE*, February 9, 1953, 20 (https://books.google.com/books?id=FkIE AAAAMBAJ&pg=PA20#v=onepage&q&f=false).

[20] Jewish Women's Archive. "Golda Meir speech raises $50 million for Haganah." https://jwa.org/thisweek/jan/21/1948/golda-meir.

[21] https://en.wikipedia.org/wiki/Altalena_Affair as derived from Daniel Gordis, *Menachem Begin: The Battle for Israel's Soul* (NY: Schocken, 2014); Eric Silver, *Begin: A Biography* (Worthington, UK: Littlehampton Book Services Ltd, 1984), 107; Joanna Saidel, "Fire in the hole: Blasting the Altalena," *Times of Israel*, June 20, 2013 (http://www.timesofisrael.com/fire-in-the-hole-blasting-the-altalena/); Michael Omer-Man: "This Week in History: Sinking the 'Altalena'," *The Jerusalem Post*, June 24, 2011(http://www.jpost.com/Features/In-Thespotlight/This-Week-in-History-The-sinking-of-the-Altalena).

[22] From the "Progress Report of the United Nations Mediator on Palestine" by Folke Bernadotte. 16 September 1948. United Nations General Assembly Doc. A/648. Part one, section V, paragraph 6.

[23] "194 (III). Palestine -- Progress Report of the United Nations Mediator," United Nations General Assembly, 11 December 1948 (https://unispal.un.org/DPA/DPR/unispal.nsf/0/C758572B78D1CD0085256BCF0077E51A)

[24] Mallory Brown, "Jews in Grave Danger in all Moslem Lands," *The New York Times*, May 16, 1948, E4.

[25] Myron Kaufman, *The Coming Destruction of Israel* (NY: The American Library Inc., 1970), 26–7.

[26] Edward Atiyah, *The Arabs* (London: Penguin Books, 1955), 183.

[27] Palestinian Authority TV, (July 7, 2009), quoted in *Palestinian Media Watch Bulletin* (July 23, 2009).

[28] Mahmoud Al-Habbash, *AlHayat alJadida* (December 13, 2006) quoted in Itamar Marcus and Barbara Cook, "The Evolving Palestinian Narrative: Arabs Caused the Refugee Problem," *Palestinian Media Watch* (May 20, 2008).

Chapter 10

Judaism, Zionism and the Land of Israel
1950 - 1967

REBUILDING A JEWISH STATE AFTER THE WAR OF INDEPENDENCE
With its victory in the War of Independence Israel now had to resurrect the first sovereign Jewish State in 1,878 years by putting together a functioning, responsive democratic government with a functioning economy devastated as a result of the war. There was also the daunting twin challenges of physically rebuilding many parts of Israel that were destroyed during the war, while at the same time taking in hundreds of thousands of new immigrants, known by its Biblical term as the "ingathering of the exiles."

But Israeli leaders had a distinct advantage over many of the leaders of the other states that had become independent during the 1940s and 1950s, most of whom were former British or French Colonies in Asia and Africa. This was the advantage of having experience in running a piece of territory. From 1920 on the Jewish Agency had acted as the de facto government of the Jewish *Yishuv* in the Land of Israel under the British Mandate. Many of these men and women were now running the State of Israel. Furthermore, there was a clear democratic tradition that had existed since the days of the World Zionist Organization as far as elections and representation were concerned. There was also the tradition of turning to Jewish, British and Ottoman law when it came to running a society. Finally, there was the clear tradition of making sure that the military took its orders from the civilian government. All of these combined allowed for a smooth transition from British colony to a functioning 20th century nation-state.

The Jewish population of Israel at the end of 1948 was about 600,000. In the next six years close to one million Jews would make *Aliyah*! Close to 600,000 would be Sephardic Jews fleeing from the Arab world, since after Israel's victory in 1948 the Arab world turned its frustration out on the Jews in their countries. An additional 400,000 were Ashkenazi Jews, mostly Holocaust survivors. Though Israel had just fought a devastating war and had no money or economy, it would now absorb more immigrants than it had people! All this was done without UN or international help, as every resource in Israel was tapped to absorb immigrants.

There were 160,000 Arabs who remained in Israel after the War of Independence. They became citizens of Israel—just as was stated in the Israeli Declaration of Independence. There were some security issues that had to be addressed regarding some of these Israeli Arabs' ties to enemies of the State, and there was the issue of the new government appropriating land for use for military bases and other government uses. The latter applied to Jewish citizens as well.

The first fundamental decision that was taken was to create a parliamentary system of government following the English model, a model that was very familiar to Ben-Gurion and all the founders of the modern Jewish State, since they had all lived under British rule since 1917. The specific name of the Israeli Parliament would be the Knesset, which was the name of the political governing body of the Ancient Kingdom of Judea during the time of the Second *Beit Hamikdash*. There were 120 members in the original Knesset, hence there were 120 in the modern one as well. To control the Knesset there had to be a party or a coalition of parties that controlled at least 61 seats.*

Modern Zionism has always seen itself as an extension of ancient Biblical Zionism, hence the flag is based on the *Talit—*

*For more details about the Knesset go to https://knesset.gov.il/review/ReviewPage2.aspx?kns=2&lng=3

prayer shawl—and the Israeli Declaration of Independence begins with the ancient Biblical connection between the Jewish nation and the land of Israel. When Israel was re-established and it was time to pick a national symbol, the decision was to pick the menorah that sat in the First and Second Temples.

The re-established State also established the position of president, which normally does not exist in a parliamentary system. The Israeli president is chosen by the members of the Knesset and acts as the ceremonial head of state. In the early decades of the position, the presidency was reserved for a personality that had played an important role in the Zionist movement. By the 1980s, it became a title for a personality who played an important role in the history of the re-established State of Israel.

In order for Israel to be a true Western-style democracy, a powerful judiciary branch was also created, with the Supreme Court as the final arbiter of judicial issues. This Supreme Court is called the *Beit Mishpat Elyon* and functions on the local and national level.

The one promise the newly established government failed to keep was writing and establishing a constitution to govern the Knesset and be enforced by the judiciary branch. This has come back to haunt the government in many ways. The biggest problem has been that since there is no official constitution, the Israeli Supreme Court uses Knesset laws, international laws and its own sense of "justice" to determine which laws the Knesset passes are "constitutional" or not, thus giving it enormous power. Additionally, Israeli Supreme Court justices appoint the judges that will succeed them! There is no Knesset oversight. This makes the Israeli Supreme Court the most powerful one in the Western democratic world.

The Knesset passed a series of laws in its first two years of existence that allowed Israel to function under the rule of law, and established many government agencies as well as the laws governing the Israel Defense Forces (IDF) and the concept of a drafted army. But the most important law in Israel's history was the 1950

"Law of Return." This law states that any Jew in the world who wants to make *Aliyah* has the right to become a citizen the day s/he arrives! The message was that a people who were a nation but had no homeland now have a place to call home and every Jew in the world has the right to come and pick up his passport—something members of the Jewish nation had been dreaming, praying and waiting for since the destruction of the Second Temple in 70 CE.

Law of Return 5710-1950

Every Jew has the right to come to this country as an Oleh.
Aliyah shall be by Oleh's visa.

An Oleh's visa shall be granted to every Jew who has expressed his desire to settle in Israel, unless the Minister of Immigration is satisfied that the applicant

1. is engaged in an activity directed against the Jewish people; or

2. is likely to endanger public health or the security of the State.

3a. A Jew who has come to Israel and subsequent to his arrival has expressed his desire to settle in Israel may, while still in Israel, receive an Oleh's certificate.

3b. The restrictions specified in section 2 (b) shall apply also to the grant of an Oleh's certificate; but a person shall not be regarded as endangering public health on account of an illness contracted after his arrival in Israel.

4. Every Jew who has immigrated into this country before the coming into force of this Law, and every Jew who was born in this country, whether before or after the coming into force of this Law, shall be deemed to be a person who has come to this country as an Oleh under this Law.

5. The Minister of Immigration is charged with the implementation of this Law and may make regulations as to any matter relating to such implementation and also as to the grant of Oleh's visas and Oleh's certificates to minors up to the age of 18 years.[1]

The Law of Return was the heart and essence of taking the ideals of Zionism and turning them into practice. The Jews of the world no longer had to pray for a return to the Jewish homeland, it had occurred. Now a Jew could come home if he or she chose to do so.

The Law of Return resonated with the Jews of re-established Israel, first for the Jews of Germany and later for the Jews who fell under the rule of the Third Reich. Being a member of the Jewish nation meant that s/he was marked for extermination with no country or international body doing anything substantial to save those doomed by the Nazis. Now there was a country that welcomed Jews with open arms.

RELIGION AND STATE IN ISRAEL

Israel was founded as the nation-state of the Jewish people, hence there is no complete separation of religion and state. This applies to Israel's non-Jewish citizens as well. In Israel there is a Ministry of Religious Affairs which oversees the needs of Israel's non-Jewish communities, including paying the salaries of mukhtars (Islamic rabbis) and local Islamic court judges. The same is true of the Israeli Druze and Christian communities and even the tiny Circassian community. In all of these communities the Ministry of Religious Affairs, together with the Ministry of Education, work together to insure that these communities can teach their religions and cultures to their children at the expense of the State of Israel.

The Rabbinate

There is a branch of the Israeli Government called the Rabbinate. It is a rabbinical institution, connected to the government, that was set up during the British Mandate. At that time the first chief rabbi was the iconic Rabbi Avraham Yitzchak Kook. The Rabbinate handles the following:

a) Marriage
b) Divorce
c) Conversion

d) Religious Courts
e) Ritual Baths
f) Burial
g) Circumcision
h) Sabbath observance in the public sphere
i) Kosher certificates for all government institutions and functions, like the Knesset and the IDF
j) Supporting various types of Torah study institutions
k) Local Religious Councils

When one adds all this up, the Rabbinate is there to create and maintain a sense of religious cohesion between all the different types of Jews who have returned to the Land of Israel since 1882 (the year of the First *Aliyah*).

During the 2,000-year Diaspora, many Jewish communities, not in direct contact with each other, developed different customs. Furthermore, since the Emancipation of Western European Jewry, many Jews had broken with Jewish traditions and created new Jewish entities (i.e., Reform Judaism) that were not based in Jewish Law, thus having the potential to create great divisions among the Jews of Israel. In particular, when it came to the different types of Jews marrying each other, and thus truly acting and behaving as a united nation, there was a fear that without a single accepted standard of "Jewishness" there would evolve a very divisive culture in the re-established Jewish State. The Rabbinate, in essence, is an Orthodox establishment that follows traditional *Halacha*. With all its flaws and political overtones, the Rabbinate has created a reality so that since 1949 the overwhelming majority of Israeli Jews feel comfortable marrying Jews from countries where their parents never even knew Jews lived. These marriages have created a true sense of Jewish unity and nationhood.

There are two Chief Rabbis for the entire State of Israel, one Ashkenazic (Jews of European descent) and one Sephardic (Jews of Middle Eastern/Spanish descent). Every city and town has its own Rabbinate rabbis.

One of the agreements reached by Israel's first government included the creation of the Ministry of Religious Affairs and the Chief Rabbinate, but also a very significant one on military deferment for rabbinic students.*

THE INGATHERING OF THE EXILES (1949 - 1959)

There were two refugee stories that took place as a result of Israel's War of Independence: The Palestinian Arab one and the one of Jews from Arab and Islamic countries, as well as the story of the European Jews in DP camps finally having a country that wanted them.

As for the Jewish refugees from European and Arab countries and those from DP camps, from November 30 1947-January 1948 Israel was a battleground whose towns and cities had maintained serious damage, and all able-bodied men and women were either fighting or involved in preparing items for the IDF, running families and/or small businesses. As a whole, there was barely an Israeli economy during this entire period as Israel was still fending off Arab and Islamic states' ongoing promise to eliminate the Jewish State. Hence, while Israel was working to accept these one million refugees she was also trying desperately to get back on her feet economically and rebuild her heavily damaged infrastructure. Unlike the Palestinian Arab refugees who were abandoned by their brethren and had to be taken care of by the UN, Israel took on

---

* At the time of the Agreement in 1949, there were four hundred full-time rabbinic students studying in *yeshivot*. This was something even the very secular, but very Jewish David Ben-Gurion could live with and agree to since he understood the historical and traditional role that full-time, high level Torah studies played in the history of the Jewish nation. But as is the case with many agreements and laws, there is the law of unintended consequences. In this case, many members of the Haredi community became concerned that service in the IDF would seriously compromise the religious integrity of their community. Hence, almost all men, once they turned eighteen, have been encouraged by their community leaders to declare themselves to be full-time rabbinic students. At present there are about 60,000 Haredi men of military age who sit and learn in *yeshivot* who never serve in the IDF. This has become a very sore social, political, religious and economic issue in present-day Israel.

its enormous refugee problem as the nation-state of the Jewish people. Thus, she turned to the Jews of the United States and other first-world countries to help bankroll this massive endeavor.

As part of that endeavor, the government also ordered that there be rationing of many food staples, such as milk, eggs, chicken and beef, so as to insure that the new immigrants would have enough protein in their diets. Regardless of how much money a person had, there was simply a limit on how much one could purchase.

In the early 1950s there were close to two dozen refugee camps spread throughout Israel that were set up for the thousands of refugees pouring in monthly. The Israeli government set up temporary health clinics, schools, recreational centers, kindergartens, stores, synagogues, adult education centers, etc. In essence, the inhabitants were made to feel as new citizens of the re-established State of Israel, not as refugees who were to be set apart from the population. Within a few years Israel set up temporary towns that had homes made of prefabricated wood. These homes had plumbing and electricity with paved roads and sewage lines installed. These were called "*Ma'abarot*," literally a bridge between a refugee camp and a permanent town. Again there was a huge investment of manpower and construction materials. On top of all of this there were hundreds of new schools opened all over Israel in and near the refugee camps and *Ma'abarot* so that the children of the new Israelis could be assimilated into Israeli society as quickly as possible.

There is no doubt that there were serious mistakes made during this period of mass immigration. Some of them were due to insensitivity and stupidity and some were more calculated. For example, Jews from Iraq were thrown into a home in a *Ma'abara* next door to a Polish family. This was done without any "cultural" sensitivity training. This created a clash of cultures on a micro and macro level throughout Israel.

Since Israel was very interested in creating a new anti-Diaspora Jewish persona, there was a sense of disdain for Holocaust survivors for their alleged crime of being "passive" during the Holocaust, which led to them being labeled with the repulsive nickname of "*Sabon*" (soap), in this context the soap that the Nazis made out of human fat.

The Sephardic newcomers, who were overwhelmingly religious, were ridiculed at times by the Israelis for their backward ways, or made to feel that in Israel just being Israeli was sufficient and they should drop many of their Diaspora religious trappings. In addition, the housing in the *Ma'abarot* were not conducive to the extended Sephardic family structure where it was very common back in their countries of origin for three generations to live together in one large dwelling. This housing set-up created a serious social and ultimately a religious gap between the grandparents, parents and the younger Sephardic generation that was away from their families most of the day and were busy becoming Israeli. Furthermore, the schooling that most of the new immigrant children received was purposely non-religious, thus contradicting and eroding these young immigrants' ties to Orthodox Judaism and, by extension, to their parents. There were no social workers or psychologists dealing with all the traumas that these new immigrants had faced in Nazi Europe or in the antisemitic Arab Middle East, not to mention their difficult resettlement and acculturation to Israel.

But when all was said and done, these one million Israeli newcomers more often than not became proud and integrated Jewish Israeli citizens. Eventually, many members of the younger generation who were brought up non-religious either returned to their religious roots or decided to send their children to religious schools later on.

By 1960, "development towns," new cities and towns that had been built all over Israel, replaced the *Ma'abarot*.

THE IDF AND ITS ROLE IN ISRAELI SOCIETY

Since the day Israel was re-established she has not known a period of real peace with all her neighbors. Thus, the idea of having a strong, well-trained, well-equipped and proportionally large military has always been a priority. Israel took the following steps to insure that she will always be capable of fielding a large, well-prepared fighting force:

1) There is a compulsory draft in Israel for all Israelis who turn 18. This applies to men and women. The two exceptions to this rule were Israeli Arab citizens and members of the Haredi community.

2) Men were drafted for three years of service (as of 2016 the period of service has been cut to 32 months).

3) Women were drafted for two years of service. (In a step to promote equality, women's length of service has been increased to 28 months.)

4) Men do on average between 15 to 45 days a year of reserve service from the ages of 22 to 50. Officers can do as much as 100+ days a year. This is modeled after the Swiss Army model where all male citizens do military service and then do reserve duty. This allows the IDF to field a very large professional army when the need arises.

5) Israeli Arabs are not drafted into the IDF for two reasons:

a) Israel is literally at war with their relatives. This creates a moral issue for Israeli Arabs;

b) it also creates a security concern for the IDF.

6) Israeli Druze, an ethnic Arab non-Muslim community that has been persecuted by the Islamic world, has requested to be drafted into the IDF alongside their Jewish countrymen.

7) Israeli Bedouin men are not drafted but many volunteer for service, especially as trackers.

8) No Druze, Bedouin or Israeli Arab women are drafted into the IDF, though a handful volunteer.

9) There is an alternative for women who don't want to serve in the IDF. It is called "*Sherut Leumi*," National Service. This involves serving in hospitals, schools, nursing homes, etc. for the benefit of Israeli society. Many Orthodox Jewish women choose this option.

10) Since it must be prepared for combat missions at all times, the IDF spends a great deal of time on combat readiness and much less time on spit and polish.

11) The IDF also serves as a social gathering place for all elements of Israeli society. Since it is a drafted army, all types of citizens—rich, poor, well-educated, poorly educated, dark skinned, light skinned, religious Jews, secular Jews, Druze Israelis, Bedouin Israelis and Arab Israelis—must interact on a daily basis. This helps break down many social barriers and helps create a sense of social and national cohesiveness.

12) The IDF also serves as an educational center. Many soldiers learn more about Israel, Zionism and Judaism in the IDF. Some even finish their high school degrees in the IDF.

13) Druze, Muslim and Christian IDF soldiers receive all the special accommodations that their religions require. For example, whereas Jewish soldiers are sworn in with a Tanach—the Jewish Bible—Muslim soldiers are sworn in with a Quoran, and Christian soldiers with a New Testament.

14) Most Israelis will do around 20 years of reserve duty, thus also allowing them to form close friendships with fellow soldiers who come from very different backgrounds but who serve together in the same units.

15) Most Haredi men do not serve in the IDF, but that is slowly changing.

16) The IDF is the one national institution that is held in high regard by an overwhelming majority of Israelis.

The Issue of German Reparations in the early 1950s

On top of establishing a functioning democratic government and taking in one million refuges, Israel began secret talks with the new, democratic, Western-oriented West Germany on the emotional issue of German reparations to Jewish Holocaust survivors. The Chancellor of West Germany, Konrad Adenauer, one of the few men of his generation who was publicly known to have been anti-Nazi during World War II, was very interested in showing the Jewish nation and their newly re-established State of Israel that West Germany felt remorse and contrition for the actions of Nazi Germany. There were several ways that Adenauer planned on doing this. First and foremost, he purged West Germany of all public officials who were openly proud Nazis during World War II. At the same time, the Israeli government was looking for German compensation for the cost of the absorption of 500,000 Holocaust survivors (when one counts those who snuck in during 1940-1948, as well as the 400,000 that immigrated after the re-establishment of the State). The monetary amount that Moshe Sharett, Israel's Foreign Minister, was speaking about was $1.5 billion, or $3,000 per survivor who made *Aliyah*. There were secret negotiations held between the West German government and the Israeli government that was represented by a confidant of Prime Minister David Ben-Gurion, Nachum Goldmann. An agreement was reached in early 1952. This agreement spoke about the payment of $1 billion over a fourteen-year period.

In January 1952 the stormy debates in the Knesset over this proposal began. Menachem Begin, the former head of the Irgun and now head of the opposition Herut Party, was the main opponent. He felt that Israel should not take one penny from the West German government, for it would be viewed as either blood money, or worse, a "fee" for the crimes of Nazi Germany—as if any amount of money could wipe away the guilt and responsibility of Germany for the horrors of the Holocaust. Begin also organized street demonstrations, which included Holocaust survivors wearing their concentration camp uniforms. When all was said and done, the Knesset voted 61-50 to accept the reparations deal.

The Israeli government also helped negotiate a deal that would have all Jews who were victims of Nazi Germany receive reparations for their immense and horrific suffering. The deal was struck, and depending on where you were during the Holocaust—ghettos, concentration camps, slave labor camps, hiding in forests, and how long you were in one or a combination of these situations—a monetary sum was affixed. This sum did not include Jewish property that had been confiscated and was not meant to be a tradeoff for what was done, but rather, as in the case of the reparations to the State of Israel, it was meant as a tangible form of penance by the government of Germany. This reparations deal went through, but as opposed to the deal that transferred cash and goods to the State, in this deal every individual Holocaust survivor had the option of going through the process of applying for reparations. There was also the option for those who did apply and qualify to either be paid one lump sum or to be paid monthly over their lives. Again, this was a very emotional and controversial decision that each Holocaust survivor had to make.

In hindsight, the decision by the Ben-Gurion-led Israeli government to accept West German reparations was the correct choice for the fledgling Jewish State. Besides the heavy taxation of the population and the generous donations coming from the Jewish communities of the Western World, it was German reparations that helped keep Israel afloat financially during the 1950s and early 1960s.

WHY DID THE SOVIET UNION SUPPORT ISRAEL FROM 1947-1949, BUT THEN, IN THE EARLY 1950S, TURN TO HER ENEMIES?

It was Andrei Gromyko, the Soviet Ambassador to the United Nations, who stunned the UN in a session on November 26, 1947 (three days before the 1947 Partition Plan was voted on and accepted) by making a case for the establishment of a Jewish State. This speech certainly helped the cause of Israeli statehood.

During the Israeli War of Independence, it was the Soviet Union who told its satellite Czechoslovakia to sell the fledgling State of Israel weapons on the black market during the crucial June 11, 1948 cease-fire period. These weapons clearly helped give the IDF the edge it needed when the fighting resumed after the cease-fire was broken by Arab armies. As we have seen, the ammunition, along with the ammunition purchased on the black markets of Europe and the U.S., proved to have helped the IDF greatly in the War of Independence. So why did the Soviet Union, on one hand quite antisemitic in its internal polices, support Zionism in its foreign affairs policy in that 1947-1949 period?

Soviet leadership, since the days of Lenin, had always pursued a foreign policy that it considered in its interest regardless of whom the deal was with. Witness the famous Ribbentrop-Molotov Non-Aggression Pact of 1939 that had the Soviet Union work as an ally of Nazi Germany. After World War II, when the temporary alliance between the "decadent" West and the Soviet Union was no longer needed, the Soviet Union entered into a Cold War with the Western democracies. In 1947, the chief ally of the Arab States was Great Britain. Hence, the fact that the Zionist movement was an enemy of Great Britain created an opportunity for the Soviet Union to thwart Great Britain's plans for a one-dimensional Pan-Arab, pro-Great Britain, pro-Western Middle East. Also, it didn't hurt that the leading political entity in Israel at that time was the pro-Socialist Labor Zionist Movement, a movement viewed by the Soviet leadership as a potential natural ally.

The defeat of the Arab armies after their invasion of the one-day-old State of Israel turned out to be a turning point in the history of the Arab Middle East. All the leaders of the Arab States that lost to Israel were forced to flee, were killed, or removed from office. Their replacements were often more bellicose toward Israel and more suspicious of the Western democracies whom they partially blamed for their loss in the 1948-49 war.

The man who would rise as the undisputed leader of the Arab Middle East was Gamal Abdel Nasser, who led a revolution in Egypt in 1952, and officially became its president in 1956. Nasser made it clear that he was open to do business with either the West or the Soviet Union, depending on who offered him the best deal. This was great news for the Soviet Union, for it finally opened the Middle East to Soviet intervention.

It also became apparent that Prime Minister David Ben-Gurion of Israel and his coalition, though socialist in ideology, were not going be the type of one party, authoritarian socialist state that the Soviet Union preferred. Finally, there was an event that took place in the Soviet Union in 1949 that apparently soured the Soviet leadership on Zionism and the re-established State of Israel. That year, Golda Meir, Israel's new Ambassador to the Soviet Union, went on her first trip there. One must remember that since the Soviets took complete power in 1922 and declared the Union of Soviet Socialist Republics (USSR), they had done everything they could to suppress all public practice of religion and of support for any non-Soviet form of nationalism. Judaism was particularly repressed since there was a pre-Soviet history of antisemitism. Yet when Meir appeared, tens of thousands of Soviet Jews lined the streets with homemade Israeli flags, waving and greeting her! Meir was very moved, having been born in Russia in 1898 and having left with her family to the U.S. in 1906. She saw the effect that the re-establishment of a Jewish State had on an oppressed very large Jewish community that, for the most part, survived the Holocaust. The Soviet officials were appalled and frightened by this unabashed display of Zionism and Jewish identity.

When one adds all these factors together, by the early 1950s the Soviet Union was no longer in need of Zionism or Israel. She thus turned her attention to the Arab States of the Middle East who, for the most part, were no longer under British or Western influence.

THE 1948-49 WAR DID NOT CHANGE ANYTHING FROM THE PERSPECTIVE OF ISRAEL'S ARAB NEIGHBORS

There was hope that after the huge defeat Arabs suffered at the hands of the State of Israel that this would perhaps cause the Arab world to begrudgingly accept Israel as a neighbor. Not only was Israel victorious in the war, but she was magnanimous during the cease-fire negotiations. Israel returned to Egypt several hundreds of miles of Sinai that she had captured and a few square miles to Lebanon as well. But such hope was based on the hope that there was actually something that would change the conflict. In reality, the last ten decades have made it clear that the crux of the hostility to Zionism and to Israel is that its enemies simply did not believe the Jewish people had a right to any form of sovereignty. As the late General Yehoshafat Harkabi wrote in his groundbreaking book *Arab Attitudes Towards Israel*: "The objective which has been proclaimed day and night by the Arab Leaders is the liquidation of the State of Israel."[2]

As an Arab leader stated after 1949:

> "It is well known and understood that the Arabs, in demanding the return of the refugees to Palestine, mean their return as masters of the Homeland and not as slaves. With greater clarity, they mean the liquidation of the State of Israel." (Muhammad Salah al-Din, Foreign Minister of the Egyptian Government, quoted in *Al-Misri*, October 11, 1949).[3]

On April 12 1954 he made another clear statement regarding what the Arabs should do to Israel: "We should not be satisfied except by the final obliteration of Israel from the Map of the Middle East." (*Al-Masri*, April 12, 1954).[4]

From the commander of the Egyptian Third Division from a speech he gave on February 15, 1956:

> Every Commander is to prepare himself and his subordinates for the inevitable campaign with Israel in which we are fully immersed, for the purpose of the fulfilling our exalted aim, namely, the annihilation of Israel and her extermination in the shortest possible time, in the most brutal and cruel battles.[5]

Thus, while Israel was busy in its early years establishing a viable democratic country that was absorbing more immigrants than it had citizens, the Arab world was ignoring all of its own political, social, and economic problems and focusing on what could be done to annihilate the Jewish State. In the 1950s this took the form of four different approaches:

1) economic boycott;

2) cutting off Israel from the Suez Canal in 1949, then blockading the Gulf of Eliat/Gulf of Aqaba in 1955;

3) arming terrorists to attack and kill Israeli civilians; and

4) preparing for another war against Israel, this time a

successful one that would destroy Israel and avenge the loss of 1948-49.

THE ECONOMIC BOYCOTT OF ISRAEL

The Arab boycott was formally declared by the newly formed Arab League Council on December 2, 1945:

"Jewish products and manufactured goods shall be considered undesirable to the Arab countries." All Arab "institutions, organizations, merchants, commission agents and individuals" were called upon "to refuse to deal in, distribute, or consume Zionist products or manufactured goods."[6]

The Arab League used the word Jewish and Zionist interchangeably, being honest in its definition of whom and what was hated. The Mufti and his ilk never distinguished between Jews and Zionists. Neither did the Arab leaders who spoke about the genocidal war they were preparing to wage against Israel in 1948. In fact, it was only during the 1980s when the Arab world realized that if it separated its hatred of Jews from its hatred of Zionism it would be able to gain a much broader appeal in the Western world.

Be that as it may, the Arab League was dedicated to boycotting Israel economically even before the re-establishment of the State of Israel.

The boycott, as it evolved after 1948, is divided into three components. The primary boycott prohibits direct trade between Israel and the Arab nations. The secondary boycott is directed at companies that do business with Israel. The tertiary boycott involves the blacklisting of firms that trade with other companies that do business with Israel.

The blacklisting process is capricious; it is unclear whether boycott officials collect any evidence at all before placing an individual or company on the blacklist. No two countries have identical lists, and six countries—Algeria, Mauritania, Morocco, Somalia, the Sudan and Tunisia—do not enforce the secondary boycott. Egypt's policy changed from strict enforcement to unofficial complicity after the signing of the peace treaty with Israel, despite the provision whereby Egypt agreed to the "termination of economic boycotts and discriminatory barriers to the free movement of people and goods. . . ."

Once on the list, it is sometimes difficult to get off, since the company or some Arab sponsor must initiate the request. A firm might be required to supply proof that it no longer has any business with Israel and/or might be asked to make investments in Arab countries equal to those made earlier in Israel. Bribery is another means of becoming "de-listed."

The objective of the boycott has been to isolate Israel from its neighbors and the international community, as well as to deny it trade that might be used to augment its military and economic strength. Israel's capacity to reach its full economic potential was hindered for decades by the actions of Great Britain, Japan and other countries that cooperated with the boycott. It has undoubtedly enhanced Israel's isolation and separated the Jewish State from its most natural markets, but the boycott failed to undermine Israel's economy to the degree intended.[7]

CLOSING THE SUEZ CANAL TO ISRAELI SHIPPING AND COMMERCE

Even after the 1949 Armistice Agreement with Egypt was signed, Egypt, like all the other Arab states who signed their own armistice agreement with Israel, all made it clear that Israel did not exist as far as they were concerned and that they were all waiting for the next chance to wipe Israel off the map. Since Egypt controlled which ships entered the Suez Canal, she made it clear that no Israeli ships could pass through the Canal, and neither could any ships bringing cargo to or from Israel. This was another attempt to strangle Israel economically.[8]

TERROR ATTACKS AGAINST ISRAELI BETWEEN 1950 - 1956

Since the Arab Armies were soundly defeated in 1948-49, which meant frontal war against Israel was not a viable option, in the early 1950s the Arab world resorted to using terrorists in order to try to destabilize Israel. These terrorists were overwhelmingly recruited from the Palestinian refugee camps in Jordan, Syria and the Gaza Strip that were created by the Arab States' failed war. These terrorists were armed and trained by their host Arab states—Syria and Jordan, but in particular, Egypt. It is ironic that these same Arab states had no money to resettle Palestinians or improve conditions in refugee camps, but they did have money for arming and training terrorists. These terrorists were called "*fedayeen*" (freedom fighters). During this period there were thousands of *fedayeen* raids into Israel, which killed hundreds of Israeli civilians, and caused a great deal of damage.

Immediately after the declaration of independence of the state of Israel in 1948, the neighboring Arab countries together with the local Palestinian community provoked an overall war against the newborn state. After the cessation of the hostilities, Israel had to deal with a new type of military challenge—the intrusion of fedayeen into Israeli territory. These were Palestinian refugees, terrorists, and criminals who infiltrated Israel for the purposes of agricultural cultivation, theft, robbery, looting, killing, assassination, and sabotage. From 1951 to 1955, more than 800 Israeli civilians and soldiers were injured by fedayeen penetrating the border (mostly from Jordan), with the casualty count rising every year. These penetrations into Israel over the years challenged Israel's sovereignty within its territory and tarnished the status quo Israel was attempting to achieve through stabilizing its borders.

Against this backdrop, the idea began to develop that there was a need to conduct offensive retributions against various targets in Arab countries, in order to alleviate, at least partially, the anxiety and low morale of Israeli citizens affected by the infiltrations. Thus, efforts were directed towards deterrence and retaliation against Arab and Palestinian targets outside Israeli territory, consistent with the notion of "an eye for an eye and a tooth for a tooth." Initially, these operations were carried out by one local commander or another and were usually directed against Arab or Palestinian targets that had a direct or symbolic connection with the preceding attacks, or against the bases from which the attacks were launched.

In an attempt to formalize the sporadic military activity, in 1953 the Israeli Defense Forces (IDF) established a military unit trained for special missions under the command of Major Ariel Sharon. This unit came to be called Unit 101. Its successes and Israel's retaliatory actions strengthened morale amongst the Israeli public and IDF soldiers, who began to volunteer for the unit. After several months of activity and dozens of reprisals, Unit 101 consolidated with the paratroopers' battalion in early 1954. The Israeli retaliatory operations at that time were not necessarily designed to deter the fedayeen but to punish them and their supporters as an end unto itself.

One retaliatory operation that drew widespread criticism and protest took place against the village of Kibiya on October 1, 1953. It followed a month of attacks on Israel that had killed twelve people, culminating two days earlier when infiltrators from Jordan threw a hand grenade into a house in the Jewish town of Yehud, killing a mother and her two young children. The response was immediate. Unit 101, reinforced by paratroopers, raided three Jordanian villages, including Kibiya, the main target of the operation since it was an established fedayeen base. The paratroopers blew up several houses and dozens of villagers were killed, despite claims by the force commanders that the residents had been warned before the attack.

The Kibiya operation was a turning point, spurring the Jordanian Legion into intensive efforts to curb infiltration: Jordanian forces in the West Bank were increased, more ambushes and patrols were carried out to prevent fedayeen infiltrations, orders were given restricting the activities of citizens along the border, and penalties were imposed for those who violated these orders. In the years that followed, the number of thefts, robberies and casualties along this border decreased.[9]

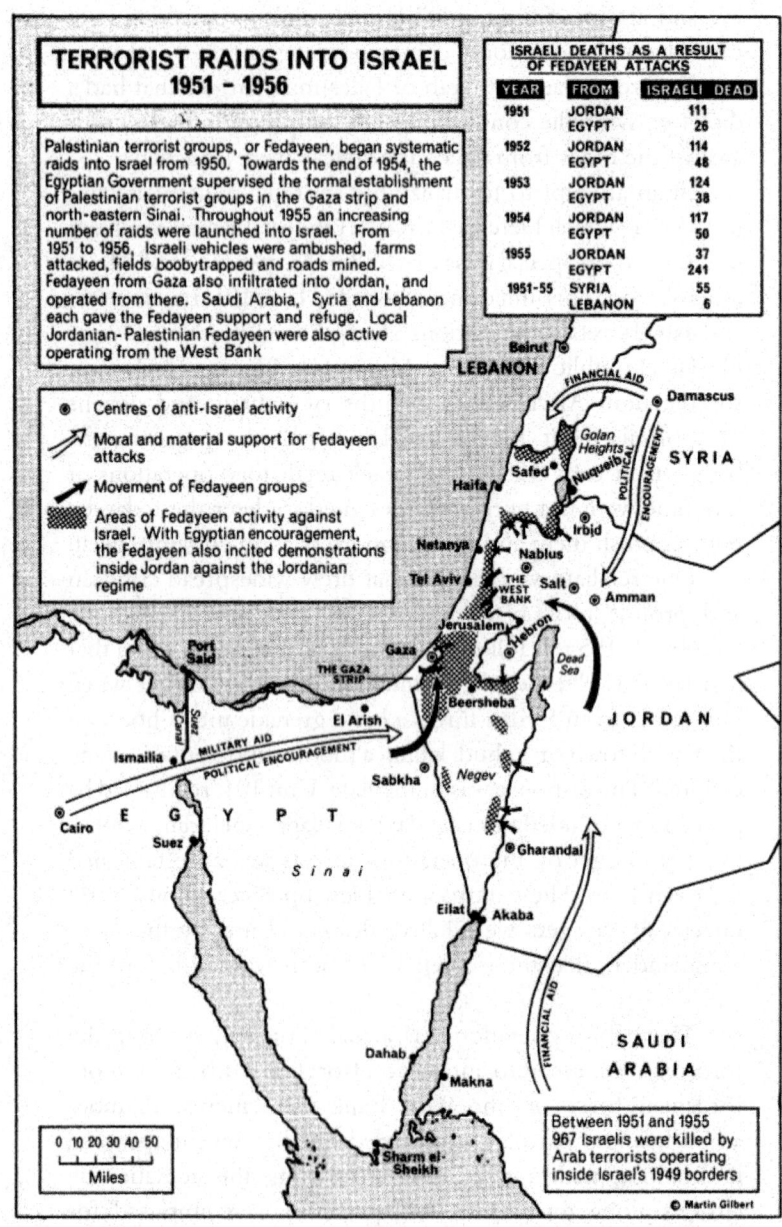

TERRORIST RAIDS INTO ISRAEL 1951 - 1956

Palestinian terrorist groups, or Fedayeen, began systematic raids into Israel from 1950. Towards the end of 1954, the Egyptian Government supervised the formal establishment of Palestinian terrorist groups in the Gaza strip and north-eastern Sinai. Throughout 1955 an increasing number of raids were launched into Israel. From 1951 to 1956, Israeli vehicles were ambushed, farms attacked, fields boobytrapped and roads mined. Fedayeen from Gaza also infiltrated into Jordan, and operated from there. Saudi Arabia, Syria and Lebanon each gave the Fedayeen support and refuge. Local Jordanian-Palestinian Fedayeen were also active operating from the West Bank

ISRAELI DEATHS AS A RESULT OF FEDAYEEN ATTACKS		
YEAR	FROM	ISRAELI DEAD
1951	JORDAN	111
	EGYPT	26
1952	JORDAN	114
	EGYPT	48
1953	JORDAN	124
	EGYPT	38
1954	JORDAN	117
	EGYPT	50
1955	JORDAN	37
	EGYPT	241
1951-55	SYRIA	55
	LEBANON	6

● Centres of anti-Israel activity

↗ Moral and material support for Fedayeen attacks

➤ Movement of Fedayeen groups

▨ Areas of Fedayeen activity against Israel. With Egyptian encouragement, the Fedayeen also incited demonstrations inside Jordan against the Jordanian regime

Between 1951 and 1955 967 Israelis were killed by Arab terrorists operating inside Israel's 1949 borders

© Martin Gilbert

Sir Martin Gilbert, © 2010. Reproduced by permission of Taylor & Francis Books UK. www.martingilbert.com

Typically, the UN never condemned a single *fedayeen* attack but always condemned Israeli reprisal attacks!*

1955 - 1956 Tensions with Egypt Grow

Following a failed attempt by then-Prime Minister Moshe Sharett to initiate a peace deal with Egypt,** *fedayeen* attacks increased from the Gaza Strip while they declined from other Arab states. For Jordan and Syria the Israeli reprisals were becoming too costly, hence they stopped the *fedayeen* attacks. For Egypt, on the other hand, since Gaza was 200 miles away from most of Egypt, the Egyptian government didn't seem to mind Israeli reprisals as long as they were aimed at Gaza. For this reason, Egypt ramped up its support of *fedayeen* terror attacks.

At the same time, the Soviet Union had found a very willing partner in Egypt's president. Under Nasser, Egypt turned on her old colonial allies, England and France, who had built and maintained the Suez Canal. This was great news for the Soviet Union. The Soviets thus agreed to build a huge power station, known as the Aswan Dam, which would harness the power of the mighty Nile River. In addition, Egypt signed a $200 million weapons deal with Czechoslovakia, with the blessings of the Soviet Union as well, which allowed the Egyptian army to be totally re-equipped with modern Soviet equipment. This included brand new Soviet jet fighters, tanks, artillery, missiles and naval vessels. In one swift stroke the Egyptian Army was totally modernized. Most of this new materiel found its way to the border with Israel.

Now prepared for war, Nasser fired the first round by closing the Straits of Tiran in 1955 to Israeli shipping, thus blockading Eilat. (The Straits of Tiran lie about one hundred miles due south of the Port of Eilat where the Gulf of Aqaba spills into the Red Sea.

---

* It must be noted that Judea, Samaria and Gaza were in Arab hands during this period of attacks against Israeli civilians. Which occupied territories were the *fedayeen* trying to liberate? Clearly, the Israel that existed within the 1949 Armistice lines.

** See Jerome Chanes, "The Lessons of the Lavon Affair," *The Forward*, May 16, 2014 (http://forward.com/opinion/198375/the-lessons-of-the-lavon-affair/)

From the Red Sea, traveling east, you reach the Indian Ocean and eventually the Pacific Ocean.) By blockading the Straits of Tiran, Egypt was cutting off Israel from all of its potential African and Asian trade routes. By blockading Eilat, Egypt, by international law, was effectively declaring war on Israel. So by the middle of 1955 Israel found itself being slowly bled to death by *fedayeen*, facing a rearmed Egyptian army and its economy suffering badly due to the blockade. Israel, throughout this period, received no support from either the UN or the U.S.

THE SUEZ CRISIS WITH ENGLAND AND FRANCE AFFECTS ISRAEL

Nasser had become the face of the Arab world in the 1950s since Egypt was the most populous Arab country, and Nasser was a very flamboyant and charismatic leader who spoke of creating a true Pan-Arab movement that would unite the Arab World. He did not see himself as a religious figure, but rather as a nationalistic and military leader. He was also seen as the leader of the new emerging block of Third World non-aligned nations, essentially the former colonies of the European powers that were granted independence after World War I, who decided that if they'd ban together at the UN they could actually be a formidable voting block that both the Western countries and the communist countries would have to pay close attention to. Nasser used this newly-found position of power to let it be known that Egypt saw the presence of the large British force that controlled the Suez Canal (Britain and France being the project's builders who completed the canal in 1869) as a foreign occupying power that must leave Egypt. The Suez Canal had been a linchpin in British and French military, foreign and economic policies since the canal's completion because it connected Europe to Asia and West Africa, as well as to the Persian Gulf oil fields beginning in the 1930s. The Suez Canal was also a source of great revenue since hundreds of ships passed through it every year each paying a user's fee. Nasser had already been hinting since 1954 that he intended to make the Suez Canal purely an Egyptian asset.

In July of 1955 Nasser wanted to make a clear statement to the British, French, the entire Western World, as well as the entire Arab and Third World that he was the one who dictated policy in all of Egypt, including the Suez Canal. Hence, he formally nationalized the Canal and gave the British and the few French there a short timetable to evacuate the area. For its own foreign policy reasons, the U.S. at the time fresh off the Korean War and in a Cold War with the USSR, chose not to involve itself in this Middle East quagmire. The Soviet Union was delighted since this was yet another blow to the Western democracies.*

The fact that England and France were angry at Egypt and felt they had no U.S. or UN support opened up the door for them to listen to the State of Israel, who was at the same time having its own very different set of problems with Egypt. Though Israel had managed to purchase some weapons from France prior to 1955 to update its arsenal, most of its materiel inventory was comprised of either refitted World War II surplus, second tier-French equipment and U.S. Sherman tanks. But once Nasser ordered the British and French out of the Suez Canal zone, then France finally was prepared to sell Israel some top-of-the line French equipment that included French jet fighters and bombers. Israel worked hard to integrate all the new military equipment into the IDF.

---

* "Well into the 1940s, Egypt, along with most of the rest of the Middle East, remained a lesser global concern, still in the thrall of the European powers that imposed their will on the area decades before. That began to change at the end of World War II with the discovery of vast new oil fields in the region, and with the collapse of the British and French colonial empires. The pace of change greatly accelerated when Nasser and his Free Officers Movement of junior military officers overthrew Egypt's Western-pliant king in 1952.

"Championing 'Arab socialism' and Pan-Arab unity, Nasser swiftly became a galvanizing figure throughout the Arab world, the spokesman for a people long dominated by foreigners and Western-educated elites. Just as crucial to the strongman's popularity was what he opposed: colonialism, imperialism and that most immediate and enduring example of the West's meddling in the region, the state of Israel.

"Nasser's success inspired many other would-be Arab leaders, nowhere more so than in the artificial states of the Middle East formed by the (cont'd)

By 1956 it was clear that England and France were not going to leave the Suez Canal without a fight. The British, in fact, had one the world's largest military installations in and around the Suez Canal, in excess of 80,000 troops. A secret plan was worked out between Israel, France and Britain regarding how each would attack Egypt at the same time, at different locations for completely different reasons. Israel was fighting for her life and England and France were fighting for what was left of their international influence and power. Even though this was distasteful to Ben-Gurion, Israel did not have any alternatives. With no allies or support in the UN, Israel had to break out of the stranglehold she was in.

The eventual plan had the IDF attack Gaza and Sinai, which would allow Israel to destroy the *fedayeen* bases, as well as the Egyptian army in Sinai, thus ending the blockade of the Straits of Tiran. The IDF, if successful, would stop ten miles distant from the Suez Canal, thus leaving the British and French armies with the task of securing the two large port cities at the opening of

---

European powers. By 1968, military officers espousing the Baathist ('renaissance') philosophy—a quasi-socialist form of Pan-Arabism—had seized power in Iraq and Syria. They were joined the following year by the Libyan lieutenant Muammar el-Qaddafi, and his somewhat-baffling 'third universal theory,' which rejected traditional democracy in favor of rule by 'people's committees.' In all three countries, just as in Egypt, Western-favored monarchs or Parliaments were neutered or cast aside.

"But Nasser possessed an advantage that his fellow autocrats in the region did not. With a sense of national identity that stretched back millenniums, Egypt never seemed in danger of being torn apart; the centrifugal pull of tribes or clans or sectarian identity simply didn't exist there to the degree it did in Syria or Iraq. At the same time, Egypt's long tradition of relative liberalism had given rise to a fractious political landscape that ran the spectrum from secular communists to fundamentalist Islamists.

"Part of Nasser's genius was his ability to bridge these divides, and he did so by appealing both to Egyptian national pride and to a shared antipathy for the West, a vestige, perhaps, of 70 years of heavy-handed rule by Britain. Thus, even when Islamist conservatives became alarmed by Nasser's moves toward greater secularism, most still saw him as a hero for nationalizing Western businesses, and for besting Britain, France and Israel in the 1956 Suez crisis. (cont'd)

the Canal—Port Said and Port Fouad—from Egyptian control, thus giving them total control of the zone. The fact that the IDF would be ten miles east of the Suez Canal was supposed to be a justification for the British and French armies to enter the Sinai and separate the forces.

SINAI CAMPAIGN "MIVTZA' KADESH":
OCTOBER 29, 1956 - NOVEMBER 5, 1956

On October 29, 1956, Israel launched a pre-emptive war against Egypt in order to solve her three major problems: a) *fedayeen* attacks; b) the build-up of the newly equipped Egyptian army, and c) the Egyptian blockade of the Straits of Tiran. In an exceptionally well planned and well-executed attack involving IDF infantry, armor, artillery, air and naval power, the Israeli army achieved all of its goals. In addition, Israel captured the Sinai Desert, including the Gaza Strip, in 100 hours of combat but was careful to stay ten miles east of the Suez Canal as agreed upon with England and France. The Chief of Staff of the IDF at the time was one of the young heroes of the 1948-49 War of Independence, Moshe Dayan. The Egyptian Army suffered a devastating defeat in terms of the amount of territory it lost, the amount of men killed, wounded and captured, as well as the vast amount of brand new Soviet equipment that was destroyed by the IDF.

"Similarly, urban liberals like the Soueif family who disdained Nasser's strong-arm rule—his was a military dictatorship, after all—also cheered him for his leadership in the international Nonaligned Movement, for proudly thumbing his nose at the threats and enticements of the United States as it sought to compel Egypt into its orbit during the Cold War. This became the means by which Nasser and his successor, Anwar Sadat, maintained their grip on power: play left and right off each other as a matter of course; bring them together when needed by focusing on an external foe." (Scott Anderson, "Fractured Lands: How the Arab World Came Apart," New York Times, August 11, 2016 ((http://www.nytimes.com/interactive/2016/08/11/magazine/isis-middle-east-arab-spring-fractured-lands.html?action=click&contentCollection=Olympics&module=Trending&version=Full&region=Marginalia&pgtype=article))

Once again the Arab world threatened Israel and did not grasp the effect these threats had on the behavior of the Jewish State. Nasser and Egypt were stunned by the defeat.

The British and French attacks against Port Said and Port Fouad were a total disaster. They were partially repulsed by the Egyptian Army, and the United States condemned the British and French attack and brought in the UN to condemn France and Britain with the support of the Soviet Union, no less. With the exception of British and French air attacks on Egyptian bases, the entire operation was a total fiasco. It would be the last time these two countries would be perceived as world powers.

The Israeli war against Egypt in 1956 was a different and separate war from the one England and France fought. As mentioned earlier, the motives of the parties were quite different. The Israeli victory was yet another message to the Arab world that Israel was an indigenous local country fighting for its existence and not the colonialist straw man they had been claiming Zionism and Israel represented. Subsequently, France was to be Israel's main ally and weapons supplier from 1956 to 1967.

March 1957 - Israel Completes Withdrawal from Sinai

The UN reaction to the Sinai Campaign was to condemn Israel as the aggressor. There was no mention of the *fedayeen* terror attacks, the Egyptian calls to annihilate the State of Israel, nor any reference to the huge Egyptian military buildup in Sinai that began in 1955.

Because of the intense pressure from the UN, the U.S. and the Soviet Union, Israel was told that she must immediately withdraw from all of Sinai and Gaza in the second week of November 1956. In essence, Israel was told to cooperate in her own destruction; for, to return Sinai to Egypt would have meant a return of the *fedayeen*, a re-initiation of the blockade of the Straits of Tiran and an eventual buildup of the Egyptian Army back in Sinai threatening Israel once again. Though Israel was a small country in the early

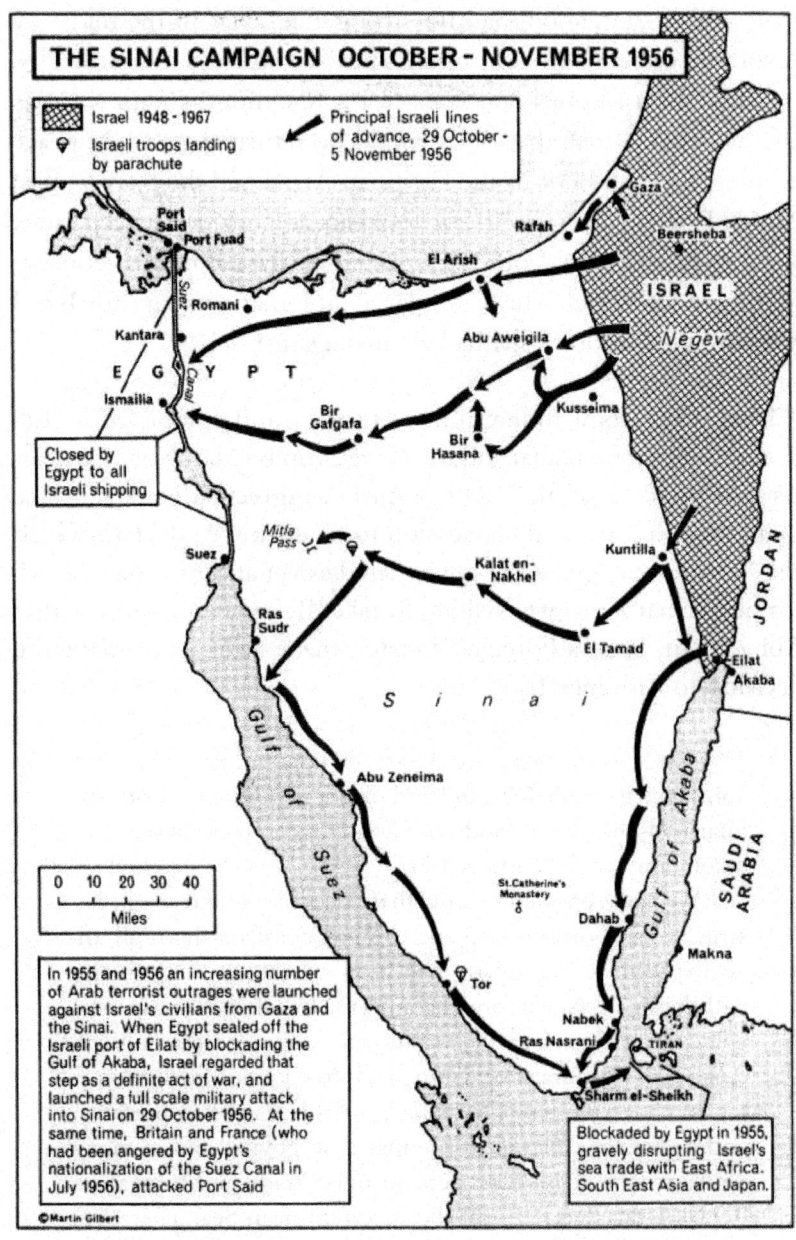

THE SINAI CAMPAIGN OCTOBER – NOVEMBER 1956

Israel 1948 - 1967

Israeli troops landing by parachute

Principal Israeli lines of advance, 29 October – 5 November 1956

Port Said
Port Fuad
Gaza
Rafah
Beersheba
El Arish
Romani
ISRAEL
Kantara
Abu Aweigila
Negev
E   G   Y   P   T
Ismailia
Bir Gafgafa
Kusseima
Bir Hasana

Closed by Egypt to all Israeli shipping

Mitla Pass
Suez
Kalat en-Nakhel
Kuntilla
JORDAN
Ras Sudr
El Tamad
Eilat
Akaba
S i n a i
Gulf of Suez
Gulf of Akaba
SAUDI ARABIA
Abu Zeneima

0 10 20 30 40
Miles

St.Catherine's Monastery
Dahab
Makna
Tor
Nabek
Ras Nasrani
TIRAN
Sharm el-Sheikh

In 1955 and 1956 an increasing number of Arab terrorist outrages were launched against Israel's civilians from Gaza and the Sinai. When Egypt sealed off the Israeli port of Eilat by blockading the Gulf of Akaba, Israel regarded that step as a definite act of war, and launched a full scale military attack into Sinai on 29 October 1956. At the same time, Britain and France (who had been angered by Egypt's nationalization of the Suez Canal in July 1956), attacked Port Said

Blockaded by Egypt in 1955, gravely disrupting Israel's sea trade with East Africa, South East Asia and Japan.

©Martin Gilbert

Sir Martin Gilbert, © 2010. Reproduced by permission of Taylor & Francis Books UK. www.martingilbert.com

stages of its statehood, had no strong allies, was in the midst of absorbing one million new immigrants, she still said no to the UN. Israel held on to Sinai and Gaza for a few months until she was able to strike a deal that Sinai would be returned to a UN peace keeping force and not to the Egyptian Army and the *fedayeen*. [See Appendix XII.] This UN force would act as a buffer between Israel and Egypt that could only be withdrawn by the mutual consent of Egypt and Israel. This was a large diplomatic victory for Israel considering the forces she had aligned against her.

I srael began its withdrawal in early 1957 and completed its full withdrawal from Sinai and the Gaza Strip by March of that year. As was the case of the 1949 Armistice Agreements, Israel once again made a territorial concession to an enemy Arab state, which also was not recognized or appreciated as yet another tangible risk for peace that Israel was willing to take. Below is the speech that Abba Eban, Israel's Foreign Minister, made after Israel made the decision to withdraw from Sinai:

> The Government of Israel is now in a position to announce its plans for a full and prompt withdrawal from the Sharm el-Sheikh area and the Gaza Strip, in compliance with resolution I of 2 February 1957.
> We have repeatedly stated that Israel has no interest in the strip of land overlooking the western coast of the Gulf of Aqaba. Our sole purpose has been to ensure that, on the withdrawal of Israeli forces, continued freedom of navigation will exist for Israeli and international shipping in the Gulf of Aqaba and the Straits of Tiran. Such freedom of navigation is a vital national interest for Israel, but it is also of importance and legitimate concern to the maritime Powers and to many States whose economies depend upon trade and navigation between the Red Sea and the Mediterranean Sea. There has recently been an increasingly wide recognition that the Gulf of Aqaba comprehends international waters in which the right of free and innocent passage exists. On 11 February

1957, the Secretary of State of the United States of America handed to the Ambassador of Israel in Washington a memorandum dealing, among other things, with the subject of the Gulf of Aqaba and the Straits of Tiran. This statement discusses the rights of nations in the Gulf of Aqaba and declares the readiness of the United States to exercise those rights on its own behalf and to join with others in securing general recognition of those rights. My Government has subsequently learnt with gratification that other leading maritime Powers are prepared to subscribe to the doctrine set out in the United States memorandum of 11 February and have a similar intention to exercise their rights of free and innocent passage in the Gulf and the Straits. The General Assembly's resolution (II) of 2 February 1957 contemplates that units of the United Nations Emergency Force will move into the Straits of Tiran area on Israel's withdrawal. It is generally recognized that the function of the United Nations Emergency Force in the Straits of Tiran area includes the prevention of belligerent acts. In this connection, my Government recalls the statements by the representative of the United States in the General Assembly on 28 January and 2 February 1957, with reference to the function of the United Nations Emergency Force units which are to move into the Straits of Tiran area on Israel's withdrawal. The statement of 28 January, repeated on 2 February, said: "It is essential that units of the United Nations Emergency Force be stationed at the Straits of Tiran in order to achieve there the separation of Egyptian and Israeli land and sea forces. This separation is essential until it is clear that the non existence of any claimed belligerent rights has established in practice the peaceful conditions which must govern navigation in waters having such an international interest." (AIPV 645, pages 35) My Government has been concerned with the situation which would arise if the United Nations Emergency Force, having taken up its position in the Straits of Tiran area for the purpose of assuring nonbelligerency, were to be withdrawn, in conditions which might give rise to interference with free and innocent navigation and, therefore, to the renewal of

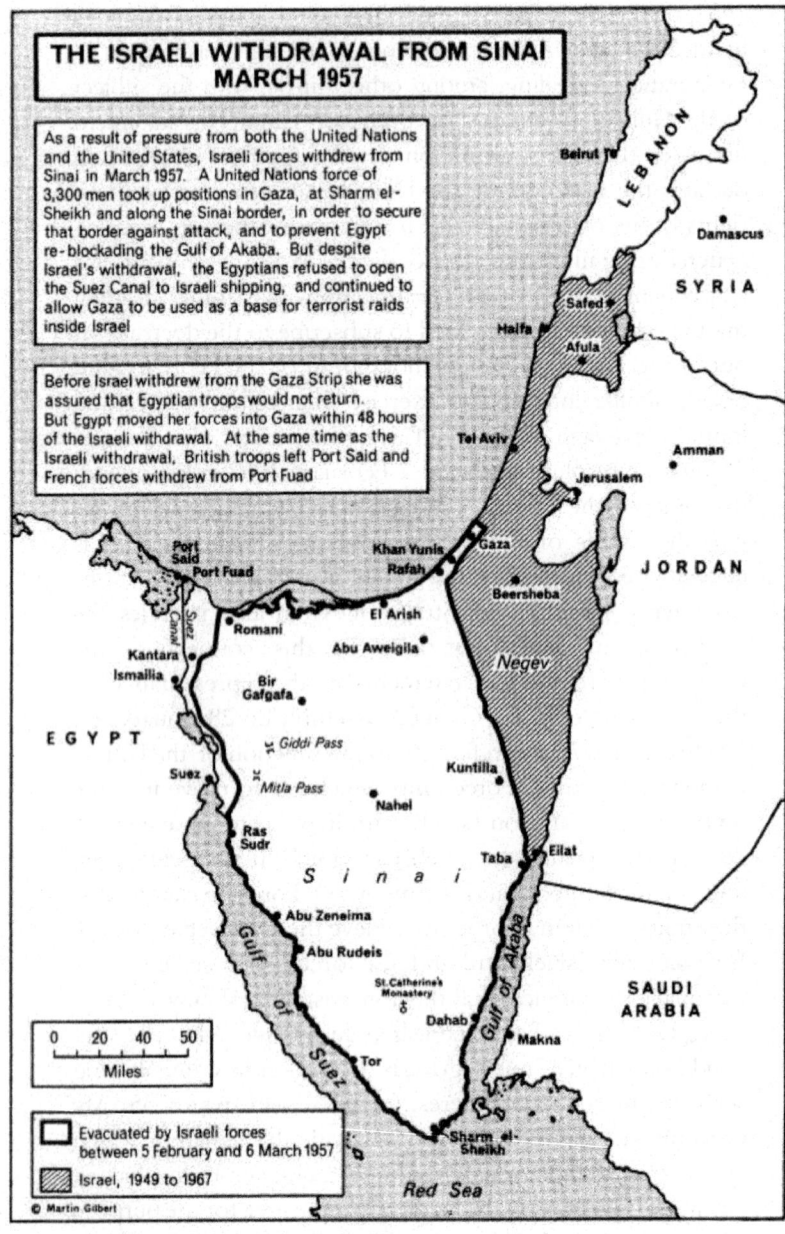

THE ISRAELI WITHDRAWAL FROM SINAI
MARCH 1957

As a result of pressure from both the United Nations and the United States, Israeli forces withdrew from Sinai in March 1957. A United Nations force of 3,300 men took up positions in Gaza, at Sharm el-Sheikh and along the Sinai border, in order to secure that border against attack, and to prevent Egypt re-blockading the Gulf of Akaba. But despite Israel's withdrawal, the Egyptians refused to open the Suez Canal to Israeli shipping, and continued to allow Gaza to be used as a base for terrorist raids inside Israel

Before Israel withdrew from the Gaza Strip she was assured that Egyptian troops would not return. But Egypt moved her forces into Gaza within 48 hours of the Israeli withdrawal. At the same time as the Israeli withdrawal, British troops left Port Said and French forces withdrew from Port Fuad

LEBANON

Beirut

Damascus

SYRIA

Safed

Haifa

Afula

Tel Aviv

Amman

Jerusalem

JORDAN

Port Said
Port Fuad

Khan Yunis
Rafah
Gaza

Beersheba

El Arish

Romani

Negev

Kantara
Ismailia

Abu Aweigila

Bir
Gafgafa

EGYPT

Giddi Pass

Kuntilla

Suez

Mitla Pass

Nahel

Ras
Sudr

Sinai

Taba
Eilat

Abu Zeneima

Gulf
of
Suez

Abu Rudeis

St.Catherine's
Monastery

SAUDI
ARABIA

Dahab

Gulf of Akaba

Makna

| 0 | 20 | 40 | 50 |

Miles

Tor

Sharm el-
Sheikh

Red Sea

Evacuated by Israeli forces
between 5 February and 6 March 1957

Israel, 1949 to 1967

© Martin Gilbert

Sir Martin Gilbert, © 2010. Reproduced by permission of Taylor
& Francis Books UK. www.martingilbert.com

hostilities. Such a premature cessation of the precautionary measures taken by the United Nations for the prevention of belligerent acts would prejudice important international interests and threaten peace and security. My Government has noted the assurance embodied in the Secretary General's report of 26 February 1957 that any proposal for the withdrawal of the United Nations Emergency Force from the Gulf of Aqaba area would first come to the Advisory Committee, which represents the General Assembly in the implementation of its resolution of 2 November 1956. This procedure will give the General Assembly an opportunity to ensure that no precipitate changes are made which would have the effect of increasing the possibility of belligerent acts. We have reason to believe that in such a discussion many members of the United Nations would be guided by the view expressed by Ambassador Lodge on 2 February in favour of maintaining the Emergency Force in the Straits of Tiran until peaceful conditions were in practice assured. In the light of these doctrines, policies and arrangements by the United Nations and the maritime Powers, my Government is confident that free and innocent passage for international and Israeli shipping will continue to be fully maintained after Israel's withdrawal. It remains for me now to formulate the policy of Israel both as a littoral State and as a country which intends to exercise its full rights of free passage in the Gulf of Aqaba and through the Straits of Tiran. The Government of Israel believes that the Gulf of Aqaba comprehends international waters and that no nation has the right to prevent free and innocent passage in the Gulf and through the Straits giving access thereto, in accordance with the generally accepted definition of those terms in the law of the sea. In its capacity as a littoral State, Israel will gladly offer port facilities to the ships of all nations and all flags exercising free passage in the Gulf of Aqaba. We have received with gratification the assurances of leading maritime Powers that they foresee a normal and regular flow of traffic of all cargoes in the Gulf of Aqaba. Israel will do nothing to impede free and innocent passage by ships of Arab countries bound to Arab ports or to any other destination. Israel is resolved, on behalf of vessels of Israeli registry, to exercise the right of free and innocent passage and is prepared to join with others to secure universal respect of this right. Israel will protect ships of its own flag exercising the right of free and innocent passage on the high seas and in international waters. Interference, by armed force, with ships of Israeli flag exercising free and innocent passage in the Gulf of Aqaba and through the Straits of Tiran will be regarded by Israel as an attack entitling it to exercise its inherent right of selfdefence under Article 51 of the Charter and to take all such measures as are necessary to ensure the free and innocent passage of its ships in the Gulf and in the Straits. We make this announcement in accordance with the accepted principles of international law under which all States have an inherent right to use their forces to protect their ships and their rights against interference by armed force. My Government naturally hopes that this contingency will not occur. In a public address on 20 February, President Eisenhower stated: "We should not assume that if Israel withdraws, Egypt will prevent Israeli shipping from using the Suez Canal or the Gulf of Aqaba." This declaration has weighed heavily with my Government in determining its action today. Israel is now prepared to withdraw its forces from the Gulf of Aqaba and the Straits of Tiran in the confidence that there will be continued freedom of navigation for international and Israeli shipping in the Gulf of Aqaba and through the Straits of Tiran. We propose that a meeting be held immediately between the Chief of Staff of the Israel Defence Forces and the Commander of the United Nations Emergency Force in order to arrange for the United Nations to take over its responsibilities in the Sharm elSheikh area. The Government of Israel announces that it is making a complete withdrawal from the Gaza Strip in accordance with General Assembly resolution (I) of 2 February 1957 (A/RES/460). It makes this announcement on the following assumptions: (a) That on its withdrawal the United Nations Forces will be deployed in Gaza and that the takeover of Gaza from the military and civilian control of Israel will be exclusively by the United Nations Emergency

Force. (b) It is further Israel's expectation that the United Nations will be the agency to be utilized for carrying out the functions enumerated by the Secretary General, namely: "safeguarding life and property in the area by providing efficient and effective police protection as will guarantee good civilian administration; as will assure maximum assistance to the United Nations refugee programme; and as will protect and foster the economic development of the territory and its people." (AIPV. 659, page 17) (c) It is further Israel's expectation that the aforementioned responsibility of the United Nations in the administration of Gaza will be maintained for a transitory period from the takeover until there is a peace settlement, to be sought as rapidly as possible, or a definitive agreement on the future of the Gaza Strip. It is the position of Israel that if conditions are created in the Gaza Strip which indicate a return to the conditions of deterioration that existed previously, Israel would reserve its freedom to act to defend its rights. Accordingly, we propose that a meeting be held immediately between the Chief of Staff of the Israel Defence Forces and the Commander of the United Nations Emergency Force in order to arrange for the United Nations to take over its responsibilities in the Gaza area. For many weeks, amidst great difficulty, my Government has sought to ensure that, on the withdrawal from the Sharm elSheikh and the Gaza areas, circumstances would prevail which would prevent the likelihood of belligerent acts. We record with gratitude the sympathetic efforts of many Governments and delegations to help bring about a situation which would end the insecurity prevailing in Israel and among its neighbours these many years. In addition to the considerations to which I have referred, we place our trust in the vigilant resolve of the international community that Israel, equally with all member-States, enjoy its basic rights of freedom from fear of attack; freedom to sail the high seas and international waterways in peace; freedom to pursue its national destiny in tranquillity without the constant peril which has surrounded it in recent years. In this reliance we are embarking upon the course which I have announced today.

May I now add these few words to the States in the Middle East area and, more specifically, to the neighbours of Israel: We all come from an area which is a very ancient one. The hills and the valleys of the region have been witnesses to many wars and many conflicts. But that is not the only thing which characterizes that part of the world from which we come. It is also a part of the world which is of an ancient culture. It is that part of the world which has given to humanity three great religions. It is also that part of the world which has given a code of ethics to all humanity. In our countries, in the entire region, all our peoples are anxious for and in need of a higher standard of living, of great programmes of development and progress. Can we, from now on, all of us turn a new leaf and, instead of fighting with each other, can we all, united, fight poverty and disease and illiteracy? Is it possible for us to put all our efforts and all our energy into one single purpose, the betterment and progress and development of all our lands and all our peoples? I can here pledge the Government and the people of Israel to do their part in this united effort. There is no limit to what we are prepared to contribute so that all of us, together, can live to see a day of happiness for our peoples and see again from that region a great contribution to peace and happiness for all humanity."[10]

While the UN focused on an Israeli withdrawel from the Sinai and Gaza, it failed to act on an act of aggression being perpetrated by the Soviet Union. That event was the invasion of Hungary that lasted from October 23-November 10, 1956. Hungary tried to declare itself independent, and its Soviet masters would have none of it. The USSR invaded Hungary with tens of thousands of Soviet troops, killed several thousand Hungarians and caused over 200,000 Hungarians to flee. Other than the creation of a committee after the fact, the UN reaction was nonexistent.

ADOLF EICHMANN, ARCHITECT OF THE FINAL SOLUTION, CAPTURED (1960-1961)

No one man was more responsible (other than Hitler) for the

deaths of six million Jews than Adolf Eichmann, the architect of the Final Solution who came up with the entire plan and how it should be carried out. He laid out these plans at the infamous Wannsee Conference held in January 1942. In 1960 he was tracked down by Israel's Mossad in Argentina, captured, and brought to Israel to stand trial for crimes against the Jewish people. The trial was held in Jerusalem in the spring of 1961 and lasted until late that summer. This was not a show trial. Israeli prosecutors had collected thousands of documents, and hundreds of Holocaust survivors testified. Eichmann himself had a defense team and sat in a bullet proof glass booth while in court, because of the fear of an assassination attempt by relatives of Holocaust victims. At the end, Eichmann was found guilty and remains to this day the only person to be put to death by the State of Israel.

There were a few reasons to have this trial. (Had they just wanted Eichmann dead, the Mossad agents could have easily killed him in Argentina.)

1) Israel sent a message to the world: The re-established Jewish State of Israel is, and will continue to be, the defender of the Jewish people.

2) Antisemitism will no longer be a painless pursuit. He who kills Jews just because they are Jews was put on notice that the State of Israel will hold them responsible.

3) Israel's youth needed to receive a lesson in the history of the Holocaust, and the trial was a perfect vehicle.

4) The world needed to be reminded of the Holocaust; again, the trial was the perfect vehicle for this kind of lesson.

5) The testimony that was collected at this trial, which was held only 16 years after the Holocaust, created a vast library of first-hand taped evidence by survivors, who each gave personal, heart wrenching detailed testimony as they stood 30 to 40 feet away from their former tormenter.

The Eichmann trial represented a form of justice that the Jewish people had been unable to receive from their many tormentors over their 2,000-year journey in the Diaspora. The trial itself was at once a remarkable testament to the new status of the once stateless and defenseless Jewish nation while at the same time was the greatest punishment a man like Eichmann could be subjected to. The idea that the architect of the most thought out premeditated murder of a nation, who back in 1942 in Wannsee thought he was doing the most just thing in the world—cleansing the world of the subhuman Jews—was now sitting in a court room in their state, adorned with the symbol of that state, the Menorah, while sitting in a bullet proof booth, being tried by Jewish judges speaking to him in Hebrew.

QUIET YEARS OF GROWTH AND DEVELOPMENT (1957 - 1967)

After the 1956 Sinai Campaign, Israel was to have one of her quietest decades. This occurred because the Arab world was simply incapable during that time of launching any meaningful military or terror actions. The 1956 War humbled and, to an extent, scared Israel's neighbors. During this decade Israel was involved in settling its new immigrants, mass construction projects that included building new cities for all of these new Israelis, and building up a manufacturing capacity, power plants, hospitals, schools, *yeshivot*, research centers and universities. Furthermore, Israel built an irrigation canal bringing water from the Kinneret in the Galil down to the Northern Negev. This project was called the "*Movil Ha'artzee,*" the National Water Carrier.

By 1967 the Jewish population of Israel had reached two million and its Arab population was 500,000. The country was now on its way up economically and at peace. In the spring of 1967 all of this was about to change in a very dramatic way!

Footnotes

[1] "The Law of Return," The Jewish Agency (http://www.jewishagency.org/first-steps/program/5131)

[2] Yehoshafat Harkabi, *Arab Attitudes Towards Israel* (Jersualem: Keter Publishing, 1972), 1

[3] *Ibid.*, 28.

[4] *Ibid.*

[5] *Ibid.*, 38.

[6] Mitchel Bard, "Arab League Boycot: Background and and Overview," Jewish Virtual Library (http://www.jewishvirtuallibrary.org/jsource/History/Arab_boycott.html)

[7] *Ibid.*

[8] *Ibid.*

[9] Boaz Ganor, "Israel and the Palestine Liberation Organization," in *The Routledge History of Terrorism*, ed. Randall D. Law (Florence, KY: Taylor & Francis Group, 2014), 239-240. (239-257).

[10] "The Sinai-Suez Campaign: Israel Agrees to Withdrawal, March 1, 1957," Israeli Foreign Ministry, Jewish Virtual Library (http://www.jewishvirtuallibrary.org/jsource/History/iswithdraw.html).

Chapter 11

The Six-Day War
June 1967

THE LEAD UP TO THE 1967 SIX-DAY WAR

While Israel was busy in turning herself into a functional democratic Jewish State, her neighbors were busy creating repressive dictatorships that kept their people united and distracted by trying to outdo each other in anti-Israel behavior and rhetoric. Lost in all of this were the Palestinian Arabs who lived in the surrounding Arab countries and those who lived in what was called the West Bank* and the Gaza Strip. These refugees were treated as pariahs who needed to stay in their UN-sponsored refugee camps where they could be a tangible exhibit of "Israeli aggression" against the Arab world in particular and the Palestinian Arabs specifically. There was no attempt to integrate them into society or to allow them to feel wanted and accepted. Jordan, who illegally annexed the West Bank, pretended that there was never supposed to be an Arab Palestinian state based on the November 29, 1947 UN Partition Plan. Egypt had a similar attitude with regard to the Gaza Strip; as far as Egypt was concerned the Gaza Strip was a military district belonging to Egypt and the Arab Palestinians who lived

---

*"The name *West Bank* is a translation of the Arabic term *ad-Diffah I-Garbiyyah*, given to the territory west of the Jordan River that fell, in 1948, under occupation and administration by Jordan, which claimed subsequently to have annexed it in 1950...The term was chosen to differentiate the west bank of the River Jordan from the "east bank" of this river." (https://en.wikipedia.org/wiki/West_Bank)

there were treated as if they were prisoners. They were not allowed to leave the Gaza Strip to enter Sinai or Egypt, though they were not forgotten when it came to be recruited as terrorists to attack Israeli civilians in the 1950s.*

From 1949 to 1967 the Arab countries that bordered Israel, with the exception of Lebanon, chose to engage in activities to weaken or destroy Israel. In the 1950s the *fedayeen* came from Syria, Jordan and Egypt. Egypt attempted to strangle Israel with a blockade of Eilat, and Syria decided to use the Golan Heights as a base for attacks against Israeli *kibbutzim* and towns in the area.**

ELI COHEN

Eli Cohen was born in Egypt in 1928 to Syrian Jewish parents. They made *Aliyah* in 1949, but Cohen remained in Egypt where he worked as an agent for the State of Israel. He made *Aliyah* in 1953, returned to Egypt in 1956 as a spy for the Mossad, and was expelled from Egypt in 1957. For the next few years he drifted from job to job until he was rehired by the Mossad to be a special agent. Since

---

*What is most interesting is the lack of any concern at all by the Arab world, the UN, Western Europe, the Vatican, the block of Third World Nations, the Communist nations or the American Left in establishing an Arab Palestinian State during the period of 1949-1967. It was alright for Jordan to be illegally governing the West Bank, and Egypt illegally ruling the Gaza Strip. The world outcry for Palestinian rights only occurred in 1967 after Israel conquered these territories.

**The Golan Heights is an area that rises to the east of the Hula Valley and the Sea of Galilee. It is made of mountains of mostly basalt and ancient volcanic ash that tower over the Hula Valley and the Kinneret by an average of 2,000 to 3,000 feet. The highest point is the pinnacle of Mt. Hermon that is close to 9,000 feet above sea level. From 1949 to 1967 the Syrian government pursued a policy of turning the Golan into a massive series of fortified military positions literally dug into the Golan mountains. At the same time, since the Kinneret lay at the base of the Golan and was Israel's only sweet water lake, Syria tried to build canals and dams to divert the creeks and small rivers that flowed downwards from the Heights, and especially Mt. Hermon (which is snow covered twelve months a year), from reaching the Kinneret. In addition, this region was under constant artillery shelling, mortar and sniper fire.

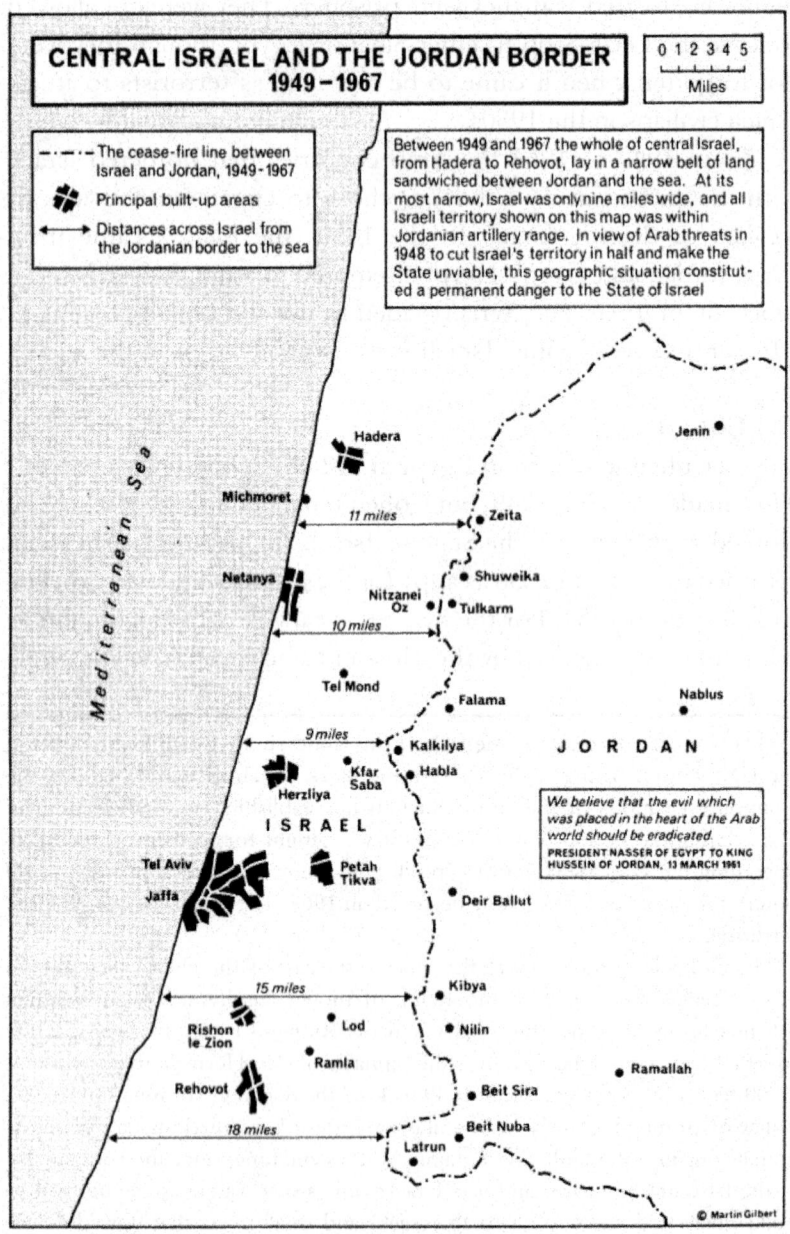

CENTRAL ISRAEL AND THE JORDAN BORDER 1949–1967

0 1 2 3 4 5 Miles

–·–·– The cease-fire line between Israel and Jordan, 1949-1967

Principal built-up areas

Distances across Israel from the Jordanian border to the sea

Between 1949 and 1967 the whole of central Israel, from Hadera to Rehovot, lay in a narrow belt of land sandwiched between Jordan and the sea. At its most narrow, Israel was only nine miles wide, and all Israeli territory shown on this map was within Jordanian artillery range. In view of Arab threats in 1948 to cut Israel's territory in half and make the State unviable, this geographic situation constituted a permanent danger to the State of Israel

Mediterranean Sea

Jenin

Hadera

Michmoret

11 miles — Zeita

Netanya

Shuweika

Nitzanei Oz — Tulkarm

10 miles

Tel Mond

Falama

Nablus

9 miles

Kalkilya

J O R D A N

Kfar Saba — Habla

Herzliya

I S R A E L

We believe that the evil which was placed in the heart of the Arab world should be eradicated.
PRESIDENT NASSER OF EGYPT TO KING HUSSEIN OF JORDAN, 13 MARCH 1961

Tel Aviv

Petah Tikva

Jaffa

Deir Ballut

15 miles — Kibya

Rishon le Zion

Lod

Nilin

Ramla

Ramallah

Rehovot

Beit Sira

18 miles

Beit Nuba

Latrun

© Martin Gilbert

Sir Martin Gilbert, © 2010. Reproduced by permission of Taylor & Francis Books UK. www.martingilbert.com

he was fluent in Arabic and knew a great deal about Syrian culture and geography from his parents, he was given an assignment to penetrate the Syrian government at the highest levels.

Cohen's cover was that he was an expatriate Syrian who became a successful businessman in Argentina and was returning to Syria to open up businesses there. With this cover he became exceptionally successful. He gained access to Syrian military bases and strategic sites. Cohen was especially interested in what was going on in the Golan Heights. In 1964 Cohen saw firsthand the large canal the Syrian Army was building to divert the waters from the Banias Stream, a main feeder of the Kinneret. Using a secret radio transmitter, he passed this information on to Israel. Several months later the Israeli Air Force, in a well-planned and precise raid, bombed the entire canal. The damage was so extensive it was too expensive for the Syrian Army to restart the project.

During this same period Cohen got a tour of all the Syrian fortifications in the Golan Heights. After the tour he made a suggestion to the Syrian commanders that since it was very sunny and hot in all these positions they should plant large trees at each fortification to offer the soldiers shade. His advice was taken. Cohen was thus able to pass on to the IDF that all they needed to spot was a cluster of trees to know where the Syrian fortifications were located. This became a vital piece of information for the IDF during the 1967 Six-Day War.

Sadly, Cohen was caught transmitting to Israel on his secret radio by Syrian security officials. He was tortured, given a show trial, and then hanged publicly in Damascus.

INSTABILITY IN THE ARAB WORLD AND ITS EFFECT ON THE ARAB WAR AGAINST ISRAEL, 1958 – 1967

In 1958 there was a brutal coup in Iraq wherein the ruling King Feisal was executed, along with his uncle Abdul Illah, and then their bodies dragged through the streets of Baghdad. At the same time, the legendary father of modern Iraq, Nuri Said, was also brutally murdered by a rampaging mob. The new leader was a pro-

Soviet general, Abdul Karim Kassem, who gave the Soviet Union its first foothold in the strategic Persian Gulf area.

At the same time, President Nasser of Egypt, who was working on becoming the leader of the entire Arab World under the banner of Pan Arabism (uniting all the Arab States that were mostly formed right before or after World War II), began to foment problems in both Lebanon and Jordan. In Lebanon his intervention in internal politics was so great that there was a civil war in 1958 that caused then-President Eisenhower, at the invitation of the Lebanese President Camille Nimr Chamoun (1900-1987), to send a large contingent of Marines into Beirut to reestablish order and stability. At the same time in Jordan, and at the invitation of the young King Hussein, who had assumed the throne after his grandfather, King Abdullah, was assassinated in 1951, the British Army flew in forces to protect the Hashemite leadership.

Similarly, in the same year, after a revolution in Syria brought to power the Baath Party, Nasser forged an alliance creating a new Arab country consisting of Egypt and Syria called the United Arab Republic (U.A.R.) and then encouraged the Syrian branch to heat up the Golan Heights/Israeli border. Hamstrung to an extent by the UN presence in Sinai and Gaza, but realizing that creating hostilities with Israel was a great way to unify almost any Arab country having internal issues, Nasser saw the Golan Heights incursion as a way to reinforce his position as the new head of the U.A.R.

In 1960 his thirst for political power made him attempt to destabilize Jordan. Condemning King Hussein as a lackey of the West, he had the Jordanian prime minister, Haza al Majali, assassinated.[1] But Nasser had overplayed his hand and Syria began to see him as an occupying ruler. As a result, the U.A.R. was dissolved.

In February of 1966 there was yet another bloody revolution in Syria which brought to power a radical branch of the Baath Party. This new government wanted to move closer to the Soviet

Union, but it had many enemies in Syria. The best way to deflect attention away from itself was to ramp up hostilities with Israel. One of those tactics was to ramp up *fedayeen* activities.

Beginning in early 1967 there was an uptick in Syrian attacks against the Israeli towns that bordered the Golan Heights. The IDF was forced to respond with its own artillery fire and bombing of Syrian positions. The Syrian population stopped worrying about the radical nature of the new Baath government and instead rallied behind it as a champion of the anti-Israel cause.

On April 7th 1967, after a particularly extensive artillery barrage that covered almost all of northeastern Israel, the IDF replied with a proportional artillery barrage and a large scale air strike on Syrian fortifications in the Golan Heights. The Syrian air force had seven of its Russian made MIG fighter planes shot down. At the same time, the Chief of Staff of the IDF, Yitzchak Rabin, offered a warning to the new Baath regime in Damascus: If it would continue to shell northeastern Israel, then the IDF would retaliate in such a way that would endanger the existence of the regime.

The Soviet Union, Syria's powerful patron, saw an opportunity in the Israeli April 7th operation. Moscow, aware that it became more essential when its clients needed military aid and political cover at the UN, determined it was in its best interest to exaggerate the intentions of the IDF response. Thus, the Soviet Union informed the Syrian government that its satellites had detected a massive movement of IDF soldiers and equipment to the Golan Heights border. As a result, Syria began to mobilize her reserve soldiers and put the country on a war footing. By late May, the Syrian army was ready for war with Israel.

During this period Israel still had diplomatic relations with the Soviet Union. The Israeli prime minister at the time, Levi Eshkol, was aware that the Soviet Union's lies were the reason that Syria was on the brink of attacking Israel. Hence, he invited the Soviet ambassador to Israel at the time to accompany him personally to the Israel-Syria Border to see for himself if there was any Israeli mobilization. The Soviet ambassador rejected the offer. Since there was no Soviet retraction, the Syrian Army continued its preparations for war throughout April and May.

On May 13 a Soviet delegation arrived in Egypt to meet with Nasser and inform him of its assessment of the Israeli threat to Syria. Nasser, at the time, was at a low point politically since his ascension to power. Egypt had been soundly defeated by Israel in the 1956 War; the side Egypt had chosen to support in the 1962 civil war in Yemen was doing poorly, and the Saudis, supporting the other side in the Yemen civil war, were growing very angry and frustrated with Nasser. With the Soviets and the Syrians asking him for assistance in the battle against the Israelis, here was opportunity for Nasser to set all of his troubles aside and once again become the champion of the Arab world.

Thus, on May 14, Nasser mobilized the Egyptian Army. On May 16, Egyptian forces began moving through the streets of Cairo towards the Suez Canal and Sinai. On that same day, Egypt demanded the withdrawal of all UN peace keeping forces that had been stationed in Sinai since Israel's withdrawal in 1957. On May 17 1967, there was a mass demonstration in Cairo supporting Nasser as the Arab leader who would once and for all destroy Israel. On May 19, Nasser's demand that the UN immediately withdraw from Sinai was honored by then-Secretary General U Thant without even bringing it up to the UN Security Council, let alone Israel, who had predicated its 1957 withdrawal on the legal basis that there would be no UN withdrawal without its approval.

On May 20 the Egyptian army began pouring into Sinai. The UN peace keeping forces had departed so quickly that they left warm meals on the tables in their dining rooms. On May 22 Nasser declared the Straits of Tiran closed to Israeli shipping, an outright act of war.

THE NOOSE TIGHTENS, MAY 25 – JUNE 4 1967
On May 25 Nasser requested that Jordan put its military under

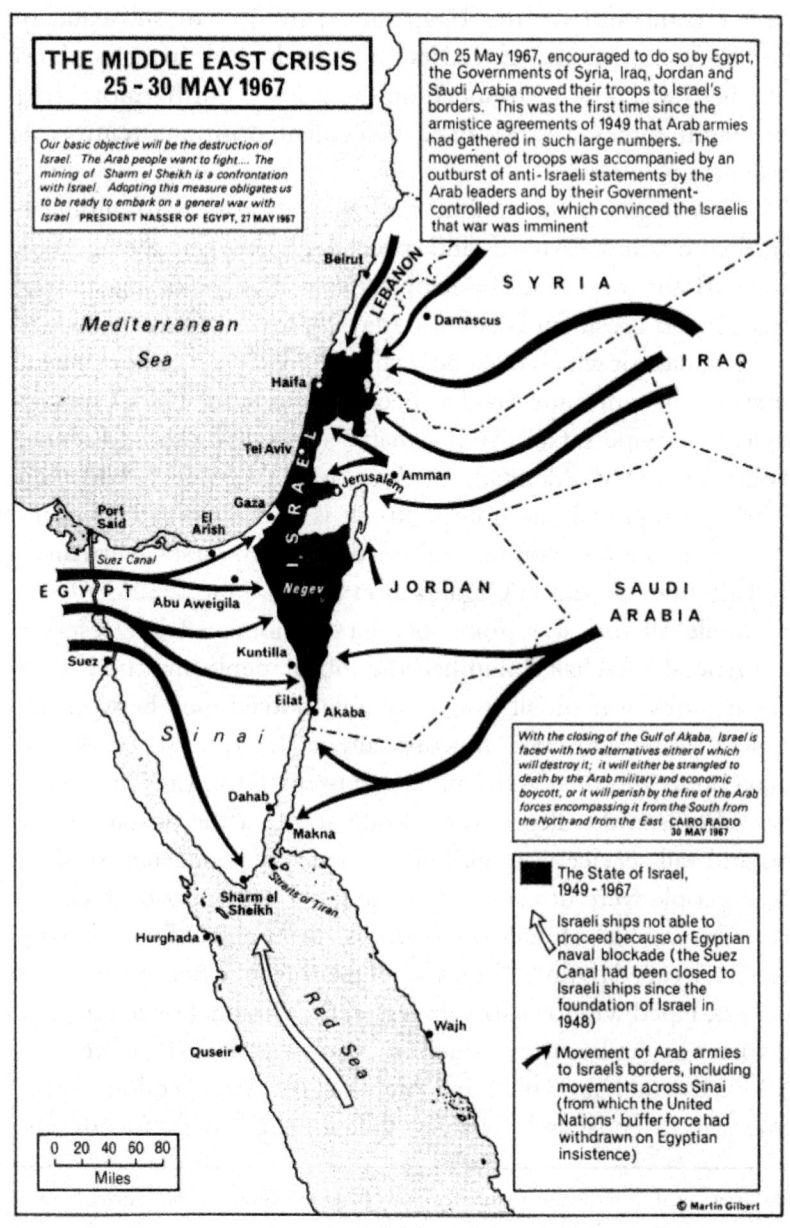

**THE MIDDLE EAST CRISIS
25 - 30 MAY 1967**

Our basic objective will be the destruction of Israel. The Arab people want to fight.... The mining of Sharm el Sheikh is a confrontation with Israel. Adopting this measure obligates us to be ready to embark on a general war with Israel PRESIDENT NASSER OF EGYPT, 27 MAY 1967

On 25 May 1967, encouraged to do so by Egypt, the Governments of Syria, Iraq, Jordan and Saudi Arabia moved their troops to Israel's borders. This was the first time since the armistice agreements of 1949 that Arab armies had gathered in such large numbers. The movement of troops was accompanied by an outburst of anti-Israeli statements by the Arab leaders and by their Government-controlled radios, which convinced the Israelis that war was imminent

Mediterranean Sea

Beirut

LEBANON

S Y R I A

• Damascus

Haifa

I R A Q

Tel Aviv

I S R A E L

Jerusalem • Amman

Gaza

Port Said

El Arish

Suez Canal

E G Y P T

Abu Aweigila

Negev

J O R D A N

S A U D I
A R A B I A

Suez

Kuntilla

Eilat • Akaba

S i n a i

Dahab

With the closing of the Gulf of Akaba, Israel is faced with two alternatives either of which will destroy it; it will either be strangled to death by the Arab military and economic boycott, or it will perish by the fire of the Arab forces encompassing it from the South from the North and from the East CAIRO RADIO 30 MAY 1967

Makna

Straits of Tiran

■ The State of Israel, 1949 - 1967

Sharm el Sheikh

Hurghada

⇧ Israeli ships not able to proceed because of Egyptian naval blockade (the Suez Canal had been closed to Israeli ships since the foundation of Israel in 1948)

Red Sea

Wajh

Quseir

➤ Movement of Arab armies to Israel's borders, including movements across Sinai (from which the United Nations' buffer force had withdrawn on Egyptian insistence)

0 20 40 60 80
Miles

© Martin Gilbert

Sir Martin Gilbert, © 2010. Reproduced by permission of Taylor & Francis Books UK. www.martingilbert.com

a joint command of the Egyptian Army. Jordan subsequently mobilized its army and moved its forces to the 1949 armistice lines. Jerusalem was now surrounded on three sides. Furthermore, Iraqi and Saudi forces also assumed belligerent positions reinforcing Jordanian positions.

Then began a very public call by Arab leaders to annihilate Israel with rallies, cartoons and speeches all with one theme: Wipe Israel off the map. "Our basic objective will be the destruction of Israel,"[2] said President Nasser on May 27, 1967. "The existence of Israel is an error which must be rectified. This is our opportunity to wipe out the ignominy that has been with us since 1948. Our goal is clear: to wipe Israel off the map."[3] (President Abdul Rahman Mohammed Arif Aljumaily of Iraq, May 31, 1967.) And then, "This is a fight for the homeland—it is either us or the Israelis. There is no middle ground."[4] (Ahmed Shukairy, First Chairman of the Palestine Liberation Organization (PLO), June 1, 1967.)

While all this was going on, Israel mobilized her reserves. Lt. General Yitzchak Rabin had the job of deploying the IDF to prepare for a war on all fronts. All able-bodied men between the ages of 22-50 who were not officially in the IDF Reserves were called up to join their active units and prepare for war. This meant that schools and colleges were closed and that the postal service, bus and rail service were all but non-existent, since almost all of these people were now on active duty. A large portion of Israel's economy was also shut down as tens of thousands of working-age men were called to duty. High school teenagers helped set up bomb shelters, taped windows to help lessen the shrapnel once the Arab air forces began bombing Israeli cities and towns, and dug trenches and filled sand bags. Israel thus prepared for Armageddon.* Many American friends and relatives called their Israeli friends and

---

*My great aunt, a Holocaust survivor who lived in Herzelia only thirteen miles from the border with Jordan, was so frightened by the situation that she went down to the local drug store and purchased cyanide pills for herself and her three children should the Jordanian Army break through. She simply could not bear the thought of going through another Holocaust.

relatives and offered to take their children to the U.S. for fear that all of Israel would be a battleground.

Prime Minister Eshkol sent his Foreign Minister, Abba Eban, on a desperate mission to find a sympathetic ally to help diplomatically avert a catastrophic war. He visited France, West Germany, England, Canada and the U.S. An openly hostile French president, Charles de Gaulle (1890-1970), made it clear that France, Israel's main weapons supplier since 1955, would no longer sell Israel any military materiel. The message from the other Western countries was that none were in a position to offer any assistance. Even though President Lyndon Baines Johnson (1908-1973) was quite sympathetic, his attention was totally focused on the growing U.S. war in Vietnam. When Abba Eban returned to Israel on June 3rd, his message was quite clear: The state of Israel was on her own and must do what she must to survive.

Prime Minister Eshkol was a wise and cautious man but he did not come across well on TV. When he addressed the nation in late May he appeared nervous and unsure, sowing further panic among part of the population. Hence it was decided to bring in a very familiar, confident face to be the new Minister of Defense, one who could be the face of the forthcoming battle: Moshe Dayan. A former Chief of Staff and hero of the 1956 Sinai Campaign, Dayan's trademark eye patch and steely demeanor was just what the country needed. Since the plans for the upcoming war were already made by IDF chief Rabin, Dayan's appointment made no difference in the planning of the war but made a huge psychological difference for the people of Israel. Furthermore, seeing that Israel was backed into a corner and had some very tough decisions to make, the Labor-led government took the extraordinary step of creating a national unity alliance which entailed bringing in Menachem Begin and his Gachal (later to be known as Likud) Party.

On June 4, after seven hours of discussion, the Cabinet, having heard from Rabin and Dayan, had a clear picture of what the only option was: Israel had to launch a pre-emptive strike or would be either strangled by the Arab noose tightening around Israel or find herself fighting battles in the street of every major Israeli city. The vote was unanimous.

THE SIX-DAY WAR AND ITS AFTERMATH, JUNE 5 - JUNE 10 1967

On June 5, early in the morning, the Israeli Air Force launched a daring and dangerous attack on all the surrounding Arab army air bases, concentrating on the Egyptian Air Force. This plan involved almost every single combat and training Jet the IDF had at its disposal, with very few jets left to defend the skies of Israel. It was clear that any Arab airstrike against an Israeli city would have devastating consequences, and since Israel was so narrow and small, Arab jets could reach almost any Israeli city within ten to fifteen minutes of flying time. There was no margin for error. The skies of Israel and of the Arab countries around her had to be controlled by the IDF.

Thus the IAF flew under enemy radar and attacked many Arab bases in Jordan, Syria and Iraq. The IAF targeted every Egyptian airbase in Sinai and in Egypt. The goal was to destroy all enemy aircraft on the ground. This meant the IAF flew very low and was able to literally see their targets. By the morning of June 5 the skies of the Middle East belonged to the Israeli Air Force. Close to eighty percent of Egypt's Air Force was destroyed and about fifty percent of Jordan's, Syria's and Iraq's air forces as well. That having been achieved, the IDF went on the offensive to take on the Egyptian Army in Sinai and Gaza. By June 7th almost all of Sinai and Gaza were once again in Israel's hands; the Egyptian Army, with all its Soviet equipment, was routed.

Using U.S. diplomats as a go-between, Jordan was warned to stay out of the war. But King Hussein was both bound by a military pact he had signed with Nasser on May 25th and also received misleading information from Nasser that the Egyptian Army had entered Tel Aviv. At 11 a.m. on June 5th, King Hussein gave the order to open fire across the entire Israel-Jordan cease-fire lines. This would prove to be a huge mistake. Israel responded by attacking the West Bank. The Jordanian Army was a well-trained and highly motivated army, but the IDF was better prepared and fighting for the existence of its homeland.

On the morning of June 7, Eshkol sent one last appeal to Hussein: If you agree to peace talks, we won't invade. Hussein didn't respond and the government ordered the paratroopers to enter the Old City.

Even at this late stage, the paratroopers had little idea of what awaited them in the narrow alleys within the walled Old City. In fact, most of the Jordanian troops stationed inside the walls had slipped out the night before; the Old City lay open.

[Lt. Gen. Mordechai "Motta"] Gur's half-track led the attack, crashing through the massive bronze doors onto the Via Delarosa, then turning left and onto the Temple Mount. Gur and Achmon [Major Arik Achmon, chief intelligence officer for Brigade 55 of Israel's paratrooper reservists] rushed up a flight of stairs leading to a large plaza—the golden Dome of the Rock and the silver-domed al-Aqsa. Gur radioed headquarters: "The Temple Mount is in our hands." He wasn't just making a military report, but staking a historic claim. The focus of centuries of Jewish longing, the place toward which Jews prayed no matter where they lived, was now in Israeli hands.

The brigade's chief communications officer, Ezra Orni, retrieved an Israeli flag from his pouch and asked Gur whether he should hang it over the Dome of the Rock. "*Yalla*," said Gur, "Go up." [Achmon] accompanied him into the Dome of the Rock. They climbed to the top of the building and victoriously fastened the Israeli flag onto a pole topped with an Islamic crescent.

Except then the flag was quickly and unceremoniously lowered. Defense Minister Moshe Dayan, watching the scene through binoculars from Mount Scopus, urgently radioed Gur and demanded: Do you want to set the Middle East on fire? Gur told Achmon to remove the flag. But Achmon couldn't bear the notion of lowering the Israeli flag, and so he instructed one of his men to do it instead.[5]

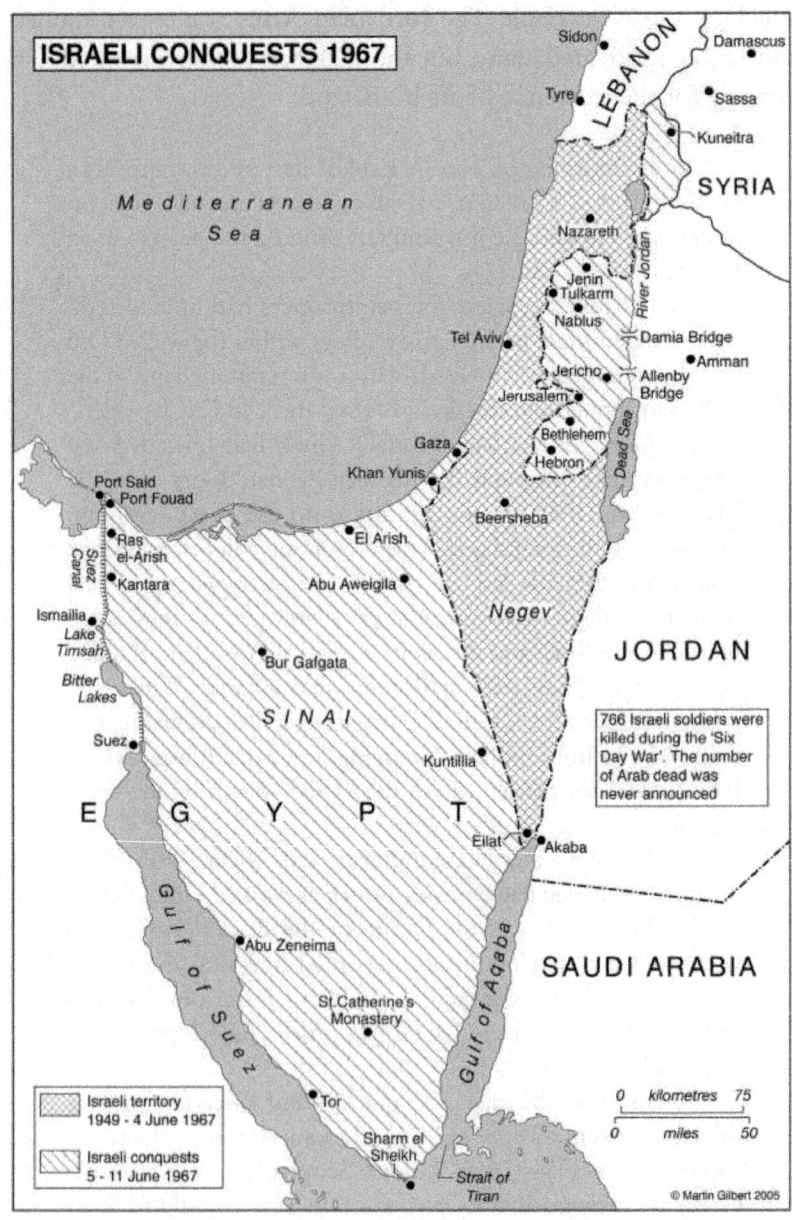

ISRAELI CONQUESTS 1967

Sidon
Damascus

Tyre
LEBANON
Sassa
Kuneitra

SYRIA

*Mediterranean
Sea*

Nazareth

Jenin
Tulkarm

Nablus

Tel Aviv
Damia Bridge
Amman

Jericho
Allenby
Bridge

Jerusalem

River Jordan

Gaza
Bethlehem

Khan Yunis
Hebron

Dead Sea

Port Said
Port Fouad
Beersheba

Ras
el-Arish
El Arish

Suez Canal
Kantara
Abu Aweigila

Ismailia
Negev

Lake
Timsah
JORDAN

Bitter
Lakes
Bur Gafgata

S I N A I

Suez
766 Israeli soldiers were
killed during the 'Six
Day War'. The number
of Arab dead was
never announced

Kuntillia

E   G   Y   P   T
Eilat
Akaba

Abu Zeneima

Gulf of Suez
Gulf of Aqaba
SAUDI ARABIA

St.Catherine's
Monastery

Tor
	kilometres 75
0	
0	miles 50

Israeli territory
1949 - 4 June 1967

Israeli conquests
5 - 11 June 1967

Sharm el
Sheikh
Strait of
Tiran

© Martin Gilbert 2005

Sir Martin Gilbert, © 2010. Reproduced by permission of Taylor
& Francis Books UK. www.martingilbert.com

By June 8 all of the West Bank was in Israel's hands. The greatest prize was the liberation of the Old City of Jerusalem during which one hundred eighty-three IDF soldiers were killed. It was the first time a sovereign Jewish State had control of all of the Jewish holy sites in Jerusalem since the days of the Maccabees.* The return to all of these places had a profound religious and psychological effect on the people of Israel and on Jews all around the world.

The one front that had been dealt with in the first four days of the war, ironically, was the Syrian front, the crisis point first triggered in April. By June 8, the IDF had conquered all of Sinai and Gaza from Egypt and sat on the eastern shore of the Suez Canal. The IDF had also captured all of the West Bank from Jordan and was sitting on the Jordan River. Still, the IDF had not launched an assault on the Golan Heights during this period, simply returning Syrian artillery fire that was pounding northeastern Israel, and hardly making a dent in the Golan's fortifications. Hence, on June 9th, with the Egyptian and Jordanian fronts pacified, Israel was able to turn her full attention to the Syrian front. Sending armored bulldozers, tanks, halftracks and infantry straight at the Syrian fortifications while the Israeli Air Force provided cover from above, the audacity and ferocity of the IDF assault caused many Syrian soldiers to flee. Within twenty-four hours the IDF had captured an area approximately forty miles north to south and fifteen miles west to east that became the Israeli portion of the Golan Heights.

The UN Security Council, pushed by the Soviet Union, called for an immediate cease fire that went into effect on the evening of

---

*The list of the Holy Biblical sites captured from Jordan included: The oldest (3,000 years old) Jewish cemetery in the world, the Mount of Olives, where Jewish kings and prophets, among others, were buried; the Tomb of the Patriarch's—Maarat Ha Machpela—in Hevron, where Jews had lived until 1929 when they fled as a result of a horrible pogrom; the Burial Place of Rachel, one of the four Jewish Matriarchs, in Bet Lechem; the Tomb of Joseph, the son of the Patriarch Jacob, in Shechem. There were dozens of other places of Biblical significance, for the West Bank was the heartland of ancient Israel and Judea.

June 10. By then Israel was sitting in Kuneitra, the capital of the Golan Heights, and had captured the peak of Mt. Hermon.

The Six-Day War was equivalent to Israel's second war of independence. Israel was literally looking into the abyss in early June and preparing for a possible war in every Israeli city and town with tens of thousands of casualties. But by June 10th Israel had captured over 26,500 square miles of territory, an area totaling over three times the size of pre-1967 Israel. Besides the religious and psychological results of Israel returning to so much of Biblical Israel, there was the immediate sense of incredible relief which turned into a sense of euphoria, for now all of Israel's enemies had been driven far away from its main population centers. Israel finally had some strategic depth. For Israelis this was a time of great joy, thankfulness and optimism. Though Israel had no clear plans on what to do with all the areas she had just captured, she did know one thing: Jerusalem would no longer be a divided city where Jews were forbidden from having access to their holiest sites. Hence, two weeks after the war, the Israeli government voted to annex Jerusalem. All 40,000 Jordanian Arab residents were offered Israeli residency, with all the entitlements that come with that: voting in municipal elections; being part of the Jerusalem municipality; free public education; free medical insurance; welfare; social security, and food stamps.

For Nasser and the leaders of the Arab combatants, theirs was a world of complete shock. Instead of wiping Israel off the map, the Six-Day War created an even stronger non-Arab Middle East presence. The Arab League, convening in Khartoum in the summer of 1967, to decide how to react to the Six-Day War, issued its famous Khartoum Resolution that came to be referred to as "the three no's":

THE KHARTOUM RESOLUTIONS—SEPTEMBER 1, 1967

1. The conference has affirmed the unity of Arab ranks, the unity of joint action and the need for coordination and for the elimination of all differences. The Kings, Presidents

and representatives of the other Arab Heads of State at the conference have affirmed their countries' stand by and implementation of the Arab Solidarity Charter which was signed at the third Arab summit conference in Casablanca.

2. The conference has agreed on the need to consolidate all efforts to eliminate the effects of the aggression on the basis that the occupied lands are Arab lands and that the burden of regaining these lands falls on all the Arab States.

3. The Arab Heads of State have agreed to unite their political efforts at the international and diplomatic level to eliminate the effects of the aggression and to ensure the withdrawal of the aggressive Israeli forces from the Arab lands which have been occupied since the aggression of June 5. This will be done within the framework of the main principles by which the Arab States abide, namely, no peace with Israel, no recognition of Israel, no negotiations with it, and insistence on the rights of the Palestinian people in their own country.

4. The conference of Arab Ministers of Finance, Economy and Oil recommended that suspension of oil pumping be used as a weapon in the battle. However, after thoroughly studying the matter, the summit conference has come to the conclusion that the oil pumping can itself be used as a positive weapon, since oil is an Arab resource which can be used to strengthen the economy of the Arab States directly affected by the aggression, so that these States will be able to stand firm in the battle. The conference has, therefore, decided to resume the pumping of oil, since oil is a positive Arab resource that can be used in the service of Arab goals. It can contribute to the efforts to enable those Arab States which were exposed to the aggression and thereby lost economic resources to stand firm and eliminate the effects of the aggression. The oil-producing States have, in fact, participated in the efforts to enable the States affected by the aggression to stand firm in the face of any economic pressure.

5. The participants in the conference have approved the plan proposed by Kuwait to set up an Arab Economic and Social Development Fund on the basis of the recommendation

of the Baghdad conference of Arab Ministers of Finance, Economy and Oil.

6. The participants have agreed on the need to adopt the necessary measures to strengthen military preparation to face all eventualities.

7. The conference has decided to expedite the elimination of foreign bases in the Arab States.[6]

This effectively closed the door on any possible negotiations with any Arab state regarding the future relations between Israel and her Arab neighbors.

UN RESOLUTION 242

On November 22, 1967, the UN Security Council passed UN Resolution 242 as its response to the Six-Day War:

> The Security Council,
>
> Expressing its continuing concern with the grave situation in the Middle East,
>
> Emphasizing the inadmissibility of the acquisition of territory by war and the need to work for a just and lasting peace in which every State in the area can live in security,
>
> Emphasizing further that all Member States in their acceptance of the Charter of the United Nations have undertaken a commitment to act in accordance with Article 2 of the Charter,
>
> 1. Affirms that the fulfillment of Charter principles requires the establishment of a just and lasting peace in the Middle East which should include the application of both the following principles:
>
> (i) Withdrawal of Israel armed forces from territories occupied in the recent conflict;
>
> (ii) Termination of all claims or states of belligerency and respect for and acknowledgment of the sovereignty, territorial integrity and political independence of every State in the area and their right to live in peace within secure and recognized boundaries free from threats or acts of force;
>
> 2. Affirms further the necessity

(a) For guaranteeing freedom of navigation through international waterways in the area;

(b) For achieving a just settlement of the refugee problem;

(c) For guaranteeing the territorial inviolability and political independence of every State in the area, through measures including the establishment of demilitarized zones;

3. Requests the Secretary-General to designate a Special Representative to proceed to the Middle East to establish and maintain contacts with the States concerned in order to promote agreement and assist efforts to achieve a peaceful and accepted settlement in accordance with the provisions and principles in this resolution;

4. Requests the Secretary-General to report to the Security Council on the progress of the efforts of the Special Representative as soon as possible.[7]

ANALYSIS OF RESOLUTION 242

Regarding the statement that Israel withdraw from territories captured, the Arab League and the Soviet Union lobbied for months to have the word *all* added before the word *territories*. Their reason was simple. Without the word *all* Israel would not have to withdraw from all of the 24,000 square miles she captured during the war. The reason the word *all* was not included by the principal author of the document (Hugh Mackintosh Foot, Baron Caradon of England, the UK's ambassador to the United Nations) was because the United States and England, in particular, did not think it was rational to expect Israel to withdraw to militarily indefensible borders. Furthermore, the 1949 cease-fire lines were never recognized as borders by any of Israel's Arab neighbors.* The

---

* The issue of Israel's return to its pre-1967 armistice lines sits at the heart of UN Resolution 242. These were the cease fire lines that were negotiated between Israel and its Arab neighbors following the 1948-49 War of Independence. But these pre-1967 lines were never recognized borders by any Arab state; they were merely the lines that demarcated where the fighting in 1949 stopped. If anything, Arab countries made a point throughout 1949-1967 that they did not recognize the existence of the State of Israel, referring instead to the "Zionist Entity," the "Zionist Cancer," "Occupied Palestine," etc. Thus, today, it is interesting to hear the Arab world and its supporters demand that Israel return to borders that they themselves never recognized.

paragraph that stated, *"Termination of all claims or states of belligerency and respect for and acknowledgment of the sovereignty, territorial integrity and political independence of every state in the area and their right to live in peace within secure and recognized boundaries free from threats or acts of force,"* meant that the Arab world would have to recognize the existence of the sovereign Jewish State of Israel and that every country, including Israel, would no longer have to live behind artificial lines but rather have recognized secure borders.

"Guaranteeing the right of freedom of navigation through international waterways," a *casus belli* of both the '56 and '67 wars, sought relief from this sort of attack on Israel's economic viability.

And, *"for achieving a just settlement to the refugee problem,"* was the only mention of what would become a major sticking point for the next half century. In 1967 the West Bank was viewed as Jordanian territory, and Sinai and Gaza were viewed as Egyptian territory. In November of 1967 the international community did not view the Palestinians as a separate national entity. Rather, they were an Arab people whose interests would be handled by existing sovereign Arab states.

In totality, Resolution 242 was not a one-dimensional document that just called for unconditional Israeli withdrawal from all the territories captured in the Six-Day War. The resolution was clearly one that promulgated a framework for peace that had all sides to the conflict making serious changes in their perceptions.*

THE HISTORY OF ISRAEL'S MILITARY OCCUPATION

A major downside of the Six-Day War was that Israel now controlled not only more area—Sinai, the Golan, Gaza and the

---

* Still, the Arab States demanded that Israel must return every inch of land that she had won in the Six-Day War to Egypt, Jordan and Syria. There was no talk at the time of creating another Arab state called Palestine. It was only in the late 1970s, when Palestinian Arabs began to be treated by the world community as a separate entity, that the Arab world demanded that before there could be talk of peace with Israel she must hand over all of Judea, Samaria and Gaza to the Palestinian Arabs, citing UN Resolution 242 as the legal source for their demand.

West Bank—but it had also inherited the large hostile Arab population in these areas. Approximately 400,000 Arabs lived in the Gaza Strip and about 600,000 Arabs in the West Bank. The total population of the State of Israel in 1967 was 2.5 million citizens, of whom 500,000 were Arabs. Since Israel was unsure of what the status would be of these areas and their inhabitants, she decided to keep security control through short-term military occupation, viewing this as an interim measure that would last until some agreement was reached with the Arab world. Only in May of 1994, when Israel withdrew from the Gaza Strip and the city of Jericho, has that occupation ceased. Regrettably, for the rest of the West Bank, that occupation persists.

Shortly after the war, Israel began to allow Jews to move into certain parts of the West Bank, now recognized as the biblical Judea and Samaria. Having great religious and historical significance to the Jewish people, Israel's position was that the land was not really "occupied" territory as defined by international law since the West Bank and Gaza were not sovereign areas, but rather areas that Egypt and Jordan illegally occupied after the 1948-49 War of Independence. These areas were supposed to be part of the Palestinian state that the UN wanted to establish when it passed its November 29, 1947 resolution calling for the partition of Mandate Palestine. Hence, Israel viewed these areas as "disputed" territories, areas whose final status had yet to be determined.

Thus, the Gush Etzion bloc (south of Jerusalem and north of Hevron) was reclaimed, since Jewish towns had existed there prior to 1948. At the same time, other Israelis went to live near the second holiest city to the Jewish people, Hevron, a city where the biblical patriarchs and matriarchs were buried, a city where Jews had lived until 1929, when they were forced to flee after an Arab pogrom.

Since the Israeli government did not want to displace the local Arab population or even upset daily lives, Israelis were not allowed to live in any areas with Arab populations. Thus a new Jewish town was created near Hevron called Kiryat Arba, a Hebrew biblical name that refers to the four holy Jewish couples buried in the Tomb of the Patriarchs in Hevron (Adam and Eve, Abraham and Sarah, Isaac and Rivka, and Jacob and Leah.)

Finally, for security reasons, agricultural settlements were set up in the Jordan River Valley, Israel's new eastern boundary with Jordan. In total, in the ten years following the Six-Day War, some 10,000 Israelis moved to the West Bank, once again called Judea and Samaria.

GUSH EMUNIM

In the aftermath of the war a Religious Zionist revival took place. The Religious Zionist movement was always very prominent in taking a proactive stance in the resurgence of a Jewish presence in their ancient homeland. From the days of the founding of the Mizrachi Party in 1902, Religious Zionists always saw the return to the Land of Israel as a clear sign from the Almighty that the promises of the Jewish prophets regarding the return of the Jewish nation had begun to be realized.

The most prominent and influential leader of the Religious Zionist Movement in the early 20th century was Rabbi Avraham Yitzchak Kook. It was clear to him that all the events that had occurred since the early 1800s all pointed to a change in the status of the Jewish nation with regard to *Eretz Yisrael*. Though he died in 1935, he left a remarkable legacy with his written works, his lessons, speeches, his son and his many students. Many of these students and his son, Rabbi Tzvi Yehuda Kook, saw the return to the Old City, especially the Temple Mount, the Kotel, and all of biblical Judea and Samaria as further proof of the Almighty's plan to return the Land of Israel to the nation of Israel. Hence, they would be at the forefront of the movement to have Jews live in Judea and Samaria.

Rabbi Hanan Porat (1943-2011) and Rabbi Moshe Levinger (1935-2015) were among those who took Rabbi Kook's lessons to heart and became instrumental in the Gush Emunim movement:

After the Six-Day War, Rabbi Hanan Porat became a founder of the movement instrumental in the establishment of over 100 Israeli settlements in Samaria and the Golan Heights.

> His personal philosophy: [T]he Land of Israel for the people of Israel according to the Torah of Israel; the Land of Israel in its entirety, with all its regions, to the entire Jewish people, with all its branches and committees, in the light of a complete Torah of life that embraces the individual and the public, society and state.[8]

> Mr. Porat opposed the removal of Jews from any land in exchange for peace with Israel's neighbors..."He who lends a hand in uprooting settlements," he said, "hurts not only the settlers themselves but the Jewish legacy and the prayers of generations as well."[9]

Porat served in five Knessets as a representative from different religious parties.

Rabbi Moshe Levinger was a legend of the Gush Emunim movement for his "liberation" of Hebron and the establishment of the Kiryat Arba settlement. As Benjamin Netanyahu stated:

> Levinger's name will be forever linked with the movement for renewed Jewish settlement in Hebron and other areas of the country where our patriarchs walked thousands of years ago. He was an outstanding example of a generation that sought to realize the Zionist dream, in deed and in spirit, after the Six-Day War...[10]

His lionization outside of religious settler circles, however, was mitigated by his propensity for vigilantism and his multiple arrests and convictions for assault and "negligent homicide" of affronting Arabs.[11]

ISRAEL TAKES A STEP TOWARDS THE ARAB AND ISLAMIC WORLD IN JERUSALEM

Even though Israel annexed the eastern parts of Jerusalem, in a gesture of reconciliation to the Arab and Muslim world Defense Minister Moshe Dayan…

> …decided to leave the mount and its management in the hands of the Muslim Wakf, while at the same time insisting that Jews would be able to visit it (but not pray at it!) without restriction. Dayan thought, and years later even committed the thought to writing, that since for Muslims the mount is a "Muslim prayer mosque" while for Jews it is no more than "a historical site of commemoration of the past…one should not hinder the Arabs from behaving there as they now do." The Israeli defense minister believed that Islam must be allowed to express its religious sovereignty—as opposed to national sovereignty—over the mount; that the Arab-Israeli conflict must be kept on the territorial-national level; and that the potential for a conflict between the Jewish religion and the Muslim religion must be removed. In granting Jews the right to visit the mount, Dayan sought to placate the Jewish demands for worship and sovereignty there. In giving religious sovereignty over the mount to the Muslims, he believed he was defusing the site as a center of Palestinian nationalism.[12]

THE FIRST DECADE OF ISRAELI MILITARY OCCUPATION, 1967-1977

The Israeli Military occupation was initially meant as a stopgap measure until such time as there would be a viable Arab negotiating partner. If Israel truly wanted to crush the Arabs of Gaza, Judea and Samaria then Israel could have annexed all these areas right after the Six-Day War and not offered citizenship, expelled most, if not all, of the Arabs of these areas and, used its overwhelming military superiority to fight a "total war."

Instead, during this first decade of Israeli occupation, several guiding principles prevailed: Israel wanted to show its Arab population that the image it had of Israel, Israelis and Jews was not true; it wanted to create a humane relationship between Israelis and Arabs; Israel did not want to disrupt the established cultural routines that existed, but to share the benefits of a modern culture, i.e., better health care, access to electricity and water, better agricultural techniques, better education, freedom of religion, freedom of the press, a judicial system guaranteeing legal rights, etc. As such, Israel paved new roads, connected villages to the power grid, dug wells, put in sewage lines, and brought in telephone lines. On the ideological level, Israel opened universities, created equal rights for women and made education until age 14 compulsory. The government also opened clinics and introduced new methods to fight certain widespread diseases. All in all, though the Arabs resented Israel's presence, life overall was better than it had been under Jordanian rule.

But after the 1977 election victory of the Likud Party, there came about a dramatic shift in the policies of the Israeli Government regarding the territories. The Likud actively declared a commitment to the idea that since Judea and Samaria were the heartland of biblical Israel, that the new Israel should encompass as much of this territory as possible. Thus, the Likud government began to pour hundreds of millions of dollars into building new towns and encouraging tens of thousands of Jews to move there.

Footnotes

¹ "1960: The assassins of Hazza Majali," ExecutedToday. com. December 31st, 2009 (http://www.executedtoday. com/2009/12/31/1960-the-assassins-of-hazza-majali/)

² Martin Gilbert, *The Routledge Atlas of the Arab Israeli Conflict*, 10th ed. (London: Routledge Taylor & Francis Group, 2012) 66.

³ *Ibid.*, 67.

⁴ *Ibid.*

⁵ Yossi Klein Halevi, "The Astonishing Israeli Concession of 1967," *The Atlantic*, July 7, 2017 (https://www.theatlantic.com/ international/archive/2017/06/israel-paratroopers-temple- mount-1967/529365/)

⁶ "Khartoum Resolution" (https://en.wikipedia.org/ wiki/Khartoum_Resolution)

⁷ "Chapter 3: The 1967 And 1973 Wars" (http://www.un.org/ Depts/dpi/palestine/ch3.pdf)

⁸ "Porat Hanan" (http://www.news1.co.il/Archive/006D-1091-00. html?tag=14-27-38)

⁹ Ethan Bronner, "Hanan Porat, Jewish Settlement Leader, Dies at 67," *New York Times*, October 4, 2011 (http://www.nytimes. com/2011/10/05/world/middleeast/hanan-porat-jewish-settle- ment-leader-dies-at-67.html)

¹⁰ Ami Pedazhur and Arie Perliger, *Jewish Terrorism in Israel* (NY: Columbia University Press, 2009), 72.

¹¹ JNS.org, "Rabbi Moshe Levinger, Jewish Settlement Movement Pioneer, Dies at 80,' *The Algemeiner*, May 17, 2015 (https://www. algemeiner.com/2015/05/17/rabbi-moshe-levinger-jewish-settle- ment-movement-pioneer-dies-at-80/)

¹² Nadav Shragai, "The 'Al Aksa is in Danger" Libel; The History of a Lie," Jerusalem Center for Public Affairs (http://jcpa.org/al- aksa-is-in-danger-libel-temple-mount/)

Chapter 12

The PLO and Preamble to the '73 War
1964-1973

THE PALESTINIAN LIBERATION ORGANIZATION – PLO

After the Six-Day War a new entity entered the Arab-Israeli Conflict: the PLO. The PLO was founded in 1964 by the Arab League in a meeting in Cairo. The goal was to collect the various Palestinian Arab terror groups, which the Arab world referred to as resistance movements, together under one umbrella. The largest of the groups was Fatah, then run by Egyptian-born Yasser Arafat. It is interesting to note that the PLO was founded by the Arab League and operated under Egyptian control. Normally an indigenous movement to reclaim one's homeland from an enemy springs up from the aggrieved group. In this case, an outside entity created a liberation movement for another group of people.*

---

* It is easy to surmise that both the Arab League and Egypt were very well aware of the value of having a "Palestinian Liberation Organization" as a sword over Israel's head, but not because they were truly interested in helping Palestinian Arab refugees. If the Arab League and Egypt truly wanted to help aggrieved Palestinian Arabs they could have taken the following concrete steps as early as 1949: declared an Arab Palestinian State in Gaza and in Judea and Samaria; dismantled all the refugee camps in Gaza and Judea and Samaria and offered these people citizenship in what could have been an Arab State of Palestine, and allowed the Palestinian Arabs who lived in the refugee camps in Arab States to have the same rights as that of the local Arab citizens, instead of forcing their continued habitation in said refugee camps.

FATAH

Fatah* is the largest faction of the multi-party Palestine Liberation Organization (PLO). Its name is...

> ...a reverse acronym of the Arabic *Harekat at-Tahrir al--Wataniyyeh al Falastiniyyeh*, meaning "conquest by means of jihad [Islamic holy war]." The Fatah flag features a grenade with crossed rifles superimposed on the map of Israel....This emphasizes the dedication of Fatah, along with the other "liberation" groups, to the "armed struggle"—a euphemism for terrorism—against Israel.[1]

Fatah was founded in 1959 by a group of Cairo and Beirut University alumni who felt that Palestinians would only achieve true liberation by taking matters into their own hands. Yasser Arafat was one of its original founders.

Born in Cairo in 1929, Arafat joined the Muslim Brotherhood, whose main goal is to make Islam a universal way of life. He served as the president of the Union of Palestinian Students at the University of Cairo from 1952-1956 and later served in the Egyptian Army during the 1956 Sinai War. He then moved to Kuwait in 1957 where he became an engineer and subsequently helped found Fatah.

In 1964 Fatah began to carry out terrorist attacks against Israel from Jordan, Lebanon and the Gaza Strip. It was also the

---

* Fatah, which is commonly referred to as a secular movement, is anything but. It is an Arab Islamic group that is dedicated to the eradication of the State of Israel. It is not a reaction to the 1967 Six-Day War, but rather a reaction to the results of the 1948-49 War, which resulted in a staggering defeat for the Arab world. In essence, all Arab and Islamic terror groups that have Israel as their target are interested in but one outcome: The destruction of the State of Israel. It's not a part of Israel they are looking to destroy, but all of it. The narrative about trying to liberate the "occupied territories" conquered by Israel in the Six-Day War is a post-1967 spin on the original argument. This new spin was used because it resonated with the Western world, since in theory it means pre-1967 Israel will be left alone. But that never was the true aim of Fatah or the PLO.

year in which the first draft of the PLO Covenant was produced, later finalized in 1968. This document is the cornerstone of the Palestinian Arab movement which, since 1993, when the Oslo Agreements were signed, became known as the Palestinian Authority as opposed to the Palestine Liberation Organization.

THE PALESTINIAN NATIONAL CHARTER RESOLUTIONS OF THE PALESTINE NATIONAL COUNCIL
JULY 1 TO 17 1968

Article 1:

Palestine is the homeland of the Arab Palestinian people; it is an indivisible part of the Arab homeland, and the Palestinian people are an integral part of the Arab nation.

Article 2:

Palestine, with the boundaries it had during the British Mandate, is an indivisible territorial unit.

Article 3:

The Palestinian Arab people possess the legal right to their homeland and have the right to determine their destiny after achieving the liberation of their country in accordance with their wishes and entirely of their own accord and will.

Article 4:

The Palestinian identity is a genuine, essential, and inherent characteristic; it is transmitted from parents to children. The Zionist occupation and the dispersal of the Palestinian Arab people, through the disasters which befell them, do not make them lose their Palestinian identity and their membership in the Palestinian community, nor do they negate them.

Article 5:

The Palestinians are those Arab nationals who, until 1947, normally resided in Palestine regardless of whether they were evicted from it or have stayed there. Anyone born, after that date, of a Palestinian father—whether inside Palestine or outside it—is also a Palestinian.

Article 6:

The Jews who had normally resided in Palestine until the beginning of the Zionist invasion will be considered Palestinians.

Article 7:

That there is a Palestinian community and that it has material, spiritual, and historical connection with Palestine are indisputable facts. It is a national duty to bring up individual Palestinians in an Arab revolutionary manner. All means of information and education must be adopted in order to acquaint the Palestinian with his country in the most profound manner, both spiritual and material, that is possible. He must be prepared for the armed struggle and ready to sacrifice his wealth and his life in order to win back his homeland and bring about its liberation.

Article 8:

The phase in their history, through which the Palestinian people are now living, is that of national (watani) struggle for the liberation of Palestine. Thus the conflicts among the Palestinian national forces are secondary, and should be ended for the sake of the basic conflict that exists between the forces of Zionism and of imperialism on the one hand, and the Palestinian Arab people on the other. On this basis the Palestinian masses, regardless of whether they are residing in the national homeland or in diaspora (mahajir) constitute - both their organizations and the individuals - one national front working for the retrieval of Palestine and its liberation through armed struggle.

Article 9:

Armed struggle is the only way to liberate Palestine. This it is the overall strategy, not merely a tactical phase. The Palestinian Arab people assert their absolute determination and firm resolution to continue their armed struggle and to work for an armed popular revolution for the liberation of their country and their return to it . They also assert their right to normal life in Palestine and to exercise their right to self-determination and sovereignty over it.

Article 10:

Commando action constitutes the nucleus of the Palestinian popular liberation war. This requires its escalation, comprehensiveness, and the mobilization of all the Palestinian popular and educational efforts and their organization and involvement in the armed Palestinian revolution. It also requires the achieving of unity for the national (watani) struggle among the different groupings of the Palestinian people, and between the Palestinian people and the Arab masses, so as to secure the continuation of the revolution, its escalation, and victory.

Article 11:

The Palestinians will have three mottoes: national (wataniyya) unity, national (qawmiyya) mobilization, and liberation.

Article 12:

The Palestinian people believe in Arab unity. In order to contribute their share toward the attainment of that objective, however, they must, at the present stage of their struggle, safeguard their Palestinian identity and develop their consciousness of that identity, and oppose any plan that may dissolve or impair it.

Article 13:

Arab unity and the liberation of Palestine are two complementary objectives, the attainment of either of which facilitates the attainment of the other. Thus, Arab unity leads to the liberation of Palestine, the liberation of Palestine leads to Arab unity; and work toward the realization of one objective proceeds side by side with work toward the realization of the other.

Article 14:

The destiny of the Arab nation, and indeed Arab existence itself, depend upon the destiny of the Palestine cause. From this interdependence springs the Arab nation's pursuit of, and striving for, the liberation of Palestine. The people of Palestine play the role of the vanguard in the realization of this sacred (*qawmi*) goal.

Article 15:

The liberation of Palestine, from an Arab viewpoint, is a national (qawmi) duty and it attempts to repel the Zionist and imperialist aggression against the Arab homeland, and aims at the elimination of Zionism in Palestine. Absolute responsibility for this falls upon the Arab nation—peoples and governments—with the Arab people of Palestine in the vanguard. Accordingly, the Arab nation must mobilize all its military, human, moral, and spiritual capabilities to participate actively with the Palestinian people in the liberation of Palestine. It must, particularly in the phase of the armed Palestinian revolution, offer and furnish the Palestinian people with all possible help, and material and human support, and make available to them the means and opportunities that will enable them to continue to carry out their leading role in the armed revolution, until they liberate their homeland.

Article 16:

The liberation of Palestine, from a spiritual point of view, will provide the Holy Land with an atmosphere of safety and tranquility, which in turn will safeguard the country's religious sanctuaries and guarantee freedom of worship and of visit to all, without discrimination of race, color, language, or religion. Accordingly, the people of Palestine look to all spiritual forces in the world for support.

Article 17:

The liberation of Palestine, from a human point of view, will restore to the Palestinian individual his dignity, pride, and freedom. Accordingly the Palestinian Arab people look forward to the support of all those who believe in the dignity of man and his freedom in the world.

Article 18:

The liberation of Palestine, from an international point of view, is a defensive action necessitated by the demands of self-defense. Accordingly the Palestinian people, desirous as they are of the friendship of all people, look to freedom-loving and peace-loving states for support in order to restore their legitimate rights in Palestine, to re-establish peace and security in the country, and to enable its people to exercise national sovereignty and freedom.

Article 19:

The partition of Palestine in 1947 and the establishment of the state of Israel are entirely illegal, regardless of the passage of time, because they were contrary to the will of the Palestinian people and to their natural right in their homeland, and inconsistent with the principles embodied in the Charter of the United Nations; particularly the right to self-determination.

Article 20:

The Balfour Declaration, the Mandate for Palestine, and everything that has been based upon them, are deemed null and void. Claims of historical or religious ties of Jews with Palestine are incompatible with the facts of history and the true conception of what constitutes statehood. Judaism, being a religion, is not an independent nationality. Nor do Jews constitute a single nation with an identity of its own; they are citizens of the states to which they belong.

Article 21:

The Arab Palestinian people, expressing themselves by the armed Palestinian revolution, reject all solutions which are substitutes for the total liberation of Palestine and reject all proposals aiming at the liquidation of the Palestinian problem, or its internationalization.

Article 22:

Zionism is a political movement organically associated with international imperialism and antagonistic to all action for liberation and to progressive movements in the world. It is racist and fanatic in its nature, aggressive, expansionist, and colonial in its aims, and fascist in its methods. Israel is the instrument of the Zionist movement, and geographical base for world imperialism placed strategically in the midst of the Arab homeland to combat the hopes of the Arab nation for liberation, unity, and progress. Israel is a constant source of threat vis-á-vis peace in the Middle East and the whole world. Since the liberation of Palestine will destroy the Zionist and imperialist presence and will contribute to the establishment of peace in the Middle East, the Palestinian people look for the support of all the progressive and peaceful forces and urge them all, irrespective of their affiliations and beliefs, to offer the Palestinian people all aid and support in their just struggle for the liberation of their homeland.

Article 23:

The demand of security and peace, as well as the demand of right and justice, require all states to consider Zionism an illegitimate movement, to outlaw its existence, and to ban its operations, in order that friendly relations among peoples may be preserved, and the loyalty of citizens to their respective homelands safeguarded.

Article 24:

The Palestinian people believe in the principles of justice, freedom, sovereignty, self-determination, human dignity, and in the right of all peoples to exercise them.

Article 25:

For the realization of the goals of this Charter and its principles, the Palestine Liberation Organization will perform its role in the liberation of Palestine in accordance with the Constitution of this Organization.

Article 26:

The Palestine Liberation Organization, representative of the Palestinian revolutionary forces, is responsible for the Palestinian Arab people's movement in its struggle—to retrieve its homeland, liberate and return to it and exercise the right to self-determination in it—in all military, political, and financial fields and also for whatever may be required by the Palestine case on the inter-Arab and international levels.

Article 27:

The Palestine Liberation Organization shall cooperate with all Arab states, each according to its potentialities; and will adopt a neutral policy among them in the light of the requirements of the war of liberation; and on this basis it shall not interfere in the internal affairs of any Arab state.

Article 28:

The Palestinian Arab people assert the genuineness and independence of their national (wataniyya) revolution and reject all forms of intervention, trusteeship, and subordination.

Article 29:

The Palestinian people possess the fundamental and genuine legal right to liberate and retrieve their homeland.

The Palestinian people determine their attitude toward all states and forces on the basis of the stands they adopt vis-á-vis to the Palestinian revolution to fulfill the aims of the Palestinian people.

Article 30:

Fighters and carriers of arms in the war of liberation are the nucleus of the popular army which will be the protective force for the gains of the Palestinian Arab people.

Article 31:

The Organization shall have a flag, an oath of allegiance, and an anthem. All this shall be decided upon in accordance with a special regulation.

Article 32:

Regulations, which shall be known as the Constitution of the Palestinian Liberation Organization, shall be annexed to this Charter. It will lay down the manner in which the Organization, and its organs and institutions, shall be constituted; the respective competence of each; and the requirements of its obligation under the Charter.

Article 33:

This Charter shall not be amended save by [vote of] a majority of two-thirds of the total membership of the National Congress of the Palestine Liberation Organization [taken] at a special session convened for that purpose.[2]*

---

*Analysis of The PLO Charter/Covenant:

Article 9 and 15 both make it exceptionally clear that armed struggle against Zionism is not a phase but a basic tenet of Palestinian nationalist ideology. The Zionist entity must be destroyed and replaced by an Arab Palestinian State. (The idea that the PLO, or post-Oslo the PA, can repudiate armed struggle is absurd. It is asking the Palestinian Nationalist Movement to go against one of its fundamental tenets. The use of armed struggle is not connected in any way to the 1967 Israeli victory in the Six-Day War, it is rather about eliminating the Zionist State, period. That means every inch of Israel needs to be liberated/destroyed and replaced by an Arab Palestinian State. Once again, many in the West who believe that all political speech is mere hyperbole and subject to negotiation don't grasp the depth of Palestinian Arab animosity for the idea of Jewish nationalism. Hence, this document is not a political platform (cont'd)

In the wake of the Six-Day War the PLO was transformed. First, its original leader, Ahmed Shukairy (handpicked by the Egyptian leadership), was disgraced as he had made many statements leading up to the war as to how the Palestinian Liberation Army would annihilate Israel. He was replaced by Yahya Hamoudeh, a former deputy of the General Refugee Council, who then headed the PLO Executive from December 24, 1967 to February 2, 1969 following the resignation of Shukeiri.[3] He was succeeded by Yasser Arafat, the more popular, flamboyant and younger leader of Fatah.

---

drafted for a Palestinian Arab electoral convention. Rather, it is the equivalent of a Palestinian constitution and a clear blueprint of what they believe and stand for.

Article 19 nullifies the existence of the State of Israel and all international declarations that helped establish the State legally, like the Balfour Declaration and the November 29, 1947 Partition Plan. It speaks about the Palestinian right for self-determination while in the same breath denying that same right to the Jewish nation—a remarkable act of hypocrisy.

In Article 20 it is clear that the PLO, today the PA, does not consider the Jewish people as a nation and thus denies their right to sovereignty. As opposed to the PLO Constitution, there is no Zionist document that states that Palestinian Arabs have no right to sovereignty. The fact that Israel accepted the November 29, 1947 partition plan meant that, de facto, it recognized the creation of yet another Arab State, this one to be called Palestine. It was the Mufti and the Arab leaders who rejected the partition plan because it pushed the idea of a sovereign Jewish State.

Article 20 states that the Jews are a religious group and hence have no national rights. This is the heart and soul of the conflict. To ignore this basic tenet of Palestinian Arab ideology is to willfully ignore a very unpleasant but true reality. It is not the size of the Jewish State that is the problem, it is the mere fact that it exists.

Article 21 states clearly that there can be no peace or justice until all of Palestine is liberated, read Israel is destroyed. Hence any Israeli/Zionist withdrawal from any piece of territory is merely a step towards the eventual defeat or collapse of the Zionist entity.

Article 22 makes it clear that Zionism is an imperialist, colonialist movement that must be defeated and destroyed. Furthermore, it is a racist and fascist movement. In short, it is the modern embodiment of evil. The choice of the words *racist* and *fascist* were not random choices. The reason the UN was formed was to combat these twin forces of evil. In essence, the PA is beholden to an ideology that believes the Zionist movement and Israel must be destroyed.

Back in the mid-'60s Arafat began using the subversive terror tactics he had learned in the Soviet Union in his quest to exterminate Israel. As part of his tactic, many radical Palestinian Arab terror factions, like the Popular Front for the Liberation of Palestine (PFLP), were welcomed as allies in the war against Israel and Zionism. Finally, he felt that dramatic actions had to begin to let the Zionists, the Arab States and the Palestinians themselves know that there remained but one force that would actively fight the Zionists and cause them pain, his organization, the PLO.*

The PLO thus began to carry out terror attacks emanating from the Gaza Strip and from Judea and Samaria. The PLO and its allies opened up a two-front terror war: terror in Israel itself and against Israeli targets globally. Between June 1967 and December 1968 there were one hundred fifty-nine terrorist attacks inside Israel. The targets were civilian: buses, bus stations and markets— the casualty toll in 1968 alone reaching one hundred seventy-seven Israeli dead and seven hundred wounded, with six hundred sighty-one Palestinians killed and wounded in attacks and reprisals.[4] During the same period there were one thousand twenty-nine terror attacks from across the borders into Israel. The IDF rooted out PLO terrorists operating out of Judea and Samaria and Gaza by the end of 1968 and also responded to the terror attacks from Lebanon, Syria and Jordan by launching raids into these countries, targeting the bases of the PLO and groups like the PFLP.

The largest and most famous Israeli anti-terror raid took place on March 21, 1968 in the Jordanian town of Karameh*, which Arafat was using as a jumping-off point for terror raids into Israel. As a result, the IDF created a fenced, mined border across the entire Jordan River Valley border to keep PLO terrorists from entering Israel.

---

* "Karameh was a Fatah base in Jordan. The town thus became the target of an Israeli assault planned in reprisal for a terrorist attack against a school bus full of children that killed two and wounded 28 on March 18, 1968... When the Israeli forces arrived, they met unexpected resistance from forces of the regular Jordanian army [which believed the large Israeli battle group was seeking to make territorial gains in Jordan]. In the ensuing battle, from which (cont'd)

Consequently, Arafat was forced to move his base of operations across the Jordan River into Western Jordan, an area that had many refugee camps as a result of the 1948-49 Israeli War of Independence, hence a friendly environment for the PLO.

The arrival of the PLO into Western Jordan by early 1968 started a trend that continues. Wherever the PLO gains a foothold, it brings with it a gangster-like mentality as its means of governing. It shows no respect for the population it rules over as it is all about the needs of the PLO rulers who then hide behind the "cause" that is supposedly operating in the best interest of the Palestinian people. As such, PLO henchmen demand protection money, raid public coffers, impose their own brand of justice against anyone who disagrees with them, while excusing themselves from the scrutiny of a free press or an independent judiciary.

Arafat fled after distributing weapons, the Israelis said they suffered 28 dead and 90 wounded, whereas the Jordanians had 100 dead and 90 wounded and 170 terrorists had been killed and 200 captured. The Jordanian account virtually reversed these figures, claiming 200 Israeli dead compared to only 20 of their soldiers. The Palestinian version presented an entirely different picture, claiming their heroic resistance had caused 500 Israeli casualties…" ("Yasser Arafat (1929 -2004)" (http://www.jewishvirtuallibrary.org/yasser-arafat) For the Israelis, despite having destroyed much of Karameh, the battle was a military and political disaster. Even so, "Both military and political decision makers responsible for the operation worked to make sure the public never knew of the debacle. Instead, in newspaper interviews and speeches, the politicians and generals made Karameh sound like a smashing success." (Muki Betser, *Secret Soldier* (NY: Grove Atlantic, 2011), 200.) The battle over Karameh resulted in a huge psychological win for the PLO. Despite losing its headquarters, the black eye it gave the IDF resulted in exponential enlistment. (A.I. Dawisha, *Arab Nationalism in the Twentieth Century: From Triumph to Despair* (NJ: Princeton University Press, 2003), 258. The chief of bureau of the then Israeli Foreign ministry Gideon Rafael later said that "The operation gave an enormous lift to Yasser Arafat's Fatah organization and irrevocably implanted the Palestine problem onto the international agenda, no longer as a humanitarian issue of homeless refugees, but as a claim to Palestinian statehood" (Donald Neff, "Battle of Karameh Establishes Claim of Palestinian Statehood," *Washington Report on Middle East Affairs* (March 1998), 87–88 (https://www.wrmea.org/1998-march/middle-east-history-it-happened-in-march.html)

While this was going on in or near Israel, the PLO, from 1968 to 1972, began a series of dramatic terrorist attacks across Europe against Israeli targets:

July 22, 1968: PFLP hijackers commandeered an El Al plane in Rome. The plane was diverted to Algiers, where the Israeli passengers were held hostage for five weeks.

February 18, 1969: PLO terrorists attacked an El Al aircraft while it was on a Zurich runway. One pilot and three passengers were killed.

February 10, 1970: PLO terrorists tried to hijack an El Al plane during which one passenger was killed and eleven wounded.

September 6, 1970: The PFLP hijacked three planes that were on their way to New York from different European cities. The terrorists then forced the planes to land in Dawson's Field, an airfield in Western Jordan that was under the control of the PLO. Arafat and George Habash—the head of the PFLP—held a joint news conference at the airfield announcing that they were putting the Palestinian Arab agenda on the top of the world's list of priorities. They separated the Jewish hostages from the non-Jewish ones and also held six Americans they felt had some diplomatic titles they presumed would be good bargaining chips. The hijackers then demanded the release of fellow terrorists who were sitting

---

* *Analysis of the Dawson's Field Hijacking and the Black September War*

Yasser Arafat and George Habash learned the power of having the media's attention. The hijacking of the three planes to Dawson's Field and the attention it was given was a propaganda bonanza for the PLO. People in the West equate "desperate measures" with some sort of a legitimate grievance, otherwise why would anyone take such a risky and outlandish move? It was no longer necessary to make the "historical case" against the Zionist enemy, which is not one that stands up to historical scrutiny. But acts of terror that are explained as acts of desperation do buy a great deal of sympathy and certainly raise questions as to why people take such desperate measures. Arafat understood already in 1968 that the media was interested in compelling pictures and narratives, not an Oxford-style debate based on facts and documents. Hence, even though he lost this round militarily, it was a great propaganda victory. He and Habash had succeeded in placing the Palestinian Arab agenda front and center to the Western World. (cont'd)

in Israeli and European jails. The deadline for their release was September 13, yet in another dramatic move on September 12 all three planes were blown up. All of this unfolded in front of the world media.

On September 16 Jordan's King Hussein declared martial law and began a full scale military operation, subsequently known as Black September, to oust the PLO and the PFLP from the state within-a-state these organizations had created in Western Jordan. The Jordanian Army was successful and the PLO and the PFLP fled to Lebanon, the only Arab State that had a border with Israel and an indigenous Palestinian population (as a result of the 1948-1949 War of Independence). It also didn't hurt that Lebanon had a very weak central government and army.

May 8, 1972: One Israeli passenger was killed when IDF commandos stormed a Belgian airliner that was hijacked on the runway at Israel's Lod Airport (renamed Ben Gurion Airport in 1973). Two of the four Black September hijackers were killed in this IDF commando raid.

May 30 1972: The PFLP, together with members of a Japanese terrorist group called the Red Army, carried out the deadliest terror

---

On the other hand, Arafat learned that you can only push an Arab State and its leader so far before you become the target of its ire. And that an Arab army that is pitted against you will not fight you the same way the IDF does. They will fight you the way you fight your enemies: no rules, no holds barred.

A very radical group of Palestinian terrorists broke off from the PLO and the PFLP as a result of their crushing defeat by the Jordanian Army during the September 1970 War known as Black September. This group swore vengeance against Jordan, Israel and the West. Calling itself Black September, in the coming years the group would carry out the bloodiest and boldest terror attacks. Arafat would now be able to practice the art of plausible deniability, essentially enjoying the fruits of another group's actions while disavowing any and all responsibility for them.

Finally, Arafat learned that he must operate from an area where he would have full independence and not be beholden to some Arab State that inevitably had different interests. Hence, Arafat opened a new base of operations and took control of yet another region: South Lebanon. At first this appeared to be a great strategic move for Arafat and the PLO, but eventually it led to a very severe blow in Operation Peace for Galilee in 1982.

attack ever committed at Lod Airport. Twenty-six people, eight of them Israelis, were killed and 78 wounded when the terrorists took out machine guns that had been hidden in their luggage and began to open fire in the passenger terminal. Two of the terrorists were killed and one captured. (He was later released as part of the Jibril Agreement of 1985.)

September 5, 1972: Black September terrorists attacked the Israeli Olympic team during the Summer Olympics in Munich, Germany. Eleven Israeli athletes and one German police officer were murdered.[5]

> Olympic competition was suspended for 24 hours to hold memorial services for the slain athletes...After a memorial service was held for the athletes at the main Olympic stadium, International Olympic Committee President Avery Brundage ordered that the games continue, to show that the terrorists hadn't won.[6]

Thus, Palestinian terror, under the direct or indirect control of Yasser Arafat, became a serious threat to Israelis at home and abroad as well as a new propaganda tool used effectively by the PLO. Instead of being totally discredited, there began to be some in the West who felt there must be something very compelling pushing the PLO and its allies to take such desperate measures. For Israel it meant that she now had to revamp her army, security forces and her diplomatic approach to fight the growing audacity of Palestinian terror.

THE WAR OF ATTRITION: OCTOBER 1968 - AUGUST 1970

Nasser and Egypt were left reeling and dumbfounded by the extent of the Israeli military victory in the Six-Day War. Both Egypt and its Soviet patron were embarrassed by the scope of the Israeli victory. The USSR had to find a way to win back its credibility while at the same time not exposing Egypt to a direct military confrontation with Israel. The solution was for the Soviets to supply Egypt with massive amounts of military aid, but specifically long-range artillery and many sophisticated top-of-the line anti-aircraft missiles. The new round of fighting that Egypt would initiate would be very conducive to its type of fighting—a long drawn out war of attrition that would take place from behind the safety of the Suez Canal. The goal of the war would not be to capture territory in Sinai or push the IDF out of any of its positions. Rather, the goal was to force Israel to spend huge sums of money building fortifications on its side of the Suez Canal, pin down the IDF in a long, drawn-out war that would cause weekly Israeli casualties—which the Egyptians and the Soviets knew upset the Israeli population a great deal—and cause the IDF to constantly rotate forces involving many reserve units thereby disrupting family and work life, further bleeding the Israeli economy. Since the goal would not be to capture territory, this war of attrition could go on indefinitely. Egypt could easily absorb a steady stream of casualties while Israel could not. Finally, should the IDF want to use its air force in the Suez Canal zone, the Egyptians would not scramble their jets to intercept them, but would rather fire volleys of Soviet anti-aircraft missiles, causing loss of planes and lives.

On October 26, 1968 Egypt began with a massive artillery barrage from its side of the Suez Canal launching a drawn-out duel across the Canal. Egypt used its artillery as its weapon of choice, inducing Israel to respond with air strikes deep into Egypt, as well as firing its own artillery. In addition, Israel was forced to spend hundreds of millions of dollars building a chain of forts along the Suez Canal to protect its frontline soldiers. This line of forts was named after its architect, General Chaim Bar Lev, hence the name, the Bar Lev Line. The Israelis were thus able to withstand the Egyptian heavy artillery shelling since they could now sit in their bomb-proof fortifications.

But that was not a way to win a war. The way to win a war of attrition is to turn the tables on your enemy and make the war too costly for the opposition. So while the Egyptians were pounding the Bar Lev Line and sending in commandos via helicopter, Israel began to bomb targets deeper and deeper into Egypt, thus no

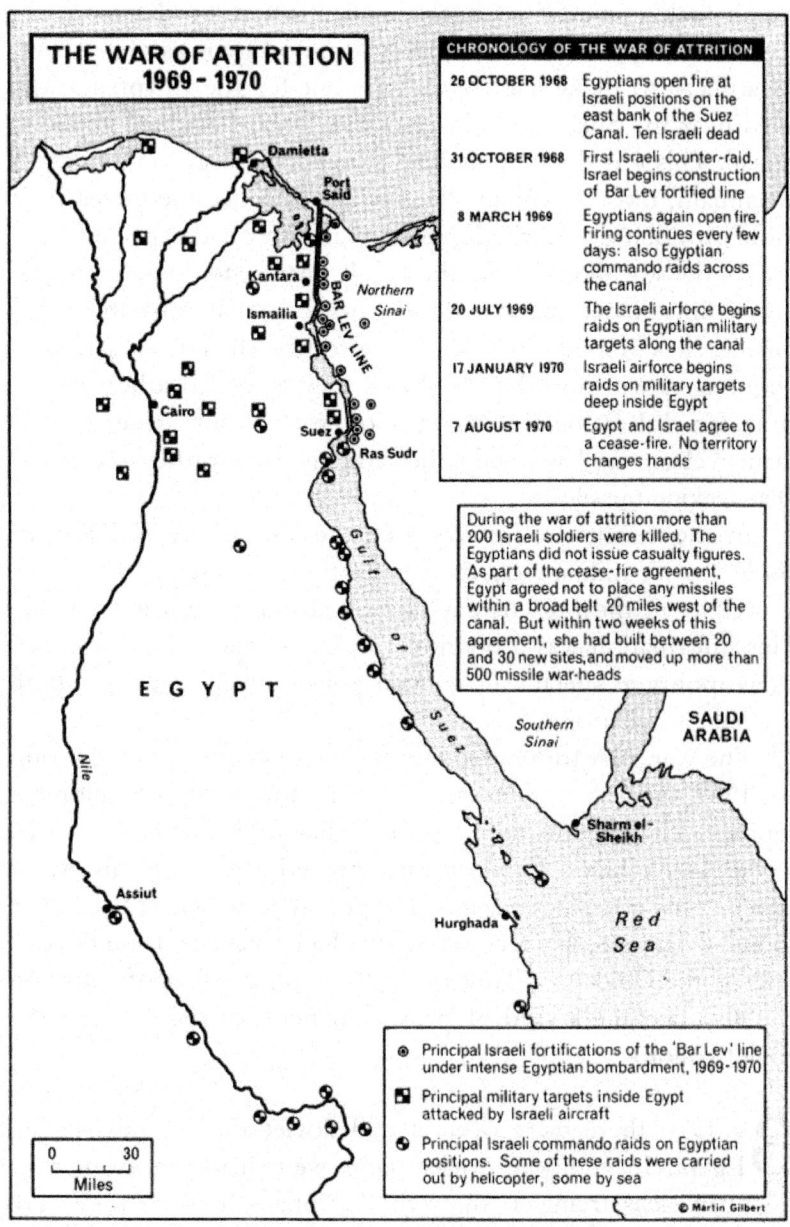

THE WAR OF ATTRITION 1969-1970

CHRONOLOGY OF THE WAR OF ATTRITION

26 OCTOBER 1968	Egyptians open fire at Israeli positions on the east bank of the Suez Canal. Ten Israeli dead
31 OCTOBER 1968	First Israeli counter-raid. Israel begins construction of Bar Lev fortified line
8 MARCH 1969	Egyptians again open fire. Firing continues every few days: also Egyptian commando raids across the canal
20 JULY 1969	The Israeli airforce begins raids on Egyptian military targets along the canal
17 JANUARY 1970	Israeli airforce begins raids on military targets deep inside Egypt
7 AUGUST 1970	Egypt and Israel agree to a cease-fire. No territory changes hands

During the war of attrition more than 200 Israeli soldiers were killed. The Egyptians did not issue casualty figures. As part of the cease-fire agreement, Egypt agreed not to place any missiles within a broad belt 20 miles west of the canal. But within two weeks of this agreement, she had built between 20 and 30 new sites, and moved up more than 500 missile war-heads

Damietta

Port Said

Kantara

Ismailia

Northern Sinai

BAR LEV LINE

Cairo

Suez

Ras Sudr

EGYPT

Nile

Gulf of Suez

Southern Sinai

SAUDI ARABIA

Assiut

Hurghada

Sharm el-Sheikh

Red Sea

⊚ Principal Israeli fortifications of the 'Bar Lev' line under intense Egyptian bombardment, 1969-1970

▪ Principal military targets inside Egypt attacked by Israeli aircraft

◉ Principal Israeli commando raids on Egyptian positions. Some of these raids were carried out by helicopter, some by sea

0   30
Miles

© Martin Gilbert

longer making it a Suez Canal war of attrition. Furthermore, the IDF launched its own commando raids into Egypt, as well as using its artillery to make life very unpleasant for the Egyptians who lived near the Suez Canal in cities like Suez, Port Said and Port Fouad. This was done by shelling closer and closer to these cities. Eventually, most Egyptians fled, as the pain became increasingly more pronounced for the Egyptians than they had expected.

As the war dragged on, the USSR once again had its prestige on the line. Soviet military advisors began to man the anti-aircraft missile sites hoping to be more effective than the Egyptians. Shooting down more Israeli planes, they extracted a heavy price from Israel. But the IDF pilots soon learned how to use special maneuvers, as well as ejecting heated targets to confuse the Soviet heat-seeking missiles.

In the meantime, Israel shared the secrets she had learned about Soviet military equipment captured in the Six-Day War, as well as in the present day war of attrition, with its U.S. ally. This information was a boon to the U.S. military as it revamped its weaponry to specifically counter Soviet materiel in use in both Vietnam and Europe.

The War of Attrition was a turning point in U.S.-Israel relations. By 1969 the U.S. had become Israel's top military equipment supplier delivering the then top-of-the line F4 Phantom Jet as well as the A4 Skyhawk. Israel, in turn, proved itself to be an expert at using this equipment against Egypt and even against her Soviet sponsor. The U.S. also recognized that Israel was clearly on the U.S. side of the Cold War. Thus, by 1969-1970, the War of Attrition had also become a kind of proxy war between the U.S. and the Soviet Union.

By 1970 there were over 20,000 Soviet military advisors in Egypt. In addition, Soviet pilots were flying missions over Egyptian skies trying to show the Egyptians how far they were willing to go to protect them. But even that did not work. The IDF pilots still got to their targets and some Soviet pilots were shot down as well. Fearing an "East vs. West" Cold War confrontation,

U.S. president Richard Nixon sent his Secretary of State, William Rogers, to formulate a plan to obtain a ceasefire.

In essence, both sides would cease all hostile activities against each other with the Egyptians having to push back their anti-aircraft batteries fifty kilometers west of the Suez Canal. Had there not been this stipulation, the Egyptians could have created a thick missile umbrella near the Suez Canal that would cover the first 40 to 50 kilometers of Israeli-held Sinai, thus giving the Egyptians a very dangerous military edge. Eventually, the plan indicated that...

> Israel will withdraw to agreed borders taking into account its security, and not to the borders prior to the Six Day War, and the withdrawal will be executed following the signing of a binding bilateral agreement; the solution suggested regarding the refugees will not harm Israel's characteristic as a Jewish state; the United States guarantees Israel's sovereignty, security and territorial entirety; and the balance of arms will be preserved. The Israeli Government gave its basic consent to the plan on July 31st 1970, causing the Herut-Liberal Bloc to resign from the coalition.
>
> The Israeli-Egyptian new ceasefire came into affect [sic] on August 7th, but Israel suspended the...talks shortly thereafter due to Egypt's violation of the Ceasefire Agreement and stationing of anti-aircraft warfare alongside the Suez Canal.[7]

Thus Egypt's ceasfire violation and Rogers' failure to sanction Egypt for its perfidy led to a further impasse in continued negotiations with Egypt. This impasse, and the leaving of Egyptian batteries alonside the Canal, would have disastrous effects on the IDF in the opening days of the Yom Kippur War, October 6-24, 1973.

YEARS OF PEACE AND PROSPERITY: AUGUST 1970 - OCTOBER 1973

After the War of Attrition, and even though Egypt openly violated the 1970 Cease Fire Agreement, Israeli hubris fomented a sense of superiority over the leadership and military forces of its

Arab neighbors. It was thought that the Arab world would not dare start up with Israel again, at least for ten to fifteen years, and in all probability would try to negotiate a settlement. Thus, the army and government began to slack off—they did not make sure to keep the army sharp, well-equipped and always ready to fight, as was the case prior to the Six-Day War. The new strategic depth Israel enjoyed, its overwhelming victory in 1967, its defeat of Egypt and to an extent the Soviets in the War of Attrition, left the Israeli leadership deluded about its sense of security.

COUNTDOWN TO THE YOM KIPPUR WAR

On September 28, 1970 Gamel Abdul Nasser died of a heart attack. Nasser had been the Egyptian leader since 1953, having led his country in three wars against Israel: 1956 Sinai Campaign, the 1967 Six-Day War and the 1968-1970 War of Attrition. His replacement was the little known, uncharismatic Anwar Sadat. In aggregate, the Israeli government and military analysts thought this combination of quiet in the South and the death of Nasser would guarantee a long period of peace and quiet. Nothing could have been further from the truth. The unassuming Sadat turned out to be a much smarter and more formidable enemy leader that Nasser ever was.

Sadat began by slowly consolidating power in Egypt and winning the trust of the Egyptian Army, which was essential for any Egyptian leader seeking successful rule. Then Sadat made the demand that Israel withdraw from Sinai and in return Egypt would permit Israeli use of the Suez Canal. To Sadat, Israeli withdrawal was a pre-condition to what was hinted could be a form of peace. Furthermore, Sadat made it clear that the Egyptian Army would enter any area that the IDF withdrew from. This plan, referred by many Middle East commentators as "the Peace Plan," was rejected.

Essentially, Israel was being asked to withdraw from an area that she had twice captured because of Egyptian threats to destroy her, with Sinai as the springboard for an invasion. Eilat, on the southern end of Sinai, had been blockaded twice by Egyptian forces when they had control of the area. Israel's prime minister at the time, Golda Meir, did not see Sadat's demands as a peace plan, but rather more of a threat. Either Israel withdraw from Sinai and hand it over to the Egyptian Army, or the Egyptians would be forced to conquer it. There was no discussion of normalization and the start of diplomatic and trade relations, or how that would be achieved. Sadat had used this "peace plan" and Israel's so called "rejection" as the pretext for his threat to take Sinai back by force in 1972.

Sadat called 1972 the "Year of Decision." By this he meant that Egypt would no longer tolerate the Israeli occupation of Sinai and that the time had come for Egypt to take it back by force. He even went on to say that he was prepared to sacrifice one million Egyptian soldiers to regain this territory. But, since 1971, Sadat had been threatening Israel that he was prepared to go to war to end Israeli control of Sinai, but nothing concrete had happened yet. Thus his current threat was taken with a grain of salt. Apparently, this form of disinformation was all part of a brilliant plan that Sadat deployed to totally throw Israel off balance regarding how to react to his threats.

In 1972 Sadat seemingly lost patience with his Soviet patrons who were not being responsive to his requests for more and better military materiel. With Egypt threatening to go to war against Israel, she would need to be armed with the best weaponry the Soviets had. But the world was changing and this affected the Soviet attitude toward Sadat and Egypt. At the time, the U.S.A. had opened the door to much better relations with Communist China and had signed a détente agreement with the Soviet Union. Détente precluded the Soviets from openly trying to support Sadat's bid to start a war with Israel, a clear U.S. ally.

After the Soviets kept rebuffing Sadat's requests for more and better equipment, he grew so frustrated that in a surprise move he kicked out all 20,000 Soviet advisors from his country. Sadat thus signaled the U.S. that he was willing to switch sides if the U.S. was willing to pressure Israel into handing over Sinai.

Sadat was no Nasser; Nasser was an in-your-face bull in a china shop and Sadat was a chess player, leaving his friends and foes wondering what his next move would be. Thus 1972 came and went and there was no real "decision" vis-á-vis Sinai and a war with Israel. In the eyes of Israeli leaders, Sadat was but an erratic Arab leader who made statements he was not able to back up, nor did he seem to have a coherent policy.

In the spring of 1973 Sadat ordered the mobilization of the Egyptian Army and had it deployed right on the Suez Canal, seemingly prepared to carry out his threats to take back Sinai by force. In response, the then-Chief of Staff of the IDF, David Elazar, requested permission for a partial call-up of IDF reserves to be sent to Sinai in and around the Canal region. Golda Meir approved the request. For close to two weeks the IDF eyeballed the Egyptian Army that was sitting right across the Suez Canal. Then, suddenly, the Egyptian Army was moved away from the Canal and its reserves sent home. The message conveyed was that Sadat was just a man who threatened and bluffed. Even when he deployed the Egyptian Army on the Canal, it didn't mean anything.*

---

* I was a teenager volunteer in the summer of 1973 on Kibbutz Yavneh. I remember one night in August watching Israeli News in the kibbutz collective TV room/den. There was a segment about the Egyptian army practicing to cross the Suez Canal to invade Sinai. They were using the Nile as their "fake" Canal. The exercise involved thousands of Egyptian soldiers and was a re-enactment of what would happen a mere two months later when the Yom Kippur War actually was initiated by Egypt and Syria. I distinctly remember all the kibbutz members watching the segment and laughing. It was as if they were watching a comedy skit. Sadat had gained the reputation of a deluded man who made outrageous claims, so even when he publicly showed his war plans the Israelis looked at it and laughed. This sentiment was not limited to the members of Kibbutz Yavneh; it was a universal sentiment in Israel. Sadat had mastered the idea of feeding into the false narrative that Israelis wanted to believe: Israel was a military juggernaut and no Arab army would dare risk war with her. This allowed Sadat to say and do things right in front of everyone's nose and be ignored. Sometimes the best place to hide something is right in front of everyone!

During this period, Israel was far more consumed with the growing threat of Palestinian terror. And thus the cagey Sadat correctly analyzed that Israel was overconfident from her victories in the Six-Day War and the War of Attrition and that she saw him as a deluded Arab leader who had no stomach for war. As a result of this reasoning, since early 1972 Sadat was able to plan the most devastating surprise attack against the State of Israel in her entire history, a plan that would not only return Sinai and other captured territories, but would initiate a war that could finally realize the Arab dream of annihilating Israel.

Sadat thus convinced Hafez Assad of Syria to work together with him in planning a well-coordinated attack on Israel at a time that the Israelis would least expect it. Sadat had analyzed all the reasons that Arab Armies had lost to Israel since 1948 and believed the time was right for a war that would finally vanquish Israel:

1) Israel's overconfidence was her greatest liability;

2) Sadat created an atmosphere where what he said and even did vis-á-vis his threats against Israel were not taken seriously.

3) Even the movement of Egyptian troops to the front line, the Suez Canal, was not something Israel had to worry about.

4) Make it appear as if the Soviets were kicked out completely from Egypt, thus losing its main supplier of armaments. In reality, however, the Soviets were equipping both Egypt and Syria with a great deal of sophisticated arms, as well as promising them diplomatic cover at the UN. This also created the false impression to the U.S. that Sadat could be won over if it just put enough pressure on Israel. (Soviet ships full of armaments were docking in Syrian ports on the third day of the Yom Kippur War, even though it's a seven-day journey from the closest Russian port. This was further evidence of Soviet involvement in the planning and execution of the Yom Kippur War.)

5) Coordinate an attack with other Arab states. Sadat approached Syria and Jordan, but King Hussein was still licking his wounds from the devastating loss he suffered in the Six-Day War. He also remembered very clearly that Syria was prepared to join

the PLO against him in September of 1970, and it was Israel, in fact, that helped save his kingdom. But Assad of Syria was happy to be part of this historic coordinated attack against Israel.

6)   Sadat picked October 6, 1973 as the day to attack Israel for a variety of reasons:

a) It was the 9th of Ramadan that year on the Islamic calendar. Ramadan is a holy month.

b) On the 17th of Ramadan Islamic armies won their greatest victory in Islamic history, the Battle of Badr. Mohammed himself led the army that won this battle. Having a war coincide with that date would be a great honor and sure sign of victory.

c) October 6th in 1973 was the Jewish holy day of Yom Kippur, the Day of Atonement, the holiest day on the Jewish calendar, with most Israelis in synagogue for the day. The IDF commonly granted extra leave on that day so soldiers could be home with their families.

7)   Since the coordinated attack was schedules to begin at 2 p.m., in the Golan the sun would blind the Israeli defenders, and it would be well into the fast day, which would probably affect the fighting effectiveness of the IDF.

8)   Egypt, in violation of the 1970 War of Attrition Cease Fire Agreement, had spent over three years creating the world's thickest anti-aircraft network near the Suez Canal. The Soviet-equipped anti-aircraft missiles were able to cover 20 miles deep into Sinai with so many missile launchers it was virtually impossible for an IDF plane not to be shot down. The Syrians had also created an almost identical missile umbrella east of the Golan Heights that the Israelis mistakenly attributed to the Syrian Defense of Damascus network.

9)   In addition, the Soviets had given the Egyptian and Syrian armies a brand new top-of-the-line anti-tank missile, the Sagger, that was exceptionally accurate and deadly. This would nullify the fact that the Israeli Armored Corps was made up of better soldiers and better tanks.

Having done all this preparation, Sadat launched the most effective and devastating attack on Israel that had ever occurred. Already, in late September 1973, the Egyptian Army had massed along the Suez Canal, and the Syrian Army had done the same across from the Golan Heights. The misinformation spread by both the Egyptian and Syrian armies was that these were late summer maneuvers. As a result, IDF Intelligence interpreted all the information that forward IDF positions were relaying to them about Egyptian and Syrian troop concentrations as nothing to worry about. It was only on October 5th that the Chief of Staff of the IDF, David Elazar, reached the conclusion that Israel was about to be attacked. He requested permission from Prime Minister Golda Meir to call up some of the reserves and to keep all air force personnel on base, effectively cancelling all Yom Kippur leaves. In addition, he requested permission to initiate a pre-emptive strike. Golda Meir, for a variety of reasons—including pressure from U.S. Secretary of State Henry Kissinger not to be the side that began hostilities—rejected Elazar's requests.*

---

* "Prime Minister Golda Meir, Minister of Defense Moshe Dayan, and Chief of General Staff David Elazar met at 8:05 am the morning of Yom Kippur, six hours before the war began. Dayan opened the meeting by arguing that war was not a certainty. Elazar then presented his argument in favor of a pre-emptive attack against Syrian airfields at noon, Syrian missiles at 3:00 pm, and Syrian ground forces at 5:00 pm. 'When the presentations were done, the prime minister hemmed uncertainly for a few moments but then came to a clear decision. There would be no preemptive strike. Israel might be needing American assistance soon and it was imperative that it would not be blamed for starting the war. "If we strike first, we won't get help from anybody", she said.' Prior to the war, Kissinger and Nixon consistently warned Meir that she must not be responsible for initiating a Middle east war. On October 6, 1973, the war opening date, Kissinger told Israel not to go for a preemptive strike, and Meir confirmed to him that Israel would not.

"Other developed nations, being more dependent on OPEC oil, took more seriously the threat of an Arab oil embargo and trade boycott, and had stopped supplying Israel with munitions. As a result, Israel was totally dependent on the United States for military resupply, and particularly sensitive to anything that might endanger that relationship. After Meir had made her decision, (cont'd)

Elazar, on his own, still cancelled all leaves for the air force, but could not do much more. This decision by Meir was to haunt her for the rest of her life.

---

at 10:15 am, she met with American ambassador Kenneth Keating in order to inform the United States that Israel did not intend to preemptively start a war, and asked that American efforts be directed at preventing war. An electronic telegram with Keating's report on the meeting was sent to the United States at 16:33 GMT (6:33 pm local time).

"A message arrived later from United States Secretary of State Henry Kissinger saying, 'Don't preempt.' At the same time, Kissinger also urged the Soviets to use their influence to prevent war, contacted Egypt with Israel's message of non-preemption, and sent messages to other Arab governments to enlist their help on the side of moderation. These late efforts were futile. According to Henry Kissinger, had Israel struck first, it would not have received "so much as a nail".' (https://en.wikipedia.org/wiki/Yom_Kippur_War as derived from Abraham Rabinovich (2004). *The Yom Kippur War: The Epic Encounter That Transformed the Middle East* (NY: Schocken Books, 2004), 498; William B. Quandt, *Decade of Decisions: American Policy Toward the Arab–Israeli Conflict, 1967–1976* (Berkeley: University of California Press, 1977) 169; http://nsarchive.gwu.edu/NSAEBB/NSAEBB98/octwar-10.pdf; "Government of Israel Concern about possible Syrian and Egyptian attack today," United States Department of State. October 6, 1973.

Footnotes

[1] "Fatah: History & Overview," *Jewish Virtual Library* (http://www.jewishvirtuallibrary.org/jsource/Terrorism/Fatah.html)

[2] "The Palestinian National Charter: Resolutions of the Palestine National Council July 1-17, 1968," Yale Law School, Lillian Goldman Law Center, *The Avalon Project* (http://avalon.law.yale.edu/20th_century/plocov.asp)

[3] "Palestinian Liberation Organization (PLO)," *Encyclopedia of the Modern Middle East and North Africa* (http://www.encyclopedia.com/history/asia-and-africa/middle-eastern-history/palestine-liberation-organization)

[4] "Yasser Arafat (1929 - 2004), *Jewish Virtual Library* (http://www.jewishvirtuallibrary.org/jsource/biography/arafat.html)

[5] Wm. Robert Johnston, "Chronology of Terrorist Attacks in Israel Introduction," 8 January, 2017 (http://www.johnstonsarchive.net/terrorism/terrisrael.html); "Japanese kill 26 at Tel Aviv airport," *On This Day 1950-2005*, BBC (http://news.bbc.co.uk/onthisday/hi/dates/stories/may/29/newsid_2542000/2542263.stm)

[6] This Day in History, "1972: Massacre begins at Munich Olympics," (http://www.history.com/this-day-in-history/massacre-begins-at-munich-olympics)

[7] "Rogers Plan" (https://www.knesset.gov.il/lexicon/eng/rogers_eng.htm)

Chapter 13

The Yom Kippur War
October 6 - October 24, 1973

All of Sadat's planning paid off on October 6, 1973* as Israel was attacked simultaneously on two fronts. First, the Syrian Army began a devastating artillery barrage of the Golan, together with low flying jets bombing Israeli positions.

"At the onset of the battle, the Israeli brigades of some 3,000 troops, 180 tanks and 60 artillery pieces faced off against three infantry divisions with large armor components comprising 28,000 Syrian troops, 800 tanks and 600 artillery pieces."[1] By the second day, two more Syrian armored divisions joined the fray.

It cannot be emphasized enough how it important it was for the Israeli forces to hold their position on the forty mile-long, fifteen-mile wide Golan—failure meant an open doorway to major Israeli cities such as Tiberias, Safed, Haifa and Netanya and, ultimately, a destruction of the State.

---

* "President Gamal Abdel Nasser of Egypt died in September 1970 and was succeeded by Anwar Sadat. A peace initiative led by UN intermediary Gunnar Jarring failed to produce a lasting peace agreement. While both parties reaffirmed their desire for a peace agreement, the Israelis refused any preconditions to negotiations; the Egyptians, on the other hand, refused to enter into negotiations before Israel withdrew their troops from the Sinai peninsula to the 1967 ceasefire lines. In one instance, in response to a letter sent by Jarring to governments of Israel and Egypt, Sadat wrote that Egypt would be 'ready to enter into a peace agreement with Israel' if Israel committed itself to 'withdrawal of its armed forces from Sinai and the Gaza Strip', to 'achievement of a just (cont'd)

In the south, the same scenario was being played out: Egypt began a devastating artillery barrage across the entire Suez Canal, while Egyptian planes bombed the entire Bar Lev Line. Because

---

settlement for the refugee problem', and to implementation of other provisions of UN Security Council Resolution 242. In addition, the Egyptian response included a statement that the lasting peace could not be achieved without 'withdrawal of the Israeli armed forces from all the territories occupied since 5 June 1967'. The UNSC resolution called for 'withdrawal from territories occupied' intentionally omitting 'all', and 'the'; the Israeli response included a statement that they were not willing to 'withdraw to the pre-June 5, 1967 lines.'

Sadat hoped that by inflicting even a limited defeat on the Israelis, the status quo could be altered. Hafez al-Assad, the leader of Syria, had a different view. He had little interest in negotiation and felt the retaking of the Golan Heights would be a purely military option. After the Six-Day War, Assad had launched a massive military buildup and hoped to make Syria the dominant military power of the Arab states. With the aid of Egypt, Assad felt that his new army could win convincingly against Israel and thus secure Syria's role in the region. Assad only saw negotiations beginning once the Golan Heights had been retaken by force, which would induce Israel to give up the West Bank and Gaza, and make other concessions.

Sadat also had important domestic concerns in wanting war. 'The three years since Sadat had taken office...were the most demoralized in Egyptian history.... A desiccated economy added to the nation's despondency. War was a desperate option.' In his biography of Sadat, Raphael Israeli argued that Sadat felt the root of the problem was the great shame over the Six-Day War, and before any reforms could be introduced, he believed that that shame had to be overcome. Egypt's economy was in shambles, but Sadat knew that the deep reforms that he felt were needed would be deeply unpopular among partsof the population. A military victory would give him the popularity he needed to make changes. A portion of the Egyptian population, most prominently university students who launched wide protests, strongly desired a war to reclaim the Sinai and was highly upset that Sadat had not launched one in his first three years in office.

The other Arab states showed much more reluctance to fully commit to a new war. Jordanian King Hussein feared another major loss of territory, as had occurred in the Six-Day War, in which Jordan lost all of the West Bank, territory it had conquered and annexed in 1948-49, which had doubled its population. Sadat also backed the claim of the Palestine Liberation Organization (PLO) to the West Bank and Gaza and, in the event of a victory, promised Yasser Arafat that he would be given control of them. Hussein still saw the West Bank as part of Jordan and wanted it restored to his kingdom. Moreover, during the Black September crisis of 1970, a near civil war had broken out between the (cont'd)

it was Yom Kippur and many leaves had been granted, there were a grand total of four hundred eighty-eight IDF soldiers manning the fortification. While the Bar Lev Line was being pounded, thousands of Egyptian soldiers stormed across the Suez on dozens of pontoon bridges and hundreds of rubber dinghies. In total, 80,000 Egyptian soldiers would be involved in this first wave assault. Unlike the Golan Heights, the Sinai is one hundred eighty miles wide and in order to get into the Israeli Negev you must cross through one of three mountain passes that control Sinai: Gidi, Mitla and Khatmia. Sitting in these three passes, about twenty-five miles behind the Bar Lev Line, was an IDF armored division and an IDF paratrooper brigade.

Although Israel had anticipated an attack*, it was caught flatfooted and there was a real fear that the Egyptian and Syrian armies would quickly make their way into pre-1967 Israel and

---

PLO and the Jordanian government. In that war, Syria had intervened militarily on the side of the PLO, estranging Hussein.

Iraq and Syria also had strained relations, and the Iraqis refused to join the initial offensive. Lebanon, which shared a border with Israel, was not expected to join the Arab war effort because of its small army and already evident instability. The months before the war saw Sadat engage in a diplomatic offensive to try to win support for the war. By the fall of 1973, he claimed the backing of more than a hundred states. These were most of the countries of the Arab League, Non-Aligned Movement, and Organization of African Unity. Sadat had also worked to curry favor in Europe and had some success before the war. Britain and France for the first time sided with the Arab powers against Israel on the United Nations Security Council. (https://en.wikipedia.org/wiki/Yom_Kippur_War as derived from Elie Podeh, Elie (2015). Chances for Peace: Missed Opportunities in the Arab-Israeli Conflict (Austin: University of Texas Press, 2015) 104–105; Meir Rosenne, "Understanding UN Security Council Resolution 242". Jerusalem Center For Public Affairs (http://jcpa.org/security_council_resolution_242/); "The Jarring initiative and the response", Israel's Foreign Relations, Selected Documents, vols 1–2, 1947–1974; Abraham Rabinovich, *The Yom Kippur War: The Epic Encounter That Transformed the Middle East* (New York, NY: Schocken Books, 2005), 13.

*Ashraf Marwan was an Egyptian billionaire and the husband of Mona Gamal Abdel Nasser, daughter of former Egyptian president Gamal Abdel Nasser. Since 1969 Marwan [had] served in the Presidential Office, first under (cont'd)

destroy the country! Air raid sirens began to blare all over the country. Radio stations that were silent because of Yom Kippur all came on line broadcasting coded messages where reserve soldiers from different units should assemble to join their units to help the overwhelmed IDF regular army forces.

But Sadat had made two mistakes:

1) Yom Kippur is not the ideal day to invade Israel since roads are all empty because most Israelis are in synagogue. Hence, it was easy for reservists to run out of their synagogues, hop onto vehicles and drive to their bases. And it was easy for large military convoys to make their way to the front.

2) Like the Mufti, Nasser and other Arab leaders, he underestimated the nature of the Jews who live in Israel, their relationship to the land and to what extent they will go to defend it.

The forces on the front lines realized what was at stake and that the entire Nation of Israel was depending on them. The soldiers responded and fought with incredible bravery. Since in the Golan there was no rear to retreat to, a decision was made by the IDF general staff to send eighty percent of the reserves up north to engage the Syrian Army. Although the IDF can mobilize all its reserves within 48 hours, the standing forces didn't have 48 hours to wait for reinforcements, thus increasing the pressure to hold their positions. The outmanned two Israeli brigades were thus committed to stopping the Syrian divisions, though at a terrible

---

Nasser and, then as a close aide to his successor, President Anwar Sadat. In 2002 it became known that, during the period leading up to the October 1973 Yom Kippur War, Marwan spied for Israel (under the Mossad code-name "The Angel"), disclosing some of Egypt's best-kept secrets. His warning on 5 October 1973 that "war will start tomorrow", triggered an emergency Israeli military mobilization and prevented a complete surprise on 6 October and the complete occupation of the Golan Heights by the Syrian Army a day later. (https:// en.wikipedia.org/wiki/Ashraf_Marwan, see Simon Parkin, "Who killed the 20th cenury's greatest spy?" *The Guardian*, 15 September 2015 (https://www. theguardian.com/world/2015/sep/15/who-killed-20th-centurys-greatest-spy-ashraf-marwan))

cost of lives—in two days of bloody fighting the Syrian Army captured a little less than half of the Golan Heights, paying a frightful price.

On the third day of the war the first IDF reserve forces began to arrive to support the remnants of the defenders. By the end of that day, the IDF had pushed the Syrian Army out of the Golan. By the fourth day, the IDF began to push the Syrian Army back into Syria, and by the fifth day, in the Valley of Tears, routed the Syrian Army in one of the largest and fiercest tank battles in the history of modern warfare. After that battle the IDF began to chase the Syrian Army towards Damascus, all the while capturing more Syrian territory.

Down south the situation was very different. The Bar Lev Line's four hundred eighty-eight fighters were fighting 80,000 Egyptian soldiers. They held on for forty-eight hours and then fell. The Egyptian Army took pictures of their soldiers storming the fortification, planting the Egyptian flag, and falling to the ground and praying, giving thanks for their incredible victory. These pictures were forever enshrined in a museum in Cairo that celebrates the "victory" of the Egyptian Army in the "War of Ramadan" against Israel. There were also pictures of dead Israeli soldiers strewn all over the Bar Lev Line, as well as pictures released to the world media by the Egyptian Army of captured, bewildered-looking Israeli soldiers. The goal was to create a sense of victory in Egypt and the entire Arab world and to sow a sense of fear and panic in Israel. While the former did occur, the latter did not; if anything it motivated the IDF citizen-soldier to fight with even more tenacity seeing what the enemy had in store.

By October 8th the Egyptian Army, though having suffered heavy losses, now controlled the eastern side of the Suez Canal—with the exception of one Israeli fort called "Budapest"—and began streaming thousands of soldiers, hundreds of tanks and artillery pieces, as well as anti-aircraft missile batteries, into Sinai. There it established a beachhead on the entire eastern side of the Suez Canal.

On that date, some of the IDF forces that were stationed in the Sinai passes moved westward toward the Suez Canal beachhead to counterattack. Those forces did not break through the Egyptian lines but appeared to have stopped the advance. The Egyptian army now controlled an area around 100 miles long (north to south) and around seven miles deep. The following day, October 9th, there was another unsuccessful counterattack, this one led by General Ariel Sharon.

In essence, a stalemate was developing in Sinai: The Egyptians had their beachhead well established but were unable to push eastward deeper into Sinai and toward the strategic passes they needed to capture to control Sinai and eventually enter pre-1967 Israel. The IDF, in turn, was unable to dislodge the Egyptian Army from its beachhead. By October 12 the northern front had been stabilized with most of the Syrian Army destroyed or on the run and the IDF chasing them to Damascus. This allowed the IDF to shift its focus to Sinai and move thousands of reservists down south.

On October 14th, Israel, having learned how to cope with the Russian Sagger Anti-Tank Missile threat, used different tactics and launched a very effective counterattack on the Egyptian Army that had attempted to breakout of their beachhead and move toward the Sinai passes. The IDF destroyed over two hundred fifty tanks while losing only ten. General Sharon then executed a daring plan which would decisively determine the outcome of the war.

THE TURNING POINT OF THE WAR ON THE SOUTHERN FRONT: OCTOBER 15-16

After the first few days of the Yom Kippur War there were over 100,000 Egyptian soldiers on the eastern side of the Suez Canal divided into two armies: the Second Army sitting in the northern sector and the Third Army in the southern sector. General Sharon sent scouts to see where the lines of the Second Army ended and the Third Army began. They reported that there was a seam between the two armies around one kilometer wide. Sharon decided to launch a nighttime attack directed at widening the seam and creating an Israeli bridgehead between the two Egyptian armies. Securing this area, he then utilized Israeli pontoon bridges across the Suez Canal to allow the IDF to come up behind the Egyptians and surround them, cut them off from supplies, and, equally important, destroy their anti-aircraft umbrella that had been causing so much grief to the IDF. This plan was executed on October 15-16. Composed mainly of paratroopers, commandos, combat engineers and the armored corps, it was a bloody battle, but the IDF achieved all of its goals. By the night of October 16th there was a large IDF fighting force operating in North Africa. This force grew in strength by the hour as more and more men and equipment were sent over the Suez Canal along the secured route.

With the two Egyptian armies cut off from each other, the IDF began operating behind their lines. With the Egyptian anti-aircraft batteries systematically destroyed, the Israeli Air Force soon established full air superiority. Sadat, who had seen the UN as his ally up until October 15, on October 16 begged the USSR to convene the UN Security Council and demand an immediate ceasefire. But the U.S., led by President Richard Nixon, was not so quick to have Soviet clients Egypt and Syria be saved by the UN from the consequences of a war they had initiated. By October 21 the IDF had encircled the Egyptian Third Army, a force in excess of 40,000 men. At the same time, IDF forces in North Africa were now only forty miles from Cairo, while IDF forces in the north had captured a part of Syria and were fifteen miles away from Damascus. Finally, on October 22, the IDF recaptured the strategic peak of Mt. Hermon that was lost on the first day of the war.

THE UN AND THE END OF THE YOM KIPPUR WAR: OCTOBER 22-24, 1973

By the end of October both Syria and Egypt were pressing the USSR to force the UN Security Council to save them from a defeat that would be worse than the defeat of 1967. By October 22 the U.S. decided that Egypt and Syria had suffered enough for their belligerence, especially since Egypt was still viewed as a potential country that could be pulled from the Soviet orbit. Israel, for her part, wanted to continue to fight for the following reasons:

a) In one or two more days of fighting the IDF could encircle the Egyptian Second Army as well;

b) The Egyptian First Army that was stationed in North Africa had retreated closer to Cairo to defend the capitol. The IDF wanted the Egyptian people and the Arab world to know that the IDF was now in North Africa and a stone's throw from Cairo.

Nevertheless, the U.S. agreed with the USSR and a UN Cease Fire Resolution, Security Council Resolution 338, was passed on October 22.

Security Council Resolution 338

The Security Council,

1. Calls upon all parties to present fighting to cease all firing and terminate all military activity immediately, no later than 12 hours after the moment of the adoption of this decision, in the positions after the moment of the adoption of this decision, in the positions they now occupy;

2. Calls upon all parties concerned to start immediately after the cease-fire the implementation of Security Council Resolution 242 (1967) in all of its parts;

3. Decides that, immediately and concurrently with the cease-fire, negotiations start between the parties concerned under appropriate auspices aimed at establishing a just and durable peace in the Middle East.[2]

Resolution 338, in essence, called for a cessation of fighting and the implementation of Resolution 242, which had called for the recognition of Israel, its right to live in secure boundaries, and its right to use all local international waterways. The only negative aspect of this resolution was that it robbed Israel of delivering a devastating blow to the Egyptian Army. Ironically, the Egyptian

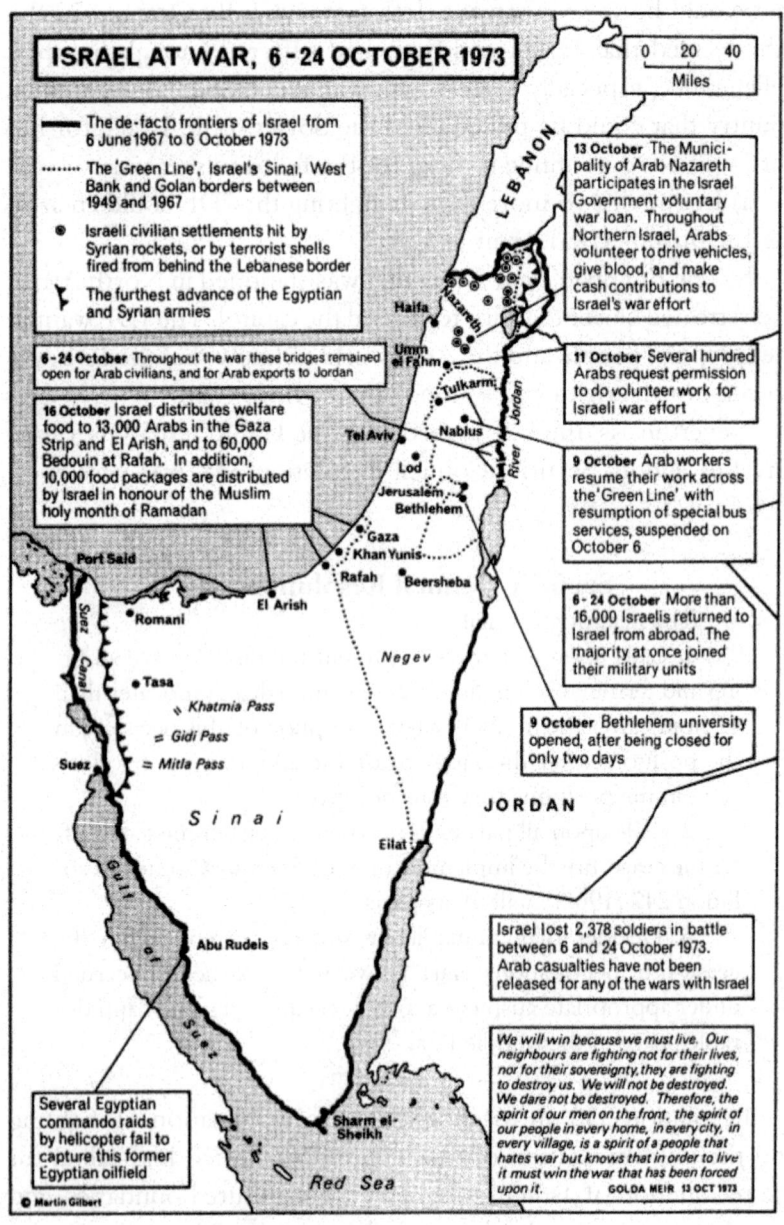

ISRAEL AT WAR, 6-24 OCTOBER 1973

0   20   40
Miles

▬▬▬ The de-facto frontiers of Israel from 6 June 1967 to 6 October 1973

········ The 'Green Line', Israel's Sinai, West Bank and Golan borders between 1949 and 1967

● Israeli civilian settlements hit by Syrian rockets, or by terrorist shells fired from behind the Lebanese border

⌐ The furthest advance of the Egyptian and Syrian armies

6-24 October Throughout the war these bridges remained open for Arab civilians, and for Arab exports to Jordan

16 October Israel distributes welfare food to 13,000 Arabs in the Gaza Strip and El Arish, and to 60,000 Bedouin at Rafah. In addition, 10,000 food packages are distributed by Israel in honour of the Muslim holy month of Ramadan

13 October The Municipality of Arab Nazareth participates in the Israel Government voluntary war loan. Throughout Northern Israel, Arabs volunteer to drive vehicles, give blood, and make cash contributions to Israel's war effort

11 October Several hundred Arabs request permission to do volunteer work for Israeli war effort

9 October Arab workers resume their work across the 'Green Line' with resumption of special bus services, suspended on October 6

6 - 24 October More than 16,000 Israelis returned to Israel from abroad. The majority at once joined their military units

9 October Bethlehem university opened, after being closed for only two days

LEBANON

Haifa

Umm el Fahm

Tulkarm

Tel Aviv   Nablus

Lod

Jerusalem

Bethlehem

Gaza

Khan Yunis

Rafah   Beersheba

Port Said

Suez Canal

Romani

El Arish

Negev

Tasa

Khatmia Pass

Gidi Pass

Suez   Mitla Pass

S i n a i

Eilat

JORDAN

River Jordan

Nazareth

Abu Rudeis

Gulf of Suez

Israel lost 2,378 soldiers in battle between 6 and 24 October 1973. Arab casualties have not been released for any of the wars with Israel

We will win because we must live. Our neighbours are fighting not for their lives, nor for their sovereignty, they are fighting to destroy us. We will not be destroyed. We dare not be destroyed. Therefore, the spirit of our men on the front, the spirit of our people in every home, in every city, in every village, is a spirit of a people that hates war but knows that in order to live it must win the war that has been forced upon it.   GOLDA MEIR 13 OCT 1973

Several Egyptian commando raids by helicopter fail to capture this former Egyptian oilfield

Sharm el-Sheikh

Red Sea

© Martin Gilbert

Sir Martin Gilbert, © 2010. Reproduced by permission of Taylor & Francis Books UK. www.martingilbert.com

Army violated the cease fire and on October 23, the IDF captured the large Egyptian city of Suez.

The UN Security Council issued another call for an immediate cease fire on October 24, but sporadic fighting still continued. The Soviets, desperate to stand up for their Egyptian client, threatened to send a division of paratroopers to North Africa to aid the Egyptians and engage the Israelis. President Nixon responded by putting U.S. forces in the Mediterranean on nuclear alert, thereby transmitting the willingness to use nuclear weapons should the Soviets intervene. The Soviets backed down, and the Yom Kippur War thus officially ended on October 24, 1973.

RESULTS AND ANALYSIS OF THE YOM KIPPUR WAR
ISRAELI PERSPECTIVE

From a purely military perspective this war had been the IDF's greatest military victory. Considering the conditions the IDF had found itself in on Yom Kippur and how things ended up on October 24, it was a remarkable turn of events that involved a great deal of fierce determination, incredible sacrifice and heroism, as well as brilliant military adaptation to the ever-changing battlefield conditions. The IDF captured 1,000 square miles of Egyptian territory in North Africa, and were one hundred one kilometers away from Cairo. The IDF also controlled a two hundred fifty-square-mile wedge it captured from Syria.

But Israel paid a frightful price for the fighting that took place in this eighteen-day war. If one takes into account all those who eventually died of their wounds, close to 3,000 soldiers were killed and another 10,000 wounded. Also, four hundred IDF soldiers were taken prisoner by the Egyptian Army and sixty-three by the Syrian Army. Almost every Israeli family lost a relative in this war.

There was also a great deal of anger at the political leadership, in particular Prime Minister Golda Meir, and her defense minister, Moshe Dayan. Both emerged from this war with a tarnished image. How did they not see the signs of war? How did they let it happen? Why was the IDF so surprised and so unprepared? By association, the Labor Party, which was running the government, was also blamed for the failures associated with the Yom Kippur War.

Finally, on the economic front, since all its reserves were called up, the work force was cut dramatically. In addition, there was an enormous cost of the war in terms of war materiel. Also, since the war did not end with any agreement, a large part of the IDF reserves remained mobilized for months, further crippling the economy.

EGYPTIAN PERSPECTIVE

For Egypt, the highlight of the war was the first forty-eight hours. The images of Egyptian soldiers storming the Bar Lev Line, planting the flag, kissing the ground and praying all exist as huge pictures in the Ramadan War Victory Museum in Cairo. But the Egyptian population never heard of the staggering defeat its army ultimately suffered, having received all its information from government-controlled media outlets. Since there was a ceasefire that relatively quickly removed the IDF from North Africa and allowed the Egyptian Army to control the entire east side of the Suez Canal, there was no evidence that the IDF had won the war as far as most Egyptians were concerned. Sadat and his commanders knew otherwise, and that was the reason there would eventually be a peace process.

Egypt never released its casualty figures.*

SYRIAN PERSPECTIVE

Syria didn't have a shining moment in the war. Though it did

---

* "There are few ways to document the casualties of this war. Historians, however, generally concede the following: All told, the Egyptians/Syrians lost some 15,600 men, with 35,000 wounded and 8,700 captured, to Israel's losses of 2,687, with 7,251 wounded and 314 taken prisoner. The Arabs lost 440 planes to Israel's 102. They lost 2,250 tanks to Israel's 400 destroyed, and 600 needing repairs. They lost 770 cannons to Israel's 25. 12 missile boats were sunk, the Israelis lost none. The Israelis took ground, the Arabs lost it." ("reddit Ask Historians" ((https://www.reddit.com/r/AskHistorians/comments/27ou8w/is_the_egyptian_claim_of_being_victorious_in_the/))

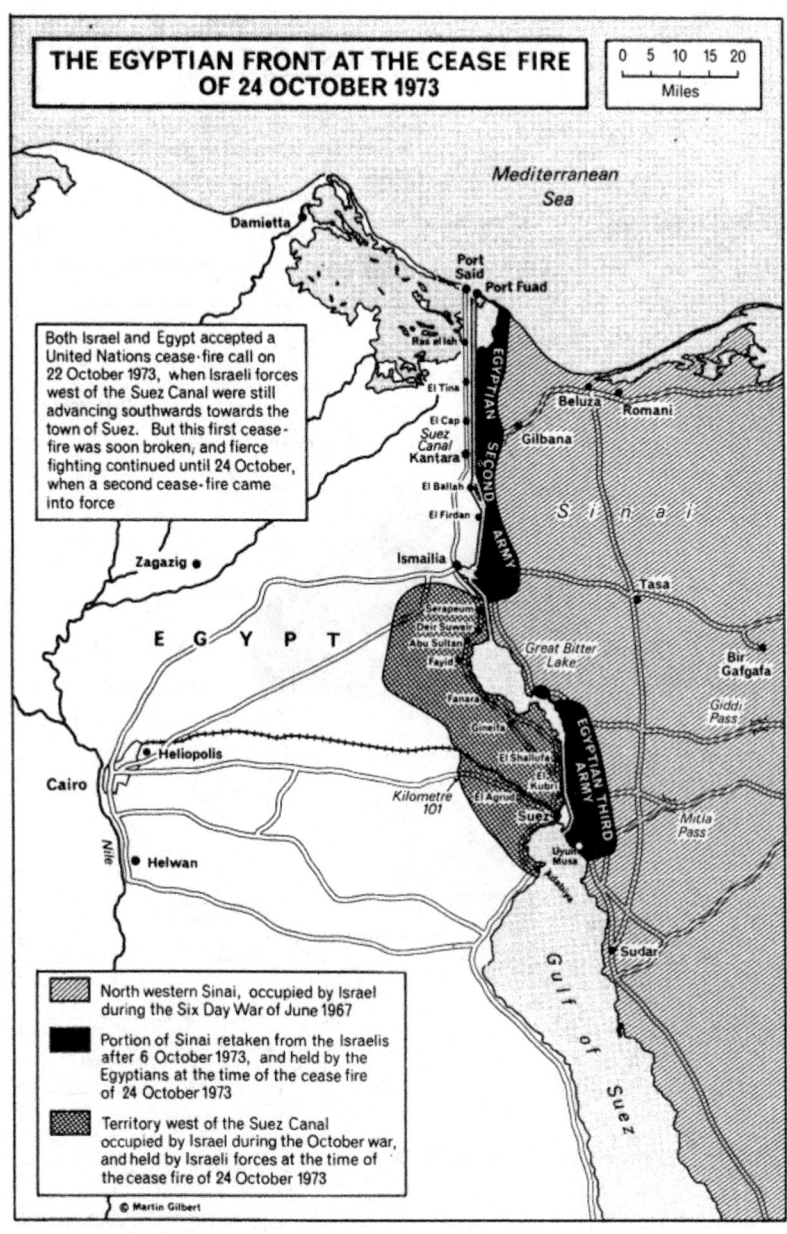

THE EGYPTIAN FRONT AT THE CEASE FIRE OF 24 OCTOBER 1973

0 5 10 15 20
Miles

Both Israel and Egypt accepted a United Nations cease-fire call on 22 October 1973, when Israeli forces west of the Suez Canal were still advancing southwards towards the town of Suez. But this first cease-fire was soon broken, and fierce fighting continued until 24 October, when a second cease-fire came into force

North western Sinai, occupied by Israel during the Six Day War of June 1967

Portion of Sinai retaken from the Israelis after 6 October 1973, and held by the Egyptians at the time of the cease fire of 24 October 1973

Territory west of the Suez Canal occupied by Israel during the October war, and held by Israeli forces at the time of the cease fire of 24 October 1973

© Martin Gilbert

Sir Martin Gilbert, © 2010. Reproduced by permission of Taylor & Francis Books UK. www.martingilbert.com

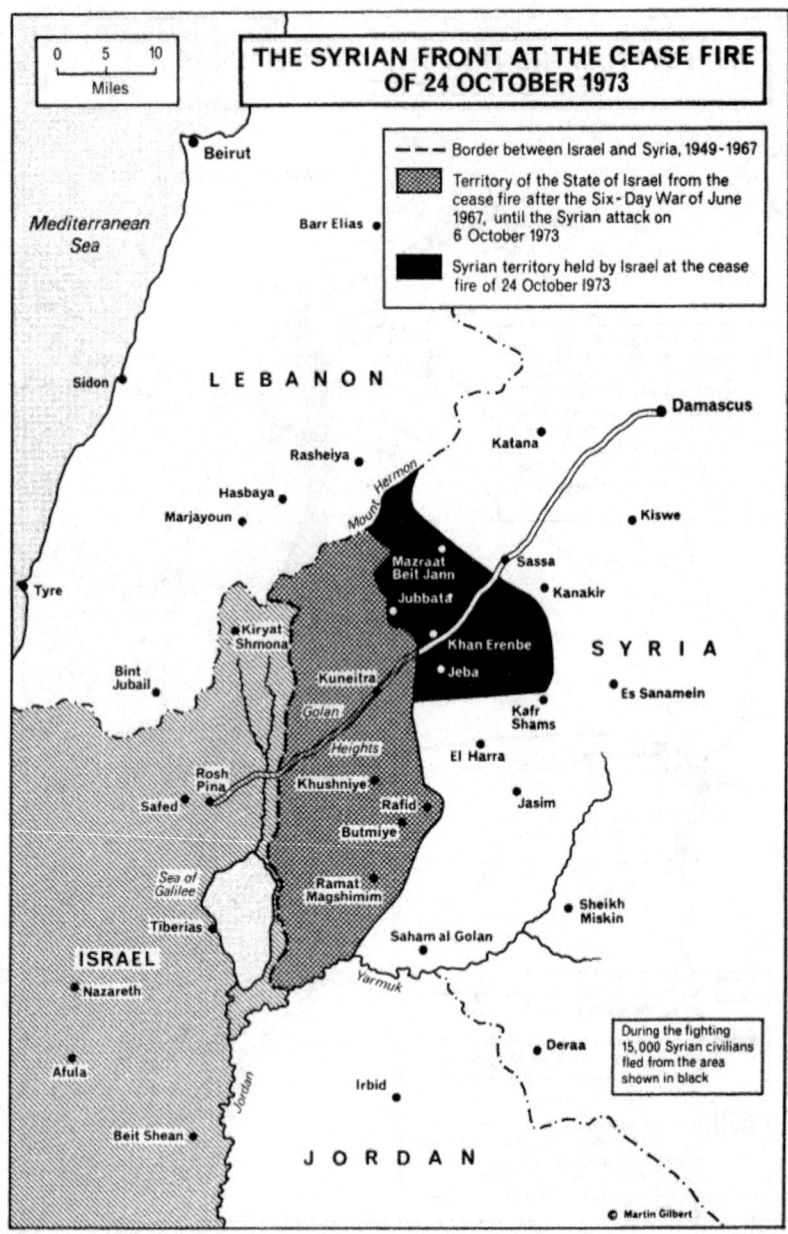

THE SYRIAN FRONT AT THE CEASE FIRE
OF 24 OCTOBER 1973

0 5 10
Miles

– – – Border between Israel and Syria, 1949-1967

Territory of the State of Israel from the
cease fire after the Six-Day War of June
1967, until the Syrian attack on
6 October 1973

Syrian territory held by Israel at the cease
fire of 24 October 1973

Mediterranean
Sea

Beirut

Barr Elias

Sidon

L E B A N O N

Damascus

Katana

Rasheiya

Hasbaya

Marjayoun

Mount Hermon

Kiswe

Sassa

Tyre

Mazraat
Beit Jann

Jubbata

Kanakir

Kiryat
Shmona

Khan Erenbe

S Y R I A

Bint
Jubail

Kuneitra

Jeba

Es Sanamein

Golan

Kafr
Shams

Heights

Rosh
Pina

Khushniye

El Harra

Safed

Rafid

Jasim

Butmiye

Sea of
Galilee

Ramat
Magshimim

Sheikh
Miskin

Tiberias

Saham al Golan

ISRAEL

Nazareth

Yarmuk

Deraa

During the fighting
15,000 Syrian civilians
fled from the area
shown in black

Afula

Irbid

Jordan

J O R D A N

Beit Shean

© Martin Gilbert

Sir Martin Gilbert, © 2010. Reproduced by permission of Taylor
& Francis Books UK. www.martingilbert.com

capture a bit less than 50 percent of the Golan Heights, it was barely able to hold it for 24 hours before the IDF counterattacked and push its army all the way back to a town called Sassa, around fifteen miles from Damascus.

The Syrian Army was decimated in this war. Over 3,500 of its soldiers were killed, close to 12,000 were wounded, five hundred sixty-three of its soldiers were taken prisoner and most of its command centers in Syria were destroyed. But the Syrians had two cards to play at the end of the war:

1) They had sixty-three Israeli POW's and they refused to allow the Red Cross to visit them. It was no secret that these Israelis were being tortured; and

2) Syria could still force the IDF to stay mobilized and make its "stay" in the two hundred fifty-square-mile Syrian wedge unpleasant. Hence, the Syrian army began a war of attrition with the IDF where it kept shelling IDF positions in the Syrian wedge for months after the war was officially over.

Assad, being in no hurry to bring anything to a resolution, continued to dangle the 63 Israeli POW's until he got something in return that he felt was significant.

THE ROLE OF THE SUPERPOWERS—U.S.A. AND USSR

It is clear that the USSR played a very important role in giving Sadat and Assad the confidence to carry out their well-coordinated invasion of Israel. The Soviets supplied them with the armaments and the battle plans—deemed a classic Russian military-style invasion—and gave both Egypt and Syria political cover at the UN. Finally, the Soviets were ready to rearm them very quickly even though both countries had an overwhelming advantage in frontline weaponry when the war began. Soviet supply ships unloaded armaments in Syria on the third day of the war and in Egypt, which is further south from the USSR, on the fourth day of, even though they were a seven- and eight-day sail, respectively, from the closest Soviet port. Soviet support was so serious that it even threatened to send troops to join the war on Egypt's behalf.

Yet, when all was said and done, the Soviets were forced to back down.

The United States kept Israel from opening up with a preemptive strike on October 5th, probably because this would have ruined any chance for the U.S. to have any leverage with Sadat. Though "in bed" with the Soviets, Sadat was clearly intimating that he could be persuaded to become allied with the U.S. if it put enough pressure on Israel to cede Sinai to Egypt, without necessarily normalizing relations.

But as the war progressed, and it became clear that this was a war that could lead to the destruction of the State of Israel, the view in the White House changed. The Yom Kippur War saw the largest tank battles since World War II take place in much smaller spaces and in shorter periods of time. While the Soviets were rapidly supplying Egypt and Syria with war materiel, Israel was quickly running out of tanks, planes and ammunition. The main reasons for this reality were:

1) the unprecedented thick anti-aircraft missile umbrella that existed in Egypt right near the Suez Canal in direct violation of the 1970 Rogers Cease Fire Agreement. The Syrian missile umbrella was less thick, but it took its toll on Israeli fighter planes that were acting as flying artillery in the first few days of the war to help slow down both the invading Egyptian and Syrian armies;

2) the introduction of the Russian Sagger Anti-Tank Missile that was exceptionally deadly knocking out Israeli tanks. Again, the Egyptian and Syrian armies had so many of them they were firing dozens of them at each tank, and

3) the sheer volume of the forces the Egyptian and Syrian armies used in their invasion of Israel.

Hence, on the fifth day of the war, President Nixon personally gave the order for the U.S. Army to begin resupplying the IDF. It hadn't hurt that...

American intelligence had signs that Israel had put its Jericho missiles, which could be fitted with nuclear warheads, on high alert (the Israelis had done so in an easily detectible way, probably to sway the Americans into preventive action")[3].

On October 10, U.S. Galaxy C5A aircraft—the largest U.S. military cargo plane at the time—began a non-stop air train to Ben Gurion Airport. With a C5A Galaxy landing every fifteen to twenty minutes around the clock, they came loaded with fighter planes, tanks and ammunition.

When all was said and done, the U.S. ended up in a better position with both Israel and Egypt. Israel, though restrained from striking first, was kept armed during this ferocious war. The U.S. also did not allow the UN to stop Israel from winning a decisive victory. Yet, on the other hand, the U.S. did not allow Israel to totally humiliate Egypt by ultimately defeating the Egyptian Second and Third armies, and then threatening Cairo as well. Sadat was allowed to walk away claiming he had beaten the Israelis and returned Egypt its honor. That gift came from the U.S., not the USSR.

Footnotes

[1] https://en.wikipedia.org/wiki/Yom_Kippur_War as derived from USMC Major Michael C. Jordan, "The 1973 Arab–Israeli War: Arab Policies, Strategies, and Campaigns" (1997) GlobalSecurity.org.; Major George E. Knapp, "4: Antiarmor Operations on the Golan Heights," *Combined Arms in battle since 1939* (Leavenworth, KS: U.S. Army Command and General Staff College, 1992; Peter Caddick-Adams, "Golan Heights, battles of", *The Oxford Companion to Military History*, ed. Richard Holmes (Oxford: Oxford University Press, 2001); Edgar O'Ballance, *No Victor, No Vanquished: The Yom Kippur War* (London: Barrie & Jenkins Publishing, 1979), 119-146.

[2] "Chapter 3: The 1967 and 1973 Wars" (http://www.un.org/Depts/dpi/palestine/ch3.pdf)

[3] Avner Cohen, "The Last Nuclear Moment," *New York Times*, Oct. 6, 2003 (http://www.nytimes.com/2003/10/06/opinion/the-last-nuclear-moment.html)

Chapter 14

The Beginning of Peace with Egypt

On October 28, 1973, for the first time since armistice agreements were signed with Egypt in 1949, IDF and Egyptian officers sat together face-to-face to discuss implementing the UN October 24 Cease Fire Resolution in the field. Though the UN facilitated the talks, there were no UN representatives present, just Israeli and Egyptian commanders. Each side had an interest in finding a way to de-escalate the very tense situation. They met in a tent set up at the edge of the IDF zone in North Africa, 101 kilometers away from Cairo. Hence, these talks came to be known as the "Kilometer 101 Talks." The head of the IDF delegation was General Aharon Yariv, the Egyptian, General Mohamed Abdel Ghani el-Gamasy. The talks lasted for a very intense three weeks and led to a six-point agreement that was signed on November 11, 1973. The agreement contained political as well as military aspects.

THE NOVEMBER 11, 1973 AGREEMENT
BETWEEN ISRAEL AND EGYPT

1. Egypt and Israel agree to observe scrupulously the cease-fire called for by the UN Security Council.

2. Both sides agree that discussions between them will begin immediately to settle the question of the return to the 22 October positions in the framework of agreement on the disengagement and separation of forces under the auspices of the United Nations.

3. The town of Suez will receive daily supplies of food, water and medicines. All wounded civilians in the town of Suez will be evacuated.

4. There shall be no impediment to the movement of non-military supplies to the east bank of the Suez Canal.

5. The Israeli checkpoints on the Cairo-Suez road will be replaced by UN checkpoints. At the Suez end of the road, Israeli officers can participate with the UN in supervising the non-military nature of the cargo at the bank of the Canal.

6. As soon as the UN checkpoints are established on the Cairo-Suez road, there will be an exchange of all prisoners of war, including wounded.[1]

Israel's reasons for negotiating with Egypt:

1) Though Israel was sitting in a militarily superior position, the IDF could not remain mobilized for months on end. The strain on IDF personnel and the economy was too great.

2) The new supply lines running into Egyptian territory in the south and fifteen miles from Damascus in the north were a logistical problem for the IDF.

3) The IDF wanted to get back its POW's as soon as possible.

4) The fact that Egypt, the largest Arab state, was interested in negotiating with Israel was a remarkable breakthrough that had to be taken advantage of. One third of the Arab world is Egyptian, and no other Arab state had fought Israel as often as had Egypt.

Egypt's reasons for negotiating with Israel:

1) Sadat was smart enough to plan the Yom Kippur War in a way that everything was set up to go Egypt's way. Yet, despite the element of surprise, total Russian backing, coordination with Syria, still Egypt had to be saved by Russia, and to an extent by the U.S., from being totally humiliated by Israel. Finally, Egypt had paid an extraordinary price in dead and wounded. Sadat had given it his best shot. If Israel could not be destroyed under the conditions that existed on October 6, 1973, then, logically, it could not be achieved for a very long time, if ever. Hence, the next logical

alternative was to speak to the Israelis and see what could be done to create a situation that Egypt could live with.

2) Egypt had 40,000 soldiers of its Third Army totally surrounded by the IDF and needed to find a way to keep it from having to surrender.

3) Egypt had 15,000 POW's being held by the IDF.

4) The IDF was sitting on 1,000 square miles of Egyptian territory in North Africa. At the closest point, the IDF was one hundred one kilometers from Cairo. Even with a total news blackout, and the Egyptian Army closing that area off to all, the longer the IDF remained there the greater the risk that the Egyptian public would find out that the IDF was in Egypt.

What this agreement did was create a direct line between Israel and Egypt to solve issues. The IDF agreed to allow the surrounded Egyptian Third Army to be supplied with food, water and other non-military supplies. In order for the Egyptians not to feel humiliated, the actual delivery would be done by UN Forces and not the IDF. Furthermore, the IDF would hand over its checkpoints on the Cairo to Suez highway to the UN. Once again this step was taken not to humiliate the Egyptians. After the UN took over the checkpoints and began delivery of supplies to the Egyptian Third Army, both sides exchanged prisoners of war. Thus, Israel and Egypt saw that by direct negotiations much could be accomplished.

Sinai I and Sinai II Agreements between Israel and Egypt: 1974 & 1975

Israeli and Egyptian negotiating teams continued to negotiate to tackle the bigger issue of the IDF presence in North Africa and the Egyptian need to save face regarding its Third Army. After weeks of very intensive negotiations, Israel and Egypt signed another agreement, called "The Separation of Forces Agreement." This agreement was signed by the chiefs of staff of both armies. It is also referred to as the "Sinai I Agreement."

Separation of Forces Agreement Between Israel and Egypt—January 18, 1974

A. Egypt and Israel will scrupulously observe the cease-fire on land, sea, and air called for by the UN Security Council and will refrain from the time of the signing of this document from all military or paramilitary actions against each other.

B. The military forces of Egypt and Israel will be separated in accordance with the following principles:

1. All Egyptian forces on the east side of the Canal will be deployed west of the line designated as Line A on the attached map. All Israeli forces, including those west of the Suez Canal and the Bitter Lakes, will be deployed east of the line designated as Line B on the attached map.

2. The area between the Egyptian and Israeli lines will be a zone of disengagement in which the United Nations Emergency Force (UNEF) will be stationed. The UNEF will continue to consist of units from countries that are not permanent members of the Security Council.

3. The area between the Egyptian line and the Suez Canal will be limited in armament and forces.

4. The area between the Israeli line (Line B on the attached map) and the line designated as Line C on the attached map, which runs along the western base of the mountains where the Gidi and Mitla Passes are located, will be limited in armament and forces.

5. The limitations referred to in paragraphs 3 and 4 will be inspected by UNEF. Existing procedures of the UNEF, including the attaching of Egyptian and Israeli liaison officers to UNEF, will be continued.

6. Air forces of the two sides will be permitted to operate up to their respective lines without interference from the other side.

C. The detailed implementation of the disengagement of forces will be worked out by military representatives of Egypt and Israel, who will agree on the stages of this process. These representatives will meet no later than 48 hours after the signature of this agreement at Kilometre 101 under the aegis of the United Nations for this purpose. They will complete this task within five days. Disengagement will begin within 48 hours after the completion of the work of the military representatives and in no event later than seven days after the signature of this agreement. The process of disengagement will be completed not later than 40 days after it begins.

D. This agreement is not regarded by Egypt and Israel as a final peace agreement. It constitutes a first step toward a final, just and durable peace according to the provisions of Security Council Resolution 338 and within the framework of the Geneva Conference.

For Egypt:

General Abdul Gani al Gamasy

For Israel:

David Elazar, Lt. Gen., Chief of Staff of I.D.F[2]

Basically, Israel agreed to withdraw from all of North Africa to a line east of the Bar Lev Line. The Egyptian Third Army was now no longer surrounded. Egypt could keep an area in Sinai that was where their forces were prior to General Sharon's game-changing breakthrough on October 16 when he split the Egyptian forces. But Egypt would be restricted as to how many men and how much military equipment would be allowed in this area. In essence, on the map, Egypt got to keep what she conquered in the first two days of the Yom Kippur War. Most importantly, both sides agreed to keep talking and work towards implementing a framework for a real peace between the two countries based on UN Security Council Resolutions 242 and 338.

Subsequent negotiations between Israel and Egypt were no longer held at Kilometer 101 since Israel had withdrawn from Egyptian North Africa. But Israeli and Egyptian diplomats continued their discussions. After over a year of negotiations and the involvement of the U.S., which both Israel and Egypt trusted, a more comprehensive and substantial agreement was signed on September 4, 1975 called the "Interim Agreement Between Egypt and Israel." It was also known as the "Sinai II Agreement."

The Sinai II Agreement was signed by diplomats as opposed to military personnel, which meant this was a step closer towards normalizing relations between the two countries. In this agreement Israel agreed to withdraw eastward deeper into Sinai. Furthermore, Israel, as a show of good faith, handed over the three strategic passes that controlled Sinai to a special U.S. force that would monitor them and make sure that neither side began to move forces near the passes or start a military buildup in Sinai. The U.S. was involved because Israel had no faith that the UN would or could carry out such an important mission faithfully. Furthermore, Israel handed over to Egypt the Abu Rudeis oil field that she had developed during her eight-year stay in Sinai. Once again, Israel was trying to send to Sadat and Egypt a message: Negotiations and contact with Israel would be far more fruitful than constant warfare. Egypt, for her part, then agreed to let Israeli cargo pass through the Suez Canal. Egypt also agreed that she would continue to negotiate with Israel towards the goal of establishing a true peaceful relationship between the two countries.

THE SYRIAN FRONT POST-THE YOM KIPPUR WAR

Unlike Egypt, Syria was left with no sign of any victory, only the very visible signs of being totally defeated. As mentioned earlier, Syria had no interest in any peace process, for that would make it appear to be capitulating to the hated Zionist State that had just humiliated it militarily. Instead, Syria began a war of attrition against the IDF sitting on the new Syrian wedge at Sassa. Syria determined to bleed Israel slowly and not allow her to demobilize her army. The second move by Syria was to dangle the sixty-three Israeli POWs as bait. Syria refused these prisoners any visits from the Red Cross, or any organization for that matter. Should Israel want her soldiers back, she would need to pay dearly for them. With the exception of the Israeli-Egyptian prisoner swap (400 for 15,000) Arab terrorist entities always use captured Israelis—or even their bodies—as bargaining chips, since they are keenly aware of how sensitive Israelis are to the well-being, health and safety of their citizens, as well as for the sanctity of the body.

Israel was able to deal with the war of attrition by simply making Syria pay a heavy price for its actions. Whenever the IDF was bombarded, it returned fire that was felt in Damascus, including the occasional bombing carried out over Syrian skies. What eventually caused Israel to submit was the pressure exerted on the Israeli government by the families of the POWs.

It took months of shuttle diplomacy by American Secretary of State Henry Kissinger, who flew between Jerusalem and Damascus many times, to broker a ceasefire agreement between Israel and Syria. This agreement was signed in Geneva by their representatives on May 31, 1974.

ISRAEL-SYRIA SEPARATION OF FORCES AGREEMENT: MAY 31, 1974

The title of the agreement made it clear that this was not the road to any peace settlement. Rather, it was a formal way to conclude the Yom Kippur War. By the terms of the agreement:

1) Israel agreed to return the Syrian wedge she had conquered.

2) Israel agreed, as a sign of good faith, to hand over the city of Kuneitra that Israel had captured in the 1967 Six-Day War.

3) Israel also agreed to return five hundred sixty-three Syrian POWs and all the bodies of Syrian soldiers she had in her possession.

4) In turn, Syria would return Israeli POWs and all the bodies of IDF soldiers she had in her possession.

5) Israel and Syria agreed to have a UN force of 1,200, called the United Nations Disengagement Observer Force (UNDOF), to be in control of a one to two mile buffer zone separating the Israeli Golan Heights from Syria. Its task would be to observe and make sure both sides kept the cease fire agreement of October 24, 1973.

6) Israel and Syria further agreed to thin out military forces on both sides of the ceasefire line (around fifteen miles in each direction). The UNDOF force was authorized to insure that this was honored. The idea was that less forces on each side lessens the chance of war breaking out.

7) The agreement needed to be renewed every six months.

Shortly after the agreement was signed, all of its aspects were implemented. Until the Syrian Civil War of 2011, the agreement was renewed and the Golan Heights-Syrian "border" was quiet.

In Israel there was deep relief when her POWs returned home, though sadly all of them had suffered physical and psychological torture.*

OTHER RAMIFICATIONS OF THE YOM KIPPUR WAR

At the end of the war the Arab world was so upset by its results that they decided to punish all countries that had either directly or indirectly assisted Israel. It did so by using its immense reserves of oil—the life blood of the industrialized world—as a weapon. Many European countries, fearing such a move, thus did not allow U.S. military aircraft involved in the massive airlift to Israel during the Yom Kippur War to even fly over their airspace en route to Israel, thus forcing U.S. planes to use more fuel and add precious time to their flights. This was especially true of Spain and France.

On October 17, 1973 the Organization of Petroleum Exporting Countries (OPEC) announced a full oil boycott of the U.S., The Netherlands, Portugal and South Africa, among others. Oil prices quadrupled in a matter of weeks creating an economic nightmare in the U.S. and other affected countries. (Signs screaming "Burn Jews, not oil," became commonplace among the long lines of those seeking fuel for their autos.) It wasn't until March that the Arab-dominated OPEC countries decided to end the embargo.

Meanwhile, in Israel, a special commission headed by Supreme Court Justice Shimon Agranat was set up by the Knesset to investigate Israel's unpreparedness in the first few hours of the

---

*Syria was handed a propaganda and strategic victory by this agreement. It turned a Syrian rout into a semi-victory, as Syria walked away from the Yom Kippur War with extra territory—the city of Kuneitra, and the removal of IDF forces from the Syrian wedge. Israel, on the other hand did get back its POWs and went on to enjoy 37 years of quiet on the Golan Heights-Syria border.

war. The Agranat Commission's initial report was issued on April 1, 1974, with a final report issued on January 30, 1975. In essence, it was a scathing condemnation of the IDF Intelligence branch, as well as the leadership of the IDF and the arrogance and incompetence that existed in many of its segments. There were many recommendations made, including the removal of the head of IDF Intelligence, General Eliyahu Zeira, and restructuring the country's intelligence gathering services, as well as the IDF's ability to maintain all of its standing units in battle readiness. Surprisingly, the report did not blame Prime Minister Golda Meir or Defense Minister Moshe Dayan. But their stature in the eyes of the Israeli public had been close to destroyed. Golda Meir handed in her resignation on April 11, 1974. She never returned to public office. The Labor Party chose Yitzchak Rabin, the hero of the Six-Day War, as Israel's next prime minister. He was officially installed on June 3, 1974. Rabin was careful not to include Moshe Dayan in his new cabinet.

The PLO, which came into its own after the Arab defeat of the Six-Day War, once again ramped up its terrorist activities after the defeat of Egypt and Syria in the Yom Kippur War. As they had before, they made claim that they were the only Arabs capable of taking the fight to the hated Zionists and inflicting damage, as well as "standing up" for the Palestinian people. Now operating out of South Lebanon, a sample of their post-Yom Kippur War terror attacks included:

April 11, 1974 in Kiryat Shemona: Three members of the PFLP-GC cross the Israeli border from Lebanon, enter an apartment building and kill all eighteen residents there, half of whom are children..

May 15, 1974 in Ma'alot: Palestinian militants of the Democratic Front for the Liberation of Palestine cross the Israeli border from Lebanon. They attack a van killing two Israeli Arab women then enter an apartment building in the town of Ma'alot and kill a couple and their 4-year-old son. After that they take over a local school and hold 105 students and 10 teachers hostage. The hostage-takers demanded the release of 23 Palestinian militants from Israeli prisons or they would kill the students. On the second day of the standoff a unit of the elite Golani Brigade stormed the building. During the assault the hostage-takers detonated their grenades and shot the children. Ultimately, 25 hostages were killed, including 22 children; 68 more were injured.[3]

THE RABAT SUMMIT: OCTOBER 1974

In the aftermath of the 1973 Yom Kippur War, negotiations commenced between Israel and its Arab neighbors. These talks were mostly focused on a cease-fire, but there were serious attempts to progress further. Even the Soviet Union co-sponsored the first Geneva Conference in 1973 to resolve the Arab-Israeli dispute.

Consequently, the Palestine Liberation Organization (PLO) was concerned that Arab regimes might make peace with Israel over its head. The PLO also worried about the possibility of having the West Bank return to the Jordanian rule that was lost in the Six Day War in 1967, a development which would eliminate any hope of Palestinian control over that territory. A proposal fielded by the Democratic Front for the Liberation of Palestine (DFLP), led by the Jordanian-born Nayif Hawatmeh, suggested the solution for the PLO. The DFLP proposal was to establish a secular, democratic state where Arabs and Jews would both have an equal role as individuals. This aspect was rejected by the PLO. But the DFLP plan had a second part, which became the cornerstone of the PLO's whole approach from then on. This plan suggested that the PLO announce its readiness to take any part of Mandatory Palestine that was up for grabs. In short, if Israel was to withdraw from the West Bank and Gaza, that territory should go to the PLO and not to Jordan or Egypt. This avoided the unthinkable (to the PLO) question of making peace with Israel, it was merely a claim to any available land. In the same time period, Arafat sought contacts with the United States. He sent two messages to the Nixon administration requesting clarification of the US position on key diplomatic issues. The US agreed to a meeting, and on

November 3, 1973, Vernon Walters, then deputy director of the CIA, met secretly in Rabat, Morocco with a top Arafat aide. Henry Kissinger described that Rabat meeting in the second volume of his memoirs, *Years of Upheaval*. Walters was instructed to say that the question of who represented the Palestinians—Jordan or the PLO—was an "inter-Arab concern." The PLO took this as an American invitation to seek Arab backing as the sole representative of the Palestinians, and they obtained this status at the Arab summit meeting in Rabat in 1974. Arafat expected, wrongly, that this would also lead to prompt American recognition of the PLO. In 1974, the 12th session of the Palestine National Council followed Arafat's script when it called for the establishment of a "national authority" on any portion of Palestinian land liberated. The Rabat Summit conference in October 1974 brought together the leaders of twenty Arab states and representatives of the PLO, whose leaders threatened a walkout if their demands for unconditional recognition were not met. The PLO required a statement from the conference that any Palestinian territory liberated by Arab forces would be turned over to the "Palestinian people" as represented by the PLO. Jordan protested, pointing out that recognition on these terms would give the PLO sovereignty over half of the population in the East Bank and that in fact the annexation of the West Bank by Jordan had been approved by popular vote. A compromise solution was adopted that nonetheless favored PLO interests. The conference formally acknowledged the right of the Palestinian people to a separate homeland, but without specifying that its territory was restricted to the West Bank. Most important, the PLO was for the first time officially recognized by all the Arab states as the "sole legitimate representative of the Palestinian people." The Arab heads of state also called for close cooperation between the front-line states and the PLO but prohibited interference by other Arab states in Palestinian affairs. The Rabat Summit declaration conferred a mantle of legitimacy on the PLO that was previously absent. It gave official Arab recognition to PLO territorial claims to the West Bank and unambiguously put the fate of the Palestinian people solely in the hands of the PLO. Jordanian King Hussein opposed the declaration, although he eventually signed it under intense Arab pressure and after the Arab oil-producing states promised to provide Jordan with an annual subsidy of $US 300 million. The Rabat statement allowed Arafat to proceed against Israel without worrying about other Arab countries (e.g. Jordan) grabbing the prize. At the same time, the message to Israel was clear: The resolution clearly states that the conflict would continue until Israel's destruction. Indeed, it explicitly states that any land the PLO took over would be used primarily as a base for attacking Israel. The continued subsequent use of terrorism against Israeli civilians made it clear that this resolution did not mean favoring any kind of compromise with Israel. Nevertheless, there have been attempts made by Arafat and various Western writers to rewrite history and misrepresent what happened in 1974 as some kind of major peace initiative.[4]

ATTACKING ISRAEL AND ZIONISM AT THE UN

Since the Arab world had failed again to destroy Israel on the battlefield, other ways had to be found to hurt and punish her and those who supported her. In the fall of 1974, after months of work by Arab, Islamic, Third World and communist states, Yasser Arafat, a guerilla fighter in his own eyes and a terrorist in the eyes of many in the West, spoke at the UN as a world leader. This invitation paved the way for what eventually would be the non-voting nation status that the Palestinian Authority enjoys today.

On November 13 Arafat, the mastermind and/or supporter of hundreds of terrorist attacks against Israel and Jews, addressed the United Nations General Assembly. Refusing to relinquish the revolver that was always present at his side, Arafat spoke about the olive branch he held in one hand and the freedom fighter's gun he held in the other. His speech was laced with anti-Zionist rhetoric and historical fabrications and his vision of peace included the withdrawal by Israel to the November 29, 1947 partition lines, lines that had been rejected by the entire Arab world in 1947. To round out his vision of peace, Israel had to accept all Palestinian refugees and their decedents and return to them their homes, property and, of course, their Palestine. In essence, Arafat's olive branch was a peace without a Jewish State in the Middle East. Arafat received a standing ovation. This was the beginning of a serious downward spiral for the UN, which apparently no longer stood for the noble ideas enshrined in its charter, but rather a politicized international body where the tyranny of the majority would be the new order of the day.

UNITED NATIONS RESOLUTION CALLING ZIONISM RACISM: NOVEMBER 11, 1975

On November 11, 1975, an emboldened Palestinian propaganda machine launched a new attack upon Israel at the United Nations. Submitting a proposal that Zionism was essentially a form of racism, its action was a political attempt to isolate the State of Israel and ultimately cause its demise. The Arab world worked hard to convince the other Islamic, Communist and Third World countries to vote with them on this resolution. Israel and the United States were outraged.*

The resolution was the culmination of a twenty-seven-year effort. In essence, by calling Zionism a form of racism, Israel, the Zionist state, had become an outlaw. According to the UN Charter, the UN was formed at the end of World War II to fight against the horrors of Nazism, the then-ultimate form of racism. According to the Charter, member states were obligated to fight against all forms of racism. And, prior to 1975, the UN had legally classified two movements as racist and had dedicated itself to fight against them: Nazism and apartheid. Nazism was defeated and apartheid was in the process of being defeated. Now Zionism was added to the list. As such, actions against Israel, including terrorist actions, could now be officially legitimate acts of self-defense!

---

* Thanks to a big effort by the U.S. this was overturned in 1991. But its message was revived at the 2002 U.N. Human Rights Conference held in Durban, South Africa.

The passing of this resolution was a dark moment in the history of the UN and a chilling moment for Israel and the Jewish people. It acknowledged the Orwellian logic that now pervaded the UN: Zionism, the national liberation movement of the ancient Jewish Nation, was now made equivalent to racism while the truly racist views of the PLO and most Arab states were absolved of condemnation.

UNITED NATIONS GENERAL ASSEMBLY
RESOLUTION 3379 (XXX)

Elimination of All Forms of Racial Discrimination

THE GENERAL ASSEMBLY,

RECALLING its resolution 1904 (XVIII) of 20 November 1963, proclaiming the United Nations Declaration on the Elimination of All Forms of Racial Discrimination, and in particular its affirmation that "any doctrine of racial differentiation or superiority is scientifically false, morally condemnable, socially unjust and dangerous" and its expression of alarm at "the manifestations of racial discrimination still in evidence in some areas in the world, some of which are imposed by certain Governments by means of legislative, administrative or other measures",

RECALLING ALSO that, in its resolution 3151 G (XXVIII) of 14 December 1953, the General Assembly condemned, inter alia, the unholy alliance between South African racism and Zionism,

TAKING NOTE of the Declaration of Mexico on the Equality of Women and Their Contribution to Development and Peace 1975, proclaimed by the World Conference of the International Women's Year, held at Mexico City from 19 June to 2 July 1975, which promulgated the principle that "international co-operation and peace require the achievement of national liberation and independence, the elimination of colonialism and neo-colonialism, foreign occupation, Zionism, apartheid and racial discrimination in all its forms, as well as the recognition of the dignity of peoples and their right to self-determination",

TAKING NOTE ALSO of resolution 77 (XII) adopted

by the Assembly of Heads of State and Government of the Organization of African Unity at its twelfth ordinary session, held at Kampala from 28 July to 1 August 1975, which considered "that the racist regime in occupied Palestine and the racist regime in Zimbabwe and South Africa have a common imperialist origin, forming a whole and having the same racist structure and being organically linked in their policy aimed at repression of the dignity and integrity of the human being",

TAKING NOTE ALSO of the Political Declaration and Strategy to Strengthen International Peace and Security and to Intensify Solidarity and Mutual Assistance among Non-Aligned Countries, adopted at the Conference of Ministers for Foreign Affairs of Non-Aligned Countries held at Lima from 25 to 30 August 1975, which most severely condemned Zionism as a threat to world peace and security and called upon all countries to oppose this racist and imperialist ideology,

DETERMINES that Zionism is a form of racism and racial discrimination.

2400th plenary meeting
10 November 1975[5]

The response of Israel's UN Ambassador at the time, Chaim Herzog, defended the Jewish Nation's right to self-determination:

It is symbolic that this debate, which may well prove to be a turning point in the fortunes of the United Nations and a decisive factor as to the possible continued existence of this Organization, should take place on 10 November. This night, 37 years ago, has gone down in history as the Kristallnacht, or the Night of the Crystals. This was the night of 10 November 1938 when Hitler's Nazi Storm Troopers launched a co-ordinated attack on the Jewish community in Germany, burnt the synagogues in all the cities and made bonfires in the streets, of the Holy Books and the Scrolls of the Holy Laws and the Bible. It was the night when Jewish homes were attacked and heads of families were taken away, many of them never to return. It was the night when the windows of all Jewish businesses and stores were smashed, covering the streets in the cities of Germany with a film of broken glass which dissolved into millions of crystals, giving that night the name of Kristallnacht, the Night of the Crystals. It was the night which led eventually to the crematoria and the gas chambers, to Auschwitz, Birkenau, Dachau, Buchenwald, Theresienstadt, and others. It was the night which led to the most terrifying holocaust in the history of man.

It is indeed fitting, that this draft, conceived in the desire to deflect the Middle East from its moves towards peace, and born of a deep, pervading feeling of anti-Semitism, should come up for debate on this day which recalls one of the tragic days in one of the darkest periods of history. It is indeed fitting that the United Nations, which began its life as an anti-Nazi Alliance, should, 30 years later, find itself on its way to becoming the world centre of anti-Semitism. Hitler would have felt at home on a number of occasions during the past year, listening to the proceedings in this form and, above all, to the proceedings during the debate on Zionism.

It is a sobering reflection indeed to consider to what this body has been dragged down, if we are obliged today to contemplate an attack on Zionism. For this attack constitutes not only an anti-Semitic attack of the foulest type, but also an attack in this world body on Judaism, one of the oldest-established religions in the world, a religion which has given the world the human values of the Bible, a religion, from which two other great religions, Christianity and Islam, sprang —a great and established religion that has given to the world the Bible with its Ten Commandments; the great prophets of old, Moses, Isaiah, Amos; the great thinkers of history, Maimonides, Spinoza, Marx, Einstein; many of the masters of the arts; and as high a percentage of Nobel Prize winners in the world, in the sciences, the arts and the humanities, as has been achieved by any other people on earth.

One can but ponder and wonder at the prospect of countries, which consider themselves to be part of the civilized world, joining in this first organized attack on an established religion since the Middle Ages. Yes, to these depths are we being dragged by those who propose this draft resolution to the Middle Ages.

The draft resolution before the Third Committee was originally a resolution condemning racism and colonialism, a subject on which consensus could have been achieved, a consensus which is of great importance to all of us and to our African colleagues in particular. However, instead of this being permitted to happen, a group of countries, drunk with the feeling of power inherent in the automatic majority, and without regard to the importance of achieving a consensus on this issue, railroaded the Committee in a contemptuous manner by the use of the automatic majority, into bracketing Zionism with the subject under discussion. Indeed, it is difficult to speak of this base move with any measure of restraint.

I do not come to this rostrum to defend the moral and historical values of the Jewish people. They do not need to be defended. They speak for themselves. They have given to mankind much of what is great and eternal. They have done for the spirit of man more than can readily be appreciated in a forum such as this one.

I come here to denounce the two great evils which menace society in general and a society of nations in particular. These two evils are hatred and ignorance. These two evils are the motivating force behind the proponents of this draft resolution and their supporters. These two evils characterize those who would drag this world organization, the idea of which was first conceived by the prophets of Israel, to the depths to which it has been dragged today.

The key to understanding Zionism lies in its name. In the Bible, the westernmost of the two hills of ancient Jerusalem was called Zion. The period was the tenth century B.C. In fact, the name "Zion" appears 152 times in the Old Testament referring to Jerusalem. The name is overwhelmingly a poetic and prophetic designation. The religious and emotional qualities of the name arise from the importance of Jerusalem as the Royal City and the City of the Temple. "Mount Zion" is the place where God dwells according to the Bible. Jerusalem or Zion, is a place where the Lord is King according to Isaiah, and where he has installed his King David, as quoted in the Psalms.

King David made Jerusalem the capital of Israel almost 3,000 years ago, and Jerusalem has remained the capital ever since. During the centuries the term "Zion" grew and expanded to mean the whole of Israel. The Israelites in exile could not forget Zion.

The Hebrew psalmist sat by the waters of Babylon and swore "If I forget thee, O Jerusalem, let my right hand forget her cunning". This oath has been repeated for thousands of years by Jews throughout the world. It is an oath which was made over 700 years before the advent of Christianity, and over 1,200 years before the advent of Islam.

In view of all these connotations, Zion came to mean the Jewish homeland, symbolic of Judaism, of Jewish national aspirations.

Every Jew, while praying to his God, wherever he is in the world, faces towards Jerusalem. These prayers have expressed for over 2,000 years of exile the yearning of the Jewish people to return to its ancient homeland, Israel. In fact, a continuous Jewish presence, in larger or smaller numbers, has been maintained in the country over the centuries.

Zionism is the name of the national movement of the Jewish people and is the modern expression of the ancient Jewish heritage. The Zionist ideal, as set out in the Bible, has been, and is, an integral part of the Jewish religion.

Zionism is to the Jewish people what the liberation movement of Africa and Asia have been to their peoples. Zionism is one of the most stirring and constructive national movements in human history. Historically, it is based on a unique and unbroken connection, extending some 4,000 years, between the People of the Book and the Land of the Bible.

In modern times, in the late 19th century, spurred by the twin forces of anti-Semitic persecution and nationalism, the Jewish people organized the Zionist movement in order to transform its dream into reality. Zionism, as a political movement, was the revolt of an oppressed nation against the depredations and wicked discrimination and oppression of the countries in which anti-Semitism flourished. It is indeed no coincidence at all, and not surprising, that the sponsors and supporters of this draft resolution include countries which are guilty of the horrible crime of anti-Semitism and discrimination to this very day.

Support for the aim of Zionism was written into the League of Nations Mandate for Palestine, and was again endorsed by the United Nations in 1947, when the General Assembly voted by an overwhelming majority for the restoration of Jewish independence in our ancient land.

The re-establishment of Jewish independence in Israel, after centuries of struggle to overcome foreign conquest and exile, is a vindication of the fundamental concepts of the equality of nations and of self-determination. To question the Jewish people's right to national existence and freedom, is not only to deny to the Jewish people the right accorded to every other people on this globe but is also to deny the central precepts of the United Nations.

For Zionism is nothing more—and nothing less—than the Jewish people's sense of origin and destination in the land, linked eternally with its name. It is also the instrument whereby the Jewish nation seeks an authentic fulfilment of itself. And the drama is enacted in the region in which the Arab nation has realized its sovereignty in 20 States, comprising a hundred million people in four and a half million square miles, with vast resources. The issue therefore is not whether the world will come to terms with Arab nationalism. The question is, at what point Arab nationalism, with its prodigious glut of advantage, wealth and opportunity, will come to terms with the modest but equal rights of another Middle Eastern nation to pursue its life in security and peace.

The vicious diatribes on Zionism voiced here by Arab representatives, may give this Assembly the wrong impression, that while the rest of the world supported the Jewish national liberation movement, the Arab world was always hostile to Zionism. That is not the case. Arab leaders, cognizant of the rights of the Jewish people, fully endorsed the virtues of Zionism. Sheriff Hussein, the leader of the Arab world during the First World War, welcomed the return of the Jews to Palestine. His son, Emir Feisal, who represented the Arab world in the Paris Peace Conference had this to say about Zionism on 3 March 1919:

"We Arabs, especially the educated among us, look with deepest sympathy on the Zionist movement... We will wish the Jews a hearty welcome home... We are working together for a reformed and revised Near East, and our two movements complement one another. The movement is national and not imperialistic. There is room in Syria for us both. Indeed, I think that neither can be a success without the other."

It is perhaps pertinent at this point to recall, that in 1947, when the question of Palestine was being debated in the United Nations, the Soviet Union strongly supported the Jewish independence struggle. It is particularly relevant to recall some of Mr. Andrei Gromyko's remarks on 14 May 1947, one year before our independence:

"As we know, the aspirations of a considerable part of the Jewish people are linked with the problem of Palestine and of its future administration. This fact scarcely required proof.. During the last war, the Jewish people underwent exceptional sorrow and suffering. Without any exaggeration, this sorrow and suffering are indescribable. It is difficult to express them in dry statistics on the Jewish victims of the fascist aggressors. The Jews in the territories where the Hitlerites held sway, were subjected to almost complete physical annihilation. The total number of Jews who perished at the hands of the Nazi executioners is estimated at approximately six million ...".

"The United Nations cannot and must not regard this situation with indifference, since this would be incompatible with the high principles proclaimed in its Charter, which provides for the defence of human rights, irrespective of race, religion or sex..."

The fact that no Western European State has been able to ensure the defence of the elementary rights of the Jewish people and to safeguard it against the violence of the fascist executioners, explains the aspirations of the Jews to establish their own State. It would be unjust not to take this into consideration and to deny the right of the Jewish people to realize this aspiration. Those were the words of Mr. Andrei Gromyko at the General Assembly session on 14 May 1947.

How sad it is, to see here a group of nations, many of whom have but recently freed themselves from colonial rule, deriding one of the most noble liberation movements of this century, a movement which not only gave an example of encouragement and determination to the people struggling for independence, but also actively aided many of them during the period of preparation for their independence or immediately thereafter.

Here you have a movement, which is the embodiment of a unique pioneering spirit, of the dignity of labour, and of enduring human values, a movement which has presented to the world an example of social equality and open democracy, being associated in this resolution with abhorrent political concepts.

We, in Israel, have endeavored to create a society which strives to implement the highest ideals of society—political, social and cultural—for all the inhabitants of Israel, irrespective of religious belief, race or sex. Show me another pluralistic society in this world in which, despite all the difficult problems among which we live, Jew and Arab live together with such a degree of harmony, in which the dignity and rights of man are observed before the law, in which no death sentence is applied, in which freedom of speech, of movement, of thought, of expression are guaranteed, in which even movements, which are opposed to our national aims, are represented in our Parliament.

The Arab delegates talk of racism. It lies not in their mouths. What has happened to the 800,000 Jews who lived for over 2,000 years in the Arab lands, who formed some of the most ancient communities long before the advent of Islam? Where are those communities? What happened to the people, what happened to their property?

The Jews were once one of the important communities in the countries of the Middle East, the leaders of thought, of commerce, of medical science. Where are they in Arab society today? You dare talk of racism when I can point with pride to the Arab Ministers who have served in my Government; to the Arab deputy speaker of my Parliament; to Arab officers and men serving of their own volition in our defence, border and police forces, frequently commanding Jewish troops; to the hundreds of thousands of Arabs from all over the Middle East crowding the cities of Israel every year; to the thousands of Arabs from all over the Middle East coming for medical treatment to Israel; to the peaceful coexistence which has developed; to the fact that Arabic is an official language in Israel on a par with Hebrew; to the fact that it is as natural for an Arab to serve in public office in Israel as it is incongruous to think of a Jew serving in any public office in any Arab country, indeed being admitted to many of them. Is that racism? It is not. That is Zionism.

It is our attempt to build a society, imperfect though it may be—and what society is perfect?—in which the visions of the prophets of Israel will be realized. I know that we have problems. I know that many disagree with our Government's policies. Many in Israel, too, disagree from time to time with the Government's policies, and are free to do so, because Zionism has created the first and only real democratic State in a part of the world that never really knew democracy and freedom of speech.

This malicious resolution, designed to divert us from its true purpose, is part of a dangerous anti-Semitic idiom which is being insinuated into every public debate by those who have sworn to block the current move towards accommodation and ultimately towards peace in the Middle East. This, together with similar moves, is designed to sabotage the efforts of the Geneva Conference for peace in the Middle East...

We are seeing here today but another manifestation of the bitter anti-Semitic, anti-Jewish hatred which animates Arab society. Who would have believed that in the year of 1975 the malicious falsehoods of the Elders of Zion would be distributed officially by Arab Governments? Who would have believed that we would today contemplate an Arab society which teaches the vilest anti-Jewish hate in the kindergartens? Who would have believed that an Arab Head of State would feel obliged to indulge publicly in anti-Semitism of the cheapest nature when visiting a friendly nation? We are being attacked by a society which is motivated by the most extreme form of racism known in the world today. This is the racism which was expressed so succinctly in the words of the leader of the Palestine Liberation Organization (PLO), Yasser Arafat, in his opening address at a symposium in Tripoli, Libya, and I quote: "There will be no presence in the region except for the Arab presence". In other words, in the Middle East, from the Atlantic Ocean to the Persian Gulf, only one presence is allowed, and that is the Arab presence. No other people, regardless of how deep are its roots in the region, is to be permitted to enjoy its right of self-determination.

Look at the tragic fate of the Kurds of Iraq. Look at what happened to the black population in southern Sudan. Look at the dire peril in which an entire community of Christians finds itself in Lebanon. Look at the avowed policy of the PLO, which calls, in its Palestine Covenant, for the destruction of the State of Israel, which denies any form of compromise on the Palestine issue, and which, in the words of its representative only the other day in this building, considers Tel Aviv to be occupied territory. Look at all this and you see before you the root cause of the pernicious resolution brought before this Assembly. You see the twin evils of this world at work: the blind hatred of the Arab proponents of this resolution, and the abysmal ignorance and wickedness of those who support them.

The issue before this Assembly is not Israel and is not Zionism. The issue is the fate of this Organization. Conceived in the spirit of the prophets of Israel, born out of an anti-Nazi alliance after the tragedy of the Second World War, it has degenerated into a forum which was this last week described by one of the leading writers in a foremost organ of social and liberal thought in the West as, and I quote:

"rapidly becoming one of the most corrupt and corrupting creations in the whole history of human institutions... almost without exception those in the majority come from States notable for racist oppression of every conceivable hue..."

"Israel is a social democracy,...its people and Government have a profound respect for human life, so passionate indeed that, despite every conceivable provocation, they have refused for a quarter of a century to execute a single captured terrorist. They also have an ancient but vigorous culture, and a flourishing technology. The combination of national qualities they have assembled in their brief existence as a State is a perpetual and embittering reproach to most of the new countries whose representatives swagger about the United Nations building. So Israel is envied and hated, and efforts are made to destroy her. The extermination of the Israelis has long been the prime objective of the Terrorist international; they calculate that if they can break Israel, then all the rest of civilization is vulnerable to their assaults".

And then he goes on to conclude:

"The melancholy truth, I fear, is that the candles of civilization are burning low. The world is increasingly governed not so much by capitalism, or communism, or social democracy, or even tribal barbarism, as by a false lexicon of political cliches, accumulated over half a century and now assuming a kind of degenerate sacerdotal authority... We all know what they are..."

Over the centuries it has fallen to the lot of my people to be the testing agent of human decency, the touchstone of civilization, the crucible in which enduring human values are to be tested. A nation's level of humanity could invariably be judged by its behaviour towards its Jewish population. It always began with the Jews but never ended with them.

The anti-Jewish pogroms in Czarist Russia were but the tip of the iceberg which revealed the inherent rottenness of the regime which was soon to disappear in the storm of revolution. The anti-Semitic excesses of the Nazis merely foreshadowed the catastrophe which was to befall mankind in Europe.

This wicked resolution must sound the alarm for all decent people in the world. The Jewish people, as a testing agent, has unfortunately never erred. The implications inherent in this shameful move are terrifying indeed.

On this issue, the world as represented in this hall has divided itself into good and bad, decent and evil, human and debased. We, the Jewish people, will recall in history our gratitude to those nations, who stood up and were counted, and who refused to support this wicked proposition. I know that this episode will have strengthened the forces of freedom and decency in this world and will have fortified them in their resolve to strengthen the ideals they so value. I know that this episode will have strengthened Zionism as it has weakened the United Nations.

As I stand on this rostrum, the long and proud history of my people unravels itself before my inward eye, I see the oppressors of our people over the ages as they pass one after another in evil procession into oblivion. I stand here before you as the representative of a strong and flourishing people which has survived them all and which will survive this shameful exhibition and the proponents of this resolution. I stand here as the representative of a people one of whose prophets gave to this world the sublime prophecy which animated the founders of this world Organization and which graces the entrance to this building:

"...nation shall not lift up sword against nation, neither shall they learn war any more." (Isaiah ii, 4)

Three verses before that, the Prophet Isaiah proclaimed

"And it shall come to pass in the last days... for out of Zion shall go forth the law, and the word of the Lord from Jerusalem." (Isaiah, ii, 2 and 3)

As I stand on this rostrum, the great moments of Jewish history come to mind as I face you, once again outnumbered and the would-be victim of hate, ignorance and evil. I look back on those great moments. I recall the greatness of a nation which I have the honour to represent in this forum. I am mindful at this moment of the Jewish people throughout the world wherever they may be, be it in freedom or in slavery, whose prayers and thoughts are with me at this moment.

I stand here not as a supplicant. Vote as your moral conscience dictates to you. For the issue is not Israel or Zionism. The issue is the continued existence of the Organization which has been dragged to its lowest point of discredit by a coalition of despotisms and racists.

The vote of each delegation will record in history its country's stand on anti-Semitic racism and anti-Judaism. You yourselves bear the responsibility for your stand before history, for as such will you be viewed in history. But we, the Jewish people, will not forget.

For us, the Jewish people, this is but a passing episode in a rich and an event-filled history. We put our trust in our Providence, in our faith and beliefs, in our time-hallowed tradition, in our striving for social advance and human values, and in our people wherever they may be. For us, the Jewish people, this resolution, based on hatred, falsehood and arrogance, is devoid of any moral or legal value. For us, the Jewish people, this is no more than a piece of paper, and we shall treat it as such.[6]

THE RAID AT ENTEBBE – OPERATION THUNDERBOLT: JUNE 27-JULY 4, 1976

On June 27, 1976 a group of PFLP and German terrorists hijacked an Air France plane en route to Israel. They diverted the plane to Entebbe, Uganda, where they were warmly greeted by Idi Amin, the then-ruler. "On 28 June, a PFLP-EO hijacker issued a declaration and formulated their demands: In addition to a ransom of $5 million USD for the release of the airplane, they demanded the release of fifty-three Palestinian and pro-Palestinian militants, forty of whom were prisoners in Israel."[7] Failure to meet their demands would result in the execution of the hostages.

On 30 June, the hijackers released 48 hostages picked from among the non-Israeli group—mainly elderly and sick passengers and mothers with children. 47 of them were flown to Paris, and one passenger was treated in hospital for a day. On 1 July, after the Israeli government had conveyed its agreement to negotiations, the hostage-takers extended their deadline to noon on 4 July and released another group of 100 non-Israeli captives who again were flown to Paris a few hours later. Among the 106 hostages staying behind with their captors at Entebbe airport were the 12 members of the Air France crew, about ten young French passengers, and the Israeli group of some 84 people.[8]

The Israeli government, led by Prime Minister Yitzchak Rabin, Defense Minister Shimon Peres and IDF Chief of Staff Mordechai Gur gave the green light for perhaps the most daring commando raid in modern military history. Named "Operation Thunderbolt"...

...[t]he operation took place at night. Israeli transport planes carried 100 commandos over 2,500 miles (4,000 km) to Uganda for the rescue operation. The operation, which took a week of planning, lasted 90 minutes. 102 hostages were rescued. Five Israeli commandos were wounded and one, the unit commander, Lt. Col. Yonatan Netanyahu, was killed. All the hijackers, three hostages and 45 Ugandan soldiers were killed, and [a number of] Soviet-built MiG-17s and MiG-21s of Uganda's air force were destroyed.[9]*

The surviving hostages were flown back to Ben-Gurion Airport

Analysis of the IDF Commando Rescue Mission to Entebbe
1. This event lifted Israel and Israelis from the deep depression that seemed to have descended upon the country after the Yom Kippur War. It was truly a remarkable military operation.
2. Israel sent a message that collecting passports and checking as to who is Jewish or Israeli and then making a "Holocaust-like" selection, where non-Jews get to live and Jews are marked for death, is no longer a risk-free endeavor. Those who hunt the Jews in the post-1948 world would quickly find themselves being the hunted.
3. Israel became the leader in the war against terror.

where they were greeted by tens of thousands of cheering Israelis. As a result of the raid,

> ...The United Nations Security Council convened on 9 July 1976, to consider a complaint from the Chairman of the Organization of African Unity charging Israel with an "act of aggression". The Council allowed Israel's ambassador to the United Nations, Chaim Herzog, and Uganda's foreign minister, Juma Oris Abdalla, to participate without voting rights. UN Secretary General Kurt Waldheim told the Security Council that the raid was "a serious violation of the sovereignty of a Member State of the United Nations" though he was "fully aware that this is not the only element involved ... when the world community is now required to deal with unprecedented problems arising from international terrorism." Abdalla, the representative of Uganda, alleged that the affair was close to a peaceful resolution when Israel intervened while Herzog, the representative of Israel, accused Uganda of direct complicity in the hijacking. The USA and UK sponsored a resolution which condemned hijacking and similar acts, deplored the loss of life arising from the hijacking (without condemning either Israel or Uganda), reaffirmed the need to respect the sovereignty and territorial integrity of all States, and called on the international community to enhance the safety of civil aviation. However, the resolution failed to receive the required number of affirmative votes due to 2 abstentions and 7 absences. A second resolution sponsored by Benin, Libya and Tanzania, that condemned Israel, was not put to the vote.[10]

THE FALL OF THE RABIN GOVENRMENT: MAY 1977

Though Rabin was not directly involved in any way in the government that led Israel during the Yom Kippur War, in the next election, held on May 17, 1977, there was a shock to the Israeli electoral system. After 29 years of Labor dominance, the Revisionist Zionist Party, now known as Likud and led by Menachem Begin, won. There were many factors that led to the victory of Likud;

one of them was clearly the dissatisfaction of the Sephardic Jewish community which felt that Labor, at best, had a very paternalistic view of them and, at worse, viewed them with contempt. But the chief reason that Likud won was the sense that it was Labor that led Israel into the suffering of the Yom Kippur War.

THE PEACE TREATY BETWEEN EGYPT AND ISRAEL: 1977-1979

By the end of 1975 Israel and Egypt had negotiated face-to-face and signed three significant agreements that moved the two countries closer to a peaceful relationship. Egypt had received land, oil and honor from Israel, while Israel had received goodwill, the use of the Suez Canal and a pledge by Egypt to solve problems through negotiations, rejecting war as an option. Through 1976 there continued to be contact between the two countries, as well as adherence to the Sinai II Agreement.

In the spring of 1977 Menachem Begin was elected as the new prime minister of Israel. While Begin was known to be a hardliner when it came to security, he understood the significance of having Egypt, the world's largest and most powerful Arab country, be at peace with Israel. Hence, shortly after being elected, Begin invited Sadat to come to Israel to meet with him and offered to fly to Egypt to meet with Sadat in order to push to the next level a process that had begun on October 28, 1973.

In the fall of 1977 the newly-elected president of the U.S., Jimmy Carter, who was looking to improve relations with the USSR through the mechanism of détente (established by his predecessor Richard Nixon), issued a joint statement on October 1, 1977 calling for a Middle East peace conference in Geneva. This caught Begin and Sadat by surprise. Bringing in the Soviets to the peace process would be a big step backwards for both Israel and Egypt, as would bringing in other Arab entities who were officially at war with Israel and did not even accept her right to exist. In such a setting the most radical anti-Israel states would control the conference; for, they would set the bar for what constitutes "peace", thus publicly daring any other Arab country to behave in a more conciliatory fashion towards Israel, a treasonous act in the eyes of all the Arab states.

Israel and Egypt were able to accomplish what they had since 1973 only because they had negotiated bilaterally, and when an outside actor was needed both countries trusted the U.S. to play that role. To insure that this Geneva conference would not take place, Sadat accepted Begin's invitation to come to Israel and meet with the Israeli leadership.*

This dramatic move did indeed end the talk of any Geneva peace conference, and catapulted the Sadat visit to Israel as the most dramatic news story of that period. The leader of Egypt, a nation that had been at war with Israel five times, was coming to visit Israel and meet her leaders and speak to her people. It was an unbelievable event. Sadat was about to break every taboo that had existed in the Arab world since the days of Mufti Haj Amin Al-Husseini.

Sadat landed in Israel on November 19, 1977. He was greeted

---

* "The story is briefly told, and it begins a little over a month before Sadat's initiative, when a severe controversy erupted over Carter's decision to bring the Soviets into the planned Geneva conference. The world learned of this new partnership suddenly and without warning on October 1, 1977, with the release of a joint Soviet-American communiqué. The document elicited a storm of outrage, especially from Israel and its American supporters, who complained, among other things, about the communiqué's support for 'Palestinian rights.' This phrase, combined with the fact that the Soviets would be co-chairing the conference, generated a fear in Israel that a plan was afoot to impose a settlement by rolling the Israelis out of the West Bank and establishing a political entity there... Anwar Sadat fully shared the Israelis' distaste for Geneva. Not only was Carter bringing the Soviets into the diplomacy as equals, but he also aspired to involve Moscow's clients, Syria and the Palestinian Liberation Organization (PLO). The grand plan was the stuff of Sadat's worst nightmares. The Egyptian leader saw no reason why, when his two goals were to reclaim the Sinai and move Egypt into the American sphere, he should be locked into a room with the Soviets and the Syrians, who would bar the door whenever he sought to talk to the Israelis and Americans alone. Sadat went to Jerusalem, therefore, to scuttle Geneva." (Michael Doran, "What Carter Owes Begin" in *Menachem Begin's Zionist Legacy* (New Milford, CT: The Toby Press, 2015), 7-9.

by Begin and all of Israel's political and military leadership. Golda Meir, Moshe Dayan—now serving as the Foreign Minister—and Ariel Sharon were among the many dignitaries there. Sadat specifically wanted to meet these three because of the Yom Kippur War. Hundreds of thousands of Israelis lined the road from Ben-Gurion Airport to Jerusalem waving Egyptian flags. There was a true sense of euphoria in Israel.

Sadat came to Jerusalem, laid a wreath at Yad Vashem, Israel's national monument to the Holocaust, prayed at the Al Aqsa Mosque in Jerusalem (the first Arab leader to do so since King Abdullah was assassinated there in 1952) and, perhaps most importantly, addressed the Israeli Knesset that was broadcast live to the entire world. He also met with Begin. Finally, Sadat also met with sixty non-PLO Palestinian Arab political and local leaders from Judea, Samaria and Gaza.

Israel and Egypt continued to negotiate and sent a message to President Carter that if the U.S. wanted to be helpful it should act as a facilitator between the two countries. That meant keeping the USSR, other Arab countries and even the UN out of the peace-making process. Jimmy Carter got the message. When after months of negotiations Israel and Egypt were faced with some intractable issues, the U.S. became the honest broker. President Carter invited Prime Minister Begin and President Sadat and their respective negotiating teams to spend 10 days "locked away" with him and his negotiating team at the presidential retreat at Camp David, Maryland, in September of 1978.

CAMP DAVID AGREEMENTS BETWEEN ISRAEL & EGYPT SIGNED: SEPTEMBER 1978

After ten days of intense negotiations at Camp David, Israel and Egypt signed the first comprehensive framework for peace involving participants in the Arab-Israeli conflict. The main points were: Israel agreed to withdraw from the entire Sinai Desert—an area three times larger than Israel! Israel did insist and receive the concession that the Sinai would have to be demilitarized with only a token Egyptian military force present, and with a special multinational force patrolling the Sharm El-Sheikh area to insure there would not be another blockade of the Gulf of Eilat (Aqaba). This multinational force would not be a UN entity because of its clearly established hostility and unreliability. Israel also offered the Egyptians Gaza, but the Egyptians politely refused. Israel also offered the Arabs of Gaza, Judea and Samaria autonomy—a way to end the stalemate that existed since the Arab League had passed the "Three No's" in September of 1967 [No Recognition of Israel, No Peace with Israel, and No Negotiations with Israel]. The autonomy plan would bring about an end to Israeli rule of the Arabs who lived there, offering self-government in all the following areas: education, health, business, civil law, construction, garbage and sewage. This status of autonomy would last five years and then a final status would be negotiated between Israel, Egypt, Jordan and the Palestinian Arab autonomous area.

In return for all of Sinai, the Egyptians offered Israel full recognition and peace, the first peace with any Arab country. It took close to a full year to hammer out all the details of the peace agreement, but finally there was an Arab country that recognized the State of Israel, and there would be a recognized boundary between Israel and Egypt, not a ceasefire line.

Unfortunately, the Arabs of Gaza, Judea and Samaria, who were officially represented by the PLO, refused any dealings with or recognition of Israel, so the autonomy talks never got off the ground. Furthermore, the PLO branded Egypt and Sadat as traitors to the Arab nation, and the Palestinian cause in particular. Once again, Palestinian leadership missed another opportunity that could have led to Palestinian statehood and peace with Israel. It was more important to Palestinian leadership to focus on a way to destroy Israel than it was to create a functioning Palestinian State.

ISRAEL & EGYPT PEACE TREATY SIGNED ON WHITE HOUSE LAWN: MARCH 26, 1979

A peace process that had begun on October 28, 1973 at

Kilometer 101, finally reached its goal on March 26, 1979. A formal peace treaty between Israel and Egypt was signed. The 22,000-square-mile Sinai that served as a natural buffer for Israel's southern border was returned to Egypt. Furthermore, Israel handed over numerous oil wells it had developed and moved out of over three hundred IDF bases that included twelve air bases, relocating them to the Negev. Finally, Israel forcefully evacuated 3,000 Israelis from the Yamit Settlement bloc, twelve towns set up in the northwest part of Sinai. This was the first time in the history of the state that Jews were forcibly evicted from their homes. It was a painful and very divisive step that the Begin government felt was part of the heavy price Israel had to pay for peace with its former greatest foe.

All in all, Israel made huge sacrifices—economically, security-wise, ideologically and psychologically—to achieve peace with Egypt. Sadat, personally, took a huge risk in signing this peace treaty, as Arafat and the Egyptian-based Muslim Brotherhood branded him a traitor and demanded his death. Also, as a consequence, Egypt was thrown out of the Arab League.

The U.S., as honest broker and then as facilitator of the treaty, paid for the construction of two new top-of-the line air bases in the Negev, the Uvda and Ramon Air Bases. Egypt also received substantial economic assistance from the U.S. as Sadat had to deliver to his people some tangible results for the deal, since Egypt was now treated as a pariah by the rest of the Arab world.

Israel and Egypt then formally exchanged ambassadors and set up embassies in each other's countries. In April of 1982 Israel finished its phased withdrawal from all of Sinai. Tragically, Sadat did not live to see the final implementation of the peace treaty. He was assassinated by members of the Muslim Brotherhood during the annual Operation Badr (Yom Kippur War) Victory Parade in Cairo on October 6, 1981. Dressed as soldiers, they jumped out of their military vehicles during the parade and ran to the reviewing stands and gunned him down and ten others; twenty-eight were injured. Sadat's vice president, Hosni Mubarak, former commander of the

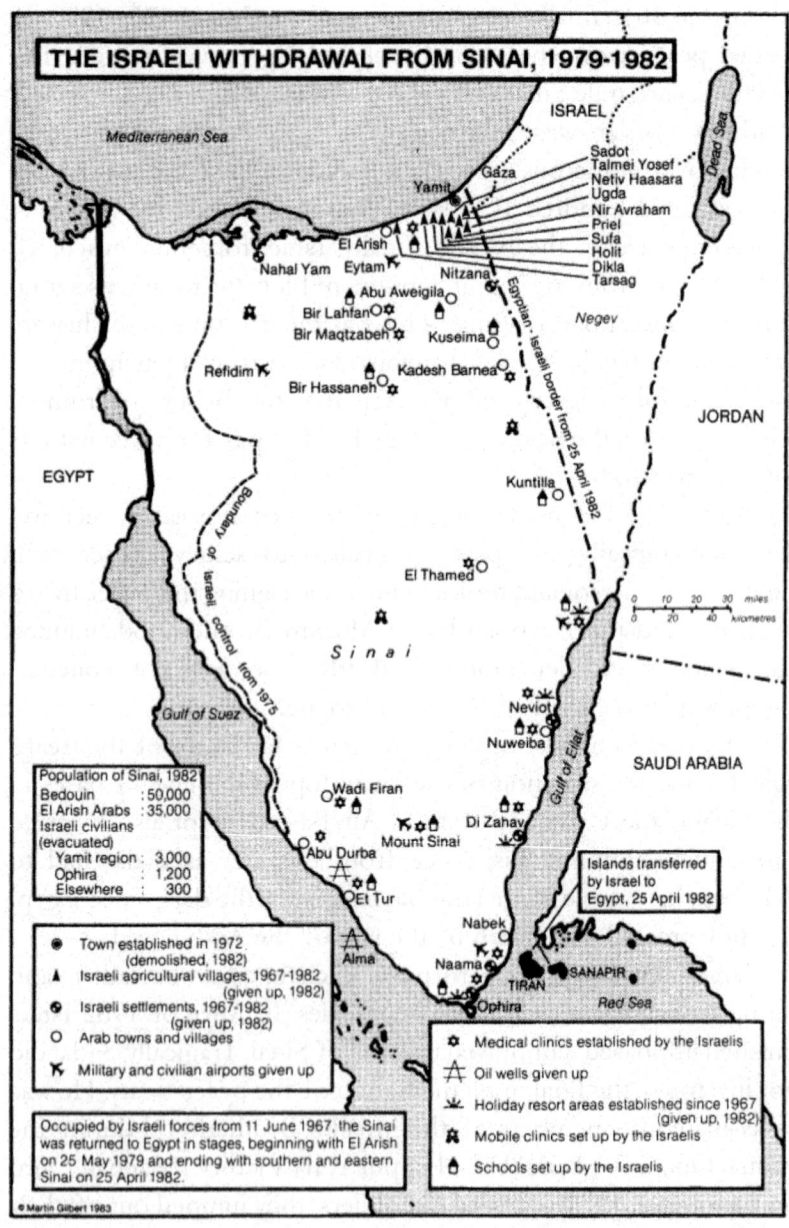

THE ISRAELI WITHDRAWAL FROM SINAI, 1979-1982

Mediterranean Sea

ISRAEL

Sadot
Talmei Yosef
Netiv Haasara
Ugda
Nir Avraham
Priel
Sufa
Holit
Dikla
Tarsag

Yamit Gaza

Dead Sea

El Arish
Nahal Yam Eytam Nitzana

Abu Aweigila
Bir Lahfan
Bir Maqtzabeh Kuseima

Negev

Egyptian-Israeli border from 25 April 1982

Refidim Kadesh Barnea
Bir Hassaneh

EGYPT

Boundary of Israeli control from 1975

JORDAN

Kuntilla

El Thamed

0 10 20 30 miles
0 20 40 kilometres

S i n a i

Gulf of Suez

Neviot
Nuweiba

Gulf of Eilat

SAUDI ARABIA

Population of Sinai, 1982
Bedouin : 50,000
El Arish Arabs : 35,000
Israeli civilians
(evacuated)
  Yamit region : 3,000
  Ophira : 1,200
  Elsewhere : 300

Wadi Firan
Di Zahav
Mount Sinai

Abu Durba
Et Tur

Islands transferred
by Israel to
Egypt, 25 April 1982

Nabek
Alma
Naama SANAPIR
TIRAN
Ophira Red Sea

● Town established in 1972
   (demolished, 1982)
▲ Israeli agricultural villages, 1967-1982
   (given up, 1982)
✿ Israeli settlements, 1967-1982
   (given up, 1982)
○ Arab towns and villages
✗ Military and civilian airports given up

✿ Medical clinics established by the Israelis
⚓ Oil wells given up
✹ Holiday resort areas established since 1967
   (given up, 1982)
⚑ Mobile clinics set up by the Israelis
⚑ Schools set up by the Israelis

Occupied by Israeli forces from 11 June 1967, the Sinai
was returned to Egypt in stages, beginning with El Arish
on 25 May 1979 and ending with southern and eastern
Sinai on 25 April 1982.

© Martin Gilbert 1983

Egyptian Air Force during the Yom Kippur War, took over. He honored the peace treaty until he was removed from office in 2011.

Israel and Egypt did not become friends, and certainly not allies, but they did become neighbors who could deal with each other via diplomatic means as opposed to war.

THE RISE OF THE MUSLIM BROTHERHOOD: 1978

> The Muslim Brotherhood is a fundamentalist international organization or organizations originating in Egypt, whose goals are the conversion of Muslim countries into states ruled by Sha'aria law, the reestablishment of the Caliphate and ultimately, world dominion. The Muslim Brotherhood's ideology, which insists that Islam is prescription for governance as well as a religion, is the prototypical example of Islamism. ...Different factions of the Muslim Brotherhood believe that an Islamic society can be achieved by violent means in the near term, or by education and "preparation" of society and "democratic" takeover. The Muslim Brotherhood was founded formally in March 1928 in Egypt by Hassan al-Banna, but it may have existed before in a less formal framework.[11]

Within a year of his election as prime minister, Menachem Begin sought for a means to negate the power that Arafat had attained in the Arab world as a result of the Rabat Summit of 1974 and his subsequent terrorist attacks upon Israel. Adopting a plan promulgated by Ariel Sharon, the Israeli government began creating and funding a system of local Palestinian councils called the "Village Leagues." These leagues were managed by hand-picked Palestinians to adminster their localities and thus eliminate potential PLO influence should Arafat return to the area from his exile in Tunisia.

> Israel saw benefits in the leagues which became a breeding ground for Palestinian collaborators who were blackmailed or bribed into reporting on the activities of other Palestinians.

Many of them held positions of leadership in the Village Leagues and were friendly to Israel.

The Israeli military gave the League members protection and widespread powers. As many as 200 of the league members were given weapons training by Israel. Israel's Shin Bet recruited paid informers from this network and Israeli sources estimated the number of informants were in the thousands.

Israel Military Government employed as many as 19,000 Palestinians, with 11,000 of them working as teachers, clerks and administrators.[12]

In addition, in 1973 a quadraplegic cleric named Sheik Ahmed Yassin founded a Muslim Brotherhood-affiliated social services agency called the Mujama al-Islamiya. As Yassin's influence grew in Gaza and the West Bank, Sharon viewed the Islamic cleric as a religious alternative to the secular Arafat, an alternative that promised to be less threatening. Thus, in 1979, over the objections of Palestinian leaders, Israel registered Yassin's "Islamic Association."

With Israeli funds that were funneled through the Village Leagues, and through his own fundraising, Yassin built mosques, schools, and medical institutions in Gaza, thus endearing him to a Palestinian population that had only known the corrupt, kleptocratic and rapacious PLO. He also established social service and job agencies. Despite initially avowing the Brotherhood's long-term position of peaceful activism, Yassin proved to be a wolf in sheep's clothing. In 1983 he was convicted of the illegal possession of weapons and the creation of a military organization and sentenced to thirteen years in prison.[13] But in 1985 he was released under the terms of the Jibril Agreement.

The Jibril Agreement was a prisoner exchange deal which took place on May 21, 1985 between the Israeli government, headed by Shimon Peres, and the Popular Front for the Liberation of Palestine - General Command. As part of the agreement, Israel released 1,150 security prisoners held in Israeli prisons in exchange for three Israeli prisoners (Yosef Grof, Nissim Salem, Hezi Shai) captured during the First Lebanon War. This was one of several prisoner exchange agreements carried out between Israel and groups it classified as terrorist organizations around that time...The Israeli government faced harsh public criticism for agreeing to release 1,150 security prisoners, among them those sentenced to life imprisonment and responsible for the killing of many Israeli citizens, particularly since the exchange did not include Israelis who were captured in the Battle of Sultan Yacoub [which took place on June 10, 1982 during the Lebanon War]. One of the Israeli negotiators resigned in protest against the agreement.[14]

In December of 1987, when an IDF truck accident in the Jabalia Refugee Camp resulted in the death of four Palestinians, the First Intifada was born. Yassin thereupon transformed his Islamic Association into a new militant group, Hamas.

Footnotes

[1] "The Six-Point Agreement- 11 November 1973 ," Israel Ministry of Foreign Affairs (http://www.mfa.gov.il/mfa/foreignpolicy/mfadocuments/yearbook1/pages/17%20the%20six-point%20agreement-%2011%20november%201973.aspx

[2] "Israel-Egypt Separation of Forces Agreement-1974," Israel Ministry of Foreign Affairs (http://www.mfa.gov.il/mfa/foreignpolicy/peace/guide/pages/israel-egypt%20separation%20of%20forces%20agreement%20-%201974.aspx)

[3] "1967-1993: Major Terror Attacks," Israel Ministry of Foreign Affairs (http://www.mfa.gov.il/mfa/aboutisrael/maps/pages/1967-1993-%20major%20terror%20attacks.aspx); "Timeline of Jewish History: Modern Israel & the Diaspora (1970 - 1979)" (http://www.jewishvirtuallibrary.org/timeline-of-modern-israel-1970-1979); BBC, On This Day: "1974: Dozens die as Israel retaliates for Ma'alot," May 16, 1974 (http://news.bbc.co.uk/onthisday/hi/dates/stories/may/16/newsid_2512000/2512399.stm)

[4] "October 1974 Rabat Arab Summit Conference" (http://www.palestinefacts.org/pf_1967to1991_rabat_1974.php)

[5] United Nation General Assembly (https://unispal.un.org/DPA/DPR/unispal.nsf/0/761C1063530766A7052566A2005B74D1)

[6] Chaim Herzog, "The United Nations: Israeli Statement in Response to 'Zionism Is Racism' Resolution (November 10, 1975)" (http://www.jewishvirtuallibrary.org/jsource/UN/herzogsp.html)

[7] Simon Dunstan, *Entebbe: The Most Daring Raid of Israel's Special Forces* (New York: Rosen, 2011), 17–18.

[8] https://en.wikipedia.org/wiki/Operation_Entebbe as derived from Bill McRaven, "Tactical Combat Casualty Care – November

2010," MHS US Department of Defense; Terence Smith, "Hostages Freed as Israelis Raid Uganda Airport; Commandos in 3 Planes Rescue 105-Casualties Unknown Israelis Raid Uganda Airport And Free Hijackers' Hostages," *New York Times*, July 4, 1976; Eyal Ben, "Special: Entebbe's unsung hero," Ynetnews (http://www.ynetnews.com/articles/0,7340,L-3270314,00.html); "Israel's Wars & Operations: The Entebbe Rescue Mission," Israel Defense Forces, July 3, 2006, Jewish Virtual Library (http://www.jewishvirtuallibrary.org/the-entebbe-rescue-operation)

[9] Michael Brzoska and Frederic S. Pearson, *Arms and Warfare: Escalation, De-escalation, and Negotiation* (Columbia, SC: Univ. of S. Carolina Press, 1994), 203.

[10] *Op. cit.*

[11] "Muslim Brotherhood ," *Encyclopedia of the Middle East* (http://www.mideastweb.org/Middle-East-Encyclopedia/muslim_brotherhood.htm)

[12] Ray Hanania, "Sharon and Hamas," *Counterpunch*, January 18, 2003 (https://www.counterpunch.org/2003/01/18/sharon-and-hamas/)

[13] Gil Sedan, "The life of Hamas leader Sheik Ahmed Yassin," *JTA World Report*, March 23, 2004 (pdfs.jta.org/2004/2004_03_23.pdf)

[14] "Jibril AGreement," *World Heritage Encyclopedia* (http://self.gutenberg.org/articles/Jibril_Agreement)

Chapter 15

The PLO in South Lebanon: 1970-1982

The history of Palestinian organizations that ostensibly exist to help further the cause of Palestinian sovereignty—starting with the *fedayeen* of the 1950s up until the Palestinian Authority and Hamas of 2017—seem to have one clear goal: the eradication of Israel. Even when they either take territory by force or are given territory in formal agreements, their behavior always remains the same: They do very little, if anything, to improve the lives of Palestinians. Rather, they focus on causing damage to Israel and, in the process, always seem to hurt their own people.

In September of 1970 King Hussein of Jordan literally declared war on the PLO because it had taken over Western Jordan and turned it into a terror state within-a-state. After Black September, Yasser Arafat moved the PLO and its affiliates to South Lebanon, where a weak government and inefficient military could not hope to challenge their presence.

Once again the appearance of Yasser Arafat in a sovereign Arab state became an issue for the "host" state. The PLO did not consider itself a guest in South Lebanon but rather a landlord that operated out of Palestinian refugee camps, as well as local cities and towns. The PLO once again became an occupation force.

By 1975 the PLO's terror war against Israel had become something that forced all Lebanese to choose sides. Lebanon, whether she chose to or not, became the staging ground for hundreds of terrorist attacks against Israel, which also meant many Israeli reprisal incursions to destroy known PLO terror facilities.

From the moment of Lebanon's liberation from French mandatory control in 1943, the country had been divided along religious and ethnic lines. The Christian population tended to be pro-Western, and after 1948-49 had no reason to fight Israel. The Sunnis tended to be more pro-Palestinian; the Shiites actually tended to side with the Christians. The Druze wanted to be left alone living in their Shouf Mountains. Still, in 1958, Lebanon had its first civil war, causing then-U.S. President Dwight Eisenhower to send U.S. military personnel to Beirut to restore order.*

By 1975 Lebanon's Christian leadership was appalled at the amount of control the PLO had gained in Southern Lebanon. Using extortionist tactics, the PLO set up checkpoints stopping Lebanese citizens on their way to work or vacation and collected "taxes" for its "revolution." In addition, it took over Western Beirut and turned it into PLO operational headquarters.

Fighting broke out between Christian and PLO forces in Beirut in April 1975, and the fighting quickly spread to other parts of Lebanon. Democratic, tranquil, scenic, cosmopolitan Beirut became a horrific war zone with the city being divided in half: West Beirut PLO-dominated and East Beirut Christian-dominated. Lebanon, as a whole, became a war zone.

On January 18, 1976 an estimated 1,000-1,500 people were killed by Maronite forces in the Karantina Massacre, followed two days later by a retaliatory strike on Damour by Palestinian militias. These two massacres prompted a mass exodus of Muslims and Christians, as people fearing retribution fled to areas under the control of their own sect. The ethnic and religious layout of the residential areas

* U.S. Marines were landed in Lebanon July 15 to honor formal requests by President Camille Chamoun for armed assistance against Moslem rebels said to be supported by the United Arab Republic [UAR]....The landings were ordered by President Eisenhower after Iraqi Army officers had overthrown the pro-Western monarchy of King Faisal II July 14 and had proclaimed a republic friendly to the UAR. (web.stanford.edu/group/tomzgroup/pmwiki/uploads/2331-1958-07-16-FF-a-ctd.doc)

of the capital encouraged this process, and East and West Beirut were increasingly transformed into what was in effect Christian and Muslim Beirut. Also, the number of Maronite leftists who had allied with the Lebanese National Movement (LNM), and Muslim conservatives with the government, dropped sharply, as the war revealed itself as an utterly sectarian conflict. Another effect of the massacres was to bring in Yassir Arafat's well-armed Fatah, and thereby the Palestine Liberation Organization, on the side of the LNM, as Palestinian sentiment was by now completely hostile to the Maronite forces.[1]

Sadly, there were to be many more massacres and the switching of alliances by many Lebanese actors and Syria, which had always seen Lebanon as part of its domain. In 1976, in order to try to put an end to the Lebanese Civil War, the Arab League voted to send in 40,000 Syrian soldiers as peace keepers. In essence, the Arab League de facto permitted Syria to become the new ruler of most of Lebanon.

OPERATION LITANI: MARCH-APRIL 1978

In March of 1978 PLO operatives from Lebanon slipped into Israel by ship and took over a bus on the Tel Aviv-Haifa highway.

The Coastal Road massacre of 1978 was an attack involving the hijacking of a bus on Israel's Coastal Highway in which 38 Israeli civilians, including 13 children, were killed, and 71 were wounded. The attack was…carried out by the PLO faction Fatah. The plan was to seize a luxury hotel in Tel Aviv and take tourists and foreign ambassadors hostage in order to exchange them for Palestinian prisoners held by Israel.[2]

This attack in the heart of Israel was the straw that broke the camel's back. Israel decided to respond with not merely a reprisal raid or a preemptive strike at a specific PLO staging ground. Rather, Israel launched a small-scale invasion of South Lebanon involving thousands of IDF troops, and entered about 10 miles into Lebanon, captured PLO weapons and men in their way and killed about five hundred terrorists. The IDF stopped at the Litani River. The UN, which never condemned PLO terror against Israel and which had never done anything to stop the massacres that had taken place in Lebanon during the civil war, condemned Israel, this time with U.S. support. While President Jimmy Carter did play a major role in helping Israel and Egypt complete their peace process, he was not seen as a friend of Israel. Thus, Israel was forced to withdraw from South Lebanon. A UN force of 7,000, called the United Nations Interim Force in Lebanon (UNIFIL), was deployed to act as a buffer.*

Since Israel had had so many negative experiences with the UN, the most recent being the 1975 UN Resolution equating Zionism with racism, Israel did not expect anything good to come from the UNIFIL presence. Hence, Israel helped set up a pro-Israel Arab militia in South Lebanon called the South Lebanon Army (SLA) commanded at the time by Major Sa'ad Hadaad. This 2,000-man force controlled a strip directly north of Israel, an area about seven miles deep and 50 miles wide, wherein about 250,000 Arabs lived. These Lebanese Arabs were a collection of Christian, Muslim and Druze who found that since the Lebanese Civil War (1975-1976) had devastated their once serene and prosperous homeland, the area directly north of Israel was the safest and most stable part of Lebanon. Furthermore, since many of these Lebanese Arabs entered Israel as day laborers, there had developed a growing trade between Israel and this region. Hence the IDF and the SLA became close allies. This area became known as the Israeli security zone, and Israel opened up the border to these 250,000 Arabs and

---

*To put this in perspective, in 1957 the UN sent 5,000 peace keepers to monitor 22,000 square miles of territory and 7,000 soldiers to Lebanon in 1978 to an area that was around 60 square miles in size!

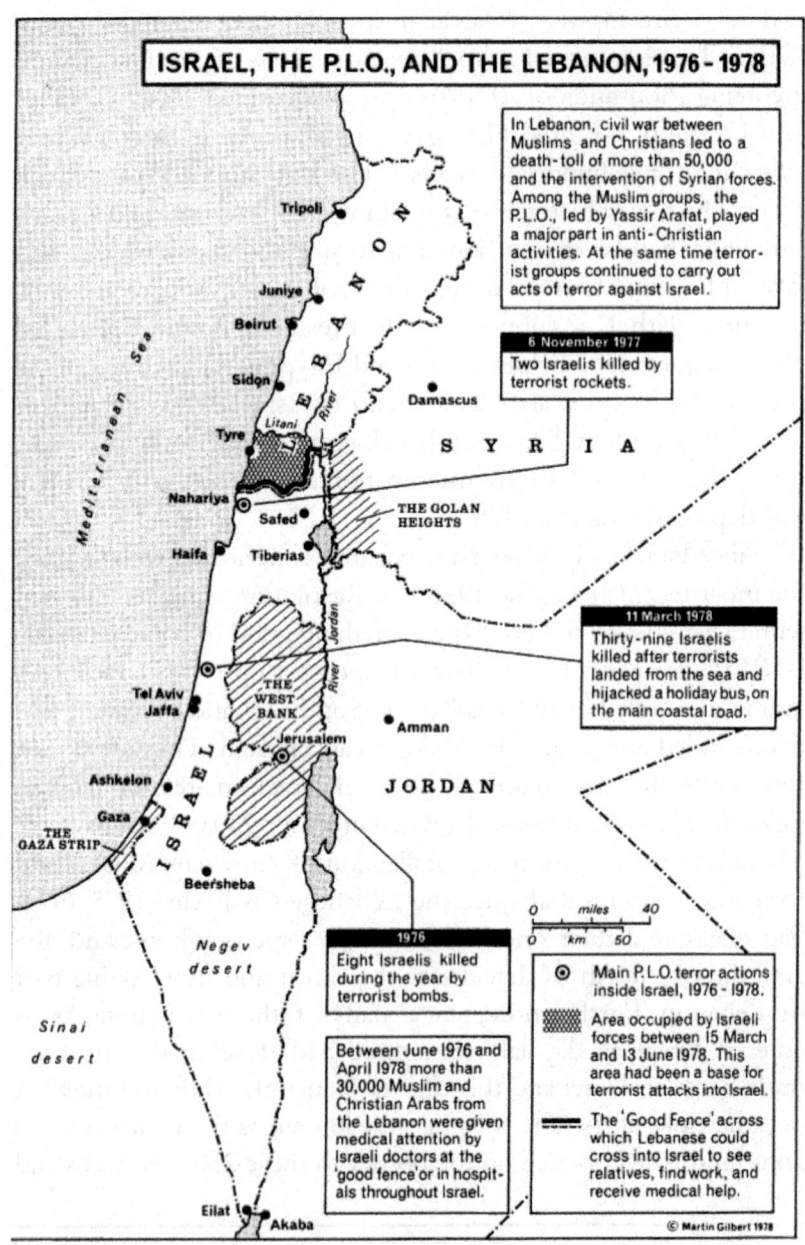

ISRAEL, THE P.L.O., AND THE LEBANON, 1976 – 1978

In Lebanon, civil war between Muslims and Christians led to a death-toll of more than 50,000 and the intervention of Syrian forces. Among the Muslim groups, the P.L.O., led by Yassir Arafat, played a major part in anti-Christian activities. At the same time terrorist groups continued to carry out acts of terror against Israel.

6 November 1977
Two Israelis killed by terrorist rockets.

11 March 1978
Thirty-nine Israelis killed after terrorists landed from the sea and hijacked a holiday bus, on the main coastal road.

1976
Eight Israelis killed during the year by terrorist bombs.

Between June 1976 and April 1978 more than 30,000 Muslim and Christian Arabs from the Lebanon were given medical attention by Israeli doctors at the 'good fence' or in hospitals throughout Israel.

Tripoli

Juniye

Beirut

Sidon

Tyre   Litani   River   Damascus

S Y R I A

Nahariya
Safed   THE GOLAN HEIGHTS
Haifa   Tiberias

Tel Aviv   THE WEST BANK
Jaffa   Amman
Jerusalem

Ashkelon   JORDAN
Gaza
THE GAZA STRIP
Beersheba

Negev desert

Sinai desert

Mediterranean Sea

River Jordan

L E B A N O N

I S R A E L

Eilat   Akaba

miles   40
0
0   km   50

⊙ Main P.L.O. terror actions inside Israel, 1976 - 1978.

Area occupied by Israeli forces between 15 March and 13 June 1978. This area had been a base for terrorist attacks into Israel.

The 'Good Fence' across which Lebanese could cross into Israel to see relatives, find work, and receive medical help.

© Martin Gilbert 1978

the SLA. The main cross-point, located in Metula, became known as the "Good Fence." This remained the situation until the IDF unilaterally withdrew from Lebanon in 2000.

OPERATION PEACE FOR GALILEE: JUNE-AUGUST 1982

In 1981 the PLO added a new form of terror to its arsenal: rockets—thus becoming the world's first terrorist army having rockets, tanks, missiles, anti-tank and anti-aircraft missiles. As such, the PLO was able to blanket northern Israeli towns and cities with volleys of rocket fire from South Lebanon, safely behind the blind eye of the UNIFIL buffer zone. After 12 years of PLO raids and attacks, after four years of an ineffective UN presence, after the PLO had the time and opportunity to build up a military infra-structure which included training bases, operational headquarters, supply areas and 25,000 armed men operating in army brigades, and after the PLO had several hundred artillery pieces and rocket launchers used to bombard northern Israel, Israel decided to solve its South Lebanon PLO problem.

In 1981 Israel had to contend with the PLO firing volleys of Katyusha (Russian made and supplied) rockets at northern Israeli cities like Ma'alot and Kiryat Shmona. It reached the point where thousands of Israelis had abandoned their homes since they simply could not live under the shadow of constant rocket fire. As the escalation between PLO rocket and artillery fire into northern Israel intensified, so did the Israeli responses. The U.S. became concerned and sent a special negotiator, Philip Habib, who brokered a ceasefire between the PLO and Israel.

> The cease-fire arrangement took an intricate form because of the refusal of Israel and the United States to talk to the P.L.O. and the refusal of Lebanon to talk to Israel. The understandings were between Israel and the United States and between the United States and Lebanon, which dealt with the P.L.O. through the United Nations. Mr. Habib negotiated with Israeli, Saudi Arabian and Lebanese leaders, but not with the Palestinians.... The only on-the-record elaboration

was provided by Justice Minister Moshe Nissim. "This is an arrangement," he said, "by which the Government of Lebanon commits itself to stop any act of violence against Israel, and Israel has agreed to this challenge and will cease acts of hostility."[3]

Shortly after the agreement was reached, the PLO began to violate the ceasefire in two significant ways: 1) It launched terror attacks from Lebanon, Gaza, Judea and Samaria at Israeli civilians; and 2) it used the cease fire to rearm and bring in more sophisticated armaments into South Lebanon. The PLO claimed since they were not firing rockets and artillery shells into northern Israel, that it was not violating the ceasefire. Israel obviously did not see it that way.

By June of 1982, 11 months after the Habib ceasefire had been brokered, Israel felt that the agreement it had signed only served to tie the hands of the IDF while giving the PLO freedom to do greater damage to Israel at the time of its choosing, all the while behind the protection of UNIFIL.

On June 4th, Abu Nidal, a group allied with the PLO, attempted to assassinate the Israeli ambassador to England. Though seriously wounded, miraculously he did not die. Nevertheless, this attempt on a high-ranking Israeli diplomat could not go unanswered. The IDF retaliated with a series of pinpoint air force strikes on PLO strongholds in Lebanon. The PLO responded by firing hundreds of rockets and shells on northern Israel, sending hundreds of thousands of Israelis into bomb shelters.

On June 6, 1982 Israel launched Operation Peace for Galilee to clean up South Lebanon. A full-scale military invasion involving some 40,000 Israeli soldiers and every branch of the IDF by June 11th conquered all of South Lebanon and was sitting on the hills surrounding Beirut, just south of the Damascus to Beirut highway. The PLO had its bases and command centers smashed, close to 4,000 PLO terrorists killed, 6,000 taken prisoner, and $2.5 billion worth of ammunition taken—a staggering dollar amount for a group whose main constituents were residents of refugee camps.

The Syrian Army, which ruled most of eastern and northern Lebanon since 1976 and a PLO ally, also engaged in this war and was pushed back to the Damascus to Beirut highway. The IDF additionally dealt with the long-range sophisticated ground-to-air anti-aircraft missile batteries in the Bekka Valley Syria had installed in 1981. These advanced anti-aircraft missile batteries not only threatened Israel's ability to operate over Lebanese skies, but also threatened Israel's ability to patrol over the skies of northern Israel. As a result, all of these missile batteries were destroyed. The Israeli Air Force also engaged Syria in one of the largest post-World War II aerial battles, shooting down ninty Syrian jets.

THE CONSEQUENCES OF OPERATION PEACE FOR GALILEE: THE CALUMNY OF THE WORLD PRESS

This was the first true war against a terrorist entity. Since terrorists do not abide by the Geneva Convention—the set of rules of war set up by countries in 1949—the PLO had introduced a new type of warfare wherein one side, the non-state actor who abides by no rules, expects its enemy, an organized nation state, to abide by the civilized world's rules of engagement. The only way such a scenario can play out to the benefit of the non-state actor is if the international community, led by the UN and the international media, allows this to occur. Sadly, this is exactly what happened in Operation Peace for Galilee. The UN and the Western media acted as cheerleaders for the PLO while at the same time doing everything in their power to have the IDF appear as brutal as possible.

In the post-Yom Kippur War era the Arab, Islamic, Communist and Third World countries had banded together in the UN to form a massive voting bloc. Thus, the UN international community readily lined up behind the PLO in the 1982 Lebanon War. In addition, Western media as a whole—the Western European media in particular—went to great pains to frame the IDF attack against the PLO in Lebanon as an unprovoked attack by the bully of the

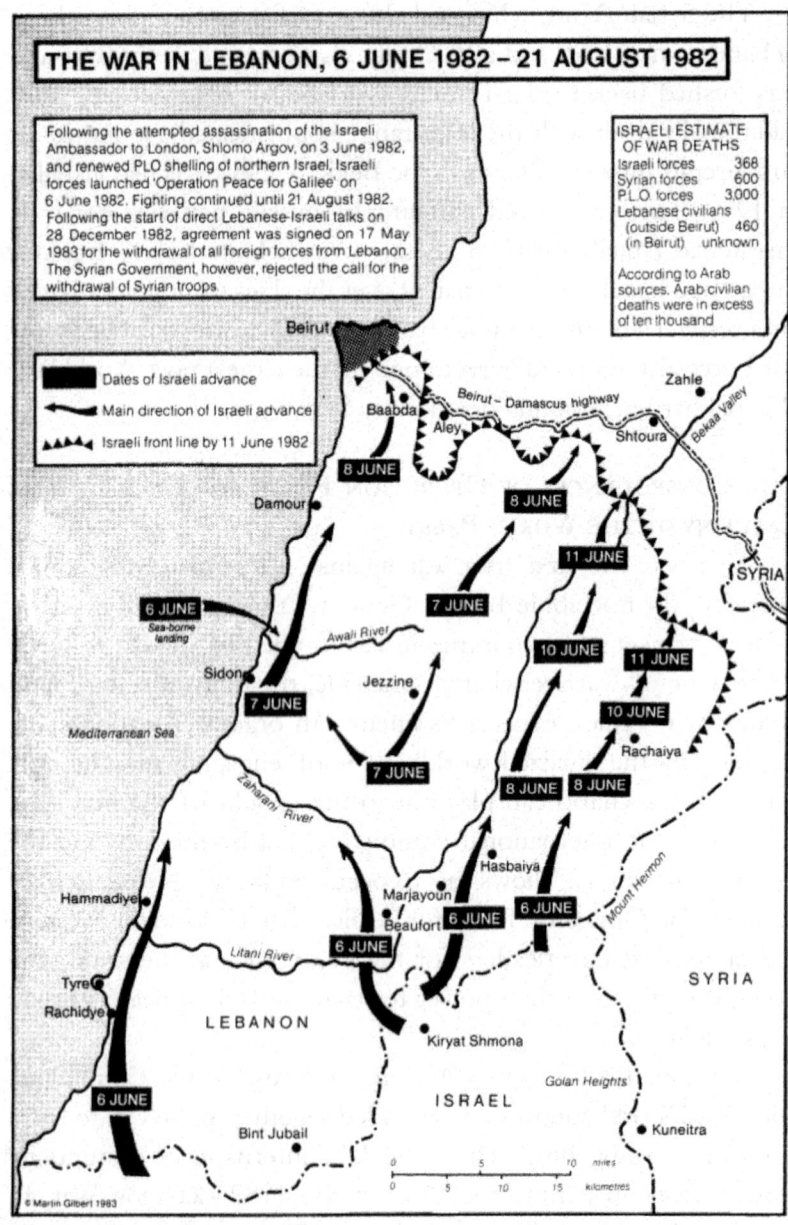

THE WAR IN LEBANON, 6 JUNE 1982 – 21 AUGUST 1982

Following the attempted assassination of the Israeli
Ambassador to London, Shlomo Argov, on 3 June 1982,
and renewed PLO shelling of northern Israel, Israeli
forces launched 'Operation Peace for Galilee' on
6 June 1982. Fighting continued until 21 August 1982.
Following the start of direct Lebanese-Israeli talks on
28 December 1982, agreement was signed on 17 May
1983 for the withdrawal of all foreign forces from Lebanon.
The Syrian Government, however, rejected the call for the
withdrawal of Syrian troops.

ISRAELI ESTIMATE
OF WAR DEATHS
Israeli forces   368
Syrian forces   600
P.L.O. forces   3,000
Lebanese civilians
  (outside Beirut)   460
  (in Beirut)   unknown

According to Arab
sources, Arab civilian
deaths were in excess
of ten thousand

Beirut

Dates of Israeli advance

Main direction of Israeli advance

Israeli front line by 11 June 1982

Zahle

Beirut – Damascus highway

Baabda
Aley
Shtoura
Bekaa Valley

8 JUNE

8 JUNE

Damour

11 JUNE

SYRIA

7 JUNE

6 JUNE
Sea-borne
landing

Awali River

10 JUNE

11 JUNE

Sidon

7 JUNE

Jezzine

10 JUNE

Mediterranean Sea

7 JUNE

Rachaiya

Zaharani River

8 JUNE   8 JUNE

Hasbaiya

Hammadiye

Marjayoun

Mount Hermon

Beaufort   6 JUNE   6 JUNE

Litani River

6 JUNE

SYRIA

Tyre

Rachidye

LEBANON

Kiryat Shmona

Golan Heights

6 JUNE

ISRAEL

Bint Jubail

Kuneitra

0   5   10   miles
0   5   10   15   kilometres

© Martin Gilbert 1983

Sir Martin Gilbert, © 2010. Reproduced by permission of Taylor
& Francis Books UK. www.martingilbert.com

Middle East whose only goal was to humiliate Palestinian Arabs, destroy them and grab more Arab territory. The term *blitzkrieg* (lightning war), a term coined by the Nazis in World War II when they overwhelmed their opponents with overwhelming force, brutality and speed, was applied by many in the Western European press to describe the IDF push into Lebanon. And this became the new "norm" in coverage of Israeli actions.*

As Edward Alexander noted in his *NBC's War in Lebanon: The Distorting Mirror*,

> It probably took several centuries from the time printing was invented for the belief to die out that 'whatever is in print must be true.' Now, in the age of television, we face a parallel danger in the widespread belief that "pictures don't lie." In fact...pictures, like words, can and do lie, for pictures, like words, are created and manipulated by men, whose reputation for probity has been open to question since the expulsion from Eden. The injunction to "hold the mirror up to nature" sounds sensible enough until we remember that mirrors may be dirty or clean, concave or convex, cracked or whole; and that everything depends upon which portion of nature you choose to reflect, how often you reflect it, and how much you reveal of the history of the reflected images.[4]

---

*By definition, the media shapes how the general public sees events. In Israel's case this form of media bias has created a Western European public that has a view of Israel that is horrifically distorted. At the same time, this form of media bias, though supposedly motivated by the media's attempt to assist the "persecuted" Palestinians, really operates under a very subtle yet clear form of bigotry. Referred to as "the soft bigotry of low expectations," it essentially holds certain actors to a lower standard of behavior than one would more "civilized" or "developed" groups. Hence, ignored is brutal, uncivilized, unacceptable behavior that allows the perpetrators to get away with reprehensible acts precisely because there are such low expectations of them. This has allowed Palestinians and their allies to get away with real and metaphorical murder, shielding them from the need to be reflective, looking at their own behavior and implementing needed reforms and changes.

Thus, elements of the Western media became the propaganda arm of the PLO. For example, if one followed the non-Israeli media during Operation Peace for Galilee one would never have known that the IDF dropped millions of warning leaflets hours before any IDF airstrike on a PLO target. Obviously, this also gave PLO terrorists time to prepare for the strike and the ground assault that was to follow. One would never know that the IDF specifically targeted only PLO command, communications, training, and munitions centers in Lebanon, leaving the overwhelming majority of cities where the PLO had embedded itself untouched. Thus, in the name of "getting access to the story," distortions were liberally broadcast and printed. These reporters knew very well that if they wanted access to the story on the PLO side of the battle they needed to follow the "script" handed them.[5]

Western media also exaggerated the casualty and refugee numbers that were supposedly caused by the IDF *blitzkrieg*. These numbers were handed to them by the Palestinian Red Crescent, which was at the time headed by Yasser Arafat's brother, Fathi. Not connected to the Lebanese Red Crescent, the Palestinian Red Crescent was part of the PLO disinformation war. As such, after the first week of the war, the Western media was reporting that over 10,000 Palestinian and Lebanese civilians had been killed by the IDF, as well as 600,000 Palestinian Arab and Lebanese civilians made homeless by the Israeli attack. No one fact checked that there were no 600,000 Arabs living in South Lebanon.*

One of the most outrageous examples of media ignorance was evidenced when an NBC reporter had a film crew in the destroyed town of Damour and droned on in front of the rolling cameras that Damour was just one example of a Lebanese city destroyed by the Israeli war machine. The fact that Damour was a Christian Lebanese city destroyed in the 1975-1976 Lebanese Civil War by the PLO was conveniently omitted.

---

* For an examination of the misleading and biased reporting perpetrated by the Western media see: Edward Alexander's "NBC's War in Lebanon: The Distorting Mirror" (http://www.afsi.org/pamphlets/NBC_war_in_lebanon_alexander[1].pdf)

Contributing to the overt anti-Israeli "objectivity" was the media's cowardly failure to admit that a good deal of its reporting was controlled by the very forces Israel was combatting.

> On February 22, 1982, John Kifner, *New York Times* correspondent in Beirut, wrote:
>
> To work here as a journalist is to carry fear with you as faithfully as your notebook. It is the constant knowledge that there is nothing you can do to protect yourself and that nothing has ever happened to any assassin. In this atmosphere, a journalist must often weigh when, how, and sometimes even whether, to record a story. . .
>
> In February 1982 Zeev Chafetz, then director of Israel's Government Press Office, charged that substantial segments of the western news media follow a double standard in reporting and commentary on the Arab-Israeli conflict because they fear and respect Arab terror, but take for granted and abuse the freedom allowed them in Israel's open society. He explicitly charged that terror prevented critical reporting on the PLO and Syria...[6]

There were a handful of brave souls in the American media in particular who spoke up and attempted to give some balance to the alarmingly distorted view of the war coming out of most of the media. Two that come to mind are George Will, the syndicated columnist who has always been an admirer of Israel, and David K. Shipler of the *New York Times*, who was anything but sympathetic to Israel. Nevertheless, he too spoke out against the media's biased and exaggerated anti-Israel claims. On July 25, 1982 he wrote:

> The PLO was not on a campaign to win friends among the Lebanese. Its thrust was military. The huge sums of money the PLO received from Saudi Arabia and other Arab countries seems to have been spent primarily on weapons and ammunition, which was placed strategically in densely populated civilian areas in the hope that this would either deter Israeli attacks or exact a price from Israel in world

opinion for killing civilians. Towns and camps were turned into vast armories as crates of ammunition were stacked in underground shelters and antiaircraft guns were emplaced in schoolyards, among apartment houses, next to churches and hospitals.[7]

But the most famous, detailed and vigorous defense of Israel in the U.S. media was mounted by the then-editor-in-chief of the *New Republic*, Martin Peretz. The piece began with the now famous sentence: "Much of what you have read in the newspapers and newsmagazines about the war in Lebanon, and even more what you have seen and heard on television is simply not true."[8]

THE GREATEST AIR BATTLE IN MODERN HISTORY: JUNE 9-10, 1982

In April of 1981, Syria, in respponse to the loss of two of its attack helicopters at the hands of Israeli aircraft, introduced surface-to-air (SAM) batteries in Syrian-occupied Lebanon's Bekaa Valley as a means to protect the border.

Said David Ivry, head of the IAF:

> From our point of view," ..."the movement of SAM brigades into the Bekaa Valley was 'crossing the red line' because it threatened Israel's air superiority over its border with Lebanon. SAMs in the Bekaa Valley restricted the IAF's ability to conduct reconnaissance or to provide air cover for ground operations.[9]

Thus Israel undertook Operation Mole Cricket to eliminate the SAM threat.

> Operation Mole Cricket was a SEAD (suppression of enemy air defenses) campaign launched by the Israeli Air Force against Syria on June 9th, 1982. This was due to the breakout of hostilities during the 1982 Lebanon War, which saw Israel yet again at war with its neighbors. To pre-empt any Syrian intervention as well as cripple the Syrian Air Force, Israel or-

ganized a pre-emptive strike against various SAM installations and radar stations scattered throughout the Beqaa Valley in Lebanon.

Israel launched over 96 aircraft including F-15 Eagles, the world's best operational aircraft having an unbeaten combat record, along with supporting F-4 Phantoms (the ground pounders) and F-16 Falcons (escort fighters) into Syria to begin the operation.

In turn, Syria sent up over 100 aircraft of its own to counter the Israeli onslaught, mostly concentrated in antiquated Soviet fighters such as the MiG-23, MiG-21 and Su-20.

Over 2 hours of combat followed when these forces clashed and the end results weren't pretty; 86 Syrian planes were shot down that day with a loss of over 19 SAM batteries to boot with the Israelis suffering 0 lost planes.

To date, Operation Mole Cricket 19 remains one of the most lopsided air battles in history while also being the largest jet battle by the sheer number of aircraft involved and the complete calamity that became of it for the Syrian Air Force.[10]

THE SECOND PART OF OPERATION PEACE FOR GALILEE: JUNE 13-AUGUST 21, 1982

Operation Peace for Galilee achieved the overwhelming majority of its goals by June 12, 1982. That is when the IDF declared a unilateral cease fire. The PLO was routed and no longer possessed an army with bases and armaments that could threaten all of northern Israel. Similarly, the Syrian Army was routed in East Lebanon. The non-Palestinian Arabs of South Lebanon actually felt liberated. That is how badly the PLO treated civilians in the areas they had ruled since 1970. Even Shiite Muslim Lebanese greeted the IDF as liberators.

No longer under PLO hegemony, reports now poured out about the treatment of Lebanese civilians between 1970-1982:

Testimony of Father John Nasser, a priest of Aishiye, a Christian village:

"Nearly 1,000, PLO terrorists attacked our village on

October 19, 1976. They rounded up all the people—100 families—and locked them up in the church. Over 60 were left outside. We heard successive machine gun fire followed by dead silence. We were imprisoned for two days. When the church doors were opened we saw a horrible picture: 65 bodies of men, women, and children lying in a pool of blood. Among them were my brother Ibrahim, and my cousin Antony. Then the big looting began. A convoy of trucks entered the village and they took virtually everything away. Lebanon is full of such Oradour-like hair raising atrocities (Oradour-sur was a French village where the Nazis committed atrocities during World War II)... The world ought to know what this blood thirsty foul organization called the PLO did to my poor beloved country."[11]

Testimony of Mukhtar Salah Shafro, head of the Muslim village of Burg-Bachel, near Sidon:

"While searching for a citizen of the town, the PLO found on him Israeli money and a pair of shoes made in Israel. He was sentenced to death. His hand and legs were chained to the fenders of four vehicles. When a Fatah officer signaled with his pistol, the four cars raced away tearing the body apart while the horrified spectators screamed. The cars raced through the streets with the body parts dangling. People fainted. There were hundreds of witnesses to this terrible thing. But no paper reported it. The world did not hear about it. For seven years we lived a life not worth living. Now it is over."[12]

Even though the IDF had achieved very significant goals in seven days, the war was not yet over. The official goal of Operation Peace for Galilee was to wipe out the PLO's ability to harm Israel. To do that the IDF had to enter 40 kilometers (25 miles) into South Lebanon. And there was a national consensus for this type of operation. However, by June 12, 1982, the IDF was already eighty kilometers deep into Lebanon and sitting on the outskirts of Beirut. Arafat was now hiding in West Beirut with close to 10,000 terrorists who had fled with him, holed up behind women and children who they were using as human shields. If the IDF wanted Arafat and the remainder of his terrorist army, it would have to go through West Beirut and hundreds of thousands of civilians.

A part of the Israeli public was dismayed at where the IDF found itself, and it is not clear to this day if Prime Minister Begin was fully aware of the scope of the plan behind Operation Peace for Galilee that was put together by Minister of Defense Ariel Sharon. Sharon wanted to turn Lebanon into a PLO-free state, with a Syrian Army that would be humbled and thus less capable of running Lebanon as a vassal state. In short, Sharon sought for a Lebanon dominated by the Christian Lebanese who were friendly to Israel and who would be happy to sign a real peace treaty. This was a very ambitious plan that made a great deal of strategic sense, but it was executed in a way that kept most of the country's leadership and the country itself in the dark.

In addition to now sitting on a large segment of Lebanon, around 1,500 square miles, the IDF had Arafat trapped in West Beirut, which it began to lay siege to on June 13. Slowly but surely the IDF tightened its grip by capturing small slivers of land near West Beirut, thus getting closer and closer to Arafat and his army of terrorists. But Arafat just went deeper into the city and made sure his civilian shield could not leave. In essence, the Lebanese civilian population were his hostages.

Now Israel was under the magnifying glass of the media which didn't have to worry about being in the middle of a war, but rather in the middle of a siege that it could dramatically film. Of course the PLO continued its policy of allowing reporters to film in their area only what they allowed them to, using them as their propaganda arm. There was no context, no background of who the PLO was and what they were doing in South Lebanon and in West Beirut. Sadly, Israel, and specifically the IDF, continued to be made to look like an unprincipled vicious army. The media had no interest in being confused by the facts. As a result, there was great pressure on Israel from the U.S. and Western Europe to ease up on its siege.

From a military perspective there is no half siege; it is like being half pregnant. You either are or you are not. For close to seven weeks the IDF was involved in a half siege that only brought misery to all sides. Arafat and his PLO army were trapped with hundreds of thousands of Lebanese civilians as hostages. The IDF couldn't go in and get them because it could lead to a blood bath, and while this halfhearted siege was going on the IDF was still being portrayed on a daily basis by most of the Western media as a war mongering juggernaut. It was a lose-lose proposition.

Finally, on August 4th, Sharon gave the order to capture the Beirut Airport and some southern neighborhoods in West Beirut. On August 12th Israel had run out of patience and was probably no longer concerned about the public relations hit she was taking. At least she should achieve her strategic goals. So the IDF had the IAF selectively pound the parts of West Beirut where Arafat and his PLO terror army were hiding. It was then that Arafat suddenly had an epiphany and was willing to work out a deal that would have him leave West Beirut and Lebanon.

With the assistance of U.S. negotiator Philip Habib, the siege of West Beirut was about to come to an end that would strategically please Israel, Christian Lebanese and many Muslim Lebanese who had suffered under the PLO occupation. Habib worked out that a multinational force of 8,000 U.S. Marines, French and Italian combat soldiers would come to Beirut to act as a buffer between the IDF and the PLO. Under the protection of this multinational force Arafat and the PLO would be evacuated by boat to Arab countries far away from Lebanon. (Most of the PLO army and Arafat himself ended up in Tunisia.) Part of the deal permitted Arafat and his men to receive new uniforms and that they could drive to the port of Beirut from their hideouts in West Beirut as a victorious army.

Bill Moyers commented on the *CBS Evening News* on August 23, 1982 about this grotesque victory parade Arafat orchestrated for the Arab world and the Western media.

Watching scenes of the Beirut evacuation this weekend, I was struck by how it is possible for the cameras to magnify a lie. These Palestinian troops left town as if they'd just won a great victory. Arafat, they praised as a conquering hero. In fact, they have lost the battle. In fact, they are leaving in defeat. And in fact, Arafat led them to this cul-de-sac where they made their last stand behind the skirts of women and among the playground of children. The only victory they won was to give General Sharon an excuse for total war and so bring upon Israel the condemnation of world opinion and to many Jews, a tormented conscience. But the world was condemning Israel before Beirut, and will for time to come. And the anguish of Jews at the suffering caused by their own war machine comes from the bitter experience that those who die by the sword must live by the sword. Carnage, indeed, and no one's hand is clean. But it could have been otherwise if Arafat and his allies accepted the reality of Israel, if they had not established in Lebanon a terrorist state sworn to Israel's destruction, and if Arab governments had not found it useful to nurture the PLO in the bloody illusion that Israel one day can be pushed into the sea. Argue as you might about the events leading up to the establishment of Israel. Weep as you must for the Palestinian refugees. But a fact is a fact, and Israel is a fact. Yet, the guerillas leaving Beirut this week are vowing to fight until victory. Well, there will be no peace in the Middle East until the Arabs stop asking their young men to die for a lie.

SABRA AND SHATILA

After Arafat, under the protection of the multinational force, left Beirut with the PLO to exile in different Arab states, Lebanon held an election. The new president-elect was a Christian named Bashir Gemayel, who was an advocate of peaceful coexistence with Israel. He was supposed to take office on September 23, 1982, but on September 14th was assassinated by Syrian and Palestinian gunmen who blew up the headquarters of Gemayel's Phalangist Party in East Beirut. What had seemed like the last piece in the puzzle of Sharon's plan to turn Lebanon into a peaceful, friendly

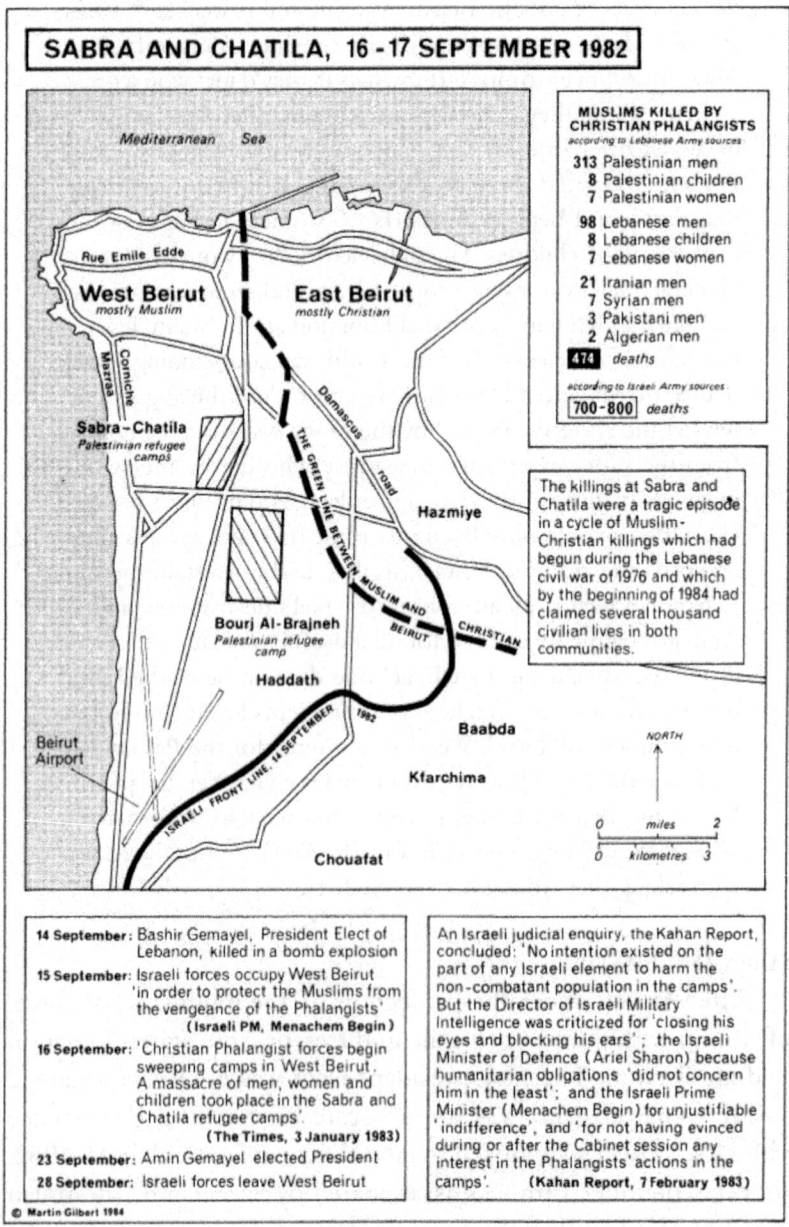

SABRA AND CHATILA, 16 - 17 SEPTEMBER 1982

Mediterranean Sea

Rue Emile Edde

West Beirut
mostly Muslim

East Beirut
mostly Christian

Corniche Mazraa

Damascus road

THE GREEN LINE BETWEEN MUSLIM AND

Sabra - Chatila
Palestinian refugee camps

Hazmiye

BEIRUT   CHRISTIAN

Bourj Al-Brajneh
Palestinian refugee camp

Haddath

Beirut Airport

1982

ISRAELI FRONT LINE. 14 SEPTEMBER

Baabda

NORTH

Kfarchima

Chouafat

0   miles   2
0   kilometres   3

MUSLIMS KILLED BY CHRISTIAN PHALANGISTS
according to Lebanese Army sources

313 Palestinian men
8 Palestinian children
7 Palestinian women

98 Lebanese men
8 Lebanese children
7 Lebanese women

21 Iranian men
7 Syrian men
3 Pakistani men
2 Algerian men

474 deaths

according to Israeli Army sources

700 - 800 deaths

The killings at Sabra and Chatila were a tragic episode in a cycle of Muslim-Christian killings which had begun during the Lebanese civil war of 1976 and which by the beginning of 1984 had claimed several thousand civilian lives in both communities.

14 September: Bashir Gemayel, President Elect of Lebanon, killed in a bomb explosion

15 September: Israeli forces occupy West Beirut 'in order to protect the Muslims from the vengeance of the Phalangists' **(Israeli PM, Menachem Begin)**

16 September: 'Christian Phalangist forces begin sweeping camps in West Beirut. A massacre of men, women and children took place in the Sabra and Chatila refugee camps'. **(The Times, 3 January 1983)**

23 September: Amin Gemayel elected President

28 September: Israeli forces leave West Beirut

An Israeli judicial enquiry, the Kahan Report, concluded: 'No intention existed on the part of any Israeli element to harm the non-combatant population in the camps'. But the Director of Israeli Military Intelligence was criticized for 'closing his eyes and blocking his ears'; the Israeli Minister of Defence (Ariel Sharon) because humanitarian obligations 'did not concern him in the least'; and the Israeli Prime Minister (Menachem Begin) for unjustifiable 'indifference', and 'for not having evinced during or after the Cabinet session any interest in the Phalangists' actions in the camps'. **(Kahan Report, 7 February 1983)**

© Martin Gilbert 1984

Sir Martin Gilbert, © 2010. Reproduced by permission of Taylor & Francis Books UK. www.martingilbert.com

neighboring state had literally been blown up. Now the situation would take a radical turn for the worse.

The Christian Lebanese and, in particular, the Phalangist Party, prepared to extract a price from those who were behind the bombing. For Israel this created not only a depressing new political reality but a very dangerous security situation. It meant that the Syrians and PLO, though defeated, still had the ability to carry out terrorist attacks in the heart of Christian East Beirut, and that now Lebanon was on the verge of another civil war.

Israel thus took the following actions: The IDF entered West Beirut and captured some remaining PLO terrorists, confiscated more ammunition and secured the entire Western half of Beirut. The IDF had the Palestinian refugee camps located in Southwest Beirut surrounded, but purposely did not enter because of the threats to its forces that would be encountered. The two large Palestinian refugee camps in this area were called Sabra and Shatila. The reasoning not to have the IDF enter Sabra and Shatila was based on experience. In the early days of the war the IDF had encountered many armed young non-uniformed terrorists in these camps, including boys as young as 12. Firing RPG's (rocket propelled grenades)—earning them the nickname "RPG Kids"—these 12-year-olds had been trained by PLO commanders to be part of the PLO terror army. Given Israel's already vicious image in the world press, having to fight children was not a welcome prospect.

The IDF thus preferred that an Arab military force enter Sabra and Shatila. Negotiating with the Lebanese Army to take responsibility for the Palestinian refugee camps in the parts of Lebanon that were now under the control of the IDF, it appeared that this was about to come to fruition. However, once President-Elect Bashir Gemayel was assassinated, the Lebanese Army had no interest in taking responsibility for the refugee camps. The IDF was now left in a quandary: Which force should go in to take responsibility for Shatila and Sabra since PLO terrorists could still be there and hence an already volatile situation might intensify.

At this point, on September 15th, the IDF gave permission to Christian Lebanese Forces aligned with the Phalangist Party to enter Sabra and Shatilla to disarm any armed combatants. On the evening of September 16th these forces entered the two refugee camps. They were warned not to harm any non-combatants but it soon became apparent that the Phalangist forces were not just involved in a cleanup operation. Rather, their motive was one of revenge. By September 17th the IDF had reached the conclusion that there was a massacre going on. Right away the commander of the IDF Northern Front, General Amir Drori, summoned the representatives of the Phalangist forces and demanded they leave Sabra and Shatila. They withdrew from the camps by the morning of September 18.

But it was too late. What had occurred was a massacre of some 700-800 people. Most were Palestinian Arabs, but not all. Most of the victims were men, but women and children were killed as well. Israeli society was shocked and sickened when the story broke all over the Israeli media. One of the largest demonstrations in the history of Israel took place in Tel Aviv in which 400,000 people participated. They called for an independent commission to investigate how this could occur under Israel's watch. There were calls for Begin, Sharon and other members of the government to resign. The pressure of this giant rally had its intended effect. A special commission was set up to investigate the events that led up to the Phalangist massacre at the camps. The president of the Israeli Supreme Court, Justice Yitzchak Kahan, was named as chairman. The Kahan Commission had the power to subpoena, and Begin, Sharon, Foreign Minister Shamir, IDF Chief-of-Staff Raful Eitan and many others were called in to testify.

By February of 1983 the Kahan Commission issued its findings. In brief, its conclusions were that there was no intention by anyone on the Israeli side, military or government, to have any civilian harmed in the Sabra and Shatila refugee camps, but that it had been a very bad error in judgment to allow the Phalangist forces to enter these camps. Furthermore, it recommended that

Defense Minister Sharon resign, that the Director of Military Intelligence, General Yehoshua Saguy, be removed, that Brigadier General Amos Yaron be relieved of command positions for three years, and that the tenure of Rafael "Raful" Eitan, one of the most respected chiefs-of-staff in the history of the IDF, not be renewed. While the commission clearly did not believe that anyone in the IDF had acted in a way that would have given the Phalangist forces approval for their actions, it did make clear that there was a serious lack of oversight and very bad judgment on the part of the IDF chain of command and its civilian overseers, i.e., the prime minister and the minister of defense.[13] Subsequently, many lessons were learned and changes implemented in the IDF.

A few days after the publication of the Kahan Report there was an anti-Begin demonstration near the prime minister's residence in Jerusalem. They were not satisfied with the conclusions of the report and wanted Begin and Sharon to resign. By this point the country was spilt between those who were in support of Operation Peace for Galilee, who focused on the achievements of the IDF and how the Galilee was now safe. In fact, thousands of Israelis who had left the Galil began to return to their abandoned homes a few weeks after the end of the war. On the other hand, there was the segment of the country that focused on the eighty kilometer incursion as opposed to the 40 kilometer incursion that was the official plan. They also focused on the IDF's entering an Arab capitol for the first time and the massacres at Sabra and Shatila and the quagmire it had caused for Israel and the IDF. The country had not been this split on a major issue since the early 1950s when there was the debate on accepting German reparations.

At this demonstration a pro-government fanatic, Yonah Avrushmi, was so angry at the anti-Begin/Sharon demonstrators that he threw a grenade into the crowd. The grenade killed Emil Grunzweig, a 33-year-old IDF veteran (Avrushmi received a life prison sentence). Over 10,000 people attended his funeral. This was the first war ever fought by the IDF that created a rift within the nation. But the strength of Israeli society and democracy prevailed and eventually people's emotions were channeled into political parties and election results.

When the news of the Sabra and Shatila massacre became common knowledge, the world media reaction was not nuanced, honest, or even remotely objective. There were headlines screaming that the IDF had committed a massacre of epic proportions, or that the IDF had sent in the Phalangist forces to do the dirty work for them. Israel, and Jews in general, were chastised for being behind this massacre in one way or another. There were articles, editorials and demonstrations around the world against Israel. The massacre at Sabra and Shatila became yet another "atrocity" committed by the violent Zionists. There was no interest in the details of what had happened. And to this day not one of the members of the Phalangist militia that committed the massacre has stood trial or has been punished for his role in the massacre.

ISRAEL AND LEBANON: OCTOBER 1982-JUNE 1999

A week after Bashir Gemayel was assassinated his brother Amin was elected president. Amin, unfortunately, was much closer to the Syrians than he was to Israel, having learned the lesson of what happens to Arab leaders who are too close to Israel. Though Israel had achieved many of its strategic goals in Operation Peace for Galilee, the assassination of Bashir Gemayel and the Phalangist massacres at Sabra and Shatila had radically changed the security and political landscape of Lebanon.

The IDF soon found itself in the middle of a shooting war in the Shouf Mountains by early 1983. There was also great instability in and around Beirut itself, which was now under the control of the multinational force comprised of U.S., Italian, French and Lebanese personnel.

On April 18, 1983, a suicide bomber driving a van devastated the U.S. embassy in Beirut, killing 63 people, including 17 Americans. Then, on October 23, a Lebanese terrorist plowed his bomb-laden truck through three guard posts, a barbed-wire fence, and into the lobby of the Marines Corps headquarters in Beirut, where he detonated a massive bomb, killing 241 marine, navy, and army personnel.[14]

This led to the withdrawal of the U.S. contingent of the multinational force; thereafter, the Italians and French left as well.

After the election of Amin Gemayel as president of Lebanon, Israel began negotiating with the new government on what was hoped to be a formal peace treaty between the two countries. Eventually, on May 17, 1983, an agreement was signed that would have created a peaceful relationship between Israel and Lebanon, with a full withdrawal of all foreign forces including the IDF and the Syrian Army. Syria refused to recognize the treaty.

UNIFIL had been sitting in South Lebanon since 1978 after Operation Litani, and had been, at best ineffective and, at worst, an impediment to peace by turning a blind eye to the PLO military buildup in South Lebanon. The multinational force brought in in August of 1982 to help create a buffer between East and West Beirut and between the IDF and Beirut was, similarly, too small and not sufficiently armed to insure that there would be quiet and peace in Beirut, let alone a larger part of Lebanon. In essence their main job became to protect themselves from anti-Western forces operating in and around Beirut. When they couldn't even do that, they left—another example of a failed agreement imposed upon Israel.

Shortly after Bashir Gemayel's assassination, fighting began between Syrian and Phalangist forces, and Phalangist forces and the Druze who lived in the Shouf Mountains south of Beirut. This created more of a headache for the IDF who did not enter Lebanon to act as a policeman between its warring factions. After the IDF had one its headquarters in Sidon blown up in June of 1983, the decision was made to withdraw from the Shouf Mountains and redeploy behind the Awali River, twenty-seven kilometers north of the Israeli-Lebanese ceasefire lines established in February of

1983. The IDF remained in this position for two more years. But this redeployment created a set of new problems: 1) The IDF was still sitting in a large area of South Lebanon and was no longer seen as the liberator it was in 1982, but rather as an occupying force. 2) A new Shiite organization, Hezbollah, picked up on the theme of ending the Israeli occupation of South Lebanon and began to launch attacks against the IDF, causing many casualties. 3) There was still inter-Lebanese fighting going on in this large area where the IDF was deployed. Again, not the role the IDF had planned for itself in Lebanon.

Thus, in June of 1985, the IDF withdrew from the Awali River line to the area that had been the Israeli Security Zone since 1978. In the summer of 1985 the IDF deployed forces there that worked together with the SLA until the summer of 1999 when then-prime minister Ehud Barak decided to withdraw the IDF in response to pressure from several Leftist groups in Israel, chief among them the Four Mothers.* This group's main argument for withdrawal was the casualties the IDF incurred in South Lebanon—around

* "Four Mothers-Leaving Lebanon in Peace, according to journalistic and academic sources, was a remarkably successful antiwar movement—"probably the most influential protest movement in the history of Israel.".... Between 1997 and 2000, movement activists helped turn Israeli public opinion against a counterinsurgency war that Israel had been fighting in Lebanon since 1982. The group, which was the only national grassroots movement active against the war at the time... Movement leaders... used both religious and secular nationalist imagery to appeal to Jewish Israeli public opinion, which, in the course of the Four Mothers protest, shifted from less than 35 percent in favor of unilaterally ending Israel's military presence in Lebanon to more than 70 percent in favor. This opinion shift was attributable not only to the movement's demonstrations, lobbying, petitions, and media and public education campaigns: Increasing Israeli casualties in Lebanon, some dramatic military disasters, and the government and military's inability to articulate attainable goals and strategies for the war were also important factors. However, as the Four Mothers protest expanded into a national movement, it managed to garner considerable media and public attention to its message: that Israel's 16-year-long war in southern Lebanon had failed to protect the northern communities—the war's ostensible purpose at that stage—and had pointlessly endangered two generations of Israeli (cont'd)

35 IDF soldiers killed annually and over 100 wounded. What was not spoken about by the group was the peace for northern Israel that the Security Zone had provided. Between 1985-1999 there had been perhaps only two to three successful terrorist attacks in that area with hundreds of terrorists killed on their way to Israel through the Security Zone. It had been a very effective deterrent. Northern Israel had enjoyed a quiet 14-year period which had fostered economic and demographic growth.

Unfortunately, the withdrawal was poorly managed and not coordinated with the SLA. Many SLA men were subsequently captured by Hezbollah and many others fled the country. Sadly, SLA and IDF equipment fell into Hezbollah's hands. Israel had signaled weakness by withdrawing hastily and unilaterally.

At the time the UN praised the Israeli withdrawal and even sent inspectors to the Israel-Lebanon ceasefire lines to insure that Israel had actually withdrawn from every last centimeter of Lebanon. Subsequently, the UN declared that Israel was in full compliance with UN Security Council Resolution 425 which was passed in 1978 after Operation Litani. But within a few weeks the UN was back to condemning Israel for anything any Arab country would bring up as a real or perceived Israeli infractions, while never condemning Arab states or Islamic terror groups for their actions against Israelis.

Finally, Barak had hoped that Hezbollah would now have no reason to fight Israel since it was no longer an "occupying" force

soldiers as well...In 1999, in the context of national elections and antiwar trends in public opinion, Labor party leader Ehud Barak pledged to withdraw the army, if he were elected prime minister. Barak was elected prime minister and then in May 2000 ordered the soldiers' return to Israel. Four Mothers-Leaving Lebanon in Peace, as an ad hoc movement focused on ending Israel's military involvement in Lebanon, voted to dissolve itself soon afterward." (Rachel Ben Dor Daniel Lieberfeld, "Mission Accomplished? Israel's Four Mothers and the Legacies of Successful Antiwar Movements," *International Journal of Peace Studies*, Vol 13:1, Spring/Summer 2008 (85-97), 86 (https://www.gmu.edu/programs/icar/ijps/vol13_1/IJPS13n1%20BenDor&Lieberfeld.pdf))

in South Lebanon. But, alas, that was not to be. Hezbollah made two new claims: 1) Hezbollah claimed that an area called Shebaa Farms*, which lies adjacent to the Golan Heights near the Lebanese side, belonged to Lebanon and since Israel was still occupying it, she would continue her resistance to Israel, and 2) Hezbollah announced its solidarity with the Palestinian people and their cause to liberate all of Palestine. Hence, they would continue to fight the Zionist oppressor even if Israel did return Shebaa Farms.

Once again Israel was shown by her Arab neighbors that no matter what she did to appease them comity was illusory.

---

* "Shebaa Farms is a small strip of disputed land at the intersection of the Lebanese-Syrian border and the Israeli-occupied Golan Heights. The territory is about 11 kilometres (7 mi) long and 2.5 kilometres (2 mi) wide.

The dispute over ownership of Shebaa Farms resulted in part from the failure of the French Mandate administrations, and later the Lebanese and Syrian governments, to demarcate the border between Lebanon and Syria. Documents from the 1920s and 1930s indicate that inhabitants paid taxes to the Lebanese government. However, from the early 1950s until Israel's occupation of the Golan Heights in the Six-Day War, Syria was the de facto ruling power.

In 1981, the Golan Heights, which include Shebaa Farms, were annexed by Israel, a move not recognized by the international community. The territory has been a flashpoint for violence since Israel withdrew from Lebanon in May 2000. Hezbollah claimed that the withdrawal was not complete because Shebaa was on Lebanese – not Syrian – territory. After studying 81 different maps, the United Nations concluded that there is no evidence of the abandoned farmlands being Lebanese." (https://en.wikipedia.org/wiki/Shebaa_farms as derived from Asher Kaufman, "Understanding the Sheeba Farms dispute," *Palestine-Israel Journal*, 11 (1), 2004; Greg Myre and Hassan M. Fattah, "Israel and Militants Trade Fire Across Lebanese Border," *New York Times*, May 29, 2006 (http://www.nytimes.com/2006/05/29/world/middleeast/29mideast.html?_r=0); Yaniv Berman, "Shebaa Farms - nub of conflict, Ynet news.com, 10.8.06 (http://www.ynetnews.com/articles/0,7340,L-3289532,00.html); Herb Keinon, "Har Dov Withdrawl Not on the Table," *Jerusalem Post*, July 26, 2006 (http://www.jpost.com/Israel/Har-Dov-withdrawal-not-on-the-table)

Footnotes

1 https://en.wikipedia.org/wiki/Lebanese_Civil_War

2 https://en.wikipedia.org/wiki/Coastal_Road_massacre as derived from Richard Ernest Dupuy, Trevor Nevitt Dupuy (chamel), "1978, March 11. The Coastal Road Massacre," *The Encyclopedia of Military History from 3500 B.C. to the Present* (NY: Harper & Row, 1986), 1362; Gregory S. Mahler, "Operation Litani is launched in retaliation for that month's Coastal Road massacre." *Politics and Government in Israel: The Maturation of a Modern State* (Lanham, MD: Rowman & Littlefield, 2004), 259; Moshe Brilliant, "Israeli officials Say Gunmen Intended to Seize Hotel," *New York Times*, March 13, 1978.

3 David K. Shipler, "Cease-Fire In Border Fighting Declared By Israel and P.L.O.; U.S. Sees Hope For Wider Peace," *New York Times*, July 25, 1981 (http://www.nytimes.com/1981/07/25/world/cease-fire-border-fighting-declared-israel-plo-us-sees-hope-for-wider-peace.html)

4 Edward Alexander, *NBC's War in Lebanon: The Distorting Mirror.* (http://www.afsi.org/pamphlets/NBC_war_in_lebanon_alexander[1].pdf, 1.)

5 The best insight into one of the key phenomena at play here comes not from a local reporter but from the journalist and author Philip Gourevitch. In Rwanda and elsewhere in Africa, Gourevitch wrote in 2010, he was struck by the ethical gray zone of ties between reporters and NGOs. "Too often the press represents humanitarians with unquestioning admiration," he observed in *The New Yorker*. "Why not seek to keep them honest? Why should our coverage of them look so much like their own selfrepresentation in fundraising appeals? Why should we (as many photojournalists and print reporters do) work for humanitarian agencies between journalism jobs, helping them with their official reports and

institutional appeals, in a way that we would never consider doing for corporations, political parties, or government agencies?"

This confusion is very much present in Israel and the Palestinian territories, where foreign activists are a notable feature of the landscape, and where international NGOs and numerous arms of the United Nations are among the most powerful players, wielding billions of dollars and employing many thousands of foreign and local employees... The dominant characteristic of nearly all of these people is their transience. They arrive from somewhere, spend a while living in a peculiar subculture of expatriates, and then move on. In these circles, in my experience, a distaste for Israel has come to be something between an acceptable prejudice and a prerequisite for entry. I don't mean a critical approach to Israeli policies or to the hamfisted government currently in charge in this country, but a belief that to some extent the Jews of Israel are a symbol of the world's ills, particularly those connected to nationalism, militarism, colonialism, and racism—an idea quickly becoming one of the central elements of the "progressive" Western zeitgeist, spreading from the European left to American college campuses and intellectuals, including journalists. Philip Gourevitch "What the Media Gets Wrong About Israel," *The Atlantic*, 12/4/2014 (http://www.theatlantic.com/international/ print/2014/11/howthemediamakestheisraelstory/383262/ 4/11)

[6] *Op. cit.*, 8.

[7] David K. Shipler, "Lebanese Tell of Anguish of Living Under the P.L.O.," *New York Times*, 7/25/82.

[8] Martin Peretz, "Lebanon Eyewitness," *New Republic*, August 2, 1982, 15 (15-23)

[9] Rebecca Grant, "The Bekaa Valley War," *Air Force Magazine*, June 2002 (http://www.airforcemag.com/MagazineArchive/Pag-es/2002/June%202002/0602bekaa.aspx)

[10] "What was the largest air-to-air jet battle in history?," *Quora* (https://www.quora.com/What-was-the-largest-air-to-air-jet-battle-in-history)

[11] "PLO: Now the Story Can Be Told," ed. Eliyahu Tal (Tel Aviv: Achduth, 1982)

[12] *Los Angeles Examiner*, July 13, 1982; *Maariv*, July 16 1982

[13] "First Lebanon War: The Kahan Commission of Inquiry (February 8, 1983)" Israel Ministry of Foreign Affairs (http://www.jewishvirtuallibrary.org/jsource/History/kahan.html)

[14] "October 23, 1983: Beirut barracks blown up," *The History Channel* (http://www.history.com/this-day-in-history/beirut-barracks-blown-up)

Chapter 16

Major Events: 1981-1993

ISRAEL'S DESTRUCTION OF IRAQ'S NUCLEAR REACTOR: MAY 1981

After a falling out with the Soviet Union that entailed the loss of a Russian-promised nuclear reactor, Saddam Hussein, the volatile dictator of Iraq since 1979, was about to have his now French-supplied nuclear reactor in Osirak completed. On many occasions Saddam had publicly stated that when his nuclear plant was operational he would manufacture nuclear weapons and use them to destroy Israel,* his hatred of Israel, Zionism and Jews being a driving force behind his desire to see Israel annihilated.

> On March 27, 1979, Saddam Hussein...laid out his vision for a long, grinding war against Israel in a private meeting of high-level Baathist officials. Iraq, he explained, would seek to obtain a nuclear weapon from "our Soviet friends," use the resulting deterrent power to counteract Israeli threats of nuclear retaliation, and thereby enable a "patient war"—a war

---

*Following the U.S. invasion of Iraq in 2003, American forces captured a number of documents detailing conversations that Saddam Hussein had with his inner sanctum. In a 1982 conversation Hussein stated that, "Once Iraq walks out victorious [over Iran], there will not be any Israel." Of Israel's anti-Iraq endeavors he noted, "Technically, they [the Israelis] are right in all of their attempts to harm Iraq." (Michael R.Gordon, "Papers From Iraqi Archive Reveal Conspiratorial Mind-Set of Hussein," *New York Times*, 25 October 2011.)

of attrition—that would reclaim Arab lands lost in the Six Day War of 1967. As Saddam put it, nuclear weapons would allow Iraq to "guarantee the long war that is destructive to our enemy, and take at our leisure each meter of land and drown the enemy with rivers of blood...."[1]

Saddam's animus toward Israel flowed from several factors. There was, of course, opportunism—haranguing the Zionists always played well in Iraqi politics and the Arab world. There was also the long history of conflict between Israel and its Arab neighbors, a struggle that had flared during the early years of the Baathist regime. The Baathist government contributed one division to the Syrian front during the Yom Kippur War of 1973; Israel, for its part, sought to bleed and distract the radical Baathist government by supporting an insurgency among Iraq's Kurdish population. These events, as well as the broader legacy of Arab-Israeli strife, weighed heavily on Saddam's perceptions."[2]

Ever since Saddam began construction on the nuclear reactor, Israel's top leaders had begun to plan how to keep Iraq from becoming an existential threat to the homeland. As a result of such planning, and in recognition of the potential commencement of operations at the Osirak plant, in late May 1981 the Israeli Air Force launched a daring raid from an airbase in southern Israel and wiped out the reactor,* setting back Saddam's nuclear weapons program by at least 10 years. (One of the pilots in this historic raid was Ilan Ramon, who later became Israel's first astronaut and tragically died in the 2003 Atlantis shuttle disaster.)

At the time Israel was roundly condemned by the world community, but by the 1991 Gulf War the same complainants began to view the raid in a more positive light.

---

* Eight F-16s, belonging to both 117 and 110 Squadrons both based at Ramat David, took off from Etzion, the best placed base for the attack, escorted by six F-15s while an E-2C Hawkeye provided airborne early warning and control and several CH-53s for SAR duties were deployed near the Iraqi border. Two more Fighting Falcons were kept as a reserve.

The F-16s were armed with two 2,000 pounds Mk. 84, two AIM-9J (cont'd)

[In fact, in 1991] U.S. Secretary of Defense Dick Cheney sent the Israeli Air Force commander who oversaw the operation, David Ivri, an enlarged black-and-white U.S. satellite photograph of Osirak, taken a few days after the IAF raid. Cheney wrote an inscription: "For Gen. David Ivri, with thanks and appreciation for the outstanding job he did on the Iraqi nuclear program in 1981—which made our job much easier in Desert Storm."[3]

It was clear to many members of the vast coalition that lined up against Saddam after his August 1990 invasion and attempted annexation of Kuwait that had he had nuclear weapons at his disposal the events of 1990 and 1991 would have played out very

---

Sidewinders, two 370 gal. external tanks under the wings and one 300 gall tank under the belly.

...[T]he Israeli jets flew more than 600 miles in the skies of three supposedly enemy nations: to reach the target, the first country that the aircraft overflew was northern Saudi Arabia and its deserts.

The route over Iraq was planned not only to avoid the radar coverage but also the airfields; inbound to the target the F-16s flew at an altitude between 150 and 300 ft.

At 17:35 with the sun at their back complicating any intercept attempt, the aircraft arrived over the target: before releasing their bombs the F-16s lit their afterburners at about 12.5 miles from the nuclear plant, climbed to 8,000 ft and then dived at 600 kts releasing their Mk. 84s at 3,500 ft.

The weapons were delivered on target by two waves of four Falcons each.

Even if two bombs missed the target the others were able to destroy and damage the reactor and several facilities. Some Mk. 84s had very long delayed fuzes to avoid any attempts to repair or rebuild the plant.

The attackers remained on the reactor site for less than two minutes and the only opposition they faced were an inefficient AAA fire and some SAM launches which missed the F-16s.

On their way home, the Fighting Falcons climbed to 40,000 ft to save fuel and overflew the third hostile country, Jordan, which however didn't show any opposition against them.

One F-15 and one F-16 diverted from the planned route to complicate any intercept attempts, while all the aircraft landed at Etzion after a 3 hours of mission, during which no aircraft was damaged. ("Operation Opera: how 8 Israeli F-16s destroyed an Iraqi nuclear plant 33 years ago today," The Aviaionist, Jun 07 2014 (https://theaviationist.com/2014/06/07/operation-opera-explained/)

differently and could have very well led to a Saddam-dominated Persian Gulf and Middle East—a nightmare scenario.

ISRAEL ANNEXES THE GOLAN HEIGHTS: DECEMBER 14, 1981

Fourteen years after the Six-Day War Israel changed the legal status of the Golan Heights from occupied territory to Israeli territory on December 14, 1981. Syria, unlike Egypt, was seen as a deadly foe whose goal (which had been articulated by the Syrian leadership in print and in speeches) was the annihilation of the State of Israel. Thus, Syria was not a country with which Israel could even hope of negotiating a peace settlement. Hence, Israel "annexed" the Golan, granting citizenship to the 15,000 Druze who lived there.

> It was Syria's hard-line stance that Mr. Begin cited as an immediate reason for his action. He quoted a report in the Kuwaiti newspaper Al Rai Al Amm ... that President Hafez al-Assad of Syria had expressed the determination to refuse to recognize Israel "even if the Palestinians deign to do so."[4]

Though the world community refused to acknowledge Israel's annexation (on December 17, 1981 the United Nations Security Council unanimously declared the annexation null and void in Resolution 497), Israel's most recent government avows that the Golan will remain a part of Israel in perpetuity.[5] And considering the ongoing civil war in Syria wherein the breakup of the former state is now being discussed as a strong possibility, international law may swing in Israel's behalf to legally accept Israel's annexation of the Golan.*

---

* "The purpose of international law is to protect the international order, one in which states exist within secure and recognized borders. When the law provides no clear answers, it should be interpreted in the spirit of bolstering this international order. If the international community wishes to do this, nothing can legally stop it. The only way to bolster this international order and resolve the open question of the Golan is to recognize Israeli control over the territory.

From the Israeli perspective, this is obvious. Realistically speaking, (cont'd)

OPERATION MOSES: THE RESCUE OF ETHIOPIAN JEWRY: 1984-85

In 1955 Graenum Berger, an American communal administrator and institutional and community planner from The Bronx, New York, went to Israel and met Ethiopian Jewish students who were studying there. The encounter led to a decade-long study of the Ethiopian tribe known as the Beta Israel/Falasha. In 1965 he traveled to the country where he found an "outsider" people, impoverished and discriminated against in the most terrible ways. As a result, he came back to the States and founded the American Association for Ethiopian Jews. At first he thought that his Jewish community colleagues would help him set up a system with the Israelis to rescue the Beta Israel from their awful fate. He was wrong. It took him and his supporters 20 years to convince the global Jewish community and the Israelis to bring some 25,000 Jews to the land they had prayed for and had dreamed about for centuries.

Despite the continued debate in the Israeli-Ashkenzi community about the authenticity of the purported lost tribe of Dan, the Sephardi community had long accepted Ethiopia's Beta Israel as legitimate Jews entitled to Israeli citizenship under the law of return. As the 16th century Chief Rabbi of Egypt, Rabbi David Ben Solomon Ibn Zimra, also known as the Radnaz, declared, "[These [Jews] who come from the Land of Cush are without a doubt of the tribe of Dan."[6]

---

there is no longer any incentive for Israel to return the Heights to Damascus. Until recently, some in Israel hoped to offer the Golan in order to seduce Syria away from the Iranian axis, a bold gamble to thwart Tehran's push for regional hegemony. But with Iran emboldened by the recent nuclear deal and Syria now firmly under its domination, that possibility is foreclosed. (Eylon Asan-Levy, "The Case for Israeli Sovereignty in the Golan Heights," *The Tower*, Issue 38, May 1926 (http://www.thetower.org/article/the-case-for-israeli-sovereignty-in-the-golan-heights/)

Why then didn't Israel respond sooner to the Beta Israel's plight? Because of religion and politics. Religiously, the Beta Israel had for 2,500 years been separated from the main thrust of Ashkenzi and Sephardic Jewry, and thus their practices and rituals were different. Because they had not been exposed to Rabbinic Judaism (the *Talmud, Shulchan Aruch,* etc.) they did not practice the Jewry observed by the modern-day world. As such, despite the Radnaz's declaration, there was great debate among the Israeli rabbinate as to the Jewish legitimacy of this "lost tribe." Still, in 1973, Israel's Sephardic Chief Rabbi [Ovadia Yosef] decided they were Jews and deserved repatriation to the Jewish homeland. To this day, however, there are many in Israel's *rabbanut* who question their authenticity and discriminate against them in education and incorporating them as part of mainstream Orthodox communities.[7]

Politically, Ethiopian Emperor Haile Selassie was one of the few allies Israel had in North Africa, and he did not want the Beta Israel/Falasha to leave. Because they were one of many diverse ethnic groups in the country, he feared that once the doors were open everyone else would leave as well, causing chaos and making it harder for him to control his subjects. The Israelis accommodated him by not bringing the Falasha to Israel until after he was dethroned.[8] Selassie was deposed in 1974 by the Derg, a Soviet-backed Marxist–Leninist military dictatorship led by Mengistu Haile Mariam.[9]

Once Haile Selassie was gone, those Beta Israel who could then fled to Sudan seeking relief from famine and a way to the Promised Land. Berger's group, the American Association for Ethiopian Jewry, tried to rescue them with little result, complaining that the Israelis were not doing enough. But Israeli Mossad agents were already there. Because Sudan was at war with Israel, Israel needed eyes on the ground. Once the Mossad discovered the size of the population of Beta Israel living in Sudanese refugee camps and their dire condition, they began quietly creating an infrastructure to smuggle Ethiopian Jews into Israel.[10]

And so, by 1984, when large numbers of Beta Israel were dying of hunger in Sudanese refugee camps, the Israelis, with funding from the organized diaspora Jewish community, began to implement Operation Moses, the rescue of the Jews of Ethiopia. Working with the the U.S.'s Central Intelligence Agency (CIA) in Khartoum, the Mossad made arrangements with the security services of the Sudanese government to begin airlifts to Israel. The refugees were moved first to a Sudanese town called Gedaref and from there to Khartoum. The Israelis chartered the flights through a Belgian airline, and the first flight left Khartoum (where a special runway was built) on November 21, 1984. In that first "operation," more than 8,000 Ethiopian Jews were rescued. All went well until January 5, 1985, when Israeli Prime Minister Shimon Peres confirmed published reports about the airlifts and effectively brought the operation to a halt. Fearing retaliation from other countries in the Arab bloc, Sudan ended the flights and 800 people were left stranded in Khartoum. Eight weeks later, with the approval of then-U.S. President Ronald Reagan and the active efforts of Vice-President George H.W. Bush, the Sudanese president was convinced to finish the airlift. Thus began Operation Sheba.* At a special runway near the refugee camps in Sudan,

---

*As the economic and political conditions inside Ethiopia deteriorated [in the 1970s], tens of thousands of people began to cross the border to neighboring Sudan. Many Ethiopian Jews joined the exodus. In 1979, the Israelis and, to a smaller degree, private groups began to evacuate the Ethiopian Jews from Sudan by various covert means and bring them to Israel. As word reached the Jewish villages in Ethiopia that the route to Israel lay through Sudan, the flow of Jewish refugees across the border increased dramatically.

After cleaning out the refugee camps of most of the Ethiopian Jews by the winter of 1984, the Israelis discovered that the camps were soon being overwhelmed by new Jewish refugees. It became clear to the Mossad that their previous methods of rescue would not allow them to evacuate the Ethiopian Jews fast enough to prevent them from dying in large numbers in the squalid camps. In addition, the primary method employed by the Mossad—periodic flights from a secret airstrip in the desert near the refugee camps—could not be continued because the risk of being caught and exposing the entire operation had become too great.

Israeli officials then apparently approached the United States and asked for

Mossad agents drove them to the airfield where U.S. transport planes and Israeli C-130 Hercules aircraft, working in twenty-minute shifts, picked them up and took them to Tel Aviv.[11]

As the Mengistu regime faltered in 1991 and rebel forces began to take control, a deal was made for the emigration of some 15,000 Beta Israel still living in Ethiopia. Again with the help of now-President George H.W. Bush[12], the new Shamir government developed a plan to move the entire group to Israel within a 36-hour time frame. Using an armada of El Al planes and IAF C-130s, and flying on the Sabbath with special rabbinic dispensation in compliance with the Jewish law of *pikuach nefesh* (saving a life),

---

help in rescuing the Ethiopian Jews from Sudan. This request created a major dilemma for the United States because, unlike Israel which was technically at war with Sudan, the United States enjoyed very close relations with President Gaafar el-Numeiry.... The United States provided Sudan with large amounts of aid and, consequently, had a great deal of leverage over Numeiry. In 1984, the Sudanese president was in urgent need of further U.S. aid because of his country's failing economy, civil unrest, and the need to take care of the nearly half million refugees living there. The problem was that, as a member of the Arab League, Numeiry could not afford to be seen helping the "Zionists." U.S. officials were well aware of the instability of Sudan and were hesitant to do anything that might further endanger Numeiry's regime.

It was in this context that a representative of Sudan came to the United States in June 1984 to ask for additional economic aid. In a meeting with Richard Krieger and Ambassador Eugene Douglas of the State Department, Krieger decided to play on the anti-Semitic feelings of his visitor and suggest that the approval of the omnipotent Jewish lobby would be necessary to obtain congressional support for an increase in aid. He suggested that Sudan could help by allowing the United States to take the Ethiopian Jews out of the refugee camps. "Besides," Krieger added, "these people are nothing but a burden on the Sudan." The Sudanese official found this line of argument appealing and steps were put into motion to arrange a rescue operation.

Krieger later flew to Jerusalem to inform the Israelis that an understanding had been reached and then finalized plans with the Sudanese official in Geneva. The refugee affairs coordinator at the U.S. embassy in Khartoum, Jerry Weaver, met with Sudanese Vice President and Security Chief Omar Tayeb and secured his agreement to a plan for evacuating the Ethiopian Jews. Weaver, the Israeli Mossad, and the Sudanese secret police then devised the secret operation.

That operation, later known as "Operation Moses," began on November 21, 1984, and continued until January 5, 1985. Every night during that period,

on May 24, 1991 Operation Solomon began to airlift 14,324 Beta
Israel to reunite with family and to become citizens of *Eretz Yisrael*.
Though the flight was but 1,000 miles, it nevertheless became a
trip of 2,500 years for an agrarian community now faced with life
in a multi-ethnic, high-tech society. Assimilation has not been easy
for the Beta Israel, but progress proceeds apace, as does Israel's

except the Sabbath, buses would pick up groups of about fifty-five Ethiopian
Jews from the refugee camps and take them to Khartoum where they would
board Boeing 707s. The planes belonged to Trans European Airlines, a Belgian
company owned by an Orthodox Jew, and were used routinely as charter planes
to carry Muslim pilgrims to Mecca. Altogether, thirty-six flights carrying approximately 220 passengers flew first to Brussels and then on to Tel Aviv. A total
of 7,800 Ethiopian Jews was rescued by this method.

News of the airlift eventually leaked out. When the Israeli government confirmed the stories, the Sudanese ordered the operation stopped. The Ethiopian
government was outraged, but most Americans reacted jubilantly and shared
the feeling of admiration aptly expressed by William Safire: "For the first time
in history, thousands of black people are being brought into a country not in
chains but as citizens."

Sources say that all of the Jews in the Sudanese refugee camps would have
reached Israel if the airlift had continued for only two more days. Instead, officials believed, perhaps as many as two thousand Jews were left behind in the
camps.

Almost immediately, Israeli and American officials began to look for ways
to resume the rescue. Senators Alan Cranston and Alfonse D'Amato gathered
signatures of all one-hundred senators on a letter to President Reagan urging
him to use American influence with Sudan to encourage the resumption of the
airlift. The president called Cranston and told him, "We'll take care of what's
going on."

According to Richard Krieger, by the time the letter reached the president
on February 21, 1985, plans had already been made to finish the rescue. Vice-
President George Bush was scheduled to visit Numeiry in March and was given
approval by Reagan to raise the issue of another airlift with the Sudanese leader.

U.S. officials had considered resuming Operation Moses, but, when Bush
met with Numeiry on March 3, 1985, he found that Numeiry did not want a
repeat of the earlier fiasco. Instead, he agreed to a quick, one-shot operation.
Numeiry insisted, however, that the planned operation be carried out secretly by
the Americans and not the Israelis and that the flights not go directly to Israel...
Bush met with Weaver and the CIA station chief in Khartoum to discuss means
for carrying out the president's order to rescue the Ethiopian Jews remaining in

continued attempt to locate more of those claiming to be Jews still remaining in Ethiopia.

PLO CLAIMS READINESS TO RECOGNIZE ISRAEL

[On November 15, 1988, in Algiers,] Yasir Arafat, the chairman of the Palestine Liberation Organization, early today declared the establishment of an independent Palestinian state as part of a broad political program that recognizes Israel, at least implicitly, for the first time.

In a speech to the Palestine National Council, the parliament in exile of the Palestinian movement, Mr. Arafat declared, "The Palestine National Council announces in the name of God, in the name of the people, of the Arab Palestinian people, the establishment of the state of Palestine in our Palestinian nation, with holy Jerusalem as its capital."

He did not indicate the borders of such a state, although he said a 1947 United Nations partition plan, which provided for a Jewish state and an Arab state in Palestine, still offers a basis for "international legitimacy."

The state envisioned by Mr. Arafat is assumed to include the West Bank of the Jordan River and the Gaza Strip, which are occupied by Israel, and the Arab sector of Jerusalem,

---

Sudan. To avoid the possibility of disclosure, Reagan wanted the operation carried out within three to four days. Weaver took an embassy plane to check out the runway of a remote airstrip near Gedaref, midway between the camps where most of the Ethiopian Jews were living, and found that it would be acceptable for the operation.

On March 28, 1985, the operation, codenamed "Sheba," began with Ethiopian Jews from Israel working for the Mossad identifying the Ethiopian Jews in the camps and taking them by truck to the airstrip. The airstrip itself was eight miles outside of Gedaref, just far enough so that it would be difficult to spot the planes from the town.

Planes designed to hold ninety passengers each were prepared at the American base near Frankfurt, West Germany. Planes filled with food, water, and medical supplies were flown from an Israeli military base near Eilat to the airstrip in Sudan. These camouflaged U.S. Hercules transports landed at twenty-minute intervals to pick up their passengers. Sudanese security officers cordoned off the area and, by 9:00 a.m., all of the Ethiopian Jews were evacuated. Instead

which Israel considers its own. Thus, the announcement was mainly a political declaration of hope and intent without immediate practical meaning.[13]

But another of Arafat's attempts to gain power and vilify Israel, the proclamation of statehood was readily accepted by an all too-willing United Nations as Palestinian recognition of Israel and an end to the persistent turmoil in the region. While the document speaks of resolutions 242 and 338, which recognize Israel as a Jewish State that has the right to live in secure and recognized boundaries, on the other hand this same document speaks of the Zionist entity—a pejorative term—and affirms that the Intifada must continue until the Zionist entity ends its occupation, an occupation that began in 1948, as the land it seeks to reclaim are all those won in Israel's three major wars. Furthermore, it was also all to easy to disregard the proviso...

> The National Council also renews its commitment to the United Nations resolutions that affirm the right of peoples to resist foreign occupation, imperialism and racial discrimination, and their right to fight for their independence....[14]

—which by no means prevents the PLO from further engagement in terrorist acts against Israel in its "right to fight for independence."

---

of going to an intermediate destination, the planes flew directly to an Israeli air force base outside Eilat where the passengers were greeted by Prime Minister Shimon Peres. The organizers had prepared to airlift as many as two thousand Ethiopian Jews from the camps, but they found only 494, so three planes returned from Sudan empty....

Soon after Operation Sheba, Numeiry was overthrown. The timing was largely coincidental, since his fall had been expected by U.S. officials for some time. Vice-President Tayeb and other Sudanese suspected of cooperating with the rescue of the Ethiopian Jews were either imprisoned or executed. (Mitchell Bard and Howard Lenhoff, "Ethiopian Jewry: America's Role in the Rescue of Ethiopian Jewry," Jewish Virtual Library (http://www.jewishvirtuallibrary.org/america-s-role-in-the-rescue-of-ethiopian-jewry)

Thus, in its perpetual wisdom as related to the State of Israel, the UN General Assembly...

...adopted a resolution in which it "acknowledg[ed] the proclamation of the State of Palestine by the Palestine National Council on 15 November 1988," and, further, decided that "the designation 'Palestine' should be used in place of the designation 'Palestine Liberation Organization' in the United Nations system." One hundred and four states voted for this resolution, forty-four abstained; only the United States and Israel voted against.[15]

On the heels of the November proclamation, in December 1988 five Jews from the International Center For Peace in the Middle East met with Arafat in Switzerland in an attempt to further Israeli-Palestinian relations. While they returned all aglow with what they assumed were positive negotiations—although they represented no one but themselves—their euphoria eventually dimmed. As one of the participants, Menachem Rosensaft later wrote:

"We believed him," Rosensaft wrote in the Washington Post, "when he said that he and the PLO were committed to a political solution to the Israeli-Palestinian conflict. We believed him when he proclaimed an end to terrorism. We were wrong. . . . Of course the Palestinians were entitled to self-determination—even independence—but only on terms of mutual respect. The Palestinians' claims of nationhood could not stand separate and apart from their acknowledgment that Israelis are entitled to precisely the same rights. Arafat and his colleagues gave lip service to these lofty sentiments. We believed them. We were wrong. . . . Perhaps, in time, the Palestinians will realize that a different leader will better serve them and their cause. Perhaps they will realize that stabbing and stomping Israeli soldiers to death and then parading their mutilated bodies in an obscene triumph is not acceptable behavior in the 21st century. Perhaps. But then, we also believe in the eventual arrival of the Messiah. In the meantime, those of us who wanted so desperately to see Arafat as a positive, constructive presence of any kind must reiterate over and over again: We were wrong."[16]

1989-2000: OPERATION EXODUS

Upon the initiation of perestroika and the easing of emigration laws, over 900,000 Jews—and some non-Jews posing as Jews to escape from a crumbling USSR—made *Aliyah* to Israel.

"To appreciate the impact on this small country, this is comparable to the arrival of 60 million new immigrants to the United States over a period of three to five years."[17]

This was the largest influx of new *olim* since the 1950s. The *Aliyah*, clearly a blessing because of the number of university graduates, scientists, medical personnel, etc. among the new immigrants, caused Israel severe economic and social problems as it had to provide housing, economic support, job placement and education for the new arrivals. Israel's Jewish population hit the 4 million mark for the first time since the days of the *Second Beit Ha'Mikdash*.

JANUARY-FEBRUARY 1991: IRAQI INVASION OF KUWAIT AND OPERATION DESERT STORM

After Saddam Hussein's invasion and annexation of Kuwait in August of 1990, the rest of the Arab world—led by a Saudi regime that feared it was Saddam's next target—supported a U.S.-led coalition to liberate Kuwait. Though Israel was not invited to be part of the coalition, Saddam's history of anti-Israel belligerence caused a flurry of activity in Israel's defense forces. From the day of the Iraqi invasion, the military equation for the IDF changed. Since the Iraqis had so easily conquered Kuwait and were now threatening Saudi Arabia, it was conceivable that the massive Iraqi forces could have some of its army turn west and march through Jordan towards Israel. That would mean Israel would be fighting Iraq along most, if not all, of its eastern border. This also meant that the IDF would have to move units and other resources to the Jordanian border, just in case.

This was further complicated by U.S. action. As much as the U.S. was clearly an ally of Israel's during the Gulf War it was equally clear that the two countries' national security interests were not the same. For the U.S., Israel was an ally that presented a problem since President George H.W. Bush had assembled a global coalition against Saddam Hussein that included the entire Arab world. Many Arab states that had very bad relations with each other were able to put these differences aside for the greater good of defending Saudi Arabia, liberating Kuwait and teaching Saddam Hussein a lesson. The only thing from the perspective of President Bush that could break apart this coalition was if Israel entered the war against Saddam; for, as much as the Arab world hated Saddam, apparently there was much greater hatred for Israel. Hence, Israel entering the war could cause some, many or all of the Arab members of the coalition reversing their positions and siding with Saddam in his war against the Zionist entity. This meant that Bush had to make it very clear to Israel's leader that no matter how hard Israel might get hit by Saddam, under no circumstances could Israel retaliate against Iraq.

Fearing possible Israeli intervention should Saddam indeed seek to involve Israel and thus undermine the solidarity of the coalition's Arab participants, Bush sent Secretary of State Lawrence Eagleburger to coordinate policy with Israeli Prime Minister Yitzhak Shamir. Under their subsequent agreement, which included that the U.S. supply Patriot missile batteries for Israeli protection should Saddam actually launch a missile attack upon Israel, the Prime Minister promised that the Israelis would defray involvement in the Gulf War. Shamir's action was a radical departure from usual Israeli policy, a policy which had always involved pre-emptive action or retaliation whenever there was an attack on the homeland. But because Shamir would not outright promise not to retaliate against Iraq should it seek to engage Israel in the war—a political non-starter vis-à-vis Israel's national security—Eagleburger turned down Shamir's request for coordination between Israeli and U.S. troops in the Gulf.[18]

Of major concern to the Israelis was the fact that Saddam had already launched eight Scud missiles onto Haifa and Tel Aviv, though there was little damage. But by not being permitted to react to Saddam's provocation there was a hue and cry as to why there was no reaction on Israel's part. To defray the population's angst, then-Defense Minister Moshe Arens, in an emergency meeting, broached the subject of accepting the batteries of Patriot missiles promised by the U.S. The IDF didn't like them very much, but public pressure for protection was high so IDF Chief of Staff Dan Shomron recommended accepting them. Arens called Dick Cheney, the then-U.S. Secretary of Defense, who immediately agreed to send them. But when five more Scuds landed in Tel Aviv on January 19, the public demanded retaliation for its dead and wounded. Shamir's military advisors asked him to hold off, and they convinced him, Shomron believing that the Americans were already doing a good job of destroying Iraqi materiel and infrastructure. But if Israel continued to take heavy hits, Israel might have to intervene,* especially if the Iraqis used chemical weapons.[19]

Since there was a fear of Iraqi use of poison gas, every Israeli was issued a gas mask, and babies had special covered cribs. Civilians were advised on how to protect their homes and create safe rooms. This was a psychological nightmare because of the association with gas and the deaths of millions of Jews at the hands of the Nazis and their collaborators during WWII, the most

---

*After Shamir's death in 2012, Moshe Arens indicated that Shamir intended to retaliate against Saddam despite his agreement with the Americans. "At the beginning of the war we couldn't launch an attack without coordination with the Americans, but with the continued missile fire, Yitzhak Shamir sent me to Washington to announce that we would take action," Arens told Israel Radio. "But it was exactly at that moment that the American president announced a ceasefire." (PTI, "Israel was prepared to attack Iraq in 1991: Moshe Arens," *Economic Times*, Jul 01, 2012 (http://economictimes.indiatimes.com/news/politics-and-nation/israel-was-prepared-to-attack-iraq-in-1991-moshe-arens/articleshow/14561599.cms)

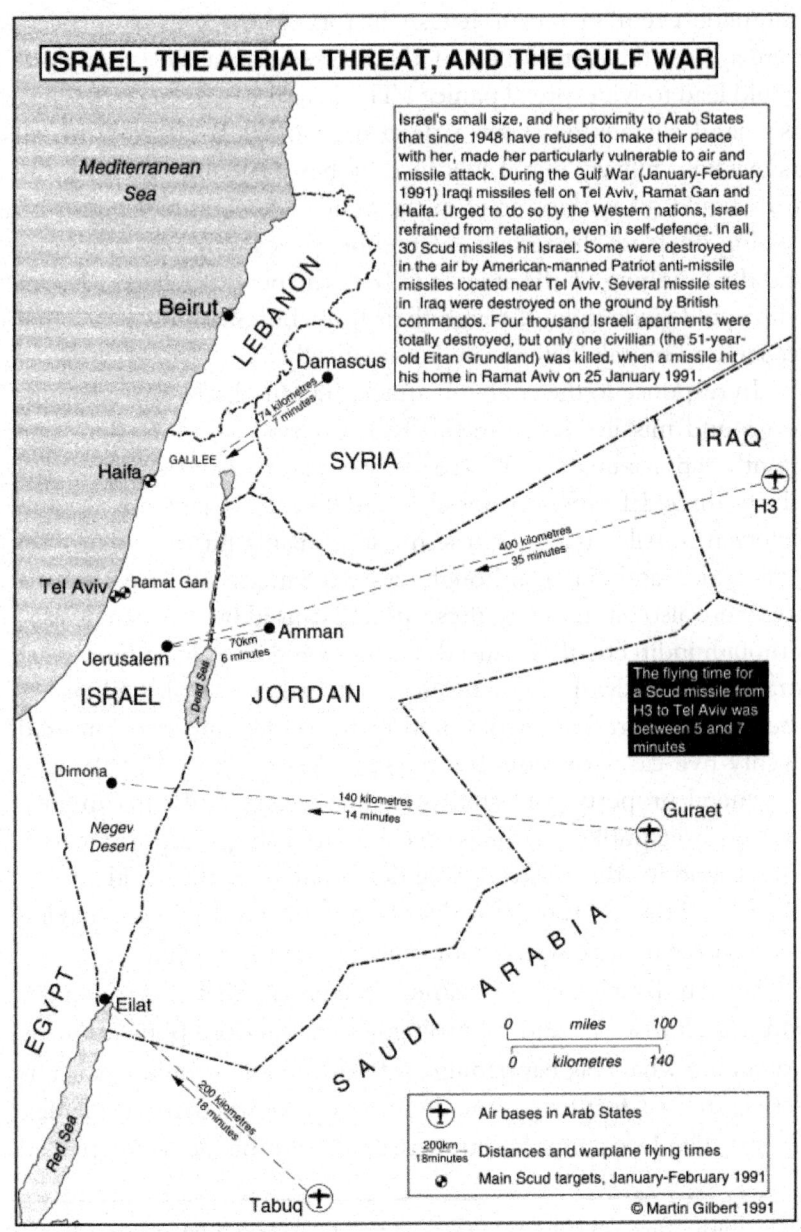

ISRAEL, THE AERIAL THREAT, AND THE GULF WAR

Israel's small size, and her proximity to Arab States that since 1948 have refused to make their peace with her, made her particularly vulnerable to air and missile attack. During the Gulf War (January-February 1991) Iraqi missiles fell on Tel Aviv, Ramat Gan and Haifa. Urged to do so by the Western nations, Israel refrained from retaliation, even in self-defence. In all, 30 Scud missiles hit Israel. Some were destroyed in the air by American-manned Patriot anti-missile missiles located near Tel Aviv. Several missile sites in Iraq were destroyed on the ground by British commandos. Four thousand Israeli apartments were totally destroyed, but only one civilian (the 51-year-old Eitan Grundland) was killed, when a missile hit his home in Ramat Aviv on 25 January 1991.

The flying time for a Scud missile from H3 to Tel Aviv was between 5 and 7 minutes

Air bases in Arab States

Distances and warplane flying times

Main Scud targets, January-February 1991

© Martin Gilbert 1991

Sir Martin Gilbert, © 2010. Reproduced by permission of Taylor & Francis Books UK. www.martingilbert.com

traumatic event in recent Jewish history. Many military officers were against the distribution of the masks because they thought it would lead to widespread panic.[20] The inability of Israel to protect its inland citizens did have a deep psychological effect. With all its existing military might, because of her deal with America, the army could do nothing to stop the Scuds.* Spoiled by legends of derring-do, from the rescue at Entebbe, the capture of Eichmann, and the bombing of the reactor in Iraq, the people needed a leader who could guide them through their fears, but Shamir was not that leader, and morale deteriorated dramatically.[21]

In response to the coalition attack, Iraq fired salvos of ground-to-ground missiles into Israel. Over a period of more than one month, approximately 38 Iraqi versions of Scud missiles fell (thirty-three El Hussein missiles and five El Tijara missiles) in nineteen missile attacks. These missiles mainly hit the greater Tel Aviv region and Haifa, although western Samaria and the Dimona area were also hit. Directly, these attacks caused two civilian deaths, although indirectly they caused the following casualties: four heart attacks, seven deaths as a result of incorrect use of biological/chemical warfare kits, twohunred eight injured and two hundred twenty-five cases of unnecessary injection of atropine. Damage to general property consisted of 1,302 houses, 6142 apartments, twenty-three public buildings, two hundred shops and fifty cars.[22] The reason for this relatively low death rate were threefold:

a) All the pre-war drills, distribution of gas masks and having people prepare safe sealed rooms was an enormous plus.

b) An Israeli general named Nachman Shai was on radio and TV almost day and night literally calming the population by explaining what was happening and how people should react. His very matter-of-fact reassuring demeanor won him many accolades.

c) The U.S.-supplied anti-missile Patriot missile was deployed

---

* The Bush Administration had promised to prevent Iraq from attacking Israel, but the U.S. troops assigned to scour the desert for Scud missiles had poor intelligence and failed to destroy a single real missile (they did destroy several decoys) in nearly 2,500 missions (*Jerusalem Post*, January 30, 2003).

throughout Israel and though militarily not terribly effective, psychologically they did a great job of reassuring the Israeli population.

While Israel and the U.S. had different national security issues as regards the Gulf War, Israel still played the role of a reliable and capable ally. Israel did many things that helped the U.S. military:

a) The IDF presence in the Jordan River Valley kept Saddam from attempting to invade Jordan.

b) The U.S. air force used Israeli special enhanced fuel tanks on its F-15s.

c) The US air force used Israeli-made Have Nap Missiles launched from B-52 bombers.

d) Israeli-made night vision goggles were used by U.S. combat infantry soldiers.

e) An Israeli-made enhanced targeting system was used by U.S. air force Cobra attack helicopters.[23]

f) "In January 1991, Pioneer surveillance drones…from Israel, were used in the First Gulf War by the US Navy, to guide shells fired from battleships."[24]

Unfortunately, despite Israel's compliance with the request that she stay out of the war, the Gulf War changed the dynamic between Israel and America.

> …Throughout the Gulf crisis and the war that followed it, there was tension in the triangular relationship between America, Israel and the Arabs. Gradually,… under the impact of the crisis, America continued to move away from reliance on Israel to reliance on her old and new Arab allies to attain her objectives in the region. In this important respect, Israel was to emerge not as a winner but as an ultimate loser from the Gulf conflict. Nothing demonstrated this more clearly than the pressure applied by the Bush administration on Israel to engage in peace negotiations with the Arabs as soon as the guns in the Gulf fell silent.[25]

As for the Palestinians in Kuwait, over 400,000 were deported for being "Iraqi collaborators."

The narrative in historical sources indicate that the Palestinians in Kuwait, under PLO influence, sided with Iraq, which was used as the excuse to deport them. But the Palestinian community there was not monolithic, and different groups responded differently. Many did favor Iraq because they were allies against Israel in the 1948 War of Independence and again in 1967. Iraq was a Palestinian sanctuary, had never signed the armistice after the *Nakba* and had remained in open war with Israel. Iraq's Baathists put Palestine on their front burner, after they had been neglected by other Arab allies since the 1979 Camp David Accords. They blamed lack of Arab unity for the failure of the first Intifada to earn political advantage, and appreciated Saddam Hussein's support. But they were surprised at how Iraq looted Kuwait and imposed draconian laws, throwing the Palestinian community into confusion. As the largest Palestinian community outside of Jordan, there were cultural and class differences within the community itself, and the older, established community had everything to lose. Not so the poorer classes, who had the PLO mentality. But the undemocratic PLO had no structure to encourage discussion and was a reactionary body that took advantage of "opportunities." Two days after the war began in the Gulf, Arafat was meeting with Saddam in Baghdad, and a week or so later voted against cooperation with Saudi Arabia, the U.S. and Western forces to push back the invasion. It was a decision that would be devastating to the Palestinian Kuwaiti community. In short order the U.S. built Arab/Western coalition was victorious and Iraq was hit hard with harsh sanctions applied. By the time the war ended, the Palestinians were gone from Kuwait, deported by force and terror. "Of the 400,000 Kuwaiti Palestinians, 300,000 settled in Jordan, 2,200 went to the US; 21,000 moved to Canada and other western countries, and the rest settled in the occupied territories."[26]

The expulsion of some 400,000 Palestinians caused Arafat himself to declare... "[W]hat Kuwait did to the Palestinian people is worse than what has been done by Israel to Palestinians in the occupied territories."

> [Despite such protest]...it was largely ignored by the international community with neither the U.N. Security Council nor the General Assembly doing anything to assist the newly displaced refugees and punish their ethnic cleanser....The General Assembly-established Committee on the Exercise of the Inalienable Rights of the Palestinian People did record twenty-four statements on expulsions and deportations of Palestinians during 1990-91, but not one of these statements was about the 400,000 Palestinians deported by Kuwait. Instead, all twenty-four statements were angry protestations objecting to Israel's deportation of four convicted Palestinian terrorists with blood on their hands.[27]

In the war against Iraq dubbed Operation Desert Storm, the U.S.-led coaltion achieved a resounding victory against Iraq and Saddam Hussein. Kuwait was liberated; Saudia Arabia and the Gulf States were spared an Iraqi invasion. But Saddam remained in power and took out his anger on the defenseless Kurds in the North and the Shiite Swamp Arabs in the South. He was only removed from power when the U.S. invaded and "liberated" Iraq from Saddam's clutches in 2003.

OCTOBER 1991: MADRID PEACE CONFERENCE

With the American victory against Iraq fresh in allied minds, U.S. president H.W. Bush saw an opening for negotiations between Israel and her Arab neighbors to settle the Israeli-Palestinian issue. Thus, after forty-three years of non-stop war and hostility, a number of Arab countries agreed to meet with the Israelis face-to-face.

> The Conference, co-chaired by [U.S. pesident George H. W.] Bush and Soviet President Mikhail Gorbachev, was attended by Israeli, Egyptian, Syrian, and Lebanese delegations, as well

as a joint Jordanian-Palestinian delegation. For the first time, all of the parties to the Arab-Israeli conflict had gathered to hold direct negotiations—a historically unprecedented event.[28]

In Madrid, Israeli and Arab leaders sat together and began a process of negotiations to lead to a solution to the Arab-Israeli conflict. Israel, having rejected any participation by the PLO, was mollified by the presence of Palestinians not affiliated with Arafat. Even so, though not invited, the PLO was still represented at the conference.[29]

Eventualy little came of the Madrid Peace Conference as far as Israel and the Arabs moving towards a resolution of their decades-old conflict. But a psychological barrier had been broken.

Frustrated by the Palestinian delegation's inability to move forward without Arafat's approval, the Israelis decided to negotiate directly with the PLO, culminating in the signing of the Declaration of Principles on September 13, 1993. King Hussein and the Israelis likewise decided to move forward independently of the Madrid framework, holding direct talks which produced a peace treaty by October 1994.[30]

THE PALESTINIAN INTIFADA: 1987-1992

Between 1977 and 1987 the Israeli policy in Judea, Samaria and Gaza was one of enlightened occupation. Israel continued to try to improve the living conditions of the Arab population and even introduced municipal elections in the major cities. On the foreign policy front Israel continued to operate under the correct assumption that since the Arab League continued to refuse to recognize the State of Israel and the PLO openly called for Israel's destruction there was no one to talk to regarding the "Territories." Hence, Israel continued to rule these areas under the rubric of military occupation and politically felt that these were still "disputed territories." But in 1978 Israel saw that it did have a potential Arab partner to talk to regarding the future of these lands. That partner was Egypt. Since right after the Yom Kippur War of 1973 Israel and Egypt had begun to talk to each other face-to-face, by 1978 they had negotiated a formula for peace for the Israeli-Arab conflict at Camp David, Maryland. This was to become the Israel-Egypt Peace Treaty signed in March 1979.

Besides dealing with the specifics of the Israeli and Egyptian peace process, a blueprint for solving the issue of the status of Judea, Samaria and Gaza was included. In essence, Israel would offer full autonomy to the Arabs of these areas, i.e., education, economy, construction, law, welfare, health, etc., in short everything except a military and a state department. The plan called for a five-year period of full Palestinian autonomy that included local elections, followed by negotiations between the Israelis and the Palestinians as to the final status of Judea, Samaria and Gaza.

Egypt was fully on board with this proposal. As a matter of fact, a year earlier in 1977, when Sadat visited Israel, he met with a group of sixty local Palestinian leaders. During that meeting he floated the idea of getting Israel to offer the Palestinians autonomy, and many in the audience were receptive. The reason that the autonomy plan never moved forward was its complete and total rejection by Yasser Arafat and the PLO. The PLO's position was clear and unequivocal: Any plan that recognized the sovereignty of the Jewish State was unacceptable—the same rationale the PLO used against the Israeli-Egyptian Peace Treaty. Since there was no Palestinian partner for peace, the Israeli military occupation continued under the 1967 temporary stop-gap measure that was in force until the Arab world recognized Israel and entered into peace negotiations. Since the occupation continued far beyond the five to ten years that were originally intended, there would be many unforeseen consequences of the longer Israeli military presence.

After Likud won the election in 1977, a policy of settling "Greater Israel" was set, with the intent of moving Jews into Judea, Samaria and Gaza. It was based on the tenets of Religious Zionism introduced into the Israeli body politic by the Gush Emunim,

> ...whose beliefs were based...on the teachings of Rabbi
> Abraham Isaac Kook and his son, Rabbi Tzvi Yehuda Kook.
> [They] taught that secular Zionists, through their conquests of
> Eretz Israel, had unwittingly brought about the beginning of
> the Messianic Age, which would culminate in the coming of
> the messiah, which Gush Emunim supporters believe can be
> hastened through Jewish settlement on land they believe God
> has allotted to the Jewish people as set forth in the Hebrew
> Bible.[31]

By 1987, more than 100,000 Jews had been inserted into those
areas to become "facts on the ground" for security purposes and
to create the foundations of a "settlement enterprise."

The Labor government of Levi Eshkol and Moshe Dayan,
having initiated the settling of the Jordan River Valley in the post-
Six-Day War period, accepted the claims of the Gush Emunim
Movement as being consistent with its political and ideological
agenda.

A very clear articulation of Labor's view was the Allon Plan,
made public in 1970 by then Labor Government Deputy Prime
Minister Yigal Allon. The plan was based on the premise that Israel
could work out a real peace treaty with Jordan, seen as a potential
partner for peace because of the actions of its leader, King
Hussein. Furthermore, Jordan was already viewed as the Arab state
that was responsible for the Arabs who lived in Judea, Samaria
and Gaza since some two-thirds of its inhabitants were Palestinian.
The Allon Plan had Israel annexing the overwhelming majority
of Judea/Southern West Bank, most of the Jordan River Valley,
a small part of Samaria—north and east of Jerusalem including
the area that today is Maale Adumim—and the southern half of
the Gaza Strip. The areas not annexed would be handed over to
Jordan in the context of a formal peace treaty. It was thus obvious
that Israel's Labor government did not consider returning to the
1967 ceasefire lines. The idea that any Israeli government prior to

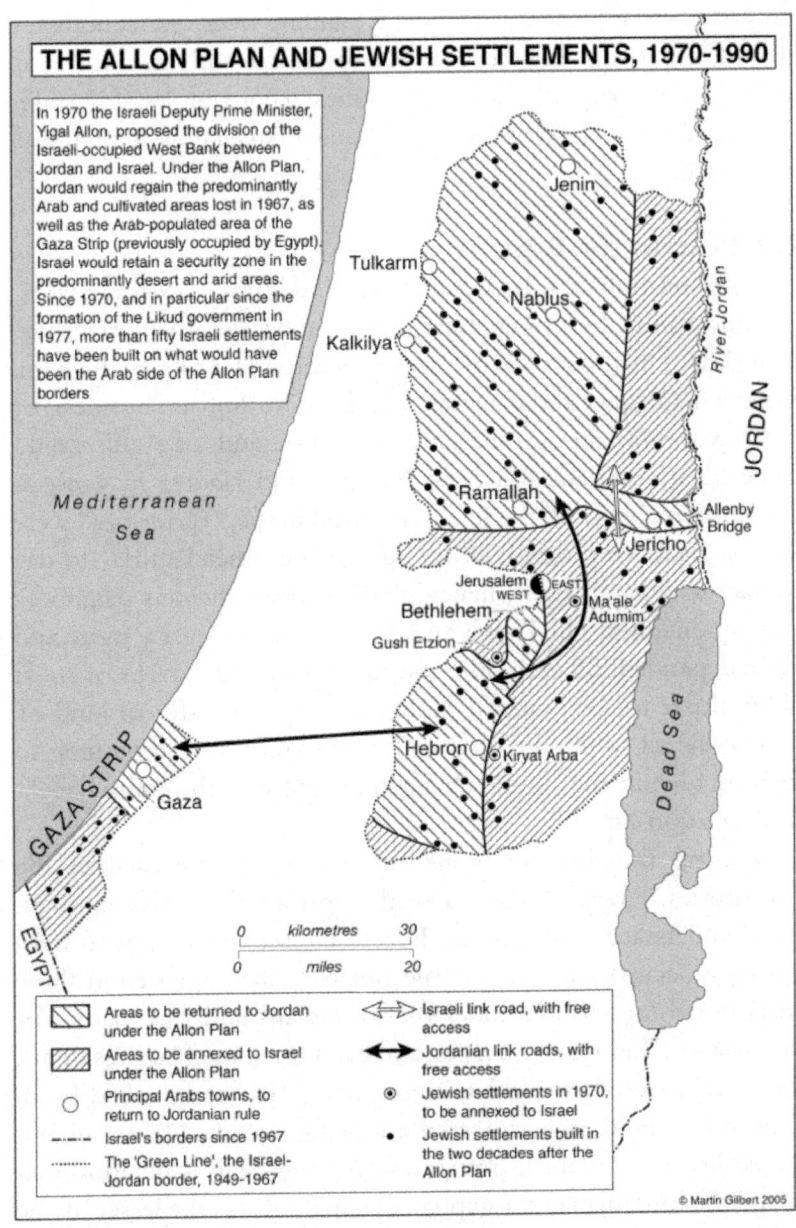

THE ALLON PLAN AND JEWISH SETTLEMENTS, 1970-1990

In 1970 the Israeli Deputy Prime Minister, Yigal Allon, proposed the division of the Israeli-occupied West Bank between Jordan and Israel. Under the Allon Plan, Jordan would regain the predominantly Arab and cultivated areas lost in 1967, as well as the Arab-populated area of the Gaza Strip (previously occupied by Egypt). Israel would retain a security zone in the predominantly desert and arid areas. Since 1970, and in particular since the formation of the Likud government in 1977, more than fifty Israeli settlements have been built on what would have been the Arab side of the Allon Plan borders

Mediterranean
Sea

JORDAN

Jenin

Tulkarm

Nablus

Kalkilya

River Jordan

Ramallah

Allenby
Bridge

Jericho

Jerusalem
WEST EAST

Bethlehem

Ma'ale
Adumim

Gush Etzion

Dead Sea

Hebron Kiryat Arba

GAZA STRIP

Gaza

EGYPT

| 0 | kilometres | 30 |
| 0 | miles | 20 |

Areas to be returned to Jordan under the Allon Plan

Areas to be annexed to Israel under the Allon Plan

Principal Arabs towns, to return to Jordanian rule

Israel's borders since 1967

The 'Green Line', the Israel-Jordan border, 1949-1967

Israeli link road, with free access

Jordanian link roads, with free access

Jewish settlements in 1970, to be annexed to Israel

Jewish settlements built in the two decades after the Allon Plan

© Martin Gilbert 2005

the Oslo Accords would dream of handing over one centimeter of Judea, Samaria or Gaza to Yasser Arafat and the PLO was unthinkable, for good reason: The track record of Yasser Arafat and the PLO was horrendous as far as any Israeli government was concerned.

THE ROAD TO THE INTIFADA

The relationship between Jews and Arabs was complex. On one hand, the Green Line representing the 1949 Armistice disappeared as thousands of Israelis entered Hevron, Bethlehem, Ramallah, Qalqilya and Gaza on daily basis to shop, do business, or visit Jewish holy sites. At the same time, thousands of Arabs would come into Jerusalem, Tel Aviv, Netanya and Hadera to work as day laborers. Many of the Jews who lived in the "Territories" were on one hand very nationalistic, but on the other had day-to-day contact with local Arabs, hence tending to see them as neighbors and not enemies. The Israeli and Arab economies grew more and more dependent on each other during this period. Israelis of most political persuasions viewed the territories as a different kind of part of Israel, while the Arabs of these areas were beginning to form an identity that would change the nature of the entire Israeli-Arab relationship.

During the first ten years of the Israeli presence in the "Territories," local Arabs enjoyed a positive relationship with Israel and Israelis. Because of Israel's conscious attempt to have a benign occupation, life for Palestinian Arabs improved in these areas in contrast to life under the Jordanians and Egyptians. For the Arabs of Judea and Samaria, and even for some Gaza residents, the Israelis were better rulers than their Arab brothers had been. True, they would have preferred not being occupied by Israel, but the reality of the Israeli occupation for the Arab generation that tasted the Jordanian and Egyptian occupation was the lesser of the evils. Furthermore, day-to-day life for this generation was not as much of a hardship when compared to what they had previously experienced between1949-1967; if anything, life on many levels was better. As a matter of fact, many of the Israeli police who kept the peace and order in the "Territories" were local Palestinian Arabs! During the 1987-1991 Intifada, this reality came to an end.

All that changed as another Arab generation reached maturity while under Israeli occupation. Arabs born after 1962—those who had no real recollection of Jordanian and Egyptian rule—would undergo profound changes during the second decade of Israel's rule. First and foremost, this generation did not compare its reality under Israel to any prior reality, since they did not have any prior reality to compare it to. Israeli rule was all they had ever known. Hence, all the improvements that Israel made—paving roads, connecting villages to the power grid and water, opening up health clinics, opening up universities and allowing freedom of the press—were seen by the younger generation as givens, rights, entitlements, not some sort of gift from Israel. If anything, from their perspective, the measuring stick they used to evaluate the quality of their lives had nothing to do with a comparison to some other Arab state. Rather, this generation compared its day-to-day reality with that of the Israelis. This thus became a crucial turning point in the evolution of what would become a Palestinian agenda and identity. Israeli society had become the new yardstick to measure the quality of life for an Arab in Judea, Samaria and Gaza. Israelis had nicer houses, better paved roads, better medical care, better schools, better wages, etc. That is what these younger Arabs aspired to. In short, they wanted what Israeli's had; anything short of that was unacceptable. And so began a revolution of rising expectations.

This younger generation resented the fact that they lived a worse life than the Israelis. They saw this disparity as the result of Israeli occupation. When they would return from a day at work in Jerusalem—where they earned ten times what their fathers earned when they were their age and returned to a home that had running water, electricity, phone service, a TV and a car parked in front of their homes—they did not think of the days when such things didn't exist. Instead, they were resentful—resenting that the luxury they saw in Jerusalem did not exist in their village, and blaming Israel for this. They were resentful of the relative freedom of movement in Israeli cities as opposed to Judea, Samaria and Gaza where they would, on occasion, have to show their ID at a checkpoint. Keep in mind that until the rampant terror of the 1990s there were very few Israeli checkpoints in the territories. Yet these younger Arabs felt the difference. They did not want to see the Israelis on "their" land anywhere, anytime, for any reason. They wanted the Israelis out. Period!

More importantly, during these 20 years, 1967-1987, the Arabs of Judea, Samaria and Gaza began to form a true Palestinian identity. Prior to that, the term Palestinian was more of a political "straw man" used to describe the Arabs who were homeless because of the Arab loss of the War of 1948-49, and whose grievance could only be settled by allowing them to return and flood Israel—what the Palestinians call the "Right of Return." Certainly those Arabs who lived in Judea, Samaria or Gaza from 1949-1967 saw themselves as part of either Jordanian or Egyptian society. However, that began to change during the period of Israeli rule. The Arabs of the "Territories" were no longer part of Jordan or Egypt and they were also not part of Israel, since these areas were under military occupation. So what were they? In the wake of this identity vacuum, the Arabs of Judea, Samaria and Gaza came to see themselves as Palestinians with their own political identity. This new generation did not want to be incorporated into an existing Arab State, if anything as much as they disliked Israel they also did not find much to admire in the Arab world either. This new generation thus saw themselves as Palestinian. In essence, inadvertently, the overextended Israeli occupation became the midwife of a true Palestinian nationalism. The Palestinians were no longer a stick to hit Israel over the head with; they had gained their own voice.

By 1987, the younger generation of self-aware Palestinians became fired up by the vision of an independent Palestine. These younger Palestinians took courses at Bir Zeit University (established

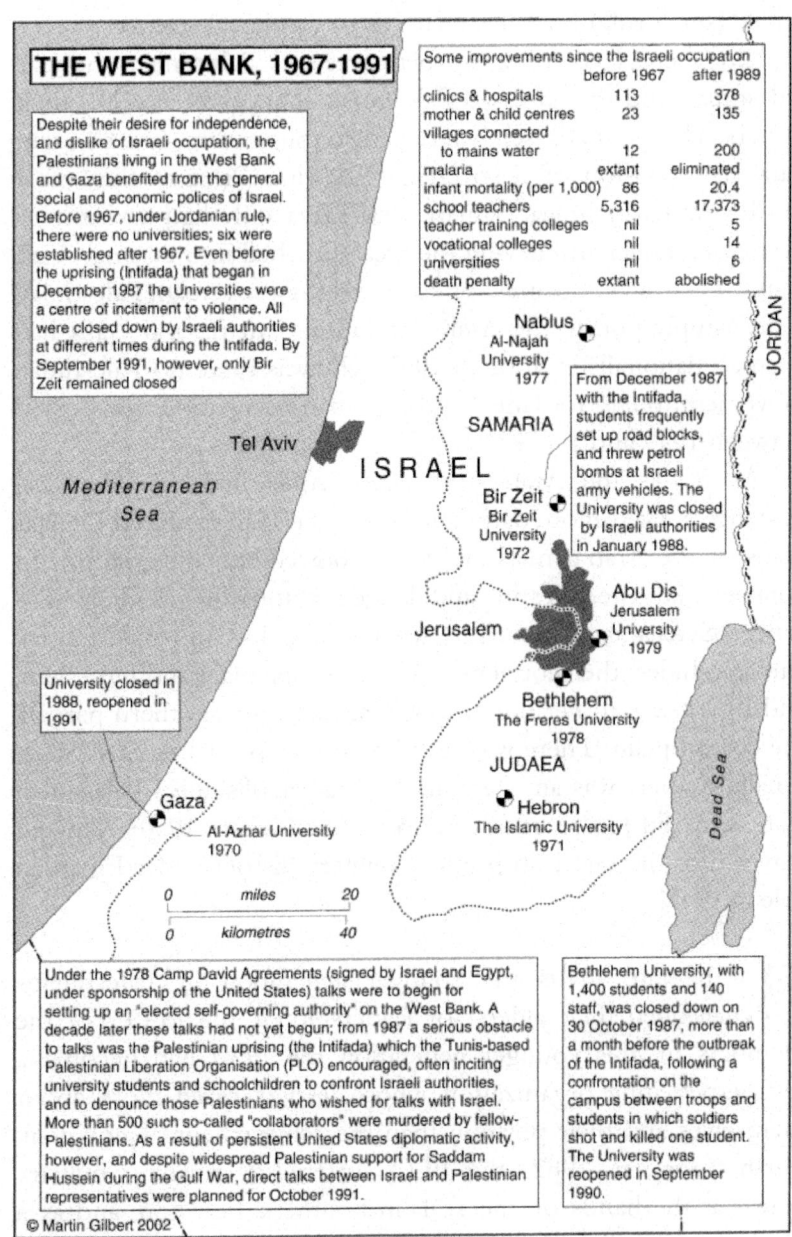

THE WEST BANK, 1967-1991

Despite their desire for independence, and dislike of Israeli occupation, the Palestinians living in the West Bank and Gaza benefited from the general social and economic polices of Israel. Before 1967, under Jordanian rule, there were no universities; six were established after 1967. Even before the uprising (Intifada) that began in December 1987 the Universities were a centre of incitement to violence. All were closed down by Israeli authorities at different times during the Intifada. By September 1991, however, only Bir Zeit remained closed

Some improvements since the Israeli occupation	before 1967	after 1989
clinics & hospitals	113	378
mother & child centres	23	135
villages connected to mains water	12	200
malaria	extant	eliminated
infant mortality (per 1,000)	86	20.4
school teachers	5,316	17,373
teacher training colleges	nil	5
vocational colleges	nil	14
universities	nil	6
death penalty	extant	abolished

JORDAN

Nablus
Al-Najah
University
1977

SAMARIA

Tel Aviv

I S R A E L

Mediterranean
Sea

Bir Zeit
Bir Zeit
University
1972

From December 1987, with the Intifada, students frequently set up road blocks, and threw petrol bombs at Israeli army vehicles. The University was closed by Israeli authorities in January 1988.

Abu Dis
Jerusalem
University
1979

Jerusalem

University closed in 1988, reopened in 1991.

Bethlehem
The Freres University
1978

JUDAEA

Gaza

Al-Azhar University
1970

Hebron
The Islamic University
1971

Dead Sea

0 — miles — 20
0 — kilometres — 40

Under the 1978 Camp David Agreements (signed by Israel and Egypt, under sponsorship of the United States) talks were to begin for setting up an "elected self-governing authority" on the West Bank. A decade later these talks had not yet begun; from 1987 a serious obstacle to talks was the Palestinian uprising (the Intifada) which the Tunis-based Palestinian Liberation Organisation (PLO) encouraged, often inciting university students and schoolchildren to confront Israeli authorities, and to denounce those Palestinians who wished for talks with Israel. More than 500 such so-called "collaborators" were murdered by fellow-Palestinians. As a result of persistent United States diplomatic activity, however, and despite widespread Palestinian support for Saddam Hussein during the Gulf War, direct talks between Israel and Palestinian representatives were planned for October 1991.

Bethlehem University, with 1,400 students and 140 staff, was closed down on 30 October 1987, more than a month before the outbreak of the Intifada, following a confrontation on the campus between troops and students in which soldiers shot and killed one student. The University was reopened in September 1990.

© Martin Gilbert 2002

Sir Martin Gilbert, © 2010. Reproduced by permission of Taylor & Francis Books UK. www.martingilbert.com

under Israeli rule) on Palestinian history, political science, poetry, sociology, etc. Everything in their lives was Palestinian; they ate Palestinian and they dressed Palestinian. They were not like their fathers. This younger, self-aware generation was the first one that truly had a vision of a sovereign Palestine. Prior to this, most of the Arabs in Judea, Samaria and Gaza only had a vision of destroying Israel and having the area absorbed into existing Arab states. They never dreamed or clamored for a sovereign Palestinian state. Simply put, if the Arabs of Judea, Samaria and Gaza had been so nationalistic prior to 1967, why was there no Palestinian movement to end Jordanian and Egyptian occupation that existed between 1949 and 1967?

As far as the Arab states were concerned, the historical evidence is even more damning. When the IDF captured the war plans of the Arab armies in 1948 it showed that the goal was to conquer Mandate Palestine and divide it among the invading Arab armies. Syria was supposed to get the Galil; Jordan would receive Samaria, Judea, the central part of the coastal plain and Jerusalem, and Egypt was to get the Negev, Gaza and the southern part of the coastal plain. There was no plan to set up a Palestinian State. Finally, if there was any Arab interest in establishing a Palestinian state, why did Jordan annex Judea and Samaria in 1950? Why did Egypt turn the Gaza Strip into a military district under Egyptian rule in 1949?

By the late 1970s the younger generation of Palestinians challenged their elders for leadership of the PLO. For the members of this younger generation the PLO had become a self-perpetuating organization whose leaders cared more about themselves and their position than the achievement of any goal. Furthermore, in 1982, the PLO suffered a crushing military defeat at the hands of the IDF in Southern Lebanon, and as a result most of the PLO leadership, including Arafat, was exiled tin Tunisia, more than a thousand miles from Judea, Samaria and Gaza. These PLO leaders there lived as exiled heads of state in the lap of luxury, totally removed from the day-to-day reality of the Palestinians who lived under Israeli rule. By the mid-1980s, all these factors converged as Palestinians between the ages of 15-25 looked to have their grievances against Israel and the older PLO leadership addressed.

In early December 1987, Ahmed Jibril, the head of the Popular Front for the Liberation of Palestine (PFLP)—one of the more radical and violent of the Palestinian groups—planned and executed a very successful attack against an Israeli army base near Kiryat Shemona. Crossing from Lebanon undetected into Israel on engine powered gliders, several PFLP terrorists killed five Israeli soldiers. Many believe that this event created a rush of pride among the younger radical Palestinians since it was the first time that any Palestinian terrorist group had entered an Israeli army base and killed soldiers. The Zionist enemy was not as invincible as their parents had thought.

The stage was now set for what became known as the Intifada, which in Arabic means to shake off, like a dog shakes off fleas. In this context, the Palestinians would shake off the Israelis, first from the territories, then from all of Palestine.

The Intifada was a local Palestinian "uprising"; Yasser Arafat and his cohorts in Tunis had nothing to do with it. The actual event that is credited as being the beginning of the Intifada was a car accident in Gaza between an Israeli truck and a Palestinian car in which four Palestinians were killed. Shortly thereafter riots broke out throughout the Gaza Strip. The Palestinians claimed that the Israeli truck purposely rammed into the Palestinian car, an accusation that inflamed the "Palestinian street." Thousands of Palestinians, mostly youths, began to converge on Israeli Army outposts and pelt the few soldiers there with rocks and Molotov cocktails. (It should be noted that due to the nature of the Israeli Palestinian relationship up until that point there were very few Israeli soldiers stationed in and around Judea, Samaria and Gaza.)

The riots soon spread all over Judea, Samaria and Gaza and involved the use of rocks, Molotov cocktails, pieces of concrete that had razor blades cemented inside, and eggs that had their contents siphoned out and injected with lye to burn and blind. The purpose was to wound or kill, not to just make a political statement. The IDF was not equipped to deal with this type of violent rioting. Hence, at first, the soldiers who typically were facing situations which had 20 of them facing 1,000 violent rioters, used live ammunition to keep the crowd from overwhelming their positions. Very quickly the Intifada took aim at Israeli civilians as well. Many Israelis who were driving in the territories had their vehicles stoned and hit by Molotov cocktails. Finally there began a rash of stabbings in Israeli cities by Palestinians. By mid-1988 the Intifada was in full swing.

ISRAEL'S IMAGE AND THE MEDIA

Israel's media image took a big hit during the 1982 War in Lebanon. As was mentioned earlier, Israel was portrayed as a war mongering juggernaut that recklessly attacked its peaceful neighbor. Throughout the war most media outlets spoke of the Israeli blitzkrieg, Israeli massacres and unrestricted warfare by the IDF. Overall, the damage to Israel's image was severe. Israel was no longer the brave little "Dosh" (an Israeli cartoon character) fighting the giants of the Arab world, but a militaristic Goliath threatening all its frightened Arab neighbors.

The media images from the Intifada picked up where the 1982 War left off. TV screens were filled with images of Palestinian teens throwing rocks, while heavily armed Israeli soldiers fired at them. These TV scenes were always tight shots that didn't show ten to fifteen Israelis being attacked by a mob of well over 1,000 rioters. Furthermore, it would have been clear that the Israelis were stationed at an entrance to an Arab city and that the mobs came out of the city to confront them. So biased was the coverage that rarely were there any pictures of the damage done by the "rock throwing youths". Many Israeli soldiers received burns on their faces and hands, many lost an eye and some were killed. Also, the horrible scenes of Israeli civilians, including children, being maimed, burned and killed were also rarely seen on TV screens outside of Israel.

THE END OF THE INTIFADA AND ITS AFTERMATH

By early 1989 the IDF had learned how to manage the Intifada. Special Israeli undercover units were formed that would operate behind enemy lines. Dressed as Arab rioters they would infiltrate Arab villages and cities and create fear among the leaders of the Intifada who were being neutralized. Military and civilian vehicles were armored, special operations were carried out by the IDF, and the media had once again reached a level of surfeit from too much Arab-Israeli violence. All of these factors finally brought about a decrease in Intifada activities. But by now the nature of the Intifada had changed.

By mid-1989 the Intifada was a more violent and professional production. Instead of mobs of thousands, it was now composed of small well-armed groups of terrorists carrying out attacks on Israeli vehicles, buses, civilians and Palestinians who were considered collaborators. By 1990, more Palestinians were being killed by these professional terrorists than were being killed by the IDF. Nevertheless, by 1991 the Intifada had all but died out.

There were some very profound results of the Intifada. For the Palestinians the entire relationship with Israel had changed. There was no longer any possibility of coexistence in Judea, Samaria and Gaza between Israelis and Palestinians as there had been too much blood spilled. The world that had existed in the "Territories" between 1967 and 1987 ceased to exist. Israel was hated as were Israelis, but a special hatred was now reserved for the Israeli settlers who lived in Judea, Samaria and Gaza. The Palestinians were now committed to eradicating Israeli rule, first in the "Territories" and then in pre-1967 Israel. In essence, the Palestinian Arabs were ready to start implementing the PLO 1974 Ten Point Program*:

> Following the failure of the armies of Egypt and Syria to
> defeat Israel in the Yom Kippur War, the Palestinian leadership
> began formulating a strategic alternative.
>
> The PLO's Phased Plan did not stipulate clear operational
> measures and only repeated the principles of the policies
> which the Palestinian National Council had accepted in
> the past: the denial of United Nations Security Council
> Resolution 242 (adopted after the Six Day War), the denial
> of the existence of the State of Israel and the demand of
> the return of all Palestinian refugees to their original homes
> and the establishment of an Arab-Palestinian state in the
> entire region of Palestine within the pre-1948 borders. The
> innovation of PLO's Phased Plan was in the assertion that
> each step which would lead to the fulfillment of these goals
> would be a worthy step. It also states that any territory, from
> the region of Palestine, which would be transferred to an
> Arab rule should be transferred to Palestinian control, also if
> the takeover of other territories would be delayed as a result.
> Some interpret these series of decisions as a realization of the

---

* "The Ten Point Program met with opposition from other hardline factions
such as the Popular Front for the Liberation of Palestine (PFLP), which fought
to eliminate Israel. As a result, the Ten Point Program led to several radical PLO
factions (such as the PFLP, PFLP-GC and others) breaking out to form the
Rejectionist Front, which would act independently of PLO over the following
years. The Rejectionist Front was mainly worried that the Ten Point Program
could potentially turn into a peace agreement between the Palestinian leadership
and the State of Israel. Suspicion between the Arafat-led mainstream and
more hard-line factions, inside and outside the PLO have continued to (cont'd)
dominate the inner workings of the organization ever since, often resulting in
paralysis or conflicting courses of action. A temporary closing of ranks came
in 1977, as Palestinian factions joined with hard-line Arab governments in
the Steadfastness and Confrontation Front to condemn Egyptian attempts to
reach a separate peace with Israel (eventually resulting in the 1979 Camp David
Accords).

"Israel perceived the Ten Point Program as a dangerous policy, mainly because
it implied that any future compromise agreement between Israel and (cont'd)

council in the fact that it cannot fulfill all its goals at once, but rather it would be able to do so in gradual small steps, and as a recognition of the council in the possibility of initiating political and diplomatic measures and not just an "armed struggle" (although PLO's Phased Plan does not consist of a denial of the use of an armed struggle).[32]*

On the other hand, the Palestinians were quite depressed that the Intifada did not yield the intended results of shaking off Israeli rule. In the first few weeks of the Intifada the Palestinians had tasted victory. World sympathy had shifted towards them, and it was believed that Israel would soon be chased from the "Territories." Once again the Palestinians underestimated Israeli resolve. The Palestinians failed to grasp that Zionism was in fact Jewish nationalism, and that the Jews would fight tenaciously to defend their homeland.

For Israel the Intifada was a pivotal moment in history. In its three-plus years thousands of Israeli reservists served in the "Territories" and had a very close look at the Palestinians, especially the younger generation. It was very clear to the overwhelming majority of them that the "Territories" were no longer worth keeping. The Judea, Samaria, and Gaza that they used to visit and shop in were gone; the Palestinians they used to haggle with or buy pita and zata from were replaced with a generation of Palestinians who hated Israelis with a passion. The idea that Likud had been pushing since 1977 for a Greater Israel—which implied the incorporation of Judea, Samaria and Gaza into Israel—seemed out of touch with reality. There was no way that these Palestinians could ever become part of Israeli society. It became clear that even though there was no one to speak to regarding the future of the "Territories" Israel had to find a way to stop ruling over an angry,

---

the Palestinian leadership would not be honored by the PLO. It raised the fear among Israelis that the Palestinian leadership might be under the intention of exploiting future Israeli territorial compromises in order to "improve positions" for attacking Israel. (https://en.wikipedia.org/wiki/PLO%27s_Ten_Point_Program)

hateful Palestinian population for two basic reasons: Zionism must focus on building a Jewish State, not on controlling the Palestinians, and in order to control the Palestinians Israel would have to resort to more and more oppressive measures, which would ultimately destroy the moral fabric of Israeli society.

So while the Palestinians did not kick out the Jews from the "Territories," they did cause a fierce debate in Israeli society regarding the future of Judea, Samaria and Gaza. On one hand, many Israelis were still deeply connected to these areas for all the same reasons they had been since 1967. On the other hand, many Israelis now saw Judea, Samaria and Gaza as dangerous places to travel, places they should avoid going near. Compounding this reality was that by 1992 around 170,000 Jews lived in these areas, some in towns of over 20,000 people. So while one group of Israelis was now frightened to enter these areas, more and more Israelis were calling them home. For people on the right of the Israeli political spectrum the Intifada showed that there was no one to speak to on the Arab side. For many on the Left it was felt that Israel must find a way to divorce itself from Judea, Samaria and Gaza. The fact that because of the Intifada most Israelis ceased to set foot in the territories, created a de facto reality that separated the "Territories" from the rest of Israel in the minds of most Israelis. These new realities set the stage for the Olso Agreements.

THE OSLO PEACE PROCESS: 1992 – 2000

By 1992 it was clear that the debate in Israeli society over the future of the "Territories" had moved to the top of the nation's agenda. The fact that the Left-leaning Labor Party won the 1992 election was evidence of this feeling, though in all fairness to the Israeli voters Yitzhak Rabin did run as a Labor hawk in 1992. But the other top people on the Labor list were openly dovish on the future of the "Territories."

Besides the Intifada and its aftermath, other events had happened in the Middle East and around the world that profoundly changed the political status quo and hence affected the Israeli-Palestinian conflict:

1) The Soviet Union collapsed by late 1989, thus leaving the U.S. as the sole global superpower, and depriving most of the Arab hardliners and the PLO of their most important and powerful ally.

2) Saddam Hussein, in August of 1990, invaded a neighboring Arab state, Kuwait, and declared it to be the 19th district of Iraq. This caused a panic among the other Arab Gulf oil-producing states, especially Saudi Arabia, who assumed that it would be next.

3) During the term of President George H. W. Bush the U.S. led a worldwide military coalition that included almost every Arab state to oust Saddam Hussein and the Iraqis from Kuwait. In January-February 1991 the Gulf War liberated Kuwait.

4) During the Gulf War Saddam Hussein launched 38 Scud long-range missiles at Israel. Each missile was capable of carrying either an unconventional (chemical or biological) or a regular (explosive) warhead. The Iraqis targeted Israel's population centers, in particular the Tel Aviv metropolitan area where twenty-five percent of Israel's population resided. Regardless of the type of warhead the Scuds had, the impact of one direct hit in the middle of a populated city could have been hundreds if not thousands of casualties.

5) Since September of 1990 the Israeli military had been preparing the country for an Iraqi missile strike. As a result, every Israeli citizen had been handed a gas mask, including "crib covers" for babies; every Israeli household was told to prepare a "sealed room" to run to and received a vile of atropine in case of a chemical attack. All of Israel's hospitals were prepared for mass casualties. When the Scuds began to hit Israel during the Gulf War in many subplots unfolded:

a. It was the first time since the 1948 War of Independence that Israeli cities were under attack.

b. Even though most of the Scuds hit buildings in densely populated areas, there were very few casualties.

c. Israel wanted to respond with a devastating retaliatory strike but was stopped by the U.S., who felt that such a strike would cause the Arab members of the coalition to withdraw.

d. Israeli Jews, some of whom were Holocaust survivors, were sitting in rooms with their gas masks waiting for a "gas" attack, and feeling helpless. This scenario went against every fiber of post-Holocaust Zionist philosophy.

e. The Palestinian Arabs in Judea, Samaria and Gaza were dancing on the roofs of their homes, hoping that entire Israeli cities would be wiped out.

6) When the war ended, the U.S., having accumulated many "chips" from the Arab world, sponsored an Arab-Israeli Peace Conference in Madrid. All the Arab parties to the conflict attended and sat for the first time in the same room with the Israeli delegation.

7) Kuwait published a two-page ad in the *New York Times* thanking the U.S. The ad featured a map of the Middle East. For the first time a map of the Middle East published publicly by an Arab state included Israel.

8) After the war Kuwait expelled 400,000 Palestinians because:

a. Yasser Arafat had publicly backed Saddam Hussein.

b. The Palestinians in Kuwait had collaborated with the Iraqi occupiers.

9) Yasser Arafat and the PLO became pariahs in the Arab world because of Arafat's support of Saddam. Gulf State Arabs, the PLO's main contributors, stopped sending money.

10) Yasser Arafat and the PLO were not invited to the Madrid Peace Conference and no Arab state objected!

As a result of these events, the Israeli Labor-led government and the PLO unexpectedly found that they needed each other. Israel was looking for a partner to talk to about ending its occupation of Judea, Samaria and Gaza and the PLO had become an almost irrelevant player in the politics of the Middle East, as younger leadership that lived in the "Territories" had gained popularity during the Intifada. Hence Yossi Beilin and Shimon Peres of the newly elected Labor government began to secretly meet with PLO leaders to see if there could be a historic breakthrough that could serve the interests of both peoples. In short, if the PLO changed its tune and recognized Israel as a Jewish State then Israel could negotiate with them about the future of Judea, Samaria and Gaza.

Israel would have peace with the Palestinians, and the PLO and Arafat would become the key players that they once were, perhaps even the leadership of a sovereign Palestinian State.

These secret contacts ultimately became secret negotiations. Oslo, Norway was chosen as the unlikely setting for long-term negotiations between a team of Israelis and a team of Palestinians who would not only negotiate a treaty, but would form a relationship with each other over close to a year of negotiations. After a year, by September, 1993, the two sides were ready to go public with the historic announcement that became known as the Oslo Peace Agreement.

Once the process became public there were many people on the Right of the Israeli political spectrum who felt that the Israeli government was operating out of a sense of desperation. True, Israel needed peace, and it could use a negotiating partner to help bring about a resolution to the ambiguous position of Judea, Samaria and Gaza. But just because Israel needed this, one should not see the PLO or Arafat as anything but what they had been since 1967: terrorists bent on Israel's destruction. These critics urged people to read Arafat's interviews, to listen to his Arabic speeches, or to read the PLO Covenant that clearly called for the eradication of the Jewish State. These Cassandras warned that Israel was going to create a Palestinian terrorist entity in all the areas that she intended to hand over to the Palestinians, and that Israel would suffer greatly as a result. Finally, they argued that though the status quo was far from perfect it would prove to be far better than what Oslo would bring. At the time, most Israeli politicians and political pundits branded these voices as enemies of peace.

Oslo I Agreement: September 13, 1993

On September 13, 1993, Israel and the PLO signed an agreement on the White House Lawn. President Bill Clinton, PM Yitzhak Rabin, and PLO Chairman Yasser Arafat were all present, as were hundreds of dignitaries from all over the world, especially from Arab countries. There was a declaration of mutual recognition and a promise to negotiate a settlement. The agreement called for granting the PLO autonomy over some of the areas captured by Israel in the Six-Day War, with a withdrawal from the Gaza Strip and from Jericho as a first stage.

The Oslo Agreement was built on the premise that there should be no attempt to solve all the serious outstanding issues separating the Israelis and the Palestinians, like Jerusalem, the Right of Return, Jewish settlements in Judea, Samaria and Gaza, and the final borders of Israel and Palestine. The theory was that these issues were too difficult, and emotional and trying to tackle them would destroy the peace process. Hence, it was decided to deal with steps that would create good faith between the two sides. The basic formula for the first few years of the Oslo Peace Process was that Israel would turn the PLO from a terrorist organization into a legitimate political entity called the Palestinian Authority (PA). This PA would have all the trappings of a government—departments, agencies, and an elected assembly. Israel would lobby the U.S. and Western European countries to fund the new Palestinian Authority in order facilitate the necessary infrastructure of what would be a functioning, organized peaceful Palestinian State. Finally, the PA would also have an armed police and paramilitary force that would be responsible for security in all the newly acquired Palestinian areas. Israel would do everything in her power to help create a functioning PA, including actually arming the new PA police and paramilitary force. The PA, for its part, would act as a good neighbor to Israel, one that would fight terror—something very significant from Israel's point of view. In short, the Palestinians would receive political legitimacy, large amounts of American and Western European money, territory, and power, while Israel would receive peace, security and a peaceful neighbor.

ANALYSIS OF THE OSLO I 1993 AGREEMENT

The Oslo I Agreement set up a mechanism by which the State of Israel, an existing nation state with a functioning government and infrastructure, helped a former Arab terror organization morph into a governing entity over a piece of territory that at first would include most of Gaza, the city of Jericho, and areas surrounding it.

Gaza, since 1949, had been a hotbed of anti-Israel propaganda and ideology. Thousands of terror attacks against Israelis had been carried out from there since the days of the *fedayeen* in the early 1950s. Hence, this area was one that most Israelis were happy to be rid of.

Jericho, on the other hand, since 1967 and even through the Intifada, was a quiet, friendly and peaceful place. Thus, Israel was prepared to have Jericho be the first place the IDF would leave and hand over to the Palestinian Authority.

The principals laid down in UN Resolution 242 and reaffirmed in UN Resolution 338 were a cornerstone of the Oslo I Agreement. As was previously mentioned, these two resolutions speak of recognition of Israel as a state in the Middle East that had the right to live in peace behind secure boundaries, while Israel would have to withdraw from to-be-determined territories captured in the 1967 Six-Day War. This was always acceptable to Israel; the Peace Treaty with Egypt signed in 1979 offers proof of this position as was Israel's offer of autonomy to the Palestinian Arabs in 1978, with the blessings of Egypt under the Camp David Accords. For the PLO Olso meant a 180 degree about face. They would have to recognize Israel's right to exist as a Jewish State within secure boundaries. It also meant the PA would have to shift its focus from terror attacks against Israel, Israelis and Jews worldwide and focus on becoming a responsible governing entity that dealt with the realities of education, policing, infrastructure, tax collection, settling business disputes, etc. Oslo was set up to help the PA make this very difficult transition. The PA would have an elected council and an elected president—not a selected one. This would also constitute a huge change for the former PLO and its head, Yasser Arafat, who had always ruled as a dictator from behind the barrel of a gun, and whose main focus was inflicting pain and suffering on Israelis, while not improving the lives of Palestinian Arabs. Now the PA would find itself as a ruling governing entity that would be charged with running the day-to-day lives of hundreds of thousands of Palestinian Arabs.

The PLO would be aided in its historical transformation by Israel, who would use her diplomatic, political, economic and even military power to help the PLO become the PA. Oslo I created a framework for the beginning of a historical process both for the PLO and the Palestinian Arabs and for transforming the entire relationship and dynamic between the Palestinian Arabs and Israelis. But there would have to be a scrupulous adherence to the Oslo I agreement if all of these goals were to be achieved.

As in the case of UN Resolution 242 there are those who attribute all sorts of quotes, understandings and obligations that simply are not found in the Oslo I agreement. For example, it has almost become an article of faith among the critics of Israel that the Oslo I Accords obligated Israel to begin dismantling the settlements that were built in the disputed territories of Judea, Samaria and Gaza as soon as the agreement was signed. Furthermore, these people claim that Israel obligated herself to withdraw from all of Judea, Samaria and Gaza as a first step to create peace. Both of these assertions are simply untrue; they do not exist in the Oslo I Agreement by design. It was clear that the PLO and Israel had many trust hurdles to get over before each side could view the other as a truly peaceful neighbor and partner. Hence, the document is all about setting up a small PA proto-state in most of Gaza and the Jericho area. This proto-state would be a test case of how the newly-formed PA did as far as living up to its obligations: being a good neighbor to Israel and a fair and just ruler of the people under its jurisdiction. Once this would be established, the process would move on to the next phase, which would include more territory being handed over to the PA and creating more trust between the PA and Israel.

The Oslo I Agreement was unlike any peace agreement signed by Israel before or since. In the Egyptian and Jordanian peace agreements, peace and trust were established first on the ground, and then the peace agreement came to formalize the reality that already existed. Since the PLO and Israel were such mortal enemies, the thinking process was that first let there be trust and some tangible fruits from the agreement and then hopefully peace on the ground would follow later. Tragically, this gamble did not pay off, and peace on the ground has yet to be established. Many would argue that the evidence points to the fact that peace on the ground between the PA and Israel is no closer today.

Footnotes

[1] "Revolutionary Command Council Meeting," March 27, 1979, Conflict Records Research Center, Washington, D.C. Kevin M. Woods, David D. Palkki, and Mark E. Stout, eds., *A Survey of Saddam's Audio Files, 1978-2001: Toward an Understanding of Authoritarian Regimes* (Alexandria, Va.: Institute for Defense Analyses, 2010), 262-263. As derived from Hal Brands, David Palkki, "Why Did Saddam Want the Bomb? The Israel Factor and the Iraqi Nuclear Program," *Foreign Policy Research Institute*, August 3, 2010 (http://www.fpri.org/article/2011/08/whydidsaddamwantthebombthe-israelfactorandtheiraqinuclearprogram/)

[2] *Ibid.*, 93.

[3] Mitchell Bard, "Israeli Attack on Iraqi Reactor Offers History Lesson for Obama," March 16, 2010, *Encyclopedia Britannica* Blog (http://blogs.britannica.com/2010/03/israeli-attack-on-iraqi-reactor-offers-history-lesson-for-obama/)

[4] David K. Shipler, "The Golan Heights Annexed by Israel in an Abrupt Move," *New York Times,* December 15, 1981, 1 (http://www.nytimes.com/learning/general/onthisday/big/1214.html)

[5] "UN rejects Israel's claim over Syria's Golan Heights," 26 Apr 2016 (http://www.aljazeera.com/news/2016/04/rejects-israel-claim-syria-golan-heights-160426195853040.html)

[6] David Bleich, *Contemporary Halakhic Problems*, Vol.1 (Hoboken, NJ: KTAV Publishing, 1977), 302.

[7] Ibrahim Omer, "The Forgotten Origin of Ethiopian Jews; From Northern Sudan," *The Jewish Magazine*, April 2013. (http://www.jewishmag.com/174mag/ethiopian_jews_origin/ethiopian_jews_origin.htm)

[8] Mitchell Bard, "The Ethiopian Exodus, Part I, *Think Tank* (http://www.pbs.org/thinktank/transcript1252.html)

[9] Raul Valdes Vivo, *Ethiopia's Revolution* (New York: International Publishers, 1977), 25.

[10] *Op. cit.*

[11] Michael Omer-Man, "This Week in History: Operation Moses Begins," *The Jerusalem Post*, November 19, 2010 (http://www.jpost.com/Features/In-Thespotlight/This-week-in-History-Operation-Moses-begins)

[12] Mitchell G. Bard, "Operation Solomon: The Daring Rescue of the Ethiopian Jews," *The Middle East Quarterly*, Spring 2006, Vol 13:2 (http://www.meforum.org/961/operation-solomon)

[13] Youssef M. Ibrahim, P.L.O. Proclaims Palestine to be an Independent State; Hints at Recognizing Israel," *New York Times*, November 15, 1988 (http://www.nytimes.com/1988/11/15/world/plo-proclaims-palestine-to-be-an-independent-state-hints-at-recognizing-israel.html?pagewanted=all)

[14] http://www.jewishvirtuallibrary.org/palestinian-national-council-declaration-of-independence-november-1988

[15] John Quigley, "The Palestine Declaration to the International Criminal Court: The Statehood Issue," *Rutgers Law Record*, Vol. 35, Spring 2009 (https://web.archive.org/web/20110716143235/http://www.lawrecord.com/files/35-rutgers-l-rec-1.pdf)

[16] Menachem Z. Rosensaft, "Wrong About Arafat," *The Washington Post*, October 14, 2000, page A23

[17] http://jcpa.org/article/operation-exodus-soviet-jewry-comes-home/, p. 2

[18] Avi Shlaim, "Israel and the Conflict" in Alex Danchev and Dan Keohane, eds., *International Perspectives on the Gulf Conlict, 1990-91* (London: St Martin's Press, 1994) 59-79 (http://users.ox.ac.uk/~ssfc0005/Israel%20and%20the%20Conflict.html)

[19] *Ibid.*

[20] *Ibid.*

[21] *Ibid.*

[22] Israel Ministry of Foreign Affairs, "The Gulf War, 1991" (http://www.mfa.gov.il/mfa/aboutisrael/history/pages/the%20gulf%20war%20-%201991.aspx)

[23] Mitchell Bard, "The Arab/Muslim World: The Gulf War, August 1990 – February 1991 (http://www.jewishvirtuallibrary.org/the-gulf-war)

[24] Mary Dobbing and Chris Cole, "Drone Wars UK," (Oxford: Peace House, 2014), 9 (https://dronewarsuk.files.wordpress.com/2014/01/israel-and-the-drone-wars.pdf)

[25] Avi Shlaim, "Israel and the Conflict"

[26] Toufic Hadad, "Palestinian Forced Displacement from Kuwait: The Overdue Accounting," *Badil Resource Center* (http://www.badil.org/en/component/k2/item/1514-art07.html)

[27] Steven J. Rosen, "Kuwait Expells Thousands of Palestinians," *The Middle East Quarterly*, Fall 2012. vol. 19:4 (http://www.meforum.org/3391/kuwait-expels-palestinians)

[28] U.S. Department of State, Office of the Historian, "The Madrid Conference, 1991" (https://history.state.gov/milestones/1989-1992/madrid-conference)

[29] Clyde Haberman, "Palestinian Says His Delegation Will Assert P.L.O. Ties at Talks," *New York Times*, October 22, 1991 (http://www.nytimes.com/1991/10/22/world/palestinian-says-his-delegation-will-assert-plo-ties-at-talks.html)

[30] *Op. cit.*

[31] https://en.wikipedia.org/wiki/Gush_Emunim as derived from Eliezer Don-Yehiya, "The Book and the Sword: the Nationalist Yehivot and Political radicalism in Israel," in Martin E. Marty, R. Scott Appleby (eds.), *Accounting for Fundamentalisms: The Dynamic Character of Movements*, (Chicago, IL: University of Chicago Press, 2004) 264-310, p.274.

[32] https://en.wikipedia.org/wiki/PLO%27s_Ten_Point_Program (see NSW Jewish Board of Deputies, "The Ten-Point Program," *Israel & Judaism Studies* (http://www.ijs.org.au/The-Ten-Point-Program-/default.aspx))

Chapter 17

Major Events:
1993-1999

THE IMPLEMENTATION OF THE OSLO I ACCORDS

In order to implement the Oslo I Accords Israel had to change the status of Yasser Arafat, the entire PLO leadership and thousands of PLO terrorists. All of these individuals were criminals in the eyes of Israeli law and its security forces. As a result of the Oslo Accords they would all become peace partners. There was not just a legal status change, which was in and of itself a large step by Israel, but by the agreement Israel allowed Arafat and the PLO leadership, presently exiled in Tunisia, to return to Gaza and Jericho. This meant entry to these areas via Israel, or Israeli-controlled crossing points like the Allenby Bridge. In addition, thousands of future PA policemen were all wanted former PLO terrorists. Israel also began to release some PLO security prisoners from Israeli prisons. These were mostly men who were directly or indirectly involved in terror attacks against Israelis, most of them during the 1987-1991 Intifada. The last step Israel took before she began to withdraw from most of Gaza and the Jericho area was to make sure the new PA police force, essentially a mini army, was properly trained—mostly by the Jordanian Army—and armed by the IDF. The last step was the most controversial. Many right of center politicians and pundits felt arming former terrorists was suicidal. But the record shows that Israel took very concrete and risky steps to begin the transformation of the PLO from terrorist enemy organization to the PA, peace partner and neighbor.

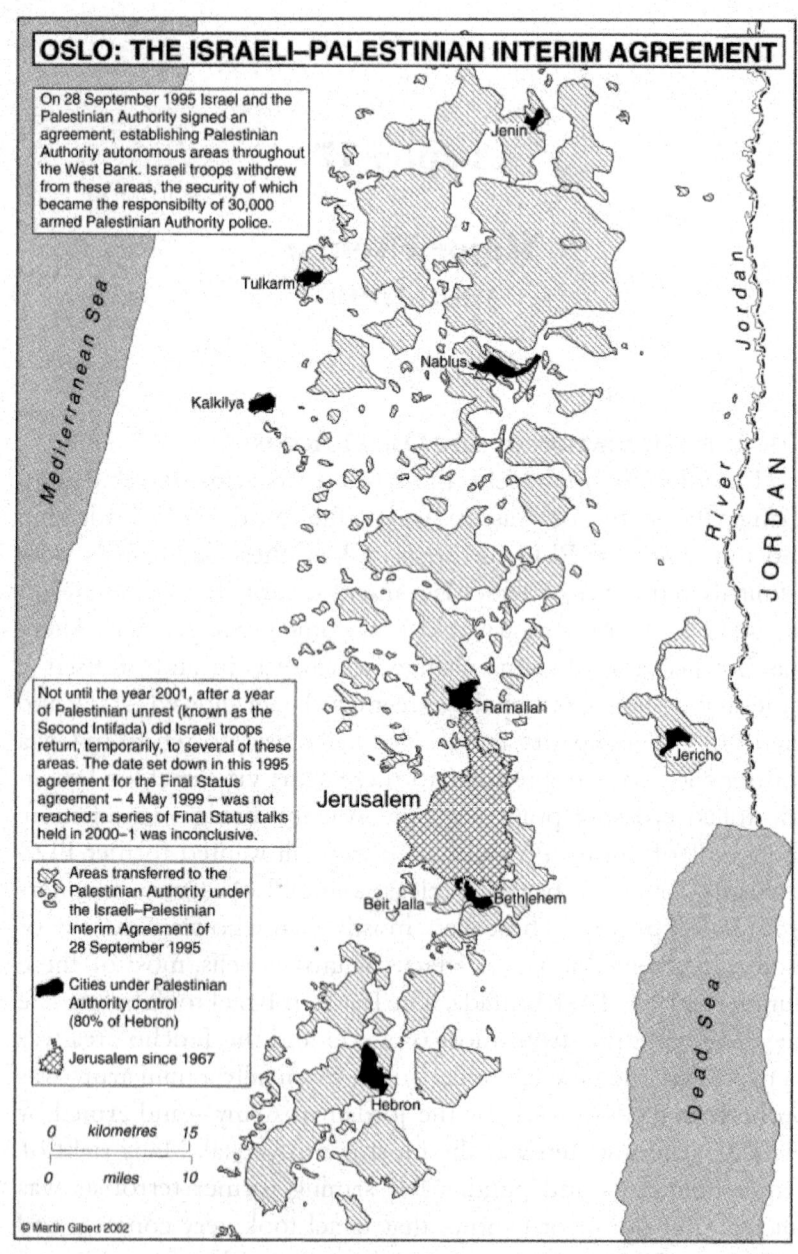

OSLO: THE ISRAELI–PALESTINIAN INTERIM AGREEMENT

On 28 September 1995 Israel and the Palestinian Authority signed an agreement, establishing Palestinian Authority autonomous areas throughout the West Bank. Israeli troops withdrew from these areas, the security of which became the responsibilty of 30,000 armed Palestinian Authority police.

Jenin

Mediterranean Sea

Tulkarm

Nablus

Kalkilya

River Jordan

JORDAN

Not until the year 2001, after a year of Palestinian unrest (known as the Second Intifada) did Israeli troops return, temporarily, to several of these areas. The date set down in this 1995 agreement for the Final Status agreement – 4 May 1999 – was not reached: a series of Final Status talks held in 2000–1 was inconclusive.

Jerusalem

Ramallah

Jericho

Areas transferred to the Palestinian Authority under the Israeli–Palestinian Interim Agreement of 28 September 1995

Cities under Palestinian Authority control (80% of Hebron)

Jerusalem since 1967

Beit Jalla — Bethlehem

Dead Sea

Hebron

| 0 | kilometres | 15 |
| 0 | miles | 10 |

© Martin Gilbert 2002

Sir Martin Gilbert, © 2010. Reproduced by permission of Taylor & Francis Books UK. www.martingilbert.com

During this initial period the big steps the PLO took towards Israel were in the form of speeches and statements, mostly to Western audiences. Arafat had to do very little, if anything concrete, to show that the PLO was transforming itself from a terror organization into the governing body that would be the PA.

On May 4, 1994 the IDF began to redeploy from most of Gaza, the city of Jericho and some of the area surrounding the city. The IDF remained in control of the Jewish settlements in Gaza, known as Gush Katif, in accordance with the Oslo I Accord. These settlements were founded in the 1970s and many of the settlers were those that had been removed from Yamit in April 1982, when Israel made her last withdrawal from Sinai in accordance with the terms of the Israel-Egypt Peace Agreement. As before, the IDF tried to stage as orderly a withdrawal as possible to make sure that the new PA police force would have bases, police stations and headquarters to begin administrating Gaza and Jericho.

Though the new PA police had new uniforms, PA insignia and military grade weapons from the IDF, their behavior at the handover of both areas was that of an unruly militia at best. There was non-stop firing in the air once the IDF departed, in fact so much ammunition was used that PA policeman found themselves short of bullets. Moreover, the PA police in both areas proved not interested in controlling the local crowds that came to pelt with rocks the IDF soldiers who were involved in the handover. They apparently wanted to make the point that the IDF was chased out as opposed to withdrawing by agreement.[1]

Both the behavior of the Palestinian Arabs in Gaza and Jericho and that of the PA police was to be an omen of how the Oslo Accords would be adhered to over the next two decades.

HAMAS

A few weeks after the Olso Accords were signed and Israel began preparing for the withdrawal of its military forces and working on the transfer of authority to the newly-formed PA, there began to be a steady uptick in Palestinian terror attacks against

Israelis. Most of these attacks were carried out by Hamas in Gaza. Hamas, a Sunni Islamic terrorist organization founded in 1987 by Sheikh Ahmad Yassin, had added a new dangerous dimension to the Israeli-Palestinian conflict.

The roots of Hamas go all the way back to the oldest radical Muslim organization in the modern Middle East: the Muslim Brotherhood.

The Muslim Brotherhood (*Hizb al Ikhwan al Muslimeen* (The Party of the Muslim Brothers) or *Jamaat al-Ikhwan al-Muslimun* (Society of the Muslim Brotherhood) is a fundamentalist international organization originating in Egypt, whose goals are the conversion of Muslim countries into states ruled by Sha'aria law, the reestablishment of the caliphate and ultimately, world dominion. The Muslim Brotherhood's ideology, which insists that Islam is a prescription for governance as well as a religion, is the prototypical example of Islamism. Its slogan is self-explanatory: "God is our purpose, the Prophet our leader, the Qur'an our constitution, Jihad our way and dying for God's cause our supreme objective."[2]*

The Muslim Brotherhood has given birth to many radical Sunni movements over the last 50 years, including Al Qaeda,

---

* Since its very beginning, the Muslim Brotherhood was based on ideological foundations that first emerged as a result of disenchantment with the idea of "Islamic reformism". Advocates of the idea, which appeared in the second half of the 19th and early 20th century, sought to have Muslim society undergo a rapid Western modernization and reform the religion of Islam.

According to Jamal al-Din al-Afghani (1838-1897) and Muhammad Abduh (1849-1905), the founders of this school of thought, the modernization they sought was to be based on a comprehensive adoption of technology, social structure, and even way of life prevailing in the West at the time, only clothed in Islamic garb. This required deep, substantial reforms in Islam and its institutions.

As part of the proposed changes, the reformists sought to abolish the principle of "taqlid" ("tradition", i.e., blind imitation of past customs) and adopt the principles of Islamic religious law to modern demands. They considered the religious-legal restraints that interfere with modernization to be "harmful additions" added to Islam over the centuries, believing that Islam should be liberated from them through innovations (some of them far-reaching) in religious law.

For example, Muhammad Abduh wanted to grant equal rights to (cont'd)

ISIS, Taliban, Islamic Jihad, Hamas and many others. Hamas was formally founded in 1988. Briefly, it is a Sunni Islamic Palestinian organization that feels that all of Palestine is holy Islamic territory and must be conquered from the Jews who are non-believers/infidels and tools of the Christian West. Israel must be destroyed and all of Palestine must be under Islamic rule. This new Islamic Palestinian state that Hamas dreams of setting up will be an Islamic Republic.

The founder of Hamas, Sheik Ahmad Yassin, used a very successful tactic that is proscribed by the Muslim Brotherhood

---

women, particularly in education, and argued for the need to draw know-how and technology from the West without considering it to be "bid'ah" (a change that contradicts religious law and is therefore prohibited).

The ideas of Afghani and Abduh may be viewed as an attempt to promote a gradual process of Westernization, stemming from their belief that Western societies were the most advanced and that emulating them was a goal to be achieved. These ideas, however, did not gain extensive support in the Islamic world. It was their successor, Muhammad Rashid Rida (in 1865-1935) who started calling for a reexamination of his predecessors' ideas. Like them, he considered the Muslim world to be weak compared to the West, yet his suggested method of rectifying the situation was different: instead of Westernization, a return to the roots of Islam, the implementation of Islamic religious law (Sharia), and the establishment of a Sharia state.

Hassan al-Banna, the founder of the modern Muslim Brotherhood movement, was highly influenced by Rashid Rida's thought, and developed his ideas into a social organization dedicated to the implementation of those principles. Alongside the Muslim Brotherhood's rapid expansion in the 1930s, Al-Banna wrote five risalat (letters) to his young, educated supporters. The ideas he set forth in the letters are still the pillars of the movement's worldview.

In his ideological messages, Al-Banna defined his movement as a group of believers on a quest for the revival of Islam, seeking to establish a Sharia state based on the Quranic "law of Allah". It is an objective Al-Banna hoped to achieve by liberating the Muslim world from any kind of foreign rule, followed by shaping a state governed by Islamic religious law. According to Al-Banna, the establishment of such a state is not the final goal. On the contrary, the new Sharia state must realize its social order in accordance with Islamic religious law and become a basis for the worldwide spread of Islam, eventually culminating in the emergence of Islamic hegemony around the globe. (cont'd)

when he began Hamas. In 1978 Yassin, an Israeli Arab citizen founded an Islamic organization called Mujama al-Islamiya. It acted as a social/civic organization which focused on helping the poor. Being a religious organization, it also built a network of mukhtars to run mosques throughout Gaza. In its beginning the organization focused on the Palestinian Arab refugees who lived in Gaza. Between 1978 and 1988 Sheikh Yassin and his Islamic Association thus developed a large and loyal following. It had a good reputation as an organization that really cared about the day-to-day realities of indigenous Palestinian Arab refugees. In 1988 Sheikh Yassin was confident enough to state the real goals of his organization, hence there was a name change to Hamas* and the issuing of the Hamas Charter. The veil had been lifted; Hamas was ready to be crystal clear as to what it believed in.

Up until the PLO signed the Oslo I Accord in September 1993 there was really no difference between the two organizations as far as the destruction of Israel and Zionism. But this all changed once the Oslo I Accord was signed. From Hamas's perspective, the

---

Al-Banna listed seven stages to achieve these objectives, each to be carried out in a gradual fashion. The stages are divided into social and political: the first three are based on educating the individual, the family, and the entire society of the Muslim world to implement Sharia laws in every aspect of daily life. The next four stages are political by nature, and include assuming power through elections, shaping a Sharia state, liberating Islamic countries from the burden of (physical and ideological) foreign occupation, uniting them into one Islamic entity ("new caliphate"), and spreading Islamic values throughout the world

The principle of liberating the world of Islam from the occupation of foreign powers has particular implications for the Muslim Brotherhood's stance towards Israel, whose establishment is considered by the movement members an integral part of the Western plot to conquer and bring division into the world of Islam. They categorically deny Israel's right to exist, and express vociferous opposition to any indication of normalization in relations with it. ("The ideology of the Muslim Brotherhood," *Crethi Plethi*, June 19, 2011 ((http://www.crethiplethi. com/the-ideology-of-the-muslim-brotherhood/global-islam/2011/))

* Hamas is an acronym of the Arabic phrase *Harakat al-Muqāwama al Islāmiyya*, meaning Islamic resistance ovement. The Arabic word *hamas* means courage or zeal.

PLO had sold out Palestinian Arabs and Islam itself. Hamas would become a foe of the PA on many levels and on other levels an ally in the war against Israel and Zionism.

As soon as the Oslo I Accord was signed Hamas sent a message to both Israel and the newly-formed PA that Israel under the best of conditions had signed a binding peace agreement with a Palestinian organization that did not speak for Hamas.* If anything, Oslo I would be rallying cry for war against Israel. It was also a challenge to the PA.

How would the PA react to Hamas terror? Would they act as the "Israelis watch dog" or would they support their "brother" Palestinian organization? Besides the doubts that had already existed regarding the sincerity of Arafat and the PLO/PA, as far as their commitment to live in peace with Israel, Hamas's declaration of war against Oslo and those who supported it in the Palestinian Arab world would really put Arafat and the PA to the test. Would they be able to stand up to Hamas and honor their core commitment to fight terror? As mentioned, Hamas began to ramp up its terror attacks against Israelis very shortly after Olso I was signed.

---

* Analysis of the Hamas Charter

Hamas took the PLO Covenant and surpassed it in its hatred of Israel and Zionism. This is because Hamas is an Islamic organization that couches the entire conflict in religious terms. To Hamas it is very clear and simple: The struggle with Israel is really a struggle between Islam and Judaism, between the believers and the unbelievers, between the righteous and the wicked. Since the Arab world, and the Gazan universe, in particular, are quite religious, by framing the conflict in religious terms—in contrast to the secular PLO—it sought to repurpose the conflict in a way the Grand Mufti described back in the 1920s, namely that it is a religious conflict that obligates Muslims to be involved in a jihad (holy war) to liberate the Islamic land of Palestine from the evil Jewish usurpers. Thus, Israel must be destroyed; there is no possibility of any sort of compromise or recognition of Israel.

Finally, Hamas developed two branches: the political wing and the military wing. When it suits its political needs it tells the West that its military wing—the Izz ad-Din al-Qassam Brigades—is responsible for terror attacks and did not have the approval of the political branch. But, in reality, the Izz ad-Din al-Qassem Brigades take their orders from the Hamas political leadership.

Baruch Goldstein and the Ma'arat HaMachpela Massacre: February 25, 1994

Besides an uptick in Hamas terror attacks in Gaza, there was also an increase in Hamas terror activities in and around the city of Hevron. Since the 1929 Massacre of Jews, Hevron had earned a well-deserved reputation as a hotbed of anti-Jewish, anti-Zionist, and anti-Israeli sentiment, most of it being religiously driven. Many Israelis were killed in the Hevron area between December 1993 and the summer of 1994. There were even credible reports that there was a plan to repeat the 1929 massacre against the Jews of Hevron and Kiryat Arba. But the Israeli government now treated these terrorist attacks in a very different light than it had done in the past.

In the post-Olso I Accord period the Israeli government had invested so much time, energy, prestige—not to mention constant reassuring Israelis that they would now be safer since Arafat and the PLO had become Israel's partners in fighting terror—that it was very hard for it to reconcile the rising body count of Israelis killed by Palestinian terrorists with the picture it had painted. Hence, the Israeli government found itself playing down these growing terrorist attacks, especially those that occurred in and around Jewish towns in Judea and Samaria. This was not merely turning a blind eye, but ignoring a very unpleasant reality.

In Kiryat Arba, a town right next door to Hevron, there lived an American-born physician named Baruch Goldstein who had made *Aliyah* in 1983. Goldstein had moved specifically to Kiryat Arba because of its religious and historical significance to Jews. There, Goldstein earned a reputation as a diligent and caring doctor. A fellow Kiryat Arba resident, Danny Wilder, wrote about his friend:

> I knew Goldstein. He was my friend. He was also a doctor. A very good one. He treated both Arabs and Jews. His trauma treatment was legendary in Israeli medical circles. His on-the-spot diagnoses were, after weeks of hospital tests, found to be 100% on the mark.

He was also the only on-duty doctor in Kiryat Arba, just about 24 hours a day, seven days a week. During the first intifada, following drive-by shootings and terror attacks, he was frequently the first medical person at the scene. As such, he witnessed horrible sights. It is said that he would sleep at night with earphones in his ears, allowing him to hear reports of attacks, without disturbing his wife's sleep.[3]

Goldstein was an admirer of Meir Kahane, the founder of the militant New York-based Jewish Defense League (JDL) that had earned a reputation in the 1960s for both standing up to antisemites and harassing Soviet officials and Soviet-related presentations in New York. But the JDL crossed the line at times and was involved in illegal violent incidents. As such, Meir Kahane and the JDL were both very controversial in the eyes of most American Jews. In 1971 Kahane made *Aliyah*, where shortly afterwards he founded Kach (Hebrew for "Thus"), an extreme, right-wing political party whose main platform was based on finding a way to remove the vast majority of Israel's Arab citizens he viewed as an indigenous fifth column. He subsequently served in two Knessets before he and his party were ruled racist by the Israeli Supreme Court and thus made ineligible to run or be members of Israel's parliament. In 1990 Kahane was assassinated in New York by an Egyptian Arab who was a member of the Muslim Brotherhood.*

Goldstein's admiration for Kahane was not the central theme of his life. Living in Kiryat Araba and being a doctor was.

Goldstein had never been involved in any violent act against Arabs, but the post-Olso terror attacks in the Hevron area affected him greatly—several of his close friends had been murdered on the road to Kiryat Arba. As a result, apparently he snapped. Like many Israelis, Goldstein was an IDF reservist, and like many Israelis who

* It is worth noting that Kahane was a minor political gadfly who never achieved the status of a powerful political figure in Israeli politics, while in the Arab world people like Yasser Arafat and Sheik Ahmed Yassin, who led the PLO and Hamas respectively and were involved in ordering thousands of terror attacks against Israeli Jews, were and remain revered figures in the Arab and Islamic world.

lived in areas deemed dangerous he was allowed to keep an IDF-issued M16 rifle in his home. Shortly after yet another of his close friends was murdered, Goldstein put on his IDF reserve uniform, took his M16 and several clips of ammunition and walked into Maarat HaMachpela (The Tomb of the Patriarchs). The day was February 25, 1994. At Maarat HaMachpela there exists a synagogue and a mosque. Since 1967 Jews were once again allowed to pray at the second holiest Jewish shrine, but a schedule was set up to allow for separate Jewish and Muslim services. Dressed as a soldier, he easily gained entry into the back of the mosque while local Muslims were praying. Once inside, he began to shoot into the crowd. By the time he ran out of ammunition and was subsequently beaten to death, he had killed 29 Palestinian worshipers and wounded 125.

This was the single largest Jewish terrorist attack against Arabs in the entire history of the Arab-Israeli conflict. Unlike the Palestinian Arab world that glorifies those who murder Jews and/or Israelis, the Israeli government and Jews all over the world publicly condemned the massacre. Since Goldstein had been a product of the Orthodox Jewish educational system in New York, ads were placed condemning the massacre and contending that his educational background played no part in his actions that day. In the ad it was also asked that Palestinian Arabs do the same for each of the many terrorist attacks carried out by terrorists against Jews and Israelis.

This massacre is now on the short list of "Zionist Atrocities", even though every Israeli political, religious, educational and military leader, with the exception of the Kach Party, condemned this massacre. It became the latest excuse for Palestinian terror that was to increase after this event. In a sense, Goldstein handed Hamas and the PA a propaganda gift.

ISRAEL - JORDAN DECLARATION OF NON-BELLIGERENCY: AUGUST 10, 1994

Israel's eastern neighbor, Jordan, a country that Israel enjoyed a de facto peace with since 1970—and had many secret contacts with over the years—openly pledged no more war with Israel. The reason Jordan was finally prepared to do so was the signing of the Oslo Accords. If the Palestinians, the putatively most "injured" Arab party in the conflict with Israel were talking about peace, certainly the Arab world could not fault Jordan for making peace as well. In a ceremony in the Arava near Eilat, the two countries held an elaborate ceremony to commemorate the start of the Israel-Jordan peace process.

ISRAEL JORDAN PEACE TREATY SIGNED: OCTOBER 26, 1994

On October 26, 1994, Prime Minister Yitzhak Rabin and Prime Minister Abdul-Salam Majali signed the Treaty of Peace between the State of Israel and the Hashemite Kingdom of Jordan, the second peace treaty Israel has signed since its independence.

The peace treaty with Jordan comprises 30 articles, five annexes which address boundary demarcations, water issues, police cooperation, environmental issues and mutual border crossings, and six maps.

The main provisions of the treaty are as follows:

1. International boundary

The Agreement delimits the agreed international boundary between Israel and Jordan including territorial waters and airspace. This boundary is delimited with reference to the Mandate boundary and is shown on the maps attached to the agreement. The Agreement provides for some minor mutual border modifications which will enable Israeli farmers in the Arava to continue to cultivate their land.

The Naharayim/Baqura Area and Zofar Area will fall under Jordanian sovereignty with Israeli private land use rights. These rights include unimpeded freedom of entry to, exit from and movement within the area. These areas are not subject to customs or immigration legislation. These rights will remain in force for 25 years and will be renewed automatically for the same period unless either country wishes to terminate the arrangement, in which case consultations will be taken.

2. Security

The two parties will refrain from any acts of belligerency or hostility, will ensure that no threats of violence against the other party originate from within their territory, and undertake to take necessary and effective measures to prevent acts of terrorism. They will also refrain from joining a coalition whose objectives include military aggression against the other party. Israel and Jordan will abstain from hostile propaganda and will repeal all discriminatory references and expressions of hostility in their respective legislation.

The two countries will establish a Conference on Security and Cooperation in the Middle East (CSCME) which will be modeled after the Conference on Security and Cooperation in Europe (CSCE). This is an ambitious attempt to replace the more classical view of security by substituting the old notions of deterrence and military preparedness with confidence building measures. In due time, confidence will lead to the establishment of mutual trust and institutions aimed at preventing war and enhancing cooperation.

3. Water

Israel and Jordan have agreed on allocations of water from the Jordan and Yarmouk Rivers and from Araba/Arava groundwaters. Israel has agreed to transfer to Jordan 50 million cubic meters of water annually from the northern part of the country. In addition the two countries have agreed to cooperate to alleviate the water shortage by developing existing and new water resources, by preventing contamination of water resources, and by minimizing water wastage.

4. Freedom of Passage

Nationals from both countries and their vehicles will be permitted freedom of movement through open roads and border-crossings. Vessels from either country will have the right to passage through territorial waters, and will be granted access to ports. Negotiations are underway towards a Civil Aviation Agreement. The Strait of Tiran and the Gulf of Aqaba are considered international waterways, open to all nations for freedom of navigation and overflight.

5. Places of Historical and Religious Significance

There will be freedom of access to the places of religious and historical significance. In accordance with the Washington Declaration, Israel respects the present special role of the Hashemite Kingdom of Jordan in Muslim Holy shrines in Jerusalem. When negotiations on the permanent status, as detailed in the Declaration of Principles, will take place, Israel will give high priority to the Jordanian historic role in these shrines.

6. Refugees and Displaced Persons

The parties recognize the human problems caused by the conflict in the Middle East, and agree to alleviate them on a bilateral level and to try to resolve them through three channels:

The quadripartite committee with Egypt and the Palestinians with regard to displaced persons.

The Multilateral Working Group on Refugees.

Negotiations in a framework to be agreed upon - bilateral or otherwise in conjunction with permanent status negotiations detailed in the Declaration of Principles.

7. Normalization of Relations between Israel and Jordan

The peace treaty deals not only with an end to war, but also normalization. Various articles of the treaty deal with practical issues of normalization in such matters as culture and science, the war against crime and drugs, transportation and roads, postal services and telecommunications, tourism the environment, energy, health, agriculture, and the development of the Jordan Rift Valley and the Aqaba/Eilat area. Economic cooperation is seen as one of the pillars of peace, vital to the promotion of secure and harmonious relations between the two peoples.

Diplomatic relations between Israel and Jordan were established on November 27, 1994, including the appointment of ambassadors and the opening of embassies.[4]

The Israeli Jordanian Peace Treaty was realized in the opposite way that Oslo was conceived. Israel and Jordan had had a de facto peace since September 1970, and after 24 years of slowly and quietly creating an air of trust and cooperation on certain matters the two countries formalized their existing relationship in the form of a treaty. Oslo was an agreement between two warring parties that were hoping by taking a huge leap of faith and ignoring all the real issues that separated them that they could achieve peace. It was a leap of faith that failed miserably.

TERROR ATTACKS BEGIN TO UNDERMINE THE OSLO PEACE PROCESS: 1994-1995

During the 16-month post-Oslo period there began to emerge a very disturbing pattern. While the diplomats and politicians in Israel and the West spoke of a peace process, the average Israeli citizen was beginning to sense that s/he was much more susceptible to Palestinian terror than at any time in their lives. It was the opposite of a peace process on the ground; instead it was the beginning of a period of an exponential growth of terror.

Nevertheless, Israel moved ahead with the Oslo process and did its best to put a positive spin on the growth of terror. The Israeli government was at times arguing that Arafat and the PA simply had not had enough time to take control of the security situation, and given more time, support, political power and territory there would be good results. Still, there were many in the Israeli public who began to have serious doubts about Oslo.

OSLO II ACCORD SIGNED:
SEPTEMBER 28, 1995

A 420-page document, the Oslo II Accord delineated the Israeli plan for withdrawal from major Arab population centers in Judea and Samaria (such as Shechem, Ramallah, Jenin, etc.). It outlined what areas Israel was withdrawing from, and set up an elaborate system of joint Palestinian-Israeli cooperation, i.e., security, economic, trade, etc. It also outlined what the Palestinian Authority's responsibilities were in great detail.

A very complex map was drawn up to define areas under autonomy and areas still under the jurisdiction of the Israeli Army. The map divided Judea and Samaria into three zones: Areas A, B and C.

Area A was designated as under the full control of the PA. In this area were the main urban centers where the overwhelming majority or Palestinian Arabs resided. Once it redeployed, the IDF could not enter Area A without the approval of the PA. In essence, this area became a mini-independent Palestinian State.

Area B contained most of the Arab villages that comprised the suburbs near the large Arab population centers in Judea and Samaria. In area B the PA would have full control of the day-to-day lives of the Palestinian Arab population, no different than in area A. The main difference. however, was that while there would be PA police deployed in these areas, the IDF was permitted to enter Area B to maintain safety and security for Israeli settlements in the vicinity as well as for security for pre-1967 Israel as well.

Area C encompassed all the existing Israeli settlements, IDF bases and what was Jordanian land prior to 1967. All of Area C remained under the full control of Israel and the IDF.

There was not much about Gaza in the agreement since with the exception of the Gush Katif area, a few Jewish settlements in the northern part of Gaza and one settlement called Netzarim in the middle of Gaza, the area had been under PA jurisdiction since May of 1994.

This second Oslo agreement also created the apparatus for the PA to have its first elections for an 88-person council as well as for a president.

Redeployment was completed by January 1996 in all cities except Hevron, where there was an issue concerning some 400 Jews who lived in the city proper. The agreement also stated that Israel and the PA were to begin negotiations on the final status of Judea, Samaria, Gaza and on the status of Jerusalem. The target date for a full comprehensive final agreement was set for May of 1999.

There was now a new map of Judea and Samaria with the PA controlling the day-to-day lives of over 95 percent of the Palestinian Arab population in Judea and Samaria. For all practical purposes, the Israeli occupation ended in January of 1996.

CONSEQUENCE OF THE OSLO II ACCORD

Despite the rise of Hamas and the PA's inability or disinterest in stopping its terror attacks, Israel still felt committed to continue the Oslo peace process. Israel fleshed out what was missing from the Oslo I Accord in terms of the details of how the PA would operate, be organized and under what principles it would administer the areas that were being handed over. Area C would be something to negotiate about in the future. Oslo II truly created the best opportunity the Palestinian Arabs ever had for building the foundations of a functioning, healthy, democratic state.

This agreement made it abundantly clear that both sides were obligated to creating an environment among their respective populations that would foster neighborly and peaceful relations. This meant actively working to project positive images about the other side, and certainly not to disseminate any negative propaganda. This was a very crucial point. Oslo was built on a unusual premise: There had never been a history of peaceful relations between the sides, in fact they were enemies. Oslo was designed to create an atmosphere of trust and positive feelings between these two enemies. Once a positive atmosphere was created, then Israel and the PA would hopefully be comfortable tackling the very difficult issues that separated them and come up with acceptable compromises.

For many Israelis who were directly or indirectly affected by the rise in terror, there soon developed a growing sense that Arafat and the PA were not exactly true peace partners.* But this was not so easily accepted by the Labor-led government and most of the Israeli media that had both invested so much effort in Oslo. This led to a very uneasy reality developing in Israel. It was almost forbidden to speak out against the Oslo Peace Process, regardless of how much proof one had that perhaps it was not all that it

---

* "Although some Palestinian factions have expressed readiness for a peace treaty based on the Green Line, all the factions are agreed that the conflict will not end until an Arab majority has been created in Israel by flooding the country with the refugees of 1948 and their millions of descendants. Reunion (cont'd)

was supposed to be. For a very open, opinionated, democratic society like Israel, this caused more anger at the government and the media than there would have been had the growing dissent not been marginalized and referred to as enemies of peace.

THE ASSASSINATION OF PRIME MINISTER YITZCHAK RABIN: NOVEMBER 4, 1995

On November 4, 1995, "Prime Minister Yitzhak Rabin, who led Israel to victory in 1967 and began the march toward peace a generation later, was shot dead by a lone assassin...as he was leaving a vast rally in Tel Aviv."[5] It is the first time in its 47-year history that an Israeli political figure is murdered by a fellow Jew.

> Yigal Amir [Rabin's assassin] focuse[d] on...two tenets of religious law—in Hebrew it is *din moser* and din *rodef*. And

---

with Gaza and the West Bank would then follow. Likewise, opinion polls have testified that the vast majority of the Palestinian population views the 'two-state solution' as acceptable only as a stage toward a unitary state on the territory of the British Mandate.

"As for Arafat himself, despite his speeches in English from 1988 on, he clearly never abandoned the struggle to eliminate the State of Israel. In early 1996, details of a speech emerged that he had given to a closed audience of Arab ambassadors in Stockholm on January 30. There he explained that the Oslo accords signed with Israel in 1993 and 1995 were a ruse to give the PLO a base in Palestine from which it could make the lives of Jews so miserable that they would all want to leave. This strategy he put into action, in vain, during the Second Intifada of 2000-2005, after refusing Israeli-American offers to create a Palestinian state that satisfied all Palestinian demands except the "right of return" for Palestinian refugees.

"When the Israel Defense Force (IDF) occupied Arafat's headquarters in Ramallah during 2002-2004, it found documents signed by Arafat authorizing money for bomb belts for suicide bombers. Arafat was aware of what he was signing, as he had personally crossed out the sums requested and replaced them with smaller sums. So much in secret; his public speeches in Arabic included a ditty that sang of 'a million martyrs marching on Jerusalem.' It made meaningless his commitments in the Oslo accords to cease terrorism and incitement." (Malcom Lowe, "Israeli Settlements, the Violet Line and the Cheshire Cat," Gatestone Institute, September 7, 2016 ((https://www.gatestoneinstitute.org/8865/israel-settlements))

essentially what these say are—is that if someone is pursuing Jews with the intent of harming them, or if someone is handing over Jews to the enemy and that will cause them harm, then you have the right, or even the obligation…to prevent it and to prevent it even by killing the pursuer. And Amir determines pretty early on that these Jewish laws apply to Rabin and that there is a death sentence hanging over Rabin…Later, it comes out [that] in the religious seminaries, in the yeshivas in Israel and the Orthodox schools, rabbis are talking about these issues. And as the Oslo process progresses, they're talking quite a lot about it.[6]

Subsequent to the assassination, Israel entered a period of shock and deep introspection. How did this happen? A period of deep polarization occurred in Israel because Amir wore a *kippah* and represented a very alienated and angry segment of the Religious Zionist movement. Even though the murder was condemned by every leader in the State of Israel, regardless of party or religious affiliation, because Amir came from a Religious Zionist background there was an exceptionally great deal of condemnation from Religious Zionist rabbis and leaders, as well as a great deal of soul searching.

The years following the assassination of Rabin were very rocky ones as far as the relationship between the Religious Zionist Movement and many in the secular Left of Israeli society but it might be said that by 1999, when Ehud Barak was elected prime minister, things had returned to the way they were before this hideous act.

As mentioned earlier, the architects and advocates of the Oslo process were so invested in its success that they willfully ignored early signs that suggested Arafat and the newly-formed PA would not be the peace partners hoped for. By doing so, they not only ignored acts of terror, the rise of Hamas and the duplicity of Arafat, but they ignored a growing segment of the

Israeli population that felt totally disenfranchised, frightened and threatened by the Oslo agreements.

Rabin—one of Israel's greatest patriots, warriors and statesmen—by dint of his history and accomplishments had managed to push through Oslo despite the distrust of many reactionary groups. But the events between late 1993 and early 1995 had already cast serious doubts as to how the Oslo process could succeed. To those victimized by terrorism, much like Baruch Goldstein, there were those who snapped. Though inexcusable, Rabin represented for these extremists the wrong direction the country was headed, a direction that threated Jewish life in the homeland.

The case of Yihyeh Ayash was an early example of why Oslo was doomed to fail. Ayash was a Hamas "engineer" whose specialty was making bombs.

> Ayyash built the bombs used in a number of Hamas suicide attacks: the Mehola Junction bombing, the Afula Bus massacre, the Hadera central station massacre, the Tel Aviv bus 5 massacre, the Egged bus 36 bombing, the Ramat Gan bus 20 bombing, and the Jerusalem bus 26 bombing. As part of a strategic alliance between Hamas and Palestinian Islamic Jihad, Ayyash built the bombs used by Islamic Jihad at the Beit Lid massacre.[7]

After a long and arduous manhunt the Israeli Shabak—Israel's internal security agency—caught up to Ayash. Though Ayash's only contribution to the Palestinian "cause" was his construction of instruments of death, his neutralization was touted as one of martyrdom. It was reported that over 100,000 Palestinians attended his funeral. Arafat himself gave a eulogy and paid a very public condolence call to Ayash's mother. Even streets were named after him. These overt signs of PA transgression were ignored by the Israeli government and its consorts in the media. For them Oslo had become an article of faith, almost a religion unto itself. They appeared not to want to be confused by unpleasant facts.*

PALESTINIAN ELECTIONS: JANUARY, 1996

In its first-ever election, eighty-eight representatives were installed in the PA Assembly. Yasser Arafat was elected president of the Authority. One of the only democratic elections ever held in the Arab world, it was the beginning of Palestinian self-rule. The PA subsequently deployed a very large police force in Judea and Samaria, approximately 30,000 men, with another 10,000 men in Gaza. On one hand, this was very promising and exciting. On the other hand, it came one month after the funeral of Yihyeh Ayash and was to be followed by one of the bloodiest months in Israeli history—as far as civilian casualties caused by terror attacks were concerned. Hamas suicide bombers pulled off four very bloody suicide bombings in Israel in the span of two weeks. In Ashkelon, Jerusalem twice, and Tel-Aviv, sixty-three Israelis were killed and hundreds more wounded.

---

* In retrospect, the naysayers were correct: "[T]he Oslo 'peace process' between Israel and the Palestine Liberation Organization (PLO) stands as one of the worst-ever calamities to have hit Israelis and Palestinians. For Israel, it has been the starkest strategic blunder in the country's history—establishing an ineradicable terror entity on Israel's doorstep, deepening its internal cleavages, destabilizing its political system, and weakening its international standing.

For West Bank and Gaza Palestinians, it has brought about subjugation to corrupt and repressive PLO and Hamas regimes—regimes that have reversed the hesitant advent of civil society in these territories, shattered their socioeconomic wellbeing, and made the prospects for peace and reconciliation with Israel ever more remote.

This abject failure is a direct result of the Palestinian leadership's perception of the process as a pathway not to a two-state solution—meaning Israel alongside a Palestinian state in the West Bank and Gaza—but to the subversion of the State of Israel; not to nation-building and state creation, but to the formation of a repressive terror entity that would perpetuate conflict with Israel while keeping its hapless constituents in constant and bewildered awe as its leaders line their pockets from the proceeds of this misery." (Efraim Karsh, "The Oslo Disaster," *Mideast Security and Policy Studies* No. 123 (The Begin-Sadat Center for Strategic Studies, Bar-Ilan University, 2016), 8.)

As a result, public opinion began to shift toward the Benjamin Netanyahu-headed Likud Party, which took a harder line toward the PA and Hamas. In the meantime, the Labor government now headed by Shimon Peres closed off all PA areas from Israel proper. In addition, Arafat was pressured to begin a crackdown on Hamas in the areas under PA jurisdiction. Unfortunately, this crackdown was short-lived. Many of the Hamas operatives who were arrested were released in a matter of days.

Israeli Election: May 29, 1996

After taking over from Yitzhak Rabin following his assassination, Peres decided to call early elections in order to give the government a mandate to advance the peace process...Labour and Peres were comfortably ahead in the polls early in 1996, holding a lead of 20%. However, the country was hit by a spate of suicide attacks by Hamas including the Jerusalem bus 18 massacres and other attacks in Ashkelon and the Dizengoff Center, which killed 59 people, [which] severely damaged Peres' election chances. Polls taken in mid-May showed Peres ahead by just 4-6%, whilst two days before the election his lead was down to 2%.

Several leading ultra-orthodox [r]abbis, including Elazar Shach, called on their followers to vote for Netanyahu, whilst Leah Rabin, Yitzhak's widow, called on Israelis to vote for Peres so that her husband's death "would not be in vain." Netanyahu also warned that a Peres victory would lead to the division of Jerusalem in a final peace deal with the Palestinians.

Despite the national trauma which the assassination of Rabin caused, and although many blamed at the time the leaders of Israeli political right for the incitement that preceded the assassination, due to the series of suicide bombings carried out in Israel, and due to the failed military operation "Grapes of Wrath" conducted in Lebanon that caused many casualties among Lebanese civilians, a significant change occurred in the position of the Israeli voters which resulted eventually in

50.5% percent of voters supporting Netanyahu on election day. A significant number of Israeli Arabs boycotted the elections amidst rising Lebanese casualties, which became an advantage for Netanyahu as the vast majority of Arabs would have supported Peres but declined to vote. In addition, the intensive campaign conducted by Netanyahu versus the failed campaign of Shimon Peres, as well as the support Netanyahu got at the last moment from the Chabad movement, were all in Netanyahu's favor.[8]

For the first time in Israel's history, Israelis had gotten to vote for the Knesset and the prime minister on separate ballots. The main issues debated in this election were: the future of the Oslo Accords, and could the PA and Arafat be trusted? Was there even a chance that the PA could really become a true partner for peace? What about the tough issues that were cast aside by Oslo, but would eventually have to be tackled—Jerusalem, the settlements, final borders and the Arab refugees?

Once in power, at the head of a right of center coalition, Netanyahu proceeded to scale back the speed of the Oslo process.

As Prime Minister Netanyahu raised many questions about many central premises of the Oslo peace process. One of his main points was disagreement with the Oslo premise that the negotiations should proceed in stages, meaning that concessions should be made to Palestinians before any resolution was reached on major issues, such as the status of Jerusalem, and the amending of the Palestinian National Charter. Oslo supporters had claimed that the multi-stage approach would build goodwill among Palestinians and would propel them to seek reconciliation when these major issues were raised in later stages. Netanyahu said that these concessions only gave encouragement to extremist elements, without receiving any tangible gestures in return. He called for tangible gestures of Palestinian goodwill in return for Israeli concessions. Despite his stated differences with the

Oslo Accords, Prime Minister Netanyahu continued their implementation, but his Premiership saw a marked slow-down in the Peace Process.[9]

ARAB SUMMIT HELD TO REACT TO THE VICTORY OF NETANYAHU: JUNE 1996

For the first time since the Gulf War (1991) the majority of the Arab World's twenty-two heads of state met together to discuss the Arab response to the Netanyahu victory. Many of the delegates represented Arab countries that to this day do not recognize Israel and would like to see it wiped off the map. Interestingly enough, the summit's conclusion was that Israel better be prepared to create a Palestinian State and to make Jerusalem the capital of that state. Furthermore, it was mandated that Israel withdraw from the Golan Heights. If Israel failed to commit herself to these demands, then the Middle East would return to a situation of implacable enmity between the Arab World and Israel.

The Israeli government responded that peace is not dictated by threats, and that the outcome of negotiations could not be pre-determined. Let each side present its position at the negotiating table.

TUNNEL RIOTS IN ISRAEL: SEPTEMBER 1996

There is an ancient, 300-yard-long tunnel running north to south parallel to the Western Wall that is approximately 30-40 feet below the area where people pray at the Kotel. The tunnel dates back to the period of the Second Temple remodeling (some 2,000 years ago.) The tunnel has been studied and excavated by archeologists since the late 1970s. Opened to the general public for guided tours since 1989, the tunnel has great religious and historical significance to the Jewish people due to its proximity to the Temple Mount. But there was only one way to get in and out, so groups had to wait to enter until one group doubled back and left.

In late September of 1996, "Netanyahu and Jerusalem's mayor Ehud Olmert decided to open an exit in the Arab Quarter for the

Western Wall Tunnel, which prior Prime Minister Shimon Peres had instructed to be put on hold for the sake of peace."[10] The new opening allowed visitors to walk out into the Via Delarosa in the Christian Quarter of the Old City and not have to double back to the entrance near the Kotel. The entrance had nothing to do with the Temple Mount, the Al-Aqsa Mosque, or the Dome of the Rock, yet the Palestinian Authority chose to turn the opening of the new entrance into a reason to go to war. They presented the issue in the following way: Israel has just dug a tunnel underneath the holy Al-Aqsa Mosque. This was a religious offense as well as a danger to the Mosque itself, which now may collapse!

When this version of events was delivered to the Palestinian population they began attacking the Israeli checkpoints separating the zones from Israeli-held territory. The Palestinian Police at first let them attack the Israelis—they just moved out of the way—and then joined in themselves. But unlike the rioters the Palestinian police were armed. Fierce gun battles erupted between Tzahal (IDF) and the Palestinian police. The riots lasted for three days! Over seventy Palestinians were killed and twelve Israelis. Israel eventually had to deploy tanks and artillery around the autonomy zones to calm the situation.

This mini-war caused the Israeli public and government to further lose confidence in their new peace partners, who they held directly responsible for the misinformation about the tunnel, encouraging the riots and allowing their police to open fire on the Israelis.

PEACE SUMMIT IN WASHINGTON: OCTOBER 1-3 1996

In light of the mini-war, U.S. President Bill Clinton invited the sides to Washington to calm the situation.

Marathon negotiations between Israeli and Palestinian leaders failed to resolve bitter differences that exploded in Mideast violence and jeopardized the fragile peace process. But the two sides agreed to press ahead with nonstop talks... Israeli Prime Minister Benjamin Netanyahu proclaimed a feeling of greater trust with Palestinian leader Yasser Arafat as discussions ended yesterday. But he added, "I don't have any illusions whatsoever about the difficulties ahead. It's a very tense period fraught with dangers right now." Closing the White House-sponsored talks, President Clinton said somberly, "We have not made as much progress as I wish we had."

He said he was not certain the Mideast crisis was over but expressed confidence that violence would subside. "Please, please give us a chance to make this thing work in the days ahead," Clinton implored Palestinians and Israelis... Netanyahu and Arafat sat stone-faced, side by side in the East Room with Jordan's King Hussein at the wrapup of the talks. By prearrangement, they declined an opportunity to talk there. Leaving the White House, Netanyahu vigorously shook Arafat's hand, clasping it with both hands for several seconds. Clinton beamed. Arafat saluted Clinton before stepping into his car. The president returned the gesture. Netanyahu said the summit "cemented the principle that the path to peace is through negotiations and not through violence." He added, "The children of Israel are safer tonight."

Nabil Shaath, a top aide to Arafat, said the summit's failure was Israel's fault. "There is no agreement about anything. President Clinton did his best to put the peace process back on track, but the Israelis wouldn't let him," Shaath said.[10]

HEVRON AGREEMENT: JANUARY 15, 1997

As a result of Oslo II, Israel withdrew from all major Palestinian population centers by January 1996 with the exception of Hevron, because there was a Jewish population living in the city itself (as opposed to a Jewish town nearby). A very detailed agreement was signed. The Palestinian Authority ended up controlling eighty percent of the city of about 80,000 Palestinians and Israel retained twenty percent of the city with about 18,000 Palestinians, as well as the 500 Jews. Ma'arat HaMachpela remained under Israeli control. By the end of January the redeployment was carried out.

Unfortunately, within a day, the PA began violating the agreement; instead of 400 police they brought in 1,200.

HELICOPTER ACCIDENT AT SH'AR YASHUV: FEBRUARY 4, 1997

The worst air disaster in Israeli history occurred when two large helicopters that were on their way to the Israeli security zone in South Lebanon collided. All seventy-three soldiers on board were killed. The entire country was in mourning for seven days.

> To this day, the cause of the crash has yet to be definitively ascertained. A government commission of inquiry failed to come to a conclusion, although it did rule out any mechanical or technical malfunction in the helicopters.
>
> ...The commission also failed to find evidence of health-related ailments or psychological distress that could have played a role.
>
> Investigators ruled out other possible factors, including the use of mobile devices, weather conditions, or enemy fire.
>
> "The events in the final few seconds will remain a mystery," the panel's report said.[12]

ISRAEL ANNOUNCES PLANS TO BEGIN CONSTRUCTION OF HAR HOMA: MARCH 1997

Har Homa was a barren hill on the southern edge of Jerusalem near Bet-Lechem and right across the road from Gilo. It is in an area captured by Israel in the Six-Day War. In 1997, after paying both Arab and Jewish owners of the property (albeit after winning Supreme Court decisions granting eminent domain rights to the State), the Netanyahu government authorized construction on the site despite internation clamor. Citing language similar to that of Itzhak Rabin, Netanyahu stated:

> .. the land expropriations in Jerusalem were not designed to usurp anyone's property, but rather to turn uncultivated areas into construction projects for both Arabs and Jews. (Prime Minister Rabin, Ma'ariv, 12 May 1995)

***

I want to make clear that we will build in all of Jerusalem, and we will build also in Har Homa... First of all because there is a big housing deficit in Jerusalem, there will be construction for both Jews and Arabs. (Prime Minister Netanyahu, AP, 25 February 1997)[13]

Again, as in the case of the Kotel tunnel, the Palestinian Authority sought to create an incident. The PA thus proceeded to claim that Israel was building a settlement in the heart of Arab East Jerusalem in direct violation of the Oslo II Accord.

Israel counterclaimed...

...that Har Homa is within Jerusalem, and construction work does not constitute a change in the status of Jerusalem, in accordance with the Oslo Accords. Furthermore, the land was unoccupied and undeveloped prior to the current construction; both Jewish and Arab landholders were compensated for the land; and residents of Beit Sahour would not be able to develop the land in any event as the Oslo agreements specifically barred Palestinian jurisdiction over Jerusalem for the time being, and also excluded settlements as an issue, leaving it for permanent status negotiations.[14]

This started a wave of demonstrations, riots, and violence that went on through July of 1997. After cogent analysis the following was determined:

The land for Har Homa was not stolen from Palestinians.

The Israeli administration, with typical lack of foresight, failed to make decisions and explain them to the world in a manner that was not easy to misconstrue.

The Palestinian objection was actually a desire to prevent Israel building because it might strengthen Israel's bargaining position.

Palestinians do not explain that, but say, or allow their supporters to believe, that the land was stolen.

Advocates for the Palestinian cause eagerly make their accusations against Israel on the basis of a convenient misunderstanding (a lie if one were to be blunt).[15]

The initial project was completed in 2005.

THE STRATEGIC SIGNIFICANCE OF HAR HOMA

Har Homa, established in 1997, is another Jewish neighborhood on Jerusalem's southern flanks. With an estimated 6,000 residents, the suburb is a strategic impediment to Palestinian attempts to link up northern Bethlehem with Jerusalem. Google Earth's maps of the area show Har Homa about a kilometer from the Palestinian Authority-controlled town of Bethlehem. Just north of Har Homa are several Arab neighborhoods of east Jerusalem, and the Old City of Jerusalem lies just 5.5 kilometers beyond...The city of Jerusalem is ringed by neighborhoods built after 1967. They house about one-third of Jerusalem's burgeoning population, and they also serve to protect the city. The neighborhood of Ramot serves as a buffer to the north; Mount Scopus, French Hill, Ramat Eshkol, and Sanhedria protect Jerusalem's east; and Gilo and Har Homa serve as a buffer to the south.[16]

HAMAS BOMBS MACHNE YEHUDA MARKET IN JERUSALEM: JULY/SEPTEMBER 1997

A pattern that began shortly after the Oslo I Accord was signed continued.

On Wednesday, 30 July 1997 at 1:15 pm, two Palestinian suicide bombers who carried bags laden with explosives and nails detonated their explosive devices 45 meters (150 feet) apart almost simultaneously in a central alley in the popular outdoor market, killing 16 civilians, among them an Arab resident of Eilabun, and injuring 178 people, many of them teenagers and tourists.

Thirteen Israelis were killed immediately and three others died later from their injuries. The Mahane Yehuda attack was followed by a triple suicide bombing on the Ben Yehuda pedestrian mall in downtown Jerusalem on 4 September, which killed five Israelis and wounded over 190.[17]

To the Palestinian Authority, when talks move slowly and its demands are not being met, a message must be sent to the Israeli side. The message is that terror is not an inconceivable option; if all else fails there is always the threat of terrorist activities against the Israeli civilian population. Though Hamas takes responsibility, the PA, by allowing Hamas to operate almost unmolested, and itself inciting antisemitic and anti-Israeli behavior in its speeches, TV spots, radio broadcasts, newspapers, etc., is responsible as well.

Israel responded by closing off all of Judea, Samaria and Gaza from pre-1967 Israel to create a separation between Israelis and Palestinians. In addition,

> ... [i]n retaliation for these and other attacks, a decision was reached to target Hamas leaders. According to an Israeli press release, Mossad agents tried to poison chairman Khaled Mashal, who resided at the time in Jordan. The assassination attempt failed and the Mossad agents were captured by the Jordanian authorities. They were later released in exchange for the release of Sheikh Ahmed Yassin, the founder and "spiritual leader" of Hamas who was serving a life sentence in an Israeli prison.[18]

The appearance of Sheik Yassin was an unmitigated disaster from an Israeli perspective. A man who was all but forgotten when he was sitting in Israeli prison received a second life. Hundreds of thousands of Gazans came out to greet the founder of Hamas. His reception was a clear message that the people of Gaza viewed him as a true hero since he spoke of the destruction of Israel and Zionism openly and unabashedly unlike Arafat who did speak that way to Palestinian audiences but paid lip service to peace with

Israel when speaking to Western leaders and the Western media. Thanks to Yassin's freeing from jail and hero's welcome in 1997 Hamas appeared to be far more popular than the PA.

Dani Yatom, who up until this debacle in Jordan had had a thirty-five-year stellar career in the IDF and Mossad, was forced to step down.

WYE RIVER AGREEMENT: OCTOBER 1998

Ever Since the Hevron Agreement was signed in January of 1997 a stalemate existed between Israel and the PA with regard to the Oslo peace process. In an effort to breakthrough this logjam President Bill Clinton invited Prime Minister Benjamin Netanyahu and PA Chairman Yasser Arafat to join him in an intense series of face-to-face negotiations at the Wye Plantation in Maryland. All three leaders came with their top aides, and after almost two weeks of non-stop negotiations the parties held a public signing ceremony at the White House. King Hussein of Jordan, who was terminally ill at the time, came from his hospital bed to urge all the sides to work out an agreement.

The agreement basically set up a framework for moving the Oslo process forward. Besides the twenty-seven percent of Judea and Samaria that the PA had been controlling since the Hevron Agreement, Israel agreed to hand over an additional thirteen percent. These land transfers would come in stages and only after the PA complied with promises made in the past: a) The PA must stop the anti-Israel and antisemitic propaganda in the PA-controlled media; b) collect the thousands of weapons in the hands of Palestinians who were not police and were not part of the Palestinian security forces; c) disarm Hamas; d) arrest known Hamas activists wanted for acts of violence against Israelis, and e) trim the police and security forces down to the original numbers agreed upon in the 1995 Oslo II Accord.

Israel also agreed to release more Palestinian prisoners from Israeli jails. The U.S. CIA was inserted as the monitoring organization that everybody trusted. It was detailed to verify the PA's compliance to the deal. Finally, once the agreement was fully implemented, then Israel and the PA would begin the final status negotiations on all outstanding issues.

COLLAPSE OF THE LIKUD GOVERNMENT: DECEMBER 1998

After two and a half years the coalition government led by Benjamin Netanyahu came apart.

> The most significant aspect of the Wye Accords was not the agreement itself but, rather, Netanyahu's reluctant acceptance of the principle of exchanging occupied land for peace and security. However much he sought to distance himself from this portion of the Accords, the fact remained that he had accepted it on behalf of Israel. In doing so, he created deep rifts within the ruling Likud coalition, which had consistently demanded the establishment of Greater Israel and denounced all compromises on withdrawal from West Bank territory. As his government teetered on the brink of collapse, Netanyahu sought to appease his critics on the religious right with an announcement that Israel would suspend its scheduled withdrawal from an additional 13 percent of the West Bank. This was a violation of the Wye Accords he had signed only a month earlier. Riddled by dissension within and pressured by the United States from without, the Netanyahu government fell in December 1998 during a raucous session of the Knesset, which rejected the Wye Accords and voted to dissolve itself. Netanyahu's coalition of rightists and nationalists simply could not endorse the principle of returning occupied land to the Palestinians. At the same time, political moderates and leftists condemned Netanyahu for failing to implement the Wye agreement. Netanyahu's attempt to satisfy the United States and the Israeli moderates by signing the Wye Accords and to mollify the religious Right by refusing to carry them out had failed. He now had to submit his government's record to the Israeli electorate.

> ...[I]t should be noted that Likud's domestic policies also contributed to its downfall. Netanyahu's failure to further

the peace process cost Israel the economic gains it had
made in the immediate aftermath of Oslo 1. Unemployment
continued to rise and with it constant labor unrest. In the
bitter contest over the role of religion in the state, Netanyahu
catered to the religious Right. The government posed as the
protector of Israel's Jewish identity in the face of secular
assaults from within Israel and from the homogenizing effects
of globalization on cultural distinctiveness in general. In a
gesture of support for the religious conservatives, Netanyahu
allowed the Knesset to debate a proposed Conversion Bill that
would provide the Orthodox rabbinical establishment with
greater power in determining who was a Jew in Israel. His
government also increased state subsidies to ultra-Orthodox
educational and social programs. Netanyahu's courting of the
religious Right led secular Israelis to view him as a figure who
was prepared to tilt Israel toward becoming a state controlled
by Orthodox religious circles and served to intensify the
cultural war that was already dividing Israeli society.[19]

ISRAELI ELECTION: MAY 17, 1999

The 1999 election became a referendum on Prime Minister
Netanyahu's ability to lead the country and his ability to lead
a coalition. The election centered on the issue of personal
accountability and trustworthiness. Other issues were the future
of the Oslo peace process, the economic recession that had
been going on since 1996, the growing rift between the religious
and secular communities in Israel, the growing rift between the
different Jewish ethnic groups in Israel, i.e., Russians, Ethiopians,
Moroccans, etc., and finally Israeli Arab demands to have a bigger
say in Israeli politics.

As in the previous two elections Israelis once again sent a
message to their elected officials and to the world at large.

The election campaign, vituperative even by Israeli
standards, pitted Netanyahu and his Likud bloc against
Ehud Barak, a former army chief of staff, and his expanded
Labor coalition known as One Israel. When Israelis went to

the polls on May 17, 1999, they delivered a harsh verdict on Netanyahu's leadership. Barak received 56 percent of the votes for prime minister to Netanyahu's 44 percent. In the context of Israeli politics, this constituted a landslide victory for Barak and showed that Israelis had become disenchanted with Netanyahu's political machinations, with the divisiveness associated with his leadership, and with his failure to pursue a true peace agreement with the Palestinians.

Israel's new prime minister has been described as a dovish hawk in the image of his mentor, the late Yitzhak Rabin. Barak endorsed the resumption of peace negotiations with the Palestinians and recognized the need for compromise. He wished to avoid the confrontational posture adopted by his predecessor and to employ a more conciliatory approach to the Palestinian leadership. But as a career military man and the most decorated soldier in Israeli history, he possessed a keen sense of Israel's security needs and was expected to be a tough negotiator.

If Barak's victory represented the desires of the majority of Israelis for a revival of the peace process, the results of elections to the Knesset revealed a society deeply divided on domestic issues. Beginning with the elections of 1996, Israeli voters cast two ballots, one for prime minister and another for the party list. In the 1999 elections, an unprecedented thirty-three parties received official authorization to field candidates, and fifteen of these parties ended up with representation in the Knesset. The problem this proliferation of parties presented to the formation of a stable governing coalition was compounded by several competing domestic agendas among them. For example, the two parties that made the biggest gains in the Knesset held firm—and opposing—views on the role of religion in the state. One was a new rigorously secular party, Shinui, and the other was Shas, an ultra-Orthodox religious party that became the third largest party in the Knesset. Shas did not object to the peace process, but it rejected the concept of a secular legal system and insisted instead that Israel should be governed by Jewish law. The growth of these two parties suggested that the issue of peace with the Palestinians was less divisive than the differences between secular and religious sectors of Israeli society.

In seeking to rise above this rift and pose as the leader of all of Israel, Barak formed a coalition that included not just Labor's natural center-left partners but also Shas. This raised the possibility that Barak would be forced to make the same kind of domestic religious concessions that all of his predecessors had made in order to achieve consensus on such other issues as peace, economic policy, and social programs. Israel's electoral system, instead of providing the foundation for unified government under a popularly acclaimed prime minister, appeared to contain the seeds for further factionalism and stalemate.[20]

Footnotes

[1] Clyde Haberman, "Israel Finishes Withdrawing Troops from the Gaza Strip," *New York Times*, May19, 1994.

[2] Gary M. Servold, "Know Thy Enemy: Profiles of Adversary Leaders and Their Strategic Cultures," edited by Barry R. Schneider and Jerrold M. Post, USAF Counterproliferation Center (CPC), July 2003, 14.

[3] David Wilder, "I Was Baruch Goldstein's Friend," *Jewish Press. com*, February 28, 2014 (http://www.jewishpress.com/indepth/opinions/i-was-baruch-goldsteins-friend/2014/02/28/)

[4] Israel Ministry of Foreign Affairs, "Main Points of Israel-Jordan Peace Treaty, 26 Oct 1994" (http://www.mfa.gov.il/mfa/foreignpolicy/peace/guide/pages/main%20points%20of%20israel-jordan%20peace%20treaty.aspx)

[5] Serge Schmemann, "Assassination in Israel: The Overview; Rabin Slain After Peace Rally in Tel Aviv; Israeli Gunman Held; Says He Acted Alone," *New York Times*, Novembere 5, 1995 (http://www.nytimes.com/1995/11/05/world/assassination-israel-overview-rabin-slain-after-peace-rally-tel-aviv-israeli.html?pagewanted=all)

[6] Terry Gross, "Revisiting Rabin's Assassination, And The Peace That Might Have Been," *NPR*, October 13, 2015 (http://www.npr.org/2015/10/13/448269886/revisiting-rabins-assassination-and-the-peace-that-might-have-been)

[7] Samuel Katz (2002). *The Hunt for the Engineer* (Augusta,GA: Lyons Press, 2002), 77 (Bet El), 106–109 (Afula and Hadera), 147 (#5 bus), 167 (Biet Lid), 191 (#20 bus), 197 (#26 bus)

[8] https://en.wikipedia.org/wiki/Israeli_general_election,_1996 as derived from: "Israeli elections will test support for peace," *CNN*, 11 February 1996; "Suicide bombings scar Peres' political ambitions," *CNN*, May 28, 1996; "Pivotal Elections: Candidates," *CNN*, 1996; "Israeli election is a dead heat," *CNN*, 28 May 1996; "Israeli race for prime minister narrows," *CNN*, 27 May 1996;

"Rabin's widow tells Israelis: Vote for Peres," *CNN*, 30 May 1996.

[9] "Benjamin Netanyahu," (https://en.wikipedia.org/wiki/Benjamin_Netanyahu)

[10] Nomi Morris and Eric Silver, "Israel Opens Disputed Tunnel," *Maclean's*, October 7, 1996, in *The Canadian Encyclopedia* (Historica Foundation, 2012) (https://web.archive.org/web/20121020014235/http://www.thecanadianencyclopedia.com/articles/macleans/israel-opens-disputed-tunnel)

[11] "Summit Makes Little Progress," *The Stanford Daily*, Vol. 210, Issue 10:3, October 1996 (http://stanforddailyarchive.com/cgi-bin/stanford?a=d&d=stanford19961003-01.1.3&e=01-01-1990-31-12-1999--en-20--1--txt-txTI-radio------#)

[12] Noam Amir and Maariv Hashavua, "Israel Remembers 73 Soldiers Killed in Helicopter Disaster 19 Years Ago," *Jerusalem Post*, February 5, 2016 (http://www.jpost.com/Israel-News/Israel-remembers-73-soldiers-who-died-in-helicopter-disaster-19-years-ago-444000)

[13] Alexander Safian, "Building in Har Homa," CAMERA, February 27, 1997 (http://www.camera.org/index.asp?x_context=7&x_issue=3&x_article=37)

[14] https://en.wikipedia.org/wiki/Har_Homa as derived from "Building in Jerusalem," Israel Ministry of Foreign Affairs, 8 February, 1997 (http://mfa.gov.il/MFA/MFA-Archive/1996-1997/Pages/Building%20in%20Jerusalem.aspx); Alexander Safian, "Building in Har Homa," CAMERA, February 27, 1997 (http://www.camera.org/index.asp?x_context=7&x_issue=3&x_article=37)

[15] "Har Homa," *Wild Olive* (http://www.wildolive.co.uk/Har%20Homa.htm)

[16] Lenny Ben-David, "The Strategic Significance of Har Homa," *The Jerusalem Post*, December 15, 2007 (http://www.jpost.com/Opinion/Op-Ed-Contributors/The-strategic-significance-of-Har-Homa)

[17] https://en.wikipedia.org/wiki/1997_Mahane_Yehuda_Market_bombings (see also "14 killed in Jerusalem suicide bombings," CNN, June 30, 1977 (http://edition.cnn.com/WORLD/9707/30/

jerusalem.noon/); "Mahane Yehuda attack toll up to 16." *JTA*, October 5, 1997 (http://www.jta.org/1997/10/05/news-opinion/ mahane-yehuda-attack-toll-up-to-16))

[18] https://en.wikipedia.org/wiki/1997_Mahane_Yehuda_Market_ bombings as derived from *Report of the Commission Concerning the Events in Jordan September 1997* (Jerusalem Government Press Office, 17 February 1998); Annamarie Rowe, Paul Cossali, David Lea and Cathy Hartley, *Survey of Arab-Israeli Relations* (Oxford: Taylor & Francis, 2004), 231; Jonathan Schanzer, *Hamas vs. Fatah: The Struggle for Palestine* (NY: St. Martin's Press, 2008), 45.

[19] William L. Cleveland, "Israeli-Palestinian Relations Since the Gulf War," *A History of the Modern Middle East.* 2nd edition (Boulder, CO: Westview Press, 2000) (http://acc.teachmideast. org/texts.php?module_id=3&reading_id=1026&sequence=8)

[20] *Ibid.*

Chapter 18

Major Events:
2000-2006

THE SECOND INTIFADA: SEPTEMBER 2000 -2006

In a bold attempt to end once and for all the Israeli-Palestinian conflict, U.S. President Bill Clinton invited Ehud Barak and Yasser Arafat to Camp David, Maryland, for a ten-day intense conference in July 2000. Since 1992 the model that was used by peace negotiators was the incremental approach: build rapprochement by taking small confidence-building steps. Most significantly, this approach, known as the Oslo Peace Process, avoided all the major points of contention between the two sides. The philosophy was that if trust could be built up between the Israelis and the Palestinians, then and only then would they be able to tackle the heart and soul of the conflict.

As of the signing of the first Oslo Accords in September 1993 these were the thorniest issues:

A. Palestinian refugees from the 1948-49 War of Independence, together with all their decedents—numbering about four million people—should have the right to return to their former homes in what today is the State of Israel.

B. Israel's return to its pre-1967 borders à la Resolution 242.

C. The status of Israeli cities, towns/settlements built in Judea, Samaria and the Gaza Strip after 1967.

D. The issue of Jerusalem.

Jerusalem must be the capitol of the new Palestinian State, which will be made up of the Gaza Strip and the entire West Bank. At the very least, all of Eastern Jerusalem, including the entire Old City (which includes the Temple Mount, the Western Wall and the

Jewish Quarter), and all the new post-1967 Jewish neighborhoods (Ramot, Gilo, East Talpiot, Ramat Eshkol, etc.) must be handed over. Finally, the Palestinians assert that there are no historical links between the Jews and Jerusalem, and that Jerusalem is and has always been an Arab-Muslim city.

OFFER MADE BY EHUD BARAK AT CAMP DAVID

Between 1993-2000 all the basic core issues were sidestepped in favor of a "land for security" formula. This formula failed as more Israeli civilians were killed by Palestinian terrorists than in the entire post-1967 Six-Day War period. Thus, in July of 2000, Ehud Barak made Yasser Arafat the following offer:

1. Israel would withdraw from one hundred percent of the Gaza Strip. This also meant that Israel would remove the 8,000 Jews who lived predominantly in the Gush Katif area (southwestern part of the Gaza Strip).

2. Israel would withdraw from approximately ninty-five percent of Judea and Samaria. This would entail moving some 70,000 Jews who lived in dozens of Jewish towns spread throughout the area.

3. Israel would retain five percent of Judea and Samaria. This percent contains the four large Jewish settlement blocs where approximately 250,000 Jews live. These areas would formally become part of the State of Israel.

4. Israel would "compensate" the Palestinians for this five percent by giving up parts of the Negev.

5. Israel would break a decades-old pledge made to its own citizens and divide the city of Jerusalem, handing over most of the eastern part of the city to the PA. Thus the PA could claim that Jerusalem was the capitol of the emerging Palestinian State.

6. The Temple Mount in the Old City of Jerusalem would be under Palestinian sovereignty, while the Western Wall/Kotel remained in Israeli hands.

7. The PA would have to recognize in writing the Jewish historical and religious connection to the Temple Mount.

8. A commission would be set up to work out financial

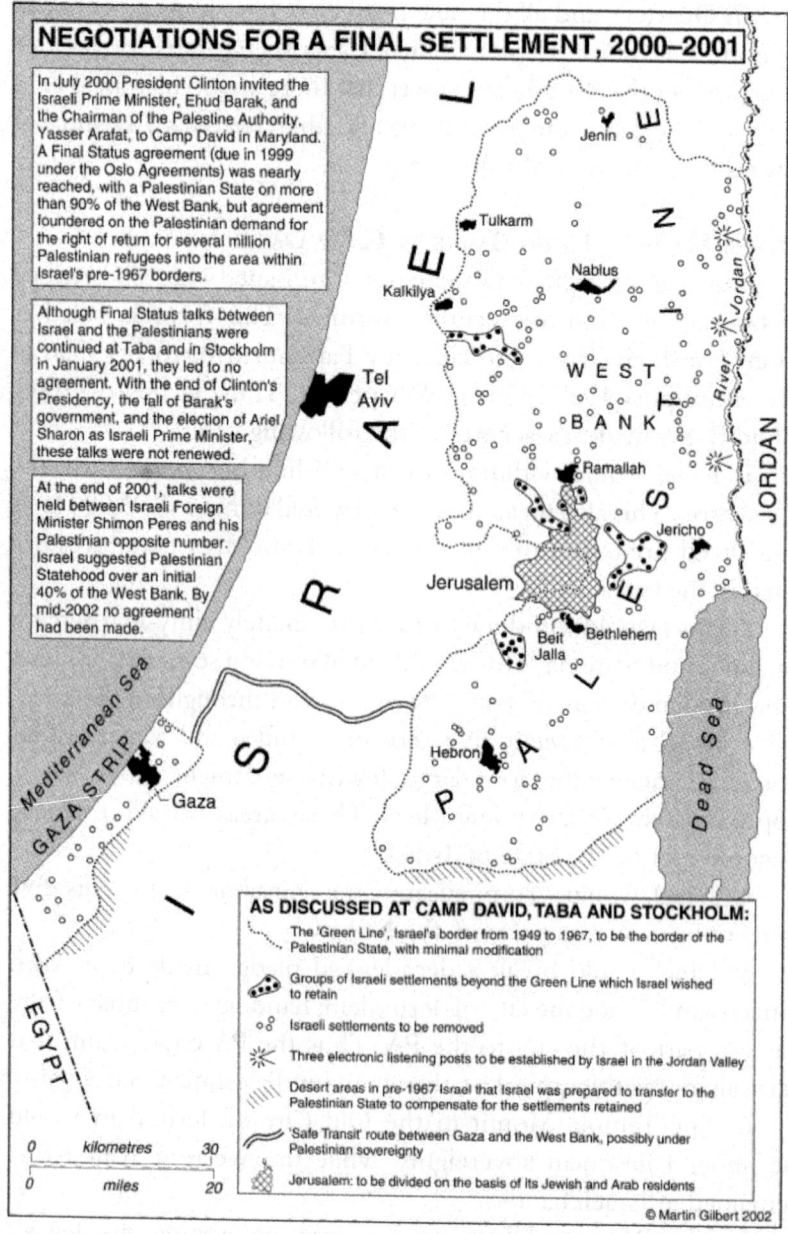

NEGOTIATIONS FOR A FINAL SETTLEMENT, 2000-2001

In July 2000 President Clinton invited the Israeli Prime Minister, Ehud Barak, and the Chairman of the Palestine Authority, Yasser Arafat, to Camp David in Maryland. A Final Status agreement (due in 1999 under the Oslo Agreements) was nearly reached, with a Palestinian State on more than 90% of the West Bank, but agreement foundered on the Palestinian demand for the right of return for several million Palestinian refugees into the area within Israel's pre-1967 borders.

Although Final Status talks between Israel and the Palestinians were continued at Taba and in Stockholm in January 2001, they led to no agreement. With the end of Clinton's Presidency, the fall of Barak's government, and the election of Ariel Sharon as Israeli Prime Minister, these talks were not renewed.

At the end of 2001, talks were held between Israeli Foreign Minister Shimon Peres and his Palestinian opposite number. Israel suggested Palestinian Statehood over an initial 40% of the West Bank. By mid-2002 no agreement had been made.

Jenin

Tulkarm

Nablus

Kalkilya

W E S T

B A N K

Tel Aviv

Ramallah

Jericho

Jerusalem

Beit Jalla · Bethlehem

Hebron

Gaza

Mediterranean Sea

GAZA STRIP

EGYPT

River Jordan

JORDAN

Dead Sea

AS DISCUSSED AT CAMP DAVID, TABA AND STOCKHOLM:

The 'Green Line', Israel's border from 1949 to 1967, to be the border of the Palestinian State, with minimal modification

Groups of Israeli settlements beyond the Green Line which Israel wished to retain

Israeli settlements to be removed

Three electronic listening posts to be established by Israel in the Jordan Valley

Desert areas in pre-1967 Israel that Israel was prepared to transfer to the Palestinian State to compensate for the settlements retained

'Safe Transit' route between Gaza and the West Bank, possibly under Palestinian sovereignty

Jerusalem: to be divided on the basis of its Jewish and Arab residents

0 kilometres 30
0 miles 20

© Martin Gilbert 2002

Sir Martin Gilbert, © 2010. Reproduced by permission of Taylor & Francis Books UK. www.martingilbert.com

compensation for Palestinian refugees. As a symbolic and real gesture, Israel would accept approximately 50,000 Palestinian refugees into the State of Israel, and grant them Israeli citizenship.

9. This agreement would signify the end of the Israeli-Palestinian conflict. There would be no more incremental steps to take; the conflict would be resolved!

But Barak had made greater concessions than he was authorized to by his government or the people of Israel. In fact, many in Israel were stunned by the offer and its ramifications! But the most unbelievable piece of news coming out of Camp David was Arafat's total rejection of the accords because ithey did not allow for the "right of return" of Palestinians to present-day Israel, a concept essentially entailing the self-destruction of a Jewish State.

Finally, Arafat did not even make a counteroffer. Contrary to some who claim that Arafat was ambushed at Camp David, Barak, after years of Palestinian claims of Israeli intransigence, had called Arafat's bluff. Arafat had no intention of signing any sort of deal that would have left a sovereign Jewish State as part of the Middle East. It was then apparent to the overwhelming majority of Israelis that the Oslo Peace Process was not only dead, but it was an illusion. In fact, the then-President himself laid the collapse of the talks at Arafat's feet. In the context of discussing the failure of the Camp David 2000 Peace Summit, Bill Clinton is quoted as telling Arafat, "I am a colossal failure, and you made me one."[1]

Several weeks after the collapse of the Camp David 2000 talks it was clear to many Israeli Palestinian affairs experts that Arafat was not to be trusted on any level whatsoever. They realized that Olso was an immense subterfuge just as Arafat had planned. Arafat wanted land and power so he could sit in Gaza, Judea and Samaria running a proto-Palestinian terror state. And he achieved his goal. Between the years 1994-2000 Israel had handed over to the PA eighty percent of Gaza, which included one hundred percent of its Palestinian Arab population, as well as forty-two percent of Judea and Samaria, which included ninty-five percent of the Palestinian Arabs who lived in these areas. Thanks to Israel he was now President Arafat, treated like a head of state. He had a government apparatus, a huge budget donated mostly by Western countries, and a very large and well-armed network of paramilitary organizations that included many terrorist groups. Arafat was able to create a reality where the world spoke about the "Oslo Peace Process" in admiring and hopeful tones at the same time that Israel had more civilians killed by terror attacks (in 1993-1999, the ostensible peace process period) than she had during the war period between 1980 and 1992.[2]

Yasser Arafat and the PLO/PA had looked at the Oslo Process as a way to get concessions from the more powerful Israeli side via negotiations since it had been proven that through military means and terror Israel was not handing over any territory to the PLO! At the same time, he attempted to insure through international agreements (e.g., the Oslo Accords) that Israel could not use its force against the newly created PA, certainly in areas A. That is why after the failure at Camp David in July of 2000 it made sense that Arafat would revert to his other form of dealing with Israel, terror and violence to gain more concessions. Since Israel had gone as far as she could possibly go in making concessions to the PA, Arafat would have to use terror and violence on a much larger scale than at any time in the past to "get the point across" to the Israelis that the PA would never agree to anything less than in the Zionist State ceasing to exist.[3]

As one of Fatah's leaders indicated speaking in Araft's name:

> We are undergoing a struggle through which we can compel the Zionist society to get rid of Zionism, because there can be no coexistence between Zionism and the Palestinian national movement. The Jews must get rid of the Zionism that rules them, that forces them into conflict after conflict, and that does not serve their interests. They must become citizens of the state of the future, the democratic Palestinian state.[4]

THE SECOND INTIFADA

Using as a pretext Ariel Sharon's visit to the Temple Mount

on September 28, riots "erupted" first in the Jerusalem area and then spread to the West Bank, Gaza and even to the Israeli Arab Wadi Ara area in the Southern Galilee. These riots were to quickly morph into a well-coordinated war of terror against Israelis that involved mostly suicide bombers and drive-by shootings. This war would have two different names: the Al Aqsa Intifada (preferred by the Arab world) and, for many Israelis, the Oslo War. To the world at large it was referred to as the Second Intifada.

This would be the first war since Israel's War of Independence in which Israeli civilians would be killed in large numbers. It would also be the first war that Israel fought against an enemy who did not field a uniformed army, had no real bases, and did not operate out of military formations, an enemy that was essentially the Palestinian civilian population, operated out of densely populated areas, and which preferred to slip suicide bombers into Israeli buses, malls, restaurants, and clubs one at a time. The targets of choice were Israeli civilians.

The suicide bomber thus turned the Israeli home front into the frontline of the war. Every time another suicide bomber murdered Israelis, thousands of Palestinians would take to the streets to cheer. Finally, it became clear that Palestinian culture had morphed into one that celebrated suicide bombers; *shaheeds* (martyrs) had become the new superstars as posters with their faces adorned school yards, markets and apartments. Palestinian media treated the *shaheeds* as if they were celebrities, and worse, encouraged Palestinians to become *shaheeds* as well!*

---

* Unfortunately, in some part of the more Leftist Western media, there began to be some moral justification for suicide bombing on the grounds that the Palestinians were responding to years of Israeli occupation and humiliation. In analyzing this phenomenon one should consider:

1) As events have unfolded it has become apparent that Israel was the "canary in the coal mine." The plague of suicide bombing that began as an Israeli/Jewish problem ultimately spread to Iraq, Chechnya, Indonesia, Pakistan, India, and of course the U.S. on September 11, 2001. (cont'd)

SHARON'S VISIT TO THE TEMPLE MOUNT AND THE "OUTBREAK" OF THE INTIFADA

The Temple Mount was liberated by Israeli forces in the Six-Day War. In a gesture of conciliation to the Muslim world (to Muslims the area is known as the Haram El Sharif), day-to-day control was handed over to the Muslim religious council known as the Waqf. Not only was this gesture never seen for what it was, it was interpreted as a sign of weakness. As such, this action has come back to haunt Israel time and again.

Israeli politicians have been visiting the Temple Mount since its liberation. The reason most of them go there is to make a

---

2) When the Palestinians began "resorting" to this desperate method in 1995 they were beginning to taste a freedom they had never had! Israel had withdrawn from the Gaza Strip and Jericho and a Palestinian Authority had been established to govern the new autonomous Palestinian areas. Did it make sense that precisely at this time in their history when they were beginning to taste the end of Israeli occupation and the beginning of self-rule that they felt humiliated?

3) The Palestinians returned to suicide bombing as the chief weapon against Israel in the fall and winter of 2000/2001.

4) The use of suicide bombing against Israelis had nothing to do with humiliation. Unfortunately, every time Israel made what it considered a concession to the Palestinians—motivated by a genuine hope of resolving the conflict, be it transfer of territory, or release of prisoners, etc.—many Palestinians interpreted these moves as weakness on Israel's part. For groups such as Hamas, Islamic Jihad, Al Aqsa Martyr Brigades, Israel is seen as a Crusader state—powerful, foreign and decaying. The suicide bomber was a weapon that sowed terror in the heart of the Zionist enemy like nothing else. It was not an act of desperation; rather, it was the use of an effective terror weapon against an enemy.

5) All radical Palestinian organizations are affected by the teachings of radical Islamic philosophies in one way or another. The fact that suicide bombers are referred to as *shaheeds*, holy martyrs who will earn a special place in heaven, turned them into holy people. Unlike the secular West, where most people would never dream of committing an act of violence in the name of their religion, in the religious Islamic Middle East bestowing such a religious honor for one who commits such an act is a huge endorsement and motivating factor. *Shaheeds* are not desperate humiliated people, they are religious zealots striking at the hated infidel.

political, cultural or religious statement. And Israel, as it always did, coordinated the Sharon visit with the local Palestinian religious authorities, so Sharon's appearance was no surprise. Using Sharon's visit as a ploy for instigating an Intifada was just that, another cynical Arafat ploy to evade censure for his unwillingness to make peace with the Israelis. As PA Minister of Communications Imad Al-Faluji stated in a speech at the Ain Hilwa Palestinian Refugee Camp in South Lebanon:

> Whoever thinks that the Intifada broke out because the despised Sharon's visit to the Al-Aqsa Mosque, is wrong, even if this visit was the straw that broke the back of the Palestinian People.
> This Intifada was planned in advance, ever since President Arafat's return from the Camp David negotiations, where he turned the table upside down on President Clinton. (Arafat) remained steadfast and challenged (Clinton). He rejected the American terms and he did it in the heart of the U.S.[5]

Arafat came back from Camp David 2000 exposed as someone with whom Israel could no longer negotiate. The Palestinians could have had their state along with ninty-plus percent of their demands met, but instead he came back empty handed. Arafat once again snatched defeat from the jaws of victory! Needing a war to forestall criticism, Arafat initiated the Al Aqsa Intifada. Using Jerusalem as the centerpiece turned this new Intifada into a religious war to "liberate" Jerusalem. Palestinians would now show Israel and the world that they would fight for "their" Jerusalem and "their" Palestine.

By unleashing an unprecedented wave of terror against Israelis, Arafat was hoping for one of two things to occur: Israel would implode, since the Israelis were a weak-willed, foreign, colonial group and could not take having their buses, malls, restaurants and schools turned into fields of carnage. Israelis would thus "surrender" to the Palestinians and many would start leaving the country. The other option was that Israel would respond to the Palestinian terror wave with a massive military invasion of the Palestinian areas. That would either cause a full-scale military confrontation with Israel's Arab neighbors or possibly induce the international community to send a multinational force to "save" the Palestinians from the Israeli "onslaught," thus circumventing any negotiations with Israel and thus unilaterally declaring, by default, a Palestinian state.

It was not a new plan either. Arafat had been planning such an adventure for a long time.

> The Oslo agreements prohibit[ed] the Palestinian Authority (PA) from procuring arms, yet they [were] smuggled into the territories for years. It is not known how much the Palestinians actually invest[ed] in illegal weapons procurement, and there is no way to know how many weapons have been smuggled successfully. There is, though, strong reason to believe that it has been a major PA activity.
>
> The Israeli capture of the Karine-A* on January 3, 2002—a ship carrying fifty or more tons of arms—is the most recent incident in the long history of smuggling arms into the territories. In May 2001, the Santorini—carrying a large load of weapons—was apprehended by Israel after having completed many trips. An even less known ship, the Calypso, was apprehended during an attempt to smuggle arms in January 2001. These three incidents share four key elements:

---

* On January 3rd, the Israeli Navy seized control over the Karine A ship that was sailing in international waters on its way to the Suez Canal.

The shipment included both 122 mm. and 107 mm. Katyusha rockets, which have ranges of 20 and 8 kilometers respectively. It also contained 80 mm. and 120 mm. mortar shells, various types of anti-tank missiles, anti-tank mines, sniper rifles, Kalashnikov rifles and ammunition. From Gaza, the 122 mm. Katyushas could have threatened Ashkelon and other coastal cities; while from the West Bank, Ben-Gurion International Airport and several major Israeli cities would have been within their range. The shipment also included rubber (cont'd)

All three attempts were linked to Hizballah or Iran in a very significant way. In each incident, members of Fatah facilitated the endeavor. The three attempts involved Palestinian naval police, the Palestinian coast guard, and members of Fatah...

boats and diving equipment, which would have facilitated seaborne attacks from Gaza against coastal cities.

Preliminary investigation of the crew members has revealed so far that the commanding officer of the ship is Colonel Omar Akawi. The ship was purchased by the Palestinian Authority, loaded with weapons by the Iranians and the Hizbullah, manned by Palestinian Authority personnel, with the aim of transfering the weapons it carried to the Palestinian Naval Police near the Gaza beaches.

Since October 2000, Adel Mughrabi, a major buyer in the Palestinian weapons purchasing system (with the assistance of the Palestinian Naval Police Commander Juma'a Ghali and his executive Fathi Ghazem), has been in contact with the Iranians and Hizbullah regarding a vast weapons smuggling operation for the use of the Palestinian Authority. This operation included the testing and purchase of ships, forming a sailing crew and appointing a commander for the team, as well as making arrangements as to how the weapons would be stored, loaded onto the vessels, and its journey until delivery to the Palestinian Authority.

Preliminary investigation of the team members arrested revealed that the Karine A ship was purchased by Adel Mughrabi in Lebanon, sailed to Sudan where it was loaded with regular cargo. The crew was then switched with the team members and in November 2001 sailed to Hodeida port in Yemen.

In December 2001 the ship sailed according to detailed instructions from Adel Mughrabi to the beaches of Iran near Qeshm Island. There a ferry approached it, most likely arriving from Iran, from which the weapons stored in 80 large wooden crates were transferred and loaded onto the ship. These weapons were stored in special waterproof containers produced only in Iran, which are floatable and are set with a special configurable system that determines how deep they are submerged, were prepared by Hizbullah personnel for smuggling to the Palestinian Authority. Included in the ferry team which transferred the weapons crates to the ship was also a Lebanese trainer, a Hizbullah operative who trained a diver from the ship's crew in configuring the floatation devices in Lebanon. The trainer was present for yet another refreshing training session prior to the sailing.

After completing the loading process of the weapons onto the ship, the ship had to divert to Hodeida port in Yemen due to technical problems. After crossing the canal, the ship was supposed to meet with three smaller (cont'd)

All three ships set sail while there was heavy U.S. involvement in brokering peace initiatives. The Calypso embarked between January 27 and 29, 2001, soon after the Taba negotiations ended. The Santorini left Lebanon on May 4, 2001, the same day Senator George Mitchell submitted the Mitchell Report to the Israeli and Palestinian governments. The Karine-A set sail during the time Gen. Anthony Zinni was heading to the region in an effort to deescalate the situation.

In light of these facts, the U.S. government cannot ignore the disappointing reality that while the United States is trying in good faith to pursue a ceasefire and peace, Yasir Arafat and the PA are involved in shipping arms.[6]

TABA: ANOTHER PEACE FAILURE, JANUARY 2001

The Oslo War-Al Aqsa Intifada had a devastating effect on Israel as a country and on its civilian population. By late January Israelis had been dealing with a wave of Palestinian terror that included suicide bombings, shootings and stabbings, as well as large very violent riots. As a result, Israelis felt very insecure, affecting their daily lives and routines. Having elected Ehud Barak to pursue a course somewhere in between the Rabin and Netanyahu governments, the Palestinian response to a major peace offer was terror on a level never before experienced. By January of 2001 Barak was fighting for his political life. His opponent from the Likud was Ariel Sharon, whose reputation as a hard-line, no-nonsense military man offered a candidate who would effectively deal with Palestinian terror. It appeared from the polls that Sharon was exactly what Israelis were looking for.

---

ships that were purchased in advance and to unload the weapons onto them. According to the plan, the smaller ships were to leave the weapons near El Arish in Gaza, where the weapons were to be taken by the commander of the Palestinian Naval Police Juma'a Ghali and his executive Fathi Ghazem. (Israel Ministry of Foreign Affairs, "Seizing of the Palestinian Weapons Ship the Karine A," January 4 2002 (http://www.mfa.gov.il/mfa/foreignpolicy/iran/supportterror/pages/seizing%20of%20the%20palestinian%20weapons%20ship%20karine%20a%20-.aspx)

Barak, in an effort to save his political career and with the help of outgoing President Clinton, put together another peace conference, this one to be held much closer to the Middle East in Taba, a small town directly south of Eilat on the shores of the Gulf of Eilat (Aqaba). The talks were held between Israel's Foreign Minister Shlomo Ben Ari and for the PA Saeb Erekat, Yasser Abed Rabbo and Mohammed Dahlan. They followed an outline called the "Clinton Parameters" which were based on where Camp David negotiations ended in the summer of 2000. With the Palestinians actually making acceptable counteroffers, they were making progress on the tough issues of borders, refugees, security and Jerusalem. And so, on January 27, 2001 a very optimistic joint statement was issued by the above mentioned negotiators.

> The Taba Talks conclude an extensive phase in the Israeli-Palestinian permanent status negotiations with the sense of having succeeded in rebuilding trust between the sides and with the notion that they were never closer in reaching an agreement between them than today. We leave Taba in a spirit of hope and mutual achievement acknowledging that the foundations have been laid both in reestablishing mutual confidence and having progresses in a substantive engagement on all core issues.[7]

But by then the words of diplomats had fallen on deaf Israeli ears. Israelis had heard many wonderful optimistic things uttered by diplomats since Oslo was signed in September 1993, but what they received in reality was unprecedented terror. Thus, as the Barak government collapsed after the resignation of its Shas contingent, the Israeli public voted in a new prime minister. On February 6, 2001, Ariel Sharon defeated Ehud Barak in a landslide of epic proportions: 62.5 percent to 37.5 percent.[8]

> Sharon said upon taking office that he would only be bound by signed agreements and not by what was discussed at either Camp David or Taba and that he would not resume negotiations from the point at which they were left at Taba.[9]

The days of diplomatic optimism had been replaced by the grim reality of an Arafat-induced Palestinian wave of terror.

ISRAEL CHANGES THE RULES OF ENGAGEMENT: OPERATION DEFENSIVE SHIELD–2002

Unfortunately for Arafat, he sorely misread his opponent. For the first few months of the Intifada it did indeed look like the Palestinians had finally found the chink in Israel's armor. The brutality of the attacks stunned and frightened many, and the suicide bomber did begin to assume the mantle of super weapon.

In his first few months in office Sharon was clearly more aggressive than Barak had been, but Israel was still responding to Palestinian terror and not dictating the terms of the battle.

Ever since Israel withdrew from Gaza and Jericho in May of 1994, Israel had treated all PA-controlled areas as no-go zones to be handled by the indigenous security forces. But after 18 months of non-stop terrorist attacks, on March 28 the Israeli Army launched Operation Defensive Shield. This was meant to be a full-scale military operation aimed at crippling the infrastructure of the terrorist organizations and entailed search-and-destroy missions targeting caches of ammunition, the "laboratories" where suicide belts were manufactured and, of course, the terrorists themselves. Israel entered every large Palestinian city in Judea and Samaria, but excluded the Gaza Strip in this operation.

> The catalyst for Operation Defensive Shield came in the form of a deadly Hamas attack carried out on March 27, 2002 – Passover – on the Park Hotel in Netanya. Casualties of the Park attack numbered...30 dead and 150 injured; and in the days following the attack then-Prime Minister Ariel Sharon green-lighted the operation and authorized the Defense Ministry to declare an emergency draft of 20,000 reservists.
> ...IDF armor, gunnery and Air Force forces made their way into West Bank cities of Jenin, Bethlehem, Nablus, Qalqilya and Ramallah, on March 29; with the most intense fighting taking place in Jenin and Nablus. One [of] the operation's first

maneuvers entailed placing a siege on the Mukataa in Ramallah, where Palestinian Authority Chairman Yasser Arafat's office was. Once the IDF took over the compound, Arafat would be unable to leave it again, until his hospitalization in 2004.

...Operation Defensive Shield came to its official end on April 21, 2002, with the IDF pulling its forces from the Palestinian cities. The military did, however, continue launching small, limited operations throughout the West Bank.

The operation saw the IDF suffer 29 fatalities and 127 casualties. The Palestinians reported...250 deaths and 400 casualties. Some 5,000 Palestinians were arrested, including former Fatah Secretary-General in the West Bank Marwan Barghouti. The IDF also seized massive quantities of weapons and explosives and uncovered 23 explosive labs.[10]

Though Israel clearly had the fire power and the forces to "level" the Palestinian terrorist enclaves generally found in the poorer, more crowded neighborhoods and in certain sections of refugee camps, she did not. Instead, Israel opted for a door-to-door operation that involved mostly infantry, and minimized the destruction of Palestinian property and civilian lives. It also meant putting many Israeli soldiers in harm's way, since door-to-door operations put infantry soldiers right in the midst of the terrorists' "turf."

Also, as the spoils of this action, Israel captured thousands of PA files, documents and computer hard drives. These documents clarified once and for all the fact that the PA was working hand in hand with many terrorist organizations by offering direct and indirect financial and political support for their terror war against Israel. Many of the captured PA documents ordering the payment of bounties to the families of suicide bombers were signed by Arafat himself.[11]

THE BATTLE IN JENIN: APRIL 2002

The harshest battle of Defensive Shield took place in the town of Jenin, a stronghold for Fatah, Hamas and Islamic Jihad. Known as the capital of suicide bombers, the tirades against Israel of a "massacre" in Jenin began almost immediately.

> Palestinian spokesmen characterized Israel's counter-terrorist operations in Jenin, right from the start, as a "massacre." Palestinian Authority negotiator Saeb Erakat charged during a CNN interview on April 10, 2002, that Israeli troops had killed "more than 500 people." On April 12, he repeated the charge on CNN: "a real massacre was committed in the Jenin refugee camp." He added that 300 Palestinians were being buried in mass graves. On April 15, Erakat continued his charges: "And I stand by the term 'massacres' were committed in the refugee camps." He also began to refer to Israeli actions as "war crimes."
>
> Erakat was not alone in hurling the charge of an Israeli "massacre" of Palestinians in Jenin. Peter Hansen, the commissioner-general of the United Nations Relief and Works Agency (UNRWA) told a Danish newspaper, the Internatavisen Jyllands-Posten, on April 19, that 300-400 Palestinians had been killed in Jenin. He told CNN: "I had, first of all, hoped the horror stories coming out were exaggerations as you often hear in this part of the world, but they were all too true" (CNN, April 19, 2002). CNN correspondent Rula Amin gave her own impressions of "a lot of destruction, a lot of devastation" (CNN, April 17, 2002).[12]

Following the war, a more realistic appraisal of KIA's took place. Israeli officials determined that only fifty-four victims, not 500, were indeed casualties of the Jenin operation. Palestinian officials eventually admitted these numbers. Mousa Kadoura, director of Yasser Arafat's Fatah organization for the northern West Bank, claimed fifty-six Palestinians died in Jenin.[13]

As for the amount of destruction that the Western media commented upon, attributing it primarily to the Israeli offensive:

> Palestinians admit that they employed large amounts of explosive devices in Jenin. There were booby-trapped

buildings and explosive devices configured as anti-personnel mines. Captured Islamic Jihad operative Tabeat Mardawi told CNN that 1,000-2,000 explosive devices had been prepared. An Islamic Jihad bomb-maker from Jenin told Al-Ahram Weekly: "We had more than 50 houses booby-trapped around the camp" (MEMRI, April 24, 2002).[14]

What emerged from Operation Defensive Shield was that once again the Palestinians had underestimated the Jews of Israel. If anything, the Intifada had created a will to fight among Israelis that had probably not been seen since the 1973 Yom Kippur War. This was a very personal war for Israelis as it was a mother, father, brother, sister or best friend that was blown to bits by a Palestinian as they were eating, shopping, riding a bus. The enemy had invaded every aspect of Israeli life, and claimed their right to kill Israelis at will. This created a backlash that changed the political landscape in Israel. Israelis wanted peace; they did not want to surrender! Operation Defensive Shield was part of a multi-pronged approach to fighting terror.

The other parts to the strategy were:

a) Targeted assassinations of leaders of terrorist organizations: Hamas, Islamic Jihad, Al Aqsa Martyr Brigades and Tanzim;

b) The arrest and capture of leaders and members of these same terrorist organizations;

c) Building a security fence that would make it very difficult for suicide bombers and other terrorists to enter pre-1967 Israel from Judea and Samaria. Prior to 2002, a terrorist could readily walk from the Palestinian city of Qalqilya to the Israeli city of Kfar Saba.

By January of 2004 the IDF was sitting in all of the Palestinian cities of Judea and Samaria. This caused a dramatic drop in fatalities and casualties on the Israeli side. Suicide bombers were now caught on their way to a target or in their villages and cities. In the eyes of most Israelis, by 2004 Israel could declare victory in its latest war.

572 ﴿﷽﴾

IMAGERY FROM THE SECOND INTIFADA

For Palestinians, the most important image from the Intifada was that of a twelve-year-old Palestinian boy named Muhammad Al Dura dying in his father's arms, ostensibly shot by Israeli soldiers and then left to bleed to death. The media replayed the image hundreds of times over the next few months with Al-Jazeera actually put the event to music with words that spoke of the Israeli massacre of Palestinian children. The image of Muhammad Al Dura came to symbolize the wickedness of the Zionist "occupiers" as streets all over the world were renamed for him, and protests were held to decry the actions of the evil Israelis. Muhammad Al Dura became the poster boy for Palestinian victimhood. But as with much of Palestinian propaganda, the incident was eventually proven to be a sham propagated by a more than willing Western media.

What the investigation found was that Muhammad Al Dura was most probably killed by Palestinian police who were firing at Israeli soldiers at the Erez Check Point (separating the Gaza Strip from pre-1967 Israel). Based on where he was shot and the Israeli and Palestinian positions, it was almost impossible for an Israeli soldier to hit the boy. Furthermore, the French TV station that filmed the entire event specifically only used footage from the angle that did not show the Palestinians firing at the Israeli position. They also excluded footage that showed that the Israeli soldiers were not firing at Muhammad and his father, but rather at the Palestinian police who were shooting at them. When all was said and done, if Muhammad Al Dura was killed by an Israeli bullet it was because he was caught in a crossfire initiated by the Palestinian police.

After a year-long investigation, the French TV station that perpetrated the Al Dura footage had to admit that its reporters did indeed frame the incident so as to have it look like an Israeli assassination of a twelve-year-old Palestinian boy. But the damage to Israel's reputation had already been done![15]

On the other hand, the symbol of the Intifada for Israelis was the lynching of two Israeli reservists who accidentally ended up in PA controlled Ramallah in October 2000. Having taken a wrong turn north of Jerusalem, two Israeli reservists ended up at a PA check point. The men were arrested by the PA police and brought to the police station in Ramallah. Based on the Oslo Accords, the PA was supposed to contact the IDF liaison and work out a return of the two men. Instead, the PA police spread the word in Ramallah that they had just captured two Israeli soldiers. Hundreds of Palestinians subsequently stormed into the police station and demanded that the soldiers be handed over. Already bludgeoned and stabbed to death, the bodies were thrown from a window and …"[t]he crowd then dragged the bodies to a central square, beating them further before setting up a victory celebration. PA police forces did not attempt to intervene and in some cases, participated in the barbarism."[16]

The most chilling scene involved a Palestinian policeman coming to that very window and raising his bloody hands drenched in the blood of the Israeli reservists as the mob cheered. This scene was filmed by many media outlets, but only one Italian crew managed to sneak the footage out; all the other cameras were destroyed or confiscated by the media-conscious PA police.

Unlike Mohammed Al Dura, who was a tragic victim of a shootout, the two Israeli soldiers were murdered in cold blood. To Israelis, this became the face of their Palestinian neighbors.

THE ISRAELI SECURITY FENCE

Besides Operation Defensive Shield that not only destroyed a good portion of the PA-supported terror infrastructure in Judea and Samaria, there were now Palestinian terror leaders who were targeted by the Israeli security forces for elimination. The tables were turned. Israelis could now leave their homes and ride buses, shop, go to restaurants and lead normal lives, while Palestinian terrorist leaders were afraid to venture outside in daylight or sleep in the same place two nights in a row. Both of these actions proved to be very effective.

Another very effective tool that Israel deployed to stem the flow of suicide bombers and other terrorists was the use of special forces working with Israel's internal security apparatus—The Shabak (Israeli FBI)—to locate, arrest and, in some cases, to kill him/her before s/he was able to carry out an attack. These operations took place throughout Areas A, B and C in Judea and Samaria. In many cases, when the operation was in Area A, there was some level of cooperation with PA security forces if the wanted terrorist was a member of Hamas or other anti-PA terror group, since it was in the PA's interest to have these terrorists captured or neutralized. When terrorists were part of PA-affiliated groups, like the Al Aqsa Martyr Brigades, the PA was not made privy to IDF moves. This form of anti-terrorist operation could only take place in an area where the IDF did not have to cross an international border or entity like Gaza. Hence, this became yet one more reason why Israel is very unlikely to make any sort of deal with the PA that gives it full control of an area, since it would very easily become another Gaza terrorist enclave.

But the Israeli security measure that created the biggest long-term change was the construction of a physical separation barrier, a security fence, that made it very hard for a terrorist from Judea and Samaria to just walk into an Israeli town or city after they'd strapped on a suicide vest and put on an Israeli disguise—a Hasid or hip 20-something secular Israeli—and walk onto a crowded bus, into a mall or restaurant, yell "Allah Ho Akbar" and then blow themselves up. Now a terrorist would have to pass through check points requiring a special Israeli ID to enter pre-1967 Israel, and even with that a vehicle could be stopped and searched. The lines at the check points would be long and people would be terribly inconvenienced. Travel time from one PA area to another could take five to ten times as long as it used to. Sometimes Palestinians had to spend a long time traveling to their place of business, field or school. But as a result, suicide bombings by the end of 2004 had dropped dramatically. In essence, the equation came down to inconveniencing the Palestinian Arab population on a daily basis or making sure that Israelis were not habitually murdered or maimed.

For most rational people that was an easy choice: Save Israeli lives. Being inconvenienced is a temporary reality; being murdered or maimed was not.

The Israeli government's decision to build the security barrier was a response to a relentless torrent of Palestinian terror attacks against Israeli citizens. The Palestinian gamble failed. While it did succeed in killing hundreds of Israeli civilians, it also raised the anger and distrust level among most Israelis for whom enough was enough. Once again the Palestinians gambled and lost, and, as always, they blamed Israel for their own poor choices. The Palestinians and their supporters began to take pictures of long lines of Palestinians standing at check points with captions that spoke about the Palestinians being "harassed" and "humiliated" by Israeli soldiers. There was no context, no explanation as to why there was a security barrier and hence, check points. The Palestinian narrative was that they just appeared because of the "vicious, cruel" nature of the Zionist "occupier." Sadly, very few people in the Western media questioned this Palestinian narrative. To add to the distortion, the pictures and stories often focused on pregnant women, ambulances, and even mentally challenged teens who were made to wait on these long lines by the check points—failing to recognize that during the wave of suicide bombings against Israelis the Palestinians used pregnant women as suicide bombers, actually placed bombs underneath the stretchers of wounded Palestinians in Red Crescent ambulances and actually paid some mentally challenged Palestinians to be suicide bombers. This is what created for every IDF soldier or member of Israeli security personnel manning a check point to suspect every Palestinian and every vehicle, including an ambulance, of being a potential suicide bomber or bomb. The Palestinians, since terror attacks began to rise in the spring of 1994, had acted as enemies of Israel, celebrating and glorifying those that killed Israelis. Why then should they be treated as wonderful, peaceful neighbors?[17]

The Israeli security fence is just that, a fence, for ninty-five percent of the 450-mile path. The original path of the security fence had Israel taking fourteen percent of Judea and Samaria and leaving the PA with eighty-six percent. Palestinian citizens and Israeli Leftists were subsequently able to bring the IDF to court claiming that it was not using only purely military considerations when building the fence, and that the path of the fence was causing undo hardships to certain Palestinian citizens. So by 2005 the Israeli Supreme Court changed the path of the security fence several times. As of 2006, the path of the fence gave Israel control of but seven percent of the West Bank and the PA ninty-three percent.

Thus, in essence, the fence is a security barrier separating Israel (mostly pre-1967 with some large Jewish population enclaves in Judea and Samaria) from PA-controlled areas. Five percent of the security barrier is a twenty-foot concrete wall, which exists when a Palestinian city bumps up against an Israeli city. The concrete wall separates Jerusalem from Palestinian Abu Dis and Bethlehem, and separates Kfar Saba from Palestinian Qalqilya. In both those areas, prior to the construction of the barrier, Palestinian suicide bombers would walk into Jerusalem or Kfar Saba and blow themselves up in a crowded bus, shopping mall or restaurant. The barrier proved to be very effective in stopping these incursions.

> The Israeli Ministry of Foreign Affairs and the Israel Security Agency report[ed] that in 2002, there were 452 fatalities from terrorist attacks. Before the completion of the first continuous segment (July 2003) from the beginning of the Second Intifada, 73 Palestinian suicide bombings were carried out from the West Bank, killing 293 Israelis and injuring over 1,900. After the completion of the first continuous segment through the end of 2006, there were only 12 attacks based in the West Bank, killing 64 people and wounding 445. Terrorist attacks declined in 2007 and 2008 to 9 in 2010.[18]

THE APARTHEID WALL

Since its inception in 2002, the Palestinians speak of an Israeli "Apartheid Wall," not a security fence, and speak of an Israeli land grab and of unbearable hardships for Palestinians.* (The hardships revolve around travel times for Palestinians to reach their fields, their work or their schools.)

Secondly, if one were to listen to the complaints without knowing how these realities play out on the map, one would assume that Israel built the fence to grab a substantial chunk of the West Bank, some forty to fifty percent. Furthermore, the mere mention of a twenty-foot tall "Apartheid Wall" conjures images of a concrete prison wall surrounding the Palestinians in the world's largest jail where "white Israeli" citizens live in economic splendor while the "dark skinned" citizens" live on the other side of the barrier in penury and degradation. All of these images remain willful distortions of reality.

As to the allegations of an "Apartheid Wall," apartheid was the official legal system that separated the races in pre-1990s South Africa. Non-whites were officially classified as second class citizens according to South African law, lived in separate sections of cities and towns, could not vote for the official South African Parliament, were segregated in every sphere of life, were paid a fraction of what whites were paid, needed special travel papers to travel beyond their towns, and more. Apartheid was legalized racism. Even though non-whites made up over eighty percent of South Africa's population they were disenfranchised citizens.

The State of Israel, on the other hand, as of 2016 has approximately 8.5 million citizens of which 6.5 million are Jewish and 2 million are non-Jewish. The Jewish portion of Israel is fifty percent non-white! That includes dark-skinned Jews from Middle Eastern countries, and Black Jews from Ethiopia. The non-

---

* Ahmad Hajihosseini, Observer for the Organization of the Islamic Conference (OIC), said that building and maintaining the wall is a crime of apartheid, isolating Palestinian communities in the West Bank and consolidating the annexation of Palestinian land by Israeli settlements. ("In Day-Long Security Council Meeting, Palestine Observer Says Israeli Security Wall Involves De Facto Annexation of Occupied Land, UN Security Council, 14 October 2003 ((http://www.un.org/press/en/2003/sc7895.doc.htm))

Jewish citizens are Israeli Arabs (Muslim and Christian), Bedouin, Druze, Bahai, and other minorities. The Druze community at its own request is drafted into the Israeli Army; the other non-Jewish citizens are exempt from military service, though some choose to volunteer. All Israeli citizens have the right to vote and are protected by Israeli law. There are Israeli Arabs and Druze in the Knesset, municipal governments, police department, unions, and all professional organizations, including the Supreme Court. In short, they are part of all Israeli life and society. Arabic is the second official language of the State of Israel. Israeli Arabs presently enjoy the highest standard of living and education in the entire Arab world. Israeli Muslims, Druze, Christians, Bahai, and other religious minorities enjoy religious and cultural autonomy. Their public schools offer instruction about their cultures, their religious institutions and leaders receive funds from Israel's Ministry of Religious Affairs, and their religious holidays appear on government printed calendars, thus enjoying the same cultural and religious freedoms that the Jewish majority enjoys.

> Malcolm Hedding, a South African minister who worked against South African apartheid and Executive Director of the International Christian Embassy in Jerusalem, said that the West Bank barrier has nothing to do with apartheid and everything to do with Israel's self-defense. He said that Israel has proven its desire to reach an accommodation with the Palestinians while granting political rights to its own Arab citizens within a liberal democratic system, but that the Palestinians remain committed to Israel's destruction. By contrast, he says, it was a tiny minority in South Africa that held power and once democracy came, the National Party that had dominated the masses disappeared.[19]

Soon after Israel began construction of the security fence, the Palestinian Authority decided to take Israel to the World Court in the Hague (a branch of the United Nations). Even though Israelis who had lost their loved ones demonstrated outside the court house, testified in front of the court, and a shell of a blown-up bus was brought to the Hague to illustrate why the security fence was being built, in early July 2004 Israel was found guilty of violating the human rights of the Palestinians. Suicide bombing was not recognized as a crime against humanity.

The Court ascertains whether the construction of the wall has violated the above mentioned rules and principles. It first observes that the route of the wall as fixed by the Israeli Government includes within the Closed Area (between the wall and the Green Line) some 80 percent of the settlers living in the Occupied Palestinian Territory. Recalling that the Security Council described Israel's policy of establishing settlements in that territory as a flagrant violation of the Fourth Geneva Convention, the Court finds that those settlements have been established in breach of international law. It further considers certain fears expressed to it that the route of the wall will prejudge the future frontier between Israel and Palestine; it considers that the construction of the wall and its associated régime create a fait accompli' on the ground that could well become permanent, in which case, ... [the construction of the wall] would be tantamount to de facto annexation. The Court notes that the route chosen for the wall gives expression in loco to the illegal measures taken by Israel, and deplored by the Security Council, with regard to Jerusalem and the settlements, and that it entails further alterations to the demographic composition of the Occupied Palestinian Territory. It finds that the construction [of the wall], along with measures taken previously, . . . severely impedes the exercise by the Palestinian people of its right to self determination, and is therefore a breach of Israel's obligation to respect that right.

The Court then considers the information furnished to it regarding the impact of the construction of the wall on the daily life of the inhabitants of the Occupied Palestinian Territory (destruction or requisition of private property, restrictions on freedom of movement, confiscation of agricultural land, cutting off of access to primary water sources, etc.). It finds that the construction of the wall and its associated régime are

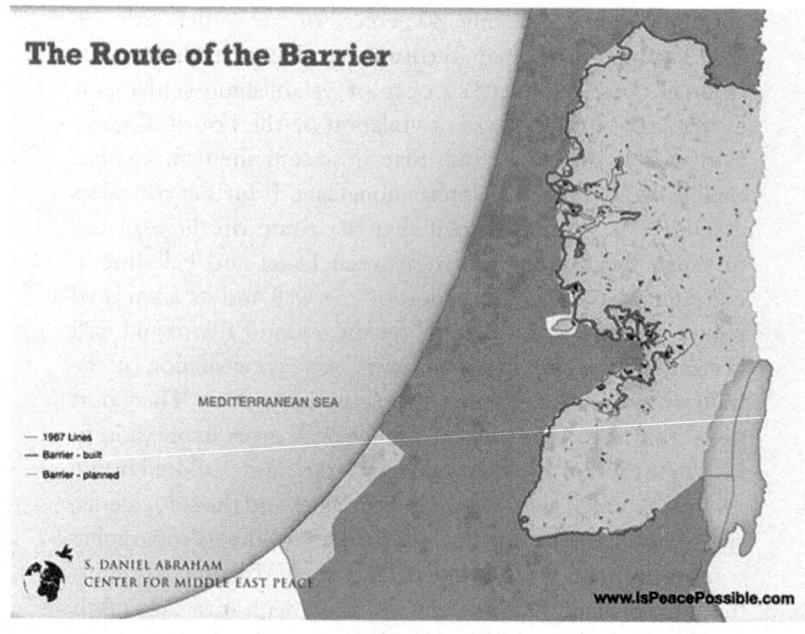

Courtesy of S. Daniel Abraham Center for Middle East Peace.

contrary to the relevant provisions of the Hague Regulations of 1907 and of the Fourth Geneva Convention; that they impede the liberty of movement of the inhabitants of the territory as guaranteed by the International Covenant on Civil and Political Rights; and that they also impede the exercise by the persons concerned of the right to work, to health, to education and to an adequate standard of living as proclaimed in the International Covenant on Economic, Social and Cultural Rights and in the Convention on the Rights of the Child. Lastly, the Court finds that this construction and its associated régime, coupled with the establishment of settlements, are tending to alter the demographic composition of the Occupied Palestinian Territory and thereby contravene the Fourth Geneva Convention and the relevant Security Council resolutions.

The Court observes that certain humanitarian law and human rights instruments include qualifying clauses or provisions for derogation which may be invoked by States parties, inter alia where military exigencies or the needs of national security or public order so require. It states that it is not convinced that the specific course Israel has chosen for the wall was necessary to attain its security objectives and, holding that none of such clauses are applicable, finds that the construction of the wall constitutes breaches by Israel of various of its obligations under the applicable international humanitarian law and human rights instruments.

In conclusion, the Court considers that Israel cannot rely on a right of self defence or on a state of necessity in order to preclude the wrongfulness of the construction of the wall. The Court accordingly finds that the construction of the wall and its associated régime are contrary to international law.[20]

Once again the world's double standard vis-á-vis Israel was on display. At the very time that Israel was being brought up on charges for building a security fence, the following countries all had security fences in place in disputed areas: India and Pakistan, Saudi Arabia and Yemen, Turkey and Syria, Turkish Cyprus and Greek Cyprus, and between Morocco and the Western Sahara region claimed by the Polisario Front guerillas. No one questioned the legality of these fences.

ROCKETS FROM GAZA AND THE DEATH OF YASSIN

Beginning in 2001 Hamas began firing Qassam rockets into Israel from Gaza. This continued into 2005 and abated somewhat in prepartion for Israel's unilateral withdrawal. In the meantime, on March 22, 2004, after a number of arrests and releases, the latest in 1997, Sheik Ahmed Yassin, the notorious founder of Hamas, finally met his end as Israeli helicopters struck his car at 5 a.m. as he was leaving morning prayers at a mosque in Gaza. The attack was in reprisal for a recent Hamas terrorist bombing that had occurrerd in Ashdod and resulted in the death of ten Israelis.[21]

Footnotes

[1] Michael Hirsh, "Clinton to Arafat: It's All Your Fault," *Newsweek*, June 26, 2001 (http://www.newsweek.com/clinton-arafat-its-all-your153779-fault-)

[2] Israeli Ministry of Foreign Affairs, "Terrorism Deaths in Israel; In Memory of the Victims of Palestinian Terror," *Jerusalem Post*, January 4, 2009 (http://www.jewishvirtuallibrary.org/number-of-terrorism-fatalities-in-israel)

[3] Lt. Col. Jonathan D.H., "Understanding the Breakdown of Israeli-Palestinian Negotiations," Jerusalem Center for Public Affairs, No. 486, 15 September-1 October 2002 (http://www.jcpa.org/jl/vp486.htm)

[4] Sakher Habash, *Al-Hayat Al-Jadida*, January 30, 2001.

[5] Palestinian Communications Minister Imad Al-Faluji, Al-Safir, 3 March 2001 (Translated by MEMRI); Simon Plosker, "New York Times' Peres Obituary Rewrites History of Second Intifada," *Honest Reporting*, September 28, 2016 (http://honestreporting.com/new-york-times-rewrites-history-of-second-intifada/)

[6] Gal Luft, "The Karine-A Affair: A Strategic Watershed in the Middle East?," The Washington Institute, January 30, 2002 (http://www.washingtoninstitute.org/policy-analysis/view/the-karine-a-affair-a-strategic-watershed-in-the-middle-east)

[7] "Taba Summit Concludes," Center for Israel Education, January 27, 2001 (https://israeled.org/taba-summit-concludes/)

[8] Richard Moriarty, "The Israeli election," *The Guardian*, February 7, 2001 (https://www.theguardian.com/world/2001/feb/07/qanda.israel?CMP=share_btn_link)

[9] *Op. cit.*

[10] "Operation Defensive Shield (2002)," *Ynet.News*, 12.3.09 (http://www.ynetnews.com/articles/0,7340,L-3685678,00.html); see also https://en.wikipedia.org/wiki/Operation_Defensive_Shield as derived from: "Suicide Bombers from Jenin," Israeli Ministry of Foreign Affairs, 2 July 2002 (https://web.archive.

org/web/20080705043647/http://www.mfa.gov.il/MFA/ MFAArchive/2000_2009/2002/7/Suicide%20Bombers%20 from%20Jenin): "Palestinian fighter describes 'hard fight' in Jenin," CNN.com/World, April 23, 2002 (https://web.archive. org/web/20080109035330/http://archives.cnn.com/2002/ WORLD/meast/04/22/jenin.fighter/index.html); Amos Harel and Avi Isacharoff, *The Seventh War* (in Hebrew) (Tel-Aviv: Yedioth Aharonoth Books and Chemed Books, 2004); Alan Dershowitz, *The Case for Israel* (Hoboken: John Wiley & Sons, 2002; Paul Wood, 'No Jenin massacre' says rights group, BBC, 3 May 2002 (http:// news.bbc.co.uk/2/hi/middle_east/1965471.stm); "U.N. report: No massacre in Jenin," *USA Today*, 8/1/2002 (https://usatoday30. usatoday.com/news/world/2002-08-01-unreport-jenin_x.htm); Matt Rees, "Untangling Jenin's Tale," TIME, May 13, 2002 (http:// content.time.com/time/magazine/article/0,9171,1002406,00. html)

[11] Dani Naveh, "Palestinian Authority: The Involvement of Arafat and PA Officials in Terrorism against Israel," Israel Ministry of Foreign Affairs, May 6, 2002, 12-15.

[12] "What Really Happened in Jenin?," Jerusalem Issue Brief, Vol. 1, No. 22, Jerusalem Center for Public Affairs, 2 May 2002 (http:// www.jcpa.org/art/brief1-22.htm)

[13] "Jenin 'massacre' reduced to death toll of 56," *The Washington Times*, May 1, 2002 (http://www.washingtontimes.com/ news/2002/may/1/20020501-023924-2910r/)

[14] *Op. cit.*

[15] Nidra Poller, "Myth, Fact, and the al-Dura Affair ," *Commentary*, Sept. 1, 2005 (https://www.commentarymagazine.com/articles/ myth-fact-and-the-al-dura-affair/)

[16] Tova Dvorin, "Details of 2000 Ramallah Lynch of IDF Soldiers Revealed," *Arutz Sheva*, December 24, 2013 (http://www.israel nationalnews.com/News/News.aspx/175494)

[17] Dani Naveh.

[18] https://en.wikipedia.org/wiki/Israeli_West_Bank_barrier as derived from: https://web.archive.org/web/20040110054951/ http://securityfence.mfa.gov.il/mfm/web/main/missionhome.

asp?MissionID=45187; Anti-Israeli Terrorism in 2007 and its Trends in 2008: Overview, Israeli Ministry of Foreign Affairs, 5 June 2008 (http://www.mfa.gov.il/mfa/foreignpolicy/terrorism/palestinian/pages/anti-israeli%20terrorism%20in%202007%20and%20its%20trends%20in%202008-%20overview.aspx); "2010 Annual Summary – Data and Trends in Terrorism" (pdf). Shin Bet. 2011. p. 4

[19] Malcolm Hedding, "Israel and Apartheid," Scholars for Peace in the Middle East, March 3, 2010 (http://spme.org/boycotts-divestments-sanctions-bds/boycotts-divestments-and-sanctions-bds-news/malcolm-hedding-israel-and-apartheid/8079/as quoted in https://en.wikipedia.org/wiki/Israeli_West_Bank_barrier)

[20] "Legal Consequences of the Construction of a Wall in the Occupied Palestinian Territory ," International Court of Justice (http://www.icj-cij.org/en/case/131)

[21] Dan Baron, "Israel defends killing of Yassin as the public braces for revenge," *JTA World Report*, March 243, 2004 (http://pdfs.jta.org/2004/2004_03_23.pdf, 1-2)

Chapter 19

Major Events:
2006-2011

WHY THE OSLO PROCESS FAILED

Israel tried to make peace with Yasser Arafat and the PLO in 1993 when the historical track record of the man and the organization pointed in one direction: Arafat was a world class terrorist, and the PLO was a terrorist organization dedicated to the destruction of Israel. When Arafat and the PLO controlled their own territory in Western Jordan in 1968-1970 and South Lebanon from 1970-1982, they ruled as autocratic gangsters extorting those they titularly controlled. To assume that Arafat and his cronies would behave any differently toward Israel was a hope for wish fulfillment at its best or delusional thinking at the other extreme. And Arafat have proven time and again his penchant for the other extreme.

The Israeli negotiators in Oslo, led by then-Deputy Minister of Foreign Affairs Yossi Beilin, were well meaning men who truly were hoping to create a two-state solution based on reconciliation and the parallel acceptance of each side of the other's rights and aspirations. But ultimately they were motivated by the bad experience that Israel had during the 1987-1992 Intifada; they wanted to end the Israeli "occupation" at almost all costs. Beilin and the other negotiators were very enamored with the peace process that began in Oslo as well as with the promise of a peaceful solution to the conflict, so enamored that they were prepared to suspend disbelief like an audience at a magician's show that pretends the laws of physics don't apply, and that the illusion of the magician is reality.

Arafat was never interested in creating a Palestinian state alongside that of Israel, and neither was his negotiating team at Olso. They wanted more than anything to receive worldwide legitimacy and a piece of territory to govern in Judea, Samaria and Gaza as a first step to "liberating" all of Palestine "from the river to the sea."

Starting with the Hamas terrorist attacks of November 1994, the canonization of Yihyeh Ayash in 1995, and the wave of suicide bombings in late 1994 and early 1995, it was abundantly clear to anyone who was not invested in the Oslo Process that Arafat and the PA were not living up to their responsibilities under the Oslo agreements. For Arafat and the PA it was all about receiving and very little, if anything, about giving. By the end of the 1996 tunnel riots that were masterminded and created by Arafat in a style that would have made the Grand Mufti proud, it was clear beyond doubt that Arafat had no intentions of abiding by Oslo. Hamas, which was supposed to be the enemy that Israel and Arafat had in common, became the new PLO that was used by Arafat to hit Israel when he felt he was not getting enough concessions. To make matters worse, Arafat had begun a very successful campaign of making statements in English to U.S. and Western leaders and audiences that sounded like those of a man who wanted to make peace while at the same time making statements in Arabic to his Palestinian constituency that called for either holy war against Israel or the destruction of all of Israel. These statements in Arabic were almost never picked up by the Western media, and sadly not by the Israeli media either, since they were also invested in having the peace process succeed.

Itamar Marcus and Nan Jacques Zilberdik, both of Palestine Media Watch (an NGO that monitors all the official media outlets, political speeches, textbooks, newspapers, and websites of the Palestine Authority) detailed PA activities that violated both the letter and the spirit of the Oslo agreements*. Here are but a few examples:

---

* Itamar Marcus and Nan Jacques Zilberdik, *Deception: Betraying the Peace Process* (Jerusalem: Palestinian Media Watch; 2nd edition, 2012)

Arafat: "This agreement [the Oslo Accords], I am not considering it more than the agreement which had been signed between our Prophet Muhammad and Quraish, and you remember the Caliph Omar had refused this agreement and considered it Sulha Dania [a despicable truce]. But Muhammad had accepted it and we are accepting now this [Oslo] peace accord."
(Audio recording of Arafat speech in Johannesburg, May 10, 1994)[1]*

Abd Al-Aziz Shahin, Palestinian Authority Minister of Supplies: "The Palestinian people accepted the Oslo Accords as a first step and not as a permanent settlement, based on the premise that the war and struggle in the land is more efficient than a struggle from a distant land [i.e., Tunisia, where the PLO was based before Oslo] ... the Palestinian people will continue the revolution until they achieve the goals of the '65 revolution...".
[Al-Ayyam, May 30, 2000]**

Arafat planned that Oslo Accords would chase away Israelis
Source: ANB TV, Feb. 16, 2006
Al-Quds al-Arabi Editor-in-Chief, Abd al-Bari 'Atwan: "After the Oslo Accords were signed, I went to Tunisia to visit him

---

* The Hudaybiyyah peace treaty was a 10-year truce that Muhammad, Islam's Prophet, made with the Quraish Tribe of Mecca. However, two years into the truce, Muhammad attacked and conquered Mecca. The PA Minister of Religious Affairs stressed in his Friday sermon that Muhammad's agreeing to the Hudaybiyyah treaty was not "disobedience" to Allah, but was "politics" and "crisis management." The minister emphasized that in spite of the peace treaty, two years later Muhammad "conquered Mecca." He ended his comparison by expressing the view that the Hudaybiyyah agreement is not just past history, but that "this is the example and this is the model." (http://palwatch.org/site/modules/print/preview.aspx?fi=157&doc_id=9401)

** The "65 Revolution" refers to the founding of the PLO and the publication of the PLO charter that calls for the destruction of Israel through armed struggle.

[Arafat] in July. I told him: 'We disagree. I don't support this agreement. It will harm us.'

[Arafat] told me: 'By Allah, I will drive them crazy. I will make these [Oslo] Accords a disaster for them [Israel]. It won't be in my lifetime, but you will see the Israelis run away from Palestine. Have a little patience.'

The Al-Aqsa Brigades [Fatah terrorist wing] were founded and armed by him [Arafat] as a reply, as a counterweight to the historic mistake of the Oslo Accords."

Ziyad Abu Ein, PA Deputy Minister of Prisoners' Affairs: "The Oslo Accords are not the dream of the Palestinian people. However, there would never have been resistance in Palestine without Oslo. Oslo is the effective and potent greenhouse whish embraced the Palestinian resistance. Without Oslo, there would never have been resistance. In all the occupied territories, we could not move a single pistol from place to place. Without Oslo, and being armed through Oslo, and without the Palestinian Authority's "A" areas, without the training, the camps, the protection afforded by Oslo, and without the freeing of thousands of Palestinian prisoners through Oslo—this Palestinian resistance and we would not have been able to create this great Palestinian Intifada." [Al-Alam TV (Iran), July 4, 2006]

Finally, one of the most famous Palestinian Authority figures during the first years of the Oslo agreement was Faisal Husseini, considered a moderate in the West. Shortly before he died in May 2001, he gave an interview where he very clearly outlined that the main purpose of the Oslo agreements was to create a Palestinian "Trojan Horse" inside Israel that would eventually destroy the Jewish State.

Q: What is happening now, unfortunately, is a natural consequence of Arafat's signing the Oslo Accords which did not explicitly state that the settlements should be removed, or even [their construction] halted... and did not explicitly determine the future of Jerusalem and the right of return... but—among other mistakes you recently admit—it did explicitly state that the PA must confiscate weapons from Palestinian civilians...

Husseini: "Following the signing of the Oslo Accords... I said three things: First: following a long period of "pregnancy" we brought a child into the world [the Oslo Accords] who is smaller, weaker, and uglier than what we had hoped for. However, despite it all, this is still our child, and we must nurture, strengthen and develop it so that he is able to stand on his own two feet.

Second, we are the Jews of the 21st century. Meaning, we the Palestinians will be the Jews of the early [previous] century. They infiltrated our country using various methods; using all kinds of passports, and they suffered greatly in the process. They even had to face humiliation but they did it all for one goal: to enter our country and root themselves in it prior to our expulsion out of it. We must act the in the same way they did. [We must] return [to the land], settle it, and develop new roots in our land from where we were expelled; whatever the price may be.

Third, the [ancient] Greek Army was unable to break into Troy due to [internal] disputes and disagreements [among themselves]. The Greek forces started retreating one after the other, and the Greek king ended up facing the walls of Troy all by himself, and he too suffered from illnesses and [internal] disputes, and ended up leading a failed assault on Troy's walls.

[Following these events] the people of Troy climbed on top of the walls of their city and could not find any traces of the Greek army, except for a giant wooden horse. They cheered and celebrated thinking that the Greek troops were routed, and while retreating left a harmless wooden horse as spoils of war. So they opened the gates of the city and brought in the wooden horse. We all know what happened next."

..."Similarly, if we agree to declare our state over what is now only 22 percent of Palestine, meaning the West Bank and Gaza—our ultimate goal is [still] the liberation of all historical Palestine from the [Jordan] River to the [Mediterranean] sea, even if this means that the conflict will last for another thousand years or for many generations.

In short, we are exactly like they are. We distinguish the strategic, long-term goals from the political phased goals, which we are compelled to temporarily accept due to international pressure. If you are asking me as a Pan-Arab nationalist what are the Palestinian borders according to the higher strategy, I will immediately reply: "from the [Jordan] river to the [Mediterranean] sea."[2]

On top of all the duplicitous behavior of Arafat and the PA there emerged a very disturbing picture of how Arafat and the PA were governing the areas under their control, which affected over 95 percent of the Palestinian Arabs who lived in Judea, Samaria and Gaza. The PA administered areas had become Third-World dictatorships where the "citizens" had far less rights than they had under Israeli rule pre-Oslo. Even more depressing was that the PA had become the world's most adept kleptocracy. While an indulgent world poured billions of dollars in aid to the Palestinian "refugees," most of that money ended up in the pockets of PA officials, their cronies and family members. Arafat alone had accumulated some $1 billion that was kept in a variety of Swiss bank accounts.* With all the billions of dollars in aid that the PA received in its first decade of existence, Judea, Samaria and Gaza could have well been on their way to becoming First World areas that could have had a robust trade going on with Israel and many other countries. Instead, they remained poor, underdeveloped and

---

* "Over the course of his 'revolutionary' career, Arafat has siphoned off hundreds of millions of dollars of international aid money intended to reach the Palestinian people.

"Estimates of the degree of Arafat's wealth differ, but are all staggering. Last year [2003], *Forbes* magazine listed Arafat in its annual list of the wealthiest 'Kings, Queens and Despots,' with a fortune of 'at least $300 million.' Israeli and US officials estimate Arafat's personal holdings at between $1-3billion. Rachel Ehrenfeld, Director of the American Center for Democracy, arrives at a figure of $1.3 billion and laments: (cont'd)

neglected by their own leadership, not to mention living under corrupt autocratic conditions.

In aggregate, by the end of 2004 there was a clear sense in Israel that the Oslo agreements were dead. Arafat was not a partner for peace and neither was the PA. In fact, they were both enemies. For these reasons, the Israeli Government headed by Prime Minister Ariel Sharon was to now act unilaterally when it came to Judea, Samaria and Gaza.

THE DISENGAGEMENT FROM GAZA: 2005

The first result of the collapse of the Oslo Accords was that the Israeli government decided that Israel should act unilaterally when it came to its next moves vis-á-vis Judea, Samaria and Gaza. Since the PA was not a peace partner, Israel would have to do what she felt was best for her. Hence, in 2005, Prime Minister Ariel Sharon made a decision that would have monumental consequences for the State of Israel.

The Israeli disengagement from Gaza, also known as "Gaza expulsion" and "Hitnatkut", was the withdrawal of the Israeli army from Gaza, and the dismantling of all Israeli settlements in

---

"This money is enough to a) feed 3 million Palestinians for 1 year, b) buy 1,000 mobile intensive care units, c) fund 10 hospitals for a decade, and d) would still leave $585 million to fund other social projects.

"And while the average Palestinian barely subsists, Arafat's wife Suha in Paris receives $100,000 a month from PA sources, as reported on CBS' *60 Minutes*. That CBS report also noted that Arafat maintains secret investments in a Ramallah-based Coca Cola plant, a Tunisian cellphone company, and venture capital funds in the U.S. and the Cayman Islands.

"Arafat also uses foreign aid funds to pay off cronies who bolster his autocracy: A recent International Monetary Fund report indicates that upwards to 8% ($135 million) of the PA's annual budget is handed out by Arafat 'at his sole discretion.' The 2003 budget for Arafat's office, which totaled $734 million, was missing $34 million that Arafat had transferred to pay unidentified 'organizations' and 'individuals.' And Ehrenfeld notes that this IMF report 'did not take into account Arafat's control of 60 percent of the security apparatus budget, which leaves him with at least an additional $360 million per year to spend as he chooses.'" ("Where Is All The Money Given To The Palestinian Authority? ((http://www.adespicabletruce.org.uk/page31.html))

the Gaza Strip in 2005. Four small settlements in the northern West Bank were also evacuated.

The disengagement was proposed in 2003 by Prime Minister Ariel Sharon, adopted by the Government in June 2004, approved by the Knesset in February 2005 and enacted in August 2005. Israeli citizens who refused to accept government compensation packages and voluntarily vacate their homes prior to the August 15, 2005 deadline were evicted by Israeli security forces over a period of several days. The eviction of all residents, demolition of the residential buildings and evacuation of associated security personnel from the Gaza Strip was completed by September 12, 2005. The eviction and dismantlement of the four settlements in the northern West Bank was completed ten days later. A total of 8,000 Jewish settlers from all 21 settlements in the Gaza Strip were relocated. The average settler received compensation of over US $200,000.[3]

The unilateral disengagement from all of Gaza was a decision made by Sharon, one of the architects of Israel's settlement policy, because of the following assessment of the "Palestinian" situation:

a) Based on Israel's experience with the PA, it was clear that a peace treaty could not be consummated. With the PA always telling its own population that it was fighting a *jihad* to liberate Palestine, terror organizations operated openly and freely in PA areas. In addition, PA owned and operated TV and radio stations constantly spewed forth antisemitic rhetoric inciting the Palestinian populace to violence.

b) The Oslo Peace Process was not only a failure, it was an illusion! The PA never intended to make peace with Israel; its goal was to weaken Israel. This the PA had proven time and again by failing to live up to its obligations under any of its signed peace agreements (Oslo I & II, Hevron, Wye River).

c) Israel did not seek to occupy the Palestinian areas. Indeed, in 1978, Israel had offered autonomy to them.

d) Since the PA could not work out a deal that accepted the

notion of two states—apparent after the rejection of the 2000 Camp David summit—Israel would end its relationship with the Palestinians unilaterally.

e) If Israel did not disengage from the Palestinians soon, it was very plausible that the new Palestinian strategy would be one state from the Mediterranean Sea to the Jordan River. They would demand that Israel annex Gaza and the West Bank and offer the three million Palestinians who lived there Israeli citizenship, thereby turning Israel into a bi-national state, which would demographically overwhelm the Jewish minority.

f) Israel had no choice but to take matters into her own hands and divorce herself from the Palestinians. Israel had to create a Palestinian "entity" apart and separate from the State of Israel.

g) Since Israel had turned over eighty percent of the area of Gaza, which included one hundred percent of the Palestinian Arab Gaza population in April 1994, there seemed to be a clear logic to disengage from this area. The overwhelming majority of this indigenous population was and remains poor and Sunni, rabidly antisemitic and anti-Israel. Severing all ties with this area could only be good for Israel.

As Sharon stated:

> [The] settlements which will be relocated are those which will not be included in the territory of the State of Israel in the framework of any possible future permanent agreement. At the same time, in the framework of the Disengagement Plan, Israel will strengthen its control over those same areas in the Land of Israel which will constitute an inseparable part of the State of Israel in any future agreement.[4]

Sharon also decided to add a small piece of northern Samaria that included four small Jewish towns—Ganim, Kadim, Sa-Nur and Chomesh—situated in and around Jenin and were straddling the borders of Areas A and B. The logic for this was because the geographic location of these towns placed them in constant danger, and Sharon argued that safeguarding them was a drain on IDF manpower. Finally, perhaps it was also a slight gesture to the PA that Israel, though disengaging unilaterally, was still potentially willing to make a deal with the PA if it would change its attitude towards Israel and what peace could really entail.

Be that as it may, while there appeared to be much logic in the points that Sharon was making regarding the case for unilateral disengagement, there were also some very glaring negative parts of the plan that did not sit well with close to half of Israel's population. Some of these were:

1) Why did Israel have to remove the three towns in the northern part of Gaza—Dugit, Alei Sinai and Nissanit? They were literally not really part of Gaza but de facto extensions of Israel.

2) The only Jewish towns that really were in the middle of Palestinian Gaza were Netzarim and Kfar Darom. The other Jewish towns (besides the three towns in northern Gaza) were all clustered together along the southern shore of Gaza called Gush Katif. These eighteen towns made up a contiguous geographic area that could be separated from PA-controlled Gaza. Hence, if Sharon really wanted to take away the friction issue and minimize the need for IDF forces that were needed to protect Netzarim and Kfar Darom, then why not just move the residents of these two towns into the Gush Katif area? Why was it necessary to kick out the residents of all 23 Jewish towns?

3) Why would Israel give up the Philadelphi Route (also called the Philadelphia Corridor), the strategic corridor separating Gaza from Sinai? This corridor (around eight miles long and half mile wide) permitted the IDF to minimize the smuggling of arms going on via tunnels from Sinai to Gaza, not to mention movement of arms and terrorists overland.

4) What strategic gain was there in handing over the four Jewish towns in northern Samaria? Not that many IDF soldiers would have been involved in securing these towns since they would have to be in areas close to Jenin because of the security issues Israel had already been facing since it handed over Jenin and the large cities in Judea and Samaria to the PA in 1994 and 1996.

5) By all objective measures the people who comprised the settlers of Gaza and northern Samaria were Religious Zionists, patriots who came to settle barren, yet strategic areas that the Israeli government had asked people to populate. They had lived difficult pioneering lives for the sake of the Zionist ideal. Furthermore, these people disproportionally served in combat and elite units in the IDF. It made one wonder whether the evacuation was about divorcing Israel from the Palestinians of Gaza or divorcing Israel from the Religious Zionist community?

6) The Gush Katif communities had created an enterprise that brought in close to $100 million of exports in flowers and vegetables. Why would the Israeli government want to hand it over to an enemy entity?

7) When all is said and done, in the eyes of the PA, Hamas and all Palestinian terror groups and their followers, Israel would appear to have been driven out of Gaza and northern Samaria by the violence directed against it by these groups. What type of message was that for Israel to send three years after Operation Defensive Shield?

Since both camps, pro- and anti-disengagement, had cogent arguments regarding what in the end was a very emotional topic, e.g., forcibly removing Jews from towns they had established and made prosper with the blessings of prior Israeli governments, the country was literally torn into two camps.

Thus, 2005 proved to be a very contentious and difficult year in Israel. The country was brought as close to an ideological civil war as a country can get to before violence enters the equation. Each side had its flag: The anti-disengagement camp adopted the orange flag, and the pro-disengagement camp adopted the blue flag. There were demonstrations near and around Gush Katif throughout July and August that pitted tens of thousands of anti-disengagement proponents against thousands of police. But Sharon's decision was written in stone. By early September, all the Gush Katif towns/settlements were emptied of their Jewish inhabitants; all were then razed/bulldozed. The synagogues that were left as "religious shrines" were subsequently burned down by mobs of jubilant Palestinians. During the actual forced evacuation, Israeli TV was full of scenes of Israeli settlers and soldiers (who were sent to remove them) hugging and crying. It was one of Israel's most traumatic events.

In addition, at the Gush Katif settlements famous for their production of flowers and a variety of hot house vegetables, a group of American Jewish businessman purchased some of the hot houses and production equipment and, as a gesture of goodwill to the Palestinian Authority, offered it gratis hoping that this would immediately create jobs and serious income for the Arab inhabitants of Gaza.[5] Upon the Israeli withdrawal, the hot houses were quickly looted and an attempt to restore their economic viability ultimately failed.

Even though the PA did not negotiate the deal that left it with control over Gaza, it nevertheless had an opportunity to demonstrate to the Palestinians and to the rest of the world that under its stewardship it could build a Palestinian Arab nation-state and take its place under the umbrella of world countries. Instead, the PA continued its policy of focusing on its war with "Occupied Palestine" and not on the well-being of the people of Gaza. Instead of attempts at social welfare, the world's eleemosynary donations wound up in the hands of weapons merchants and the PA's kleptocrats.

Also, against its wishes, due to the prodding of the U.S., Israel had had to reluctantly turn over the border crossing between Gaza and Egypt to the PA, to be monitored by a European Union observation team. In the six months following the PA control of the border, thousands of terrorists entered the Gaza Strip, including operatives from Hezbollah and Al-Qaida. More weapons were brought in during these six months than were smuggled in between 1967 and 2005!

Despite Israel's disengagement from Gaza, Hamas rocket fire into Israel increased 500 percent.[6]

In 2006, in the first real election permitted by the PA in a decade, Hamas won a majority of the vote. Fatah's worst nightmare had taken place: Hamas had become legally a dominant voice in the PA political system. At the time, many Western pundits were sure that Hamas won because it was "fighting PA corruption," an all too recognized factor of life with the thuggish PA. But a more important factor that went unrecognized was the radicalization of the Palestinian population since Oslo, and the delusion that Israel, in the eyes of Palestinians, had been kicked out of Gaza by Hamas terrorist action. Hence, it was no surprise that rocket attacks in 2006 grew exponentially.

It is fair to say that while the Israeli unilateral withdrawal from Gaza created a Palestinian mini state it also created a security nightmare for Israel, and failed to further the chances for any meaningful peace between Israel and Palestinian Arabs.

In retrospect, "Maj. Gen (ret.) Yair Naveh, then GOC Central Command [Ground Arm Command established in 1998] and later deputy chief of staff, believes reality has proven the move...failed to give Israel any security or diplomatic advantage...."

> If the disengagement from Gaza contributed anything to history, it did so by proving that terrorism has nothing to do with the settlement enterprise, and by proving that an eviction of this nature cannot be carried out in such a way again.
>
> There was no advantage to this eviction. None. Zero. Nothing has changed for the better there. It had no added value to security or to anything else. It was a frustrating event that left a feeling that it was all for nothing," he said.[7]

GILAD SHALIT

Since the early days of Oslo I the IDF was aware of Hamas's interest in kidnapping soldiers. Hamas had several "plans" for IDF soldiers unlucky enough to be captured. Sometimes they were tortured and then shot at close range, like Yehoshua Friedberg, who was kidnapped and murdered in March of 1993.[8] Or they would be beaten and their pictures disseminated to demoralize

Israelis, as in the case of Nachson Wachsman, who was held for six days in October 1994 and was killed by the terrorists in a failed rescue attempt by IDF Commandos.[9] Or in the case of Gilad Shalit, who was kidnapped by a squad of Hamas terrorists who had infiltrated Israel via a tunnel that was dug from inside Gaza on June 25, 2006. He was in his Merkava III tank positioned near the Gaza border when Hamas terrorists hit them from behind. Two of his fellow crew members were killed and one was wounded. In his own words, years later, Shalit admitted that he and his comrades had not followed IDF protocol and put up a fight.[10]

Be that as it may, Hamas had its prize: an IDF soldier to be used as trade bait for Palestinian terrorists sitting in Israeli prisons. Included on the Hamas ask list was Marwan Barghouti, captured in Operation Protective Shield (2002), who was at the time the head of the Al Aqsa Martyr Brigades and a man responsible for the death of dozens of Israelis. Normally there would have been no negotiations for Shalit and Hamas would have had to decide what their next move would be. But in this case Shalit became a national issue because of the incredible persistence of his family and his personal story, that of a nice, likeable young man from a small town in northern Israel who just wanted to serve his country. Thus, he became every Israeli's son and a great deal of pressure was applied to the government on how to handle this very sensitive situation. In response, a large scale military operation was undertaken into southern Gaza where it was believed Shalit was being held. Called Operation Summer Rain, it was carried out June 28-29 and involved both ground forces and the IAF.[11]

Hamas was thus warned that it had gone too far and would pay for its temerity. In the meantime, attempts to win Shalit's release vis-á-vis a prisoner release fomented a bitter debate in the Israeli populace:

> Here we see the basic dilemmas between the individual and the collective, and we see victim pitted against victim. Gilad Shalit is a victim who was violently kidnapped, in a way that Israelis do not consider to be a normative means of struggle.

Therefore, one side says, he should be returned at any price. But the families of those killed in terrorist attacks and the people who were wounded in those attacks are victims, too, and they say that no price should be paid to the murderers. And it is truly a dilemma, because no side is right, and no side is wrong.[12]

Nevertheless, by a vote of 26-3, the Israeli cabinet voted to approve the Hamas prisoner exchange. After five and a half years of captivity, Gilad Shalit was released on October 18, 2011 for more than a thousand terrorists, many with Israeli blood on their hands. The debate over his release triggered much anger between the pro-release Shalit camp and the families of terrorist victims.

Still, it was a very special day in Israel. Every Israeli who was old enough to be a parent felt as if their son was finally brought home. The country came to a standstill. Televisions were on literally everywhere. Israelis watched and wept with joy. Sadly, at the same time, the released Palestinian terrorists returned to a heroes' welcome in Gaza where they were greeted by tens of thousands. These freed "heroes" all spoke of their goal to return to the fight against the hated Zionist enemy and how proud they all were of their acts of murder and terror. Many of them subsequently did so and were killed or again arrested by the IDF.

The contrast between the two societies was so stark. In Israel there was a celebration of life; in Gaza there was a celebration of death. Gilad Shalit came back looking like a pale skeleton, while the Palestinian terrorists came back looking well fed and healthy.[13] It is very important to note that besides all those who opposed the Shalit deal, primarily those who had been victims of terror, there was seething anger, disbelief and depression among many combat soldiers in the IDF for two important reasons:

1) Every combat soldier had known how Gilad Shalit was captured: He and his comrades had not followed protocol and thus contributed to their own deaths or capture, Shalit going so far as not to defend himself when under attack. This went to the ethos of the IDF, and hence the complaint as to why should such a heavy price be paid for a soldier who did not do his job.

2) For the members of the elite IDF units who risked their lives to capture Palestinian terrorists, to now see these terrorists released was very demoralizing.

WAR WITH THE HEZBOLLAH: OCTOBER 2006
HEZBOLLAH: BACKGROUND

Hezbollah is a militant Shi'ite organization based in Lebanon. Its political party in the Lebanese government is called the Loyalty to the Resistance Bloc, and its paramilitary wing is the Jihad Council. The group is headed, since 1992, by its secretary general, Hassan Nasrallah.

After the 1982 war, a portion of southern Lebanon, called the Security Zone, was occupied by the Israelis, who in turn supported the primary military entity in the area, the South Lebanon Army (SLA). Iran, in its attempts to beome a power in the region, supported Shi'a Muslim clerics, followers of the Ayatollah Khomeini, who created Hezbollah to "harass" the Israelis. Hezbollah troops were trained by Iranian Revolutionary Guards who arrived via Syrian-occupied Lebanon. Though for 18 years the area enjoyed relative stability and economic prosperity, in January 2000, Hezbollah assassinated Colonel Aql Hashem, the commander of the SLA's Western Brigade. Two months later, Hezbollah began regularly attacking Israeli military outposts. As pressure mounted throughout Israel to end its deployment in Lebanon, the IDF abandoned its positions in the Security Zone and on May 24, 2000 Israel began withdrawing all troops from South Lebanon.

The Israeli pullout resulted in the collapse of the SLA and the rapid advance of Hezbollah forces into Southern Lebanon. Shi'a refugees who were thrown out of their homes and businesses came rushing back to the region, and Hezbollah gained credibility in the street. The only area they did not get back was Shebaa Farms, which remains a disputed territory. Despite the UN-backed demarcation worked out with Israelis to prove that they had fully withdrawn by June 16, the Syrian-backed Lebanese government refused to set borders.

When the Israelis left, those who thought they might be accused of helping Israel were terrified of Hezbollah vengeance and fled. More than 10,000 Lebanese Maronites and others fled into the Galilee, though Hezbollah leadership assured the Christian clergy that this was a victory for them as well. The tensions between Hezbollah and Israel continue. There have been military skirmishes and the kidnapping of Israeli soldiers in the years since.

As a result of Iran's sponsorship, Hezbollah's military strength rivals and even surpasses that of the Lebanese Army. Exercising that strength, Hezbollah has become part of the Lebanese government as a major faction in Parliament, has TV and radio stations, its own satellites, and its own social service system. When founded in 1985, the Hezbollah manifesto aimed to remove "the Americans, the French and their allies definitely from Lebanon, putting an end to any colonialist entity on our land"; demanded that the Phalangists (primarily non-Arab Christian party) be brought to justice "for the crimes they have perpetrated against Muslims and Christians," and demanded that "all the sons of our people" "pick the option of Islamic government" when given the option of choosing a government.[14]

HEZBOLLAH: CURRENT EVENTS

After the Hezbollah-instigated anti-Lebanese government riots of 2006-2008, Hezbollah and its allies gained 11 out of 30 Cabinet seats, making them a formal power in Lebanese governance. Furthermore, Hezbollah was recognized as an armed organization with permission to "liberate or recover occupied lands" (such as the Shebaa Farms).

In addition, since 2012, Hezbollah has helped the Syrian government fight the "opposition," which it describes as a Zionist plot and a "Wahhabi-Zionist conspiracy" to destroy its alliance with Assad. It has deployed in Syria and Iraq to fight or train local forces to fight ISIS. Once seen as a resistance movement throughout much of the Arab world, the group's legitimacy has been severely damaged because of the sectarian nature of the Syrian Civil War.

Hezbollah's status as a legitimate organization remains a contentious one. The Arab League, United States, France, the Gulf Cooperation Council, Australia, Canada, the Netherlands, and Israel classify Hezbollah as a terrorist organization. The European Union, New Zealand and the United Kingdom have designated Hezbollah's military wing as a terror group, distinct from Hezbollah's political wing. Russia considers Hezbollah a legitimate sociopolitical organization.[15] China remains neutral, and maintains contacts with Hezbollah.[16]

PRELUDE TO WAR

After the Israeli unilateral withdrawal from Lebanon in 2000, there were new realities in South Lebanon. Israel had lost its deterrence against Hezbollah and did not really enhance her position as a country willing to make dangerous sacrifices for the cause of peace in the eyes of the UN, and certainly not in the eyes of the Arab world. If anything, Israel was now more vulnerable on her northern front since the days leading up to the first Lebanon War in June of 1982. On October 7, 2000, Hezbollah felt comfortable enough to launch a cross border raid into Israel.

Adi Avitan, Binyamin Avraham and Omar Souad while on patrol in their jeep on the Israeli side of the border, were ambushed by Hezbollah operatives posing as UN peacekeepers. The actual UN peacekeepers present at the time did nothing to assist the Israelis.* Even though Israel had threatened serious retaliation for any violation of the Israeli border by Hezbollah, in fact, she did

---

* UNIFIL's most notorious collaboration with terrorists involved the kidnapping and murder of three Israeli soldiers, and the subsequent cover-up.

On October 7, 2000, Hezbollah terrorists entered Israel, attacked three Israeli soldiers on Mount Dov, and abducted them [to] Lebanon. The kidnapping was witnessed by several dozen UNIFIL soldiers who stood idle. One of the soldier witnesses described the kidnapping: [T]he terrorists set off an explosive which stunned the Israeli soldiers. Clad in UN uniforms, the terrorists called out, "Come, come, we'll help you."

The Israeli soldiers approached the men in UN uniforms. Then, a Hezbollah bomb detonated—apparently prematurely. It wounded the disguised Hezbollah commander, and three Israeli soldiers. (cont'd)

very little after the kidnapping, thus interpreted by Hezbollah as Israeli weakness.

Over the next six years, Hezbollah continued to prepare for a confrontation with Israel. It received hundreds of millions of dollars of military equipment from Iran, which was shipped to Lebanon via Syria. In essence, Hezbollah became a proxy Iranian army sitting on Israel's northern border. Furthermore, Hezbollah built dozens of fortifications in South Lebanon, some in heavily forested areas and some in the middle of heavily populated cities. (The reason for the latter is that Hezbollah operatives knew that operating out of civilian areas would create serious moral dilemmas for the Israelis.) During that period (2000-2006) on numerous occasions Hezbollah reminded Israel that it was a force to be reckoned with. Every now and then its people would shell Israeli military fortifications in northern Israel, and fire rockets at Israeli

---

Two other terrorists in U.N. uniforms dragged their Hezbollah commander and the three wounded soldiers into a getaway car.

According an Indian solider in UNIFIL who witnessed the kidnapping, "By this stage, there was a big commotion and dozens of UN soldiers from the Indian brigade came around." The witness stated that the brigade knew that the kidnappers in UN uniform were Hezbollah. One soldier said that the brigade should arrest the Hezbollah, but the brigade did nothing.

According to the Indian soldier, the UNFIL brigade in the area "could have prevented the kidnapping."

"I'm very sorry about what happened, because we saw what happened," he said. Hezbollah "were wearing our uniforms and it was too bad we didn't stop them."

It appears that at least four of the UNIFIL "peacekeepers," all from India, [had] received bribes from Hezbollah in order to assist the kidnapping by helping them get to the kidnapping spot and find the Israeli soldiers. Some of the bribery involved alcohol and Lebanese women.

The Indian brigade later had a bitter internal argument, as some members complained that the brigade had betrayed its peacekeeping mandate. An Indian government investigation sternly criticized the brigade's conduct.

There is evidence of far greater payments by Hezbollah to the UNIFIL Indian brigade, including hundreds of thousands of dollars for assistance in the kidnapping and cover-up.

The UN cover-up began almost immediately. (cont'd)

towns like Kiryat Shemona. The Israeli response was always tepid, further emboldening Hezbollah's resolve.

THE SECOND LEBANESE WAR: 2006

By the summer of 2006, Hezbollah had witnessed Israel withdraw unilaterally from the Gaza Strip, and the Hamas victory in the Palestinian elections. Both of these events made Israel appear even more vulnerable and weak. On the morning of July 12, 2006, a group of Hezbollah terrorists ambushed an Israeli army patrol on the Israeli side of the Lebanese-Israeli border (near Kibbutz Avivim). Three Israeli soldiers were killed and two were

---

Lebanon's The Daily Star reported the story told by a former officer of the Observer Group Lebanon (OGL), which is part of the UN Truce Supervision Organization (UNTSO). ("UN 'destroyed' evidence after abduction of 3 Israeli troops," The Daily Star, July 20, 2001.)

A few hours after the kidnapping, UNTSO learned that two abandoned cars had been discovered. One was a white Nissan Pathfinder with fake UN insignia; it had hit an embankment because it was being driven so fast that the driver missed a turn. The other was a Range Rover; it was missing a tire rim, and was still running when it was discovered.

Rather than using the very-recently-abandoned vehicles as clues to rescue the kidnap victims, the UN initiated a cover-up. The next morning, eighteen hours after the kidnapping, a team of OGL and the Indian UNIFIL began removing the contents of the cars.

The Range Rover was soaked with blood. Among the contents of the vehicles may have been a cell phone belonging to the terrorists. The UNTSO officer confirmed that the cars contained "extremely sensitive" items which included "current and relevant information that could have been easily linked to the incident."

A UNIFIL peacekeeper videotaped the removal of the contents, and attempted to tow one of the cars. According to a much-later U.N. report, there were fifty items taken from the car, seven of them blood-stained. (Report of the fact-finding investigation relating to the abduction of three Israeli soldiers on 7 October 2000 and subsequent relevant events, Aug. 2, 2001.)

The end of the UNIFIL videotape featured armed Lebanese men confronting the UN forces, and taking the cars away from the UN. The UN personnel did not resist, because, they later claimed, the cars did not belong to the UN anyway.

The UNTSO officer told The Daily Star that the UN ordered its personnel to destroy all photographs and written reports about the incident. (cont'd)

kidnapped: Eldad Regev and Ehud Goldwasser. Simultaneously, Hezbollah fired dozens of Katyusha rockets and mortar shells at Israeli towns in northern Israel.

Though the IDF had a clear plan on what to do in such circumstances, those plans were not deployed by the Olmert government. Ehud Olmert had become prime minister on April 7, 2006 when Ariel Sharon suffered a stroke that left him in an irreversible coma [he died July 11, 2014]. Unfortunately, Olmert had surrounded himself with people who did not have a firm grasp on how the IDF would need to fight Hezbollah in such a case. The minister of defense was Amir Peretz, a tough union organizer with no real military experience, and a chief of staff, Dan Halutz, a former IAF commander, the first and only IDF chief of staff who did not come from the ground forces. War looks very different from the ground, and that view is essential when it comes to having a total picture of how any war needs to be fought, certainly the wars Israel consistently found herself fighting.

The UN did not provide the Israelis with the automobile contents, or the videotape, both of which might have helped the Israelis rescue the kidnap victims. Instead, the seized contents of the cars were taken to a town in Lebanon, stored in a safe, and some were eventually returned to Hezbollah.

Israel found out about the videotape, and demanded that the UN let Israeli investigators see it. Kofi Annan and his Special Envoy denied that any videotape existed. It is not clear whether Annan was lying, or whether he was misled.

Nine months after the kidnapping, July 6, 2001, the UN admitted that it had the videotape. Annan ordered an internal UN Report, which was led by UN undersecretary-General Joseph Connor. (Connor was later implicated in the Oil-for-Food scam.) The report revealed that the UN had two additional videotapes—one of which contained still photographs from the kidnapping itself. The UN investigation declared that there was no evidence that the UNIFIL forces had been bribed, or that the UN had deliberately misled anyone.

Even after admitting the existence of the first videotape, Annan refused to allow Israel to view it. He claimed that letting Israel see evidence about the kidnapping would undermine the UN's neutrality. Thus, Annan insisted on neutrality between innocent victims and terrorists who had used fake UN insignia and who had taken vehicles from UN staff at gunpoint." (David Kopel, "United Nations an Accomplice in Hezbollah Kidnapping," *Trackbacks*, July 21, 2006 ((http://volokh.com/posts/1153523571.shtml))

These three were hesitant to use the IDF plan to end Hezbollah's rocket attacks on all of northern Israel. It would have been an ugly, bloody, costly affair grinding out a ground war, with lots of air support, which would not have played well on TV and would have cost Israel many casualties.

> The reluctance to commit ground troops to battle betray[ed] a gap between Israel's leadership and its people. Both political and military leaders misjudged the resilience of Israeli society. At the beginning of 2004, [Chief of Staff Moshe] Yaalon asserted that the weakest link in Israel's national defense was the lack of public stamina. While vice premier in 2005, Olmert said, "We are tired of fighting; we are tired of being courageous; we are tired of winning; we are tired of defeating our enemies." The current chief of the Northern Command, Maj. Gen. Benny Ganz, said that while worried about Hezbollah's missiles, he was more concerned about the ability of Israeli society to withstand the pressures of war.
>
> Such concerns were misplaced. Israeli society demonstrated high stamina, even during wars of attrition...Israeli society would have been willing to absorb greater casualties to bring an effective end to the Hezbollah threat. Even parents who had lost a child in the Hezbollah war backed its expansion. Nor did combat unit recruitment suffer because of the war.[17]

And so, Hezbollah might well have been soundly defeated, if not decimated, and the north of Israel would have been quiet for many years if Israeli leaders had trusted their own people. Instead, Olmert, Peretz and Halutz opted for using the IAF to end the rocket fire while sending in small units of ground forces to achieve inefficient results.

This mismanagement of the war extended to the home front as well. Close to one million Israelis were either stuck in bomb shelters or constantly running back and forth to them several times a day for five weeks. Hezbollah had gained the ability to fire close to two hundred rockets a day into Israel—with over one-third of Israel's cities and towns in rocket range. The largest Israeli city

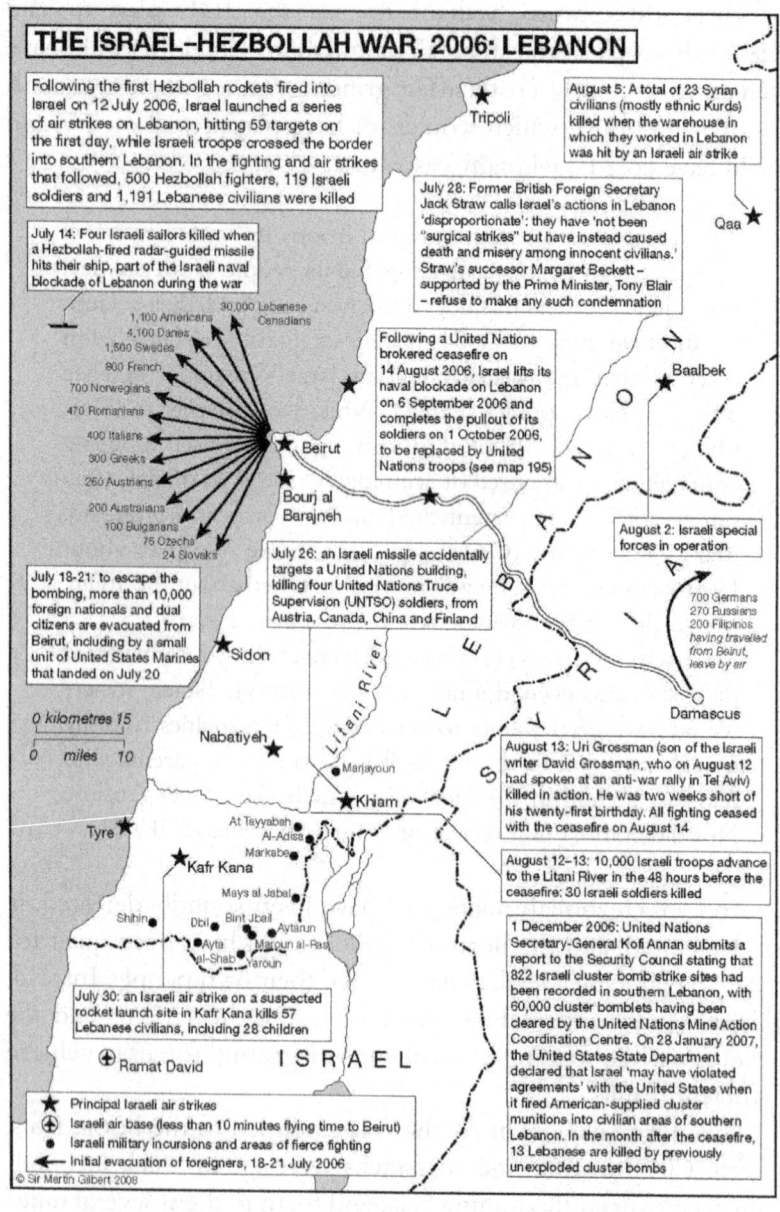

Sir Martin Gilbert, © 2010. Reproduced by permission of Taylor & Francis Books UK. www.martingilbert.com

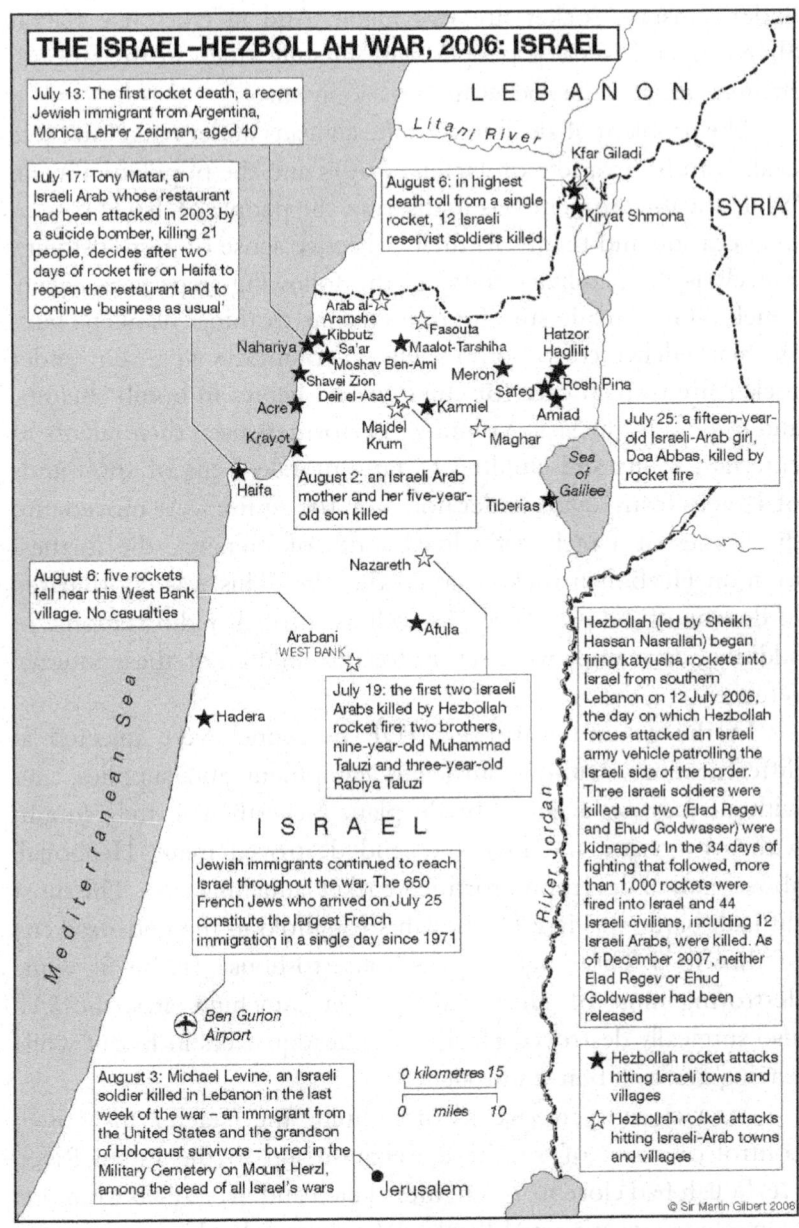

THE ISRAEL-HEZBOLLAH WAR, 2006: ISRAEL

July 13: The first rocket death, a recent Jewish immigrant from Argentina, Monica Lehrer Zeidman, aged 40

July 17: Tony Matar, an Israeli Arab whose restaurant had been attacked in 2003 by a suicide bomber, killing 21 people, decides after two days of rocket fire on Haifa to reopen the restaurant and to continue 'business as usual'

August 6: in highest death toll from a single rocket, 12 Israeli reservist soldiers killed

LEBANON

Litani River

Kfar Giladi

Kiryat Shmona

SYRIA

Arab al-Aramshe
Kibbutz
Nahariya
Sa'ar
Moshav Ben-Ami
Shavei Zion
Acre
Deir el-Asad
Krayot
Majdel Krum
Haifa

Fasouta
Maalot-Tarshiha
Meron
Karmiel

Hatzor Haglilit
Safed
Rosh Pina
Amiad
Maghar

Sea of Galilee

Tiberias

July 25: a fifteen-year-old Israeli-Arab girl, Doa Abbas, killed by rocket fire

August 2: an Israeli Arab mother and her five-year-old son killed

August 6: five rockets fell near this West Bank village. No casualties

Nazareth

Arabani
WEST BANK

Afula

July 19: the first two Israeli Arabs killed by Hezbollah rocket fire: two brothers, nine-year-old Muhammad Taluzi and three-year-old Rabiya Taluzi

Hadera

ISRAEL

Jewish immigrants continued to reach Israel throughout the war. The 650 French Jews who arrived on July 25 constitute the largest French immigration in a single day since 1971

Hezbollah (led by Sheikh Hassan Nasrallah) began firing katyusha rockets into Israel from southern Lebanon on 12 July 2006, the day on which Hezbollah forces attacked an Israeli army vehicle patrolling the Israeli side of the border. Three Israeli soldiers were killed and two (Elad Regev and Ehud Goldwasser) were kidnapped. In the 34 days of fighting that followed, more than 1,000 rockets were fired into Israel and 44 Israeli civilians, including 12 Israeli Arabs, were killed. As of December 2007, neither Elad Regev or Ehud Goldwasser had been released

River Jordan

Ben Gurion Airport

August 3: Michael Levine, an Israeli soldier killed in Lebanon in the last week of the war – an immigrant from the United States and the grandson of Holocaust survivors – buried in the Military Cemetery on Mount Herzl, among the dead of all Israel's wars

0 kilometres 15

0 miles 10

Jerusalem

Mediterranean Sea

★ Hezbollah rocket attacks hitting Israeli towns and villages

☆ Hezbollah rocket attacks hitting Israeli-Arab towns and villages

© Sir Martin Gilbert 2008

Sir Martin Gilbert, © 2010. Reproduced by permission of Taylor & Francis Books UK. www.martingilbert.com

under constant rocket fire was Haifa. And in cities like Kiryat Shemona and Ma'alot people were literally stuck in their bomb shelters because the rocket fire was so intense.

The problem of dealing with the civilians under rocket fire was dealt with by a variety of Israeli NGO's and the population itself. While the government was in disarray, the people of Israel rose to the occasion and thanks to their collective sense of responsibility, as well as their military training, the following steps were taken: Israeli NGO's made sure food, medicine, clothing, blankets, fans, etc., were delivered to bomb shelters. Volunteers were sent under rocket fire to help care for children and babies in bomb shelters, and to tend to the sick. Volunteer performers used their talents to entertain adults and children to raise morale. Tens of thousands of Israelis from towns under non-stop rocket fire were moved into the homes of Israelis who lived south of Netanya, the furthest location Hezbollah rockets could then hit. This was coordinated in dozens of NGO offices, as well as through radio stations. In addition, day camps were set up for the children of these internal refugees.

In the ground war itself IDF personnel were injected at different times without sufficient equipment and supplies, and without part of a larger battle plan. Nevertheless, they fought with great valor and ingenuity and destroyed many Hezbollah above- and underground fortified rocket launching sites. The most difficult battle was in a Hezbollah stronghold in the Lebanese city of Bint-Jbeil. There fighting was house-to-house. In the air, while destroying most of Hezbollah's rocket launching sites, the IAF also surgically destroyed Hezbollah's headquarters in Beirut while leaving most of Beirut untouched.

After close to five weeks of fighting, the Israeli army was in control of most of southern Lebanon, up to the Litani River. Hezbollah had close to 700 fighters killed and over 1,500 wounded (something not reported by the Western media. [As a matter of fact, all that was reported was that about 1,000 Lebanese had been killed, mostly civilians.[18]] Though there was a great deal of physical devastation in southern Lebanon, the Israeli Army took great pains not to willfully harm Lebanese civilians. Not only did Israel go out of its way to avoid harming civilians, but throughout the war the Israeli Air Force dropped leaflets in Arabic warning the civilian population of an impending Israeli attack, thus not only giving them time to leave, but tipping off Hezbollah fighters as well!

Finally, as was the case in the 1982 Lebanon War, and in all of Israel's military operations against Palestinian terrorist groups like Hamas, the enemy purposely had embedded itself in heavily populated civilian areas, using the local Arab population as human shields. Thus, throughout the war, the IDF and IAF operated with one hand tied behind their backs, while Hezbollah purposely targeted Israeli civilians.

In the course of the five-week war the IDF lost one hundred nineteen soldiers with forty-five civilians killed. Approximately 4,000 Hezbollah rockets had landed in Israel.[19] A great deal of damage was done to cities, towns and villages in the northern third of Israel, and many forests were burned down by the ensuing fires caused by the rockets. Hezbollah never reported its losses but it is estimated that around 700 of its fighters were killed and three times that number were wounded. More than half of all its rockets and launchers were destroyed.

But the mandated end of the war did not sit well with the Israeli populace, despite the pronounced victory.

> The fact remains, for all the losses that IDF tanks and infantry suffered at the hands of Hezbollah fighters armed with sophisticated anti-tank missiles, Israeli soldiers won every tactical engagement. There is no doubt that, if given the necessary time and freedom, the IDF would have eviscerated Hezbollah. That was the preferred course of the Israeli public: Polls show a majority wanted to continue fighting rather than accept the U.N. cease-fire....
>
> The failure (or, if you like, incomplete success) of this summer's Second Lebanon War was not the fault of ordinary Israeli soldiers and civilians. It was the fault of Israel's

current leaders, civil and military, who were shortsighted and irresponsible in their lack of preparation for this war and vacillating and irresolute in its conduct.

This fact did not sit well with the overwhelming majority of Israelis who felt that the government did not manage the war properly. That echo was shared by thousands of men who serve in the Israeli reserves, and were involved in the war up close.[20]

Many IDF officers were angry that besides not being allowed to prosecute the war the way they wanted to, that the government had signed a ceasefire agreement before the IDF finished its assigned task. So while the IDF militarily clearly won the war and Hezbollah was hurt badly, the victory should have been more decisive.

These sentiments were echoed by the Winograd Commission that was set up after the war to investigate why Prime Minister Olmert, Defense Minister Peretz and Chief of Staff Halutz did not follow the war plans prepared by the General Staff in case of such a scenario. The conclusion was that the government was afraid for political and social reasons to commit the IDF to fight a war that would cause a great deal of casualties—even though the long range results would have meant a quieter northern border with the elimination of Hezbollah and its evisceration sending a very chilling message to groups like Hamas, Islamic Jihad, ISIS and other enemies of the State of Israel. But lessons were learned and implemented in future operations, such as Cast Lead, Amood Anan (Pillar of Defense) and Defensive Edge.

As far as Hezbollah was concerned, the "death and destruction" its forces sustained caused Hassan Nasrallah, its titular head, to apologize for ever starting a war with Israel:

> "We did not believe," he said on Lebanon's New TV station, "even by one percent, that the captive operation would result in such a wide-scale war, as such a war did not take place in the history of wars. Had we known that the captive operation would result in such a war we would not have carried it out at all."

These are not the words of a man who thinks of himself as a victor. Nor are these the words of a man speaking to those who think they have won. He did not issue his apology because he hoped to appease his Christian, Sunni, and Druze opponents in Lebanon. He routinely, and absurdly, dismisses their March 14 coalition as the "Zionist hand." No. Nasrallah apologized because his Israeli adventure devastated his own Shia community.[21]

UN Security Council Resolution 1701

On August 11th, the United Nations' Security Council issued resolution 1701 for an armistice between Israel and Lebanon. It called for "a complete halt of acts of aggression, and especially those committed by Hezbollah and the military actions on behalf of Israel."

The resolution also announced the dispatch of 15,000 UN inspectors to south Lebanon, simultaneous to the Israeli withdrawal. The inspectors were authorized to use arms and instructed to vouch for "a complete stop of aggressive acts," as well as aiding the South Lebanon Army in taking over the territory and to "protect civilians from any threats of physical violence." Lebanon was asked to implement resolution 1559 dealing with disarmament of armed militias. The foreword to resolution 1701 also called for an unconditional release of the Israeli soldiers imprisoned.

Further articles of the resolution included the following: IDF's withdrawal from Lebanon and applying control to South Lebanon Army and UNIFIL; prohibition of carrying arms without consent of the Lebanese government; and the prohibition of the trade or transfer of arms to Hezbollah.[22]

When all was said and done, Israel withdrew from southern Lebanon and a UN peace keeping force took up residence to act as a buffer. However, the force was much smaller than the one stipulated in the ceasefire agreement, and it did not enforce the following aspects of the agreement: a) disarming Hezbollah; b) making sure that Syria stopped its re-supply of Hezbollah; c) physically moving Hezbollah forces north of the Litani River, and d) helping the Lebanese Army deploy along the Lebanese-Israeli border.

In essence, the cease fire agreement became yet another worthless promise in a long list of unfulfilled promises.

During the war there was one incident wherein Israel bombed a Hezbollah target that was in a building in a UN-designated safe zone in a town called Kfar Kana. The Hezbollah public relations machine right away sent out pictures of dozens of dead bodies in the rubble, including children and children's toys. These pictures, and the fact that this was in a UN-designated safe zone, created the perfect media storm against Israel. The UN and most of the Western media had a field day condemning Israel in the harshest tones.

Eventually it was found that Hezbollah did in fact fire rockets from the "safe zone" and that UN forces either let them or turned a blind eye. Equally reprehensible was that most of the bodies in the pictures that Hezbollah fed the media were killed in other places and then dragged to that site. The children's toys had also been carefully placed at the scene as well. But as Israel has learned the hard way, once something is a front page story the best of retractions only comes days later on a page buried in the newspaper in a tiny font. Once again, the damage had been done.

The day after the Kfar Kana incident, when Israel did not yet have all the evidence that denied her culpability, a powerful opinion piece, "We Will Not Capitulate," appeared on July 31, 2006, on the front page of *Maariv*. Proffered as a speech by the prime minister of Israel, journalist Ben Caspit captured the mood of Israelis when he wrote:

> In the aftermath of Kfar Kana, that would have explained to the world exactly what Israel is fighting for: Ladies and gentlemen, leaders of the world. I, the prime minister of

Israel, am speaking to you from Jerusalem in the face of the terrible pictures from Kfar Kana. Any human heart, wherever it is, must sicken and recoil at the sight of such pictures. There are no words of comfort that can mitigate the enormity of this tragedy. Still, I am looking you straight in the eye and telling you that the State of Israel will continue its military campaign in Lebanon. The Israel Defense Forces will continue to attack targets from which missiles and Katyusha rockets are fired at hospitals, old age homes and kindergartens in Israel. I have instructed the security forces and the IDF to continue to hunt for the Katyusha stockpiles and launch sites from which these savages are bombarding the State of Israel.

We will not hesitate, we will not apologize and we will not back off. If they continue to launch missiles into Israel from Kfar Kana, we will continue to bomb Kfar Kana. Today, tomorrow, and the day after tomorrow. Here, there and everywhere. The children of Kfar Kana could now be sleeping peacefully in their homes, unmolested, had the agents of the devil not taken over their land and turned the lives of our children into hell. Ladies and gentlemen, it's time you understood: the Jewish state will no longer be trampled upon. We will no longer allow anyone to exploit population centers in order to bomb our citizens. No one will be able to hide anymore behind women and children in order to kill our women and children. This anarchy is over. You can condemn us, you can boycott us, you can stop visiting us and, if necessary, we will stop visiting you.

Today I am serving as the voice of six million bombarded Israeli citizens who serve as the voice of six million murdered Jews who were melted down to dust and ashes by savages in Europe. In both cases, those responsible for these evil acts were, and are, barbarians devoid of all humanity, who set themselves one simple goal: to wipe the Jewish race off the face of the earth, as Adolf Hitler said, or to wipe the State of Israel off the map, as Mahmoud Ahmedinjad proclaims. And you – just as you did not take those words seriously then, you are ignoring them again now. And that, ladies and gentlemen, leaders of the world, will not happen again. Never again will we wait for bombs that never came to hit the gas chambers.

Never again will we wait for salvation that never arrives. Now we have our own air force. The Jewish people are now capable of standing up to those who seek their destruction – those people will no longer be able to hide behind women and children. They will no longer be able to evade their responsibility. Every place from which a Katyusha is fired into the State of Israel will be a legitimate target for us to attack. This must be stated clearly and publicly, once and for all. You are welcome to judge us, to ostracize us, to boycott us and to vilify us. But to kill us? Absolutely not.

Four months ago I was elected by hundreds of thousands of citizens to the office of prime minister of the government of Israel, on the basis of my plan for unilaterally withdrawing from 90 percent of the areas of Judea and Samaria, the birth place and cradle of the Jewish people; to end most of the occupation and to enable the Palestinian people to turn over a new leaf and to calm things down until conditions are ripe for attaining a permanent settlement between us. The prime minister who preceded me, Ariel Sharon, made a full withdrawal from the Gaza Strip back to the international border, and gave the Palestinians there a chance to build a new reality for themselves. The prime minister who preceded him, Ehud Barak, ended the lengthy Israeli presence in Lebanon and pulled the IDF back to the international border, leaving the land of the cedars to flourish, develop and establish its democracy and its economy. What did the State of Israel get in exchange for all of this? Did we win even one minute of quiet? Was our hand, outstretched in peace, met with a handshake of encouragement? Ehud Barak's peace initiative at Camp David let loose on us a wave of suicide bombers who smashed and blew to pieces over 1,000 citizens, men, women and children. I don't remember you being so enraged then.

Maybe that happened because we did not allow TV close-ups of the dismembered body parts of the Israeli youngsters at the Dolphinarium? Or of the shattered lives of the people butchered while celebrating the Passover seder at the Park Hotel in Netanya? What can you do—that's the way we are. We don't wave body parts at the camera. We grieve quietly.

We do not dance on the roofs at the sight of the bodies of our enemy's children—we express genuine sorrow and regret. That is the monstrous behavior of our enemies. Now they have risen up against us. Tomorrow they will rise up against you. You are already familiar with the murderous taste of this terror. And you will taste more. And Ariel Sharon's withdrawal from Gaza. What did it get us? A barrage of Kassam missiles fired at peaceful settlements and the kidnapping of soldiers. Then too, I don't recall you reacting with such alarm. And for six years, the withdrawal from Lebanon has drawn the vituperation and crimes of a dangerous, extremist Iranian agent, who took over an entire country in the name of religious fanaticism and is trying to take Israel hostage on his way to Jerusalem—and from there to Paris and London.

An enormous terrorist infrastructure has been established by Iran on our border, threatening our citizens, growing stronger before our very eyes, awaiting the moment when the land of the ayatollahs becomes a nuclear power in order to bring us to our knees. And make no mistake—we won't go down alone. You, the leaders of the free and enlightened world, will go down along with us. So today, here and now, I am putting an end to this parade of hypocrisy. I don't recall such a wave of reaction in the face of the 100 citizens killed every single day in Iraq. Sunnis kill Shi'ites who kill Sunnis, and all of them kill Americans—and the world remains silent. And I am hard pressed to recall a similar reaction when the Russians destroyed entire villages and burned down large cities in order to repress the revolt in Chechnya. And when NATO bombed Kosovo for almost three months and crushed the civilian population —then you also kept silent. What is it about us, the Jews, the minority, the persecuted, that arouses this cosmic sense of justice in you? What do we have that all the others don't?

In a loud clear voice, looking you straight in the eye, I stand before you openly and I will not apologize. I will not capitulate. I will not whine. This is a battle for our freedom. For our humanity. For the right to lead normal lives within our recognized, legitimate borders. It is also your battle. I pray and

I believe that now you will understand that. Because if you don't, you may regret it later, when it's too late."[23]

What Ben Caspit wrote not only reflects the vast majority of Israeli opinion today, 11 years after he wrote this powerful piece, but his warnings to the West that Israel's battle against Islamic jihadist barbarism will be the West's battle as well have also sadly become all too prophetic.

THE IAF DESTROYS A SYRIAN NUCLEAR REACTOR: SEPTEMBER 2007

In March of 2007, Mossad agents raided the home of Ibrahim Othman, the head of Syria's atomic energy commission, and downloaded top-secret information from his computer.

> The information the Mossad operatives recovered was damning: roughly three dozen color photographs taken from inside the Syrian building, indicating that it was a top-secret plutonium nuclear reactor. The reactor, called Al Kibar, was nine hundred yards from the Euphrates River and halfway between the borders with Turkey and Iraq. The photographs showed workers from North Korea at the site, which was far from Syria's biggest cities. The sole purpose of this kind of plutonium reactor, in the Mossad's analysis, was to produce an atomic bomb.[24]

After then-prime minister Ehud Olmert was briefed, he commenced a series of meetings with former prime ministers and current members of the Israeli defense establishment to discuss options. On April 18, Robert Gates, the U.S. Secretary of Defense was also informed, as well as the U.S. vice president, national security adviser and CIA director. The CIA would go on to confirm to the president that Syria was indeed building a nuclear reactor.

Although Olmert preferred that the U.S. lead a strike against this clear violation of the nuclear non-proliferation treaty to which

Syria was a signatory, President George W. Bush, already occupied with two Middle East wars in Iraq and Afghanistan, was loathe to commence a third potential war with Syria. Preferring diplomacy to an outright attack, the Bush administration demurred. However, Bush did not red light Olmert as to Israel conducting its own mission.*

---

* "There are several explanations for why Israel elected to launch a strike against the Syrian facility. The most obvious is that Israel feared the prospect of having a nuclear neighbor—particularly one with which Israel ha[d] been in a constant state of war since the Jewish state's independence in 1948. The two countries …clashed several times since the 1973 Yom Kippur war, including a major engagement in the 1982 Lebanon war and occasional skirmishes at their shared border. Moreover, Syria threatens Israel by proxy—through its support of such terrorist groups as Hamas, Hezbollah, and Palestinian Islamic Jihad.

"A second possible motivation [was] Israel's desire to re-establish deterrence in the Arab world. Israel's failures in its 2006 war with Hezbollah weakened the perceived deterrent that it held over its neighbors. The al-Kibar strike may have been an attempt to reestablish the supremacy of Israel's military apparatus in its enemies' eyes. Christopher Pang, head of the Middle East and North Africa program at the Royal United Services Institute in London, told the Associated Press, "In terms of deterrence, the effect was clear by invading Syrian airspace, by showing that Israel is not only able, but willing, to still launch strikes against Syrian targets."

"The IAF's strike may also have been intended as a warning to Iran—or even a practice run on an eventual bombing raid on Iranian nuclear facilities. Obviously, al-Kibar differed greatly from the primary nuclear targets in Iran. Indeed, al-Kibar was at least partially located above ground, and was within Israeli warplanes' striking range. Nonetheless, al-Kibar was protected by the same Russian-built Tor-M1 air defense system used to protect Iranian facilities. Thus, Israel's strike may have been a test run to find flaws in Iran's air defenses.

"If indeed Israel's strategy was to diagnose Iran's air defense weaknesses, the strategy appeared to backfire. The apparent failure of these systems prompted Iran in December 2007 to purchase the more advanced S-300 system from Russia. (Both Russia and Iran insist the deal had been in the works well before then.)

In the end, however, the Israeli operation seems to have been motivated by necessity; the pictures collected by Israel's mole depicted a nearly complete facility. Albright and Brannan argue that the late detection of the reactor, coupled with the perception of a nearly operational facility, compelled Israel to choose the military option as a measure of first resort. They write that (cont'd)

Just before midnight on September 5, 2007, four F-15s and four F-16s took off from Israeli Air Force bases, including Ramat David, southeast of Haifa. After flying north along the Mediterranean Coast, the planes turned east and followed the Syrian-Turkish border, to avoid detection by radar. Using standard electronic scrambling tools, the Israelis blinded Syria's air-defense system. In Tel Aviv, in a room of the underground I.A.F. command-and-control center known as "the pit," Olmert, Barak, Livni, and senior security officials followed the planes by radar. The room would serve as a bunker for Olmert in the event that the strike sparked a war; the Israelis had also prepared a military contingency plan.

[IAF Chief General Eliezer Shkedi] tracked the pilots by audio in an adjacent room. Sometime between 12:40 and 12:53 A.M., the pilots uttered the computer-generated code word of the day, "Arizona," indicating that seventeen tons of explosives had been dropped on their target. "There was a sense of elation," one participant recalled. "The reactor was destroyed and we did not lose a pilot."[25]

Syria subsequently announced that Israel had engaged in a military incursion but had been rebuffed by Syrian air defense systems. As for the Israelis, it was prudent to deny that any incident had taken place, even though it did brief its allies as to its actions. Syria never admitted that it was building a reactor, but under pressure to allow I.A.E.A. inspectors to visit the site, and despite burying the compound in concrete, the inspectors confirmed that nuclear material was indeed present.

Israel's 'analysis, which in hindsight must be viewed as a worst-case assessment, was that Syria could soon load uranium fuel and start the reactor.' Israel did not want to attack after the reactor was fully operational, because doing so would run the risk of spreading radioactive material. (Daveed Gartenstein-Ross and Joshua D. Goodman, "The Attack on Syria's al-Kibar Nuclear Facility," Jewish Policy CenterSpring 2009 ((https://www.jewishpolicycenter.org/2009/02/28/the-attack-on-syrias-al-kibar-nuclear-facility/))

OPERATION CAST LEAD: THE WAR AGAINST HAMAS IN GAZA: DECEMBER 2008 – JANUARY 2009

After Israel withdrew from Gaza there was the hope that the PA would now set up a mini Palestinian political entity alongside Israel, in essence to use Gaza as an incubator for a formal Palestinian State. The PA had by that point a decade of political experience, international contacts and had received billions of dollars in foreign aid. Hence running Gaza would prove to Israel and the world that the PA was up to the task of governing a sovereign state.

But that's not what occurred. Literally, as the IDF redeployed to its new border, and as 10,000 evacuated Israeli citizens were trying to rebuild their shattered lives, Qassam* rockets began to fall on most of the Israeli area around Gaza, especially the town of Sderot. And so Israel received its goodwill payment for ceding Gaza to the PA: a constant barrage of missiles that threatened the life and limb of its citizenry.

HOW DID HAMAS GET CONTROL OF THE GAZA STRIP?

Hamas was founded in 1987, soon after the outbreak of the First Intifada, the first popular uprising against the Israeli occupation. Creating Hamas to participate in the revolt was regarded as a survival measure to enable the [Muslim] Brotherhood itself, which refused to fight against Israel, to hold its own against other competing Palestinian nationalist groups. By forming a military wing distinct from its social charity organizations, it was hoped that the latter would be insulated from being targeted by Israel.[26]**

---

* Qassam rockets are manufactured by Hamas and other terrorist groups operating in Gaza. There are several types of these rockets, the smallest of which has a two-mile range and the largest a 13-mile range. The warheads vary from 11 pounds to 22 pounds of explosives and shrapnel. While they are not very sophisticated, a hit will probably kill or maim everyone inside a home and destroy a good part of the structure.

** "In truth, the creation of Hamas as a separate entity from the Muslim Brotherhood was done precisely to prevent Israeli authorities from targeting the organizations' greater activities, in the hopes that it would leave them relatively immune. Moreover, Hamas was created essentially because the Islamicists connected to the Muslim Brotherhood feared that without their direct (cont'd)

Under pressure from the U.S., Fatah was forced to hold parliamentary elections in 2006. In the elections in which it participated, Hamas won to become the dominant political party.

> While Hamas boycotted the 2005 Palestinian presidential election, it did participate in the 2005 municipal elections organized by Yasser Arafat in the occupied territories. In those elections it won control of over one third of Palestinian municipal councils, besting Fatah, which had for long been the biggest force in Palestinian politics... Hamas won the 2006 elections, winning 76 of the 132 seats to Fatah's 43. Seen by many as primarily a rejection of the Fatah government's corruption and ineffectiveness, the Hamas victory seemingly had brought to an end 40 years of PLO domination of Palestinian politics.[27]

But the unity government that was formed as a result of the election was shortlived. Hamas felt that the PA was not really abiding by the results of its election victory and that it was not officially getting the leadership positions in the government that it felt it deserved. This was compounded by the fact that PA personnel refused to take orders from Hamas superiors. So, in the summer of 2007, Hamas orchestrated a coup* in Gaza. PA leaders and security people were arrested, beaten and many were executed.

---

participation in the first Intifada, they would lose supporters to both the PIJ and the PLO, the latter of which was anxious to reassert itself in the Palestinian territories after being marginalized following its expulsion from Lebanon. As authors Mishal and Saela, explain, 'The Mujamma's decision to adopt a "jihad now" policy against "enemies of Allah" (through the creation of Hamas) was thus largely a matter of survival." (Joshua L. Gleis, Benedetta Berti, *Hezbollah and Hamas: A Comparative Study* (Baltimore: Johns Hopkins University Press, 2012, 119)

* "In an April 2008 article in Vanity Fair magazine, the journalist David Rose published confidential documents, apparently originating from the US State Department, which would prove that the United States collaborated with the Palestinian Authority and Israel to attempt the violent overthrow of Hamas in the Gaza Strip, and that Hamas pre-empted the coup.... Rose quotes former Vice President Dick Cheney's chief Middle East adviser David Wurmser (cont'd)

Since its ascension to control over Gaza,

> ...Hamas has divided its activities into three main spheres
> of operation: (1) a political section involved in Palestinian
> politics; (2) a social section (modeled on those of the Muslim
> Brotherhood and Hezbollah) that provides basic social
> services, such as hospitals, schools, and religious institutions,
> to its constituencies; and (3) a militant section, represented by
> its paramilitary wing, the Izzedine al Qassam Brigades, which
> engage in acts of terror against Israelis and also participate in
> conflict against other Palestinian factions.[28]

Gaza thus became the first modern Sunni Islamic Republic in
the Middle East. (Iran was the first Shi'ite Islamic Republic in the
Modern Middle East, established in 1979, with the overthrow of
the Shah.)

OPERATION CAST LEAD
BACKGROUND
Since 2001 Israel had been under constant rocket fire from
Gaza. Since Israel's withdrawal it had been the victim of more than
11,000 rocket attacks.[29] Despite what was essentially a *casus belli*
(a justification for war), Israel took the way of diplomacy. Over
the years it sent some one hundred petitions to the UN—to the
Secretary General and the President of the UN Security Council—
and typically got nowhere. In 2008 an Iranian-made Grad rocket
hit a mall in Ashkelon wounding ninety.[30] Again, there was no
response from the UN.

By December 2008, 40-50 rockets a day were being fired from
Gaza onto the citizens of Sderot, as well as other Israeli towns

---

accusing the Bush administration of 'engaging in a dirty war in an effort to
provide a corrupt dictatorship [led by Abbas] with victory.' He believes that
Hamas had no intention of taking Gaza until Fatah forced its hand. 'It looks to
me that what happened wasn't so much a coup by Hamas but an attempted coup
by Fatah that was pre-empted before it could happen.'" (https://en.wikipedia.
org/wiki/Battle_of_Gaza_(2007) as derived from David Rose, "The Gaza
Bombshell," *Vanity Fair*, April 2008)

and villages nearby. At this level of incitement, it was determined that simple retaliation was no longer an acceptable answer. The IDF plan to end the rocket fire was finally approved on December 27, 2008; Operation Cast Lead was launched. It began as a well-coordinated series of IAF attacks against Hamas military targets in the Gaza Strip—rocket factories, rocket and weapons storage sites, smuggling tunnels from Sinai into Gaza, command, training, and communication centers and Hamas's headquarters.

What makes fighting Hamas and other terrorist organizations so difficult to engage is that they purposely embed themselves within civilian populations. This means that a rocket factory can be in the middle of a housing complex, a rocket storage site may be in a mosque, a rocket launching area in the courtyard of a school. Since terrorist organizations are not adherents of the Geneva Convention, ironically it is only their adversaries, usually recognized states, that must suffer the international condemnation of killing civilians who become the collateral damage of the terrorist actions.

Hence, Hamas knows that its tactic of hiding behind women and children is very effective against Israel, a country that it constantly calls barbaric and Nazi-like when she responds to its attacks. In response, the IDF developed the closest thing there is to surgical air strikes. Using excellent intelligence, sophisticated smart bombs, drones and precision missiles, Israel was able to hit Hamas military targets no matter where they were.

According to the IAF, 80% of the bombs used by the IAF were precision weapons, and 99% of the air strikes hit their targets. A study by the Center for Strategic and International Studies points out that when possible, IAF executed strikes using the smallest precision-guided weapons, and coordinated air strikes and the use of artillery weapons using GPS, in a systematic effort to limit collateral damage. In a 2009 interview, Major General Ido Nehushtan said that the only use of non-precision-guided munitions from the Israeli Air Force was in open areas. He went on to say: "We had to find ways to do things as precisely and proportionately as possible, while focusing on how to differentiate between terrorists and uninvolved civilians."[31]

Where it was impossible to insure that only the target would be hit, the IDF took the unprecedented step of not just dropping tens of thousands of leaflets in Arabic in the parts of Gaza it was planning to hit, but hundreds of thousands of phone calls and texts were sent to the people of Gaza.[32] By definition this takes away the element of surprise, but insures that the civilians have the opportunity to leave the area that Hamas cynically turned into a military target. Hamas, however, responded by moving civilians into areas that Israel warned she was going to attack. One of their leaders boasted: "We love death as much as the Zionist enemy loves life!"[33]

One of the most successful techniques for preventing civilian injury was "roof knocking".

> The combination of exquisite intelligence, persistent surveillance, and precision munitions enabled very sophisticated attacks against targets. These attacks are perhaps best represented by the "roof-knocking" technique, which was employed when Hamas used human shields on top of buildings to deter IAF attacks. The following description of one such attack illustrates the IDF's detailed integration of ISR, attack, and C2:
>
> • A multistory building was identified for destruction because it contained militarymateriel.
>
> • A telephone call was placed to an occupant of the building, who was told toevacuate the building within ten minutes.
>
> • An IAF UAV, attack helicopter, and fixed-wing fighter were assigned to themission. They had the building in sight and were on a shared communicationschannel with both Southern Command and IAF headquarters in Tel Aviv.Throughout the attack, they discussed what was happening and what to do next.
>
> • A short time after the telephone call, the occupants of the building appeared onthe roof, becoming human shields intended to dissuade the Israeli attack.

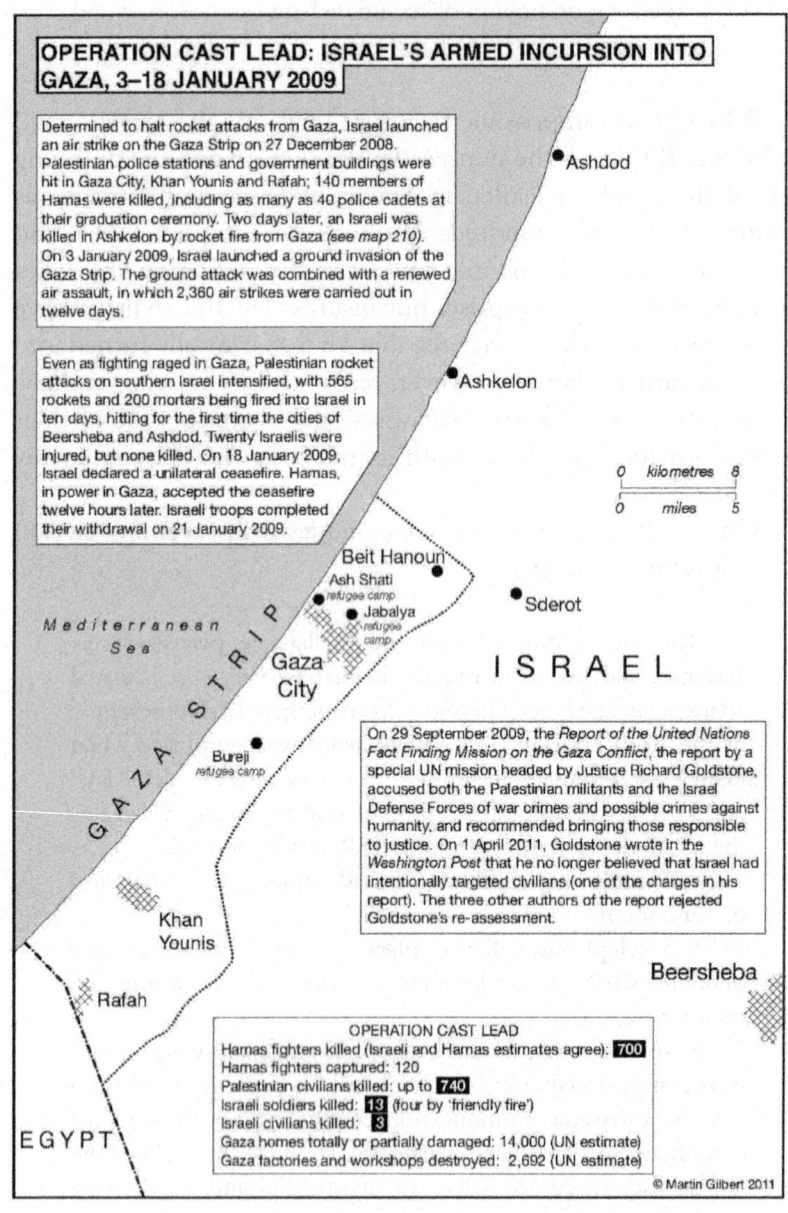

OPERATION CAST LEAD: ISRAEL'S ARMED INCURSION INTO GAZA, 3–18 JANUARY 2009

Determined to halt rocket attacks from Gaza, Israel launched an air strike on the Gaza Strip on 27 December 2008. Palestinian police stations and government buildings were hit in Gaza City, Khan Younis and Rafah; 140 members of Hamas were killed, including as many as 40 police cadets at their graduation ceremony. Two days later, an Israeli was killed in Ashkelon by rocket fire from Gaza *(see map 210)*. On 3 January 2009, Israel launched a ground invasion of the Gaza Strip. The ground attack was combined with a renewed air assault, in which 2,360 air strikes were carried out in twelve days.

Even as fighting raged in Gaza, Palestinian rocket attacks on southern Israel intensified, with 565 rockets and 200 mortars being fired into Israel in ten days, hitting for the first time the cities of Beersheba and Ashdod. Twenty Israelis were injured, but none killed. On 18 January 2009, Israel declared a unilateral ceasefire. Hamas, in power in Gaza, accepted the ceasefire twelve hours later. Israeli troops completed their withdrawal on 21 January 2009.

On 29 September 2009, the *Report of the United Nations Fact Finding Mission on the Gaza Conflict*, the report by a special UN mission headed by Justice Richard Goldstone, accused both the Palestinian militants and the Israel Defense Forces of war crimes and possible crimes against humanity, and recommended bringing those responsible to justice. On 1 April 2011, Goldstone wrote in the *Washington Post* that he no longer believed that Israel had intentionally targeted civilians (one of the charges in his report). The three other authors of the report rejected Goldstone's re-assessment.

OPERATION CAST LEAD
Hamas fighters killed (Israeli and Hamas estimates agree): 700
Hamas fighters captured: 120
Palestinian civilians killed: up to 740
Israeli soldiers killed: 13 (four by 'friendly fire')
Israeli civilians killed: 3
Gaza homes totally or partially damaged: 14,000 (UN estimate)
Gaza factories and workshops destroyed: 2,692 (UN estimate)

© Martin Gilbert 2011

Sir Martin Gilbert, © 2010. Reproduced by permission of Taylor & Francis Books UK. www.martingilbert.com

• The IAF "knocked on the roof," shooting at a corner of the building with a missile from the attack helicopter in such a way as to not injure any of the individuals on the roof. At this point, the rooftop shields rapidly vacated the roof and exited the building.

• As they left the building they were counted. When the same number who had been on the roof were out the door and away from the building, the fighter was cleared to drop a PGM to destroy the building. A video of the attack showed secondary explosions, indicating the presence of explosives in the building.[34]

For a week, the IAF hit hundreds of Hamas targets in Gaza, with Hamas responding by firing its different missiles on Beer Sheva, Ashkelon, Ashdod, Gedrea, Yavneh, Kiryat Gat, Netivot, Rechovot, Sderot and all the Israeli towns nearby. Around 1.5 million Israelis were now running in and out of bomb shelters during this time. Since Hamas rockets were aimed at Israeli civilian targets—homes, schools, shopping centers and even hospitals—it became clear that the only way to end the rocket fire would be for a full-scale military incursion, an attack into a densely populated area that Hamas had spent years fortifying with thousands of booby traps and land mines.

Hamas had planned to stand and fight, but the Qassam Brigades proved unequal to the task. Fairly early in the fighting, Hamas fighters began removing their uniforms and donning civilian clothing, further increasing the risk to the civilian population. Units in the field started to break down after a few days, then to disintegrate. Under the weight of IDF fire, ... [al-Qassam Brigade] fighters hastily withdrew to the city for cover and concealment. Even in places where they were ordered to hold their positions they abandoned them, preferring to survive rather than to fight. None of their ground combat measures worked, and while this is not surprising, given the difficulties they faced, they certainly failed to match the image Hamas tried so hard to present, of stalwart and proficient Islamic warriors.[35]

Within two weeks the IDF captured half of the Gaza Strip. This involved very dangerous urban fighting where the IDF took extraordinary steps on one hand to avoid civilian casualties and on the other hand to protect its own men. What became clear during the fighting was that most of the Hamas leaders and terrorist commanders had gone into hiding in deep underground bunkers they had prepared for themselves, leaving to their own devices the civilians they had purposely put in harm's way.

The IDF cut the northern part of Gaza from the southern part and began encircling Gaza City and Khan Yunis. Slowly but surely Hamas's military infrastructure was degraded.

> On 7 January, Israel opened a humanitarian corridor to allow the shipment of aid into Gaza. The Israeli army agreed to interrupt fighting for three hours and Hamas agreed not to launch rockets during the pause. Israel repeated the ceasefire either daily or every other day.[36]

The operation was initially supposed to last eight weeks, but political considerations, in particular the U.S. election of President Barak Obama and his inauguration on January 20, 2009, caused the IDF to unilaterally cease fighting on January 18. When Operation Cast Lead ended the IDF sat on fifty percent of the Gaza Strip. Under the terms of an Egyptian proposal, by January 21st all IDF forces left Gaza. The IDF had suffered a miraculously low amount of casualties, ten killed and around two hundred wounded.[37] Hamas suffered around 700 deaths.[38]

ASYMMETRICAL WARFARE

In the 21st century the Western world, in particular Israel and the U.S., find themselves fighting wars that are described by military experts as "asymmetrical". Essentially, this means that a well-armed, technologically advanced military finds itself fighting a terrorist entity that imbeds itself in densely populated areas and uses less sophisticated weaponry to attack the superior combatant.

This new type of terrorist enemy is banking on the technologically advanced opponent refraining from using its full military might for fear of harming civilians being used as human shields.

> ...[T]he fighting in Gaza is a case study in the fact that asymmetric warfare confronts any [soldier] actually in combat with a constant stream of hard choices and exercises in situation ethics obscured by what Clausewitz called the "fog of war." In many cases, instant choices have to be made where all of the advances in intelligence and command and control do not allow those actually fighting to know the nature of the threat forces or the number of civilians at risk.
>
> At the same time, the very nature of asymmetric warfare often forces the weaker [side] to maximize this uncertainty by not wearing uniforms, mixing in civilian areas, and using collocated civilians—often women and children—to provide support. This is no more an act of cowardice than using the protection of a tank or aircraft, but it does mean that war is evolving in ways that often increase the risk of civilian casualties and put more and more strain on the capability of armed forces to limit those casualties.[39]

In addition to the actual physical combat, a propaganda war is also involved that caters to the biases of world media. Prevented or unwilling to get first-hand information as relates to Israel, reporters have chosen to engage in showmanship rather than fact, often reporting duplicitous information supplied by Israel's opponents—invariably acknowledged terrorist organizations—without verification. In particular, there is applied...

> ..."a moral relativism between the two sides that does not exist. This is not the contest between misguided equals that many in the West seem to see. One is the region's lone democracy, which for much of its existence has faced a very real existential threat and would like, if possible, to live in peace with its neighbors. The other is a terrorist organization, bent on preventing such a future."[40]

THE GOLDSTONE REPORT

During Operation Cast Lead anti-Israel demonstrations raged throughout European cities, especially those with large Muslim populations in France, Belgium, Spain, Britain and Sweden, to name a few. These demonstrations drew thousands of angry Arab, Muslim and Leftist demonstrators who depicted Israel as a neo-Nazi country slaughtering thousands of unarmed innocent Gazans. Typically, post-1967, media outlets accepted the demonstrators' claims as "facts", though fed to them by Hamas or Hamas sympathizers.

The UN, in the meantime, busy parroting Hamas's view of the fighting, formed a special commission to "investigate" Israeli "war crimes" committed during Operation Cast Lead. Stacking the deck, the members of this commission were composed of human rights diplomats who had a history of anti-Israel activism. To give the commission an air of fairness and gravitas, a Jewish South African judge named Richard Goldstone was designated as lead actor. But because of the long and sad history of bias at the UN and the people named to be on the investigative committee, Israel refused to cooperate with the committee, though it did send it vast amounts of documentation about Hamas, the years before Operation Cast Lead and on the operation itself.

The *Goldstone Report* was issued in September 2009. Its conclusion was that the Israeli response was totally disproportionate to the threat caused by the rockets fired at Israel. And, finally, that the IDF in the way in operated in Gaza committed war crimes.*

One of the best and most detailed critiques of the *Goldstone Report* was written by Alan Dershowitz wherein he stated:

> The Goldstone Report, when read in full and in context, is much worse than most of its detractors (and supporters)

---

* The Government of Israel issued a 32-point preliminary analysis of the report, titled "Initial Response to Report of the Fact Finding Mission on Gaza Established Pursuant to Resolution S-9/1 of the Human Rights (cont'd)

believe. It is far more accusatory of Israel, far less balanced
in its criticism of Hamas, far less honest in its evaluation of
the evidence, far less responsible in drawing its conclusion,
far more biased against Israeli than Palestinian witnesses, and
far more willing to draw adverse inferences of intentionality
from Israeli conduct and statements than from comparable
Palestinian conduct and statements. It is worse than any report
previously prepared by any other United Nations agency or
human rights group.[41]

The *Goldstone Report* for Israel, its friends and allies became a
symbol of everything that is corrupt and perverse about the United
Nations, and how terrorists and extremists who have no regard for
Western laws and norms twist them to tie the hands of countries
like Israel while they are free to violate all the rules of war.

The findings of the commission so infuriated Colonel
Richard Kemp that on October 16, 2009, as a guest of the NGO
UN Monitor, Colonel Kemp addressed the UN Human Rights
Commission in Geneva:

Council". The main arguments in the analysis were the following.

1. The resolution mandating the mission was one-sided and prejudicial and
the terms of the mandate were never changed.

2. The composition of the mission and its conduct raised serious questions
about its impartiality.

3. Incidents selected for examination were cherry-picked for political effect.

4. The mission displayed double standards in acceptance of evidence: treating
even photographic evidence presented by Israel as inherently untrustworthy,
except when it could be used to condemn Israel, while uncritically accepting
statements by Hamas; reinterpreting or dismissing self-incriminating statements
by Hamas; and selectively quoting material from sources.

5. The report includes misstatements of fact: for example, it stated that
Israel discriminated against its non-Jewish citizens in providing shelter from
Palestinian rocket attacks, when the shelter was provided on the basis of
proximity to the Gaza Strip and did not discriminate between Jews and non-
Jews.

6. The report contains misstatements of law: for example, its description
of the Israeli appeals process is outdated.

7. The report fails to consider the military complexities of the war, (cont'd)

...I am the former commander of the British forces in Afghanistan. I served with NATO and the United Nations; commanded troops in Northern Ireland, Bosnia and Macedonia; and participated in the Gulf War. I spent considerable time in Iraq since the 2003 invasion, and worked on international terrorism for the UK Governments Joint Intelligence Committee. Mr. President, based on my knowledge and experience, I can say this: During Operation Cast Lead, the Israeli Defence Forces did more to safeguard the rights of civilians in a combat zone than any other army in the history of warfare. Israel did so while facing an enemy that deliberately positioned its military capability behind the human shield of the civilian population. Hamas, like Hizballah, are expert at driving the media agenda. Both will always have people ready to give interviews condemning Israeli forces for war crimes. They are adept at staging and distorting incidents. The IDF faces a challenge that we British do not have to face to the same extent. It is the automatic,

---

makes judgments lacking necessary knowledge, and ignores Israel's extensive efforts to maintain humanitarian standards and protect civilians.

8. The report unjustifiably minimizes the threat of terrorism and in effect vindicates terrorist tactics.

9. The report presents its findings as judicial determinations of guilt, despite its admission that it does not reach a judicial level of proof; it commits egregious legal errors, including unjustifiable assumptions regarding intent and commanders' states of mind, as well as misinterpretation of the willfulness requirement of responsibility under international law.

10. The report ignores Israel's own investigations into its conduct, overlooks the many independent levels of scrutiny in Israel's judicial system, misrepresents Israel's legal mechanisms and shows disdain for democratic values.

11. The report makes one-sided recommendations against Israel while making only token recommendations with respect to Palestinians: for example, recommending Israel compensate Palestinians for attacks without recommending Palestinians compensate Israelis for attacks.

The analysis concludes that the report claims to represent international law but perverts it to serve a political agenda; that it sends a "legally unfounded message to states everywhere confronting terrorism that international law has no effective response to offer them", and that it signals to terrorist groups "that the cynical tactics of seeking to exploit civilian (suffering

Pavlovian presumption by many in the international media, and international human rights groups, that the IDF are in the wrong, that they are abusing human rights. The truth is that the IDF took extraordinary measures to give Gaza civilians notice of targeted areas, dropping over 2 million leaflets, and making over 100,000 phone calls. Many missions that could have taken out Hamas military capability were aborted to prevent civilian casualties. During the conflict, the IDF allowed huge amounts of humanitarian aid into Gaza. To deliver aid virtually into your enemy's hands is, to the military tactician, normally quite unthinkable. But the IDF took on those risks. Despite all of this, of course innocent civilians were killed. War is chaos and full of mistakes. There have been mistakes by the British, American and other forces in Afghanistan and in Iraq, many of which can be put down to human error. But mistakes are not war crimes. More than anything, the civilian casualties were a consequence of Hamas' way of fighting. Hamas deliberately tried to sacrifice their own civilians. Mr. President, Israel had no choice apart from defending its people, to stop Hamas from attacking them with rockets. And I say this again: the IDF did more to safeguard the rights of civilians in a combat zone than any other army in the history of warfare.[42]

It is interesting to note that in April 2011 Judge Goldstone, in an "Op Ed" piece in the *New York Times* and the *Washington Post,* retracted most of the conclusions of the Goldstone Report stating he didn't have all the information available at the time the report was issued.

While expressing regret that Israel's failure to co-operate with the Commission had hindered its ability to gather exculpatory facts, he approved Israel's subsequent internal investigations

cont'd) for political ends actually pays dividends". (https://en.wikipedia.org/wiki/United_Nations_Fact_Finding_Mission_on_the_Gaza_Conflict   as derived from https://web.archive.org/web/20131001094449/http://www.mfa.gov.il/NR/rdonlyres/FC985702-61C4-41C9-8B72-E3876FEF0ACA/0/GoldstoneReportInitialResponse240909.pdf)

into incidents described in the report as well as their establishment of policies to better protect civilians in future conflicts. He contrasted the Israeli reaction with the failure of Hamas to investigate or modify their methods and procedures. Goldstone said he had hoped that the Commission's inquiry "would begin a new era of evenhandedness at the U.N. Human Rights Council, whose history of bias against Israel cannot be doubted".[43]

His colleagues on the commission did not change their positions.

THE MAVI MARMARA INCIDENT: THE IDF BLOCKADE OF GAZA (HAMASISTAN)

With the election of Hamas as the governing political entity in Gaza, Israel, recognizing the threat of a radical Islamist terror group on its border, within international law* initiated a blockade to insure that military supplies did not make it into its enemy's hands.

Israel surrounds Gaza on three sides. North and East Gaza are separated from Israel by a security fence and a security zone, an area where a low intensity war continues to take place between Hamas, Islamic Jihad, other radical jihadi terrorist groups and the IDF. The Israeli Navy enforces a strict blockade twenty miles offshore Gaza's west coast. Gazans are able to fish, use their beaches, build sewage treatment plants and go sailing near their coasts, but ships seeking to dock at Gaza are directed to the Israeli port of Ashdod, inspected for weapons and related contraband and then non-military supplies put on trucks and brought to Gazan crossing points at Erez, Karnei and Katif. (The southern border

---

* "The fundamental principle of the freedom of navigation on the high seas is subject to only certain limited exceptions under international law. Israel faces a real threat to its security from militant groups in Gaza. The naval blockade was imposed as a legitimate security measure in order to prevent weapons from entering Gaza by sea and its implementation complied with the requirements of international law." ("Report of the Secretary-General's Panel of Inquiry on the 31 May 2010 Flotilla Incident" ((http://www.un.org/News/dh/infocus/middle_east/Gaza_Flotilla_Panel_Report.pdf, 4))

of Gaza is with Egypt-controlled Sinai. Depending on the political situation, the level of control of that border varies. When the Muslim Brotherhood ruled Egypt from June 2012-July 2013, the border was less tightly controlled. Since the coup that took over Egypt in July of 2013, the Sinai border has been tightly controlled because the Hamas government is closely allied with the ousted Muslim Brotherhood.)

To mitigate Israel's control over military materiel reaching Gaza, then unbeknownst to Israel, Hamas began building a series of tunnels connecting Gaza to northern Sinai. The main purpose of these tunnels was to smuggle in ammunition, including missiles, rockets, small arms and explosives to be used in its ongoing terrorist war against Israel. These tunnels were also used as money makers. Hamas would rent them out by the hour to smugglers who brought in whiskey, drugs, even prostitutes. The fact that this clashed with Hama's religious ideology was conveniently overlooked.

Ironically, most of Gaza's food, basic staples, medical supplies, luxury items, electricity and phone service come either directly from or through Israel. But since most Westerners know very little about the actual facts on the ground in Israel, Gaza, Judea, Samaria or any country in the Middle East for that matter, the little they do know comes from a biased narration perpetrated by Arab propagandists.

The new story of Gaza as told by anti-Israel groups goes something like this: Gaza is still under a brutal Zionist military occupation.* The Palestinians are literally being starved by the vicious Zionist enemy. There is a lack of food, water, medicine, basic needs and there is barely electricity. Worse, the Zionist occupation army randomly bombs and rockets innocent Palestinian civilians

---

* "Israel remains an occupying Power in respect of Gaza. Arguments that Israel ceased its occupation of Gaza in 2005 following the evacuation of its settlements and the withdrawal of its troops take no account of the fact that Israel retains effective control over Gaza by means of its control over Gaza's external borders, airspace, territorial waters, population registry, tax revenues and governmental functions. The effectiveness of this control is emphasized by regular (cont'd)

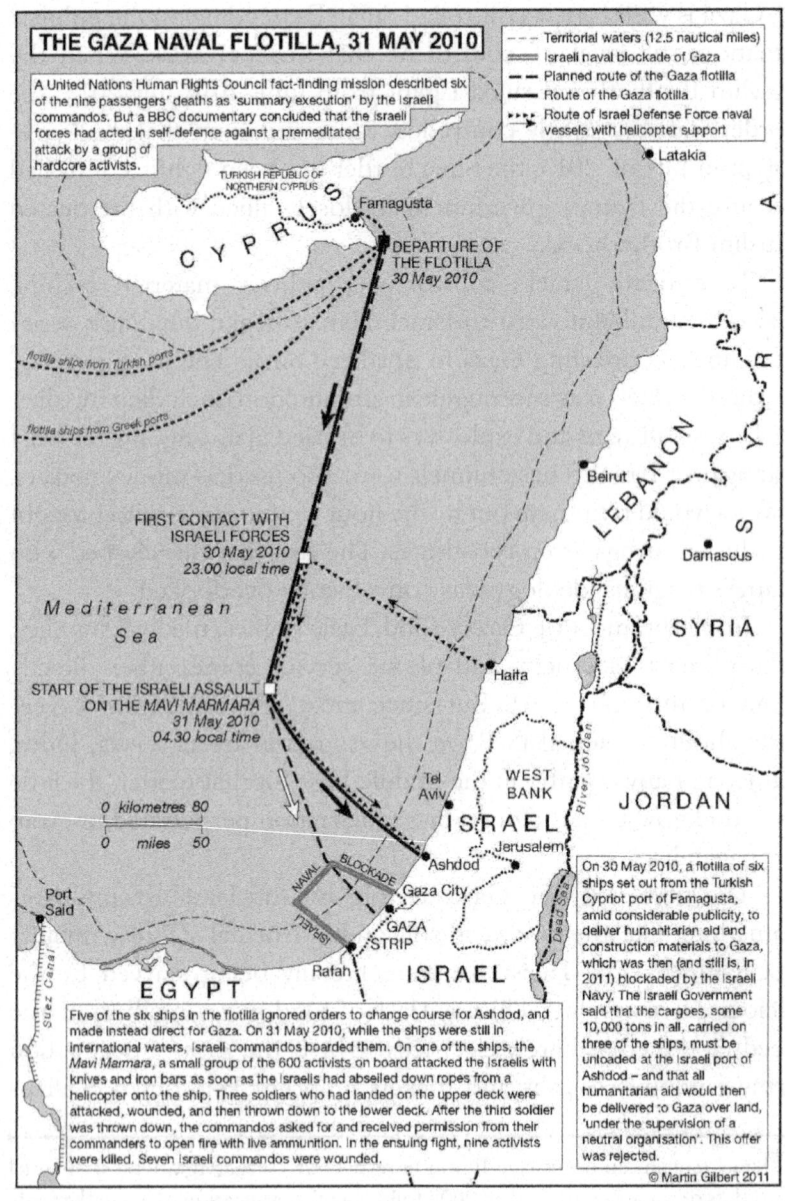

Sir Martin Gilbert, © 2010. Reproduced by permission of Taylor & Francis Books UK. www.martingilbert.com

just to let them know "who's boss". One of the ways to get the world's attention is to break the blockade of Gaza.

Hence, in May of 2010, a Free Gaza Flotilla was put together by a Turkish organization called Foundation for Human Rights and Freedoms and Humanitarian Relief (IHH) that presented itself as a humanitarian group. This flotilla of six vessels, the largest being the *Mavi Marmara*, was approached by the Israeli Navy in international waters on May 31, 2010. There they were instructed to sail to Ashdod where their cargo would be inspected and the purported humanitarian aid they carried then shipped overland to Gaza. Five of the six ships offered passive resistance but allowed members of the Israeli Navy to board their ships.

The Israeli Navy radioed Tural Mahmut, the captain of the *Mavi Marmara*, sending him this message:

> "*Mavi Marmara*, you are approaching an area of hostilities, which is under a naval blockade. The Gaza coastal area and Gaza Harbour are closed to all maritime traffic. The Israeli government supports delivery of humanitarian supplies to the civilian population in Gaza Strip and invites you to enter Ashdod port. Delivery of supplies will be in accordance with the authorities' regulations and through the formal land crossing to Gaza and under your observation, after which you can return to your home ports aboard the vessels on which you arrived." The reply was: "Negative, negative. Our destination is Gaza."[44]

The *Mavi Marmara*, carrying some 600 passengers, was not interested in a peaceful resolution. Carrying some 50 IHH activists who came looking for a confrontation[34], their mission was to create an international incident to embarrass Israel. Israeli commandos subsequently rappelled from a helicopter onto the ship. Armed with paint guns as their primary means of defense, their mission

---

military incursions and rocket attacks." (UN Special Rapporteur, "Situation of human rights in the Palestinian territories occupied since 1967" (p.2; see also pp. 8–12). 17 August 2007 (doc.nr. A/62/275))

was not to inflict casualties onboard the *Mavi Marmara*. The commandos did have firearms on them, but they were ordered not to use them unless they felt their lives were threatened. The rest became history!

The IDF, having learned from past dealings with such incidents, filmed the entire encounter. As the naval commandos rappelled onto the *Mavi Marmara* they were beaten with clubs and iron bars, one was stabbed in the stomach, and a second commando was thrown from one deck to another below. Another commando had his firearm taken from him and was shot. Subsequently, the commandos were given the green light to use deadly force to defend themselves. Within minutes nine Turkish attackers were killed and several more wounded. Shortly thereafter, the commandos took control of the ship. Upon inspection, very little was found that qualified as needed humanitarian items. Instead, they found many weapons—knives, clubs, sharpened iron bars, etc.

The *Mavi Marmara* was brought to Ashdod and all the passengers were taken off, processed by the Israeli authorities and then deported. All the humanitarian supplies brought by the six ships comprising the flotilla were eventually sent to Gaza.

Typically, the world media turned the incident yet into another Zionist massacre of innocent Muslims who were on a mission of mercy to the besieged people of Gaza. Once again Israel found itself living in a Orwellian world where she was the bad guy and Turkish radicals became peaceful protestors who were killed while on a mission of mercy. The UN immediately initiated a commission to investigate the incident. According to its *Palmer Report*:

> The commission determined Israel's naval blockade of the Gaza Strip to be legal, but stated that the "decision to board the vessels with such substantial force at a great distance from the blockade zone and with no final warning immediately prior to the boarding was excessive and unreasonable". The commission questioned the motivations of the Flotilla, stating, "There exist serious questions about the conduct, true nature and objectives of the flotilla organizers, particularly

IHH." The commission recognized that the IDF were met with "organized and violent resistance from a group of passengers" upon boarding the vessel and therefore force was necessary for purposes of self-defense, but said, "the loss of life and injuries resulting from the use of force by Israeli forces during the take-over of the Mavi Marmara was unacceptable."[45]

The greatest casualty of this incident was the Israel-Turkish relationship. Turkey for decades had been Israel's best neighbor in the region. However, since the Islamist Recep Edrogan became its prime minister in 2003, the Israel-Turkey relationship had grown cold. This incident caused a complete tear between the two countries. Edrogan demanded that the Israeli commandos who boarded the Mavi Marmara be tried as war criminals!

Israel, under international duress, set up an investigating commission to review the events of the *Mavi Marmara* incident. Chaired by retired Supreme Court Judge Jacob Turkel, who was appointed on June 14, 2010, on January 23, 2011 the commission concluded:

> The naval blockade imposed on the Gaza Strip—in view of the security circumstances and Israel's efforts to comply with its humanitarian obligations—was legal pursuant to the rules of international law. The actions carried out by Israel on May 31, 2010, to enforce the naval blockade had the regrettable consequences of the loss of human life and physical injuries. Nonetheless, and despite the limited number of uses of force for which we could not reach a conclusion, the actions taken were found to be legal pursuant to the rules of international law.[46]

Footnotes

[1] Itamar Marcus and Nan Jacques Zilberdik, "PA minister: PA agreements are modeled after Muhammad's Hudaybiyyah Peace Treaty," Palestinian Media Watch, July 22, 2013 (http://palwatch. org/site/modules/print/preview.aspx?fi=157&doc_id=9401)

[2] "Husseini's Last Interview: Oslo A Trojan Horse, *Arutz Sheva*, 10/07/01 (http://www.israelnationalnews.com/Articles/Article. aspx/317)

[3]   https://en.wikipedia.org/wiki/Israeli_disengagement_from Gaza as derived from "Jewish Settlers Receive Hundreds of Thousands in Compensation for Leaving Gaza," *Democracy Now*, 16 August 2005 (https://web.archive.org/ web/20070509035456/http://www.democracynow.org/article. pl?sid=05%2F08%2F16%2F1326221); "Demolition of Gaza Homes Completed," *Ynet news.com*, 01/01/05 (http://www. ynetnews.com/articles/0,7340,L-3136516,00.html); Paul Rivlin, *The Israeli Economy from the Foundation of the State through the 21st Century* (Cambridge: Cambridge University Press, 2010), 245.

[4] "Address by PM Ariel Sharon at the Fourth Herzliya Conference-Dec 18- 2003," Israel Ministry of Foreign Affairs (http://www. mfa.gov.il/MFA/PressRoom/2003/Pages/Address%20by%20 PM%20Ariel%20Sharon%20at%20the%20Fourth%20Herzliya. aspx)

[5] Harvey Morris, "Gaza Strip greenhouse deal breaks deadlock," Financial Times, August 13, 2005 (http://www.ft.com/cms/s/0/ ab8b7304-0b97-11da-9939-00000e2511c8.html?ft_site=falcon&d esktop=true#axzz4l1leoQqa)

[6] Dore Gold, "Israel's War to Halt Palestinian Rocket Attacks," Jerusalem Center for Public Affairs, Vol. 7:34, March 3, 2008 (http://jcpa.org/article/israel%E2%80%99s-war-to-halt-palestinian-rocket-attacks/)

[7] Mati Tuchfeld, 'Unilateral disengagement from Gaza Strip was

a mistake,' *Israel Hayom*, June 15, 2017 (http://www.israelhayom.com/site/newsletter_article.php?id=43139)

[8] Ari Fuld, "Remembering Yehoshua Friedberg, Hy"d Zt"l," *The Jewish Press*, March 8, 2017 (http://www.jewishpress.com/blogs/sword-of-israel-ari-fuld/remembering-yehoshua-friedberg-hyd-ztl/2017/03/08/)

[9] Nachshon Wachsman, Ynet news.com, March 11, 2009 (http://www.ynetnews.com/articles/0,7340,L-3684709,00.html)

[10] Ben Caspit, "Gilad Schalit's Capture: In His Own Words," *Jerusalem Post*, March 28, 2013 (http://www.jpost.com/Defense/Gilad-Schalits-capture-In-his-own-words-308015)

[11] "Operation Summer Rain: IDF enters southern Gaza Strip to secure release of abducted soldier," Israel Ministry of Foreign Affairs, 28 Jun 2006 (http://www.mfa.gov.il/mfa/pressroom/2006/pages/idf%20enters%20southern%20gaza%20strip%20to%20secure%20release%20of%20abducted%20soldier%2028-jun-2006.aspx)

[12] Eetta Prince-Gibson, "Prisoners Dilemma," *Jerualem Report*, March 25, 2009 (http://www.jpost.com/Jerusalem-Report/Prisoners-Dilemma-137099)

[13] TheLandofIsrael.com, "Gilad Shalit: Who's Blurring the Lines?," aish.com (http://www.aish.com/jw/me/Gilad_Shalit_Whos_Blurring_the_Lines.html)

[14] "The Hezbollah Program: An Open Letter, February 16, 1985," in *Israel in the Middle East: Documents and Readings on Society, Politics, and Foreign Relations, Pre-1948 to the Present (The Tauber Institute for the Study of European Jewry Series), 2nd Edition*, Itamar Rabinovich & Jehuda Reinharz, Eds. (Waltham, MA: Brandeis University Press, 2007), pp.423-429, 424-25.

[15] "Russia Says Hezbollah, Hamas Aren't Terrorist Groups," *Moscow Times*, Nov 16, 2015 (https://themoscowtimes.com/news/russia-says-hezbollah-hamas-arent-terrorist-groups-50783)

[16] Omar Nashabe, "China's Ambassador in Lebanon: Hezbollah Arms a Trade Matter," *Al-Akhbar*, 4 May 2012 (http://english.al-akhbar.com/node/6964)

[17] Efraim Inbar, "How Israel Bungled the Second Lebanon War," *The Middle East Quarterly*, Summer 2007, Vol. 14:3, 57-65 (http://www.meforum.org/1686/how-israel-bungled-the-second-lebanon-war)

[18] Max Boot, "The Second Lebanon War: It probably wont be the last," *The Weekly Standard*, September 4, 2006 (http://www.weeklystandard.com/the-second-lebanon-war/article/13751)

[19] The Knesset, "The Second Lebanese War" (https://knesset.gov.il/lexicon/eng/Lebanon_war2_eng.htm)

[20] Max Boot, "The Second Lebanon War: It probably won't be the last."

[21] Michael Totten, "Who Really Won the Second Lebanon War?" *Commentary*, January 30, 2009 (https://www.commentarymagazine.com/foreign-policy/middle-east/israel/who-really-won-the-second-lebanon-war/)

[22] The Knesset, "The Second Lebanese War" (https://knesset.gov.il/lexicon/eng/Lebanon_war2_eng.htm); "UN Security Council, Security Council Calls For End To Hostilities Between Hizbollah, Israel, Unanimously Adopting Resolution 1701 (2006)," 11 August 2006 (https://www.un.org/press/en/2006/sc8808.doc.htm)

[23] Ben Caspit, "We Will Not Capitulate," Maariv.org, July 31, 2006 http://www.nrg.co.il/online/1/ART1/457/743.html

[24] David Makovsky, "The Silent Strike," *New Yorker*, September 17, 2012 (http://www.newyorker.com/magazine/2012/09/17/the-silent-strike)

[25] *Ibid.*

[26] https://en.wikipedia.org/wiki/Hamas as derived from: *The World Almanac of Islamism: 2014*, American Foreign Policy Council (Lanham, MD: Rowman & Littlefield, 2014), 272-278; Joshua L. Gleis and Benedetta Berti, *Hezbollah and Hamas: A Comparative Study* (Balitmore: Johns Hopkins University Press, 2012), 119.

[27] Ibid. as derived from: Matthew Price, "Hamas success in Fatah heartland," BBC News, May 13, 2005; Steven Erlanger, "Hamas Routs Ruling Faction, Casting Pall on Peace Process," *New York Times*, January 27, 2006 (http://www.nytimes.com/2006/01/27/

world/middleeast/hamas-routs-ruling-faction-casting-pall-on-peace-process.html); Kristen Ess, "Why Hamas Won," ZNet, January 31, 2006 (https://zcomm.org/znetarticle/why-hamas-won-by-kristen-ess/)

[27] David E. Johnson, *Hard Fighting: Israel in Lebanon and Gaza* (Santa Monica, CA: Rand, 2011) 106

[28] *Ibid.*, 103.

[29] "Rocket Attacks Toward Israel From the Gaza Strip," IDF Blog, April 16, 2012 (https://www.idfblog.com/blog/2012/04/16/timeline-terror-2001-2012/)

[30] High Level Military Group, "An Assessment of the 2014 Conflict in Gaza," Friends of the Israel Initiative, October 2015 (http://www.jewishvirtuallibrary.org/jsource/images/hlmg2015.pdf), 19-20.

[31] https://en.wikipedia.org/wiki/Gaza_War(2008%E2% 80%9309) as derived from: Jeffrey White, "Examining the Conduct of IDF Operations in Gaza," The Washington Institute for Near East Policy, 27 March 2009 (http://www.washingtoninstitute.org/policy-analysis/view/examining-the-conduct-of-idf-operations-in-gaza); Anthony H. Cordesman, "The 'Gaza War': A Strategic Analysis" (PDF). Center for Strategic & International Studies, 3 March 2009, 7 (https://csis-prod.s3.amazonaws.com/s3fs-public/legacy_files/files/media/csis/pubs/090202_gaza_war.pdf); Barbara Opall-Rome, "Maj. Gen. Ido Nehushtan," *Defense News*, March 8, 2009

[32] United Nations Human Rights Council, *Human Rights in Palestine and Other Occupied Arab Territories: Report of the United Nations Fact Finding Mission onthe Gaza Conflict*, A/HRC/12/48, September 15, 2009. p. 152.

[33] Robert Spencer, "Hamas: We love death like our enemies love life," *Jihad Watch*, July 31, 2014 (https://www.jihadwatch.org/2014/07/hamas-we-love-death-like-our-enemies-love-life)

[34] Author's discussions with IDF officers, Tel Aviv, February 10–12, 2009,and September 2–10, 2009; author's discussions with IDF officers,Washington, D.C., February 26, 2009. The IDF posted a number of videos on its website showing attacks ontargets using

human shields; see Israel Defense Forces, "Precision Airstrikes on Hamas Terror Targets 7 Jan. 2009," web page, January 7, 2009, ff. 132-133.

[35] Yoram Cohen and Jeffrey White, *Hamas in Combat: The Military Performance of the Palestinian Islamic Resistance Movement*, Policy Focus No. 97 (Washington, DC: The Washington Institute for Near East Policy, 2009), 15.

[36] https://en.wikipedia.org/wiki/Gaza_War_(2008–0%E2% 80%9309) as derived from Sonja Pace, "Israel Opens Up Humanitarian Corridors in Gaza as Fighting Continues," VOA, July 1, 2009 (https://www.voatibetanenglish.com/a/a-28-2009-01-07-voa2-90308832/1273739.html); "Israel Declares Short 'Recess' In Gaza Fighting," *NPR*, January 7, 2009 (http://www.npr.org/templates/story/story.php?storyId=99073070)

[37] Dan Harel, "The Fire Delivery Concept in Operation 'Cast Lead,'" briefing, the Israel Fire and Combined Arms in Urban Terrain Conference, November 8–11, 2010 (as quoted in David E. Johnson, *Hard Fighting: Israel in Lebanon and Gaza* (Santa Monica, CA: Rand, 2011), 121)

[38] Yaakov Lappin, "IDF Releases Cast Lead Casualty Numbers," JPost.com, March 26, 2009 (http://www.jpost.com/Israel/IDF-releases-Cast-Lead-casualty-numbers)

[39] Anthony H. Cordesman, "The 'Gaza War': A Strategic Analysis," draft report, February 2, 2009, 3.

[40] *London Times* (August 1, 2006), as quoted in Mitchell Bard, "Myths and Facts: Chapter 24: 2008 Gaza War (Operation Cast Lead), Jewish Virtual Library (http://www.jewishvirtuallibrary.org/jsource/myths3/MFcastlead.html)

[41] Alan Dershowitz, "The Case Against the Goldstone Report: A Study in Evidentiary Bias," *Digital Access to Scholarship at Harvard* (https://dash.harvard.edu/handle/1/3593975)

[42] "Col. Richard Kemp on the IDF Performance During Cast Lead," http://www.sunlakesjewishcongregation.org/HTML/images/ColonelKemp.pdf

[43] Richard Goldstone, "Reconsidering the Goldstone Report on Israel and war crimes," *The Washington Post*, April 1, 2011

(https://www.washingtonpost.com/opinions/reconsidering-the-goldstone-report-on-israel-and-war-crimes/2011/04/01/AFg111JC_story.html?utm_term=.af2e8e91eb95)

"Gaza flotilla raid,: Wikipedia (https://en.wikipedia.org/wiki/Gaza_flotilla_raid)

"Report of the Secretary-General's Panel of Inquiry on the Flotilla Incident, 31 May 2010," September 2011 (http://www.un.org/News/dh/infocus/middle_east/Gaza_Flotilla_Panel_Report.pdf)

"Gaza Flotilla Incident: The Turkel Commission Report (January 23, 2011)," *Jewish Virtual Library* (https://www.jewishvirtuallibrary.org/jsource/Society_&_Culture/flotilla012311.html);Herb Keinon, "Palmer: Gaza Blockade Lawful, IDF Used 'Excessive' Force," *The Jerusalem Post*, September 3, 2011 (http://www.jpost.com/Diplomacy-and-Politics/Palmer-Gaza-blockade-lawful-IDF-used-excessive-force)

Chapter 20

The Arab World in Turmoil:
January 2011 - Present

THE ARAB SPRING: JANUARY 2011

In Tunisia in January of 2011, the "Arab Spring" began as a popular uprising by the people against its unpopular president, Zine El Abidine Ben Ali. It started when a fruit vendor set himself on fire as an act of protest against the repressive regime. Sadly for the Arab world, almost all of its countries have been ruled by autocrats, strongmen and monarchs since they were granted independence in the 1940s and united by a pronounced hatred of Zionism, Jews and the Jewish State, the stalking horse used to distract Islamist populations from focusing on their corrupt rulers.

But in 2011 the Arab world appeared to catch up to most of the modern world, where basic human rights and democratic principles existed on some level. It is clear that with the internet and cell phone that the flow of information was no longer something that Arab governments could totally control the way they used to. Citizens of Arab countries were able to watch and learn what was going on in the rest of the world, and what was actually going on in their own countries. Hence the riots that began in Tunisia and quickly toppled President Ben Ali soon spread to Libya (next door) which led to a civil war and the eventual downfall of Colonel Muammar Qadaffi's 42-year dictatorship. By January 2012 the fever of revolt hit the largest Arab country in the Middle East, Egypt, a country with over 80 million people, that had been run by President Hosni Mubarak since 1982.

From the very beginning of the Arab Spring two very different narratives were being given regarding where events would eventually lead the Arab world. In the United States and Western Europe, governments and most of the media were captivated by the sight of young Western-looking Arab demonstrators using Twitter and Facebook to organize demonstrations, write blogs and email pictures of what was happening. To the majority of the American and Western media the Arab world was on the cusp of a modern-day French Revolution that would usher in a wave of modern pro-Western democratic Arab governments.

The other narrative, which came mostly from Israeli Arab and a handful of conservative American Arab analysts, was more pessimistic. Both groups had a better understanding of Arab history, language and culture. In essence, they said that we cannot ignore decades of history, Arab political and religious culture and view the Middle East through the prism of Western ideals and values. They warned that while the first faces the West was seeing on TV were young, modern, tech-savvy Arab ones, they were basically but the "useful idiots" that start a revolution but are not well enough organized, nor politically powerful enough, to set up a replacement government. Once the protesters gained the Western world's attention and helped bring about the collapse of the ruling Arab autocrat, the group most likely to step in and fill the vacuum would be the Muslim Brotherhood, the most organized, disciplined and largest non-government group functioning in most Arab countries. Sadly, this is what happened in most of the Arab world.

In Tunisia the government became dominated by Islamist parties affiliated with the Muslim Brotherhood. Libya today is literally a divided country that has different factions running its different sections. Most of these factions rule by militia. Most of these groups and militias are also Islamist offshoots of the Muslim Brotherhood.

Removing Mubarak, Egypt held elections in 2012 that brought into power Mohamed Morsi, a direct representative of the Muslim Brotherhood. Morsi soon proved his mettle, as well as demonstrated the *modus vivendi* of the Moslem Brotherhood in power.

As president, Morsi issued a temporary constitutional declaration in late November that in effect granted him unlimited powers and the power to legislate without judicial oversight or review of his acts. The temporary constitutional declaration was called...a referendum, an act that his opponents called an "Islamist coup." These issues, along with complaints of prosecutions of journalists and attacks on nonviolent demonstrators, brought millions of protesters to the streets in the 2012 Egyptian protests.

On 30 June 2013, protests erupted across Egypt, which saw protesters calling for the president's resignation. In response to the events, Morsi was given a 48-hour ultimatum by the military to meet their demands and to resolve political differences, or else they would intervene by "implementing their own road map" for the country. He was unseated on 3 July by a military coup....[1]

The man who became the new president of Egypt was Abdel Fatah el-Sisi, the commander of the Egyptian Army and a foe of the Muslim Brotherhood and all radical Islamic organizations and terror groups, be they Sunni or Shi'ite. (Since 2013 the now outlawed Muslim Brotherhood has been threatening to overthrow al Sisi.)

Besides having to deal with the Muslim Brotherhood threat in Egypt proper, the Sinai Peninsula is under the control of a host of radical Islamist groups whose collective goal is to overthrow Egypt's government and to help create a worldwide Islamic Caliphate. They are well armed and organized. Presently, the Egyptian Army is trying to gain control of this area, though it looks like it will be a bitter and difficult fight. One positive note has been that Israel and Egypt have been drawn closer together in the face of the threat of these terrorist groups operating in Sinai. This seems to be the case in Gaza as well, where el-Sisi sees Hamas as a clear ally of the Muslim Brotherhood and of the many terror groups operating in Sinai.

However Sisi's rise to power created a problem not just for Egypt but Israel as well—both involving the Brotherhood's agent, Hamas. In addition to losing the support of the Brotherhood in Egypt, Hamas commited the unpardonable sin of alienating its other financial angel in the region, Iran. By endorsing the revolt against Syria's Bashar al-Assad, Iran's ally in the region, Hamas found itself in financial trouble. With support no longer in the offing, and a crackdown by el-Sisi's Egyptian regime that enforced a closure of the Rafah Crossing into Egypt thus disabling Hamas's smuggling tunnels (thereby cutting off major revenues and arms), Hamas's continued battle with Fatah now forced it into the very arms of its Palestinian opponent.

> Since 2007, the two groups have often been in a state of open conflict, interspersed by attempts at making common cause. [Thus, following the Arab Spring]...Hamas and the Palestinian Authority formed a unity government—in part a function of Hamas's increasing problems. However, President Mahmoud Abbas refused to allow Hamas the ability to participate in the Palestinian decision-making process, and he refused to pay the salaries of tens of thousands of Hamas employees in Gaza, whom he considered a threat to his own Fatah movement. As a result, Hamas's political isolation continued to be compounded by a financial squeeze putting in jeopardy its hold over its organisation and territory and posing a serious strategic challenge to the organisation.[2]

As such, Hamas had to do the only thing in its power to forestall its economic collapse and win the hearts and minds of the Arab street: It would begin a war with Israel

In the meantime, in Syria, the opponents of the repressive and dictatorial regime led by Bashir al-Assad, who inherited Syria from his father Hafez (who seized control in 1970), took to the streets to protest. At first the demonstrators where met with a brutality that was supposed to club them into submission. Instead, the outraged Syrian civilians began an open revolt against the government, which was then joined by soldiers who deserted from the Syrian Army. This led to a civil war that eventually morphed into a multilevel civil war involving many different factions who all hated the Assad regime, but did not necessarily like each other or share the same vision for a post-Assad Syria. There are close to forty different militias fighting the Syrian Army and its allies, Hezbollah and the Iranian Army. In 2015 Russia entered the fray as a Syrian ally as well. The Russians now have air and naval bases in Syria, as well as some elite commando units operating there.

Rebel forces are made up of the following types of militias:

a) The Free Syrian Army—former Syrian Army soldiers and commanders. They are hoping to establish a relatively open and democratic Syria that will respect most of the country's minorities and sects. The U.S., especially since 2017, has been the main backer of this group, supplying weapons, training, supplies and U.S. Special Forces support.

b) Jihadist Groups—There are dozens of small *jihadi* terrorist groups, Sunni Muslims fighting against the Assad regime of Alawites who are part of the Shi'ite Islamic world. The largest of these militias is an al-Qaeda offshoot called the Nusra Front, which also operates in Iraq. All these groups want to set up a Sunni Islamic Republic in Syria. Some are supported by Turkey, others by the Gulf States, and others by Saudi Arabia.

c) ISIS (The Islamic State of Iraq and Syria), the largest and best equipped anti-Assad Sunni force in Syria, is the next step in Islamic terror. As opposed to al-Qaeda, the first truly global jihadist group, ISIS, also called ISIL (the Islamic State in the Levant), has plans for more than just a state in Syria and Iraq. Its goal is not just about spreading fear and terror in the world of the infidel but in creating a 21st century version of the first Islamic State that Mohammed established in the 7th century. ISIL/ISIS and Daesh (al Dawlah al-Islameyah fi Iraq wal-Sham or literally, "Islamic State in Iraq and al-Sham") believe that they offer not merely an ideology but a complete and total "true" Islamic way of life in a "true" Islamic State. Because they have already successfully established something of an Islamic Caliphate in the Middle East, they are attracting a much larger and more broad-based following than al-Qaeda could ever dream of.

ISIS/ISIL/Daesh considers Jews, Christians, Yazidis, Kurds, Bahai, etc., as enemies of Allah and considers all Shi'ite groups and countries as apostates. ISIS/ISIL/Daesh has earned a reputation for brutality that is almost unsurpassed in the Middle East. The areas under its control are ruled in a very ruthless manner with many public executions—including beheadings, crucifixions, hangings, etc. Slavery is commonplace and women have almost no rights. They apparently have several types of followers globally: those who are prepared to join and fight with them in Syria and Iraq; those who are prepared to assist them financially, with supplies and technological support; those who are prepared to carry out attacks against the "infidels" in the countries they live in, and those who have fought with them and returned to their countries of origin with the skills and arms they acquired. This last group is reported to be numbered in the thousands in Europe and in the hundreds in the U.S. As its presently held territories are reconquered, it is investing in homegrown jihadists initiating terrorism in Europe and in the U.S.

d) Kurdish Groups—The Kurds are the true homeless people of the Middle East. They have their own language, culture and once ruled an area called Kurdistan. There are close to 30 million Kurds in the Middle East who live in Iran, Iraq, Turkey and Syria. The only country in which they have some autonomy is Iraq, and that's thanks to the U.S. liberation of Iraq from Saddam Hussein's rule. The Syrian Kurds are looking out for their own interests. They have been persecuted by the Assad regime since 1970. They live in northeast Syria and have proven to be the fiercest fighters on the ground against ISIS/ISIL/Daesh in both Syria and Iraq. The Kurds of Northeast Syria, while having some differences ideologically with the larger Kurdish entity in Iraq, are seen as being more anti-ISIS than anti-Shia. Hence, there is a kind of truce between the Syrian Kurds and the Syrian Army, since they have the same common enemy: ISIS and other Sunni jihadist groups. Israel has maintained good relations with the Iraqi Kurds since the 1970s and, by extension, has contact with the Syrian Kurds as well.

The Syrian Army's allies in the war are: Hezbollah—a Shi'ite (Shia) terrorist organization that has dominated Lebanon since the late 1980s. Though its members are Arabs because they are Shi'ite, Hezbollah has a close affinity to the Shi'ite Islamic Republic of Iran which has been its main military and political benefactor since the organization's inception. Syria has been transferring Iranian, Russian and Syrian weapons to Hezbollah since the 1980s, so it is beholden to Assad as well.

Iranian Army—The Iranian government originally sent a few teams of officers and their squads to be advisors to either the Syrian Army or to militias it set up. By the end of 2016 there were battalions of Iranian soldiers fighting in Syria, including Iranian Special Forces and high ranking field officers. Iran views the Assad regime as a key Shi'ite ally in the Middle East as it builds a Shi'ite arc that runs from Iran through Iraq, Syria and into Lebanon.

Russia—Russia has supplied both Iran and Syria with weapons before and throughout the Syrian Civil War. It is one of the reasons that President Assad has been able to cling to power. In addition, starting in 2016, Russia has deployed its air force, navy and special forces to participate in the actual fighting. As such, Russia's physical entrance into the war has been a game changer. Thanks to Russian involvement, Assad has achieved victory. He now controls most of Syria. While there are still pockets of resistance led by the Syrian Free Army, Kurds and a variety of Jihadist groups, Assad in essence has won his war.

For Israel the Arab revolutions that began in January 2011 have made the Middle East far more dangerous, unstable and volatile. To the north Israel now faces an empowered Hezbollah that is openly allied with Syria, Iran and Russia. It has accumulated close to 150,000 rockets and has gained combat experience fighting in Syria. In the northeast, Israel faces a fractured Syria that literally has been divided into many feudal areas each ruled by a different militia, terrorist group or the Syrian Army. Many times errant shells and mortars have landed in the Golan Heights, and on some occasions there have been terrorist incursions into the Israeli side of the Syrian border and at Har Dov (the part of Mount Hermon that borders Lebanon). As a result, the IAF and the IDF have had to engage in military responses in Syria and Lebanon. Furthermore, since it is completely unacceptable to Israel that either the Iranian army or Hezbollah maintain any sort of military presence in Syria—as this would clearly constitute an unacceptable threat to the homeland—the IAF continues to operate over the skies of Syria with the goal of insuring that neither Hezbollah nor Iranian forces enhance their strategic capabilities vis-à-vis Israel. That means that Israel does not allow the transfer of weapons to Hezbollah, the construction of Hezbollah or Iranian Army bases, or the construction of factories that could produce ammunition for either Hezbollah or the Iranian army.

The appearance of the Russian Air Force over the skies of Syria has clearly complicated matters for the IDF. The IDF has set up a special coordinated command with the Russian army stationed in Syria to insure that Israeli planes and Russian planes do not accidently engage. Because Russia is a global power, Israel needs to remain on decent terms with her. Furthermore, Russia understands that Israel cannot and will not allow Hezbollah to become stronger as a result of the Syrian Civil War, and so permits Israeli strikes on Hezbollah targets.

The situation is very tense and could turn into a serious confrontation very quickly. In the east, Jordan is being destabilized by close to 1 million Syrian refugees who are now in camps along the Syrian border. In addition, many *jihadi* terrorist groups in Syria have been trying to smuggle sophisticated weaponry into Judea and Samaria via Jordan. The IDF and the Jordanian Army have been working together to thwart these attempts. If such weapons should reach terrorists in Judea and Samaria, it would change the nature of the conflict with Palestinian terrorists who operate there.

Finally, in the south, Sinai over the last few years has become the new Afghanistan, with dozens of *jihadi* terrorists groups operating there with hundreds of millions of dollars' worth of rockets and missiles smuggled in from Libya when the Libyan Army disintegrated, and many more from Iran via Sudan and Egypt. Presently, Egyptian military forces have been given permission by the IDF to move into Sinai to fight the terrorists—normally not permitted because of the Israeli-Egyptian Peace Treaty.

All in all, the "Arab Spring" has really turned into an "Arab Winter" for the entire Middle East—and certainly for Israel. There is great uncertainty, and radical forces with access to advanced weaponry are multiplying.

The only positive for Israel has been that the Palestinian issue has been revealed as the red herring it has always been and not the central problem of the Middle East. For decades almost all American and Western European foreign policy makers and experts have clung to the notion that if the Israeli-Palestinian problem could be solved the Middle East would be a quiet place and there would be an end to all anti-American and anti-Western sentiments. This has been the rationale for the American and Western European obsession with one peace initiative after the next. But if one looks at the Arab uprisings since 2011 and what they have wrought, it is clear that solving the Israeli-Palestinian problem would have zero effect on the instability in Tunisia, Libya, Egypt, Mali, Somalia, Syria, Iraq and Afghanistan, and the terrorism and fighting going on in all of these countries. None of these wars are taking place because of the Palestinian issue. They are all being fought as either anti-government wars or Shi'ite vs. Sunni confrontations. The events that are taking place between Israel, Hamas and the PA have absolutely nothing to do with any of these conflicts.

THE IRANIAN THREAT

Iran is a non-Arab, Persian, Shi'ite Islamic Republic that sits 600 miles east of the State of Israel. Despite not sharing a border nor having involved itself in Israel's wars, Iran is Israel's greatest enemy and supports Hamas, Hezbollah, and the Syrian Army. Where does this hatred come from?

> In January 1963, the Shah [the monarch ruler of Iran] announced the "White Revolution", a six-point programme of reform calling for land reform, nationalization of the forests, the sale of state-owned enterprises to private interests, electoral changes to enfranchise women and allow non-Muslims to hold office, profit-sharing in industry, and a literacy campaign in the nation's schools. Some of these initiatives were regarded as dangerous, especially by the powerful and privileged Shi'a *ulama* (religious scholars), and as Westernizing trends by traditionalists...[3]

The leading *ulama* in Iran, Ayatollah Ruhollah Khomeini, opposed the secular and pro-Western programs of the Shah and openly fomented revolt, leading to his subsequent arrest and eventual exile. But in 1979, as a dying Shah left Iran for medical treatment in the United States, the Ayatollah Khomeini came back from exile in France to lead a revolution that overthrew a government rife with economic disparity and a brutal secret police (the Savak) that made dissidents painfully disappear. This Islamic revolution was a watershed event in the history of the Middle East. It literally let a genie that had been hibernating for centuries out of its bottle: Islamic hegemony. Iran became the first Islamic country in the modern period that preached spreading Islam throughout the world, and doing so by revolutionary, even violent means.

Seeing itself as the inheritor of the great Persian empires of 2,000 years ago and leading the vanguard of the Islamic revolution against the rest of the world—the non-believers—Iran's goal is to restore Islamic rule over the world. It has said since its inception

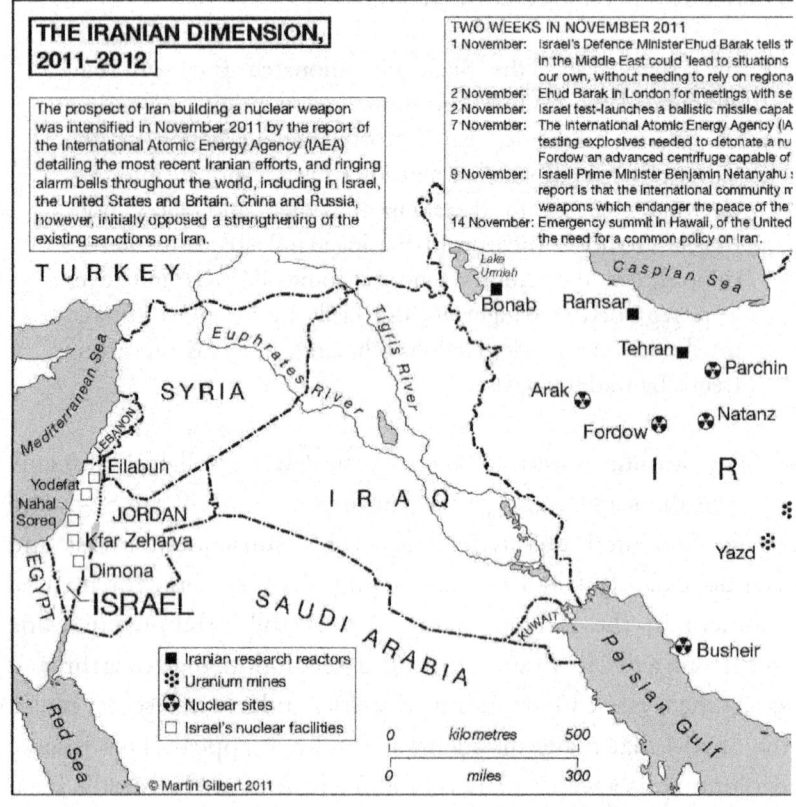

THE IRANIAN DIMENSION, 2011–2012

The prospect of Iran building a nuclear weapon was intensified in November 2011 by the report of the International Atomic Energy Agency (IAEA) detailing the most recent Iranian efforts, and ringing alarm bells throughout the world, including in Israel, the United States and Britain. China and Russia, however, initially opposed a strengthening of the existing sanctions on Iran.

TWO WEEKS IN NOVEMBER 2011

1 November: Israel's Defence Minister Ehud Barak tells th
in the Middle East could 'lead to situations
our own, without needing to rely on regiona
2 November: Ehud Barak in London for meetings with se
2 November: Israel test-launches a ballistic missile capat
7 November: The International Atomic Energy Agency (IA
testing explosives needed to detonate a nu
Fordow an advanced centrifuge capable of
9 November: Israeli Prime Minister Benjamin Netanyahu :
report is that the international community m
weapons which endanger the peace of the
14 November: Emergency summit in Hawaii, of the United
the need for a common policy on Iran.

TURKEY

Lake Urmiah

Bonab ■ Ramsar ■

Caspian Sea

Tehran ■ ☣ Parchin

Euphrates River

Tigris River

SYRIA

Arak ☣

Fordow ☣ ☣ Natanz

Mediterranean Sea

LEBANON

Yodefat □ Eilabun □

Nahal □
Soreq □

JORDAN

Kfar Zeharya □

Dimona □

I R A Q

I R

Yazd ☢

EGYPT

ISRAEL

S A U D I A R A B I A

KUWAIT

Persian Gulf

☣ Busheir

■ Iranian research reactors
☢ Uranium mines
☣ Nuclear sites
□ Israel's nuclear facilities

Red Sea

| 0 | kilometres | 500 |
| 0 | miles | 300 |

© Martin Gilbert 2011

that America is the Great Satan, Israel the small Satan, and that the Arab and Islamic countries allied with the West or unreligious were heretics and enemies of Islam and must be overthrown. While it considers Sunni Muslims to be apostates, it is willing to join forces with them in their war against the West, Christians, Jews, and the pro-Western or secular Islamic governments.

> Terrorism must be understood as an essential tool for Iran to both protect the regime and ensure the continuation of the 1979 Islamic Revolution... Iran is still a revolutionary state, built on the ideological premise of velayat-a faqih—guardianship or rule of the jurisprudent—which should be spread and adopted by other Muslim societies. Consequently, Tehran's foreign policy incorporates both hard and soft power strategies to sustain opposition to the United States, the West in general, Israel, and the rival Sunni Muslim powers, all of whom the Islamic Republic perceives as the primary political obstacles to their great national and international projects since 1979. From the early revolutionary period, the need to strike terror into the hearts of the new regime's opponents, both internal and external, was an explicit premise in the founding of the IRGC.[4]

Thus, in addition to funding, training and promoting Islamic terrorist groups, Iran has undertaken a long-term program to obtain nuclear capability. A string of Israeli governments have made it clear that Israel views the acquisition of nuclear weapons by Iran as something she cannot allow to happen. A situation wherein a sworn enemy who believes in a religious apocalypse and with a nuclear capability she would use and share with terrorist vassals is untenable. And until 2015, the U.S. sided with Israel on this issue.

After Iranian Revolutionary Guards stormed the U.S. Embassy in Tehran on November 4, 1979 and held staff hostage for 444 days, the U.S. and Iran have been on exceptionally bad terms. The U.S. froze Iranian assets in U.S. banks and imposed sanctions that severely hobbled the Iranian economy. But all this changed as in

2009 when President Obama signaled to its leadership that he was interested in reshaping the U.S. relationship with Iran as part of a larger reset that he wanted to have with the entire Islamic world. By 2012 there were secret talks going on between Secretary of State John Kerry and Iranian Foreign Minister Mohammad Javad Zarif. It was becoming clear that the deal was running counter to U.S. policy since 1979 and to the sanctions Congress had passed in 2006. Worse, it appeared that Iran was being rewarded for its quest for nuclear weapons as well as its reckless behavior in Syria, Lebanon, Iraq and Yemen. This agreement was calling for not only the end of all sanctions on Iran, but an infusion of cash into the Iranian economy and the right to inevitably build nuclear weapons, though a decade from the signing of the agreement.

This stunning about-face in U.S. foreign policy caught Israel and other Middle Eastern allies by surprise and evoked great rancor in Congress and from the Israeli prime minister. However, on July 14, 2015, the deal, called the Joint Comprehensive Plan of Action, was officially approved by the U.S. and the other four permanent members of the UN Security Council—Russia, China, Britain and France. Touted as a means of delaying Iran's nuclear capability, the deal in effect rewarded Iran for all its bad behavior with $150 billion, money then used to save its faltering economy and to finance its wars in Syria, Iraq, and Yemen, not to mention its arming of Hezbollah.

Footnotes

[1] https://en.wikipedia.org/wiki/Mohamed_Morsi as derived from Yasmine El Rashidi, "Egypt: The Rule of the Brotherhood," *New York Review of Books*, February 7, 2013 (http://www.nybooks.com/articles/2013/02/07/egypt-rule-brotherhood/);"Egypt's Mursi annuls controversial decree, opposition says not enough," *Al Arabiya*, 9 December 2012; Daniel Williams, "Muslim Brotherhood abuses continue under Egypt's military," *The Washington Post*, 15 August 2013; David D. Kirkpatrick, "President Mohamed Morsi of Egypt Said to Prepare Martial Law Decree," *The New York Times*, 26 April 2012; Stephanie McCrumen & Abigail Hauslohner, "Egyptians take anti-Morsi protests to presidential palace," *The Independent*, 5 December 2012; Asma Alsharif, "Millions flood Egypt's streets to demand Mursi quit," Reuters, 30 June 2013; Alan Taylor, "Millions March in Egyprtian Protests," *The Atlantic*, Jul 1, 2013 (https://www.theatlantic.com/photo/2013/07/millions-march-in-egyptian-protests/100543/); Salma Abdelaziz. Reza Sayah and Ben Wedeman, "Egypt's military gives Morsy ultimatum," CNN, July 2, 2013 (http://www.cnn.com/2013/07/01/world/meast/egypt-protests/index.html).

[2] High Level Military Group, "An Assessment of the 2014 Conflict in Gaza," Friends of the Israel Initiative, October 2015 (http://www.jewishvirtuallibrary.org/jsource/images/hlmg2015.pdf), 19-20.

[3] https://en.wikipedia.org/wiki/Ruhollah_Khomeinias derived from https://web.archive.org/web/20071224172550/http://www.nmhschool.org/tthornton/mehistorydatabase/arabisraeliwars.htm#white%20revolution

[4] J. Matthew McInnis, "Congressional testimony to Joint Subcommittee Hearing: Iran's Support for Terrorism Worldwide," House Foreign Affairs Committee, Subcommittee on Terrorism, Nonproliferation, and Trade, Subcommittee on the Middle East and North Africa, Mar 4, 2014 (http://docs.house.gov/meetings/

FA/FA13/20140304/101832/HHRG-113-FA13-Wstate-McInnisJ-20140304.pdf)

Chapter 21

Israel: Continued Turmoil
January 2012 - Present

⟨⟨⟨⟨⟩⟩

OPERATION PILLAR OF DEFENSE: NOVEMBER 2012

Things had been relatively quiet on the Gaza border since Operation Cast Lead, but in October of 2012 Hamas and Islamic Jihad began to ramp up rocket fire into Sderot, Ashkelon and other Israeli towns near Gaza. By early November dozens of rockets were being fired daily. As a result, Hamas military chief Ahmed Jabari was killed in a targeted air strike carried out by the Israel Defense Forces and the Shin Bet.[1] Israel further responded with a week of pinpoint aerial bombings by the IAF:

> Over the course of Operation Pillar of Defense, the IDF targeted over 1,500 terror sites including 19 senior command centers, operational control centers and Hamas' senior-rank headquarters, 30 senior operatives, damaging Hamas' command and control, hundreds of underground rocket launchers, 140 smuggling tunnels, 66 terror tunnels, dozens of Hamas operation rooms and bases, 26 weapon manufacturing and storage facilities and dozens of long-range rocket launchers and launch sites.[2]

Hamas, for its part, fired hundreds of rockets into Israel during that week, some hitting as far as Tel Aviv. The IDF anti-missile system, Iron Dome, shot down dozens of the rockets determined to have lethal effect before they reached their targets. The IDF also called up thousands of reserve soldiers and was preparing for a land invasion when, at the last minute, a ceasefire was brokered by Egypt. But the next confrontation with Hamas in Gaza was less than two years away.[3]

OPERATION MY BROTHER'S KEEPER: JUNE 2014

On June 12, 2014 three Israeli yeshiva students waiting at a bus stop/hitchhiking area near Gush Etzion—Eyal Yifrach, 16, Gilad Shaar, 16, and Naftali Fraenkel, 19—were kidnapped by two Hamas members later identified as Marwan Kawasme and Amer Abu Aysha. One of the Israeli boys managed to get a quick frantic call to Israeli 911 operators before one of the kidnappers grabbed his cell phone. The Israeli response was a massive manhunt that included close to 10,000 IDF soldiers who combed most of Judea and parts of Samaria looking for the boys. Hamas was blamed as being behind the abduction[4] and later an admission of culpability was proffered.[5] (Although this may have been after-the-fact braggadocio. The abductors were indeed Hamas members, but they had acted as a "lone cell" without leadership knowledge.[6])

The Israeli assault on the West Bank, purportedly to find the three kidnapped boys,* was named Operation My Brother's Keeper.

---

* "Only on July 1, after the boys' bodies were found, did the truth come out: The government had known almost from the beginning that the boys were dead. It maintained the fiction that it hoped to find them alive as a pretext to dismantle Hamas' West Bank operations...That evening [the evening the boys were abducted] searchers found the kidnappers' abandoned, torched Hyundai, with eight bullet holes and the boys' DNA. There was no doubt. Prime Minister Benjamin Netanyahu immediately placed a gag order on the deaths. Journalists who heard rumors were told the Shin Bet wanted the gag order to aid the search. For public consumption, the official word was that Israel was "acting on the assumption that they're alive." It was, simply put, a lie...Nor was that the only fib. It was clear from the beginning that the kidnappers weren't acting on orders from Hamas leadership in Gaza or Damascus. Hamas' Hebron branch—more a crime family than a clandestine organization—had a history of acting without the leaders' knowledge, sometimes against their interests. Yet Netanyahu repeatedly insisted Hamas was responsible for the crime and would pay for it." (J. J. Goldberg, "How Politics and Lies Triggered an Unintended War in Gaza," The Forward, July 10, 2014 (http://forward.com/opinion/israel/201764/how-politics-and-lies-triggered-an-unintended-war/))

422 terrorists were arrested during the operation, 335 of them Hamas members, 12 of them organization leaders. 56 of those arrested [had been] released during the Shalit deal and [would] go back to prison for violating the terms of their release by returning to terrorism…The IDF targeted Hamas' 'Dawa' network, a social-welfare system that fuels support for Hamas violence. The infrastructure is further used for the funneling of funds and recruitment. The IDF confiscated 1.2 M NIS in 84 operations, dealing a severe blow to Hamas' financial viability. [In addition]…2,218 homes were searched, as well as tens of caves and tunnels. During the hunt masses of weaponry were uncovered and confiscated.[7]

How Israel and the Palestinians reacted to the kidnapping was a window into the two cultures.

On the Israeli side, the entire Jewish and Druze population of Israel, as well as a minority of Israeli Arabs, became one family worried about their three boys. There were prayer vigils all over Israel, with many non-IDF personnel volunteering to help in the search. Motivation among the IDF soldiers and police looking for the three boys was exceptionally high, and thousands of Israelis from all walks of life showed up near IDF gathering points to deliver items from home to soldiers involved in the manhunt, as well as to personally thank them for what they were doing.

On the Palestinian side, both in Gaza and in PA-controlled areas, there was jubilation that three "settlers" had been kidnapped. A new three-fingered salute was initiated, symbolizing the kidnapped three Israeli teens. There were cartoons in the Palestinian press depicting the Israeli teens as rats being held on fishing lines as bait. There was total support for the "heroic" action by the Palestinian leadership, though the PA had to mute its support in English for its Western audience, while displaying its true feelings in Arabic—something learned from Yasser Arafat. The Palestinian Arab reaction in short was: Support! Pride! Heroic Action! Hoping for more of the same!

By June 30 the bodies of Yifrach, Shaar and Fraenkel were found in a field near Hevron. It was determined that they had been shot shortly after their abduction.[8]

There were three separate funerals all attended by a very large cross-section of Israelis. Many government officials and famous Israeli personalities attended as well. The tone was somber and forward looking; it was not an orgy of hate and calls for vengeance which have become the hallmark of funerals of Palestinian terrorists whose bodies are returned by Israel.

Shortly thereafter, with its operations in Judea and Samaria now degraded, Hamas, on the Gazan front, felt it needed to "respond" to appear strong and defiant, so it began to fire rockets into Israel in an effort to prove to the "Palestinian and Arab street that it represented the true "fighters" against the Israeli occupation.

OCCUPATION PROTECTIVE EDGE: JULY 2014

Following the November 12, 2012 cease fire, the next two years saw relative peace along the Gaza border. Rocket fire was reduced to its lowest levels in years.

> In the year following the ceasefire, the number of rocket and mortar attacks originating from Gaza against Israel dropped to 67 from 641 in the year prior; and there were only nine Palestinians killed in Gaza as a result of Israeli operations between December 2012 and the end of 2013, as opposed to 246 in the first eleven months of 2012 (the majority of whom were killed during Pillar of Defense).[9]

Hamas even prevented independent *jihadist* groups from launching missiles of their own.[10]

But Hamas's increased isolation in Gaza—its tunnels' efficacy (smuggling, taxation on smuggled goods, import of arms) curtailed by Egypt, Fatah refusing to sustain it economically despite their supposed "joint" government (formed in April), and its political relations with financial backers severely limited (losing the good graces of Iran and Syria by supporting Sunni opponents to the Assad regime)—following the drubbing it endured during Operation My Brother's Keeper, Hamas needed a cause to change the status quo (hoping to entice Qatar and Turkey to come to its aid financially).

Hamas achieved what it bargained for on July 8, 2014, when Israel initiated what would be called Operation Protective Edge.

> ...Hamas entered the conflict with a preexisting set of strategic objectives... [I]t sought to resolve its diplomatic and economic vulnerabilities by uniting all factions within Gaza behind its leadership, forcing its regional allies to come to its rescue and ultimately compelling Israel to accept a ceasefire that would reopen Gaza's borders... [H]amas [also] pursued a corresponding military strategy designed to compel a ceasefire in three interrelated ways: using military resources to raise the costs to Israeli civilians and military forces of continuing the conflict; deliberately provoking and exacerbating the collateral damage caused by an IDF response; and deploying a well-orchestrated information campaign of distorted facts and legal principles to create a narrative of Israeli legal culpability for civilian casualties to undermine Israel's international legitimacy. In short, Hamas found a way to redefine inevitable battlefield losses as strategic victories.[11]

Hamas began its war of "death by a thousand casualties"[12] by firing rockets into Israeli towns and cities. The targets, like always, were civilians in homes, schools, hospitals, kindergartens, shopping malls, etc. The "bigotry of low expectations" was once again on display as a compliant Western media interpreted the Hamas attacks as understandable actions: Hamas was only reacting to the onerous yoke of the Israeli occupier.

But the Israeli government could not allow Hamas to terrorize the Israeli population without a serious military response. The initial response by the IDF was pinpoint airstrikes and pinpoint fire from IDF naval boats. As in the case of Operation Cast Lead (December 2008-January 2009) and Operation Pillar of Defense (November 2012) Hamas had placed its rocket launchers deep in civilian areas, using its civilians as human shields. Facing great collateral damage if it undertook artillery shelling or mass aircraft bombardment, the IDF once again took unprecedented steps to separate the terrorists from the civilian population. Hundreds of thousands of leaflets were dropped and tens of thousands of phone calls and text messages were sent to Gazan civilians to warn them of impending IDF retaliatory strikes. Hamas responded by telling its citizens to ignore the Israeli warnings,* for as is written in the Hamas Charter:

> The day that enemies usurp part of Moslem land, Jihad becomes the individual duty of every Moslem. In face of the Jews' usurpation of Palestine, it is compulsory that the banner of Jihad be raised. To do this requires the diffusion of Islamic consciousness among the masses, both on the regional, Arab and Islamic levels. It is necessary to instill the spirit of Jihad in the heart of the nation so that they would confront the enemies and join the ranks of the fighters.[13]

Thus with every Gazan considered a combatant, it was nothing for a Hamas spokesperson to declare: "The policy of people confronting the Israeli warplanes with their bare chests... has proven effective... We in Hamas call upon our people to adopt this policy."[14]

> Offensively, Hamas employed attacks via underground tunnels, land, air and sea against Israel's military forces and civilian population centers. Most prominently, it launched its rebuilt (and improved) rocket arsenal at Israeli cities, transportation nodes and utilities. As in prior rounds of conflict, it launched large numbers of short-range Qassam and Grad rockets at

---

* "[I]n a message to Gaza residents that the messages 'are designed to weaken our resolve and to sow panic and fear among us, in light of the failures of our enemies. We call on Gaza residents not to pay attention to these messages and not to leave their homes.'" (Yosef Berger and Ari Soffer, "Seeking Human Shields, Hamas Tells Gazans to Ignore IDF Warnings," *Arutz Sheva*, 10/07/14 ((http://www.israelnationalnews.com/News/News.aspx/182741))

Israel's densely-populated southern coastline and Beersheba; furthermore, it targeted Tel Aviv and Jerusalem with medium-range rockets, as during Pillar of Defense; as well as reaching northern Israel for the first time with its longer-range rockets. Toward the end of the conflict, Hamas also used substantial mortar attacks against nearby Israeli communities. The unprecedented extent and range of Hamas's attacks, combined with their inherent inaccuracy, likely was designed to maximize the vulnerability and disruption felt by all of Israeli society. Hamas relied heavily on the well-trained artillery units of its Qassam Brigades to launch these attacks from throughout Gaza.

During the conflict, Hamas also introduced new offensive threats from special forces and unmanned aerial vehicles (UAV). The special forces, often consisting of commando teams, were to utilize assault tunnels primarily for cross-border terrorist and kidnapping raids against Israeli towns, as well as attack the vulnerable rears of IDF forces deployed around Gaza. In certain instances, these raids were conducted as seaborne operations.

In addition to supporting Hamas's preexisting tactic of taking hostages to compel Israeli political concessions, the use of tunnels and the launches of armed UAVs toward Tel Aviv was meant to compound the pressures on the Israeli government by threatening its population in startling new ways. Indeed, the profusion of assault tunnels expanded the traditional domains of Israel-Hamas warfare, to include the subterranean domain. Since Israel's 2005 withdrawal from Gaza, the two sides fought primarily on land and in the air, with Israel regularly enjoying dominance in both. Hamas's expanded use of offensive tunnels for raids, rocket and mortar attacks, and to flank IDF ground forces, created a new subterranean domain of warfare, offering the potential for new means of gaining tactical and political advantages against a materially and technologically superior foe.

Defensively, Hamas exploited Gaza's dense urban terrain to protect their forces and to maximize the military and political costs to Israel as the result of any military response. This was designed to help protect Hamas's own infrastructure, exploit Israel's aversion to casualties—its own and Gazan civilians'—trigger an international sense of urgency to pressure Israel to halt its operation prematurely and reverse the deteriorating situation inside Gaza, and undercut the legitimacy of Israeli actions.

Hamas used these asymmetric tactics in several ways. It sought to neutralize the IDF's precision-guided munitions (PGM) by covering and concealing its military leadership and forces within civilian infrastructure and underground, including tunnels. Hamas utilized parts of its expanded tunnel networks to maneuver and supply its forces while limiting the likelihood of being detected or targeted. In perhaps the most notable indication of its strategy to exploit IDF respect for the law of armed conflict (LOAC) as a force multiplier, Hamas deliberately and unlawfully placed command and control, firing positions and logistical hubs underneath, inside or in immediate proximity to structures it knew the IDF considered specially protected, to include hospitals, schools, mosques, churches and housing complexes, as well as administrative buildings formerly belonging to the Palestinian Authority, in full knowledge that this would substantially complicate IDF targeting decisions and attack options. Hamas's embedding of military capabilities amid densely populated civilian areas in Gaza was not merely an incidental consequence of the operational environment or the fog of war, but instead a deliberate and unlawful tactic utilized to exploit the presence of civilians in an effort to obtain functional immunity from attack and degrade the IDF's combat effectiveness. By locating firing positions, weapons and ammunition and command and control facilities in populated areas, Hamas provoked IDF fire on locations that increased the probability of Gazan civilian casualties. Hamas simultaneously launched rockets and attacked IDF forces from within or in direct proximity to normally protected sites—especially facilities of the United Nations Relief and Works Agency for Palestinian Refugees (UNRWA)—and from civilian buildings (sometimes forcing civilians to congregate in these areas immediately afterward), fled into these buildings after launching attacks and reportedly prevented civilians from leaving buildings after the IDF targeted them with warning communications and munitions.

By limiting Israel's willingness to counterattack by air, these tactics may have been intended to force the IDF to utilize a ground assault, while simultaneously limiting their ability to achieve a decisive victory against Hamas forces. The Qassam Brigades' infantry, artillery and armor units used mines and improvised explosive devices (IED) against tanks, anti-tank guided missiles (ATGM) against tanks and armored personnel carriers (APC), and short-range rockets and mortars against troop concentrations. In the case of rockets and mortars, Hamas fired from positions that had a high risk of causing collateral damage among their own civilian population, given the high probability of an Israeli response. In many of these engagements, Hamas fighters attempted to inflict maximum damage by attacking the vulnerable rears of IDF columns from tunnels and densely-packed civilian buildings, and by booby-trapping these buildings extensively.

The final prong of Hamas's strategy was an offensive information operations campaign. Because a conventional military or terrorist campaign was unlikely to compel Israel to meet its demands, Hamas sought to discredit Israel's actions in the eyes of the Arab and Muslim worlds, and in the international community more broadly, by portraying the IDF's use of combat power as indiscriminate and disproportional. ...Hamas undertook efforts to implicate Israel in illegal military conduct while simultaneously violating LOAC through its targeting of Israeli civilians and its exploitation of Gazan civilians to shield its military activities. By shrewdly controlling access to much of the Gaza Strip by media and international organizations, Hamas was also able to portray collateral damage resulting from its own actions as illegal IDF conduct.[15]

After many years of armed conflict, Hamas, the PA and other groups that employ terror as a means to achieve their ends have learned how to manipulate world opinion to their advantage. This included intimidating a compliant and sometimes complicit press to advance the Hamas agenda despite *prima facie* evidence that

Hamas was the egregious actor. As long as the Palestinian body count exceeded that of the Israelis it was always the Israels at fault, not the actor who set the stage for the carnage

> Deception, denial, untruthfulness, manipulation, intimidation and threat of violence against their population and media are tools readily available to these adversaries. All of these tools can be used to manipulate the information domain to influence audiences and win the contest of wills. Conversely, ...[sovereign states] must and will conduct lawful operations, and can rely only on truth as a source of information.[16]

And so Hamas accomplished its act of misinformation by forcing journalists to report just what it wanted reported, especially never showing Hamas fighters in action but only Hamas civilians who were bearing the brunt of a massive and unjujst Israeli attack. An interview with Spanish journalist evinced:

> I met today with a Spanish journalist who just came back from Gaza. We talked about the situation there. He was very friendly. I asked him how comes we never see on television channels reporting from Gaza any Hamas people, no gunmen, no rocket launcher, no policemen. We only see civilians on these reports, mostly women and children. He answered me frankly: "it's very simple, we did see Hamas people there launching rockets, they were close to our hotel, but if ever we dare pointing our camera on them [sic] they would simply shoot at us and kill us."[17]

And, as has also been noted:

> The FPA [Foreign Press Association] and its members are well aware that Israel has been and remains a paradise for the foreign media in the Middle East. They also know that, unlike many of its Arab and Islamic neighbors, Israel does not have a policy of targeting journalists. If there were such a policy, most of the foreign journalists would not be in Israel in the first place.

Their rhetorical attacks on Israel are not only a sign of hypocrisy, but should also be seen as a policy of appeasement to Arabs and Muslims—a ticket that gives you access to the Arab and Islamic countries.[18]

During the conflict that would last some fifty days, thousands of rockets were aimed at Israel. Six Israeli civilians were killed, a testament to Israeli defenses and pre-planning. Sixty-six IDF soldiers died as a result of the groundfighting.[19]

On the Palestinian side, some 2100 were killed with Hamas claiming that fifty-five percent were civilians.[20] An examination of the ages of those killed put the lie to that number, though the international press sought little impetus to accept the Israeli claims.

As far as the UN was concerned, despite Israel's continued request for assistance in stopping Hamas rocket attacks, all it could muster in its report was "Israel must break with its lamentable track record in holding wrong doers accountable," the UN Commission of Inquiry's assessment continued. "And accountability on the Palestinian side is also woefully inadequate."[21]

THE ADOPTION OF "LAWFARE"

In addition to the introduction of Vietnam War-inspired subterranean warfare, i.e., tunnels, Hamas (and the PLO) also introduced a new form of psychological warfare into their engagements with Israel.

> [T]he 2014 Gaza War...represents a successful effort by Hamas and others to leverage distorted interpretations of international law in an effort to unjustifiably constrain the militaries of nations who adhere to LOAC, and to discredit what are in fact lawful military operations. Some experts have characterized this type of distortion as "lawfare," defined as "the strategy of using—or misusing—law as a substitute for traditional military means to achieve a warfighting objective." In this case, Hamas and its supporters engaged in lawfare by substantially manipulating LOAC to allege that collateral

damage resulting from Israeli attacks against lawful military objectives was actually illegal, while concealing the fact that Hamas simultaneously encouraged that collateral damage by virtue of their deliberate and systematic LOAC violations.[22]

AN EVALUATION OF OPERATION PROTECTIVE EDGE

Following the war, a beleaguered Israel examined the results of its most recent battle with the Palestinians.

> For better or worse, there is one main person responsible for Operation Protective Edge: Prime Minister Benjamin Netanyahu. This responsibility stems from his role and status, as well as his control over setting the agenda for the government and the cabinet.
>
> In his report on Operation Protective Edge,...State Comptroller Joseph Shapira determines that "despite the fact that he was well-versed in the tunnel threat and knew that it was defined as a central and even strategic threat at the end of 2013," Netanyahu did not instruct the National Security Council and the defense establishment "to present before the cabinet the tunnel threat in a clear and detailed manner."[23]

And this disarray in the Israeli leadership and the lack of military mission was noticed by others:

> Even as the current operation began, bringing down Hamas was conspicuously not among its stated aims; instead, Netanyahu offered a vague promise to "restore calm" to southern Israel, while Defense Minister Moshe Ya'alon stated that "the aim is zero rockets." Later, Netanyahu talked of dealing "a tough blow to Hamas" to restore deterrence, while some of his ministers spoke of demilitarizing Gaza—a goal finally adopted by the prime minister three weeks into the operation. The Cabinet member Naftali Bennett, who opposes a Palestinian state, said that the goal should be to "forcefully root out Hamas' faith in its ability to win." His colleague in the Cabinet, Foreign Minister Avigdor Lieberman,

said that the operation must "end...with the IDF controlling the Gaza strip." No one mentioned the destruction of tunnels as a goal.... Since Israel's statements about its goals were both vague and shifting, it is not surprising that three weeks into the operation, Israeli media reported that "officers on the ground feel that Netanyahu and Ya'alon don't really know what their objective is."[24]

The fact that Israel bloodied Hamas and curtailed its rocket capability was the government's saving grace—one doesn't look at the costs of war when one is victorious. But in world opinion Israel had indeed lost, so much so that one writer was compelled to write:

What follows are excerpts from a June 30, 2014, news account by Tim Craig, the Washington Post's bureau chief in Pakistan:

"Pakistan's military launched a major ground offensive in the northwestern part of the country Monday, beginning what army commanders say will be a 'house-to-house search' for terrorist leaders and other militants.

"The offensive began after two weeks of airstrikes in North Waziristan. . . .

"In a statement, Pakistan's military said its soldiers discovered 'underground tunnels' and 'preparation factories' for explosives during the initial hours of the ground assault.

..."Backed by artillery and tanks, troops killed 17 terrorists Monday, the army said. Combined with the toll from airstrikes that began June 16, a total of 376 terrorists have died in the offensive, the army said. . . .

"More than a half-million residents fled North Waziristan ahead of the ground offensive. The mass evacuation of the area, which has a population of about 600,000, was intended to limit civilian casualties during the operation. The military also set up checkpoints in the area to trap militants."

***

Underground tunnels, explosives factories, weeks of airstrikes, artillery bombardment, mass displacement of civilians—leaving aside the probability that this is the first that you've heard of any of this, does it ring a familiar bell? If so, maybe the Council on American-Islamic Relations and the various self-described antiwar groups that marched near the White House on Saturday to protest Israel's military campaign in Gaza can organize another big rally outside the Pakistani embassy. No more U.S. aid to Islamabad! Boycott Pakistani products! Divest from Pakistani companies!

I'm dreaming. Over the weekend there was saturation coverage of an Israeli strike near a U.N.-run school that killed 10 people, three of them members of Islamic Jihad. U.N. Secretary-General Ban Ki-moon called the hit "a moral outrage and a criminal act" that had to be "swiftly investigated." The State Department pronounced itself "appalled." If the Secretary-General, the Secretary of State and other arbiters of international decency have expressed themselves similarly with respect to the conduct of Pakistan's army...I must have missed it. More than 1,500 Pakistani civilians have been reported killed since the government's offensive began in mid June.

Here's what else one might have missed in the midst of the media's saturation coverage of Gaza.

In Iraq, some 1,600 people were killed in the month of July. "I am concerned about the rising number of casualties in Iraq, particularly among the civilian population," U.N. envoy Nickolay Mladenov told the AFP. "Children and women are most vulnerable."

Note the verb. Not outraged or appalled, merely concerned.

In Syria, more than 1,800 people have been killed in just the last 10 days. On Monday, the London-based Syrian Network for Human Rights reported the deaths of "at least 130 people, including seven children and 10 women," at the hands of forces loyal to Bashar Assad.

As for the State Department, its only Syria-related press release from Monday was an announcement that it was funding a project to "document the current condition of cultural heritage sites in Syria and assess the future restoration, preservation, and protection needs for those sites."

In Libya, roughly 200 people were killed last month in artillery and rocket clashes between rival militias. Another 22 were killed over the weekend as Islamist groups attacked Tripoli's airport.

A joint statement by the governments of France, Italy, Germany, the U.K. and the U.S. noted only that "we strongly condemn the ongoing violence across the country...which jeopardizes the continuation of a peaceful transition and severely affects the life of the Libyan people."

In Nigeria, Boko Haram has turned its fury on Muslims who try to fight back against the jihadist group. Nearly 3,000 people have been killed so far this year, and another 500,000 have been made refugees. A spokesperson for the U.N.'s Mr. Ban issued a statement in his name, condemning Boko's attacks.

***

Since the war in Gaza began nearly a month ago, I have been bombarded with indignant letters and tweets calling me a "racist" for my views and asking whether I would like to live in Gaza.

My answer to the second point is that I would no more want to live under Hamas than I would under any other fanatical dictatorship that starts gratuitous wars, uses civilians as human shields, punishes political opposition with death, and sends others to die while its leaders hide beneath hospital sheets.

As for racism, people often point out how peculiar it is that the Jewish state seems to arouse a level of condemnation that seems to apply equally elsewhere. But perhaps the real racism is the indifference to Muslim suffering around the world when the person dropping the bomb or pulling the trigger is another Muslim. A world that makes a fetish of the alleged guilt of Israel is also a world that holds too much Muslim life cheap.[25]

Footnotes

[1] Amos Harel, Avi Issacharoff, Gili Cohen, Allison Kaplan Sommer and News Agencies, "Israel Launches Operation Pillar of Defense; Hamas Military Chief Ahmed Jabari Killed by Israeli Strike," *Haaretz*, Nov 14, 2012 (http://www.haaretz.com/israel-news/hamas-military-chief-ahmed-jabari-killed-by-israeli-strike. premium-1.477819)

[2] Consulate General of Israel in New York, "Summary of Operation Pillar of Defense," 11.21.2012 (http://embassies.gov. il/new-york/NewsAndEvents/Pages/Summary-of-Operation-Pillar-of-Defense.aspx)

[3] Israel Defense Forces, "2012 Operation Pillar of Defense," (https://www.Idfblog.Com/about-the-idf/history-of-the-idf/2012-operation-pillar-of-defense/)

[4] Ralph Ellis and Michael Schwartz, "Mom speaks out on 3 abducted teens as Israeli PM blames Hamas," *CNN*, June 15, 2014 (http://www.cnn.com/2014/06/15/world/meast/west-bank-jewish-teens-missing/index.html)

[5] "Hamas Admits To Kidnapping And Killing Israeli Teens," AP, August 22, 2014 (http://www.npr.org/2014/08/22/342318367/hamas-finally-admits-to-kidnapping-and-killing-israeli-teens)

[6] Katie Zavadski, "It Turns Out Hamas May Not Have Kidnapped and Killed the 3 Israeli Teens After All," *New York*, July 24, 2014 (http://nymag.com/daily/intelligencer/2014/07/hamas-didnt-kidnap-the-israeli-teens-after-all.html); "BBC journalist Jon Donnison quoted an Israeli police spokesperson as saying that the abduction was the act of a lone cell, operating independently of Hamas's central directions. He added that 'Israeli police spokes[person] Mickey Rosenfeld also said if kidnapping had been ordered by Hamas leadership, they'd have known about it in advance.' A similar report on Buzzfeed quoted an anonymous

Israeli intelligence official as confirming that Hamas did not carry out the abduction, adding that 'he felt the kidnapping had been used by politicians trying to promote their own agenda.' Rosenfeld later denied the statements attributed to him, but BBC's Donnison held firm to his version. The former head of Israel's internal security service (Shabak or Shin Bet), Yuval Diskin, added his own estimation that Hamas was not behind the abduction: see Julia Amalia Heyer, "Ex-Israeli Security Chief Diskin: 'All the Conditions Are There for an Explosion,'" *Der Spiegel International*, July 24, 2014; Israeli journalist and Hamas expert Shlomi Eldar had earlier surmised that the abduction was the work of the Hebron-based Qawasmeh family, which is affiliated with Hamas but operates independently: see "Accused Kidnappers Are Rogue Hamas Branch," *Al-Monitor*, June 29, 2014. Recently even *Israel Hayom* (the daily newspaper closely associated with Netanyahu) reported that Hamas did not know about the abduction: see Yoav Limor, "Interim Report," August 1, 2014 (http://www.nybooks.com/articles/2014/09/25/failure-gaza/)

[7] Aryeh Savir, "Operation Brothers Keeper Completed," *Breaking Israel News*, July 2, 2014 (https://www.breakingisraelnewscom/17503/operation-brothers-keeper-completed/#h3YFTDj1FjZQCqMa.99)

[8] The Times of Israel Staff, "Bodies of three kidnapped teens found; Netanyahu calls families," *The Times of Israel*, June 30, 2014 (http://www.timesofisrael.com/bodies-of-three-kidnapped-teens-found/)

[9] Zack Gold and Benedetta Berti, "Why is the Israel-Hamas Ceasefire Eroding?" Carnegie Endowment for International Peace, January 28, 2014 (http://carnegieendowment.org/sada/?fa=54341)

[10] Avi Issacharoff and Times of Israel Staff, "Hamas fires rockets for first time since 2012, Israeli officials say," *The Times of Israel*, June 30, 2014 (http://www.timesofisrael.com/hamas-fired-rockets-for-first-time-since-2012-israeli-officials-say/)

[11] "2014 Gaza War Assessment: The New Face of Conflict," A report by the JINSA-commissioned Gaza Conflict Task Force,

March 2015, 8-9 (http://www.jinsa.org/gaza-assessment)

[12] *Ibid.*

[13] "The Covenant of the Islamic Resistance Movement," 18 August 1988 (http://avalon.law.yale.edu/20th_century/hamas.asp)

[14] "Hamas Spokesman Encourages Gazans to Serve as Human Shields: It's Been Proven Effective," Al-Aqsa TV/translated by the Middle East Media Research Institute (July 8, 2014) (http://www.memritv.org/clip/ en/4340.htm)

[15] "2014 Gaza War Assessment: The New Face of Conflict," A report by the JINSA-commissioned Gaza Conflict Task Force, March 2015, 19-21 (http://www.jinsa.org/gaza-assessment)

[16] *Ibid.*, 53

[17] Michael Grynszpan, Facebook, July 30, 2014 (https://www.facebook.com/michael.grynszpan/posts/10152140390486065)

[18] Bassam Tawil, "The Foreign Press Association's Unlimited Bias," Gatestone Institute, August 4, 2017 (https://www.gatestoneinstitute.org/10768/foreign-press-association#continued)

[19] "Operation Protective Edge: July-August 2014," ADL (https://www.adl.org/education/resources/glossary-terms/operation-protective-edge-july-august-2014)

[20] Lenny Ben-David, "Gazan Casualties: How Many and Who They Were," Jerusalem Center for Public Affairs (http://jcpa.org/casualties-gaza-war/)

[21] "UN report cites possible war crimes by both Israel and Palestinian groups in 2014 Gaza conflict," UN News Centre (http://www.un.org/apps/news/story.asp?NewsID=51215#.WYCOAceGO1s)

[22] "2014 Gaza War Assessment"

[23] Yossi Melman, "Analysis: The Gaza Conflict Report and the Paradox of Israel's Wars," *The Jerusalem Post*, February 28, 2017 (http://www.jpost.com/Israel-News/Analysis-The-Comptroller-report-and-the-paradox-of-Israels-wars-482817)

[24] Assaf Sharon, "Failure in Gaza," *The New York Review of Books*, September 25, 2014 (http://www.nybooks.com/articles/2014/09/25/failure-gaza/)

[25] Bret Stephens, "Palestine and Double Standards: The world is outraged by Israeli self-defense but only 'concerned' when Muslims kill Muslims," *The Wall Street Journal*, Aug. 4, 2014 (https://www.wsj.com/articles/bret-stephens-palestine-and-double-standards-1407194971)

Chapter 22

The War Against Israel
in the 21st Century

Earlier we examined the reasons the Islamic and Arab worlds have very serious religious issues with Jewish nationalism and the re-establishment of Jewish sovereignty. These are all connected to Islamic theology and teachings, be they Sunni or Shia. To a lesser extent both these worlds also have a political and geographical problem with Zionism and Israel. This is connected to the dream of reestablishing a large Arab empire and an even larger Islamic Caliphate. What is clear is that these factors fuel the hundred-year war that most of the Arab and Islamic world have been waging against Zionism and Israel since the days of Haj Amin El Husseini, the Grand Mufti of Jerusalem. With the exception of the Egyptian and Jordanian peace treaties—treaties with governments and not between peoples—the overwhelming majority of the world's Arab and Islamic states are interested in seeing Israel disappear. (Even the public and intellectual cultures of both Egypt and Jordan are very antisemitic, anti-Zionist and anti-Israel.)

For one century the Arab and Islamic worlds have used every available tool they have to first bring about the abortion of a Jewish State, and after its victory in the 1948-1949 Israeli War of Independence, to bring about its destruction. Israel was supposed to be eradicated in October 1956, June 1967 and October 1973. But these wars did not go the way the Arab world had planned. So while all-out wars were one strategy to be used there was also the option of emplying terrorist acts. Terror has the option of being cheaper, aimed at civilians, can be constant and thus slowly chipping away at the sense of normalcy and safety in Israeli society. Finally, it affords the state sponsors behind them total deniability. The terrorists do not wear uniforms, show insignia and are what today are called "non-state actors". Again, the Mufti was already using terror against the Jews of Mandate Palestine in the 1920s and continued to use it as a weapon of choice before and during the Israeli War of Independence in 1948-49. This early form of terror set the stage for the terror that now seems to have washed over a large part of the globe—but mostly in the Arab and Islamic Middle East. The tactics were: car bombings, market and movie theater bombings, drive-by shootings, the bombing of buses and civilian buildings, and destroying property—farms, trees, public and private. The only aspects of modern terror the Mufti did not introduce was suicide bombers and aerial terror.

The theory behind the terror of the 1920-1949 period is the same as that which is behind Hamas, Islamic Jihad, Al Aqsa Martyr Brigades, etc.: Since the Jews are not a nation and they really come from somewhere else, e.g., Europe, if we, the Arab and Muslims, use terror against them the Jews will flee "Palestine" and return to their lands of origin. Thus, the Mufti's heirs, Yasser Arafat, Marwan Barghouti (Al Quds Martyr Brigades), Sheikh Yassin (Hamas), Kahled Mashal (Hamas), Ismail Haniyah (Hamas) and Mohammed Dief (Hamas) to mention a few, have all employed terror against Israelis/Jews in and out of the State of Israel.

In the 1950s there were the *fedayeen* who operated from Gaza, Judea, Samaria and Syria. They had the full support of Egypt, Jordan and Syria and managed to kill hundreds of Israeli civilians, but ultimately failed in their goal to chase the Jews out of their ancestral homeland. In the 1960s through the early 1980s there was the PLO that operated mostly out of Jordan and South Lebanon that was supported financially by most of the Gulf States and Saudi Arabia. The PLO added the dimension of hijacking airlines and holding Israeli and Jewish passengers hostage, as well as using heavily armed terrorists to infiltrate Israel and kill many civilians in schools, buses and residences. Finally, the PLO introduced the idea of creating a terrorist army that has tanks, artillery and rockets to fire into Israeli cities. Yet again Israel found solutions to all of these forms of terror and continued to grow its population economically, socially, educationally, culturally, etc.

By the 1990s, after the Oslo Accords were signed, the terror war against Israel, Zionism and Jews entered a new phase. Hamas, the PA-affiliated terror groups and Hezbollah added the suicide bomber and perfected the car and truck bomber. Perhaps their biggest "innovation" during this period was the introduction of the terrorist army that embeds itself in a civilian population and uses these people as shields while they focus on killing Israeli civilians. These terrorist armies also now had at their disposal short and long range missiles. This allowed them to terrorize parts, if not all, of Israel without having to penetrate her borders. Again, Israel found a myriad of new ways to defend her sovereignty and her civilians.

Arab and Islamic terror against Israel will sadly not end soon. But the leaders behind these terrorist armies know that they have not yet achieved their goals. If anything, some of them have realized that Israel has no intention of disappearing, so war and terror have not proved successful as tolls for the elimination of the Israeli state. Though these options are still being explored by Hamas, Hezbollah, *Jihadist* groups, Iran etc., they have all also been pursuing other methods to bring Israel to her knees. Their third option has been the economic boycott.

Since the first days of the Zionist effort to rebuild a Jewish state, Arab animosity has fostered economic boycotts to hinder Jewish existence in Palestine. Beginning in the 1890s,[1] assorted Arab groups have mandated the boycott of Jewish products as a means of curtailing Jewish immigration and expansion. Though none were very effective, their continued use persisted in a relative disorganized manner until the establishment of the Arab League in 1944.

The Arab boycott was formally declared by the newly formed Arab League Council on December 2, 1945: "Jewish products and manufactured goods shall be considered undesirable to the Arab countries." All Arab "institutions, organizations, merchants, commission agents and individuals" were called upon "to refuse to deal in, distribute, or consume Zionist products or manufactured goods."

As is evident in this declaration, the terms "Jewish" and "Zionist" were used synonymously by the Arabs. Thus, even before the establishment of Israel, the Arab states had declared an economic boycott against the Jews of Palestine.

The boycott, as it evolved after 1948, is divided into three components. The primary boycott prohibits direct trade between Israel and the Arab nations. The secondary boycott is directed at companies that do business with Israel. The tertiary boycott involves the blacklisting of firms that trade with other companies that do business with Israel.[2]

This economic boycott was a more sophisticated version of what the Grand Mufti practiced during the 1930s when he organized a full boycott against the Jewish segments of Mandate Palestine. The goal in the 1930s and the goal of the Arab League in the post-1945 period well into the present are all rooted in the same ideology: The Jews are not a nation and thus have no right to sovereignty. Hence, every strategy that can be used to bring about the destruction of the Jewish State must be employed.

But just like the first four major wars against Israel failed (1948-1949, 1956, 1967 and 1973), so too did the Arab League boycott. The Jewish State worked tirelessly to produce as many items and products that she could for her own economy, as well as offer products for export that would interest buyers in foreign markets. Furthermore, there were companies so large, like Coca Cola, that were not afraid of the boycott, and there were a few democratic countries, like the U.S., that made it illegal for any company to comply with this targeted attempt to damage the Israeli economy. Though Israel felt ramifications throughout the years and was hampered by it, her economy continued to grow as did her list of exports.

The Arab League boycott really began to crack after Jordan signed a peace treaty with Israel in 1994 and began to openly trade with Israel, as did several of the Arab States in the Gulf. (The Egyptian Peace Treaty with Israel signed in 1979 did not have the same positive effect because Egypt found itself thrown out of the League for signing its treaty.) As a result, the formal boycott became primarily one in name only.

> One official commented to the Egyptian newspaper Al-Ahram that, "boycotting Israel is something that we talk about and include in our official documents but it is not something that we actually carry out—at least not in most Arab states."... One reason for the bureau's [Arab Bureau for the Boycott of Israel] impotence is the lack of political will on the part of most Arab states for a boycott of Israel. "Syria, Lebanon, Libya and Iraq are the only countries that are in favour. The remainder of the Arab League's 22 members are actually opposed to the idea. They see it as a non-starter..." Moreover, boycotting Israel is something the US disapproves of utterly, the source said. Upsetting Washington is something that almost every Arab state wants to avoid.[3]

Never at a loss for ingenuity, another avenue was opened in the Arab attempt to destroy Israel. It is cloaked in the language of progressivism, the guardians of human rights, and in the language of people fighting for freedom and an end to oppression. It is called the Boycott Divestment Sanctions (BDS) movement and is essentially the old wine of antisemitism and anti-Zionism distilled and poured into a new bottle.

> The BDS movement was informally initiated in late August 2001 at the United Nations World Conference Against Racism in Durban, South Africa. An array of anti-Israel groups campaigned for language equating Zionism with racism and opposed the inclusion of language that would define anti-Semitism as a form of racism. Israel, these advocates said, was an "apartheid state" and its defensive security barrier an

"apartheid wall." They posited that BDS could impact this protracted conflict in the same way as it had been effective with the South African regime.

The final document from Durban accused Israel of genocide and apartheid. This was the opening salvo of what has become known as the "BDS movement," an effort born, in effect, in the shadow of anti-Semitism, and unable to this day to shed intolerance of Jews, Judaism, and the Jewish state from its core values. The Durban Conference's final declaration described Israel as a state that was guilty of "racist crimes including war crimes, acts of genocide and ethnic cleansing." The "Durban Strategy" promoted "a policy of complete and total isolation of Israel, the imposition of mandatory and comprehensive sanctions and embargoes, the full cessation of all links (diplomatic, economic, social, aid, military cooperation and training) between all states and Israel." While it is clearly not true that all proponents of BDS are anti-Semitic, the record of the Durban conference, and the campaign for BDS that has unfolded, have been mired by anti-Semitic tropes and in many instances by outright anti-Semitism.[4]

The Arab and Islamic war against Jewish nationalism and statehood have been relentless. All options were used: war, terror, economic boycott and, the newest avenue, delegitimization. The BDS movement employs the latter two. The old Arab League boycott of Israel was never disguised as anything moral or ethical. It was based on pure and simple unabashed hatred of Jewish nationalism/Zionism and the Jewish State. The BDS movement continues that approach by appealing to revisionist history and reverse-engineered casuistry.

According to the proponents of the BDS movement, Zionism is a colonialist, imperialist movement. It is steeped in the worst ideals and values of the "old, unenlightened" Western world that exploited and dominated Third World countries because they believed they were superior to them (i.e., dutifully fulfilling the "white man's burden"). Today, imperialism and colonialism have been defeated except in one place, "occupied Palestine, i.e. the State of Israel, not just Judea, Samaria and Gaza. Worse than merely being colonialists, the Zionists practice apartheid. As was mentioned earlier, Israeli's detractors use the security barrier/fence Israel was forced to put up after the Palestinian suicide bombing war of 1995-2003 against Israeli civilians as "proof" that Israel practices apartheid. Added to this are accusations that Israel is committing war crimes against the Palestinian people. Very selectively the leaders of BDS will focus their attention on Israeli military operations against suicide bombings, drive-by shootings, stabbings and missile and rocket attacks while all Palestinian terror is either ignored or reported as "resistance" to the "occupation". Equally appalling is BDS's acceptance of antisemitic, anti-Israel rhetoric emanating from Hamas and the PA and incitement of violence against Jews and Israelis. And when the violent acts of terror occur, the leaders and supporters of BDS explain that Israel's existence is itself an injustice, since it sits in place of "Palestine". Thus, all acts of terror are acts of resistance and justified. The Israeli right of self-defense is studiously without merit.

What makes the BDS movement different from past anti-Israel/anti-Zionist movements is that it has presented itself as a "liberal" and "progressive" grassroots movement. It proclaims that it fights injustice, occupation, apartheid, and that this is what the fight against Israel and Zionism are all about. George Orwell pointed out in *1984* how totalitarian regimes corrupted language by turning words upside down. He made the exaggerated point by describing how in these regimes they declared *slavery* to be *freedom* and *war* to be *peace*. This is how BDS is able to describe itself as a progressive movement fighting for justice! Not surprisingly, the BDS movement has not a word to say about the gross injustices that Palestinians suffer under both the PA and Hamas.[5] Thus BDS is not a moral or ethical movement. It is a political movement whose goal is to bring about the demise of the one Jewish State in the world and that this state should be replaced by a Palestinian Arab state. This has been the goal of the Arab and Islamic world since 1948.

Omar Barghouti, one of the main founders of the BDS movement and an outspoken proponent, was born in Qatar in 1964, grew up in Egypt, spent 11 years in the U.S. (1982-1993), married an Israeli Arab women in 1993 and moved to Ramallah, and then enrolled in Tel Aviv University where he earned a Masters degree in philosophy and is purportedly a doctoral candidate. His residency is in Acre, Israel. Quite an interesting background for a man who is selling the idea of Israel as one of the world's worst violators of human rights and a horrific country. He himself has made it very clear in his speeches that he is against the existence of a Jewish State, and that Israel must be replaced by a Palestinian one. Furthermore, Barghouti is not interested in "boycotting" Israeli products so Israel can be taught a lesson. Rather his goal is to have Israel blacklisted by the world's countries and peoples until it becomes a pariah state that collapses under the weight of a full-blown international condemnation. ("Barghouti may claim that the boycott movement is a 'rights' movement, but it is not. It is an effort to vilify and deny the rights of Israeli Jews. Its real agenda is to destroy Israel's image through misinformation and to enlist support for a Palestinian state without Israel."[6])

In its own words...

> Boycott, Divestment, Sanctions (BDS) is a Palestinian-led movement for freedom, justice and equality. BDS upholds the simple principle that Palestinians are entitled to the same rights as the rest of humanity to pressure Israel to comply with international law.
>
> Israel is occupying and colonising Palestinian land, discriminating against Palestinian citizens of Israel and denying Palestinian refugees the right to return to their homes. Inspired by the South African anti-apartheid movement, the BDS call urges action to pressure Israel to comply with international law.
>
> BDS is now a vibrant global movement made up of unions, academic associations, churches and grassroots movements across the world. Eleven years since its launch, BDS is having

a major impact and is effectively challenging international support for Israeli apartheid and settler-colonialism.[7]

If one did not know the history of Zionism, Israel, the Arab world and "Palestinian Arabs," then the above description does sound like a civil rights movement for some oppressed people who have been, and continue to be, colonized and discriminated against, e.g., the Tibetans by the Chinese. Even worse, Palestinians are subjected to South African apartheid. But this entire presentation is a distortion of history and reality. The Palestinians have squandered the opportunity to have a state several times in the last 100 years. The Naqba of 1948 and 1949 is a self-inflicted wound.* The treatment of Palestinian Arabs in the Arab world since 1949 has been despicable. Gaza, Judea and Samaria were occupied by Egypt and Jordan respectively between 1949-1967. As of 2017 there is a Palestinian Arab state in Gaza run by Hamas and the overwhelming majority of Palestinian Arabs in Judea and Samaria live under the control of the Palestinian Authority. Israeli Arabs or as many young Israeli Arabs now like to describe themselves, "Palestinian Arabs," living in Israel have more rights than any Arab has in any other Arab state and certainly far more than their relatives have in Hamas-controlled Gaza or in PA-controlled Judea and Samaria.[8]

The BDS Movement also ignores the economic reality of Palestinian Arabs who live in Gaza, Judea and Samaria. Gaza receives its electricity, cell phone usage, fuel, and most of its non-military supplies from Israel. The Gazan economy depends heavily on Israel for its consumer goods. In the PA-controlled sections

---

* With the opening of the archives of the founders of Israel there has arisen expostulation by "new historians" (such as Ilan Pappe) that the Naqba was a concerted Israeli plan for Arab ethnic cleansing, not a so-called "self-inflicted wound." This has been disputed as self-serving cherry-picking of specific content by other historians (such as Benny Morris) who while admitting there were some events to support such claims ("...[i]n retrospect, it is clear that what occurred in 1948 in Palestine was a variety of ethnic cleansing of Arab areas by Jews. It is impossible to say how many of the 700,000 or so Palestinians (cont'd)

of Judea and Samaria, the economic wellbeing of the Palestinian Arabs is even more tied up to the economy of Israel. Every day some 135,000 Palestinian Arabs work in pre-1967 Israel or in Israeli towns in Judea and Samaria. These workers run the gamut of blue collar workers through professionals, businessmen, contractors, managers, etc. Their incomes, as well as the money their businesses generate, are a very big part of the Palestinian economy. The better the Israeli economy, the better the Palestinian economy, and vice versa. By trying to get businesses, mutual funds, pension funds, countries, universities, etc., to stop doing business with Israel, the BDS movement is hurting Palestinians.

> Unfortunately, almost all of those so ostensibly dedicated to finding a solution have their own agendas, and these may not be to the advantage of either Palestinians or Israelis. A prime case in point is the boycott, divestment, and sanctions (BDS) movement. As a Palestinian dedicated to working for peace and reconciliation between my people and our Israeli neighbors, I do not believe that the BDS advocates are helping our cause. On the contrary, they are just creating more hatred, enmity, and polarization...."
>
> "There is no connection between the tactics and objectives of the BDS movement and the on-the-ground realities of the Middle East. Israelis continue to come to the West Bank to do business, and most Palestinians continue to buy Israeli goods. Indeed, if you ask Palestinians what they want, they'll tell you they want jobs, secure education, and health. And the people who are failing them in this regard are their own leaders: Fatah in the West Bank, and Hamas in Gaza. The focus of PA leaders is on enriching themselves and their families, rather than serving the interests of the Palestinians. They are not a generation of leaders who are able to bring about a viable end to the conflict. Indeed, they are not even interested in uplifting their own people...."

who became refugees in 1948 were physically expelled, as distinct from simply fleeing a combat zone" (Benny Morris, *1948: A History of the First Arab-Israeli War* (New Haven: Yale University Press, 2008). Thus, by and large, a claim for an organized program of ethnic cleansing is deemed *argumentum ad hominem*.

"BDS spokespeople justify calling for boycotts that will result in increased economic hardships for the Palestinians by asserting that Palestinians are willing to suffer such deprivations in order to achieve their freedom. It goes without saying that they themselves live in comfortable circumstances elsewhere in the world and will not suffer any such hardship. It would seem, in fact, that the BDS movement in its determination to oppose Israel is prepared to fight to the last drop of Palestinian blood. As a Palestinian who actually lives in east Jerusalem and hopes to build a better life for his family and his community, this is the kind of "pro-Palestinian activism" we could well do without. For our own sake, we need to reconcile with our Israeli neighbors, not reject and revile them."[9]

Pliant to the revisionist historical claims of Palestinian propagandists, the BDS movement is embraced by those on the far Left of the political and ideological spectrum. Though it lays claim to success upon success, especially on worldwide college campuses through its affiliate Palestinian Campaign for the Academic and Cultural Boycott of Israel (PACBI), mainstream political culture sees the movement for what it is: An intolerant and duplicitous endeavor whose goal is to see the Jewish State destroyed. That is why many resolutions to accept BDS have not only been rejected and defeated by many institutions, but anti-BDS legislation has been passed worldwide.

WHY DOES THE LEFT HATE JEWISH NATIONALISM AND THE JEWISH STATE?

We must go back to the aftermath of World War II to understand the intellectual underpinning of the Left's post-World War II world view. Europe and the rest of the planet had never seen the type of devastation that World War II had inflicted. The total casualty toll, including all areas of combat—both civilian and military—is estimated at between 70-85 million. Add to that 50 million refugees. Entire swaths of Europe and Asia were flattened.

As a result, the European intelligentsia began to do a great deal of soul searching. They wanted to get to the bottom of what caused Europe, in particular, and the world at large to reach such a low point that fascist regimes could gain control of otherwise sensible and cultured countries, that such societies would permit a Holocaust to occur, that the very foundations of their societies (art, books, etc.) would be irrevocably destroyed or purloined.

After careful analysis of the events that led up to World War II and the war itself, the answer they came up with was that ultra-nationalism and militarism were the two culprits that changed the trajectory of history and led to the carnage of WW II. Both Nazi Germany and Imperial Japan adopted a brand of nationalism that essentially preached that each one of their respective nations were superior to their neighbors and thus warranted their domination.

What thus emerged was a political philosophy/ideology that sought to save the world from a repeat of World War II. Hence, ultra-nationalism and militarism had to be purged from the collective mindset at any cost. If a new world order was to survive, a new approach to government had to be put in place. This new approach would be one that believes in shared values, where nation states are replaced with a sense of a united entity. In Europe there arose the concept that individual nationalities and cultures must be subordinated to a new more homogenized European identity, one which put a great deal more emphasis on conflict resolution by discussion rather than by using a military. solution One of the architects of this ideology was an Italian Communist, Altiero Spinelli, who was imprisoned by Mussolini's Fascist government for his political views. He viewed nationalism as Europe's greatest enemy. He wrote: "Men are no longer considered free citizens who can use the State in order to reach collective purposes...They are instead, servants of the State, which decides their goals."[10]

In 1957 the Treaty of Rome created the European Economic Community. This was the first step taken to unite Europe and eventually break down physical borders and the sense of national sovereignty. In 1986 Spinelli helped write the Maastricht Treaty, adopted in 1992, which created today's European Union (EU).

Between 1957 and 1992 a great deal of educational changes took place in European schools, starting from pre-school and going through university. These paved the way for the weakening of national identity and sovereignty and for the adopting of a European identity and culture. Children were taught that no culture is superior to any other, in fact all cultures are equal. One must be a true citizen of the world and not a provincial person who believes that his culture and nation are great, especially a culture that caused such suffering in the world in the form of imperialism/colonialism and eventually Nazism. Nationalism was replaced with a new ideal: multiculturalism,

> ..."the view that cultures, races, and ethnicities, particularly those of minority groups, deserve special acknowledgement of their differences within a dominant political culture. That acknowledgement can take the forms of recognition of contributions to the cultural life of the political community as a whole, a demand for special protection under the law for certain cultural groups, or autonomous rights of governance for certain cultures. Multiculturalism is both a response to the fact of cultural pluralism in modern democracies and a way of compensating cultural groups for past exclusion, discrimination, and oppression. Most modern democracies comprise members with diverse cultural viewpoints, practices, and contributions. Many minority cultural groups have experienced exclusion or the denigration of their contributions and identities in the past. Multiculturalism seeks the inclusion of the views and contributions of diverse members of society while maintaining respect for their differences and withholding the demand for their assimilation into the dominant culture.[11]

It took two generations of the revised European educational

system to view multiculturalism as their true heritage until a tipping point was reached and the people voted in a new type of political establishment that held multiculturalism above their own particular nations, culture or history. The European Union of today is a reflection of a post-nationalistic, post-military society.

But were Europeans being taught the truth? Had they gone too far? Is nationalism evil? Are all cultures really equal? Is there no upside for having a cohesive culture, history and language binding the citizens of a particular state together? Can a state or a collection of states really survive in a world where they don't have military capabilities? How did the EU experiment pan out?

Firstly, Europe was able to stand up to its dangerous, aggressive Communist neighbors—the Soviet Union and the Warsaw Pact countries (a Communist bloc of Eastern European countries that were aligned with the Soviet Union from the early 1950s until the collapse of the Soviet Union in 1989)—because their NATO ally, the USA, remained a very nationalisti ccountry and maintained a large, capable military presence in the heart of Western Europe. This U.S. military presence kept the Soviet Union at bay for close to half a century. When there was a post-Communist civil war in the Balkans in the mid 1990s, at the end it was U.S. airpower that ended the slaughter and it was U.S. ground forces that have been keeping the peace in the Balkans ever since.

With the Arab Spring turning into the Arab Winter and the disintegration of many Arab and Muslim states, there are multiple wars going on in the Near East and North Africa, a factor in millions of Muslims seeking to live in multicultural Europe. This has led to a growing Islamic population that is not allegiant or on the same page culturally or religiously with the majority of Europeans. This reality is creating a new host of security, social and economic problems that are causing many Europeans to rethink if not having a national identity or a unifying culture is a good idea or a recipe for national suicide. This dramatic debate is now taking place all over the EU.

What does this have to do with the Left in the Western world and the EU adopting the core ideology of anti-nationalism, militarism and multiculturalism and their hatred of the Jewish State? It does so because the Left sees a democratic, Western-style country moving in the opposite direction, a country that is very proud of its national history, culture and identity. Israel is a country that flies its flag proudly and teaches the history of its nation and state in all levels of its educational system. Israel highlights its history and nationalism in its holidays; its history is embedded in the country's culture. Worse, Israel drafts all its eighteen-year-olds, male and female, to serve in its military. Beyond that, its male population does reserve service until the age of fifty. Israel has proportionally one of the world's largest armies and probably the world's most active army due to the reality that it finds itself living in. The IDF is everywhere in Israel, and the overwhelming majority of Israelis are very proud of their country and their military. In essence, Israel and its Zionist ideology represent the opposite of what a truly progressive citizen of the world believes. To the Left, Israel represents all that is wrong with the world, especially since it is a First World country.

On top of all of this, the anti-Zionist and anti-Israel bias fostered by Palestinian propaganda does not accept that the Jews are a nation, and hence have no right to a form of nationalism. Only Palestinian Arabs are entitled to such nationalism. For Jews, who are at best a religious group and at worse an ethnic minority, nationhood is a false and dangerous ideology. Add to all of this that the Left has accepted the Edward Said view of Zionism, which is that Israel is the last outpost of Western imperialism in the Middle East, then as all colonial powers it subjugates indigenous people and takes their land and resources from them.

It has become useful for the anti-Zionist, anti-Israel crowd to focus on the Israeli post-1967 "occupation" of Judea and Samaria since it appears to resonate with those who have very little knowledge of the history of the Arab-Israeli conflict and who have been educated to see Zionism through the distorted prism of Orientalism. In reality, Said, his protégés and the leaders of the PA/PLO, etc., all believe that all of Israel is "occupied" Palestinian Arab land. They only use the 1967 "occupation" saga to gain a geographic foothold in an area that will allow them to eventually destroy Israel.

Finally, the Left lives by adhering to a double standard when it comes to the Jewish State, due to its adherence to the self-imposed standard of the bigotry of low expectations that gives the Arab world, the Islamic world and especially Palestinian Arabs a pass on every truly anti-liberal, anti-progressive and anti-democratic action they take.

When all is said and done, there appears to be a serious backlash taking place in the Western world against this idea of no national sovereignty, no pride in one's national history, language and culture. The cure to the horrific results of Nazism and Japanese imperialism that the intellectuals of post-World War II Europe came up with of trying to eradicate nationalism and any use of military force, in essence was trying to suppress one of the most basic human feelings of belonging to a group larger than themselves. The human race is divided into nations. There is nothing inherently evil about being loyal to your nation. The question is how do you as a member of a nation relate to other nations and the people who live and identify with those nations? Nations can exist proudly and still compete and respect each other. We see this in the Olympics and the World Cup. No one is waving an EU or NATO flag; everyone is rightfully proud of his/her own nation. Trying to suppress this inherent healthy connection to your nation does not make you dangerous or menacing, any more than being loyal to your family makes you a threat to your neighbors. The fact the we are members of the human race does not mean that the only way we can get along is if we pretend that we are citizens of Earth and have no culture, language or national loyalty. The world is a large mosaic and each nation is a small or large piece, each one a different shape, color and size. That's what gives the mosaic its beauty. Each nation can learn to respect its neighbors and fellow nations while keeping its own identity. Israel is such a nation-state. Unlike her neighbors who define themselves by their opposition to Zionism and their disdain for the Jewish State, Israel defines itself as a nation-state which is focused on fulfilling the promise of a homeland after 2,000 years of homelessness.

The idea of abandoning the military to avoid militarism has also created a cure worse than the disease. There are many actors in the world, and unlike the men and women who came up with the ideas that molded the EU, they are not enlightened but driven by either a fanatic sense of religious superiority laced with a seething resentment towards all other faiths, or a devotion to absolute power, control of natural resources, and/or fanatical hatred and fear of the "other". These actors are radical Islamic terror groups—both in its Sunni and Shiite forms—Iran, North Korea, China and Russia, to name the biggest and most dangerous forces to world peace and stability. Allowing one's country to be defenseless in the name of avoiding militarism is tantamount to collaborating with your enemies and helping make "quick work" of your own nation; for, unless every single country and actor ceases to use military force at the same time in history, the countries who live in or near dangerous areas that do abandon their military capability will find themselves defeated and or destroyed.

Nationalism and protecting one's nation with a robust and capable military are not actions that lead to Nazism or the rise of an imperial, militaristic juggernaut. They are the building blocks for a country like Switzerland, which is envied and admired by almost everyone in the world. There are very few countries prouder of their national stature, culture and language than the Swiss, and they have the military capability to insure that they remain a prosperous, beautiful, dynamic country.

Because nations existed, do exist and will exist, nationalism is an indigenous movement that will remain part of the human landscape politically and socially. To deny that is to try to deny reality. To attempt to suppress it, as the founders of the EU have done, will eventually be undone by outsides forces or actors who are ultra-nationalistic, who believe that their cultural or religion is superior, and who view violence as an extension of how one wins power and influence. Is it worth sacrificing Belgium, Holland, France etc., on the altar of multiculturalism because of the fear that should these countries remain nationalistic they would eventually become Nazi-like?

Israel is a model of what a democratic, open, truly liberal, tolerant and prosperous 21st century nation-state can be like, even while facing very determined and fanatic foes. Jewish nationalism has withstood one century of relentless opposition to the idea of a Jewish State, and to the reality of one as well. BDS will go the way of the Arab League Boycott; it will not withstand true scrutiny by intellectually honest people. It will fail because at its core it is a bigoted, anti-Jewish movement whose goal is to destroy the Jewish nation-state. It has nothing positive to offer the Arab people or Palestinian Arabs. It is based on advocating destroying Israel, not building a Palestinian Arab state. This has been and continues to be the Achilles heal of all the anti-Zionist movements. And despite these anti-Zionist attempts to disable the Jewish State, Israel continues to thrive.

As former British prime minister David Lloyd George stated in 1931:

> Zionism has brought to an old land, a renowned but a ruined old land, new wealth, new energy, new purpose, new initiative, new intelligence, a new devotion and a new hope. Zionism has not finished its task, far from it, but it has already accomplished so much as to demonstrate that the land flowing with milk and honey was no baseless legend.[12]

Footnotes

[1] Gil Feiler, *From Boycott to Economic Cooperation: The Political Economy of the Arab Boycott of Israel* (NY: Routledge, 2011), 22.

[2] Martin A. Weiss, "Arab League Boycott of Israel," Congressional Research Service, June 10, 2015 (https://fas.org/sgp/crs/mideast/RL33961.pdf).

[3] Dina Ezzat, "Boycott Israel? Not so simple," *Al-Ahram Weekly Online*, April 11-17, 2002 (http://weekly.ahram.org.eg/Archive/2002/581/ec1.htm)

[4] Ira M. Sheskin and Ethan Felson, "Is the Boycott, Divestment, and Sanctions Movement Tainted by Anti-Semitism?," *The Geographical Review*, Vol. 106(2), April 2016, 270+.

[5] Bassem Eid, "Five Facts the BDS Movement Should Learn from Bassem Eid," *InFocus*, June 27, 2016 (http://www.cameraoncampus.org/blog/5-things-for-the-bds-movement-to-learn-from-bassem-eid/#.WZXr2CiGO1s)

[6] Roberta Seid and Roz Rothstein, "Omar Barghouti's Lectures: A Case Study of Dangerous Propaganda," *StandWithUs* (https://www.standwithus.com/news/article.asp?id=2142)

[7] "What is BDS?" (https://bdsmovement.net/what-is-bds)

[8] Khaled Abu Toameh, "Palestinians' Real Tragedy: Failed Leadership," Gatestone Institute, June 15, 2017 (https://www.gatestoneinstitute.org/10526/palestinians-failed-leadership)

[9] Bassem Eid, "The Palestinian Case Against BDS," *The Washington Institute For Near East Policy*, June 25, 2015 (http://www.washingtoninstitute.org/policy-analysis/view/the-palestinian-case-against-bds)

[10] Joseph Loconte, "A Marxist Manifesto: The Birth Certificate of the European Union," *The Weekly Standard*, October 10, 2016 (http://www.weeklystandard.com/a-marxist-manifesto/article/2004627)

[11] Jennifer Egan, "Multiculturalism," *Encyclopedia Britannica* (https://www.britannica.com/topic/multiculturalism)

[12] "Mr. Lloyd George Explains Jewish National Home Policy: I Was Prime Minister when Balfour Declaration," JTA, April 13, 1931 (https://www.jta.org/1931/04/13/archive/mr-lloyd-george-explains-jewish-national-home-policy-i-was-prime-minister-when-balfour-declaration)

Selected Bibliography

⟪✺⟫

BOOKS

Abrahams, Enkel. *Juden, Christen, Muslime und die Schoa.* Niklas Günther & Sönke Zankel. eds. Stuttgart: Franz Steiner Verlag, 2006.

Achcar, Gilbert. *The Arabs and the Holocaust: The Arab-Israeli War of Narratives.* Berlin: Chastleton Travel, 2010.

Al-Dawoody, Ahmed. *The Islamic Law of War: Justifications and Regulations* London: Palgrave Macmillan, 2011.

Atiyah, Edward. *The Arabs.* London: Penguin Books, 1955.

Ben-Sasson, H. H. ed. *A History of the Jewish People.* Cambridge, MA: Harvard University Press, 1976.

Berkowitz, Michael. *The Crime of My Existence: Nazism and the Myth of Jewish Criminality.* Berkeley: Univ. of California Press, 2007.

Black, Edwin. *The Transfer Agreement: The Dramatic Story of the Pact Between the Third Reich and Jewish Palestine.* Washington, DC: Dialog Press, 2009.

———. *The Farhud: Roots of the Arab-Nazi Alliance in the Holocaust.* Washington, DC: Dialog Press, 2010.

———. *Financing the Flames: How Tax-Exempt and Public Money Fuel a Culture of Confrontation and Terror in Israel.* Washington, DC: Dialog Press, 2013.

Bleich, David. *Contemporary Halakhic Problems*, Vol.1. Hoboken, NJ: KTAV Publishing, 1977.

Bonné, Alfred. *State and Economics in the Middle East: A Society in Turmoil* London: Routledge, 2001.

Bonner, Michael. *Jihad in Islamic History: Doctrines and Practice.* Princeton: Princeton University Press, 2006.

Browning, Christopher R. *The Origins of the Final Solution: The Evolution of Nazi Jewish Policy, September 1939-March 1942.* Lincoln: University of Nebraska Press, 2007.

Brzoska, Michael and Frederic S. Pearson, *Arms and Warfare: Escalation, De-escalation, and Negotiation*. Columbia, SC: Univ. of S. Carolina Press, 1994.

Cleveland, William L. *A History of the Modern Middle East*, 2nd ed. Boulder, CO: Westview Press, 2000.

Diner, Hasia R. *The Jews of the United States, 1654 to 2000*. Berkeley, CA: University of California Press, 2004).

Dunstan, Simon. *Entebbe: The Most Daring Raid of Israel's Special Forces*. NY: Rosen, 2011.

Elon, Amos. *Understanding Israel: A Social Studies Approach*. Springfield, NJ: Behrman House, 1976.

Elpeleg, Zvi. *The Grand Mufti: Haj Amin Al-Hussaini, Founder of the Palestinian National Movement*. Shmuel Himmelstein, ed. (trans. David Harvey). London: Routledge, 2007.

Feiler, Gil. *From Boycott to Economic Cooperation: The Political Economy of the Arab Boycott of Israel*. NY: Routledge, 2011.

Feldman, Louis and Steve Mason. *Flavius Josephus*. Leiden, Netherlands: Brill Academic Publishers, 1999.

Ganor, Boaz. "Israel and the Palestine Liberation Organization," in *The Routledge History of Terrorism*. Randall D. Law, ed. Florence, KY: Taylor & Francis Group, 2014. 239-257.

Gilbert, Martin. *The Routledge Atlas of the Arab Israeli Conflict*, 10th ed. London: Routledge Taylor & Francis Group, 2012.

————. *Israel A History*. Toronto: Key Porter Books, 2008.

Harkabi, Yehoshafat. *Arab Attitudes Towards Israel*. Jersualem: Keter Publishing, 1972.

Hertzberg, Arthur. *The Zionist Idea: A Historical Analysis and Reader* Philadelphia, PA: Jewish Publication Society, 1997.

Herzog, Chaim. *The Arab Israeli Wars*. NY: Vintage Books, 1984.

Hilberg, Raul. *The Destruction of the European Jews*. NY: New Viewpoints, 1973.

Hitler, Adolf. *Mein Kampf* (NY: Reynal & Hitchcock, 1939.

Hoyland, Robert G. *Arabia and the Arabs: From the Bronze Age to the Coming of Islam*. London: Routledge, 2001.

Hyamson, Albert M., *Palestine: A Policy*. London: Methuen, 1942.

Jabotinsky, V. "A Jewish State Now" in *The Israel-Arab Reader: a documentary history of the Middle East conflict*. Walter Laqueur and Barry Rubin, eds. NY: Penguin Books, 4th revised and updated edition, 1984.

Karsh, Efraim. *Palestine Betrayed.* New Haven: Yale University Press, 2014.

———. *The Arab-Israeli Conflict: The Palestine War 1948.* London: Osprey Publishing, 2014.

Johnson, David E. *Hard Fighting: Israel in Lebanon and Gaza.* Santa Monica, CA: Rand, 2011.

Katz, Samuel. *The Hunt for the Engineer.* Augusta,GA: Lyons Press, 2002.

Kaufman, Myron. *The Coming Destruction of Israel.* NY: The American Library Inc., 1970.

Khadduri, Majid. *War and Peace in the Law of Islam.* Baltimore: Johns Hopkins Press, 1955).

Khalidi, Rashid. *Sowing Crisis: the Cold War and American Dominance in the Middle East.* Boston, MA; Beacon Press, 2009.

Laqueur, Walter. *The Changing Face of Antisemitism: From Ancient Times to the Present Day.* Oxford: Oxford University Press, 2006.

Laurens, Henry. *Une mission sacrée de civilisation. La Question de Palestine,* 2. Paris: Fayard, 2002.

Lepre, George. *Himmler's Bosnian Division; The Waffen-SS Handschar Division 1943-1945.* Atglen, PA: Schiffer Military History, 1997.

Lewis, Bernard. *Semites and Anti-Semites: An Inquiry into Conflict and Prejudice.* NY: W.W. Norton & Company, 1999.

Louër, Laurence. *To be an Arab in Israel.* NY: Columbia University Press, 2007.

Margolis, Max L. and Alexander Marx. *A History of the Jewish People* Philadelphia: The Jewish Publication Society of America, 1927.

Morris, Benny. *Righteous Victims: A History of the Zionist-Arab Conflict, 1881-1998.* NY: Random House, 1999.

———. *1948: A History of the First Arab-Israeli War.* New Haven: Yale University Press, 2008.

Nicosia, Francis R. *The Third Reich & the Palestine Question.* Piscataway, NJ: Transaction Publishers, 2000.

Parolin, Gianluca P. *Citizenship in the Arab World: Kin, Religion and Nation-State.* Amsterdam: Amsterdam Univeristy Press, 2009.

Pedazhur, Ami and Arie Perliger. *Jewish Terrorism in Israel.* NY: Columbia University Press, 2009.

Podhoretz, Norman. *Why Are Jews Liberals?* NY: Vintage Books, 2010.

Sachar, Howard M. *The History of Israel from the Rise of Zionism To Our Time.* NY: Alfred Knopf, 1996.

Said, Edward. *The Question of Palestine*. NY: Vintage Books, 1980.

Segev, Tom and Haim Watzman, *One Palestine, Complete: Jews and Arabs Under the British Mandate*. NY: Metropolitan Books, 2000.

Shapiro, Edward S. *A Time For Healing*. Baltimore, MD: The John Hopkins University Press, 1992.

Shlaim, Avi. "Israel and the Conflict" in Alex Danchev and Dan Keohane, eds., *International Perspectives on the Gulf Conflict, 1990-91*. London: St Martin's Press, 1994. 59-79.

Sklar, Marshall. *America's Jews*. Waltham, MA: Brandeis University Press, 1971.

Stillman, Norman A. "Perceptions and Understandings of Israel within Islam," in *Essential Israel: Essays for the 21st Century*. S. Ilan Troen & Rachel Fish, eds. Bloomington, IN: Indiana University Press, 2017. 311-325.

Teveth, Shabtai. *Ben Gurion and the Holocaust*. NY: Harcourt Brace & Co., 1996.

"The Hezbollah Program: An Open Letter, February 16, 1985," in *Israel in the Middle East: Documents and Readings on Society, Politics, and Foreign Relations, Pre-1948 to the Present* (The Tauber Institute for the Study of European Jewry Series), 2nd edition, Itamar Rabinovich & Jehuda Reinharz, eds. Waltham, MA: Brandeis University Press, 2007. 423-429.

Twain, Mark. *The Innocents Abroad, or The New Pilgrims' Progress, Volume 2*. NY: P. F. Collier & Son, 1911.

Vivo, Raul Valdes. *Ethiopia's Revolution*. NY: International Publishers, 1977.

Wistrich, Robert S. "Zionism and its Religious Critics in fin-de-siècle Vienna," in Shmuel Almog, et. al., *Zionism and Religion* (Waltham, MA: Brandeis University Press, 1998).

ARTICLES

"194 (III). Palestine: Progress Report of the United Nations Mediator," United Nations General Assembly, 11 December 1948. https://unispal.un.org/DPA/DPR/unispal.nsf/0/C758572B78D1CD0085285256BCF0077E51A.

"2014 Gaza War Assessment: The New Face of Conflict," A report by the JINSA-commissioned Gaza Conflict Task Force, March 2015. http://www.jinsa.org/gaza-assessment.

"Hamas Admits To Kidnapping And Killing Israeli Teens," *AP*, August 22, 2014. http://www.npr.org/2014/08/22/342318367/hamas-finally-admits-to-kidnapping-and-killing-israeli-teens.

"Husseini's Last Interview: Oslo A Trojan Horse, Arutz Sheva, 10/07/01 http://www.israelnationalnews.com/Articles/Article.aspx/317.

"Jenin 'massacre' reduced to death toll of 56," *Washington Times*, May 1, 2002. http://www.washingtontimes.com/news/2002/may/1/20020501-023924-2910r/.

"Mr. Lloyd George Explains Jewish National Home Policy: I Was Prime Minister when Balfour Declaration," JTA, April 13, 1931 (https://www.jta.org/1931/04/13/archive/mr-lloyd-george-explains-jewish-national-home-policy-i-was-prime-minister-when-balfour-declaration)

"Summit Makes Little Progress," *The Stanford Daily*, Vol. 210, Issue 10:3, October 1996. http://stanforddailyarchive.com/cgi-bin/stanford?a=d&d=stanford19961003-01.1.3&e=01-01-1990-31-12-1999--en-20--1--txt-txTI-radio------#.

"What Really Happened in Jenin?," *Jerusalem Issue Brief*, Vol. 1, No. 22. Jerusalem Center for Public Affairs, 2 May 2002. http://www.jcpa.org/art/brief1-22.htm.

"Without Settlers Initiative Rothschild Would Not Have Undertaken Colonization," *JTA*, August 13, 1928. http://www.jta.org/1928/08/13/archive/without-settlers-initiative-rothschild-would-not-have-undertaken-colonization.

Amir, Noam and Maariv Hashavua. "Israel Remembers 73 Soldiers Killed in Helicopter Disaster 19 Years Ago," *Jerusalem Post*, February 5, 2016. http://www.jpost.com/Israel-News/Israel-remembers-73-soldiers-who-died-in-helicopter-disaster-19-years-ago-444000.

Bard, Mitchell G. "Operation Solomon: The Daring Rescue of the Ethiopian Jews," *The Middle East Quarterly*, Spring 2006, Vol 13:2. http://www.meforum.org/961/operation-solomon.

Baron, Dan. "Israel defends killing of Yassin as the public braces for revenge," *JTA World Report*, March 243, 2004. http://pdfs.jta.org/2004/2004_03_23.pdf, 1-2.

Ben-David, Lenny. "The Strategic Significance of Har Homa," *The Jerusalem Post*, December 15, 2007. http://www.jpost.com/Opinion/Op-Ed-Contributors/The-strategic-significance-of-Har-Homa.

Boot, Max. "The Second Lebanon War: It probably wont be the last," *The Weekly Standard*, September 4, 2006. http://www.weeklystandard. com/the-second-lebanon-war/article/13751.

Brand, Wallace Edward. "The Exclusive Political Rights Granted To Jews In 1920 At San Remo," *Israeli Frontline*, December 30, 2012. http://www.israelifrontline.com/2012/12/the-eexclusive-political-rights-granted.html.

Bronner, Ethan. "Hanan Porat, Jewish Settlement Leader, Dies at 67," *New York Times*, October 4, 2011. http://www.nytimes. com/2011/10/05/world/middleeast/hanan-porat-jewish-settlement-leader-dies-at-67.html.

Brown, Mallory. "Jews in Grave Danger in all Moslem Lands," *New York Times*, May 16, 1948, E4.

Caspit, Ben. "Gilad Schalit's Capture: In His Own Words," *Jerusalem Post*, March 28, 2013. http://www.jpost.com/Defense/Gilad-Schalits-capture-In-his-own-words-308015.

Chanes, Jerome. "The Lessons of the Lavon Affair," *The Forward*, May 16, 2014. http://forward.com/opinion/198375/the-lessons-of-the-lavon-affair/.

Cohen, Avner. "The Last Nuclear Moment," *New York Times*, October 6, 2003 http://www.nytimes.com/2003/10/06/opinion/the-last-nuclear-moment.html.

Cohen, Shaye. "Roman Domination: The Jewish Revolt and the Destruction of the Second Temple," in *Ancient Israel*, Hershel Shanks, ed. Biblical Archaeology Society, 1999. (269-273).

Cohen, Yoram and Jeffrey White, "Hamas in Combat: The Military Performance of the Palestinian Islamic Resistance Movement," *Policy Focus*, No. 97. Washington, DC: The Washington Institute for Near East Policy, 2009.

Drews, Robert. "Canaanites and Philistines." *Journal for the Study of the Old Testament* (1998) 81: 39–61.

Dvorin, Tova. "Details of 2000 Ramallah Lynch of IDF Soldiers Revealed," *Arutz Sheva*, December 24, 2013. http://www.israel nationalnews.com/News/News.aspx/175494.

Fuld, Ari. "Remembering Yehoshua Friedberg, Hy"d Zt"l," *The Jewish Press*, March 8, 2017. http://www.jewishpress.com/blogs/sword-of-israel-ari-fuld/remembering-yehoshua-friedberg-hydztl/2017/03/08/.

Gold, Dore. "Israel's War to Halt Palestinian Rocket Attacks," *Jerusalem Center for Public Affairs*, Vol. 7:34, March 3, 2008. http://jcpa.org/article/israel%E2%80%99s-war-to-halt-palestinian-rocket-attacks/.

Goldstein, Evan R. "Rashid Khalidi's Balancing Act: The Middle-East scholar courts controversy with his Palestinian advocacy," *Chronicle of Higher Education*, March 6, 2009. http://lists.econ.utah.edu/pipermail/marxism/2009-March/045483.html.

Goldstone, Richard. "Reconsidering the Goldstone Report on Israel and war crimes," *The Washington Post*, April 1, 2011. https://www.washingtonpost.com/opinions/reconsidering-the-goldstone-report-on-israel-and-war-crimes/2011/04/01/AFg111JC_story.html?utm_term=.af2e8e91eb95.

Gourevitch, Philip. "What the Media Gets Wrong About Israel," *The Atlantic*, 12/4/2014. http://www.theatlantic.com/international/print/2014/11/howthemediamakestheisraelstory/383262/ 4/11.

Grant, Rebecca. "The Bekaa Valley War," *Air Force Magazine*, June 2002. http://www.airforcemag.com/MagazineArchive/Pages/2002/June%202002/0602bekaa.aspx.

Haberman, Clyde. "Israel Finishes Withdrawing Troops from the Gaza Strip," *New York Times*, May19, 1994 http://www.nytimes.com/1994/05/19/world/israel-finishes-withdrawing-troops-from-the-gaza-strip.html?pagewanted=all.

———. "Palestinian Says His Delegation Will Assert P.L.O. Ties at Talks," *New York Times*, October 22, 1991. http://www.nytimes.com/1991/10/22/world/palestinian-says-his-delegation-will-assert-plo-ties-at-talks.html.

Halevi, Yossi Klein. "The Astonishing Israeli Concession of 1967," *The Atlantic*, July 7, 2017. https://www.theatlantic.com/international/archive/2017/06/israel-paratroopers-temple-mount-1967/529365/.

Harel, Amos and Avi Issacharoff, Gili Cohen, Allison Kaplan Sommer and News Agencies, "Israel Launches Operation Pillar of Defense; Hamas Military Chief Ahmed Jabari Killed by Israeli Strike," *Haaretz*, Nov 14, 2012. http://www.haaretz.com/israel-news/hamas-military-chief-ahmed-jabari-killed-by-israeli-strike.premium-1.477819.

Hirsh, Michael. "Clinton to Arafat: It's All Your Fault," *Newsweek*, June 26, 2001 http://www.newsweek.com/clinton-arafat-its-all-your153779-fault-.

Hochberg, Severin A. "Arrows in the Dark: David Ben Gurion, the Yishuv Leadership, and Rescue Attempts during the Holocaust," *The Middle East Journal*, 60:2, Spring 2006. 385+.

Ibrahim, Youssef M. "P.L.O. Proclaims Palestine to be an Independent State; Hints at Recognizing Israel," *New York Times*, November 15, 1988. http://www.nytimes.com/1988/11/15/world/plo-proclaims-palestine-to-be-an-independent-state-hints-at-recognizing-israel.html?pagewanted=all.

Inbar, Efraim. "How Israel Bungled the Second Lebanon War," *The Middle East Quarterly*, Summer 2007, Vol. 14:3. 57-65. http://www.meforum.org/1686/how-israel-bungled-the-second-lebanon-war.

Israeli Ministry of Foreign Affairs, "Terrorism Deaths in Israel; In Memory of the Victims of Palestinian Terror," *Jerusalem Post*, January 4, 2009. http://www.jewishvirtuallibrary.org/number-of-terrorism-fatalities-in-israel.

Issacharoff, Avi and Times of Israel Staff, "Hamas fires rockets for first time since 2012, Israeli officials say," *The Times of Israel*, June 30, 2014 http://www.timesofisrael.com/hamas-fired-rockets -for-first-time-since-2012-israeli-officials-say/.

JNS.org, "Rabbi Moshe Levinger, Jewish Settlement Movement Pioneer, Dies at 80,' *The Algemeiner*, May 17, 2015. https://www.algemeiner.com/2015/05/17/rabbi-moshe-levinger-jewish-settlement-movement-pioneer-dies-at-80/.

Kanaana, Sharif and Nihad Zitawi, "Deir Yassin," Monograph No. 4, *Destroyed Palestinian Villages Documentation Project*. Bir Zeit: Documentation Center of Bir Zeit University, 1987.

Keinon, Herb. "Palmer: Gaza Blockade Lawful, IDF Used 'Excessive' Force," *The Jerusalem Post*, September 3, 2011. http://www.jpost.com/Diplomacy-and-Politics/Palmer-Gaza-blockade-lawful-IDF-used-excessive-force.

Lambeth, Benjamin S. "Israel's War in Gaza: A Paradigm of Effective Military Learning and Adaptation," *International Security*, 37:2. 81-118. http://www.mitpressjournals.org/doi/pdf/10.1162/ISEC_a_00099.

Landes, Richard. "Why The Arab World Is Lost In An Emotional Nakba, And How We Keep It There," *Tablet*, June 24, 2014. http://www.tabletmag.com/jewish-news-and-politics/176673/emotional-nakba.

Loconte, Joseph. "A Marxist Manifesto: The Birth Certificate of the European Union," *The Weekly Standard*, October 10, 2016. http://www.weeklystandard.com/a-marxist-manifesto/article/2004627.

Makovsky, David. "The Silent Strike," *New Yorker*, September 17, 2012. http://www.newyorker.com/magazine/2012/09/17/the-silent-strike.

Margolick, David. "Postwar Pogrom," *New York Times*, July 23, 2006. http://www.nytimes.com/2006/07/23/books/review/23margolick.html.

Medoff, Rafael. "'The Mufti's Nazi Years Re-examined," *The Journal of Israeli History*, 17 (1996). 317–333..

Melman, Yossi "Analysis: The Gaza Conflict Report and the Paradox of Israel's Wars," *The Jerusalem Post*, February 28, 2017. http://www.jpost.com/Israel-News/Analysis-The-Comptroller-report-and-the-paradox-of-Israels-wars-482817.

Moriarty, Richard. "The Israeli election," *The Guardian*, February 7, 2001. https://www.theguardian.com/world/2001/feb/07/qanda.israel? CMP=share_btn_link.

Morris, Harvey. "Gaza Strip greenhouse deal breaks deadlock," *Financial Times*, August 13, 2005. http://www.ft.com/cms/s/0/ab8b7304-0b97-11da-9939-00000e2511c8.html?ft_site=falcon&desktop=true#axzz4l1leoQqa.

Morris, Nomi and Eric Silver, "Israel Opens Disputed Tunnel," *Maclean's*, October 7, 1996, in *The Canadian Encyclopedia Historical Foundation*, 2012. https://web.archive.org/web/20121020014235/http://www.the canadianencyclopedia.com/articles/macleans/israel-opens-disputed-tunnel.

Nashabe, Omar. "China's Ambassador in Lebanon: Hezbollah Arms a Trade Matter," *Al-Akhbar*, 4 May 2012. http://english.al-akhbar.com/node/6964.

Omer, Ibrahim. "The Forgotten Origin of Ethiopian Jews; From Northern Sudan," *The Jewish Magazine*, April 2013. http://www.jewishmag.com/174mag/ethiopian_jews_origin/ethiopian_jews_origin.htm.

Omer-Man, Michael. "This Week in History: Operation Moses Begins," *The Jerusalem Post*, November 19, 2010. http://www.jpost.com/Features/In-Thespotlight/This-week-in-History-Operation-Moses-begins.

Peretz, Martin. "Lebanon Eyewitness," *New Republic*, August 2, 1982. 15-23.

Poller, Nodra. "Myth, Fact, and the al-Dura Affair ," *Commentary*, Sept. 1, 2005. https://www.commentarymagazine.com/articles/myth-fact-and-the-al-dura-affair/.

Prince-Gibson, Eetta. "Prisoners Dilemma," *Jerualem Report*, March 25, 2009. http://www.jpost.com/Jerusalem-Report/Prisoners-Dilemma-137099.

Quigley, John. "The Palestine Declaration to the International Criminal Court: The Statehood Issue," *Rutgers Law Record*, Vol. 35, Spring 2009. https://web.archive.org/web/20110716143235/http://www.lawrecord.com/files/35-rutgers-l-rec-1.pdf.

Reiss, Moshe. "Ishmael, Son of Abraham," *Jewish Bible Quarterly*, Vol. 30:4, 2002. http://jbq.jewishbible.org/assets/Uploads/304/ 304_ishmael5.pdf.

Roosevelt, Theodore. "Man in the Arena," *Citizenship in a Republic*, April 23, 1910. http://www.theodore-roosevelt.com/images/research/speeches/maninthearena.pdf.

Rosen, Steven J. "Kuwait Expels Thousands of Palestinians," *The Middle East Quarterly*, Fall 2012, vol. 19:4. http://www.meforum.org/3391/kuwait-expels-palestinians.

Rosensaft, Menachem Z. "Wrong About Arafat," *The Washington Post*, October 14, 2000. A23.

Schmemann, Serge. "Assassination in Israel: The Overview; Rabin Slain After Peace Rally in Tel Aviv; Israeli Gunman Held; Says He Acted Alone," *New York Times*, Novembere 5, 1995. http://www.nytimes.com/1995/11/05/world/assassination-israel-overview-rabin-slain-after-peace-rally-tel-aviv-israeli.html?pagewanted=all.

Sedan, Gil. "The life of Hamas leader Sheik Ahmed Yassin," *JTA World Report*, March 23, 2004. pdfs.jta.org/2004/2004_03_23.pdf.

Servold, Gary M. "Know Thy Enemy: Profiles of Adversary Leaders and Their Strategic Cultures," edited by Barry R. Schneider and Jerrold M. Post, USAF Counterproliferation Center CPC., July 2003.

Sharon, Assaf. "Failure in Gaza," *The New York Review of Books*, September 25, 2014. http://www.nybooks.com/articles/2014/09/25/failure-gaza/.

Shavit, Ari. "The Time Has Come to Open Our Eyes to the Arab Disaster," *Ha'artez*, Sept. 11, 2015. http://www.haaretz.com/opinion/.premium-1.675412?date=1441978762222.

Sheskin, Ira M. and Ethan Felson, "Is the Boycott, Divestment, and Sanctions Movement Tainted by Anti-Semitism?," *The Geographical Review*, Vol. 1062, April 2016. 270+.

Shipler, David K. "Cease-Fire In Border Fighting Declared By Israel and P.L.O.; U.S. Sees Hope For Wider Peace," *New York Times*, July 25, 1981. http://www.nytimes.com/1981/07/25/world/cease-fire-border-fighting-declared-israel-plo-us-sees-hope-for-wider-peace.html.

———. "The Golan Heights Annexed by Israel in an Abrupt Move," *New York Times*, December 15, 1981, 1. http://www.nytimes.com/learning/general/onthisday/big/1214.html.

———. "Lebanese Tell of Anguish of Living Under the P.L.O.," *New York Times*, 7/25/82.

Stephens, Bret. "Palestine and Double Standards: The world is outraged by Israeli self-defense but only 'concerned' when Muslims kill Muslims," *The Wall Street Journal*, Aug. 4, 2014. https://www.wsj.com/articles/bret-stephens-palestine-and-double-standards-1407194971.

Times of Israel Staff, "Bodies of three kidnapped teens found; Netanyahu calls families," *The Times of Israel*, June 30, 2014. http://www.timesofisrael.com/bodies-of-three-kidnapped-teens-found/.

Totten, Michael. "Who Really Won the Second Lebanon War?" *Commentary*, January 30, 2009. https://www.commentarymagazine.com/foreign-policy/middle-east/israel/who-really-won-the-second-lebanon-war/.

Tuchfeld, Mati. 'Unilateral disengagement from Gaza Strip was a mistake,' *Israel Hayom*, June 15, 2017. http://www.israelhayom.com/site/newsletter_article.php?id=43139.

Wagner, Matthew. "As NRP folds to create united front, signs of dissent emerge," *The Jerusalem Post*, Nov 19, 2008. http://www.jpost.com/Israel/As-NRP-folds-to-create-united-front-signs-of-dissent-emerge.

Weiss, Martin A. "Arab League Boycott of Israel," *Congressional Research Service*, June 10, 2015. https://fas.org/sgp/crs/mideast /RL33961.pdf.

Wesley, Yang. "The End of the Affair," *Tablet*, September 4, 2009 http://www.tabletmag.com/jewish-arts-and-culture/books/15116/the-end-of-the-affair.

Zavadski, Katie. "It Turns Out Hamas May Not Have Kidnapped and Killed the 3 Israeli Teens After All," *New York,* July 24, 2014. http://nymag.com/daily/intelligencer/2014/07/hamas-didnt-kidnap-the-israeli-teens-after-all.html.

WEB REFERENCES

"1960: The assassins of Hazza Majali," ExecutedToday.com. December 31st, 2009. http://www.executedtoday.com/2009/12/31/1960-the-assassins-of-hazza-majali/.

"1967-1993: Major Terror Attacks." Israel Ministry of Foreign Affairs.http://www.mfa.gov.il/mfa/aboutisrael/maps/pages/1967-1993-%20major%20terror%20attacks.aspx.

"Address by PM Ariel Sharon at the Fourth Herzliya Conference-Dec 18- 2003," Israel Ministry of Foreign Affairs. http://www.mfa.gov.il/MFA/PressRoom/2003/Pages/Address%20by%20PM%20Ariel%20Sharon%20at%20the%20Fourth%20Herzliya.aspx.

"Balfour Declaration: Text of the Declaration, November 2, 1917." Jewish Virtual Library. http://www.jewishvirtuallibrary.org/jsource/History/balfour.html.

"British Palestine Mandate: Text of the Peel Commission Report, July 1937." Jewish Virtual Library. http://www.jewishvirtuallibrary.org/jsource/History/peel1.html.

"British White Paper of 1939," Yale Law School, Lillian Goldman Library, The Avalon Project. http://avalon.law.yale.edu/20th_century/brwh1939.asp.

"British White Papers: The MacDonald Letter, February 13, 1931." Jewish Virtual Library. http://www.jewishvirtuallibrary.org/jsource/history/macdonaldtext.html.

"Chapter 3: The 1967 and 1973 Wars." http://www.un.org/Depts/dpi/palestine/ch3.pdf.

"Fatah: History & Overview." Jewish Virtual Library. http://www.jewishvirtuallibrary.org/jsource/Terrorism/Fatah.html.

"First Lebanon War: The Kahan Commission of Inquiry, February 8, 1983." Israel Ministry of Foreign Affairs. http://www. jewish jvirtuallibrary.org/jsource/History/kahan.html.

"Gaza Flotilla Incident: The Turkel Commission Report, January 23, 2011." *Jewish Virtual Library.* https://www.jewishvirtuallibrary.org/jsource/Society_&_Culture/flotilla012311.html.

"Hamas Spokesman Encourages Gazans to Serve as Human Shields: It's Been Proven Effective," Al-Aqsa TV. Translated by the Middle East Media Research Institute, July 8, 2014. http://www.memritv. org/clip/en/4340.htm.

"Har Homa." Wild Olive. http://www.wildolive.co.uk/Har%20Homa. htm.

"Interim Peace Agreement Sinai II., September 1, 1975." http://www. jewishvirtuallibrary.org/jsource/Peace/eginterim75.html.

"Islam: References to Jews in the Koran." Jewish Virtual Library. http://www.jewishvirtuallibrary.org/references-to-jews-in-the-koran.

"Israel War of Independence: The Capture of Deir Yassin April 9, 1948." Jewish Virtual Library. http://www.jewishvirtuallibrary.org/ the-capture-of-deir-yassin.

"Israel-Egypt Separation of Forces Agreement-1974," Israel Ministry of Foreign Affairs. http://www.mfa.gov.il/mfa/foreignpolicy/ peace/guide/pages/israel-egypt%20separation%20of%20forces%20 agreement%20-%201974.aspx.

"Israel-Palestine Liberation Organization Agreement: 1993." http:// avalon.law.yale.edu/20th_century/isrplo.asp.

"Israeli-Palestinian Interim Agreement on the West Bank and the Gaza Strip, September 28, 1995." [Abridged] http://www.mfa.gov.il/ mfa/foreignpolicy/peace/guide/pages/the%20israeli-palestinian%20 interim%20agreement.aspx.

"Japanese kill 26 at Tel Aviv airport." On This Day 1950-2005, BBC.http://news.bbc.co.uk/onthisday/hi/dates/stories/may/29/ newsid_2542000/2542263.stm.

"Jibril Agreement." *World Heritage Encyclopedia.* http://self.gutenberg. org/articles/Jibril_Agreement.

"Khartoum Resolution." https://en.wikipedia.org/wiki/Khartoum_ Resolution.

"Legal Consequences of the Construction of a Wall in the Occupied Palestinian Territory." International Court of Justice. http://www. icj-cij.org/en/case/131.

"Muslim Brotherhood." *Encyclopedia of the Middle East.* http://www. mideastweb.org/Middle-East-Encyclopedia/muslim_brotherhood. htm.

"October 1974 Rabat Arab Summit Conference." http://www. palestinefacts.org/pf_1967to1991_rabat_1974.php.

"October 23, 1983: Beirut barracks blown up." *The History Channel* http://www.history.com/this-day-in-history/beirut-barracks-blown-up.

"Operation Protective Edge: July-August 2014." ADL. https://www.adl.org/education/resources/glossary-terms/operation-protective-edge-july-august-2014.

"Operation Summer Rain: IDF enters southern Gaza Strip to secure release of abducted soldier," Israel Ministry of Foreign Affairs, 28 Jun 2006.http://www.mfa.gov.il/mfa/pressroom/2006/pages/idf%20enters%20southern%20gaza%20strip%20to%20secure%20release%20of%20abducted%20soldier%2028-jun-2006.aspx.

"Palestine 1930: The Passfield White Paper." CJPME, Factsheet No. 135, August 2011. https://d3n8a8pro7vhmx.cloudfront.net/cjpme/pages/1146/attachments/original/1433363533/135-En-Passfield-White-Paper-v3.pdf?1433363533.

"Palestinian 10 Point Program, June 8, 1974." http:// www.ijs.org.au/The-Ten-Point-Program-/default.aspx.

"Palestinian Liberation Organization PLO." *Encyclopedia of the Modern Middle East and North Africa.* http://www.encyclopedia.com/history/asia-and-africa/middle-eastern-history/palestine-liberation-organization.

"Porat Hanan." http://www.news1.co.il/Archive/006D-1091-00. html?tag=14-27-38.

"Preislamic Arabia." https://www.saylor.org/site/wp-content/uploads/2011/08/HIST351-1.1-Pre-Islamic-Arabia.pdf.

"Presence and Functions of UNEF November 1956." Jewish Virtual Library. http://www.jewishvirtuallibrary.org/jsource/History/unef1.html.

"Pre-State Israel: Feisal-Frankfurter Correspondence March 1919." Jewish Virtual Library. https://www.jewishvirtuallibrary.org/feisal-frankfurter-correspondence-march-1919.

"Pre-State Israel: The Sykes-Picot Agreement 1916." Jewish Virtual Library. http://www.jewishvirtuallibrary.org/jsource/History/sykes_pico.html.

"Quotes on Judaism & Israel: Elazar Ben Yair Speech at Masada." http://www.jewishvirtuallibrary.org/jsource/Quote/yairq.html.

"reddit Ask Historians." https://www.reddit.com/r/AskHistorians/comments/27ou8w/is_the_egyptian_claim_of_being_victorious_in_the/.

"Refugees: Key Facts." *Holocaust Encyclopedia, USHMM*. https://www. ushmm.org/wlc/en/article.php?ModuleId= 10005139.

"Report of the Secretary-General's Panel of Inquiry on the Flotilla Incident, 31 May 2010," September 2011. http://www.un.org/News/ dh/infocus/middle_east/Gaza_Flotilla_Panel_Report.pdf.

"Report of UNSCOP - 1947: September 1, 1947." Mideast Web. http://www.mideastweb.org/unscop1947.htm.

"Rocket Attacks Toward Israel From the Gaza Strip." IDF Blog, April 16, 2012. https://www.idfblog.com/blog/2012/04/16/timeline-terror-2001-2012/.

"Rogers Plan." https://www.knesset.gov.il/lexicon/eng/rogers_eng. htm.

"Separation of Forces Agreement Between Israel and Syria, May 31, 1974." http://avalon.law.yale.edu/20th_century/pal04..asp.

"Taba Summit Concludes." Center for Israel Education, January 27, 2001. https://israeled.org/taba-summit-concludes/.

"The Balfour Declaration November 2, 1917." http://www.zionism-israel.com/Balfour_Declaration_1917.htm.

"The Covenant of the Islamic Resistance Movement, 18 August 1988 [The Hamas Charter]." http://avalon.law.yale.edu/20th_century/ hamas.asp.

"The Holocaust: The Mufti's Conversation with Hitler, November 28, 1941." Jewish Virtual Library. http://www.jewishvirtuallibrary.org/ jsource/History/mufti2.html.

"The Jewish State: Theodor Herzl's Program for Zionism." http:// www.zionism-israel.com/js/Jewish_State.html.

"The Law of Return," The Jewish Agency. http://www.jewishagency. org/first-steps/program/5131.

"The Palestinian Charter." http://www.pac-usa.org/the_palestinian_ charter.htm.

"The Palestine Mandate." The Council of the League of Nations, July 24, 1922." Yale University Law School Virtual Document Library. http://avalon.law.yale.edu/20th_century/palmanda.asp.

"The Palestinian National Charter: Resolutions of the Palestine National Council, July 1-17, 1968." Yale Law School, Lillian Goldman Law Center, The Avalon Project. http://avalon.law.yale.edu/20th_ century/plocov.asp.

"The Partition Plan: United Nations Debate on Partition

November 26, 1947." Jewish Virtual Library. http://www.
jewishvirtuallibrary.org/united-nations-debate-on-partition-
november-1947.

"The Sinai-Suez Campaign: Israel Agrees to Withdrawal, March 1,
1957." Israeli Foreign Ministry. Jewish Virtual Library. http://www.
jewishvirtuallibrary.org/jsource/History/iswithdraw.html.

"The Six-Point Agreement, 11 November 1973." Israel Ministry
of Foreign Affairs. http://www.mfa.gov.il/mfa/foreignpolicy/
mfadocuments/yearbook1/pages/17%20the%20six-point%20
agreement-%2011%20november%201973.aspx.

"The Weizmann-Feisal Agreement 03 Jan 1919." Israel Ministry of
Foreign Affairs. http://www.mfa.gov.il/mfa/foreignpolicy/
peace/mfadocuments/pages/the%20weizmann-feisal%20
agreement%203-jan-1919.aspx.

"The Wye River Memorandum, October 23, 1998." http://avalon.law.
yale.edu/21st_century/wyeriv.asp.

"Timeline of Jewish History: Modern Israel & the Diaspora 1970
-1979."http://www.jewishvirtuallibrary.org/timeline-of-modern-
israel-1970-1979.; BBC, On This Day: "1974: Dozens die as Israel
retaliates for Ma'alot," May 16, 1974 http://news.bbc.co.uk/
onthisday/hi/dates/stories/may/16/newsid_2512000/2512399.stm.

"Treaty of Peace Between the State of Israel and the Hashemite
Kingdom of Jordan, October 26, 1994." http://www.mfa.gov.il/mfa/
foreignpolicy/peace/guide/pages/israel-jordan%20peace%20treaty.
aspx.

"UN rejects Israel's claim over Syria's Golan Heights," 26 Apr 2016.
http://www.aljazeera.com/news/2016/04/rejects-israel-claim-syria-
golan-heights-160426195853040.html.

"UN report cites possible war crimes by both Israel and Palestinian
groups in 2014 Gaza conflict." UN News Centre. http://www.
un.org/apps/news/story.asp?NewsID=51215#.WYCOAceGO1s.

"What is BDS?" https://bdsmovement.net/what-is-bds.

"What was the largest air-to-air jet battle in history?" *Quora*. https://
www.quora.com/What-was-the-largest-air-to-air-jet-battle-in-history.

"Yasser Arafat 1929-2004." Jewish Virtual Library. http://www.
jewishvirtuallibrary.org/jsource/biography/arafat.html.

"Zionism: BILU Manifesto." Jewish Virtual Library. https://www.
jewishvirtuallibrary.org/jsource/Zionism/BILU_Manifesto.html.

"Zionism: Socialist Zionism." Jewish Virtual Library. https://www.jewishvirtuallibrary.org/jsource/Zionism/Socialist_Zionism.html.

"Zionism." https://www.jewishvirtuallibrary.org/jsourceZionism/zionism.html.

"Zionist Congress: First Zionist Congress & Basel Program" August 1897." Jewish Virtual Library. http://www.jewishvirtuallibrary.org/jsource/Zionism/First_Cong_&_Basel_Program.html.

"Zionist Congresses: The Biltmore Conference, May 6-11, 1942." Jewish Virtual Library. http://www.jewishvirtuallibrary.org/jsource/History/biltmore.html.

Abu Toameh, Khaled. "Palestinians' Real Tragedy: Failed Leadership," *Gatestone Institute*, June 15, 2017. https://www.gatestoneinstitute.org/10526/palestinians-failed-leadership.

Adelman, Jonathan. "The Christians of Israel: A Remarkable Group," The Huffington Post. https://www.huffingtonpost.com/jonathan-adelman/the-christians-of-israel_b_8055770.html.

Alexander, Edward. "NBC's War in Lebanon: The Distorting Mirror." http://www.afsi.org/pamphlets/NBC_war_in_lebanon_alexander[1].pdf, 1.

Al-Habbash, Mahmoud. *Al-Hayat al-Jadida* (December 13, 2006) quoted in Itamar Marcus and Barbara Cook, "The Evolving Palestinian Narrative: Arabs Caused the Refugee Problem," Palestinian Media Watch. May 20, 2008.

Bard, Mitchell G. "Arab League Boycot: Background and and Overview." Jewish Virtual Library. http://www.jewishvirtuallibrary.org/jsource/History/Arab_boycott.html.

———. "The Ethiopian Exodus, Part I, Think Tank http://www.pbs.org/thinktank/transcript1252.html.

———. "The Arab/Muslim World: The Gulf War, August 1990 – February 1991. http://www.jewishvirtuallibrary.org/the-gulf-war.

———. "Israeli Attack on Iraqi Reactor Offers History Lesson for Obama," March 16, 2010. *Encyclopedia Britannica* Blog. http://blogs.britannica.com/2010/03/israeli-attack-on-iraqi-reactor-offers-history-lesson-for-obama/.

Belt, Mark. "Unsung Heroes." Horsefeathers, June 8, 2005. https://web.archive.org/web/20090611041943/http://doctor-horsefeathers.com/archives2/000437.php.

Ben-David, Lenny. "Gazan Casualties: How Many and Who They

Were." Jerusalem Center for Public Affairs. http://jcpa.org/casualties-gaza-war/.

Bernadotte, Folke. "Progress Report of the United Nations Mediator on Palestine." 16 September 1948. United Nations General Assembly Doc. A/648. Part one, section V, paragraph 6. https://msnquotations. wordpress.com/category/arab-israeli/.

Blackburn, Nicky. "65 top ways Israel is saving our planet." *Israel 21c,* April 14, 2013. https://www.israel21c.org/the-top-65-ways-israel-is-saving-our-planet/.

Caspit, Ben. "We Will Not Capitulate." Maariv.org, July 31, 2006. http://www.nrg.co.il/online/1/ART1/457/743.html.

Consulate General of Israel in New York. "Summary of Operation Pillar of Defense," 11.21.2012. http://embassies.gov.il/new-york/NewsAndEvents/Pages/Summary-of-Operation-Pillar-of-Defense.aspx.

Cordesman, Anthony H. "The 'Gaza War': A Strategic Analysis." draft report, February 2, 2009. https://csis-prod.s3.amazonaws.com/s3fs-public/legacy_files/files/media/csis/pubs/090202_gaza_war.pdf.

D.H., Lt. Col. Jonathan. "Understanding the Breakdown of Israeli-Palestinian Negotiations." Jerusalem Center for Public Affairs, No. 486, 15 September-1 October 2002. http://www.jcpa.org/jl/vp486.htm.

Dershowitz, Alan. "The Case Against the Goldstone Report: A Study in Evidentiary Bias." Digital Access to Scholarship at Harvard. https://dash.harvard.edu/handle/1/3593975.

Dobbing, Mary and Chris Cole, "Drone Wars UK." Oxford: Peace House, 2014. https://dronewarsuk.files.wordpress.com/2014/01/israel-and-the-drone-wars.pdf.

Egan, Jennifer. "Multiculturalism." *Encyclopedia Britannica.* https://www.britannica.com/topic/multiculturalism.

Eid, Bassem. "The Palestinian Case Against BDS." *The Washington Institute For Near East Policy,* June 25, 2015. http://www.washingtoninstitute.org/policy-analysis/view/the-palestinian-case-against-bds.

——— "Five Facts the BDS Movement Should Learn from Bassem Eid." *InFocus,* June 27, 2016. http://www.cameraoncampus.org/blog/5-things-for-the-bds-movement-to-learn-from-bassem-eid/#.WZXr2CiGO1s.

Elazar, Daniel J. "Deuteronomy as Israel's Ancient Constitution: Some

Preliminary Reflections." Jerusalem Center for Public Affairs. http://www.jcpa.org/dje/articles2/deut-const.htm.

Ellis, Ralph and Michael Schwartz, "Mom speaks out on 3 abducted teens as Israeli PM blames Hamas." CNN, June 15, 2014. http://www.cnn.com/2014/06/15/world/meast/west-bank-jewish-teens-missing/index.html.

Ezzat, Dina. "Boycott Israel? Not so simple." *Al-Ahram Weekly* Online, April 11-17, 2002. http://weekly.ahram.org.eg/Archive/2002/581/ec1.htm.

Feldner, Yotam. "The Revised Palestinian Account of Camp David Part III: The Palestinian Strategic Goals." MEMRI September 11, 2001. https://www.memri.org/reports/revised-palestinian-account-camp-david-part-iii-palestinian-strategic-goals.

Gold, Zack and Benedetta Berti, "Why is the Israel-Hamas Ceasefire Eroding?" *Carnegie Endowment for International Peace*, January 28, 2014 http://carnegieendowment.org/sada/?fa=54341.

Gross, Terry. "Revisiting Rabin's Assassination, And The Peace That Might Have Been." NPR, October 13, 2015. http://www.npr.org/2015/10/13/448269886/revisiting-rabins-assassination-and-the-peace-that-might-have-been.

Grynszpan, Michael. Facebook, July 30, 2014. https://www.facebook.com/michael.grynszpan/posts/10152140390486065.

Habousha, Hayim V. "The Farhud." http://www.midrash.org/articles/farhud/.

Hadad, Toufic. "Palestinian Forced Displacement from Kuwait: The Overdue Accounting." Badil Resource Center. http://www.badil.org/en/component/k2/item/1514-art07.html.

Hanania, Ray. "Sharon and Hamas," *Counterpunch*, January 18, 2003. https://www.counterpunch.org/2003/01/18/sharon-and-hamas/.

Hedding, Malcolm. "Israel and Apartheid." Scholars for Peace in the Middle East, March 3, 2010. http://spme.org/boycotts-divestments-sanctions-bds/boycotts-divestments-and-sanctions-bds-news/malcolm-hedding-israel-and-apartheid/8079/as quoted in https://en.wikipedia.org/wiki/Israeli_West_Bank_barrier.

Herzl, Theodore. "*Der Judenstaat*, 1896." Jewish Virtual Library. http://www.jewishvirtuallibrary.org/jsource/Zionism/herzl2.html.

Herzog, Chaim. "The United Nations: Israeli Statement in Response to 'Zionism Is Racism' Resolution November 10, 1975." Jewish

Virtual Library. http://www.jewishvirtuallibrary.org/jsource/UN/herzogsp.html.

High Level Military Group. "An Assessment of the 2014 Conflict in Gaza." Friends of the Israel Initiative, October 2015. http://www.jewishvirtuallibrary.org/jsource/images/hlmg2015.pdf., 19-20.

Israel Defense Forces. "2012 Operation Pillar of Defense." https://www.Idfblog.Com/about-the-idf/history-of-the-idf/2012-operation-pillar-of-defense/.

Israel Ministry of Foreign Affairs, "Main Points of Israel-Jordan Peace Treaty, 26 Oct 1994." http://www.mfa.gov.il/mfa/foreignpolicy/peace/guide/pages/main%20points%20of%20israel-jordan%20peace%20treaty.aspx.

———. "The Gulf War, 1991" http://www.mfa.gov.il/mfa/aboutisrael/history/pages/the%20gulf%20war%20-%201991.aspx.

Isseroff, Ami. "Battle of Yad Mordechai, 1948." *Zionism and Israel - Encyclopedic Dictionary.* http://zionism-israel.com/dic/Yad_Mordechai_battle.htm.

Johnston, Wm. Robert. "Chronology of Terrorist Attacks in Israel Introduction," 8 January, 2017. http://www.johnstonsarchive.net/terrorism/terrisrael.html.

Kramer, Martin. "Sykes-Picot and the Zionists." http://martinkramer.org/sandbox/2016/05/sykes-picot-and-the-zionists/

Ksharim. "The Origins of Zionism," Lesson 41. http://makomisrael.org/blog/the-origins-of-zionism-2/http://makomisrael.org/wp-content/uploads/2011/10/lesson41.pdf.

Lappin, Yaakov. "IDF Releases Cast Lead Casualty Numbers." JPost.com, March 26, 2009. http://www.jpost.com/Israel/IDF-releases-Cast-Lead-casualty-numbers.

Luft, Gal. "The Karine-A Affair: A Strategic Watershed in the Middle East?" *The Washington Institute,* January 30, 2002. http://www.washingtoninstitute.org/policy-analysis/view/the-karine-a-affair-a-strategic-watershed-in-the-middle-east.

Marcus, Itamar and Nan Jacques Zilberdik. "Arab leaders are responsible for refugee problem." Palestinian Media Watch Bulletin, July 23, 2009. http://www.palwatch.org/main.aspx?fi=157&doc_id=1102.

———. "PA minister: PA agreements are modeled after Muhammad's Hudaybiyyah Peace Treaty." Palestinian Media Watch, July 22, 2013. http://palwatch.org/site/modules/print/preview.aspx?fi=157&doc_id=9401.

———. "PA depicts a world without Israel." Palestinian Media Watch. http://www.palwatch.org/main.aspx?fi=449.

Naveh, Dani. "Palestinian Authority: The Involvement of Arafat and PA Officials in Terrorism against Israel." Israel Ministry of Foreign Affairs, May 6, 2002. Jewish Virtual Library. http://www.jewishvirtuallibrary.org/the-involvement-of-arafat-and-pa-officials-in-terrorism-against-israel.

Safian, Alexander. "Building in Har Homa," *CAMERA*, February 27, 1997. http://www.camera.org/index.asp?x_context=7&x_issue=3&x_article=37.

Savir, Aryeh. "Operation Brothers Keeper Completed," *Breaking Israel News*, July 2, 2014. https://www.breakingisraelnewscom/17503/operation-brothers-keeper-completed/#h3YFTDj1FjZQ CqMa.99.

Seid, Roberta and Roz Rothstein, "Omar Barghouti's Lectures: A Case Study of Dangerous Propaganda." StandWithUs. https://www.standwithus.com/news/article.asp?id=2142.

Shragai, Nadav. "The 'Al Aksa is in Danger" Libel; The History of a Lie," Jerusalem Center for Public Affairs. http://jcpa.org/al-aksa-is-in-danger-libel-temple-mount/.

Spencer, Robert. "Hamas: We love death like our enemies love life," *Jihad Watch*, July 31, 2014. https://www.jihadwatch.org/2014/07/hamas-we-love-death-like-our-enemies-love-life.

Tawil, Bassam. "The Foreign Press Association's Unlimited Bias," *Gatestone Institute*, August 4, 2017. https://www.gatestoneinstitute.org/10768/foreign-press-association#continued.

The Knesset. "The Second Lebanese War." https://knesset.gov.il/lexicon/eng/Lebanon_war2_eng.htm.

TheLandofIsrael.com, "Gilad Shalit: Who's Blurring the Lines?" aish.com. http://www.aish.com/jw/me/Gilad_Shalit_Whos_Blurring_the_Lines.html.

This Day in History. "1972: Massacre begins at Munich Olympics." http://www.history.com/this-day-in-history/massacre-begins-at-munich-olympics.

U.S. Department of State, Office of the Historian. "The Madrid Conference, 1991." https://history.state.gov/milestones/1989-1992/madrid-conference.

United Nation General Assembly. https://unispal.un.org/DPA/DPR/unispal.nsf/0/761C1063530766A7052566A2005B74D1.

United Nations Human Rights Council. "Human Rights in Palestine and Other Occupied Arab Territories: Report of the United Nations Fact Finding Mission on the Gaza Conflict," A/HRC/12/48, September 15, 2009. http://www.gloobal.net/iepala/gloobal/fichas/ficha.php?id=8410&entidad=Textos&html=1.

Wachsman, Nachshon. Ynet news.com, March 11, 2009. http://www.ynetnews.com/articles/0,7340,L-3684709,00.html.

Warner, Susan. "Father Naddaf–A Beacon of Light To The Christians of Israel." *Gatestone Institute*, June 19 2016. https://www.gatestoneinstitute.org/8288/gabriel-naddaf-christians-israel.

Weiss, Yf'aat. "The Transfer Agreement and the Boycott Movement: A Jewish Dilemma on the Eve of the Holocaust." Yad Vashem Shoah Resource Center. http://www.yadvashem.org/odot_pdf/Microsoft%20Word%20-%203231.pdf.

Wilder, David. "I Was Baruch Goldstein's Friend." Jewish Press.com, February 28. http://www.jewishpress.com/indepth/opinions/i-was-baruch-goldsteins-friend/2014/02/28/.

Zivotofsky, Rabbi Ari. "What's the Truth about … the Uganda Plan?" Jewish Action, March 1, 2008. https://jewishaction.com/jewish-world/history/whats_the_truth_about_the_uganda_plan/.

SUGGESTED

Websites that cover the reality of the Arab Israeli Conflict

U.N. Watch is an NGO that monitors the United Nations, and how it actually deals with Human Rights Violations, and how it is obsessed with Israel. https://www.unwatch.org/en/

Palestine Media Watch – an NGO that monitors what the Palestinian Authority and Hamas say to its people visa vis their various media outlets, social media, school text books, and sermons given in Mosques by Hamas or PA supported Imams. https://www.palwatch.org/

MEMRI | Middle East Media Research Institute - MEMRI bridges the language gap which exists between the West and the Middle East, providing timely translations of Arabic, Persian, Urdu-Pashtu, and Turkish media, as well as original analysis of political, ideological, intellectual, social, cultural, and religious trends in the Middle East. https://www.memri.org/

Honest Reporting - Defending Israel from Media Bias - An NGO that holds all forms of Journalism to their own standards of reporting. Honest Reporting makes sure that the editorial page and the news page are clearly separated, that stories and pictures are not purposely distorted to paint Israel in a negative light. http://honestreporting.com/

NGO Monitor - NGO Monitor provides information and analysis, promotes accountability, and supports discussion on the reports and activities of NGOs (non-governmental organizations) claiming to advance human rights and humanitarian agendas. https://www.ngo-monitor.org/

Jerusalem Center For Public Affairs (JCPA) - Founded in 1976, is a leading think tank focusing on Israeli security, regional diplomacy, and international law. http://jcpa.org/

Films

ISRAEL: A NATION IS BORN "is a five-part video series presented by former Israeli Foreign Minister Abba Eban. It chronicles his recollections of, and his part in, the creation of the State of Israel. The series tells the story of the events leading to the establishment of the State of Israel in 1948; the subsequent conflicts, including the 1967 Six Day War and the 1973 Yom Kippur War; the Egyptian-Israeli peace treaty; and the events of the [subsequent] decade." (https://www.amazon.com/Israel-Nation-Born-Abba-Eban/dp/B00000G3NB)

PILLAR OF FIRE: A TELEVISION HISTORY OF ISRAEL'S REBIRTH, 3 DVD set IBA DokoMedia: "Pillar of Fire focuses on the History of Zionism, beginning in 1896, in the wake of Theodor Herzl's revival of the concept of Jewish nationalism and continues to follow the Jewish People in the 20th century, the early stages of Zionism, followed by the waves of Aliyah prior to the founding of Israel, the Revival of the Hebrew language, the Ottoman Empire's rule in over the Land of Israel, the British Mandate, Anti-Semitism in Europe, the rise of Nazism and The Holocaust, the history of the Yishuv, the Jewish struggle for independence, and ends in 1948, with the Israeli Declaration of Independence." ("Pillar of fire," Wikipedia. https://en.wikipedia.org/wiki/Pillar_of_Fire_(documentary))

THE CASE FOR ISRAEL – DEMOCRACY'S OUTPOST WITH ALAN DERSHOWITZ. Doc Emet Productions: "Rising in vigorous defense of the nation-state of the Jewish people, distinguished Harvard Law School professor Alan Dershowitz presents incisive evidence from leading experts across the political spectrum to assert Israel's basic right to exist." (https://www.amazon.com/dp/B00A2P79HK)

THE FORGOTTEN REFUGEES – "The documentary explores the history, culture, and forced exodus of Middle Eastern and North African Jewish communities in the second half of the 20th century. Using extensive testimony of refugees from Egypt, Yemen, Libya, Iraq, and Morocco, the film weaves personal stories with dramatic archival footage of rescue missions, historic images of exodus and resettlement, and analyses by contemporary scholars to tell the story of how and why the Jewish population in the Middle East and North Africa declined from one million in 1945 to several thousand today." (The Forgotten Refugees," Wikipedia. https://en.wikipedia.org/wiki/The_Forgotten_Refugees)

Faith & Fate: The Miracle of Israel 1945 – 1948

Directed by Ashley Lazarus, "Berel Wein's groundbreaking documentary captures the two most monumental events in recent Jewish history: the Holocaust and the birth of the State of Israel. With original footage, ...[s]ome of the topics covered include: Nuremberg Trials, fate of Sephardic Jewry and the Exodus." (https://www.amazon.com/Miracle-Israel-1945-1948/dp/B01LTI0YKM)

Faith & Fate: A New Beginning 1948 – 1957

Directed by Ashley Lazarus, *"A New Beginning* tells of the absorption of the 850,000 Jewish refugees from Yemen, Morocco, Libya, and Egypt. The film takes us back fourteen centuries to the present-day Arab/Israeli conflict. *A New Beginning* captures the beginning of the Cold War, the Suez crisis, and the fate of Jews behind the Iron Curtain in contrast with the challenge of freedom in 1950's suburban America." (https://www.amazon.com/dp/B01NGZVK86/)

Index

"one man's terrorist, is another man's freedom fighter" 226n
"The Angel" 391n
"the soft bigotry of low expectations" 453n, 665
"We Will Not Capitulate" by Ben Caspit 614-618
"Augurers of Zion" (Mevasrei Zion) 94
"Auto-Emancipation: An Appeal to His People by a Russian Jew" 74
"Budapest" 392
"Clinton Parameters" 567
"Declaration of the Rights of Man" 85
"disputed" territories 355, 494
"Dosh" xxi, 504
"Gaza expulsion" 592
"Good Fence" 449
"Greater Israel" 495
"Hitnatkut" 592
"Initial Response to Report of the Fact Finding Mission on Gaza Established Pursuant to Resolution S-9/1 of the Human Rights Council 630n-633n
"land for security" 557
"McMahon Pledge" 115
"mission of Israel" 57
"Occupied Palestine" 597
"occupied" territory 355
"Program of the League of the Arab Fatherland" 113
"roof knocking" 625
"RPG Kids" 463
"Sussex pledge" 119
"Territories" 494, 498, 507, 508
"The Decree of Peace" 118

A

K